T0418289

MILESTONE DOCUMENTS OF THE SUPREME COURT

Exploring the Cases
That Shaped America

Milestone Documents of the Supreme Court: Exploring the Cases That Shaped America

Schlager Group Inc.

10228 E. Northwest HWY, STE 1151
Dallas, TX 75238
USA
(888) 416-5727
info@schlagergroup.com

You can find Schlager Group online at https://www.schlagergroup.com

For Schlager Group:
Vice President, Editorial: Sarah Robertson
Vice President, Operations and Strategy: Benjamin Painter
Founder and President: Neil Schlager

Printed in the United States of America 10 9 8 7 6 5 4 3 2 1
Print ISBN: 9781935306863
eBook: 9781935306870

Library of Congress Control Number: 2023934505

CONTENTS

Reader's Guide...viii

Contributors...x

Introduction..xii

Volume 1: 1803–1908

Marbury v. Madison...2

Martin v. Hunter's Lessee...23

Trustees of Dartmouth College v. Woodward...52

McCulloch v. Maryland...82

Cohens v. Virginia...107

Gibbons v. Ogden...137

Worcester v. Georgia...163

Charles River Bridge v. Warren Bridge..185

United States v. Amistad..193

Prigg v. Pennsylvania...206

Dred Scott v. Sandford...228

Ableman v. Booth..267

Ex parte Milligan..287

Slaughterhouse Cases..310

United States v. Cruikshank..351

Reynolds v. United States...366

Civil Rights Cases...382

Elk v. Wilkins..418

Plessy v. Ferguson...438

United States v. Wong Kim Ark...459

Lochner v. New York...472

Muller v. Oregon...486

Volume 2: 1915-1971

Frank v. Mangum...497

Guinn v. United States..515

Hammer v. Dagenhart..529

Schenck v. United States...542

Abrams v. United States..550

Whitney v. California..563

Olmstead v. United States...575

Powell v. Alabama...593

A.L.A. Schechter Poultry Corporation v. United States..610

United States v. Curtiss-Wright..627

National Labor Relations Board v. Jones & Laughlin Steel Corporation...644

West Coast Hotel v. Parrish..670

Cantwell v. Connecticut..687

Wickard v. Filburn..697

West Virginia State Board of Education v. Barnette...711

Korematsu v. United States...720

Sweatt v. Painter...730

Dennis v. United States...741

Youngstown Sheet and Tube Co. v. Sawyer..761

Brown v. Board of Education..772

Hernandez v. Texas...784

Gomillion v. Lightfoot...793

Mapp v. Ohio..802

Baker v. Carr..815

Engel v. Vitale...822

Gideon v. Wainwright...832

Katzenbach v. McClung...839

New York Times Co. v. Sullivan..850

Griswold v. Connecticut..857

Bond v. Floyd..868

Miranda v. Arizona...884

South Carolina v. Katzenbach...926

Loving v. Virginia 943

Tinker v. Des Moines Independent Community School District...956

New York Times Co. v. United States..967

Volume 3: 1972–2022

Flood v. Kuhn..981

Furman v. Georgia..997

San Antonio Independent School District v. Rodriguez...1010

Sierra Club v. Morton..1049

Roe v. Wade..1061

Milliken v. Bradley..1085

United States v. Nixon...1094

Craig v. Boren..1103

Regents of the University of California v. Bakke...1110

Frontiero v. Richardson..1133

Texas v. Johnson..1143

United States v. Lopez..1152

United States v. Virginia..1164

Clinton v. Jones...1173

Bush v. Gore..1187

Friends of the Earth v. Laidlaw Environmental Services..1219

Zelman v. Simmons-Harris..1234

Lawrence v. Texas..1252

District of Columbia v. Heller..1280

Citizens United v. Federal Election Commission..1322

Shelby County v. Holder...1336

Obergefell v. Hodges..1366

Bostock v. Clayton County...1380

Dobbs v. Jackson Women's Health Organization...1417

Index...1473

MILESTONE DOCUMENTS OF THE SUPREME COURT

Exploring the Cases
That Shaped America

FRANK V. MANGUM

<table>
<tr><td>DATE
1915</td><td>CITATION
237 U.S. 309</td></tr>
<tr><td>AUTHOR
Mahlon Pitney</td><td>SIGNIFICANCE
Declined to apply the due process clause to a state criminal trial that had been marked by mob intimidation and anti-Jewish sentiment; four months later, the convicted man was lynched at the jail where he was incarcerated</td></tr>
<tr><td>VOTE
7–2</td><td></td></tr>
</table>

Overview

In *Frank v. Mangum,* the Supreme Court refused to grant a writ of habeas corpus to Leo M. Frank (1885–1915), the manager of a pencil factory in Atlanta, Georgia, who had been convicted of murdering Mary Phagan, a thirteen-year-old girl who worked in the factory. The trial, in 1913, was marked by mob intimidation of the courthouse and everyone in it. In addition, some newspapers and Georgia politicians, especially Thomas Watson (a former congressman and national Populist Party candidate), vigorously called for Frank's conviction, in large part because he was Jewish. At the time, Jewish leaders called this the "American Dreyfus Case," referring the persecution of an army captain in France who was sentenced to life in prison for allegedly helping Germany win the Franco-Prussian War, when it was obvious to independent observers that his only "crime" was being Jewish. After the trial, Watson advocated lynching Frank in his newspaper. Even by the standards of the period, the trial was more a circus than a legal proceeding. The only witness against Frank was a janitor who testified he had helped move the body. Much of his testimony seemed inconsistent and false, but the judge overruled his attorneys who tried to suppress it. There was no other evidence against Frank, and modern research has shown that the murderer was in fact the janitor who testified against Frank. After losing appeals in the state courts, Frank appealed to the federal courts under the Fourteenth Amendment, arguing that he was denied due process of law in Georgia. In this period, the Supreme Court often overturned state economic regulations (such as in *Lochner v. New York*) under the Fourteenth Amendment's due process clause, but the Court refused to apply the clause to a state criminal trial. Four months after the Supreme Court rejected Frank's appeal, a mob broke into the jail where he was incarcerated and lynched him.

Leo Frank was born in Texas, raised in New York City, and earned an engineering degree at Cornell. In 1908 he moved to Atlanta to manage a factory owned by the National Pencil Company, and he was active in the local Jewish community. At the time there was some social and political anti-Semitism in Atlanta, some of which emanated from populism in rural Georgia. Accompanying increasing industrialization and foreign immigration in Georgia was a rise in child labor,

Leo Frank
(Library of Congress)

illustrated by the life of Mary Phagan (1899–1913), the daughter of rural white tenant farmers. She started working in a textile factory at age ten, and when her family moved to Atlanta, she worked in the pencil factory. On Saturday, April 26, 1913, she went to the factory to pick up a final paycheck, having been been laid off. The next day a night watchman found her body in the factory basement. She had been strangled and probably sexual assaulted. The police investigation was botched in many ways, and eventually the police concluded that Frank had committed the crime.

Two pieces of paper, later called "murder notes," appeared to have been written by the janitor, James "Jim" Conley, who was the only witness against Frank. Conley initially denied knowing anything about them; later he said he had written them at Frank's direction. Eventually, Conley told the police three different stories, with the last two implicating Frank in different ways. A local newspaper, calling for Frank's conviction, hired a lawyer to represent Conley. In late May, a grand jury indicted Frank but did not indict Conley, who had confessed to being an accessory to the murder. In addition to the district attorney, the prosecution team included the lawyer who represented Conley. Frank's attorneys

argued that Conley was the real culprit, in which case, having Conley's lawyer as part of the prosecution team clearly violated Frank's rights. Frank presented many witnesses who corroborated that although he had been at the factory that day, he could not possibly have had time to commit the crime because of when these witnesses saw him.

The prosecution and local newspapers used race, sex, ethnicity, racism, opposition to immigration, virulent anti-Semitism, and the plight of poor whites like Phagan to convince the public and the jury that Frank was guilty. There were allegations in the press and by public officials that Frank had coerced sex with other girls (and maybe boys) in his factory and that he was a "pervert." There was no evidence for any of this, but such assertions and rumors intensified the circus-like atmosphere of Frank's trial. Large crowds in the courtroom and many more outside the courtroom clamored for his conviction or even lynching him. When the presiding judge ruled in favor of the prosecuting attorney, Hugh M. Dorsey, against a motion by Frank's lawyers, spectators in the courtroom, according to one southern newspaper, "broke out in a wild uproar like a bloodthirsty mob at a bull fight." The *Atlanta Constitution* published a headline, in full capital letters, proclaiming, "SPONTANEOUS APPALUSE GREETS DORSEY'S VICTORY." When the jury announced its guilty verdict, three men carried Dorsey triumphantly out of the courtroom to a cheering crowd in the streets. The next day, the trial judge sentenced Frank to death.

Frank's lawyers initially appealed to the trial judge, arguing on numerous grounds that the trial was unfair, much of the testimony against Frank was improper and perjured, and the verdict was inconsistent with the evidence—especially that Frank was not in the factory at the time the murder took place. The judge admitted, "I am not thoroughly convinced that Frank is guilty or innocent"—that is, he did not believe Frank was guilty beyond a reasonable doubt—but he refused to reject the jury's verdict or order a new trial. An appeal to the Georgia Supreme Court was also unsuccessful. By a 4–2 vote, the state court upheld the verdict. A subsequent appeal led a stay of execution because of new evidence that had been discovered, and scientific analysis revealed that some of the evidence introduced was simply incorrect. By this time, substantial evidence had been accumulated to show that the janitor, Conley, had committed the crime.

In November 1914, the George Supreme Court once again upheld the verdict and accused Frank's lawyers of "trifling with the Court" by raising claims of newly discovered evidence.

Frank's lawyers then appealed to the U.S. Supreme Court, which rejected his appeal by a vote of 7–2.

Context

The context of the trial reflected the changing nature of American culture, with millions of immigrants from southern and eastern Europe, the Ottoman Empire, Japan, the Philippines, and other parts of Asia coming to the United States from 1890 to 1913, when the case began. This immigration of Roman Catholics, Orthodox Christians, Jews, Muslims, Buddhists, Hindus, and practitioners of other faiths seemed threatening to many white, mostly Protestant Americans. This case, which ended with Leo Frank being lynched, was one of the most violent responses to the changing nature of American society. It was not the only lynching of whites who were members of minority groups. In 1891, for example, a mob in New Orleans murdered eleven Italian immigrants in the largest mass lynching in American history. However, most lynchings, especially in the South, were of Blacks. Between 1889 and 1918 there were more lynchings in Georgia than in any other state. Of these victims, 360 were Black and 26 were white.

The Constitutional context of this case is embedded in a deeply conservative Supreme Court that was inconsistent, one might even say hypocritical, in its jurisprudence. From the 1890s to the eve of World War I, this Court was famous for overruling state laws and reversing state court decisions under the Fourteenth Amendment's due process clause, which provides: "No State shall make or enforce any law which shall abridge the privileges or immunities of citizens of the United States; nor shall any State deprive any person of life, liberty, or property, without due process of law; nor deny to any person within its jurisdiction the equal protection of the laws." Under this clause, the Court struck down legislation that sought to regulate the economy and protect workers from being forced by employers to work too many hours or accept subsistence wages. In *Allgeyer v. Louisiana* (1897), the Court held that the "liberty" in the Fourteenth Amendment included the "liberty" to make contracts, striking down a Louisiana law designed to

Mary Phagan
(Atlanta Georgian)

prevent out-of-state insurance companies from operating in the state. In *Smythe v. Ames* (1898), the Court voided a Nebraska law designed to protect shippers—mostly farmers—from excessive railroad rates. The Court held that this law deprived the railroad of its "property" without due process of law. Most famous in this line of cases was *Lochner v. New York* (1905), where the Court struck down a state law designed to protect the health of bakers (and those who bought their products) by prohibiting employers from allowing them to work more than ten hours a day and more than sixty hours a week. In a 5–4 decision, the Court concluded that this law violated the right of workers to contract for as many hours in a day or week as they wanted. In *Adair v. United States* (1908), the Court struck down a federal law that protected the rights of workers to join unions. Once again, the Court used "liberty" to protect large corporations from state laws.

At the same time, this Court had no problem upholding state laws mandating racial segregation, as in *Plessy v. Ferguson* (1896), and refusing, in *Williams v. Mississippi* (1898), to overturn a criminal conviction on "due process" grounds when the state admitted it had purposely structured its laws to prevent Blacks from serving on juries. In *Maxwell v. Dow* (1900), the Court upheld a state felony conviction where there was no grand jury indictment and a jury of only eight members rather than the traditional twelve-person jury.

Frank's lawyers appealed to the U.S. Supreme Court on the grounds that he had been denied "due process of law" and fair trial because the intimidating nature of the spectators in the courtroom, along with the mob outside the courtroom, simply made it impossible for the jury and the judge to do anything but convict him. But the Court simply refused to apply any notion of due process to state criminal cases. Justice Oliver Wendell Holmes Jr. wrote a vigorous dissent, which Justice Charles Evans Hughes joined. The Court at this time simply was unwilling to protect individual rights, civil rights, or due process rights of individuals.

About the Author

Mahlon Pitney (1858–1924) grew up on Morristown, New Jersey. His family came to America in the early eighteenth century, and he was technically Mahon Pitney IV, being the fourth family member to carry that name. He graduated from Princeton University in 1879 and earned a graduate degree three years later. Pitney studied law with his father and was admitted to the bar in 1882. He practiced law and served two terms in the U.S. House of Representatives, but in 1899 he resigned before the end of his second term when he was elected to the New Jersey state senate. He was elected president of the senate the following year. Pitney was appointed to the New Jersey Supreme Court for a seven-year term in 1901. In 1908, he was appointed chancellor, head of both law and equity branches of the court. In 1912, President William H. Taft nominated Pitney to the Supreme Court of the United States. The U.S. Senate confirmed the appointment on March 13, 1912. Most progressives in the Senate opposed his confirmation because he was notoriously hostile to labor unions and progressive reforms. Ironically, Pitney replaced the late John Marshall Harlan, who had been among the most progressive members of the Court in this period. Harlan is most famous for his dissent in *Plessy v. Ferguson*, where he denounced segregation. Pitney is most remembered for his opinion in the *Frank* case. He is also remembered for his

opinion in *Coppage v. Kansas* (1915), where he struck down a Kansas law prohibiting employers from firing workers merely because they had joined a union. He wrote this opinion three months before his opinion in *Frank v. Mangum*. In *Coppage* he had no problem reversing a decision of the Kansas Supreme Court, using the Fourteenth Amendment to protect the liberty and due process rights of a railroad. In *Frank* he would completely defer to the Georgia Supreme Court, which asserted that the mob atmosphere at Leo Frank's trial did not deny him due process of law. In *Hitchman Coal and Coke Co. v. Mitchell* (1917), Pitney would also support an injunction against a union trying to organize coal miners. Pitney retired from the Supreme Court on December 31, 1922.

Explanation and Analysis of the Document

Frank's appeal to the Supreme Court is set out in the opinion, which notes that he asserted he was denied due process of law and "did not have a fair and impartial trial, because of alleged disorder in and about the court room, including manifestations of public sentiment hostile to the defendant sufficient to influence the jury." One example of this was that Frank was not in the courtroom when the verdict was rendered, which was a departure of classic trial procedure, "because of the fear of violence that might be done the defendant were he in court when the verdict was rendered." The Supreme Court dismissed this departure of normal procedure as insignificant but did not consider that the departure illustrated—indeed proved—that the circumstances of the trial were so unfair that the defendant, the jury, and the judge all feared personal violence. Neither the jury nor the judge dared to render a verdict in favor of Frank, and in fact throughout the trial the judge, fearing violent reprisal, refused to rule in Frank's favor on a number of motions. Similarly, the Supreme Court ignored the evidence of crowd intimidation throughout the trial and especially when the verdict was read. It was clear that if any jury member had voted to acquit, there would have been violence and possibly a lynching of that juror.

Through the writ of habeas corpus, Frank was not asking the Court to overturn the state verdict, because at the time there was no procedure for that. Rather,

Frank was asking for a new trial that would be fair and unbiased. The Supreme Court in 1915 would simply not do this. While willing to strike down state laws on a variety of economic issues, this Court was unwilling to consider the problem of fair trials in state courts. The Court noted that the Georgia Supreme Court had affirmed the verdict, and that was sufficient for the U.S. Supreme Court. Justice Pitney presumed that the trial was fair because the Georgia Supreme Court said it was fair, and he would not look beyond that.

Justice Holmes, joined by Charles Evans Hughes (a future chief justice), dissented. Holmes argued that the habeas corpus process "cuts through all forms and goes to the very tissue of the structure. It comes in from the outside, not in subordination to the proceedings, and although every form may have been preserved, opens the inquiry whether they have been more than an empty shell." For Holmes, the claims of a "fair trial" by the state were transparently an "empty shell" because the court was "dominated by a mob," and the Georgia Supreme Court simply asserted that "such domination cannot be reviewed" by a federal court. Holmes put it succinctly: "Mob law does not become due process of law by securing the assent of a terrorized jury. We are not speaking of mere disorder, or mere irregularities in procedure, but of a case where the processes of justice are actually subverted."

Holmes chastised the majority for hiding behind forms of procedure rather than looking at the reality of the case:

> The single question in our minds is whether a petition alleging that the trial took place in the midst of a mob savagely and manifestly intent on a single result is shown on its face unwarranted, by the specifications, which may be presumed to set forth the strongest indications of the fact at the petitioner's command. This is not a matter for polite presumptions; we must look facts in the face. Any judge who has sat with juries knows that, in spite of forms, they are extremely likely to be impregnated by the environing atmosphere. And when we find the judgment of the expert on the spot—of the judge whose business it was to preserve not only form, but substance—to have been that if one juryman yielded to the reasonable doubt that

he himself later expressed in court as the result of most anxious deliberation, neither prisoner nor counsel would be safe from the rage of the crowd, we think the presumption overwhelming that the jury responded to the passions of the mob. Of course we are speaking only of the case made by the petition, and whether it ought to be heard. Upon allegations of this gravity in our opinion it ought to be heard, whatever the decision of the state court may have been, and it did not need to set forth contradictory evidence, or matter of rebuttal, or to explain why the motions for a new trial and to set aside the verdict were overruled by the state court.

He believed the U.S. Supreme Court had a duty "to declare lynch law as little valid when practised by a regularly drawn jury as when administered by one elected by a mob intent on death."

Unfortunately for Frank, Holmes, and the historical honor of the U.S. Supreme Court, Pitney and six of his fellow justices were unwilling to demand that the states not practice "lynch law," even when doing it through the form of a trial.

Impact

When the Supreme Court refused to overturn the verdict, Governor John Slaton commuted Frank's sentence to life in prison. By this time, many people in the state and throughout the nation realized they were watching a huge and fatal miscarriage of justice. Most newspapers in the state were now condemning the verdict, and even the pastor at the church that Mary Phagan's family attended asserted the trial was unfair. As one member of the state Prison Commission noted, Frank had been convicted on testimony of an admitted accomplice, Conley, who had persistently lied to the police and changed his story, while "the circumstances of the crime tend to fix guilt upon the accomplice." Governor Slaton received more than 1,000 death threats for commuting the sentence, further supporting the notion that the verdict was a result of mob intimidation. Slaton believed that Conley had not testified truthfully and that the new evidence showed this. He was not willing to sign a death warrant when he believed Frank was probably innocent.

After this, the Governor needed the protection of the state's National Guard and Special Police while mobs tried to attack his house. He soon left the state in fear of his life. Frank was sent to the state penitentiary in July. A month later, a carefully planned and coordinated lynching party of 28 men in eight separate cars descended on the penitentiary. They handcuffed the prison warden, cut all telephone lines from the prison, drained the gas out of all the prison vehicles, kidnapped Frank, drove him 175 miles across the state, and lynched him. One of the leaders of this lynching was Joseph M. Brown, and former governor of the state. Other public officials, including a state judge, openly participated in the lynching. No one would ever be arrested for this event, even though the leaders were well known. Pictures from the lynching were sold as postcards in Georgia.

During the trial, American Jews created the Anti-Defamation League of B'nai B'rith (known as the ADL) to fight anti-Semitism and racism. The organization still exists and has been active in fighting discrimination againt Jews, African Americans, and other minorities for more than a century. It is among the most successful civil rights litigation and lobbying organization in the country.

In 1923, in *Moore v. Dempsey*, the Court essentially rejected the precedent of the Frank case. *Moore* involved the mass trial in Arkansas of Blacks after a white man was killed while trying to attack a peaceful meeting inside a Black church. In the next few weeks, more than 200 Black people were shot and killed by police, federal troops, and white vigilantes. Eventually, authorities arrested 122 Black people, charging 73 with murder and the rest with various other crimes. Arrests were based on accusations by leading white businessmen and landowners in the town of Elaine, Arkansas, and the surrounding area. Many of those arrested were tortured into testifying against others. The trials were surrounded by mobs, whose members made it clear that anything less than a guilty verdict would lead to lynchings of the defendants and probably the uncooperative jurors. Moore and eleven other men were sentenced to death. The all-white juries usually took less than ten minutes to convict each defendant. Moore's trial lasted only 45 minutes, with his court-appointed lawyer calling no witnesses. The jury convicted him in five minutes. In the *Moore* case, the Supreme Court reversed these convictions. Justice Holmes wrote the opinion in this case, vindicating his dissent in *Frank*.

Questions for Further Study

1. How does this case reflect present-day controversies over fair trials and due process for minorities?

2. Why do you think the Supreme Court refused to act in a case that was obviously (to everyone but the prosecutor and the lynch mobs) a miscarriage of justice?

3. There is a rise in anti-Semitism in the United States today as individuals and openly neo-Nazi organizations attack Jewish synagogues, organizations, and individuals. Does this case give us insights into how to fight such intolerance?

4. For further study, you could read Justice Holmes's majority opinion in *Moore v. Dempsey* (1923). Then compare it to his dissent in *Frank v. Mangum*. How do they line up? You could also compare the dissent in *Moore* with the majority opinion in *Frank*. How do they compare?

Further Reading

Books

Dinnerstein, Leonard. *Antisemitism in America.* New York: Oxford University Press, 1994.

Dinnerstein, Leonard. *The Leo Frank Case.* Athens: University of Georgia Press, 1987.

Freedman, Eric. *Habeas Corpus: Rethinking the Great Writ of Liberty.* New York: New York University Press, 2003.

Oney, Steve. *And the Dead Shall Rise: The Murder of Mary Phagan and the Lynching of Leo Frank.* New York: Pantheon Books, 2003.

Wood, Amy Louise. *Lynching and Spectacle.* Chapel Hill: University of North Carolina Press, 2009.

Articles

Carter, Dan. "And the Dead Shall Rise: The Murder of Mary Phagan and the Lynching of Leo Frank." *Journal of Southern History* 71 (2005): 491.

Kranson, Rachel. "Rethinking the Historiography of American Antisemitism in the Wake of the Pittsburgh Shooting." *American Jewish History* 105 (2021): 247.

—Commentary by Paul Finkelman

FRANK V. MANGUM

Document Text

MR. JUSTICE PITNEY . . . delivered the opinion of the Court

The points raised by the appellant may be reduced to the following:

(1) It is contended that the disorder in and about the courtroom during the trial and up to and at the reception of the verdict amounted to mob domination, that not only the jury, but the presiding judge, succumbed to it, and that this, in effect, wrought a dissolution of the court, so that the proceedings were *coram non judice.*

(2) That Frank's right to be present during the entire trial until and at the return of the verdict was an essential part of the right of trial by jury, which could not be waived either by himself or his counsel.

(3) That his presence was so essential to a proper hearing that the reception of the verdict in his absence, and in the absence of his counsel, without his consent or authority, was a departure from the due process of law guaranteed by the Fourteenth Amendment sufficient to bring about a loss of jurisdiction of the trial court, and to render the verdict and judgment absolute nullities.

(4) That the failure of Frank and his counsel, upon the first motion for a new trial, to allege as a ground of that motion the known fact of Frank's absence at the reception of the verdict, or to raise any jurisdictional question based upon it, did not deprive him of the right to afterwards attack the judgment as a nullity, as he did in the motion to set aside the verdict.

(5) And that the ground upon which the Supreme Court of Georgia rested its decision affirming the denial of the latter motion (83 S.E.Rep. 645)—viz., that the objection based upon Frank's absence when the verdict was rendered was available on the motion for new trial, and, under proper practice, ought to have been then taken, and, because not then taken, could not be relied upon as a ground for setting aside the verdict as a nullity—was itself in conflict with the Constitution of the United States because equivalent in effect to an *ex post facto* law, since, as is said, it departs from the practice settled by previous decisions of the same court.

In dealing with these contentions, we should have in mind the nature and extent of the duty that is imposed upon a Federal court on application for the writ of habeas corpus under § 753, Rev.Stat.Comp. Stat. 1913, § 1281. Under the terms of that section, in order to entitle the present appellant to the relief sought, it must appear that he is held in custody in violation of the Constitution of the United States. *Rogers v. Peck,* 199 U. S. 425, 199 U. S. 434. Moreover, if he is held in custody by reason of his conviction upon a criminal charge before a court having plenary jurisdiction over the subject matter or offense, the place where it was committed, and the person of the prisoner, it results from the nature of the writ itself that he cannot have relief on habeas corpus. Mere errors in point of law, however serious, committed by a criminal court in the exercise of its jurisdiction over a case properly subject to its cognizance cannot be reviewed by habeas corpus. That writ cannot be employed as a substitute for the writ of error. *Ex parte Parks,* 93 U. S. 18, 93 U. S. 21; *Ex parte*

Siebold, 100 U. S. 371, 100 U. S. 375; *Ex parte Royall,* 117 U. S. 241, 117 U. S. 250; *In re Frederich, Petitioner,* 149 U. S. 70, 149 U. S. 75; *Baker v. Grice,* 169 U. S. 284, 169 U. S. 290; *Tinsley v. Anderson,* 171 U. S. 101, 171 U. S. 105; *Markuson v. Boucher,* 175 U. S. 184.

As to the "due process of law" that is required by the Fourteenth Amendment, it is perfectly well settled that a criminal prosecution in the courts of a state, based upon a law not in itself repugnant to the Federal Constitution, and conducted according to the settled course of judicial proceedings as established by the law of the state, so long as it includes notice and a hearing, or an opportunity to be heard, before a court of competent jurisdiction, according to established modes of procedure, is "due process" in the constitutional sense. *Walker v. Sauvinet,* 92 U. S. 90, 92 U. S. 93; *Hurtado v. California,* 110 U. S. 516, 110 U. S. 535; *Andrews v. Swartz,* 156 U. S. 272, 156 U. S. 276; *Bergemann v. Backer,* 157 U. S. 655, 157 U. S. 659; *Rogers v. Peck,* 199 U. S. 425, 199 U. S. 434; *United States ex rel. Drury v. Lewis,* 200 U. S. 1, 200 U. S. 7; *Felts v. Murphy,* 201 U. S. 123, 201 U. S. 129; *Howard v. Kentucky,* 200 U. S. 164.

It is therefore conceded by counsel for appellant that, in the present case, we may not review irregularities or erroneous rulings upon the trial, however serious, and that the writ of habeas corpus will lie only in case the judgment under which the prisoner is detained is shown to be absolutely void for want of jurisdiction in the court that pronounced it, either because such jurisdiction was absent at the beginning, or because it was lost in the course of the proceedings. And since no question is made respecting the original jurisdiction of the trial court, the contention is and must be that by the conditions that surrounded the trial, and the absence of defendant when the verdict was rendered, the court was deprived of jurisdiction to receive the verdict and pronounce the sentence.

But it would be clearly erroneous to confine the inquiry to the proceedings and judgment of the trial court. The laws of the state of Georgia (as will appear from decisions elsewhere cited) provide for an appeal in criminal cases to the Supreme Court of that state upon divers grounds, including such as those upon which it is here asserted that the trial court was lacking in jurisdiction. And while the Fourteenth Amendment does not require that a state shall provide for an appellate review in criminal cases (*McKane v. Durston,* 153

U. S. 684, 153 U. S. 687; *Andrews v. Swartz,* 156 U. S. 272, 156 U. S. 275; *Rogers v. Peck,* 199 U. S. 425, 199 U. S. 435; *Reetz v. Michigan,* 188 U. S. 505, 188 U. S. 508), it is perfectly obvious that, where such an appeal is provided for, and the prisoner has had the benefit of it, the proceedings in the appellate tribunal are to be regarded as a part of the process of law under which he is held in custody by the state, and to be considered in determining any question of alleged deprivation of his life or liberty contrary to the Fourteenth Amendment.

In fact, such questions as are here presented under the due process clause of the Fourteenth Amendment, though sometimes discussed as if involving merely the jurisdiction of some court or other tribunal, in a larger and more accurate sense involve the power and authority of the state itself. The prohibition is addressed to the state; if it be violated, it makes no difference in a court of the United States by what agency of the state this is done; so, if a violation be threatened by one agency of the state, but prevented by another agency of higher authority, there is no violation by the state. It is for the state to determine what courts or other tribunals shall be established for the trial of offenses against its criminal laws, and to define their several jurisdictions and authority as between themselves. And the question whether a state is depriving a prisoner of his liberty without due process of law, where the offense for which he is prosecuted is based upon a law that does no violence to the Federal Constitution, cannot ordinarily be determined, with fairness to the state, until the conclusion of the course of justice in its courts. *Virginia v. Rives,* 100 U. S. 313, 100 U. S. 318; *Civil Rights Cases,* 109 U. S. 3, 109 U. S. 11; *McKane v. Durston,* 153 U. S. 684, 153 U. S. 687; *Dreyer v. Illinois,* 187 U. S. 71, 187 U. S. 83-84; *Reetz v. Michigan,* 188 U. S. 505, 188 U. S. 507; *Carfer v. Caldwell,* 200 U. S. 293, 200 U. S. 297; *Waters-Pierce Oil Co. v. Texas,* 212 U. S. 86, 212 U. S. 107; *In re Frederich, Petitioner,* 149 U. S. 70, 149 U. S. 75; *Whitten v. Tomlinson,* 160 U. S. 231, 160 U. S. 242; *Baker v. Grice,* 169 U. S. 284, 169 U. S. 291; *Minnesota v. Brundage,* 180 U. S. 499, 180 U. S. 503; *Urquhart v. Brown,* 205 U. S. 179, 205 U. S. 182.

It is indeed settled by repeated decisions of this Court that, where it is made to appear to a court of the United States that an applicant for habeas corpus is in the custody of a state officer in the ordinary course of a criminal prosecution, under a law of the state not in itself repugnant to the Federal Constitution, the writ, in the absence of very special circumstances, ought not to be issued until the state prosecution has reached its conclusion, and not even then until the Federal questions arising upon the record have been brought before this Court upon writ of error. *Ex parte Royall,* 117 U. S. 241, 117 U. S. 251; *In re Frederich, Petitioner,* 149 U. S. 70, 149 U. S. 77; *Whitten v. Tomlinson,* 160 U. S. 231, 160 U. S. 242; *Baker v. Grice,* 169 U. S. 284, 169 U. S. 291; *Tinsley v. Anderson,* 171 U. S. 101, 171 U. S. 105; *Markuson v. Boucher,* 175 U. S. 184; *Urquhart v. Brown,* 205 U. S. 179. *And see Henry v. Henkel,* 235 U. S. 219, 235 U. S. 228. Such cases as *In re Loney,* 134 U. S. 372, 134 U. S. 376, and *In re Neagle,* 135 U. S. 1, are recognized as exceptional.

It follows as a logical consequence that where, as here, a criminal prosecution has proceeded through all the courts of the state, including the appellate as well as the trial court, the result of the appellate review cannot be ignored when, afterwards, the prisoner applies for his release on the ground of a deprivation of Federal rights sufficient to oust the state of its jurisdiction to proceed to judgment and execution against him. This is not a mere matter of comity, as seems to be supposed. The rule stands upon a much higher plane, for it arises out of the very nature and ground of the inquiry into the proceedings of the state tribunals, and touches closely upon the relations between the state and the Federal governments. As was declared by this Court in *Ex parte Royall,* 117 U. S. 241, 117 U. S. 252, applying in a habeas corpus case what was said in *Covell v. Heyman,* 111 U. S. 176, 111 U. S. 182, a case of conflict of jurisdiction:

"The forbearance which courts of coordinate jurisdiction, administered under a single system, exercise towards each other, whereby conflicts are avoided by avoiding interference with the process of each other, is a principle of comity, with perhaps no higher sanction than the utility which comes from concord; but between state courts and those of the United States, it is something more. It is a principle of right and of law, and therefore, of necessity."

And see In re Tyler, 149 U. S. 164, 149 U. S. 186.

It is objected by counsel for appellee that the alleged loss of jurisdiction cannot be shown by evidence outside of the record; that, where a prisoner is held under a judgment of conviction passed by a court having jurisdiction of the subject matter, and the indictment against him states the case and is based upon a valid existing law, habeas corpus is not an available remedy, save for want of jurisdiction appearing upon the face of the record of the court wherein he was convicted. The rule at the common law, and under the act 31 Car. II. chap. 2, and other acts of Parliament prior to that of July 1, 1816 (56 Geo. III. chap. 100, § 3), seems to have been that a showing in the return to a writ of habeas corpus that the prisoner was held under final process based upon a judgment or decree of a court of competent jurisdiction closed the inquiry. So it was held, under the Judiciary Act of 1789 (ch. 20, § 14, 1 Stat. 73, 81), in *Ex parte Watkins,* 3 Pet. 193, 28 U. S. 202. And the rule seems to have been the same under the Act of March 2, 1833 (ch. 57, § 7, 4 Stat. 632, 634), and that of August 29, 1842 (ch. 257, 5 Stat. 539). But when Congress, in the Act of February 5, 1867 (ch. 28, 14 Stat. 385), extended the writ of habeas corpus to all cases of persons restrained of their liberty in violation of the Constitution or a law or treaty of the United States, procedural regulations were included, now found in Rev.Stat. §§ 754-761. These require that the application for the writ shall be made by complaint in writing, signed by the applicant and verified by his oath, setting forth the facts concerning his detention, in whose custody he is detained, and by virtue of what claim or authority, if known; require that the return shall certify the true cause of the detention; and provide that the prisoner may, under oath, deny any of the facts set forth in the return, or allege other material facts, and that the court shall proceed in a summary way to determine the facts by hearing testimony and arguments, and thereupon dispose of the party as law and justice require. The effect is to substitute for the bare legal review that seems to have been the limit of judicial authority under the common law practice, and under the Act of 31 Car. II. chap. 2, a more searching investigation, in which the applicant is put upon his oath to set forth the truth of the matter respecting the causes of his detention, and the court, upon determining the actual facts, is to "dispose of the party as law and justice require."

There being no doubt of the authority of the Congress to thus liberalize the common law procedure on habeas corpus in order to safeguard the liberty of all persons within the jurisdiction of the United States against infringement through any violation of the Constitution or a law or treaty established thereunder, it results that under the sections cited a prisoner in custody pursuant to the final judgment of a state court of criminal jurisdiction may have a judicial inquiry in a court of the United States into the very truth and substance of the causes of his detention, although it may become necessary to took behind and beyond the record of his conviction to a sufficient extent to test the jurisdiction of the state court to proceed to judgment against him. *Cuddy, Petitioner,* 131 U. S. 280, 131 U. S. 283, 131 U. S. 286; *In re Mayfield,* 141 U. S. 107, 141 U. S. 116; *Whitten v. Tomlinson,* 160 U. S. 231, 161 U. S. 242; *In re Watts and Sachs,* 190 U. S. 1, 190 U. S. 35.

In the light, then, of these established rules and principles: that the due process of law guaranteed by the Fourteenth Amendment has regard to substance of right, and not to matters of form or procedure; that it is open to the courts of the United States, upon an application for a writ of habeas corpus, to look beyond forms and inquire into the very substance of the matter, to the extent of deciding whether the prisoner has been deprived of his liberty without due process of law, and for this purpose to inquire into jurisdictional facts, whether they appear upon the record or not; that an investigation into the case of a prisoner held in custody by a state on conviction of a criminal offense must take into consideration the entire course of proceedings in the courts of the state, and not merely a single step in those proceedings; and that it is incumbent upon the prisoner to set forth in his application a sworn statement of the facts concerning his detention and by virtue of what claim or authority he is detained—we proceed to consider the questions presented.

1. And first, the question of the disorder and hostile sentiment that are said to have influenced the trial court and jury to an extent amounting to mob domination.

The district court having considered the case upon the face of the petition, we must do the same, treating it as if demurred to by the sheriff. There is no doubt of the jurisdiction to issue the writ of habeas corpus. The question is as to the propriety of issuing it in the present case. Under § 755, Rev.Stat., it was the duty of the court to refuse the writ if it appeared from the petition itself that appellant was not entitled to it. *And see 28 U. S.* 3 Pet. 193, 28 U. S. 201; *Ex parte Milligan,* 4 Wall. 2, 71 U. S. 110; *Ex parte Terry,* 128 U. S. 289, 128 U. S. 301.

Now the obligation resting upon us, as upon the district

court, to look through the form and into the very heart and substance of the matter applies as well to the averments of the petition as to the proceedings which the petitioner attacks. We must regard not any single clause or paragraph, but the entire petition, and the exhibits that are made a part of it. Thus, the petition contains a narrative of disorder, hostile manifestations, and uproar which, if it stood alone and were to be taken as true, may be conceded to show an environment inconsistent with a fair trial and an impartial verdict. But to consider this as standing alone is to take a wholly superficial view. The narrative has no proper place in a petition addressed to a court of the United States except as it may tend to throw light upon the question whether the state of Georgia, having regard to the entire course of the proceedings, in the appellate as well as in the trial court, is depriving appellant of his liberty and intending to deprive him of his life without due process of law. Dealing with the narrative, then, in its essence and in its relation to the context, it is clearly appears to be only a reiteration of allegations that appellant had a right to submit, and did submit, first to the trial court and afterwards to the Supreme Court of the state, as a ground for avoiding the consequences of the trial; that the allegations were considered by those courts, successively, at times and places and under circumstances wholly apart from the atmosphere of the trial, and free from any suggestion of mob domination or the like; and that the facts were examined by those courts not only upon the affidavits and exhibits submitted in behalf of the prisoner which are embodied in his present petition as a part of his sworn account of the causes of his detention, but also upon rebutting affidavits submitted in behalf of the state, and which, for reasons not explained, he has not included in the petition. As appears from the prefatory statement, the allegations of disorder were found by both of the state courts to be groundless except in a few particulars as to which the courts ruled that they were irregularities not harmful in fact to defendant, and therefore insufficient in law to avoid the verdict. 141 Georgia 243, 280. And it was because the defendant was concluded by that finding that the Supreme Court, upon the subsequent motion to set aside the verdict, declined to again consider those allegations. 83 S.E.Rep. 645, 655.

Whatever question is raised about the jurisdiction of the trial court, no doubt is suggested but that the Supreme Court had full jurisdiction to determine the matters of fact and the questions of law arising out of this alleged disorder; nor is there any reason to suppose that it did not fairly and justly perform its duty. It is not easy to see why appellant is not, upon general principles, bound by its decision. It is a fundamental principle of jurisprudence, arising from the very nature of courts of justice and the objects for which they are established, that a question of fact or of law distinctly put in issue and directly determined by a court of competent jurisdiction cannot afterwards be disputed between the same parties. *Southern Pacific Railroad Co. v. United States,* 168 U. S. 1, 168 U. S. 48. The principle is as applicable to the decisions of criminal courts as to those of civil jurisdiction. As to its application, in habeas corpus cases, with respect to decisions by such courts of the facts pertaining to the jurisdiction over the prisoner, *see Ex parte Terry,* 128 U. S. 289, 128 U. S. 305, 128 U. S. 310; *Ex parte Columbia George,* 144 Fed. 985, 986.

However, it is not necessary, for the purposes of the present case, to invoke the doctrine of *res judicata;* and, in view of the impropriety of limiting in the least degree the authority of the courts of the United States in investigating an alleged violation by a state of the due process of law guaranteed by the Fourteenth Amendment, we put out of view for the present the suggestion that even the questions of fact bearing upon the jurisdiction of the trial court could be conclusively determined against the prisoner by the decision of the state court of last resort.

But this does not mean that that decision may be ignored or disregarded. To do this, as we have already pointed out, would be not merely to disregard comity, but to ignore the essential question before us, which is not the guilt or innocence of the prisoner, or the truth of any particular fact asserted by him, but whether the state, taking into view the entire course of its procedure, has deprived him of due process of law. This familiar phrase does not mean that the operations of the state government shall be conducted without error or fault in any particular case, nor that the Federal courts may substitute their judgment for that of the state courts, or exercise any general review over their proceedings, but only that the fundamental rights of the prisoner shall not be taken from him arbitrarily or without the right to be heard according to the usual course of law in such cases.

We, of course, agree that, if a trial is in fact dominated by a mob, so that the jury is intimidated and the trial judge yields, and so that there is an actual interference

with the course of justice, there is, in that court, a departure from due process of law in the proper sense of that term. And if the state, supplying no corrective process, carries into execution a judgment of death or imprisonment based upon a verdict thus produced by mob domination, the state deprives the accused of his life or liberty without due process of law.

But the state may supply such corrective process as to it seems proper. Georgia has adopted the familiar procedure of a motion for a new trial, followed by an appeal to its Supreme Court, not confined to the mere record of conviction, but going at large, and upon evidence adduced outside of that record, into the question whether the processes of justice have been interfered with in the trial court. Repeated instances are reported of verdicts and judgments set aside and new trials granted for disorder or mob violence interfering with the prisoner's right to a fair trial. *Myers v. State,* 97 Georgia 76 (5), 99; *Collier v. State,* 115 Georgia 803.

Such an appeal was accorded to the prisoner in the present case [*Frank v. State,* 141 Georgia 243 (16), 280], in a manner and under circumstances already stated, and the Supreme Court, upon a full review, decided appellant's allegations of fact, so far as matters now material are concerned, to be unfounded. Owing to considerations already adverted to (arising not out of comity merely, but out of the very right of the matter to be decided, in view of the relations existing between the states and the Federal government), we hold that such a determination of the facts as was thus made by the court of last resort of Georgia respecting the alleged interference with the trial through disorder and manifestations of hostile sentiment cannot, in this collateral inquiry, be treated as a nullity, but must be taken as setting forth the truth of the matter; certainly, until some reasonable ground is shown for an inference that the court which rendered it either was wanting in jurisdiction or at least erred in the exercise of its jurisdiction, and that the mere assertion by the prisoner that the facts of the matter are other than the state court, upon full investigation, determined them to be, will not be deemed sufficient to raise an issue respecting the correctness of that determination; especially not, where the very evidence upon which the determination was rested in withheld by him who attacks the finding.

It is argued that if, in fact, there was disorder such as to cause a loss of jurisdiction in the trial court, jurisdiction could not be restored by any decision of the Supreme Court. This, we think, embodies more than one error of reasoning. It regards a part only of the judicial proceedings, instead of considering the entire process of law. It also begs the question of the existence of such disorder as to cause a loss of jurisdiction in the trial court, which should not be assumed, in the face of the decision of the reviewing court, without showing some adequate ground for disregarding that decision. And these errors grow out of the initial error of treating appellant's narrative of disorder as the whole matter, instead of reading it in connection with the context. The rule of law that in ordinary cases requires a prisoner to exhaust his remedies within the state before coming to the courts of the United States for redress would lose the greater part of its salutary force if the prisoner's mere allegations were to stand the same in law after as before the state courts had passed judgment upon them.

We are very far from intimating that manifestations of public sentiment, or any other form of disorder, calculated to influence court or jury, are matters to be lightly treated. The decisions of the Georgia courts in this and other cases show that such disorder is repressed, where practicable, by the direct intervention of the trial court and the officers under its command, and that other means familiar to the common law practice, such as postponing the trial, changing the venue, and granting a new trial, are liberally resorted to in order to protect persons accused of crime in the right to a fair trial by an impartial jury. The argument for appellant amounts to saying that this is not enough; that, by force of the "due process of law" provision of the Fourteenth Amendment, when the first attempt at a fair trial is rendered abortive through outside interference, the state, instead of allowing a new trial under better auspices, must abandon jurisdiction over the accused, and refrain from further inquiry into the question of his guilt.

To establish this doctrine would, in a very practical sense, impair the power of the states to repress and punish crime, for it would render their courts powerless to act in opposition to lawless public sentiment. The argument is not only unsound in principle, but is in conflict with the practice that prevails in all of the states, so far as we are aware. The cases cited do not sustain the contention that disorder or other lawless conduct calculated to overawe the jury or the trial

judge can be treated as a dissolution of the court, or as rendering the proceedings *coram non judice*, in any such sense as to bar further proceedings. In *Myers v. State*, 97 Georgia 76, (5), 99; *Collier v. State*, 115 Georgia 803; *Sanders v. State*, 85 Ind. 318; *Massey v. State*, 31 Tex.Cr.Rep. 371, 381, S.C., 20 S.W. 758; and *State v. Weldon*, 91 S. C. 29, 38—in all of which it was held that the prisoner's right to a fair trial had been interfered with by disorder or mob violence—it was not held that jurisdiction over the prisoner had been lost; on the contrary, in each instance, a new trial was awarded as the appropriate remedy. So, in the cases where the trial judge abdicated his proper functions or absented himself during the trial (*Hayes v. State*, 58 Georgia 36 (12), 49; *Blend v. People*, 41 N.Y. 604; *Shaw v. People*, 3 Hun, 272, *aff'd*, 63 N.Y. 36; *Hinman v. People*, 13 Hun, 266; *McClure v. State*, 77 Ind. 287; *O'Brien v. People*, 17 Colorado 561; *Ellerbe v. State*, 75 Miss. 522) the reviewing court of the state in each instance simply set aside the verdict and awarded a new trial.

The Georgia courts, in the present case, proceeded upon the theory that Frank would have been entitled to this relief had his charges been true, and they refused a new trial only because they found his charges untrue save in a few minor particulars not amounting to more than irregularities, and not prejudicial to the accused. There was here no denial of due process of law.

2. We come, next, to consider the effect to be given to the fact, admitted for present purposes, that Frank was not present in the courtroom when the verdict was rendered, his presence having been waived by his counsel, but without his knowledge or consent. No question is made but that, at the common law and under the Georgia decisions, it is the right of the prisoner to be present throughout the entire trial, from the commencement of the selection of the jury until the verdict is rendered and jury discharged. *Wade v. State*, 12 Georgia 25, 29; *Martin v. State*, 51 Georgia 567; *Nolan v. State*, 53 Georgia 137, S.C., 55 Georgia 521; *Smith v. State*, 59 Georgia 513; Bonner v. State, *67 Georgia 510;* Barton v. State, *67 Georgia 653;* Cawthon v. State, 119 Georgia 395, 412; *Bagwell v. State*, 129 Georgia 170; *Lyons v. State*, 7 Georgia App. 50. But the effect of these decisions is that the prisoner may personally waive the right to be present when the verdict is rendered, and perhaps may waive it by authorized act of his counsel; and that where, without his consent, the verdict is received in his absence, he may treat this

as an error, and by timely motion demand a new trial, or (it seems) he may elect to treat the verdict as a nullity by moving in due season to set it aside as such. But we are unable to find that the courts of Georgia have in any case held that, by receiving a verdict in the absence of the prisoner and without his consent, the jurisdiction of the trial court was terminated. In the *Nolan* case, *supra,* the verdict was set aside as void on the ground of the absence of the prisoner; but this was not held to deprive the trial court of its jurisdiction. On the contrary, the jurisdiction was treated as remaining, and that court proceeded to exercise it by arraigning the prisoner a second time upon the same indictment, when he pleaded specially, claiming his discharge because of former jeopardy; the trial court overruled this plea, the defendant excepted, and the jury found the defendant guilty; and, upon review, the Supreme Court reversed this judgment not for the want of jurisdiction in the trial court, but for error committed in the exercise of jurisdiction. To the same effect is *Bagwell v. State,* 129 Georgia 170.

In most of the other states, where error is committed by receiving a verdict of guilty during the involuntary absence of the accused, it is treated as merely requiring a new trial. In a few cases, the appellate court has ordered the defendant to be discharged upon the ground that he had been once in jeopardy and a new trial would be futile.

However, the Georgia Supreme Court in the present case (83 S.E.Rep. 645) held, as pointed out in the prefatory statement, that because Frank, shortly after the verdict, was made fully aware of the facts, and he then made a motion for a new trial upon over 100 grounds, without including this as one, and had the motion heard by both the trial court and the Supreme Court, he could not, after this motion had been finally adjudicated against him, move to set aside the verdict as a nullity because of his absence when the verdict was rendered. There is nothing in the Fourteenth Amendment to prevent a state from adopting and enforcing so reasonable a regulation of procedure. *Dreyer v. Illinois,* 187 U. S. 71, 187 U. S. 77-80.

It is insisted that the enforced absence of Frank at that time was not only a deprivation of trial by jury, but was equally a deprivation of due process of law within the meaning of the Amendment, in that it took from him at a critical stage of the proceeding the right or oppor-

tunity to be heard. But repeated decisions of this Court have put it beyond the range of further debate that the "due process" clause of the Fourteenth Amendment has not the effect of imposing upon the states any particular form or mode of procedure, so long as the essential rights of notice and a hearing, or opportunity to be heard, before a competent tribunal, are not interfered with. Indictment by grand jury is not essential to due process (*Hurtado v. California,* 110 U. S. 516, 110 U. S. 532, 110 U. S. 538; *Lem Woon v. Oregon,* 229 U. S. 586, 229 U. S. 589, and cases cited). Trial by jury is not essential to it, either in civil cases (*Walker v. Sauvinet,* 92 U. S. 90), or in criminal (*Hallinger v. Davis,* 146 U. S. 314, 146 U. S. 324; *Maxwell v. Dow,* 176 U. S. 581, 176 U. S. 594, 176 U. S. 602, 176 U. S. 604).

It is argued that a state may not, while providing for trial by jury, permit the accused to waive the right to be heard in the mode characteristic of such trial, including the presence of the prisoner up to and at the time of the rendition of the verdict. But the cases cited do not support this contention. In *Hopt v. Utah,* 110 U. S. 574, 110 U. S. 578 (principally relied upon), the court had under review a conviction in a territorial court after a trial subject to the local Code of Criminal Procedure, which declared: "If the indictment is for a felony, the defendant must be personally present at the trial." The judgment was reversed because of the action of the trial court in permitting certain challenges to jurors, based upon the ground of bias, to be tried out of the presence of the court, the defendant, and his counsel. The ground of the decision of this Court was the violation of the plan mandate of the local statute; and the power of the accused or his counsel to dispense with the requirement as to his personal presence was denied on the ground that his life could not be lawfully taken except in the mode prescribed by law. No other question was involved. *See Diaz v. United States,* 223 U. S. 442, 223 U. S. 455, 223 U. S. 458.

The distinction between what the common law requires with respect to trial by jury in criminal cases and what the states may enact without contravening the "due process" clause of the Fourteenth Amendment is very clearly evidenced by *Hallinger v. Davis,* 146 U. S. 314, and *Lewis v. United States,* 146 U. S. 370, which were under consideration by the court at the same time, both opinions being written by Mr. Justice Shiras. In the *Lewis* case, which was a conviction of murder in a circuit court of the United States, the trial practice being regulated by the common law, it was held to be a leading principle, pervading the entire law of criminal procedure, that after indictment nothing should be done in the absence of the prisoner; that the making of challenges is an essential part of the trial, and it was one of the substantial rights of the prisoner to be brought face to face with the jurors at the time the challenges were made; and that in the absence of a statute, this right as it existed at common law must not be abridged. But in the *Hallinger* case, where a state by legislative enactment had permitted one charged with a capital offense to waive a trial by jury and elect to be tried by the court, it was held that this method of procedure did not conflict with the Fourteenth Amendment. So, in *Howard v. Kentucky,* 200 U. S. 164, 200 U. S. 175—a case closely in point upon the question now presented—this Court, finding that by the law of the state an occasional absence of the accused from the trial, from which no injury resulted to his substantial rights, was not deemed material error, held that the application of this rule of law did not amount to a denial of due process within the meaning of the Fourteenth Amendment.

In fact, this Court has sustained the states in establishing a great variety of departures from the common law procedure respecting jury trials. Thus, in *Brown v. New Jersey,* 175 U. S. 172, 175 U. S. 176, a statute providing for the trial of murder cases by struck jury was sustained notwithstanding it did not provide for twenty peremptory challenges. *Simon v. Craft,* 182 U. S. 427, 182 U. S. 435, while not a criminal case, involved the property of a person alleged to be of unsound mind, and it was held that an Alabama statute, under which the sheriff determined that Mrs. Simon's health and safety would be endangered by her presence at the trial of the question of her sanity, so that while served with notice she was detained in custody and not allowed to be present at the hearing of the inquisition, did not deprive her of property without due process of law. In *Felts v. Murphy,* 201 U. S. 123, 201 U. S. 129, where the prisoner was convicted of the crime of murder, and sentenced to imprisonment for life, although he did not hear a word of the evidence given upon the trial because of his almost total deafness, his inability to hear being such that it required a person to speak through an ear trumpet close to his ear in order that such person should be heard by him, and the trial court having failed to see to it that the testimony in the case was repeated to

him through his ear trumpet, this Court said that this was, "at most, an error which did not take away from the court its jurisdiction over the subject matter and over the person accused." In *Twining v. New Jersey,* 211 U. S. 78, 211 U. S. 101, 211 U. S. 111, it was held that the exemption of a prisoner from compulsory self-incrimination in the state courts was not included in the guaranty of due process of law contained in the Fourteenth Amendment. In *Jordan v. Massachusetts,* 225 U. S. 167, 225 U. S. 177, where one of the jurors was subject to reasonable doubt as to his sanity, and the state court, pursuant to the local law of criminal procedure, determined upon a mere preponderance of the evidence that he was sane, the conviction was affirmed. In *Garland v. Washington,* 232 U. S. 642, 232 U. S. 645, it was held that the want of a formal arraignment, treated by the state as depriving the accused of no substantial right, and as having been waived, and thereby lost, did not amount to depriving defendant of his liberty without due process of law.

Our conclusion upon this branch of the case is that the practice established in the criminal courts of Georgia that a defendant may waive his right to be present when the jury renders its verdict, and that such waiver may be given after as well as before the event, and is to be inferred from the making of a motion for new trial upon other grounds alone, when the facts respecting the reception of the verdict are within the prisoner's knowledge at the time of making that motion, is a regulation of criminal procedure that it is within the authority of the state to adopt. In adopting it, the state declares, in effect, as it reasonably may declare, that the right of the accused to be present at the reception of the verdict is but an incident of the right of trial by jury; and since the state may, without infringing the Fourteenth Amendment, abolish trial by jury, it may limit the effect to be given to an error respecting one of the incidents of such trial. The presence of the prisoner when the verdict is rendered is not so essential a part of the hearing that a rule of practice permitting the accused to waive it, and holding him bound by the waiver, amounts to a deprivation of "due process of law."

3. The insistence that the decision of the Supreme Court of Georgia in affirming the denial of the motion to set aside the verdict (83 S.E.Rep. 645) on the ground that Frank's failure to raise the objection upon the motion for a new trial amounted to a waiver of it was inconsistent with the previous practice as established

in *Nolan v. State,* 53 Georgia 137, S.C., 55 Georgia 521, 21 Am. Rep. 281, 1 Am. Crim. Rep. 532, and therefore amounted in effect to an *ex post facto* law in contravention of § 10 of article 1 of the Federal Constitution, needs but a word. Assuming the inconsistency, it is sufficient to say that the constitutional prohibition: "No state shall . . . pass any bill of attainder, *ex post facto* law, or law impairing the obligation of contracts," as its terms indicate, is directed against legislative action only, and does not reach erroneous or inconsistent decisions by the courts. *Calder v. Bull,* 3 Dall. 386, 3 U. S. 389; *Fletcher v. Peck,* 6 Cranch 87; *Kring v. Missouri,* 107 U. S. 221, 107 U. S. 227; *Thompson v. Utah,* 170 U. S. 343, 170 U. S. 351; *Cross Lake Shooting & Fishing Club v. Louisiana,* 224 U. S. 632, 224 U. S. 638; *Ross v. Oregon,* 227 U. S. 150, 227 U. S. 161.

4. To conclude: taking appellant's petition as a whole, and not regarding any particular portion of it to the exclusion of the rest—dealing with its true and substantial meaning, and not merely with its superficial import—it shows that Frank, having been formally accused of a grave crime, was placed on trial before a court of competent jurisdiction, with a jury lawfully constituted; he had a public trial, deliberately conducted, with the benefit of counsel for his defense; he was found guilty and sentenced pursuant to the laws of the state; twice he has moved the trial court to grant a new trial, and once to set aside the verdict as a nullity; three times he has been heard upon appeal before the court of last resort of that state, and in every instance the adverse action of the trial court has been affirmed; his allegations of hostile public sentiment and disorder in and about the courtroom, improperly influencing the trial court and the jury against him, have been rejected because found untrue in point of fact upon evidence presumably justifying that finding, and which he has not produced in the present proceeding; his contention that his lawful rights were infringed because he was not permitted to be present when the jury rendered its verdict has been set aside because it was waived by his failure to raise the objection in due season when fully cognizant of the facts. In all of these proceedings, the state, through its courts, has retained jurisdiction over him, has accorded to him the fullest right and opportunity to be heard according to the established modes of procedure, and now holds him in custody to pay the penalty of the crime of which he has been adjudged guilty. In our opinion, he is not shown to have been deprived of any right guaranteed to

him by the Fourteenth Amendment or any other provision of the Constitution or laws of the United States; on the contrary, he has been convicted, and is now held in custody, under "due process of law" within the meaning of the Constitution.

The final order of the District Court, refusing the application for a writ of habeas corpus, is

Affirmed.

MR. JUSTICE HOLMES, dissenting

Mr. Justice Hughes and I are of opinion that the judgment should be reversed. The only question before us is whether the petition shows on its face that the writ of habeas corpus should be denied, or whether the district court should have proceeded to try the facts. The allegations that appear to us material are these: the trial began on July 28, 1913, at Atlanta, and was carried on in a court packed with spectators and surrounded by a crowd outside, all strongly hostile to the petitioner. On Saturday, August 23, this hostility was sufficient to lead the judge to confer in the presence of the jury with the chief of police of Atlanta and the colonel of the Fifth Georgia Regiment, stationed in that city, both of whom were known to the jury. On the same day, the evidence seemingly having been closed, the public press, apprehending danger, united in a request to the court that the proceedings should not continue on that evening. Thereupon, the court adjourned until Monday morning. On that morning, when the solicitor general entered the court, he was greeted with applause, stamping of feet and clapping of hands, and the judge, before beginning his charge, had a private conversation with the petitioner's counsel in which he expressed the opinion that there would be "probable danger of violence" if there should be an acquittal or a disagreement, and that it would be safer for not only the petitioner but his counsel to be absent from court when the verdict was brought in. At the judge's request, they agreed that the petitioner and they should be absent, and they kept their word. When the verdict was rendered, and before more than one of the jurymen had been polled, there was such a roar of applause that the polling could not go on until order was restored. The noise outside was such that it was difficult for the judge to hear the answers of the jurors, although he was only 10 feet from them. With these specifications of fact, the petitioner alleges that the trial was dominated by a hostile mob, and was nothing but an empty form.

We lay on one side the question whether the petitioner could or did waive his right to be present at the polling of the jury. That question was apparent in the form of the trial, and was raised by the application for a writ of error; and although, after the application to the full Court, we thought that the writ ought to be granted, we never have been impressed by the argument that the presence of the prisoner was required by the Constitution of the United States. But habeas corpus cuts through all forms and goes to the very tissue of the structure. It comes in from the outside, not in subordination to the proceedings, and, although every form may have been preserved, opens the inquiry whether they have been more than an empty shell. The argument for the appellee, in substance, is that the trial was in a court of competent jurisdiction, that it retains jurisdiction although, in fact, it may be dominated by a mob, and that the rulings of the state court as to the fact of such domination cannot be reviewed. But the argument seems to us inconclusive. Whatever disagreement there may be as to the scope of the phrase "due process of law," there can be no doubt that it embraces the fundamental conception of a fair trial, with opportunity to be heard. Mob law does not become due process of law by securing the assent of a terrorized jury. We are not speaking of mere disorder, or mere irregularities in procedure, but of a case where the processes of justice are actually subverted. In such a case, the Federal court has jurisdiction to issue the writ. The fact that the state court still has its general jurisdiction and is otherwise a competent court does not make it impossible to find that a jury has been subjected to intimidation in a particular case. The loss of jurisdiction is not general, but particular, and proceeds from the control of a hostile influence.

When such a case is presented, it cannot be said, in our view, that the state court decision makes the matter *res judicata*. The state acts when, by its agency, it finds the prisoner guilty and condemns him. We have held in a civil case that it is no defense to the assertion of the Federal right in the Federal court that the state has corrective procedure of its own—that still less does such procedure draw to itself the final determination of the Federal question. *Simon v. Southern Ry. Co.,* 236 U. S. 115, 236 U. S. 122-123. We see no reason for a less liberal rule in a matter of life and death. When the de-

cision of the question of fact is so interwoven with the decision of the question of constitutional right that the one necessarily involves the other, the Federal court must examine the facts. *Kansas City Southern Ry. Co. v. C. H. Albers Commission Co.,* 223 U. S. 573, 223 U. S. 591; *Norfolk & West. Ry. Co. v. Conley,* March 8, 1915, 236 U. S. 605. Otherwise, the right will be a barren one. It is significant that the argument for the state does not go so far as to say that in no case would it be permissible, on application for habeas corpus, to override the findings of fact by the state courts. It would indeed be a most serious thing if this Court were so to hold, for we could not but regard it as a removal of what is perhaps the most important guaranty of the Federal Constitution. If, however, the argument stops short of this, the whole structure built upon the state procedure and decisions falls to the ground.

To put an extreme case and show what we mean, if the trial and the later hearing before the Supreme Court had taken place in the presence of an armed force known to be ready to shoot if the result was not the one desired, we do not suppose that this Court would allow itself to be silenced by the suggestion that the record showed no flaw. To go one step further, suppose that the trial had taken place under such intimidation, and that the Supreme Court of the state, on writ of error, had discovered no error in the record, we still imagine that this Court would find a sufficient one outside of the record, and that it would not be disturbed in its conclusion by anything that the Supreme Court of the state might have said. We therefore lay the suggestion that the Supreme Court of the state has disposed of the present question by its judgment on one side, along with the question of the appellant's right to be present. If the petition discloses facts that amount to a loss of jurisdiction in the trial court, jurisdiction could not be restored by any decision above. And notwithstanding the principle of comity and convenience (for, in our opinion, it is nothing more, *United States v. Sing Tuck,* 194 U. S. 161, 194 U. S. 168) that calls for a resort to the local appellate tribunal before coming to the courts of the United States for a writ of habeas corpus, when, as here, that resort has been had in vain, the power to secure fundamental rights that had existed at every stage becomes a duty, and must be put forth.

The single question in our minds is whether a petition alleging that the trial took place in the midst of a mob savagely and manifestly intent on a single result is shown on its face unwarranted, by the specifications, which may be presumed to set forth the strongest indications of the fact at the petitioner's command. This is not a matter for polite presumptions; we must look facts in the face. Any judge who has sat with juries knows that, in spite of forms, they are extremely likely to be impregnated by the environing atmosphere. And when we find the judgment of the expert on the spot—of the judge whose business it was to preserve not only form, but substance—to have been that if one juryman yielded to the reasonable doubt that he himself later expressed in court as the result of most anxious deliberation, neither prisoner nor counsel would be safe from the rage of the crowd, we think the presumption overwhelming that the jury responded to the passions of the mob. Of course we are speaking only of the case made by the petition, and whether it ought to be heard. Upon allegations of this gravity, in our opinion, it ought to be heard, whatever the decision of the state court may have been, and it did not need to set forth contradictory evidence, or matter of rebuttal, or to explain why the motions for a new trial and to set aside the verdict were overruled by the state court. There is no reason to fear an impairment of the authority of the state to punish the guilty. We do not think it impracticable in any part of this country to have trials free from outside control. But, to maintain this immunity, it may be necessary that the supremacy of the law and of the Federal Constitution should be vindicated in a case like this. It may be that, on a hearing, a different complexion would be given to the judge's alleged request and expression of fear. But supposing the alleged facts to be true, we are of opinion that, if they were before the Supreme Court, it sanctioned a situation upon which the courts of the United States should act; and if, for any reason, they were not before the Supreme Court, it is our duty to act upon them now, and to declare lynch law as little valid when practised by a regularly drawn jury as when administered by one elected by a mob intent on death.

Glossary

due process: the constitutional requirement that when the federal government acts in such a way that denies a citizen of a life, liberty, or property interest, the person must be given notice, the opportunity to be heard, and a decision by a neutral decision-maker

habeas corpus: the presentation of a person in court; the requirement that a person under arrest be brought to a court or before a judge to determine whether the person should be detained or released

nullity: something that is legally invalid

writ: a legal order

GUINN V. UNITED STATES

DATE 1915	**CITATION** 238 U.S. 347
AUTHOR Edward White	**SIGNIFICANCE** Held that certain grandfather clauses that exempted literary tests for voting rights limited Black suffrage and were therefore unconstitutional
VOTE 8–0	

Overview

 In the 1915 Supreme Court case *Frank Guinn and J. J. Beal v. United States*, Chief Justice Edward White held that the grandfather clause, an amendment to Oklahoma's constitution, limited Black suffrage and was therefore invalid. The case also applied to Maryland's constitution, which had a similar clause. The grandfather clause worked in conjunction with a literacy test to deprive African Americans of the right to vote. The literacy test stipulated that all voters be able to read, but the grandfather clause lifted literacy test requirements for anyone who was otherwise qualified to vote anywhere in the United States on January 1, 1866. The clause was particularly galling to African Americans in Oklahoma, as that state had not even existed in 1866. The literacy test additionally discriminated against African Americans, since it was very subjective and was applied by white southern registrars.

The U.S. Supreme Court held that Oklahoma's grandfather clause was unconstitutional, because it violated the spirit of the Fifteenth Amendment, ratified in 1870, which granted former slaves the right to vote. The Court's ruling had little direct effect on the exten-

sion of voting rights to African Americans in Oklahoma, however: The state simply passed a new statute, disenfranchising all those who did not register to vote during a brief, two-week window in 1916, except those who had voted in 1914. Thus, all voting whites could still vote, but all of the previously disenfranchised Blacks were still disenfranchised, unless they had been able to work their way through the system in a two-week period.

Context

The *Guinn* case was one of the first major court cases in which the National Association for the Advancement of Colored People (NAACP) played a role, filing a brief, and represented one of the few times in the early twentieth century when the federal government appeared on the side of African Americans in a legal battle. *Guinn* was also one of the first challenges to discriminatory voting laws, which had been restricting voting rights to certain segments of American society for more than forty years. The first such laws appeared in the post–Civil War Reconstruction period. African

EDDIKAZHUN
QUALIFUKAZHUN.

TH2 BLAKMAN ORTER
BE EDDIKATED BEFORE
HE KIN VOTE WITH
US WITES.

MR. SOLID SOUTH

Cartoon criticizing literacy tests
(Library of Congress)

Americans and poor whites gained allies in the White House when the Republican Party—the party of Abraham Lincoln—took power in 1860; meanwhile, southern Democrats—supporters of segregationist policies at that time—vowed to wrest their power back using any and all means to achieve their ends. Despite the fact that the ratification of the Fifteenth Amendment to the U.S. Constitution in the spring of 1870 had granted all male citizens the right to vote regardless of race, color, or prior slave status, violence and threats of violence were often used and suggested by Democrats over the next decade to keep Republicans, particularly Black Republicans, from voting. As a result, all of the southern states had Democratic legislatures by the late 1870s.

Efforts continued in subsequent years to eliminate all African Americans and many poor whites from the voting ranks, leading to the growth of the Populist movement. This biracial groundswell stemmed from a financial crisis and labor unrest in the United States that resulted in the failure of businesses throughout the country, particularly many small farms in the South and the West. Channeling the anger of America's small farmers and other laborers who wanted reform, the Populist movement pushed for policy changes that would empower the nation's workers, both Black and white, and protect small businesses from corrupt corporate interests. Reform and Fusion tickets won often in the South (and the West) in the early 1890s. Fusion politics refers to the combined power of the Republican and Populist parties at the end of the nineteenth century. In response, wealthy whites interested in seeing a resurgence of the Democratic Party organized mobs to drive African Americans from the polls. Many states adopted constitutional amendments in the late 1890s and early 1900s designed specifically to disenfranchise Blacks and to limit the voting of poor whites. All of the previous restrictions on voting rights were retained and even more were added.

It was in the midst of this political clash that Oklahoma became the forty-sixth state in the Union in late 1907. The region came late into statehood, because much of its land had been set aside for Native American reservations until the 1890s. In 1910 Oklahoma adopted a constitutional amendment that tied the voting rights of its citizens to the successful completion of a literacy test. However, certain individuals—almost always whites—were able to circumvent the literacy test requirement because of an exception known as the grandfather clause, which guaranteed descendants of eligible voters the right to vote without question. The amendment used a date of January 1 of the year after the end of the Civil War as the date for which a voter was required to prove that an ancestor—presumably a grandfather—was qualified to vote. Prospective voters who were unable to satisfy the terms of the grandfather clause were forced to prove their literacy. Maryland's grandfather clause, tested also in the case of *Guinn v. United States*, was adopted in 1908, just a couple of years before Oklahoma's.

The grandfather clause had little effect on the right to vote for most whites, but it served as a barrier to the ballot box for African American voters. Freedmen and all men of color were not guaranteed the right to vote until the passage of the Fifteenth Amendment in 1870—four years after the date specified in the grandfather clause. The Oklahoma state government claimed that the clause did not discriminate against voters on the basis of their race; the term *race* was not even mentioned in the text. Clearly, however, the voting rights of African Americans, not whites, were most threatened by the terms of the statute. In fact, the grandfather clause and similar voting restrictions generally had loopholes to protect white voters. Typically, a person who owned property or paid sufficient taxes was considered exempt from the clause; because the rate of property ownership was higher among whites than Blacks, this exception adversely affected potential Black voters.

It should be noted, however, that the grandfather clause (and the literacy test used in Oklahoma) were not the only methods employed to disenfranchise Blacks. Among other techniques was the poll tax, an annual per-person fee that had to be paid before a ballot could be cast in any election. In effect, the poll tax added an economic dimension to the social inequities encountered by African Americans seeking to exercise their right to vote. At about a dollar per person, the tax placed a financial burden on a segment of the population with little or no money to spare. In addition to making the payment, voters were required to prove that they had paid the tax each year for as long as they had resided in the state; however, records and receipts for those members of the Black community who managed to pay the poll tax were often lost or never entered in official logs. Taken together, these provisions effectively denied the right of suffrage to African Americans in the South.

It was in this context that the case of *Guinn v. United States* came to the Supreme Court. Black citizens of Oklahoma had voiced complaints to the U.S. Justice Department concerning the enormous amount of racial violence surrounding the Oklahoma elections of 1910, which served to discourage Blacks from voting. In light of the brutal and discriminatory atmosphere of the elections, U.S. Attorney John Embry, along with fellow U.S. Attorney William R. Gregg, indicted two Oklahoma elections officials, J. J. Beal and Frank Guinn, on criminal charges of depriving people of their rights under the Constitution and federal law. Contrary to most expectations, the officials were convicted of civil rights violations on September 29, 1911—despite the fact that they had been enforcing an amendment to the Oklahoma state constitution. The two officials took the case to the U.S. Court of Appeals, claiming that they should not be prosecuted for upholding the law of their state. The Court of Appeals sent the case on to the Supreme Court in 1913, and it was decided on June 21, 1915.

About the Author

Chief Justice Edward Douglass White, Jr., was born November 3, 1845, in Louisiana and served in the Confederate army during the Civil War. After that service, he returned to his parents' sugarcane plantation and began to study law. Practicing in Louisiana after joining the bar in 1868, he briefly served in the state senate and then on the Louisiana Supreme Court before returning to his legal practice in 1880. In 1891, White was elected to the U.S. Senate; three years later he was appointed to the U.S. Supreme Court, and in 1910 he became the Court's chief justice. A southern Democrat, White was the second Catholic to serve as a Supreme Court justice.

Although White had sided with the majority in the 1896 case of *Plessy v. Ferguson*, which upheld segregation in public transportation and in general by establishing the "separate but equal" clause, he went on to author the *Guinn v. United States* decision in 1915. In 1917, White agreed with the majority in *Buchanan v. Warley*, a decision that held a residential segregation law in Louisville, Kentucky, illegal. The common thread between the latter two cases, and the difference between them and *Plessy*, is that the law in the cases of both *Buchanan* and *Guinn* directly and clearly discriminated against African Americans, whereas in *Plessy* the law was explained away by the majority as being unbiased on its face. After *Guinn*, White served as chief justice for another six years. He died on May 19, 1921.

Explanation and Analysis of the Document

At issue in the U.S. Supreme Court case of *Guinn v. United States* was whether grandfather clauses had been deliberately enacted by state governments to deny African Americans their right to vote. Two Oklahoma election officials, Frank Guinn and J. J. Beal, had been charged with violating federal law by conspiring to deprive Black Oklahomans of their voting rights in a general election held in 1910. Following the convictions of both men by a jury in an Oklahoma district court a year later, the *Guinn* case was brought before the Supreme Court on appeal in 1913. *Guinn v. United States* forced the highest court in the nation to examine the combined use of grandfather clauses and literacy tests as prerequisites to voting; specifically, the application of such tests in Oklahoma and Maryland was analyzed for fairness amid charges that Black voters had been subjected to racial discrimination at the ballot box.

Before voting, a Black voter had to prove his literacy to the satisfaction of a white registrar. Whites were generally exempt from the test by the grandfather clause, which waived the need for a voter to display his literacy if his grandfather had been eligible to vote in 1866. African American voters could not satisfy this requirement because suffrage had not yet been granted to freedmen in 1866. And so Blacks, at the discretion of a white registrar, might be asked to read a book in Greek or submit to a general knowledge test about a provision in either the state's constitution or the U.S. Constitution. In some southern states, general knowledge provisions were imposed by election officials, with registrars asking prospective voters such questions as "How many bubbles are there in a bar of soap?" The adequacy of a Black voter's response to such questions was determined solely by the registrar.

Before the text of Chief Justice Edward White's opinion in *Guinn v. United States* is a syllabus summarizing the key points of the lower court's decision. Justice White then quotes the laws backing up the Fifteenth Amendment, discusses the election officials' trial, reiterates the jury instructions given at that trial, and lays out the responsibility of the Supreme Court in the case: "Let us at once consider and sift the propositions of the United States, on the one hand, and of the plaintiffs in error, on the other, in order to reach with precision the real and final question to be considered." That question, according to White, boils down to whether or not the state amendment creating the grandfather clause was valid and whether the law itself was invalid because it violated the Fifteenth Amendment. White examines the arguments on each side of the case and ends with justifications for his conclusions.

Justice White's opinion begins by noting that two election officials were charged with violating the federal law by denying "certain negro citizens" the right to vote based on the color of their skin. The Thirteenth Amendment, passed in late 1865, had abolished slavery in the United States, but the South's refusal to guarantee basic human rights to emancipated slaves forced the adoption of the Fourteenth Amendment, granting citizenship to all freedmen. Abuses continued, however, and the Republican Party in the South was seriously weakened because its large African American voting base was being denied the right to vote on a variety of technicalities. The Fifteenth Amendment to the U.S. Constitution was designed to further safeguard the rights of newly freed slaves by removing obstacles to their voting. The chief justice quotes the language of the Fifteenth Amendment, which was ratified soon after the end of the Civil War: "The right of citizens of the United States to vote shall not be denied or abridged by the United States or by any State on account of race, color, or previous condition of servitude." Black suffrage seems to be spelled out quite clearly by the text of this amendment, but that was not the case. *Guinn v. United States* tested the power of the Fifteenth Amendment against the rights of states to establish their own standards for suffrage.

After stating the law, the Court then looks back at the claims of each side represented in the original case. Representing the United States was U.S. solicitor general John Davis, who appeared before the Court to challenge the Oklahoma amendment. Davis argued that Oklahoma's provision had the effect of denying the right to vote based on race and should be struck down as a violation of the Fifteenth Amendment, regardless of whether the law was explicitly in violation of that constitutional provision. The defense, however, argued for state sovereignty—not state sovereignty in terms of states being allowed to ignore the Fifteenth Amendment, but sovereignty in terms of their being able to set their own qualifications for voting. As the law in question did not specifically use race as a standard, the state contended that it should be allowed. The federal government, the defendants argued, should not be able to read a motive into the act or state that the effect of the law made an otherwise lawful act invalid. The defendants also claimed that the fact that no Blacks qualified to vote under the law was not due to the law but due to their inability to read. It should be noted that no defense was noted by the Supreme Court as to why a date of January 1, 1866, was picked if the point were not to force all Black voters to take the test.

The Supreme Court argues here that suffrage and qualifications put upon suffrage were state issues and that their position in this case did not limit that state power in any way. Of course, state regulations like this one that blatantly violated the Fifteenth Amendment were still being challenged, but otherwise the federal government left most decisions to the states alone. The Court then considers the literacy test, stating that it would not challenge the state's right to administer such a test. The only challenge was the use of the law to try to bypass the intended meaning of the Fifteenth Amendment.

Justice White continues his opinion with the enumeration of three key questions: Did the grandfather clause law violate the Fifteenth Amendment? Did the amendment, choosing January 1, 1866 as the date to use for the grandfather clause, mean what the government said it did? And would the striking down of the grandfather clause make the rest of the literacy test invalid? The rest of Justice White's opinion sought to answer to those questions.

The Court, in answering the first question, notes that the Fifteenth Amendment still allows room for the state to manage the business of voting; state-imposed literacy tests, then, remain lawful. It is important to evaluate this decision in the proper context: It embodies an era during which states wielded great power. The reach of the Fourteenth Amendment to prohibit racial bias at the state level was still very limited, and the use of the amendment to curtail the actions of state legislatures, unless they were directly and blatantly biased, did not occur for another three decades, when the Supreme Court decided *Shelley v. Kraemer* (1948), holding that courts could not enforce racially based private restrictive covenants.

In his explanation of what the Fifteenth Amendment says about suffrage, White holds that the state still has full power over suffrage qualifications, with the exception of those qualifications based on "race, color, or previous condition of servitude." He goes on to say that while no right to vote is directly created by the amendment, that right might still result when discriminatory rules are struck down by the amendment, which the Court held to be self-executing. White takes exception to the intent of Oklahoma's grandfather clause, pointing out that for a brief period of time prior to the adoption of the clause the hurdles to African American suffrage, while still present, were actually lower. According to White, there was no doubt that the statute had been adopted as an attempt to get around the Fifteenth Amendment. For that reason, the amendment to the Oklahoma constitution ran into direct conflict with the federal constitutional amendment.

Regarding the date the amendment to the Oklahoma Constitution was adopted, White again theorizes that the only possible reason for using the date of January 1, 1866, was to bypass the rights implied in the Fifteenth Amendment. Although the language of the grandfather clause does not refer to skin color or prior slave status, its clear purpose was to avoid granting suffrage to former slaves. As White puts it, the very use of that date shows a "direct and positive disregard of the 15th Amendment." The Court also considered whether anything had occurred in 1866 other than the granting of the right to vote to Blacks in some areas (and throughout the nation four years later with the passage of the Fifteenth Amendment) that would cause a state to return its voting status to a time prior to that date. In other words, the opinion states that there was no legal change to suffrage in 1866 other than granting slaves the right to vote. If the date had been based on some other, potentially more reasonable (in the eyes of the Court) state intention, the Court might still have considered the grandfather clause law valid. No such reason was found, however.

Finally the Court examined the literacy test, but not to determine whether it disparately affected African Americans, as that was not a concern of the court at the time. Actually, at this point in history, the Court also ignored laws that produced obvious disadvantages for Black voters, such as the white primary created in Texas and other states. There, the Democratic Party was by far the majority party, and so the primary to nominate party candidates was even more important than the election, in which candidates from the various parties squared off against each other. In other decisions, the Supreme Court allowed the Democratic Party to limit primary voting to whites and ignored the connection of the party to the state. It was not until 1944 that the white primary was finally struck down. Thus, the court's decision here to consider the literacy test in the abstract is not surprising.

In *Guinn v. United States*, the literacy test used in Oklahoma was directly intertwined with the state's grandfather clause, and so the question was whether the grandfather clause could be struck down while allowing the literacy test to still operate. Justice White states that, in general, the Court would rely on state court decisions in areas like this, but he also points out that no such decision had yet been made. He asks what the impact of the decision already announced—striking down the grandfather clause—would be on the literacy test. The Court holds that the statute contradicted itself once the grandfather clause was removed, as without the grandfather clause all people would be subjected to the literacy test, which was the exact opposite of the stated goal of the legislation. The stated goal of the legislation was to limit the number of people who had to take the literacy test, and the elimination of the grandfather clause would have once again forced everyone to take the literacy test. Thus, since the legislation, as necessarily amended by the Supreme Court decision, contradicted itself, it must be struck down as a whole, even though literacy tests generally would be allowed.

Literacy tests were used to deprive African Americans of their right to suffrage through the early 1960s, as were comprehension tests covering the federal and state constitutions. Employed unfairly and disproportionately against Blacks but rarely given to whites, these tests swayed the results of elections for decades. A half century after the 1915 decision in *Guinn v. United States*, the Voting Rights Act of 1965 did away with impediments to voting by allowing the federal government to appoint registrars in any state where a significant racial disparity in voting registration existed. After the passage of this law, millions more African Americans registered to vote. In 1915, though, such advances were still fifty years in the future.

At the end of his opinion, Justice White addresses an objection made by the defendants to the charge made against them in court. This argument basically states that since the charge had presumed that the suffrage amendment to the Oklahoma constitution was unconstitutional, it should be thrown out because it had presumed their guilt. However, the Supreme Court replies that since the Fifteenth Amendment was self-executing and clearly in conflict with the suffrage amendment to the Oklahoma constitution, the charge would be allowed. The final complaint was against a conspiracy statute under which the men were arrested. However, that same day the U.S. Supreme Court had upheld the same statute in another case dealing with Oklahoma—one concerning election officials who refused to count the votes cast by African Americans. The officials were convicted, and the conviction was upheld, which in turn meant that the statute was acceptable; therefore, the conviction of the defendants in the *Guinn* case was also upheld. It should be noted that the aforementioned cases involving Oklahoma election officials were rooted somewhat in political considerations. The Republican Party was losing political ground, so party officials pushed for the thorough investigation of alleged voting rights abuses. By the end of the nineteenth century, the Republican Party had practically died out throughout the South; the adoption of new constitutions by some southern states around 1900 compounded the party's woes and proved that their concern was not an idle one. Whether motivated by the fear of the party's demise or by a real concern for the rights of those not being allowed to vote, the Republican Party's escalation of suffrage cases to the U.S. Supreme Court was a necessary step in Black enfranchisement.

Impact

The decision in the case of *Guinn v. United States* had a limited impact on Black voting rights at the time it was handed down. Only a few states had such grandfather clauses, as most preferred to restrict African American suffrage more subtly. Even national leaders who supported segregation were opposed to these clauses owing to their deliberate disregard for the spirit of the law. The voters in Oklahoma were not affected by the decision; the Oklahoma state government simply adopted a law allowing all people who had voted in 1914 to vote again, along with whoever could survive a rigorous registration process that was open for only two weeks. Those states with literacy tests could breathe a sigh of relief as well, since the Supreme Court refused to challenge them directly and generally granted full rights to the state to create their own standards for suffrage, as long as they did not blatantly challenge the Fifteenth Amendment.

The more important effect was a long-term one, as the NAACP and others saw that they could win at the Supreme Court level and so continued to press cases to the highest court. *Guinn* also saw the first brief filed by the NAACP, which helped to validate the group's efforts. The NAACP would come to be the premier organization fighting for African Americans' rights through the court system.

Questions for Further Study

1. What is a grandfather clause as it pertains to voting rights, and how did grandfather clauses interfere with the voting rights of African Americans? What was particularly unfair about Oklahoma's grandfather clause?

2. What methods besides grandfather clauses were used to interfere with Black voting rights during this era and beyond?

3. On what basis did the U.S. Supreme Court find the Oklahoma statute in question unconstitutional?

4. What was the short-term effect of the Court's decision? What, if any, was the long-term effect?

5. What role, if any, did party politics play in the events surrounding *Guinn v. United States*. Consider not only the Republican and Democratic parties but the Populist Party as well.

Further Reading

Books

Kotz, Nick. *Judgment Days: Lyndon Baines Johnson, Martin Luther King, Jr., and the Laws That Changed America.* Boston: Houghton Mifflin, 2005.

Pratt, Walter F., Jr. *The Supreme Court under Edward Douglass White, 1910–1921.* Columbia: University of South Carolina Press, 1999.

Rush, Mark E., ed. *Voting Rights and Redistricting in the United States.* Westport, CT: Praeger, 1998.

Shoemaker, Rebecca S. *The White Court: Justices, Rulings, and Legacy.* Santa Barbara, CA: ABC-CLIO, 2004.

Valley, Richard M. *The Two Reconstructions: The Struggle for Black Enfranchisement.* Chicago: University of Chicago Press, 2004.

Zelden, Charles. *Voting Rights on Trial.* Indianapolis, IN: Hackett, 2004.

Websites

"Guinn v. United States (1915)." Black Past. Accessed March 1, 2023, https://www.blackpast.org/african-american-history/guinn-v-united-states-1915/.

"The Racial History of The 'Grandfather Clause'." NPR. Accessed March 1, 2023, https://www.npr.org/sections/codeswitch/2013/10/21/239081586/the-racial-history-of-the-grandfather-clause.

—Commentary by Scott A. Merriman

GUINN V. UNITED STATES

Document Text

Mr. Chief Justice White delivered the opinion of the Court

This case is before us on a certificate drawn by the court below as the basis of two questions which are submitted for our solution in order to enable the court correctly to decide issues in a case which it has under consideration. Those issues arose from an indictment and conviction of certain election officers of the State of Oklahoma (the plaintiffs in error) of the crime of having conspired unlawfully, willfully and fraudulently to deprive certain negro citizens, on account of their race and color, of a right to vote at a general election held in that State in 1910, they being entitled to vote under the state law and which right was secured to them by the Fifteenth Amendment to the Constitution of the United States. The prosecution was directly concerned with §5508, Rev. Stat., now §19 of the Penal Code which is as follows:

> If two or more persons conspire to injure, oppress, threaten, or intimidate any citizen in the free exercise or enjoyment of any right or privilege secured to him by the Constitution or laws of the United States, or because of his having so exercised the same, or if two or more persons go in disguise on the highway, or on the premises of another, with intent to prevent or hinder his free exercise or enjoyment of any right or privilege so secured, they shall be fined not more than five thousand dollars and imprisoned not more than ten years, and shall, moreover, be thereafter ineligible to any office or place of honor, profit, or trust created by the Constitution or laws of the United States.

We concentrate and state from the certificate only matters which we deem essential to dispose of the questions asked.

Suffrage in Oklahoma was regulated by §1, Article III of the Constitution under which the State was admitted into the Union. Shortly after the admission, there was submitted an amendment to the Constitution making a radical change in that article which was adopted prior to November 8, 1910. At an election for members of Congress which followed the adoption of this Amendment, certain election officers, in enforcing its provisions, refused to allow certain negro citizens to vote who were clearly entitled to vote under the provision of the Constitution under which the State was admitted, that is, before the amendment, and who, it is equally clear, were not entitled to vote under the provision of the suffrage amendment if that amendment governed. The persons so excluded based their claim of right to vote upon the original Constitution and upon the assertion that the suffrage amendment was void because in conflict with the prohibitions of the Fifteenth Amendment, and therefore afforded no basis for denying them the right guaranteed and protected by that Amendment. And upon the assumption that this claim was justified and that the election officers had violated the Fifteenth Amendment in denying the right to vote, this prosecution, as we have said, was commenced. At the trial, the court instructed that, by the Fifteenth Amendment, the States were prohibited from discriminating as to suffrage because of race, color, or previous condition of servitude, and that Congress, in pursuance of the authority which was conferred upon it by the very terms of the Amendment to enforce its provisions, had enacted the following (Rev. Stat., §2004):

All citizens of the United States who are otherwise qualified by law to vote at any election by the people of any State, Territory, district, ... municipality, ... or other territorial subdivision, shall be entitled and allowed to vote at all such elections, without distinction of race, color, or previous condition of servitude; any constitution, law, custom, usage, or regulation of any State or Territory, or by or under its authority to the contrary notwithstanding.

It then instructed as follows:

The State amendment which imposes the test of reading and writing any section of the State constitution as a condition to voting to persons not on or prior to January 1, 1866, entitled to vote under some form of government, or then resident in some foreign nation, or a lineal descendant of such person, is not valid, but you may consider it insofar as it was in good faith relied and acted upon by the defendants in ascertaining their intent and motive. If you believe from the evidence that the defendants formed a common design and cooperated in denying the colored voters of Union Township precinct, or any of them, entitled to vote, the privilege of voting, but this was due to a mistaken belief sincerely entertained by the defendants as to the qualifications of the voters—that is, if the motive actuating the defendants was honest, and they simply erred in the conception of their duty—then the criminal intent requisite to their guilt is wanting, and they cannot be convicted. On the other hand, if they knew or believed these colored persons were entitled to vote, and their purpose was to unfairly and fraudulently deny the right of suffrage to them, or any of them entitled thereto, on account of their race and color, then their purpose was a corrupt one, and they cannot be shielded by their official positions.

The questions which the court below asks are these:

"1. Was the amendment to the constitution of Oklahoma, heretofore set forth, valid?"

"2. Was that amendment void insofar as it attempted to debar from the right or privilege of voting for a qual-

ified candidate for a Member of Congress in Oklahoma, unless they were able to read and write any section of the constitution of Oklahoma, negro citizens of the United States who were otherwise qualified to vote for a qualified candidate for a Member of Congress in that State, but who were not, and none of whose lineal ancestors was entitled to vote under any form of government on January 1, 1866, or at any time prior thereto, because they were then slaves?"

As these questions obviously relate to the provisions concerning suffrage in the original constitution and the amendment to those provisions which forms the basis of the controversy, we state the text of both. The original clause, so far as material, was this:

"The qualified electors of the State shall be male citizens of the United States, male citizens of the State, and male persons of Indian descent native of the United States, who are over the age of twenty-one years, who have resided in the State one year, in the county six months, and in the election precinct thirty days, next preceding the election at which any such elector offers to vote."

And this is the amendment:

No person shall be registered as an elector of this State or be allowed to vote in any election herein, unless he be able to read and write any section of the constitution of the State of Oklahoma; but no person who was, on January 1, 1866, or at any time prior thereto, entitled to vote under any form of government, or who at that time resided in some foreign nation, and no lineal descendant of such person, shall be denied the right to register and vote because of his inability to so read and write sections of such constitution. Precinct election inspectors having in charge the registration of electors shall enforce the provisions of this section at the time of registration, provided registration be required. Should registration be dispensed with, the provisions of this section shall be enforced by the precinct election officer when electors apply for ballots to vote.

Considering the questions in the right of the text of the suffrage amendment, it is apparent that they are two-fold, because of the two-fold character of the provisions as to suffrage which the amendment contains. The first question is concerned with that provision of the amendment which fixes a standard by which the right to vote is given upon conditions existing on January 1, 1866, and relieves those coming within that standard from the standard based on a literacy test which is established by the other provision of the amendment. The second question asks as to the validity of the literacy test and how far, if intrinsically valid, it would continue to exist and be operative in the event the standard based upon January 1, 1866, should be held to be illegal as violative of the Fifteenth Amendment.

To avoid that which is unnecessary, let us at once consider and sift the propositions of the United States, on the one hand, and of the plaintiffs in error, on the other, in order to reach with precision the real and final question to be considered. The United States insists that the provision of the amendment which fixes a standard based upon January 1, 1866, is repugnant to the prohibitions of the Fifteenth Amendment because, in substance and effect, that provision, if not an express, is certainly an open, repudiation of the Fifteenth Amendment, and hence the provision in question was stricken with nullity in its inception by the self-operative force of the Amendment, and, as the result of the same power, was at all subsequent times devoid of any vitality whatever.

For the plaintiffs in error, on the other hand, it is said the States have the power to fix standards for suffrage, and that power was not taken away by the Fifteenth Amendment, but only limited to the extent of the prohibitions which that Amendment established. This being true, as the standard fixed does not in terms make any discrimination on account of race, color, or previous condition of servitude, since all, whether negro or white, who come within its requirements enjoy the privilege of voting, there is no ground upon which to rest the contention that the provision violates the Fifteenth Amendment. This, it is insisted, must be the case unless it is intended to expressly deny the State's right to provide a standard for suffrage, or, what is equivalent thereto, to assert: a, that the judgment of the State exercised in the exertion of that power is subject to Federal judicial review or supervision, or b, that it may be questioned and be brought within the prohibitions of the Amendment by attributing to the legislative authority an occult motive to violate the Amendment or by as-

suming that an exercise of the otherwise lawful power may be invalidated because of conclusions concerning its operation in practical execution and resulting discrimination arising therefrom, albeit such discrimination was not expressed in the standard fixed or fairly to be implied, but simply arose from inequalities naturally inhering in those who must come within the standard in order to enjoy the right to vote.

On the other hand, the United States denies the relevancy of these contentions. It says state power to provide for suffrage is not disputed, although, of course, the authority of the Fifteenth Amendment and the limit on that power which it imposes is insisted upon. Hence, no assertion denying the right of a State to exert judgment and discretion in fixing the qualification of suffrage is advanced, and no right to question the motive of the State in establishing a standard as to such subjects under such circumstances or to review or supervise the same is relied upon, and no power to destroy an otherwise valid exertion of authority upon the mere ultimate operation of the power exercised is asserted. And, applying these principles to the very case in hand, the argument of the Government, in substance, says: no question is raised by the Government concerning the validity of the literacy test provided for in the amendment under consideration as an independent standard, since the conclusion is plain that that test rests on the exercise of state judgment, and therefore cannot be here assailed either by disregarding the State's power to judge on the subject or by testing its motive in enacting the provision. The real question involved, so the argument of the Government insists, is the repugnancy of the standard which the amendment makes, based upon the conditions existing on January 1, 1866, because, on its face and inherently, considering the substance of things, that standard is a mere denial of the restrictions imposed by the prohibitions of the Fifteenth Amendment, and by necessary result, recreates and perpetuates the very conditions which the Amendment was intended to destroy. From this, it is urged that no legitimate discretion could have entered into the fixing of such standard which involved only the determination to directly set at naught or by indirection avoid the commands of the Amendment. And it is insisted that nothing contrary to these propositions is involved in the contention of the Government that, if the standard which the suffrage amendment fixes based upon the conditions existing on January 1, 1866, be found to be void for the reasons urged, the other and literacy test is also void, since that contention rests not upon any assertion on the part of the Government of any abstract repugnancy of the literacy test to the prohibitions of the Fifteenth Amendment, but upon the relation between that test and the other as formulated in the suffrage amendment, and the inevitable result which it is deemed must follow from holding it to be void if the other is so declared to be.

Looking comprehensively at these contentions of the parties, it plainly results that the conflict between them is much narrower than it would seem to be because the premise which the arguments of the plaintiffs in error attribute to the propositions of the United States is by it denied. On the very face of things, it is clear that the United States disclaims the gloss put upon its contentions by limiting them to the propositions which we have hitherto pointed out, since it rests the contentions which it makes as to the assailed provision of the suffrage amendment solely upon the ground that it involves an unmistakable, although it may be a somewhat disguised, refusal to give effect to the prohibitions of the Fifteenth Amendment by creating a standard which it is repeated, but calls to life the very conditions which that Amendment was adopted to destroy and which it had destroyed.

The questions then are: (1) giving to the propositions of the Government the interpretation which the Government puts upon them and assuming that the suffrage provision has the significance which the Government assumes it to have, is that provision, as a matter of law, repugnant to the Fifteenth Amendment? which leads us, of course, to consider the operation and effect of the Fifteenth Amendment. (2) If yes, has the assailed amendment, insofar as it fixes a standard for voting as of January 1, 1866, the meaning which the Government attributes to it? which leads us to analyze and interpret that provision of the amendment. (3) If the investigation as to the two prior subjects establishes that the standard fixed as of January 1, 1866, is void, what, if any, effect does that conclusion have upon the literacy standard otherwise established by the amendment? which involves determining whether that standard, if legal, may survive the recognition of the fact that the other or 1866 standard has not, and never had, any legal existence. Let us consider these subjects under separate headings.

1. The operation and effect of the Fifteenth Amendment. This is its text:

"Section 1. The right of citizens of the United States to vote shall not be denied or abridged by the United States or by any State on account of race, color, or previous condition of servitude."

"Section 2. The Congress shall have power to enforce this article by appropriate legislation."

(a) Beyond doubt, the Amendment does not take away from the state governments in a general sense the power over suffrage which has belonged to those governments from the beginning, and without the possession of which power the whole fabric upon which the division of state and national authority under the Constitution and the organization of both governments rest would be without support and both the authority of the nation and the State would fall to the ground. In fact, the very command of the Amendment recognizes the possession of the general power by the State, since the Amendment seeks to regulate its exercise as to the particular subject with which it deals.

(b) But it is equally beyond the possibility of question that the Amendment, in express terms, restricts the power of the United States or the States to abridge or deny the right of a citizen of the United States to vote on account of race, color or previous condition of servitude. The restriction is coincident with the power, and prevents its exertion in disregard of the command of the Amendment.

But, while this is true, it is true also that the Amendment does not change, modify or deprive the States of their full power as to suffrage except, of course, as to the subject with which the Amendment deals and to the extent that obedience to its command is necessary. Thus, the authority over suffrage which the States possess and the limitation which the Amendment imposes are coordinate, and one may not destroy the other without bringing about the destruction of both.

(c) While, in the true sense, therefore, the Amendment gives no right of suffrage, it was long ago recognized that, in operation, its prohibition might measurably have that effect; that is to say, that, as the command of the Amendment was self-executing and reached without legislative action the conditions of discrimination against which it was aimed, the result might arise that as a consequence of the striking down of a discriminating clause a right of suffrage would be enjoyed by reason of the generic character of the provision which would remain after the discrimination was stricken out. Ex parte Yarbrough; Neal v. Delaware. A familiar illustration of this doctrine resulted from the effect of the adoption of the Amendment on state constitutions in which, at the time of the adoption of the Amendment, the right of suffrage was conferred on all white male citizens, since, by the inherent power of the Amendment, the word white disappeared, and therefore all male citizens, without discrimination on account of race, color or previous condition of servitude, came under the generic grant of suffrage made by the State.

With these principles before us, how can there be room for any serious dispute concerning the repugnancy of the standard based upon January 1, 1866 (a date which preceded the adoption of the Fifteenth Amendment), if the suffrage provision fixing that standard is susceptible of the significance which the Government attributes to it? Indeed, there seems no escape from the conclusion that to hold that there was even possibility for dispute on the subject would be but to declare that the Fifteenth Amendment not only had not the self-executing power which it has been recognized to have from the beginning, but that its provisions were wholly inoperative, because susceptible of being rendered inapplicable by mere forms of expression embodying no exercise of judgment and resting upon no discernible reason other than the purpose to disregard the prohibitions of the Amendment by creating a standard of voting which on its face was, in substance, but a revitalization of conditions which, when they prevailed in the past, had been destroyed by the self-operative force of the Amendment.

2. The standard of January 1, 1866, fixed in the suffrage amendment and its significance.

The inquiry, of course, here is, does the amendment as to the particular standard which this heading embraces involve the mere refusal to comply with the commands of the Fifteenth Amendment as previously stated? This leads us for the purpose of the analysis to recur to the text of the suffrage amendment. Its opening sentence fixes the literacy standard, which is all-inclusive, since it is general in its expression and contains no word of discrimination on account of race or color or any other reason. This, however, is immediately followed by the provisions creating the standard based upon the condition existing on January 1, 1866, and carving out those coming under that standard from the inclusion in the literacy test

which would have controlled them but for the exclusion thus expressly provided for. The provision is this:

> But no person who was, on January 1, 1866, or at any time prior thereto, entitled to vote under any form of government, or who at that time resided in some foreign nation, and no lineal descendant of such person, shall be denied the right to register and vote because of his inability to so read and write sections of such constitution.

We have difficulty in finding words to more clearly demonstrate the conviction we entertain that this standard has the characteristics which the Government attributes to it than does the mere statement of the text. It is true it contains no express words of an exclusion from the standard which it establishes of any person on account of race, color, or previous condition of servitude prohibited by the Fifteenth Amendment, but the standard itself inherently brings that result into existence, since it is based purely upon a period of time before the enactment of the Fifteenth Amendment, and makes that period the controlling and dominant test of the right of suffrage. In other words, we seek in vain for any ground which would sustain any other interpretation but that the provision, recurring to the conditions existing before the Fifteenth Amendment was adopted and the continuance of which the Fifteenth Amendment prohibited, proposed by, in substance and effect, lifting those conditions over to a period of time after the Amendment to make them the basis of the right to suffrage conferred in direct and positive disregard of the Fifteenth Amendment. And the same result, we are of opinion, is demonstrated by considering whether it is possible to discover any basis of reason for the standard thus fixed other than the purpose above stated. We say this because we are unable to discover how, unless the prohibitions of the Fifteenth Amendment were considered, the slightest reason was afforded for basing the classification upon a period of time prior to the Fifteenth Amendment. Certainly it cannot be said that there was any peculiar necromancy in the time named which engendered attributes affecting the qualification to vote which would not exist at another and different period unless the Fifteenth Amendment was in view.

While these considerations establish that the standard fixed on the basis of the 1866 test is void, they do not enable us to reply even to the first question asked by the court below, since, to do so, we must consider the literacy standard established by the suffrage amendment and the possibility of its surviving the determination of the fact that the 1866 standard never took life, since it was void from the beginning because of the operation upon it of the prohibitions of the Fifteenth Amendment. And this brings us to the last heading:

3. The determination of the validity of the literacy test and the possibility of its surviving the disappearance of the 1866 standard with which it is associated in the suffrage amendment.

No time need be spent on the question of the validity of the literacy test, considered alone, since, as we have seen, its establishment was but the exercise by the State of a lawful power vested in it not subject to our supervision, and, indeed, its validity is admitted. Whether this test is so connected with the other one relating to the situation on January 1, 1866, that the invalidity of the latter requires the rejection of the former, is really a question of state law, but, in the absence of any decision on the subject by the Supreme Court of the State, we must determine it for ourselves. We are of opinion that neither forms of classification nor methods of enumeration should be made the basis of striking down a provision which was independently legal, and therefore was lawfully enacted because of the removal of an illegal provision with which the legal provision or provisions may have been associated. We state what we hold to be the rule thus strongly because we are of opinion that, on a subject like the one under consideration, involving the establishment of a right whose exercise lies at the very basis of government, a much more exacting standard is required than would ordinarily obtain where the influence of the declared unconstitutionality of one provision of a statute upon another and constitutional provision is required to be fixed. Of course, rigorous as is this rule and imperative as is the duty not to violate it, it does not mean that it applies in a case where it expressly appears that a contrary conclusion must be reached if the plain letter and necessary intendment of the provision under consideration so compels, or where such a result is rendered necessary because to follow the contrary course would give rise to such an extreme and anomalous situation as would cause it to be impossible to conclude that it could have been upon any hypothesis whatever within the mind of the lawmaking power.

Does the general rule here govern, or is the case con-

trolled by one or the other of the exceptional conditions which we have just stated, is then the remaining question to be decided. Coming to solve it, we are of opinion that, by a consideration of the text of the suffrage amendment insofar as it deals with the literacy test, and to the extent that it creates the standard based upon conditions existing on January 1, 1866, the case is taken out of the general rule and brought under the first of the exceptions stated. We say this because, in our opinion, the very language of the suffrage amendment expresses, not by implication nor by forms of classification nor by the order in which they are made, but by direct and positive language, the command that the persons embraced in the 1866 standard should not be under any conditions subjected to the literacy test, a command which would be virtually set at naught if on the obliteration of the one standard by the force of the Fifteenth Amendment the other standard should be held to continue in force.

The reasons previously stated dispose of the case and make it plain that it is our duty to answer the first question No, and the second Yes; but before we direct the entry of an order to that effect, we come briefly to dispose of an issue the consideration of which we have hitherto postponed from a desire not to break the continuity of discussion as to the general and important subject before us.

In various forms of statement not challenging the instructions given by the trial court, concretely considered, concerning the liability of the election officers for their official conduct, it is insisted that as, in connection with the instructions, the jury was charged that the suffrage amendment was unconstitutional because of its repugnancy to the Fifteenth Amendment, therefore, taken as a whole, the charge was erroneous. But we are of opinion that this contention is without merit, especially in view of the doctrine long since settled concerning the self-executing power of the Fifteenth Amendment, and of what we have held to be the nature and character of the suffrage amendment in question. The contention concerning the inapplicability of §5508, Rev. Stat., now §19 of the Penal Code, or of its repeal by implication, is fully answered by the ruling this day made in United States v. Mosley, No. 180, post.

We answer the first question, No, and the second question, Yes.

And it will be so certified.

Glossary

Ex parte: a Latin term referring to a legal proceeding in which only one party is represented

necromancy: sorcery, usually involving the dead

nullity: the condition of being void

occult: secret or hidden

plaintiff in error: the plaintiff in a case on appeal, who may or may not be the plaintiff in the lower court case whose decision is being appealed

self-executing: a law that does not require further legislative or court action to take effect

Syllabus: the portion of a Supreme Court decision that summarizes the key findings and rulings

HAMMER V. DAGENHART

DATE 1918	**CITATION** 247 U.S. 251
AUTHOR William R. Day	**SIGNIFICANCE** Struck down the 1916 Keating-Owen Child Labor Act, which regulated child labor
VOTE 5-4	

Overview

 In *Hammer v. Dagenhart*, also known as the Child Labor Case, the United States Supreme Court struck down the 1916 Keating-Owen Child Labor Act by the slimmest of margins. On its face, *Hammer* seemed an easy case given its subject matter, but the later discredited 5-to-4 decision demonstrated how resistant the Court under Chief Justice Edward Douglass White could be to the Progressive legislation of the day.

Roland Dagenhart, an employee at a cotton mill in Charlotte, North Carolina, sued his employer and W. C. Hammer, the U.S. attorney for the Western District of North Carolina, on behalf of himself and his minor sons, Reuben and John, who were also employed at the cotton mill. Dagenhart sought a reversal of Keating-Owen, a federal statute aimed at ending the exploitation of underage workers by prohibiting the sale through interstate commerce of goods made using child labor. The lower district court agreed with Dagenhart's argument that Keating-Owen interfered with his sons' right to work, and the Supreme Court upheld this ruling, declaring the statute an impermissible extension of federal commerce power. While the commerce clause grants the federal government the right to regulate goods sold through interstate commerce, the Supreme Court in the *Hammer* case declared that while this power extends to goods that are inherently harmful, it cannot be used to control the process of their creation.

Context

The first two decades of the twentieth century in America were colored by initiatives spawned by the Progressive movement, a reformist agenda arising in reaction to the excesses of laissez-faire economics and social Darwinism that had dominated government policy since Reconstruction after the Civil War. The Fourteenth Amendment (1868) had been intended to codify racial equality, but a series of reactionary Supreme Court decisions interpreted the amendment's due process clause as a mechanism for restricting the governmental regulation of business activity, thereby promoting and protecting private enterprise.

The Progressive movement began as an unorganized response of middle-class consumers to the inequities

A 1916 photo showing messenger boys on strike in New York City
(Library of Congress)

of the Gilded Age, during which the few were vastly enriched at the expense of the many. In September 1891, however, after Vice President Theodore Roosevelt succeeded to the presidency following the assassination of William McKinley, the Progressives gained a champion. Roosevelt revived the dormant Sherman Antitrust Act of 1890 and sought to break up large-scale business combinations. Major trust-busting victories were achieved with cases such as *Northern Securities Co. v. United States* (1904) and *Swift & Co. v. United States* (1905). When Roosevelt was returned to office in 1904 with the largest popular majority of any previous presidential candidate, he pushed through other reforms, such as the Pure Food and Drug Act and the Hepburn Act (both passed in 1906). The Hepburn Act expanded the powers of the Interstate Commerce Commission, which regulated, among other things, railroad rates.

Roosevelt declined to run for another term, and in 1908 the Republicans nominated his handpicked successor, William Howard Taft. Taft handily beat the perennial

Democratic candidate William Jennings Bryan, and he carried on with Roosevelt's reform agenda. Still, Taft failed to galvanize his party, and he alienated Progressives with his lukewarm response to congressional and tariff reform. In the 1910 off-year election the Democrats gained control of both houses of Congress, and Roosevelt returned to lead a coalition of Republican insurgents to form a third political party, the Progressives.

In 1912 Roosevelt and Taft, the Republican Party's nominee, essentially split the Republican vote, handing the presidency to the Democratic candidate Woodrow Wilson. Wilson, formerly governor of New Jersey, already had made a name for himself as a reformer, and with his New Freedom platform he now sought to break up trusts rather than simply controlling them. He moved quickly to reform the banking system and then ushered the Federal Trade Commission Act and the Clayton Antitrust Act through Congress. Progressive social justice issues, such as women's suffrage and child labor reform, remained on a back burner until the 1914 off-year election. Amid significant Republican electoral victories and strong indications that Teddy Roosevelt would once again be a candidate in 1916, Wilson pushed through Congress workers' compensation legislation and a farm loan bill that he had previously opposed. Most significantly, Wilson personally lobbied for the passage of a child labor bill, the 1916 Keating-Owen Child Labor Act, barring the interstate transportation of goods made using underage workers. The act marked the first time Congress had used its commerce power to regulate manufacturing.

About the Author

Born on April 17, 1849, in Ravenna, Ohio, William Rufus Day came from a long line of jurists. His great-grandfather served as chief justice of the state of Connecticut, his grandfather was a member of the Ohio Supreme Court, and his father was chief justice of the Ohio Supreme Court. William R. Day, as was the custom, read law in local law offices. He then attended the University of Michigan Law School for a year before taking and passing the Ohio bar exam.

Day set up a partnership in Canton, Ohio, which quickly became the city's most prominent law firm. He did not, however, confine his activities to legal practice; he pursued an interest in politics and befriended another local attorney with political ambitions, William McKinley. McKinley's career soared, taking him from the U.S. Congress to the Ohio governor's mansion and finally to the White House. Day, meanwhile, resigned an Ohio judgeship because of low pay and declined an appointment to the federal bench, citing poor health. But when his friend McKinley summoned him to Washington in 1897, Day acquiesced. He first served as assistant to Secretary of State John Sherman, and when Sherman was eased out of office in 1898, he took Sherman's place.

Day took command of the Department of State during the Spanish-American War, and he resigned his post there in 1899 to head the American delegation to the peace conference with Spain, where he negotiated the U.S. purchase of the Philippines. President McKinley rewarded him for this coup with an appointment that same year to the Sixth Circuit Court of Appeals. After McKinley's death in 1901, Day began marking his friend's birthday with an annual memorial service.

During the January 1903 gathering, President Theodore Roosevelt made a premature announcement of his intention to appoint Day to the U.S. Supreme Court. Two months later Day was sworn in as an associate justice.

During the nearly two decades Day served on the Court, he acted primarily as a swing vote, manifesting attitudes that were alternately liberal and politically moderate. He endorsed the use of federal regulatory power embodied in the Sherman Antitrust Act, but in the opinion for which he is best remembered, *Hammer v. Dagenhart*, he declared the federal Child Labor Act unconstitutional because it violated the states' police powers. In the main, Day was overshadowed by other figures with whom he shared the high bench, such as the towering intellectual Oliver Wendell Holmes Jr. who wrote the powerful *Hammer* dissent that would later be used to overrule this decision.

Day retired from the Supreme Court on November 13, 1922. He served briefly as an umpire on the Mixed Claims Commission, which decided claims arising in the wake of World War I, before dying on Mackinac Island, Michigan, on July 9, 1923.

Explanation and Analysis of the Document

Justice Day, writing for the Supreme Court majority, opens with a brief rehearsal of the facts behind the case, including the decision of the United States District Court for the Western District of North Carolina. The district court has ruled in favor of the plaintiffs, declaring the Keating-Owen Child Labor Act unconstitutional and unenforceable. The case is now before the U.S. Supreme Court because the defendant, U.S. Attorney Hammer, has appealed the district court's judgment.

The case against the Child Labor Act rests on three arguments: 1) that it does not regulate interstate commerce or trade with a foreign country; 2) that it conflicts with the Tenth Amendment, which reserves to the states all powers not delegated to the federal government; and 3) that it conflicts with Fifth Amendment protections of due process. The question now before the Supreme Court concerns the federal government's constitutional right to regulate commerce between states: Does this power extend to prohibiting the sale of goods simply because they were produced in a factory that employs underage labor, possibly working too many hours per day, too many days per week, or after a certain hour? The federal government, for its part, cites the commerce clause of Article I of the Constitution as its authority for such control.

Seeking to define the government's commerce power, Day cites Chief Justice John Marshall's seminal opinion in *Gibbons v. Ogden* (22 U.S. 1 [1824]) : "It is the power to regulate; that is, to prescribe the rule by which commerce is to be governed." For Justice Day, this definition does not include the power to prohibit the movement of "ordinary commodities" between states. He dismisses the cases cited by Hammer, which he declares rest upon the nature of the commodities in question: *Champion v. Ames* (1903) permitted Congress to outlaw the interstate transportation of lottery tickets; *Hipolite Egg Co. v. United States* (1911) upheld the Pure Food and Drug Act because it prevented the interstate transportation of contaminated foods and drugs; *Hoke v. United States* (1913) upheld the White-Slave Traffic Act (1910), also known as the Mann Act, because it prohibited the interstate transportation of women intended to work as prostitutes. In each of these cases, Day says, interstate transportation was necessary to accomplish the harmful effects associated with the respective products. Therefore, the only way to regulate or prevent the proliferation of gambling, tainted food and drugs, and prostitution was through the exertion of the federal government's commerce power.

The *Hammer* case, by way of contrast, concerns goods that are themselves harmless, Day asserts. The Child Labor Act attempts to outlaw the use of underage workers in the production of these goods, but by the time the products are ready for interstate transport, says Day, any harmful effect on the child laborers is long past. What is more, the act itself permits the interstate transport of the goods in question thirty days after they have been removed from the factory where they were made. The manufacture of goods does not constitute "commerce" and therefore cannot be controlled by the government's commerce power. The production of goods intended for transportation between states is, instead, subject to local control; if this were not so, all goods manufactured for interstate commerce would come under federal control, thereby usurping state authority in violation of the framers' intent when writing the commerce clause into the Constitution.

Justice Day next addresses Hammer's contention that allowing the interstate transport of goods made with child labor is, in effect, an endorsement of unfair competition because some states outlaw the use of underage workers while others do not. Lower-cost goods produced in states permitting child labor that are sold in states prohibiting the use of child labor have an inherent advantage over similar native commodities. However, Congress has no authority to prevent unfair competition. The constitutional grant of the commerce power was never intended to permit Congress to usurp individual states' power to control local trade and manufacturing. Such power is, in fact, reserved to the states by the Tenth Amendment, as the Supreme Court has held in numerous earlier decisions.

Justice Day concedes that limiting the use of child labor is a desired goal; indeed, every state of the Union has passed a law addressing this subject. Furthermore, while it might be desirable to standardize such laws, writes Day, it is not within the constitutionally "enumerated" powers of the federal government to mandate such uniformity among the states. States retain control of local government. Upholding the Child Labor Act would not be a recognition of the federal government's right to regulate interstate commerce but rather a sanction of federal invasion into state control of purely local matters. If Congress, by exercising its commerce power, were permitted to control matters entrusted to local authority, not only would the free flow of interstate commerce end, he writes, but also the country's very system of government, balancing the authority of the central government with states' rights, would be "practically destroyed." For all these reasons, Justice Day concludes that the ruling of the lower court must be upheld. As a result, the Keating-Owen Child Labor Act is found to be unconstitutional.

Justice Oliver Wendell Holmes Jr. writing for a minority of four (including Joseph McKenna, Louis D. Brandeis, and John H. Clarke), penned a now-famous dissenting opinion. Holmes opens by rephrasing what is at issue in the case. For him, there is only one question: Does Congress have the power to prohibit the shipment in interstate or foreign commerce of goods manufactured less than thirty days prior to shipment using child labor, as defined by the Keating-Owen Child Labor Act? While granting that Congress does not have the authority to meddle with powers granted exclusively to the states, Holmes feels that no constitutional federal legislation should be struck down because of its indirect effects.

Holmes begins by stating that the statute in question is legitimate with regard to its immediate effects and could be considered unconstitutional only owing to some secondary consideration. For Holmes, the power to regulate interstate commerce includes the power to prohibit any part of that commerce Congress sees fit to prohibit. Unlike Justice Day, he sees decisions such as those in the Lottery Case (*Champion v. Ames*) as standing for the proposition that a law is not unconstitutional simply because it prohibits "certain transportation." Holmes is similarly firm in his belief that collateral effects on state police powers are no reason for striking down the Child Labor Act. Congress's commerce power will always trump any state's domestic controls:

> I should have thought that that matter had been disposed of so fully as to leave no room for doubt. I should have thought that the most conspicuous decisions of this Court had made it clear that the power to regulate commerce and other constitutional powers could not be cut down or qualified by the fact that it might interfere with the carrying out of the domestic policy of any State.

Holmes goes on to cite numerous cases in which the Court has declined to inquire as to the intent or the effect of various statutes: a federal tax on margarine so onerous as to prevent the manufacture and sale of this commodity was upheld; another federal tax on state banks, obviously intended to drive them out of business, was similarly sustained in *Veazie Bank v. Fenno*, in which the Court declared, "The Judicial cannot prescribe to the Legislative Departments of the Government limitations upon the exercise of its acknowledged powers" (75 U.S. 533 [1869]). In numerous cases concerning the Sherman Antitrust Act, the Court repeatedly disregarded the argument that federal exercise of the commerce power interferes with state control of production. Finally, in *Hipolite Egg Co. v. United States*, the Court went so far as to say that "no trade can be carried on between the States to which it [the power of Congress to regulate commerce] does not extend" (220 U.S. 45 [1911]). It made no difference in these cases whether the harm Congress sought to prevent preceded or followed the transportation of inherently innocuous goods across state lines; if Congress believes that this transportation itself promotes social harm, Congress is within its rights to prohibit the goods from interstate commerce. In contrast to the majority holding that the Child Labor Act violates the Tenth Amendment's reservation to the states of unenumerated powers, Holmes cites with approval an earlier case, *Leisy v. Hardin*, in which the Court stated that "a subject matter which has been confided exclusively to Congress by the Constitution is not within the jurisdiction of the police power of the State unless placed there by congressional action" (135 U.S. 100 [1890]).

In what is perhaps the most famous passage in *Hammer*, Holmes writes that he cannot understand the majority's view that goods not themselves considered harmful should not be prohibited from interstate commerce. If there is anything that civilized countries can agree is evil, he asserts, it is not something like liquor, with which American society is preoccupied at the moment, but premature and prolonged child labor. If ever there were a case for upholding the exercise of federal power, this is it.

In the past, continues Holmes, the Court has declined to substitute its judgment for that of Congress in matters of public policy or morality. He adds that it is not appropriate for the Court now to say that while the federal prohibition of liquor is permissible, the congressional prohibition of practices that ruin lives is unacceptable. The Child Labor Act does not intrude on any state prerogatives. States may run their domestic affairs as they like, but as soon as they send their products across state lines, they have lost their right to control the products. Instead of being taxed on such goods, states must cede their right to control them to the federal government, whose responsibility it is to shape public policy for the nation as a whole. The welfare of the nation may not coincide with the aims of an individual state, and the Constitution empowers Congress to use "all the means at its command" to promote the greater good.

Impact

The defeat of the Keating-Owen Child Labor Act in the Supreme Court prompted the passage of a second statute intended to protect child laborers through the exercise of Congress's taxing power. In *Bailey v. Drexel Furniture Co.* (1922), however, the Supreme Court also struck down the 1919 Child Labor Tax Act, declaring the 10 percent excise tax on the profits of companies employing children an unconstitutional penalty that usurped state authority. Two years later Congress adopted a constitutional amendment granting the federal government the power to regulate child labor. The amendment was never ratified and was eventually declared unnecessary after many states passed their own child labor laws. In 1938, however, Congress finally adopted a child labor law that passed constitutional muster: the Fair Labor Standards Act. The Supreme Court unanimously upheld this statute two years later in *United States v. Darby Lumber Co.* (1941), which also took the unusual step of specifically overruling a precedent, citing Justice Holmes's dissent in *Hammer* as the authority for this decision.

Hammer did not, however, remain dormant. Certain ambiguities in the Fair Labor Standards Act led to controversy over the applicability of the federal law to state workers. In *Maryland v. Wirtz* (1968) the Court nonetheless upheld the statute, declaring that the enforcement of its provisions on state workers did not violate state sovereignty. Just eight years later *Wirtz* was overturned in *National League of Cities v. Usury* (1976), in the process invoking *Hammer* to support the proposition that the Fair Labor Standards Act infringed upon "traditional aspects of state sovereignty."

Nine years later *National League of Cities* was itself overturned by *Garcia v. San Antonio Metropolitan Transit Authority* (1985), a 5-to-4 decision using the commerce clause to justify both the Fair Labor Standards Act and a powerful central government. The dissenters in *Garcia*, however, expressed their confidence that this case, too, would be overruled, returning power to the states. Although *United States v. Lopez* (1995) did not purport to overrule *Garcia*, it did endorse state autonomy by limiting congressional power to invoke the commerce clause when regulating matters having only a tangential relationship with interstate commerce. Profound questions remain concerning the Court's willingness to rein in the congressional assertion of its authority under the commerce clause, and the historical tension between centralized government and states' rights addressed in *Hammer* remains alive and well.

Questions for Further Study

1. In *United States v. Darby* (1941) the Supreme Court overruled *Hammer v. Dagenhart*, citing Justice Holmes's dissent in the earlier case as authority. How does the *Darby* Court turn a dissenting opinion into a controlling one?

2. A legal doctrine known as the "dormant commerce clause" does not exist in the Constitution per se but has grown out of various Supreme Court justices' attempts to interpret the commerce clause. In effect, the dormant commerce clause holds that some aspects of commerce between the states or between states and foreign countries are subject to state regulation. How might modern Internet communications be governed by this version of the commerce clause?

3. In *Lochner v. New York* (1905) the Supreme Court elevated a legal concept rooted in the due process clause of the Fourteenth Amendment and known as "substantive due process"—essentially, the right of an individual to be free from arbitrary government intrusion—into an inalienable right. How does the due process clause of the Fourteenth Amendment differ from that of the Fifth Amendment, and how might substantive due process actually work against individual liberty?

Further Reading

Books

Epstein, Lee. *Constitutional Law for a Changing America: Rights, Liberties, and Justice,* 6th ed. Washington, DC: CQ Press, 2007.

Fliter, John A. *Child Labor in America: The Epic Legal Struggle to Protect Children.* Lawrence: University Press of Kansas, 2018.

Kersch, Ken I. *Constructing Civil Liberties: Discontinuities in the Development of American Constitutional Law.* New York: Cambridge University Press, 2004.

Paddock, Lisa. *Facts about the Supreme Court of the United States.* New York: H. W. Wilson, 1996.

Schwartz, Bernard. *A History of the Supreme Court.* New York: Oxford University Press, 1993.

Articles

Sawyer, Logan E., III. "Creating Hammer v. Dagenhart." *William and Mary Bill of Rights Journal* 21 (2012): 67+.

Websites

"Hammer v. Dagenhart (1918)." Landmark Supreme Court Cases website. Accessed April 12, 2023. http://www.landmarkcases.org/gibbons/hammer.html.

"Hammer v. Dagenhart: Further Readings." Great American Court Cases, vol. 18. Law Library: American Law and Legal Information website. Accessed April 12, 2023. http://law.jrank.org/pages/13591/Hammer-v-Dagenhart.html.

"Hipolite Egg Co. v. United States, 220 U.S. 45 (1911)." FindLaw website. Accessed April 12, 2023. http://caselaw.lp.findlaw.com/cgi-bin/getcase.pl?court=US&vol=220&invol=45.

"Leisy v. Hardin 135 U.S. 100 (1890)." FindLaw website. Accessed April 12, 2023. http://caselaw.lp.findlaw.com/scripts/getcase.pl?court=US&vol=135&invol=100.

"Lochner v. People of State Of New York, 198 U.S. 45 (1905)." FindLaw website. Accessed April 12, 2023. http://caselaw.lp.findlaw.com/scripts/getcase.pl?court=US&vol=198&invol=45.

"Veazie Bank v. Fenno, 75 U.S. 533 (1869)." FindLaw website. Accessed April 12, 2023. http://caselaw.lp.findlaw.com/scripts/getcase.pl?navby=case&court=us&vol=75&invol =533.

—Commentary by Lisa Paddock

HAMMER V. DAGENHART

Document Text

MR. JUSTICE DAY delivered the opinion of the Court

A bill was filed in the United States District Court for the Western District of North Carolina by a father in his own behalf and as next friend of his two minor sons, one under the age of fourteen years and the other between the ages of fourteen and sixteen years, employees in a cotton mill at Charlotte, North Carolina, to enjoin the enforcement of the act of Congress intended to prevent interstate commerce in the products of child labor. Act Sept. 1, 1916, 39 Stat. 675, c. 432 (Comp. St. 1916, 8819a–8816f).

The District Court held the act unconstitutional and entered a decree enjoining its enforcement. This appeal brings the case here. The first section of the act is in the margin. Other sections of the act contain provisions for its enforcement and prescribe penalties for its violation.

The attack upon the act rests upon three propositions: First: It is not a regulation of interstate and foreign commerce; second: It contravenes the Tenth Amendment to the Constitution; third: It conflicts with the Fifth Amendment to the Constitution.

The controlling question for decision is: Is it within the authority of Congress in regulating commerce among the states to prohibit the transportation in interstate commerce of manufactured goods, the product of a factory in which, within thirty days prior to their removal therefrom, children under the age of fourteen have been employed or permitted to work, or children

between the ages of fourteen and sixteen years have been employed or permitted to work more than eight hours in any day, or more than six days in any week, or after the hour of 7 o'clock p.m., or before the hour of 6 o'clock a.m.?

The power essential to the passage of this act, the government contends, is found in the commerce clause of the Constitution which authorizes Congress to regulate commerce with foreign nations and among the states.

In *Gibbons v. Ogdon*, 9 Wheat. 1, Chief Justice Marshall, speaking for this court, and defining the extent and nature of the commerce power, said, "It is the power to regulate; that is, to prescribe the rule by which commerce is to be governed." In other words, the power is one to control the means by which commerce is carried on, which is directly the contrary of the assumed right to forbid commerce from moving and thus destroying it as to particular commodities. But it is insisted that adjudged cases in this court establish the doctrine that the power to regulate given to Congress incidentally includes the authority to prohibit the movement of ordinary commodities and therefore that the subject is not open for discussion. The cases demonstrate the contrary. They rest upon the character of the particular subjects dealt with and the fact that the scope of governmental authority, state or national, possessed over them is such that the authority to prohibit is as to them but the exertion of the power to regulate.

The first of these cases is *Champion v. Ames*, 188 U.S. 321, 23 Sup. Ct. 321, the so-called Lottery Case, in which it was held that Congress might pass a law having the effect to keep the channels of commerce free from use in the transportation of tickets used in the promotion of lottery schemes. In *Hipolite Egg Co. v. United States*, 220 U.S. 45, 31 Sup. Ct. 364, this court sustained the power of Congress to pass the Pure Food and Drug Act (Act June 30, 1906, c. 3915, 34 Stat. 768 [Comp. St. 1916, 8717–8728]), which prohibited the introduction into the states by means of interstate commerce of impure foods and drugs. In *Hoke v. United States*, 227 U.S. 308, 33 Sup. Ct. 281, 43 L. R. A. (N. S.) 906, Ann. Cas. 1913E, 905, this court sustained the constitutionality of the so-called "White Slave Traffic Act" (Act June 25, 1910, c. 395, 36 Stat. 825 [Comp. St. 1916, 8812–8819]), whereby the transportation of a woman in interstate commerce for the purpose of prostitution was forbidden. In that case we said, having reference to the authority of Congress, under the regulatory power, to protect the channels of interstate commerce:

> If the facility of interstate transportation can be taken away from the demoralization of lotteries, the debasement of obscene literature, the contagion of diseased cattle or persons, the impurity of food and drugs, the like facility can be taken away from the systematic enticement to, and the enslavement in prostitution and debauchery of women, and, more insistently, of girls.

In *Caminetti v. United States*, 242 U.S. 470, 37 Sup. Ct. 1 2, L. R. A. 1917F, 502, Ann. Cas. 1917B, 1168, we held that Congress might prohibit the transportation of women in interstate commerce for the purposes of debauchery and kindred purposes. In *Clark Distilling Co. v. Western Maryland Railway Co.*, 242 U.S. 311, 37 Sup. Ct. 180, L. R. A. 1917B, 1218, Ann. Cas. 1917B, 845, the power of Congress over the transportation of intoxicating liquors was sustained. In the course of the opinion it was said:

> The power conferred is to regulate, and the very terms of the grant would seem to repel the contention that only prohibition of movement in interstate commerce was embraced. And the cogency of this is manifest, since if the doctrine were applied to those manifold and important subjects of interstate commerce as to which Congress from the beginning has regulated, not prohibited, the existence of government under the Constitution would be no longer possible.

And concluding the discussion which sustained the authority of the Government to prohibit the transportation of liquor in interstate commerce, the court said:

> ... The exceptional nature of the subject here regulated is the basis upon which the exceptional power exerted must rest and affords no ground for any fear that such power may be constitutionally extended to things which it may not, consistently with the guaranties of the Constitution embrace.

In each of these instances the use of interstate transportation was necessary to the accomplishment of harmful results. In other words, although the power over interstate transportation was to regulate, that could only be accomplished by prohibiting the use of the facilities of interstate commerce to effect the evil intended.

This element is wanting in the present case. The thing intended to be accomplished by this statute is the denial of the facilities of interstate commerce to those manufacturers in the states who employ children within the prohibited ages. The act in its effect does not regulate transportation among the states, but aims to standardize the ages at which children may be employed in mining and manufacturing within the states. The goods shipped are of themselves harmless. The act permits them to be freely shipped after thirty days from the time of their removal from the factory. When offered for shipment, and before transportation begins, the labor of their production is over, and the mere fact that they were intended for interstate commerce transportation does not make their production subject to federal control under the commerce power.

Commerce "consists of intercourse and traffic ... and includes the transportation of persons and property, as well as the purchase, sale and exchange of commodities." The making of goods and the mining of coal are not commerce, nor does the fact that these things are to be afterwards shipped, or used in interstate commerce, make their production a part thereof. *Delaware, Lackawanna & Western R. R. Co. v. Yurkonis*, 238 U.S. 439, 35 Sup. Ct. 902

Over interstate transportation, or its incidents, the regulatory power of Congress is ample, but the production of articles, intended for interstate commerce, is a matter of local regulation. "When the commerce begins is determined, not by the character of the commodity, nor by the intention of the owner to transfer it to another state for sale, nor by his preparation of it for transportation, but by its actual delivery to a common carrier for transportation, or the actual commencement of its transfer to another state." Mr. Justice Jackson in Re Greene (C. C.) 52 Fed. 113. This principle has been recognized often in this court. *Coe v. Errol*, 116 U.S. 517, 6 Sup. Ct. 475; *Bacon v. Illinois*, 227 U.S. 504, 33 Sup. Ct. 299, and cases cited. If it were otherwise, all manufacture intended for interstate shipment would be brought under federal control to the practical exclusion of the authority of the states, a result certainly not contemplated by the framers of the Constitution when they vested in Congress the authority to regulate commerce among the States. *Kidd v. Pearson*, 128 U.S. 1, 21, 9 S. Sup. Ct. 6.

It is further contended that the authority of Congress may be exerted to control interstate commerce in the shipment of child-made goods because of the effect of the circulation of such goods in other states where the evil of this class of labor has been recognized by local legislation, and the right to thus employ child labor has been more rigorously restrained than in the state of production. In other words, that the unfair competition, thus engendered, may be controlled by closing the channels of interstate commerce to manufacturers in those states where the local laws do not meet what Congress deems to be the more just standard of other states.

There is no power vested in Congress to require the states to exercise their police power so as to prevent possible unfair competition. Many causes may cooperate to give one state, by reason of local laws or conditions, an economic advantage over others. The commerce clause was not intended to give to Congress a general authority to equalize such conditions. In some of the states laws have been passed fixing minimum wages for women, in others the local law regulates the hours of labor of women in various employments. Business done in such states may be at an economic disadvantage when compared with states which have no such regulations; surely, this fact does not give Congress the power to deny transportation in interstate commerce to those who carry on business where the hours of labor and the rate of compensation for women have not been fixed by a standard in use in other states and approved by Congress.

The grant of power of Congress over the subject of interstate commerce was to enable it to regulate such commerce, and not to give it authority to control the states in their exercise of the police power over local trade and manufacture.

The grant of authority over a purely federal matter was not intended to destroy the local power always existing and carefully reserved to the states in the Tenth Amendment to the Constitution.

Police regulations relating to the internal trade and affairs of the states have been uniformly recognized as within such control. "This," said this court in *United States v. Dewitt*, 9 Wall. 41, 45, "has been so frequently declared by this court, results so obviously from the terms of the Constitution, and has been so fully explained and supported on former occasions, that we think it unnecessary to enter again upon the discussion." See *Keller v. United States*, 213 U.S. 138, 144, 145 S., 146, 29 Sup. Ct. 470, 16 Ann. Cas. 1066; Cooley's Constitutional Limitations (7th Ed.) p. 11.

In the judgment which established the broad power of Congress over interstate commerce, Chief Justice Marshall said (9 Wheat. 203):

> They [inspection laws] act upon the subject, before it becomes an article of foreign commerce, or of commerce among the states, and prepare it for that purpose. They form a portion of that immense mass of legislation, which embraces everything within the territory of a state, not surrendered to the general government; all of which can be most advantageously exercised by the states themselves. Inspection laws, quarantine laws, health laws of every description, as well as laws for regulating the internal commerce of a state, and those which respect turnpike roads, ferries, etc., are component parts of this mass.

And in *Dartmouth College v. Woodward*, 4 Wheat. 518, the same great judge said:

> That the framers of the Constitution did not intend to restrain the states in the regulation of their civil institutions, adopted for internal government, and that the instrument they have given us is not to be so construed may be admitted.

That there should be limitations upon the right to employ children in mines and factories in t e interest of their own and the public welfare, all will admit. That such employment is generally deemed to require regulation is shown by the fact that the brief of counsel states that every state in the Union has a law upon the subject, limiting the right to thus employ children. In North Carolina, the state wherein is located the factory in which the employment was had in the present case, no child under twelve years of age is permitted to work.

It may be desirable that such laws be uniform, but our federal government is one of enumerated powers; "this principle," declared Chief Justice Marshall in *McCulloch v. Maryland*, 4 Wheat. 316, "is universally admitted."

A statute must be judged by its natural and reasonable effect. *Collins v. New Hampshire*, 171 U.S. 30, 33, 34 S., 18 Sup. Ct. 768. The control by Congress over interstate commerce cannot authorize the exercise of authority not entrusted to it by the Constitution. Pipe Line Case, 234 U.S. 548, 560, 34 S. Sup. Ct. 956. The maintenance of the authority of the states over matters purely local is as essential to the preservation of our institutions as is the conservation of the supremacy of the federal power in all matters entrusted to the nation by the federal Constitution.

In interpreting the Constitution it must never be forgotten that the nation is made up of states to which are entrusted the powers of local government. And to them and to the people the powers not expressly delegated to the national government are reserved. *Lane County v. Oregon*, 7 Wall. 71, 76. The power of the states to regulate their purely internal affairs by such laws as seem wise to the local authority is inherent and has never been surrendered to the general government. *New York v. Miln*, 11 Pet. 102, 139; Slaughter House Cases, 16 Wall. 36, 63; *Kidd v. Pearson*, supra. To sustain this statute would not be in our judgment a recognition of the lawful exertion of congressional authority over interstate commerce, but would sanction an invasion by the federal power of the control of a matter purely local in its character, and over which no authority has been delegated to Congress in conferring the power to regulate commerce among the states.

We have neither authority nor disposition to question the motives of Congress in enacting this legislation. The purposes intended must be attained consistently with constitutional limitations and not by an invasion of the powers of the states. This court has no more important

function than that which devolves upon it the obligation to preserve inviolate the constitutional limitations upon the exercise of authority federal and state to the end that each may continue to discharge, harmoniously with the other, the duties entrusted to it by the Constitution.

In our view the necessary effect of this act is, by means of a prohibition against the movement in interstate commerce of ordinary commercial commodities to regulate the hours of labor of children in factories and mines within the states, a purely state authority. Thus the act in a two-fold sense is repugnant to the Constitution. It not only transcends the authority delegated to Congress over commerce but also exerts a power as to a purely local matter to which the federal authority does not extend. The far reaching result of upholding the act cannot be more plainly indicated than by pointing out that if Congress can thus regulate matters entrusted to local authority by prohibition of the movement of commodities in interstate commerce, all freedom of commerce will be at an end, and the power of the states over local matters may be eliminated, and thus our system of government be practically destroyed. For these reasons we hold that this law exceeds the constitutional authority of Congress. It follows that the decree of the District Court must be

AFFIRMED.

Mr. Justice HOLMES, dissenting

The single question in this case is whether Congress has power to prohibit the shipment in interstate or foreign commerce of any product of a cotton mill situated in the United States, in which within thirty days before the removal of the product children under fourteen have been employed, or children between fourteen and sixteen have been employed more than eight hours in a day, or more than six days in any week, or between seven in the evening and six in the morning. The objection urged against the power is that the States have exclusive control over their methods of production and that Congress cannot meddle with them, and taking the proposition in the sense of direct intermeddling I agree to it and suppose that no one denies it. But if an act is within the powers specifically conferred upon Congress, it seems to me that it is not made any less constitutional because of the indirect effects that it may have, however obvious it may be that it will have those effects, and that we are not at liberty upon such grounds to hold it void.

The first step in my argument is to make plain what no one is likely to dispute that the statute in question is within the power expressly given to Congress if considered only as to its immediate effects and that if invalid it is so only upon some collateral ground. The statute confines itself to prohibiting the carriage of certain goods in interstate or foreign commerce. Congress is given power to regulate such commerce in unqualified terms. It would not be argued today that the power to regulate does not include the power to prohibit. Regulation means the prohibition of something, and when interstate commerce is the matter to be regulated I cannot doubt that the regulation may prohibit any part of such commerce that Congress sees fit to forbid. At all events it is established by the Lottery Case and others that have followed it that a law is not beyond the regulative power of Congress merely because it prohibits certain transportation out and out. *Champion v. Ames*, 188 U.S. 321, 355, 359 S., 23 Sup. Ct. 321, et seq. So I repeat that this statute in its immediate operation is clearly within the Congress's constitutional power.

The question then is narrowed to whether the exercise of its otherwise constitutional power by Congress can be pronounced unconstitutional because of its possible reaction upon the conduct of the States in a matter upon which I have admitted that they are free from direct control. I should have thought that that matter had been disposed of so fully as to leave no room for doubt. I should have thought that the most conspicuous decisions of this Court had made it clear that the power to regulate commerce and other constitutional powers could not be cut down or qualified by the fact that it might interfere with the carrying out of the domestic policy of any State.

The manufacture of oleomargarine is as much a matter of State regulation as the manufacture of cotton cloth. Congress levied a tax upon the compound when colored so as to resemble butter that was so great as obviously to prohibit the manufacture and sale. In a very elaborate discussion the present Chief Justice excluded any inquiry into the purpose of an act which apart from that purpose was within the power of Congress. *McCray v. United States*, 195 U.S. 27, 24 Sup. Ct. 769, 1 Ann. Cas. 561. As to foreign commerce see *Weber v. Freed*, 239 U.S. 325, 329, 36 S. Sup. Ct. 131, Ann. Cas. 1916C, 317; *Brolan v. United States*, 236 U.S. 216, 217, 35 S. Sup. Ct. 285; *Buttfield v. Stranahan*, 192 U.S. 470, 24 Sup. Ct. 349. Fifty years ago a tax on state banks, the obvious purpose and

actual effect of which was to drive them, or at least their circulation, out of existence, was sustained, although the result was one that Congress had no constitutional power to require. The Court made short work of the argument as to the purpose of the Act. "The Judicial cannot prescribe to the Legislative Departments of the Government limitations upon the exercise of its acknowledged powers." *Veazie Bank v. Fenno*, 8 Wall. 533. So it well might have been argued that the corporation tax was intended under the guise of a revenue measure to secure a control not otherwise belonging to Congress, but the tax was sustained, and the objection so far as noticed was disposed of by citing *McCray v. United States*; *Flint v. Stone Tracy Co.*, 220 U.S. 107, 31 Sup. Ct. 342, Ann. Cas. 1912B, 1312. And to come to cases upon interstate commerce notwithstanding *United States v. E. C. Knight Co.*, 156 U.S. 1, 15 Sup. Ct. 249, the Sherman Act (Act July 2, 1890, c. 647, 26 Stat. 209) has been made an instrument for the breaking up of combinations in restraint of trade and monopolies, using the power to regulate commerce as a foothold, but not proceeding because that commerce was the end actually in mind. The objection that the control of the States over production was interfered with was urged again and again but always in vain. *Standard Oil Co. v. United States*, 221 U.S. 1, 68, 69 S., 31 Sup. Ct. 502, 34 L. R. A. (N. S.) 834, Ann. Cas. 1912D, 734; *United States v. American Tobacco Co.*, 221 U.S. 106, 184, 31 S. Sup. Ct. 632; *Hoke v. United States*, 227 U.S. 308, 321, 322 S., 33 Sup. Ct. 281, 43 L. R. A. (N. S.) 906, Ann. Cas. 1913E, 905. See finally and especially *Seven Cases of Eckman's Alterative v. United States*, 239 U.S. 510, 514, 515 S., 36 Sup. Ct. 190, L. R. A. 1916D, 164.

The Pure Food and Drug Act which was sustained in *Hipolite Egg Co. v. United States*, 220 U.S. 45, 57, 31 S. Sup. Ct. 364, 367 (55 L. Ed. 364), with the intimation that "no trade can be carried on between the States to which it [the power of Congress to regulate commerce] does not extend."; applies not merely to articles that the changing opinions of the time condemn as intrinsically harmful but to others innocent in themselves, simply on the ground that the order for them was induced by a preliminary fraud. *Weeks v. United States*, 245 U.S. 618, 38 Sup. Ct. 219, 62 L. Ed. It does not matter whether the supposed evil precedes or follows the transportation. It is enough that in the opinion of Congress the transportation encourages the evil. I may add that in the cases on the so-called White Slave Act it was established that the means adopted by Congress as convenient to the exercise of its power might have the character af police regulations. *Hoke v. United States*, 227 U.S. 308, 323, 33 S. Sup. Ct. 281, 43 L. R. A. (N. S.) 906, Ann. Cas. 1913E, 905; *Caminetti v. United States*, 242 U.S. 470, 492, 37 S. Sup. Ct. 192, L. R. A. 1917F, 502, Ann. Cas. 1917B, 1168. In *Clark Distilling Co. v. Western Maryland Ry. Co.*, 242 U.S. 311, 328, 37 S. Sup. Ct. 180, L. R. A. 1917B, 1218, Ann. Cas. 1917B, 845, *Leisy v. Hardin*, 135 U.S. 100, 108, 10 S. Sup. Ct. 681, is quoted with seeming approval to the effect that "a subject matter which has been confided exclusively to Congress by the Constitution is not within the jurisdiction of the police power of the State unless placed there by congressional action." I see no reason for that proposition not applying here.

The notion that prohibition is any less prohibition when applied to things now thought evil I do not understand. But if there is any matter upon which civilized countries have agreed—far more unanimously than they have with regard to intoxicants and some other matters over which this country is now emotionally aroused—it is the evil of premature and excessive child labor. I should have thought that if we were to introduce our own moral conceptions where is my opinion they do not belong, this was preeminently a case for upholding the exercise of all its powers by the United States.

But I had thought that the propriety of the exercise of a power admitted to exist in some cases was for the consideration of Congress alone and that this Court always had disavowed the right to intrude its judgment upon questions of policy or morals. It is not for this Court to pronounce when prohibition is necessary to regulation if it ever may be necessary—to say

that it is permissible as against strong drink but not as against the product of ruined lives. The Act does not meddle with anything belonging to the States. They may regulate their internal affairs and their domestic commerce as they like. But when they seek to send their products across the State line they are no longer within their rights. If there were no Constitution and no Congress their power to cross the line would depend upon their neighbors. Under the Constitution such commerce belongs not to the States but to Congress to regulate. It may carry out its views of public policy whatever indirect effect they may have upon the activities of the States. Instead of being encountered by a prohibitive tariff at her boundaries the State encounters the public policy of the United States which it is for Congress to express. The public policy of the United States is shaped with a view to the benefit of the nation as a whole. If, as has been the case within the memory of men still living, a State should take a different view of the propriety of sustaining a lottery from that which generally prevails, I cannot believe that the fact would require a different decision from that reached in *Champion v. Ames*. Yet in that case it would be said with quite as much force as in this that Congress was attempting to intermeddle with the State's domestic affairs. The national welfare as understood by Congress may require a different attitude within its sphere from that of some self-seeking State. It seems to me entirely constitutional for Congress to enforce its understanding by all the means at its command.

Mr. Justice McKENNA, Mr. Justice BRANDEIS, and Mr. Justice CLARKE concur in this opinion.

Glossary

commerce clause: Article I, Section 8, Clause 3 of the Constitution provides that "Congress shall have the power . . . To Regulate Commerce with foreign Nations, and among the several States, and with the Indian Tribes"

enumerated powers: powers specifically granted in the Constitution to the various branches of federal government

jurisdiction: the power to hear and decide legal matters within a defined area of authority

police power: authority granted government, usually at the local level, to restrict individual rights in order to promote public welfare

SCHENCK v. UNITED STATES

DATE 1919	**CITATION** 249 U.S. 47
AUTHOR Oliver Wendell Holmes Jr.	**SIGNIFICANCE** Set the stage for the development of free speech law in America
VOTE 9-0	

Overview

Oliver Wendell Holmes Jr. remains one of the most influential of American legal philosophers. His formulation of the "clear and present danger" test regarding the right to free speech in his opinion in *Schenck v. United States*, which was further refined in his dissent in *Abrams v. United States,* set the stage for the development of free speech law in America. Charles Schenck, secretary-general of the Socialist Party of America, had been charged with printing and distributing antidraft literature, thus violating the Espionage Act of 1917. He appealed his conviction on First Amendment grounds, but in its 1919 decision the Supreme Court upheld the constitutionality of the Espionage Act and rejected the First Amendment protection of free speech—judging the legality of speech according to its tendency to provoke illegal acts.

Context

In 1917, the United States found itself drawn into World War I thanks in large part to the belligerency of German submarines in the Atlantic. After the sinking of the *Lu-sitania,* which had cost the lives of 128 Americans in 1915, President Woodrow Wilson continued to impress upon Germany the need to respect American sovereignty on the seas. At first, Germany acquiesced, fearing the involvement of another international power in what was rapidly becoming one of the bloodiest wars in history, but the ability of the British navy to seal off Germany from outside aid and support began to take its effect. After three years of bloodshed and near starvation on the home front, the Germans authorized their U-boat commanders to renew their attacks against civilian passenger ships, drawing the United States into the war. Coupled with Wilson's declaration that German spies were in the United States and the British revelation of the Zimmermann telegram calling for the invasion of the United States by Mexico, America found itself drawn into the war on April 2, 1917.

At the start of the war in February 1917, the U.S. Army had been a comparatively minuscule force of 133,000 men (compared with the nearly 3.8 million who would serve in the British armed forces during the war) with less than five hundred machine guns and no steel helmets or chemical warfare equipment. In order to gear up for war, the United States implemented the Selective Service Act in 1917, which called for the conscription of

2.8 million American men eighteen to forty-five years of age. This number, added to the nearly two million volunteers in the first months of the war, helped the American Expeditionary Force become a potentially powerful force against the Germans and Austrians in the war.

Not all Americans supported these efforts to get America into the war, particularly the left-wing Socialist Party, which viewed the war as further evidence of the capitalist elite's attempt to profit at the expense of imperialist goals, particularly because the United States had not been directly attacked by any German military forces. (The *Lusitania* had been a British ship.) As groups such as the International Workers of the World and the Socialist Party of America ramped up their protests against the war effort, the United States used the fear of spying to pass the Espionage Act of 1917, which included riders for those encouraging mutiny, desertion, or refusal of duty. The definition of what constituted these actions differed from state to state (as the decision was left to local federal judges and attorneys), and repercussions for engaging in these acts varied from punishment for distribution of materials promoting resistance to the draft (such as what was seen with Charles Schenck) to confiscation of movies (as with the confiscation of the film *Spirit of '76* due to the negative portrayal of British soldiers in the American Revolution and the fear that it would lead to a lack of support for America's ally in the war). Even the U.S. Postal Service became a tool for investigating possible acts of espionage, with Postmaster General Albert Burleson ordering his postmasters to monitor the mail for evidence of sedition.

It was against this backdrop that organizations calling for the end of hostilities and protests against the draft found themselves becoming the target of federal investigations and prosecution, putting the First Amendment to perhaps its greatest challenge since the passage of the Alien and Sedition Acts of 1798.

About the Author

Oliver Wendell Holmes Jr. was born in Boston in 1841, the son of a famous writer and physician and his abolitionist wife. His family was part of the prominent literary and social circles of the day, with connections to such luminaries as Ralph Waldo Emerson. Holmes counted among his lifelong friends the writer Henry James and his brother, William. In 1857, he entered Harvard College, from which

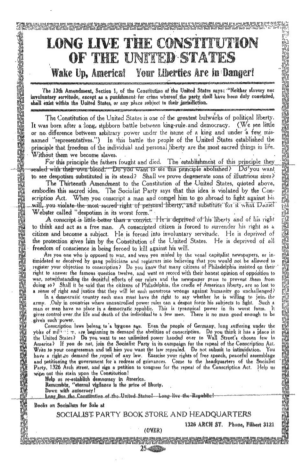

The leaflet at the center of the case
(Wikimedia Commons)

he graduated in 1861. Holmes enlisted to fight in the Civil War, and at age twenty he gained a lieutenant's commission in the Twentieth Massachusetts Volunteer Infantry and went to fight for the Union.

After mustering out, Holmes returned to Harvard, where he earned a law degree. He then worked as a lawyer and later taught at Harvard Law School, meanwhile also giving speeches and writing articles on the common law. He also served as associate and chief justice of the Massachusetts Supreme Judicial Court. In 1902 Theodore Roosevelt nominated Holmes to a seat on the U.S. Supreme Court, a position he held until 1932, when he retired at age ninety.

Holmes, the author of the opinion of the court in *Schenck v. United States*, had a reputation as being one of America's foremost legal scholars in the late nineteenth and early twentieth centuries. As a veteran of the Civil War, Holmes had seen the dangers of seditious speech when left unchecked by legal action. In an 1897 *Harvard Law Review* article, Holmes wrote that "when we speak of the rights of man in a moral sense, we mean to mark the limits of interference with individual freedom," a clear foreshadowing of his willingness to create limits to the First Amendment, as would be seen in the *Schenck* case.

Holmes's tenure as an associate justice on the Supreme Court was one that saw him consistently taking on cases related to the First Amendment, and it was through these cases that Holmes helped craft the very limits that he had written about nearly a quarter of a century earlier. In the *Schenck* case, Holmes supported the government's argument that the actions of Charles Schenck calling for refusal to serve by those summoned in the draft were a violation under the Espionage Act of 1917, contending that such actions had presented a "clear and present danger" to the United States with respect to national defense and that therefore such speech was not allowed. Less than a year later, however, Holmes wrote a dissent in the case of *Abrams v. United States* that maintained that the call for a strike in munitions plants did not constitute a violation of free speech because there did not exist a "clear and present danger" to the safety of the United States.

This seeming contradiction defined one of the great successes of Holmes as a member of the highest court in the United States: he believed strongly that there were moral limitations on the rights and freedoms guaranteed by the Constitution, but he also understood that those limitations must be in place only to protect the common good of the people. Through the artful combination of his opinion in *Schenck v. United States* and his dissent in *Abrams v. United States*, Holmes helped shape a legal precedent that would influence cases throughout the twentieth century regarding the limitations on free speech. It is for this reason that he is remembered by most legal scholars as an astute legal mind rather than a contradictory legalist.

Explanation and Analysis of the Document

Charles Schenck, secretary-general of the Socialist Party of America, was charged with printing and distributing literature urging American men to resist the draft during World War I. A federal district court found Schenck guilty of having violated the 1917 Espionage Act, which outlawed interference with conscription. Schenck appealed his criminal conviction to the U.S. Supreme Court, questioning the constitutionality of the Espionage Act on First Amendment grounds. There was, he argued, a tradition in Anglo-American law of distinguishing between opinion and incitement to illegal action. His leaflet was a reflection of the debate then raging in American society about the justness of the war and, as such, was an expression of opinion. Rather than violence, it urged that those subject to the draft assert their rights by signing an anticonscription petition that would be forwarded to Congress.

Writing for a unanimous Court, Justice Holmes upheld the constitutionality of the Espionage Act and Schenck's conviction. In considering First Amendment protection for any speech, he states, the Court must consider not only the content of the speech but also its context. Whereas in some circumstances banning speech such as Schenck's leaflet might amount to prohibited prior restraint, in the context of wartime such speech is akin to shouting "Fire!" in a crowded theater. In distributing his leaflets Schenck plainly intended to interfere with the draft, and such interference clearly violated the nation's settled right to draft citizens during time of war. Furthermore, the Espionage Act undoubtedly applied to conspiracies as well as to actual obstruction of military activities; the intended action need not have actually succeeded to be prohibited. The test, Holmes memorably declared, is whether the words at issue present a "clear and present danger" of provoking "substantive evils" that Congress is empowered to prevent.

Decided in 1919, *Schenck* was the Court's first significant attempt to define what constitutes free speech under the First Amendment. Two schools of thought about the subject grew directly out of this case: Absolutists hold that the framers meant, literally, that "Congress shall make no law . . . abridging the freedom of speech." Others believe that an individual's right to be left alone must be balanced against compelling public necessity. For his part, Holmes's subsequent refinement of the "clear and present danger" test seems to indicate that his use of the phrase in *Schenck* had been casual. In two companion unanimous decisions to *Schenck*, *Frohwerk v. United States* and *Debs v. United States*, Holmes used the same traditional "bad tendency" test—judging the legality of speech according to its tendency to provoke illegal acts—that he had employed in earlier free speech cases. It is arguable, then, that in *Schenck* he intended to equate the "clear and present danger" test with the "bad tendency" test. Within a few months, however, Holmes, together with Justice

Louis D. Brandeis, would begin the process of refining the "clear and present danger" test in *Abrams v. United States* so that it would reflect his intention of providing greater legal latitude for dissident speech.

Impact

For the *Schenck* case, the most immediate impact was felt by those who had spoken their opposition to America's war effort, as the ruling clearly limited the degree to which Americans could protest or resist a war they viewed unfavorably. More important, it empowered America's investigative agencies, such as the Bureau of Investigations (predecessor to the FBI), with a great deal of latitude in the investigation and prosecution of individuals who were suspected Socialists, which also happened to include a large number of eastern European immigrants. These investigations further fueled the growing fear in America that immigrants were attempting to subvert America's democratic government for a more liberal system like that developing in Russia. By 1919, these fears would manifest themselves in raids led by Attorney General A. Mitchell Palmer and would serve as the primary message of the resurging Ku Klux Klan in the 1920s.

The far-reaching impacts of *Schenck v. United States* lay in its creation of a precedent for defining the parameters of what constituted protected free speech. The Founding Fathers had never specifically outlined the nature of just how far the freedom of speech extended, and up until the twentieth century generally the issue had never been brought to trial unless in an utterance of rebellion or treason. With the establishment of the "clear and present danger" test, however, the Supreme Court established a more tangible understanding as to just how far the protection of speech could go.

In 1968, the Supreme Court reiterated the arguments of Holmes in the case of *U.S. v. O'Brien* in their finding that the burning of a draft card represented a dangerous protest because it threatened the ability of the United States to raise an army to defend itself. Conversely, the Court decided in *Texas v. Johnson* (1989) that the burning of an American flag was a protected form of political speech and therefore shielded by the First Amendment. With the evolution of terrorism from a local and regional issue in the late twentieth century to a global struggle at the beginning of the twenty-first century, *Schenck* once again became the precedent that defined just how far freedom of speech would be protected. In the case *Holder v. Humanitarian Law Project* (2010), the court ruled that citizens who advocated for designated terror groups were not immune from prosecution, because they represented a clear and viable threat to the safety of the United States. The case also serves as the justification for why an individual who says there is a bomb in a building or a plane can be arrested and charged for making terroristic threats, given the danger that the ensuing panic may cause.

Questions for Further Study

1. In Holmes's opinion for the Court, he writes that "we admit that in many places and in ordinary times the defendants in saying all that was said in the circular would have been within their constitutional rights. But the character of every act depends upon the circumstances in which it is done." How might the ruling in *Schenck* have been different had America not been at war at the time Schenck's literature was distributed? What impacts might that have had on the American judicial system as a result?

2. How might the *Schenck v. United States* case have helped lessen resistance to the rationing programs mandated during World War II?

3. How did the ruling in *Schenck* impact protests in unpopular wars such as Vietnam? What challenges might Holmes's ruling have faced with a war that was inherently unpopular, like Vietnam, versus a war that was substantially more popular, like World War I and World War II?

4. How might the "clear and present danger" test be applied to modern social media communications regarding support for groups deemed by the U.S. government to be terrorist organizations? What might be some challenges to this principle in the modern age?

Further Reading

Books

Work, Clemens P. *Darkest before Dawn: Sedition and Free Speech in the American West.* Albuquerque: University of New Mexico Press, 2006.

Articles

"Construction of the Espionage Act." *Virginia Law Review* 6, no. 1 (1919): 53–56.

"Criminal Law. Conspiracy. Inducing Resistance to Selective Draft Act." *Yale Law Journal* 27, no. 7 (1918): 955–956.

Johnson, Donald. "Wilson, Burleson, and Censorship in the First World War." *Journal of Southern History* 28, no. 1 (1962): 46–58.

Ragan, Fred D. "Justice Oliver Wendell Holmes, Jr., Zechariah Chafee, Jr., and the Clear and Present Danger Test for Free Speech: The First Year, 1919." *Journal of American History* 58, no. 1 (1971): 24–45.

Weinstein, James. "Anti-War Sentiment and the Socialist Party, 1917–1918." *Political Science Quarterly* 74, no. 2 (1959): 215–239.

Websites

Asp, David. "Schenck v. United States (1919)." In *The First Amendment Encyclopedia.* Accessed April 12, 2023. https://www.mtsu.edu/first-amendment/article/193/schenck-v-united-states.

"Schenck v. United States." Oyez. Accessed April 12, 2023. https://www.oyez.org/cases/1900-1940/249us47.

—Commentary by Ryan Fontanella

SCHENCK V. UNITED STATES

Document Text

MR. JUSTICE HOLMES delivered the opinion of the Court

This is an indictment in three counts. The first charges a conspiracy to violate the Espionage Act of June 15, 1917, c. 30, § 3, 40 Stat. 217, 219, by causing and attempting to cause insubordination, &c., in the military and naval forces of the United States, and to obstruct the recruiting and enlistment service of the United States, when the United States was at war with the German Empire, to-wit, that the defendants willfully conspired to have printed and circulated to men who had been called and accepted for military service under the Act of May 18, 1917, a document set forth and alleged to be calculated to cause such insubordination and obstruction. The count alleges overt acts in pursuance of the conspiracy, ending in the distribution of the document set forth. The second count alleges a conspiracy to commit an offence against the United States, to-wit, to use the mails for the transmission of matter declared to be nonmailable by Title XII, § 2 of the Act of June 15, 1917, to-wit, the above mentioned document, with an averment of the same overt acts. The third count charges an unlawful use of the mails for the transmission of the same matter and otherwise as above. The defendants were found guilty on all the counts. They set up the First Amendment to the Constitution forbidding Congress to make any law abridging the freedom of speech, or of the press, and bringing the case here on that ground have argued some other points also of which we must dispose.

It is argued that the evidence, if admissible, was not sufficient to prove that the defendant Schenck was concerned in sending the documents. According to the testimony, Schenck said he was general secretary of the Socialist party, and had charge of the Socialist headquarters from which the documents were sent. He identified a book found there as the minutes of the Executive Committee of the party. The book showed a resolution of August 13, 1917, that 15,000 leaflets should be printed on the other side of one of them in use, to be mailed to men who had passed exemption boards, and for distribution. Schenck personally attended to the printing. On August 20, the general secretary's report said "Obtained new leaflets from printer and started work addressing envelopes" &c., and there was a resolve that Comrade Schenck be allowed $125 for sending leaflets through the mail. He said that he had about fifteen or sixteen thousand printed. There were files of the circular in question in the inner office which he said were printed on the other side of the one sided circular, and were there for distribution. Other copies were proved to have been sent through the mails to drafted men. Without going into confirmatory details that were proved, no reasonable man could doubt that the defendant Schenck was largely instrumental in sending the circulars about. As to the defendant Baer, there was evidence that she was a member of the Executive Board, and that the minutes of its transactions were hers. The argument as to the sufficiency of the evidence that the defendants conspired to send the documents only impairs the seriousness of the real defence.

It is objected that the documentary evidence was not admissible because obtained upon a search warrant, valid so far as appears. The contrary is established. *Adams v. New York,* 192 U. S. 585; *Weeks v. United States,* 232 U. S. 383, 232 U. S. 395, 232 U. S. 396. The search warrant did not issueh against the defendant, but against the Socialist headquarters at 1326 Arch Street, and it would seem that the documents technically were not even in the defendants' possession. *See Johnson v. United States,* 228 U. S. 457. Notwithstanding some protest in argument, the notion that evidence even directly proceeding from the defendant in a criminal proceeding is excluded in all cases by the Fifth Amendment is plainly unsound.

The document in question, upon its first printed side, recited the first section of the Thirteenth Amendment, said that the idea embodied in it was violated by the Conscription Act, and that a conscript is little better than a convict. In impassioned language, it intimated that conscription was despotism in its worst form, and a monstrous wrong against humanity in the interest of Wall Street's chosen few. It said "Do not submit to intimidation," but in form, at least, confined itself to peaceful measures such as a petition for the repeal of the act. The other and later printed side of the sheet was headed "Assert Your Rights." It stated reasons for alleging that anyone violated the Constitution when he refused to recognize "your right to assert your opposition to the draft," and went on "If you do not assert and support your rights, you are helping to deny or disparage rights which it is the solemn duty of all citizens and residents of the United States to retain."

It described the arguments on the other side as coming from cunning politicians and a mercenary capitalist press, and even silent consent to the conscription law as helping to support an infamous conspiracy. It denied the power to send our citizens away to foreign shores to shoot up the people of other lands, and added that words could not express the condemnation such cold-blooded ruthlessness deserves, . . . winding up, "You must do your share to maintain, support and uphold the rights of the people of this country." Of course, the document would not have been sent unless it had been intended to have some effect, and we do not see what effect it could be expected to have upon persons subject to the draft except to influence them to obstruct the carrying of it out. The defendants do not deny that the jury might find against them on this point.

But it is said, suppose that that was the tendency of this circular, it is protected by the First Amendment to the Constitution. Two of the strongest expressions are said to be quoted respectively from well-known public men. It well may be that the prohibition of laws abridging the freedom of speech is not confined to previous restraints, although to prevent them may have been the main purpose, as intimated in *Patterson v. Colorado.* . . . We admit that in many places and in ordinary times the defendants in saying all that was said in the circular would have been within their constitutional rights. But the character of every act depends upon the circumstances in which it is done. . . . The most stringent protection of free speech would not protect a man in falsely shouting fire in a theatre and causing a panic. It does not even protect a man from an injunction against uttering words that may have all the effect of force. . . . The question in every case is whether the words used are used in such circumstances and are of such a nature as to create a clear and present danger that they will bring about the substantive evils that Congress has a right to prevent. It is a question of proximity and degree. When a nation is at war many things that might be said in time of peace are such a hindrance to its effort that their utterance will not be endured so long as men fight and that no Court could regard them as protected by any constitutional right. It seems to be admitted that if an actual obstruction of the recruiting service were proved, liability for words that produced that effect might be enforced. The statute of 1917 in section 4 . . . punishes conspiracies to obstruct as well as actual obstruction. If the act, (speaking, or circulating a paper,) its tendency and the intent with which it is done are the same, we perceive no ground for saying that success alone warrants making the act a crime. . . . Indeed that case might be said to dispose of the present contention if the precedent covers all media concludendi. But as the right to free speech was not referred to specially, we have thought fit to add a few words.

It was not argued that a conspiracy to obstruct the draft was not within the words of the Act of 1917. The words are "obstruct the recruiting or enlistment service," and it might be suggested that they refer only to making it hard to get volunteers. Recruiting heretofore usually having been accomplished by getting volunteers, the word is apt to call up that method only in our minds. But recruiting is gaining fresh supplies for the forces, as well by draft as otherwise. It is put as an alternative to enlistment or voluntary enrollment in this act. The fact that the Act of 1917 was enlarged by the amending Act of May 16, 1918, c. 75, 40 Stat. 553, of course, does not affect the present indictment, and would not even if the former act had been repealed. Rev.Stats., § 13.

Judgments affirmed.

Glossary

media concludendi: grounds for asserting a right

Wall Street: street in New York City where the New York Stock Exchange is located; more generally, the investment industry as a whole

---

ABRAMS V. UNITED STATES

DATE 1919	**CITATION** 250 U.S. 616
AUTHOR John Hessin Clarke	**SIGNIFICANCE** Held that the First Amendment did not uphold a defendant's free speech rights if what they uttered or printed tended to undermine the nation's defense efforts during wartime
VOTE 7–2	

Overview

 Argued October 20–21, 1919, and decided on November 10, 1919, the case of *Abrams v. United States* (titled in full *Jacob Abrams et al. v. the United States*) upheld a restriction on First Amendment freedoms if they were deemed to have attempted to impede the workings of the U.S. government and economy during the course of war. It was deemed that the actions of the defendants met the criteria of constituting a "clear and present danger" enunciated only eight months earlier, on March 3, 1919, by Justice Oliver Wendell Holmes Jr. in *Schenck v. United States*.

In 1917, a small Russian-Jewish anarchist group named Frayhayt (Yiddish for "Freedom") was formed in New York City and supported the ongoing Russian Revolution. Jacob Abrams, one of the members of Frayhayt, rented a basement apartment and purchased and installed a printing press, which turned out circulars for the group.

Seven defendants, Jacob Abrams, Mollie Steimer, Jacob Schwartz, Gabriel Prober, Hyman Lachowsky, Hyman Rosansky, and Samuel Lipman, would be arrested on charges of distributing leaflets that criticized the U.S. intervention in Russia against the Soviet regime.

One of the two leaflets in question called for a general strike designed to negatively impact war production as a means of protest against the deployment of U.S. troops in Russia. Rosansky was the first arrested on August 22, 1918, when he threw the leaflets out of a fourth-floor window of a hat factory at Houston and Crosby streets in New York. Rosansky was persuaded by police to reveal the names of his accomplices, probably in return for comparative leniency.

The first leaflet, written in English and printed under the title "The Hypocrisy of the United States and her Allies," denounced in general terms the entire policy of U.S. military intervention in Russia. The second leaflet, "Workers—Wake Up," written in Yiddish, was more specific in calling for economic action through a general strike aimed at curtailing munitions production.

The specific allegations were that the defendants violated the Espionage Act of 1917's 1918 Amendment (also referred to as the Sedition Act of 1918). The first leaflet was alleged to have illegally used language that was "abusive" to the U.S. government, and the second to have urged interference against the foreign commerce of the United States during wartime.

At the trial, held October 10–23, 1919, five of the defendants were found guilty: Abrams, Steimer, Lipman, Rosansky, and Lachowsky. Jacob Schwartz died of influenza while in prison on October 14, 1919, and Gabriel Prober was acquitted. Rosansky received the lesser sentence of three years' imprisonment; Steimer was sentenced to fifteen years, and the other three were sentenced to twenty. The defendants appealed to the Supreme Court, arguing that they had not attempted to impede the war against Germany and the other Central Powers but had focused only on protest against troop deployment in Russia, which they further argued was within their First Amendment rights.

Context

Fear of anarchism was prevalent throughout Europe and the United States during the late nineteenth to early twentieth centuries. In the wake of a series of uprisings in Europe in 1848, various radical political groups emerged espousing a complete overturning of the prevailing economic and socio-political system—some even going as far as to advocate violent revolution. Though Marxist, syndicalist, and anarchist groups often disagreed (even among themselves within their own groups) over long-term goals and strategy, they all concurred when it came to advocating destruction of "the system." Foreseeing a massive class struggle, they all focused on recruiting the working class to their movements. The anarchists were especially feared. A significant group of anarchists followed the ideas of Russian political theorist Mikhail Bakunin (1814–1876). Bakunin condemned the prevailing governmental systems as maintaining an unfair and exploitive capitalist economy, and he preached the necessity of destroying them through direct action—in the form of violent revolution and assassinations. These ideas inspired a spate of high-profile assassinations of European leaders: Tsar Alexander II of Russia (1881), President Sadi Carnot of France (1894), Prime Minister Canovas de Castillo of Spain (1897), Empress Elizabeth of Austria-Hungary (1898), and King Umberto I of Italy (1900).

The United States was not immune: the fear of anarchist agitation within European immigrant groups coming into the country was mingled with anxiety over possible domestic working-class uprisings. The

Oliver Wendell Holmes wrote a dissenting opinion.
(Wikimedia Commons)

activities of the Molly Maguires in the Pennsylvania coalfields during the 1870s, the Haymarket Square Bombing in Chicago in 1886, and the Pullman Strike of 1894 only served to intensify these apprehensions. But what truly brought it home to Americans was the death by assassination of President William McKinley on September 14, 1901, at the hands of the self-defined anarchist Leon Czolgosz, the son of Polish immigrants.

The years 1900 to 1919 witnessed an unprecedent surge of documented immigration into the United States—more than 15 million, predominantly from Eastern and Central Europe. This fanned fears that radical ideologies like anarchism were being imported into the country as well, along with the danger of their taking root. The outbreak of World War I in Europe on July 28, 1914, exacerbated these fears and fueled a backlash against the country's entry into the war. On August 4, 1914, President Woodrow Wilson initially proclaimed the United States' neutrality in the conflict, though the large volume of trade between the United States and Britain (and to a lesser extent, France) made this difficult. Germany's use of submarine warfare to break the British fleet's blockade led to a near-confrontation with the United States when several American ships were sunk by German U-boats. Germany agreed to scale back submarine attacks, and the situation eased. Newly arrived and first-generation immigrants largely took sides according to their ethnicity (German Americans gravitating toward support of the Central Powers, for example, while Italian and Russian Americans advocated for the Allies). Anti-war sentiment was still strong enough in 1916 that President Wilson ran for reelection partially on the slogan "He kept us out of war." However, on January 31, 1917, Germany announced the resumption of unrestricted submarine warfare, and on February 24, 1917, German attempts to incite Mexico to attack the United States were revealed in the intercepted Zimmermann telegram. On April 6, 1917, Congress declared war on Germany at the request of President Wilson.

By the time America entered the conflict, its Allies were in a desperate state. Britain and France were locked into a bloody stalemate against Germany in the Western Front; Italy was likewise in a deadlock with Austria-Hungary on the Alpine Front; Serbia and Romania had been overrun; and Russia was in a state of collapse. On the home front, the government assumed unprecedented power over the private sector, the economy, and the media to maximize the strength of the war effort. Anything that would tend to hamper operations or damage morale was seen as unpatriotic, if not treasonous.

The situation in Russia was particularly dire. Massive defeats, incompetent and corrupt leadership, shortages, and privations had forced the abdication of Tsar Nicholas II in March 1917, and the Duma, Russia's parliament, took over and continued Russia's participation on the side of the Allies. However, Russian defeats and starvation continued, and the Provisional Government (as the Russian Republic was called) was unable to control the Bolshevik Revolution in October 1917 and was overthrown. A Communist government was installed and opened peace negotiations with Germany and the other Central Powers to pull Russia out of the war. This would culminate in the Treaty of Brest-Litovsk on March 3, 1918, wherein Russia (now renamed the Soviet Union) ceded large tracts of territory and dropped out of the conflict. Civil war broke out between the Soviet supporters (or "Reds") and various other groups (termed "Whites").

Concerned over the possible threat of a Communist revolution spreading to the United States and the advantage that Russia's withdrawal handed to the Central Powers, the Wilson administration ordered American troops to Northern Russia and, later, Siberia, where they remained for over a year, from August 1918 to August 1919). There were protests against the deployment of troops to Russia, and on August 22, 1918, seven Russian-born immigrants distributed leaflets in New York condemning U.S. intervention in Russia. They were arrested under the 1918 Amendment to the Espionage Act of 1917, precipitating the *Abrams* case.

About the Author

John Hessin Clarke was born on September 18, 1857, in New Lisbon, Ohio, to John Clarke, an immigrant from what is now Northern Ireland, and Melissa Hessin Clarke. The father became a judge and tutored his son in the law after he had graduated from Western Reserve College, so that he was able to gain admission to the Ohio bar in 1878. In 1882 he became part owner of a newspaper, the *Youngstown Vindicator*, and was drawn into involvement in politics. He became a Progressive Democrat, aligned with the reformist mayor of Cleveland, Ohio, Tom L. Johnson. In 1903 he ran unsuccessfully for the U.S. Senate against Republican political boss Mark Hanna. In 1914, having worked for the election of Woodrow Wilson to the White House, Clarke was appointed to a U.S. District Court judgeship, and two years later he was named an associate justice for the Supreme Court. Clarke's appointment by President Wilson elicited no major opposition, and the Senate confirmed him unanimously on July 24, 1916. Contrary to the experience of many justices, Clarke did not relish his time on the Supreme Court. He found the work constricting, and he grew to be on exceptionally bad terms with one of his colleagues, James Clark McReynolds. As a justice with a more progressive stance, he often voted with Louis Brandeis and Oliver Wendell Holmes Jr.—*Abrams v. United States* was an exception to the general rule. Clarke's overall philosophy can be characterized as loose constructionist and pro-governmental interventionist.

The decline of progressivism, as manifested in the massive repudiation of the Wilsonian Democratic Party's policies in the election of 1920, and the inauguration of the ultra-conservative presidential administration of Warren G. Harding only added to Clarke's disillusionment. His final decision to resign from the Court on September 18, 1922, seems, however, to have arisen over personal family issues: the deaths of his two sisters, Ida and Alice, with whom he was close and who lived at his house. Clarke was a confirmed bachelor all his life.

Shortly after leaving the Court, Clarke became heavily involved in Woodrow Wilson's crusade to have the United States join the League of Nations. League membership had been voted down by the isolationist Republican majority Senate in 1919, and since the Republican Party was the dominant power in Washington throughout the 1920s, Clarke fought a nearly hopeless battle. During the 1930s Clarke supported President Franklin D. Roosevelt's New Deal policies and even made a speech in 1937 to a national radio audience in support of the Judicial Procedures Reform ("Court-Packing") Bill. He died on March 22, 1945.

Oliver Wendell Holmes Jr. was born on March 8, 1841, in Boston, Massachusetts, and fought in the Union Army during the Civil War, rising to the rank of Colonel. Upon graduation from Harvard Law School in 1866, he maintained a legal practice, and in 1882 he was appointed associate justice of the Massachusetts State Supreme Court, rising to the position of chief justice in 1899. On December 2, 1902, Holmes was nominated by President Theodore Roosevelt as associate justice on the U.S. Supreme Court, and he was sworn in six days later. On January 12, 1932, he retired from the Court, two months short of his ninety-first birthday, and he passed away on March 6, 1935. *Abrams v. United States* marked one of the Great Dissenter's most noteworthy dissenting opinions.

Explanation and Analysis of the Document

The Majority Opinion

Justice John Hessin Clarke wrote the majority opinion and was joined by Chief Justice Edward Douglass White and Associate Justices Willis Van Devanter, James Clark McReynolds, Mahlon Pitney, Joseph McKenna, and William R. Day. Justice Clarke opened the majority decision by listing the four counts on which the district court had convicted the defendants of vi-

olating the Espionage Act of 1917, "as amended May 16, 1918." The first two counts were only mentioned at the beginning and are ignored in the conclusion. They were that the leaflets printed and distributed by the defendants had contained, first, "disloyal, scurrilous, and abusive language about the form of government of the United States" and, second, language "intended to bring the form of government of the United States into contempt, scorn, contumely, and disrepute."

The third and fourth counts are more fully elaborated on: the leaflets contained, third, "language intended to incite, provoke, and encourage resistance to the United States in said war" (World War I) and, fourth, language intended to "incite and advocate curtailment of production of things and products, to wit, ordnance and ammunition, necessary and essential to the prosecution of war."

Justice Clarke then proceeded to lay out the political inclinations of the defendants (three of whom classified themselves opposing any and all forms of government, and a fourth as opposing the United States' government as "capitalistic"). Clarke further argued that the evidence and court testimony had established a conspiracy among the defendants to distribute the leaflets. He then addressed one of the major points raised for the defense, the argument that the Espionage Act of 1917 and its 1918 Amendment were unconstitutional on the basis of violating First Amendment freedoms of speech and of the press. Clarke dismissed this by referring to the Court's ruling in *Schenck v. United States*, backed by those in *Baer v. United States* and *Frohwerk v. United States*, which all established the Espionage Act's constitutionality during wartime.

Clarke likewise rejected the defense arguments that there was insufficient evidence to support the trial verdict and that the intent was not to break the law. In the latter context, especially, the defendants argued that their intent had not been to harm the U.S. government or to interfere with the war against Germany and the other Central Powers (explaining that they despised imperial Germany and its militarism) but to protest and act against the United States' involvement in the Russian Revolution. Clarke conceded that while the intent might possibly have focused on Russia, the inevitable effect was that it would hamper the United States' war effort and thus actually did contravene the law. In particular, Justice Clarke referred to the second leaflet, titled "Worker—Wake Up," as pushing for a general strike to impede the production of war materials as detrimental to the struggle against the Central Powers. Therefore, the conviction on the third and fourth counts would be affirmed.

The Dissenting Opinion

Justice Oliver Wendell Holmes Jr. wrote a dissenting opinion, which was joined by Justice Louis Brandeis. Justice Holmes's dissent succinctly summarized the content of the leaflets and categorized them as posing or advocating no threat to the form of government of the United States and ruled the first and second counts of conviction as being without merit. Justice Holmes then focused primarily on the fourth count, conceding that the wording in the second leaflet calling for a general strike would indeed "urge curtailment of production of things necessary to the prosecution of the war within the meaning of the Act." However, he argued that criminal prosecution could only by justified if there was proven intent to harm the United States, and Holmes alleges that such proof had not been presented. Justice Holmes went on to define and elaborate on the concept of "intent" and why he thought criminal conviction in this instance was inappropriate.

The crux of the dissent was the question as to whether the *Abrams* case passed the rigorous test of whether and to what extent Congress possessed the authority to limit First Amendment freedoms, even during wartime. In Justice Holmes's interpretation, such a drastic penalizing of free speech and the free press could only be constitutional in cases of "imminent" danger, or, as he elaborated, "danger of immediate evil or intent to carry it out," somewhat modifying his standard of "clear and present danger" articulated in *Schenck v. Ohio*. Holmes then asserted that this particular incident, which he termed "the surreptitious publication of a silly pamphlet by an unknown man," did not rise to the level of danger that could occasion a criminal penalty.

Justice Holmes touched upon the third count quite briefly and likewise dismissed it inasmuch as no intent of the use of force against the United States was advocated. Clause 57 of *Abrams* commented on what Justice Holmes believed to be the excessive severity of the sentences placed on the defendants, and Clause 58, the closing clause, expounded upon the idea of "free trade in ideas," arguing that only the most extreme and

proximate peril should occasion the suppression of even repugnant ideas. His conclusion was that the defendants had been denied their constitutional rights.

Impact

The controversy over the status of First Amendment rights in wartime did not end with *Abrams v. United States* but simmered and reemerged many times over the next half century, creating lively debate amongst jurists and legal scholars The Holmesian ideas of "clear and imminent danger" and "free trade in ideas" were never totally accepted or rejected. Instead, Justice Clarke and those justices who had reservations over the Holmesian interpretation clung to modified versions of a legal theory called the "bad tendency test," which set the lower bar for First Amendment freedom restriction at requiring proof that it would merely tend to be detrimental to the government and its functioning. The precedent had been the Supreme Court decision of *Patterson v. Colorado* (1907). The Supreme Court rulings in *Whitney v. California* (1927) and *Dennis v. United States* (1951) seemed to largely support the "bad tendency" theory at the expense of that of "imminent danger," but the issue refused to remain dormant. Justice Clarke's majority opinion notwithstanding, the *Abrams* case was ultimately best remembered for Holmes's dissenting opinion, which grew in stature as time went on. In 1969, the Supreme Court's ruling in *Brandenburg v. Ohio* reconfigured "clear and present danger" and "imminent danger" as "imminent lawless action" as the test for restriction on free speech, and it effectively overturned *Schenck v. Ohio*, *Abrams v. United States*, *Whitney v. California*, and *Dennis v. United States*. The *Brandenburg* test remains the definitive statement on the First Amendment's restrictions issue, and it was reinforced by the Supreme Court ruling in *Hess v. Indiana* (1973).

Of the *Abrams* case defendants, only Mollie Steiner (1897–1980) would achieve an appreciable level of fame. She was released from prison in 1921, on condition of her deportation back to Russia, and finally settled in Mexico and remained an active advocate for anarchism to the end of her days. Jacob Abrams also gravitated to Mexico, while Samul Lipman and Hyman Lachowsky, not as fortunate, were later executed in Russia.

Questions for Further Study

1. How might the historical background leading up to the *Abrams* case have influenced the Supreme Court's majority opinion?

2. In what ways do the interpretations of what constitutes a "clear and present danger" in the majority and dissenting opinions differ, and how is this significant?

3. What restrictions has wartime historically placed on individual freedom and actions?

Further Reading

Books

Healy, Thomas. *The Great Dissent: How Oliver Wendell Holmes Changed His Mind and Changed the History of Free Speech in America.* New York: Metropolitan Books, 2013.

Polenberg, Richard. *Fighting Faiths: The Abrams Case, the Supreme Court, and Free Speech.* Ithaca, NY: Cornell University Press, 1999.

Smith, Stephen A. "Schenck v. United States and Abrams v. United States." In *Free Speech on Trial: Communication Perspectives on Landmark Supreme Court Decisions,* edited by Richard A. Parker: 20–35. Tuscaloosa: University of Alabama Press, 2003.

Stone, Geoffrey. *Perilous Times: Free Speech in Wartime from the Sedition Act of 1798 to the War on Terrorism.* New York: Norton, 2005.

Warner, Hoyt Landon. *The Life of Mr. Justice Clarke: A Testament to the Power of Liberal Dissent in America.* Cleveland, OH: Western Reserve University Press, 1959.orton, 1972.

Websites

"Abrams et al. v. United States." Legal Information Institute, Cornell Law School. Accessed February 22, 2023, https://www.law.cornell.edu/supremecourt/text/250/616.

"Abrams v. United States (1919)." National Constitution Center. Accessed February 22, 2023, https://constitutioncenter.org/the-constitution/supreme-court-case-library/abrams-v-united-states.

Spitzer, Elianna. "Abrams v. United States: Supreme Court Case, Arguments, Impact." March 20, 2020. Accessed February 22, 2023, https://www.thoughtco.com/abrams-v-united-states-supreme-court-case-arguments-impact-4797628.

—Commentary by Raymond Pierre Hylton

ABRAMS V. UNITED STATES

Document Text

MR. JUSTICE CLARKE delivered the opinion of the Court

On a single indictment, containing four counts, the five plaintiffs in error, hereinafter designated the defendants, were convicted of conspiring to violate provisions of the Espionage Act of Congress (§ 3, Title I, of Act approved June 15, 1917, as amended May 16, 1918, 40 Stat. 553).

Each of the first three counts charged the defendants with conspiring, when the United States was at war with the Imperial Government of Germany, to unlawfully utter, print, write and publish: in the first count, "disloyal, scurrilous and abusive language about the form of Government of the United States;" in the second count, language "intended to bring the form of Government of the United States into contempt, scorn, contumely and disrepute;" and in the third count, language "intended to incite, provoke and encourage resistance to the United States in said war." The charge in the fourth count was that the defendants conspired,

"when the United States was at war with the Imperial German Government, unlawfully and willfully, by utterance, writing, printing and publication, to urge, incite and advocate curtailment of production of things and products, to-wit, ordnance and ammunition, necessary and essential to the prosecution of the war."

The offenses were charged in the language of the act of Congress.

It was charged in each count of the indictment that it was a part of the conspiracy that the defendants would attempt to accomplish their unlawful purpose by printing, writing and distributing in the City of New York many copies of a leaflet or circular, printed in the English language, and of another printed in the Yiddish language, copies of which, properly identified, were attached to the indictment.

All of the five defendants were born in Russia. They were intelligent, had considerable schooling, and, at the time they were arrested, they had lived in the United States terms varying from five to ten years, but none of them had applied for naturalization. Four of them testified as witnesses in their own behalf, and, of these, three frankly avowed that they were "rebels," "revolutionists," "anarchists," that they did not believe in government in any form, and they declared that they had no interest whatever in the Government of the United States. The fourth defendant testified that he was a "socialist," and believed in "a proper kind of government, not capitalistic," but, in his classification, the Government of the United States was "capitalistic."

It was admitted on the trial that the defendants had united to print and distribute the described circulars, and that five thousand of them had been printed and distributed about the 22nd day of August, 1918. The group had a meeting place in New York City, in rooms rented by defendant Abrams under an assumed name, and there the subject of printing the circulars was discussed about two weeks before the defendants were arrested. The defendant Abrams, although not a printer, on July 27, 1918, purchased the printing outfit with which the circulars were printed, and installed it in a basement room where the work was done at night. The circulars were distributed, some by throwing them from a window of a building where one of the defendants was employed and others secretly, in New York City.

The defendants pleaded "not guilty," and the case of the Government consisted in showing the facts we have stated, and in introducing in evidence copies of the two printed circulars attached to the indictment, a sheet entitled "Revolutionists Unite for Action," written by the defendant Lipman, and found on him when he was arrested, and another paper, found at the headquarters of the group, and for which Abrams assumed responsibility.

Thus, the conspiracy and the doing of the overt acts charged were largely admitted, and were fully established.

On the record thus described, it is argued, somewhat faintly, that the acts charged against the defendants were not unlawful because within the protection of that freedom of speech and of the press which is guaranteed by the First Amendment to the Constitution of the United States, and that the entire Espionage Act is unconstitutional because in conflict with that Amendment.

This contention is sufficiently discussed and is definitely negatived in *Schenck v. United States* and *Baer v. United States*, 249 U. S. 47, and in *Frohwerk v. United States*, 249 U. S. 204.

The claim chiefly elaborated upon by the defendants in the oral argument and in their brief is that there is no substantial evidence in this record to support the judgment upon the verdict of guilty, and that the motion of the defendants for an instructed verdict in their favor was erroneously denied. A question of law is thus presented, which calls for an examination of the record not for the purpose of weighing conflicting testimony, but only to determine whether there was some evidence, competent and substantial, before the jury, fairly tending to sustain the verdict. *Troxell v. Delaware, Lackawanna & Western R.R. Co.*, 227 U. S. 434, 227 U. S. 442; *Lancaster v. Collins*, 115 U. S. 222, 115 U. S. 225; *Chicago & Northwestern Ry. Co. v. Ohle*, 117 U. S. 123, 117 U. S. 129. We shall not need to consider the sufficiency, under the rule just stated, of the evidence introduced as to all of the counts of the indictment, for, since the sentence imposed did not exceed that which might lawfully have been imposed under any single count, the judgment upon the verdict of the jury must be affirmed if the evidence is sufficient to sustain

anyone of the counts. *Evans v. United States*, 153 U. S. 608; *Claassen v. United States*, 142 U. S. 140; *Debs v. United States*, 249 U. S. 211, 249 U. S. 216.

The first of the two articles attached to the indictment is conspicuously headed, "The Hypocrisy of the United States and her Allies." After denouncing President Wilson as a hypocrite and a coward because troops were sent into Russia, it proceeds to assail our Government in general, saying:

"His [the President's] shameful, cowardly silence about the intervention in Russia reveals the hypocrisy of the plutocratic gang in Washington and vicinity."

It continues:

"He [the President] is too much of a coward to come out openly and say: 'We capitalistic nations cannot afford to have a proletarian republic in Russia.'"

Among the capitalistic nations, Abrams testified, the United States was included.

Growing more inflammatory as it proceeds, the circular culminates in:

"The Russian Revolution cries: Workers of the World! Awake! Rise! Put down your enemy and mine!"

"Yes! friends, there is only one enemy of the workers of the world and that is CAPITALISM."

This is clearly an appeal to the "workers" of this country to arise and put down by force the Government of the United States which they characterize as their "hypocritical," "cowardly" and "capitalistic" enemy.

It concludes:

"Awake! Awake! you Workers of the World!"

"REVOLUTIONISTS"

The second of the articles was printed in the Yiddish language and, in the translation, is headed, "Workers—Wake up." After referring to "his Majesty, Mr. Wilson, and the rest of the gang; dogs of all colors," it continues:

"Workers, Russian emigrants, you who had the least belief in the honesty of *our* Government," which defendants admitted referred to the United States Government, "must now throw away all confidence, must spit in the face the false, hypocritic, military propaganda which has fooled you so relentlessly, calling forth your sympathy, your help, to the prosecution of the war."

The purpose of this obviously was to persuade the persons to whom it was addressed to turn a deaf ear to patriotic appeals in behalf of the Government of the United States, and to cease to render it assistance in the prosecution of the war.

It goes on:

"With the money which you have loaned, or are going to loan them, they will make bullets not only for the Germans, but also for the Workers Soviets of Russia. *Workers in the ammunition factories, you are producing bullets, bayonets, cannon, to murder not only the Germans, but also your dearest, best, who are in Russia and are fighting for freedom.*"

It will not do to say, as is now argued, that the only intent of these defendants was to prevent injury to the Russian cause. Men must be held to have intended, and to be accountable for, the effects which their acts were likely to produce. Even if their primary purpose and intent was to aid the cause of the Russian Revolution, the plan of action which they adopted necessarily involved, before it could be realized, defeat of the war program of the United States, for the obvious effect of this appeal, if it should become effective, as they hoped it might, would be to persuade persons of character such as those whom they regarded themselves as addressing, not to aid government loans, and not to work in ammunition factories where their work would produce "bullets, bayonets, cannon" and other munitions of war the use of which would cause the "murder" of Germans and Russians.

Again, the spirit becomes more bitter as it proceed to declare that—

"America and her Allies have betrayed (the Workers). Their robberish aims are clear to all men. The destruction of the Russian Revolution, that is the politics of the march to Russia."

"*Workers, our reply to the barbaric intervention has to be a general strike! An open challenge* only will let the Government know that not only the Russian Worker fights for freedom, but also here in America lives the spirit of Revolution."

This is not an attempt to bring about a change of administration by candid discussion, for, no matter what may have incited the outbreak on the part of the defendant anarchists, the manifest purpose of such a publication was to create an attempt to defeat the war plans of the Government of the United States by bringing upon the country the paralysis of a general strike, thereby arresting the production of all munitions and other things essential to the conduct of the war.

This purpose is emphasized in the next paragraph, which reads:

"Do not let the Government scare you with their wild punishment in prisons, hanging and shooting. We must not and will not betray the splendid fighters of Russia. *Workers, up to fight.*"

After more of the same kind, the circular concludes:

"Woe unto those who will be in the way of progress. Let solidarity live!"

It is signed, "The Rebels."

That the interpretation we have put upon these articles, circulated in the greatest port of our land, from which great numbers of soldiers were at the time taking ship daily, and in which great quantities of war supplies of every kind were at the time being manufactured for transportation overseas, is not only the fair interpretation of them, but that it is the meaning which their authors consciously intended should be conveyed by them to others is further shown by the additional writings found in the meeting place of the defendant group and on the person of one of them. One of these circulars is headed: "Revolutionists! Unite for Action!"

After denouncing the President as "Our Kaiser" and the hypocrisy of the United States and her Allies, this article concludes:

"Socialists, Anarchists, Industrial Workers of the World, Socialists, Labor party men and other revolutionary organizations, *Unite for action,* and let us save the Workers' Republic of Russia,"

"*Know you lovers of freedom that, in order to save the Russian revolution, we must keep the armies of the allied countries busy at home.*"

Thus was again avowed the purpose to throw the country into a state of revolution if possible, and to thereby frustrate the military program of the Government.

The remaining article, after denouncing the resident for what is characterized as hostility to the Russian revolution, continues:

"We, the toilers of America, who believe in real liberty, shall *pledge ourselves,* in case the United States will participate in that bloody conspiracy against Russia, *to create so great a disturbance that the autocrats of America shall be compelled to keep their armies at home, and not be able to spare any for Russia.*"

It concludes with this definite threat of armed rebellion:

"If they will use arms against the Russian people to enforce their standard of order, *so will we use arms,* and they shall never see the ruin of the Russian Revolution."

These excerpts sufficiently show that, while the immediate occasion for this particular outbreak of lawlessness on the part of the defendant alien anarchists may have been resentment caused by our Government's sending troops into Russia as a strategic operation against the Germans on the eastern battle front, yet the plain purpose of their propaganda was to excite, at the supreme crisis of the war, disaffection, sedition, riots, and, as they hoped, revolution, in this country for the purpose of embarrassing, and, if possible, defeating the military plans of the Government in Europe. A technical distinction may perhaps be taken between disloyal and abusive language applied to the *form* of our government or language intended to bring the *form* of our government into contempt and disrepute, and language of like character and intended to produce like results directed against the President and Congress, the agencies through which that form of government must function in time of war. But it is not necessary to a decision of this case to consider whether such distinction is vital or merely formal, for the language of these circulars was obviously intended to provoke and to encourage resistance to the United States in the war, as the third count runs, and the defendants, in terms, plainly urged and advocated a resort to a general strike of workers in ammunition factories for the purpose of curtailing the production of ordnance and munitions necessary and essential to the prosecution of the war as is charged in the fourth

count. Thus, it is clear not only that some evidence, but that much persuasive evidence, was before the jury tending to prove that the defendants were guilty as charged in both the third and fourth counts of the indictment, and, under the long established rule of law hereinbefore stated, the judgment of the District Court must be

Affirmed.

MR. JUSTICE HOLMES dissenting

This indictment is founded wholly upon the publication of two leaflets which I shall describe in a moment. The first count charges a conspiracy pending the war with Germany to publish abusive language about the form of government of the United States, laying the preparation and publishing of the first leaflet as overt acts. The second count charges a conspiracy pending the war to publish language intended to bring the form of government into contempt, laying the preparation and publishing of the two leaflets as overt acts. The third count alleges a conspiracy to encourage resistance to the United States in the same war, and to attempt to effectuate the purpose by publishing the same leaflets. The fourth count lays a conspiracy to incite curtailment of production of things necessary to the prosecution of the war and to attempt to accomplish it by publishing the second leaflet, to which I have referred.

The first of these leaflets says that the President's cowardly silence about the intervention in Russia reveals the hypocrisy of the plutocratic gang in Washington. It intimates that "German militarism combined with allied capitalism to crush the Russian evolution "—goes on that the tyrants of the world fight each other until they see a common enemy—working class enlightenment, when they combine to crush it, and that now militarism and capitalism combined, though not openly, to crush the Russian revolution. It says that there is only one enemy of the workers of the world, and that is capitalism; that it is a crime for workers of America, &c., to fight the workers' republic of Russia, and ends "Awake! Awake, you Workers of the World, Revolutionists!" A note adds

"It is absurd to call us pro-German. We hate and despise German militarism more than do you hypocritical tyrants. We have more reasons for denouncing German militarism than has the coward of the White House."

The other leaflet, headed "Workers—Wake Up," with abusive language says that America together with the Allies will march for Russia to help the Czecko-Slovaks in their struggle against the Bolsheviki, and that this time the hypocrites shall not fool the Russian emigrants and friends of Russia in America. It tells the Russian emigrants that they now must spit in the face of the false military propaganda by which their sympathy and help to the prosecution of the war have been called forth, and says that, with the money they have lent or are going to lend, "they will make bullets not only for the Germans, but also for the Workers Soviets of Russia," and further,

"Workers in the ammunition factories, you are producing bullets, bayonets, cannon, to murder not only the Germans, but also your dearest, best, who are in Russia and are fighting for freedom."

It then appeals to the same Russian emigrants at some length not to consent to the "inquisitionary expedition to Russia," and says that the destruction of the Russian revolution is "the politics of the march to Russia." The leaflet winds up by saying "Workers, our reply to this barbaric intervention has to be a general strike!" and, after a few words on the spirit of revolution, exhortations not to be afraid, and some usual tall talk ends, "Woe unto those who will be in the way of progress. Let solidarity live! The Rebels."

No argument seems to me necessary to show that these pronunciamentos in no way attack the form of government of the United States, or that they do not support either of the first two counts. What little I have to say about the third count may be postponed until I have considered the fourth. With regard to that, it seems too plain to be denied that the suggestion to workers in the ammunition factories that they are producing bullets to murder their dearest, and the further advocacy of a general strike, both in the second leaflet, do urge curtailment of production of things necessary to the prosecution of the war within the meaning of the Act of May 16, 1918, c. 75, 40 Stat. 553, amending § 3 of the earlier Act of 1917. But to make the conduct criminal, that statute requires that it should be "with intent by such curtailment to cripple or hinder the United States in the prosecution of the war." It seems to me that no such intent is proved.

I am aware, of course, that the word intent as vaguely used in ordinary legal discussion means no more than knowledge at the time of the act that the consequences said to be intended will ensue. Even less than that will satisfy the general principle of civil and criminal liability. A man may have to pay damages, may be sent to prison, at common law might be hanged, if, at the time of his act, he knew facts from which common experience showed that the consequences would follow, whether he individually could foresee them or not. But, when words are used exactly, a deed is not done with intent to produce a consequence unless that consequence is the aim of the deed. It may be obvious, and obvious to the actor, that the consequence will follow, and he may be liable for it even if he regrets it, but he does not do the act with intent to produce it unless the aim to produce it is the proximate motive of the specific act, although there may be some deeper motive behind.

It seems to me that this statute must be taken to use its words in a strict and accurate sense. They would be absurd in any other. A patriot might think that we were wasting money on aeroplanes, or making more cannon of a certain kind than we needed, and might advocate curtailment with success, yet, even if it turned out that the curtailment hindered and was thought by other minds to have been obviously likely to hinder the United States in the prosecution of the war, no one would hold such conduct a crime. I admit that my illustration does not answer all that might be said, but it is enough to show what I think, and to let me pass to a more important aspect of the case. I refer to the First Amendment to the Constitution, that Congress shall make no law abridging the freedom of speech.

I never have seen any reason to doubt that the questions of law that alone were before this Court in the cases of *Schenck, Frohwerk* and *Debs,* 249 U. S. 249 U.S. 47, 249 U. S. 204, 249 U. S. 211, were rightly decided. I do not doubt for a moment that, by the same reasoning that would justify punishing persuasion to murder, the United States constitutionally may punish speech that produces or is intended to produce a clear and imminent danger that it will bring about forthwith certain substantive evils that the United States constitutionally may seek to prevent. The power undoubtedly is greater in time of war than in time of peace, because war opens dangers that do not exist at other times.

But, as against dangers peculiar to war, as against others, the principle of the right to free speech is always the same. It is only the present danger of immediate evil or an intent to bring it about that warrants Congress in setting a limit to the expression of opinion where private rights are not concerned. Congress certainly cannot forbid all effort to change the mind of the country. Now nobody can suppose that the surreptitious publishing of a silly leaflet by an unknown man, without more, would present any immediate danger that its opinions would hinder the success of the government arms or have any appreciable tendency to do so. Publishing those opinions for the very purpose of obstructing, however, might indicate a greater danger, and, at any rate, would have the quality of an attempt. So I assume that the second leaflet, if published for the purposes alleged in the fourth count, might be punishable. But it seems pretty clear to me that nothing less than that would bring these papers within the scope of this law. An actual intent in the sense that I have explained is necessary to constitute an attempt, where a further act of the same individual is required to complete the substantive crime, for reasons given in *Swift & Co. v. United States,* 196 U. S. 375, 196 U. S. 396. It is necessary where the success of the attempt depends upon others because, if that intent is not present, the actor's aim may be accomplished without bringing about the evils sought to be checked. An intent to prevent interference with the revolution in Russia might have been satisfied without any hindrance to carrying on the war in which we were engaged.

I do not see how anyone can find the intent required by the statute in any of the defendants' words. The second leaflet is the only one that affords even a foundation for the charge, and there, without invoking the hatred of German militarism expressed in the former one, it is evident from the beginning to the end that the only object of the paper is to help Russia and stop American intervention there against the popular government— not to impede the United States in the war that it was carrying on. To say that two phrases, taken literally, might import a suggestion of conduct that would have interference with the war as an indirect and probably undesired effect seems to me by no means enough to show an attempt to produce that effect.

I return for a moment to the third count. That charges an intent to provoke resistance to the United States in its war with Germany. Taking the clause in the statute that deals with that, in connection with the other elaborate provisions of the act, I think that resistance to the United States means some forcible act of opposition to some proceeding of the United States in pursuance of the war. I think the intent must be the specific intent that I have described, and, for the reasons that I have given, I think that no such intent was proved or existed in fact. I also think that there is no hint at resistance to the United States as I construe the phrase.

In this case, sentences of twenty years' imprisonment have been imposed for the publishing of two leaflets that I believe the defendants had as much right to publish as the Government has to publish the Constitution of the United States now vainly invoked by them. Even if I am technically wrong, and enough can be squeezed from these poor and puny anonymities to turn the color of legal litmus paper, I will add, even if what I think the necessary intent were shown, the most nominal punishment seems to me all that possibly could be inflicted, unless the defendants are to be made to suffer not for what the indictment alleges, but for the creed that they avow—a creed that I believe to be the creed of ignorance and immaturity when honestly held, as I see no reason to doubt that it was held here, but which, although made the subject of examination at the trial, no one has a right even to consider in dealing with the charges before the Court.

Persecution for the expression of opinions seems to me perfectly logical. If you have no doubt of your premises or your power, and want a certain result with all your heart, you naturally express your wishes in law, and sweep away all opposition. To allow opposition by speech seems to indicate that you think the speech impotent, as when a man says that he has squared the circle, or that you do not care wholeheartedly for the result, or that you doubt either your power or your premises. But when men have realized that time has upset many fighting faiths, they may come to believe even more than they believe the very foundations of their own conduct that the ultimate good desired is better reached by free trade in ideas—that the best test of truth is the power of the thought to get itself accepted in the competition of the market, and that truth is the only ground upon which their wishes safely can be carried out. That, at any rate, is the theory of our Constitution. It is an experiment, as all life is an experiment. Every year, if not every day, we have to wager our salvation upon some prophecy based upon imperfect knowledge. While that experiment is part of our system, I think that we should be eternally vigilant against attempts to check the expression of opinions that we loathe and believe to be fraught with death, unless they so imminently threaten immediate interference with the lawful and pressing purposes of the law that an immediate check is required to save the country. I wholly disagree with the argument of the Government that the First Amendment left the common law as to seditious libel in force. History seems to me against the notion. I had conceived that the United States, through many years, had shown its repentance for the Sedition Act of 1798, by repaying fines that it imposed. Only the emergency that makes it immediately dangerous to leave the correction of evil counsels to time warrants making any exception to the sweeping command, "Congress shall make no law . . . abridging the freedom of speech." Of course, I am speaking only of expressions of opinion and exhortations, which were all that were uttered here, but I regret that I cannot put into more impressive words my belief that, in their conviction upon this indictment, the defendants were deprived of their rights under the Constitution of the United States.

MR. JUSTICE BRANDEIS concurs with the foregoing opinion.

Glossary

anarchists: nonbelievers in government

circulars: pamphlets, leaflets, or similar printed materials intended for wide circulation

general strike: a strike by many workers in numerous industries, intended to cease or severely curtail economic activity in a region or country, to achieve a social, economic, or political goal

WHITNEY V. CALIFORNIA

DATE 1927 **AUTHOR** Edward Terry Sanford **VOTE** 9-0 **CITATION** 274 U.S. 357	**SIGNIFICANCE** Found that the defendant's conviction under California's criminal syndicalism statute did not violate her free speech rights under the Fourteenth Amendment, because states may constitutionally prohibit speech tending to incite crime, disturb the public peace, or threaten the overthrow of government by unlawful means

Overview

Charlotte Anita Whitney was a founding member of the Communist Labor Party of California. She was prosecuted under the California Criminal Syndicalism Act of 1919 for her part in organizing a group that called for economic and political change through the use of violence. She argued in court that it was not her intent for the organization to use violence to achieve its ends and that the California law violated her free speech rights under the First Amendment. Whitney was convicted, and her conviction was affirmed by the U.S. Supreme Court.

Whitney was explicitly overruled in 1969 in the case *Brandenburg v. Ohio*.

Context

Whitney v. California was decided in the context of the fear of Communism that pervaded the United States in the wake of World War I. That fear led to "red scares"—the suddenly widespread belief that anarchists, communists, trade unionists, and foreigners, particularly those from eastern and southern Europe, were bent on fomenting a revolution that would overthrow the U.S. government. The fear grew after a bomb exploded at the home of Attorney General A. Mitchell Palmer in Washington, D.C., on June 3, 1919. The result of that event was the "Palmer raids" of 1919 and 1920, when the police rounded up and arrested as many as 10,000 people believed to be members of radical political groups. The fear was intensified when a bomb exploded at the heart of New York City's financial district at Wall and Broad Streets on September 16, 1920. The famous—or infamous— Sacco-Vanzetti case, in which two Italian immigrants were tried (in 1921) and executed (in 1927) for robbery and murder in Massachusetts, added to the hysteria.

In response to these fears, a number of states, including California, enacted criminal syndicalism laws in the late 1910s and early 1920s; California's law was enacted in 1919. These laws made it illegal for individuals or groups to advocate radical political change by criminal or violent means. Under these laws, the authorities arrested, tried, and sent to prison thousands of people who opposed capitalism and the U.S. government, even though many of those who held such views advocated them in the form of peaceful

Charlotte Anita Whitney
(Library of Congress)

protests, meetings, and distribution of literature. Many of the laws were intended to undermine the labor movement, particularly the Industrial Workers of the World (the IWW, or "Wobblies"), which was considered radical. The Supreme Court had already upheld restrictions on free speech embodied in the Espionage Act of 1917 and the Sedition Act of 1918 and in a number of earlier cases, including *Schenck v. United States* (1919), *Abrams v. United States* (1919), and *Gitlow v. New York* (1925).

Arguably the most significant of these cases was *Gitlow*, in which the Court, by a vote of 7–2, upheld the constitutionality of New York's Criminal Anarchy Statute of 1902. The statute targeted anyone or any group that advocated violent overthrow of the government. The Court held that the government may restrict or punish speech "containing or advocating, advising or teaching the doctrine that organized government should be overthrown by force, violence or any unlawful means." Benjamin Gitlow, a prominent socialist, was convicted under the New York law for producing 16,000 copies of a document called the "Left-Wing Manifesto." The manifesto called for "the proletariat revolution and the Communist reconstruction of society" through strikes and "revolutionary mass action." The Supreme Court upheld his conviction, but at the same time it identified free speech and freedom of the press as "among the fundamental personal rights and 'liberties' protected by the due process clause of the Fourteenth Amendment

from impairment by the States." The case is significant because it was the beginning of the "incorporation doctrine," which extended the reach of First Amendment rights from the actions of the federal government to those of the states.

The facts in *Whitney* were these: Charlotte Anita Whitney, who lived in Oakland, California, had been a member of the Oakland branch of the Socialist Party. At a national convention of the party in Chicago in 1919, a split occurred between the radical and more moderate wings of the party. The Oakland delegates adhered to the radicals. When they were ejected from the convention, they returned home and formed the Communist Labor Party of America. In its "Platform and Program," the party declared that it fully agreed with "the revolutionary working class parties of all countries" and stated that it adhered to the principles of Communism laid down in the manifesto of the Third International at Moscow, an association of Communist parties worldwide. The Communist Labor Party of America's purpose was "to create a unified revolutionary working class movement in America" by organizing workers in a revolutionary class struggle to overthrow capitalist rule and to establish a working-class government, the Dictatorship of the Proletariat, in place of the state machinery of the capitalists. This government would make and enforce the laws, reorganize society on the basis of Communism, and bring about a Communist Commonwealth. Workers would be organized into "revolutionary industrial unions." Propaganda would advocate strikes as a political weapon; the party recommended that strikes of national importance be supported and given a political character. It further recommended the mobilization of propagandists and organizers "who cannot only teach, but actually help to put in practice the principles of revolutionary industrial unionism and Communism."

Whitney was arrested for violating the California Criminal Syndicalism Act. The indictment stated that she did "unlawfully, willfully, wrongfully, deliberately and feloniously organize and assist in organizing, and was, is, and knowingly became a member of an organization, society, group and assemblage of persons organized and assembled to advocate, teach, aid and abet criminal syndicalism." The court of appeals upheld her conviction in county court, and she appealed to the U.S. Supreme Court.

About the Author

Edward Terry Sanford was born in Knoxville, Tennessee, on July 23, 1865. The oldest of six children, he grew up in comfortable circumstances. His father, Edward Sanford Sr., had amassed a fortune in the lumber and construction business in Knoxville. His mother, Emma Chavannes, was a refined woman of French-Swiss descent. The Sanford family attached a great deal of value to education, so as a child Edward attended private schools and then enrolled at the University of Tennessee, where in 1883 he graduated at age eighteen at the head of his class. Two years later he received another bachelor's degree from Harvard University. In 1886 he entered Harvard Law School, where he was one of the first editors of the prestigious *Harvard Law Review*. Three years later he graduated with a master's degree and a law degree. He had already passed the Tennessee bar examination, but when he left Harvard he did postgraduate study in languages in France and Germany.

Sanford returned to Knoxville to begin nearly two decades of private law practice at the prestigious firm of Andrews & Thornburgh. Just a few months after Sanford joined the firm, George Andrews died. Andrews had been scheduled to argue a number of cases before the Tennessee Supreme Court, whose new term was convening shortly. Sanford took over all of Andrews's cases, and with little preparation he was able to argue them successfully. Sanford was as active at home as he was at the office. Among other civic, charitable, professional, and educational activities, he was a trustee of the University of Tennessee, a charter member of the board of governors of the Kentucky General Hospital, a member of the board of directors at two colleges, vice president of the Tennessee Historical Society, and vice president of the American Bar Association.

Sanford's ascent to the U.S. Supreme Court began in 1905. That year he was invited to Washington, D.C., to help U.S. attorney general (and future Supreme Court justice) William Moody prosecute a fertilizer monopoly under the 1890 Sherman Antitrust Act. In 1907 he applied for and received a position as assistant attorney general when it was suggested to him that such a position could help him fulfill his ambition of becoming a federal judge. Sanford served in this post for seventeen months, frequently arguing cases before the Supreme Court. Then in 1908 President Theodore Roosevelt persuaded him to fill a vacancy on the district court in eastern and central Tennessee. Sanford remained in this post for fifteen years.

In late 1922 Supreme Court Justice Mahlon Pitney retired, and Warren Harding had the rare opportunity for a president to appoint a fourth Supreme Court justice. With the backing of the Tennessee Republican governor, the Democratic legislature, Chief Justice William Howard Taft, and virtually everyone who knew him, Sanford received the appointment and was confirmed in the Senate in January 1923. In just seven years on the high court, he delivered the opinion of the Court in 130 cases, many having to do with admiralty law, taxation, bankruptcy law, and patents.

Sanford was involved in numerous important cases. In one, the *Pocket Veto Case* (1929), he resolved a constitutional issue that had bedeviled the nation from its beginning by giving a definitive interpretation of the "pocket veto," the provision in the Constitution by which a bill becomes law if the president has not signed it "unless the Congress by their Adjournment prevent its Return." In the area of civil rights, his record was mixed. In a number of cases, he recognized the existence of noneconomic rights under the due process clause of the Fourteenth Amendment. He voted, for example, to invalidate all-white primary elections in Texas, but he also voted to uphold school desegregation and wrote an opinion upholding racially restrictive covenants, or agreements by property owners not to sell their property to non-whites.

One of the most important civil liberties cases in which Sanford was involved was *Gitlow v. New York* (1925). The case was important for establishing the principle "that freedom of speech and of the press . . . are among the fundamental personal rights and 'liberties' protected by the due process clause of the Fourteenth Amendment." The Court served notice that it would apply the Bill of Rights not just to federal questions but to state questions. Gitlow may have lost, but freedom of speech won.

Sanford was on his way to a birthday celebration for Oliver Wendell Holmes Jr. in Washington, D.C., when he stopped to have a tooth pulled. Almost immediately he fell victim to uremic poisoning and died on March 8, 1930. His passing went almost unnoticed, for Justice and former president William Howard Taft died the same day and it was his name, not Sanford's, that dominated the headlines.

Explanation and Analysis of the Document

After tracing the procedural history of the case, summarizing the pertinent provisions of the California statute at issue, examining the legal technicalities surrounding the Court's jurisdiction in the case, and citing relevant case law on these matters, Sanford proceeds to "the determination, upon the merits, of the constitutional question." Sanford then provides an exhaustive review of the facts of the case, in particular of the viewpoints held by the organization of which Whitney was a member.

Sanford then examines the particulars of the case. He starts by addressing the statement of the appeals court that the syndicalism act and its application "is repugnant to the due process and equal protection clauses of the Fourteenth Amendment." Sanford responds by stating that "the argument entirely disregards the facts." The pertinent facts, in his view, were that Whitney was a member of the national party; that the resolution she supported "did not advocate the use of the ballot to the exclusion of violent and unlawful means of bring about the desired changes in industrial and political conditions"; that the national program was accepted after the constitution of the California Communist Party had been adopted; that Whitney not only remained at the convention but later "manifested her acquiescence by attending as an alternative member of the state executive committee and continuing as a member of the Communist Labor Party."

Sanford proceeds to the question of whether the act is "repugnant to the due process clause by reason of its vagueness and uncertainty of definition." He concludes:

> The Act, plainly, meets the essential requirement of due process that a penal statute be "sufficiently explicit to inform those who are subject to it, what conduct on their part will render them liable to its penalties," and be couched in terms that are not "so vague that men of common intelligence must necessarily guess at its meaning and differ as to its application."

In other words, as Sanford writes, the act "required of the defendant no 'prophetic' understanding of its meaning."

Sanford takes up the technical question of whether the act is "repugnant" to the equal protection clause by arbitrary discrimination between those who advocate the use of violent and unlawful methods to *change* conditions and those who advocate these methods simply to *maintain* such conditions. Sanford answers this contention by stating that "a statute does not violate the equal protection clause merely because it is not all-embracing." He goes on to argue that "the statute must be presumed to be aimed at an evil where experience shows it to be most felt." It is "not to be overthrown merely because oth-

er instances may be suggested to which also it might have been applied." He further states that "the Syndicalism Act is not class legislation; it affects all alike, no matter what their business associations or callings, who come within its terms and do the things prohibited."

The Freedom of Speech Issue

Sanford then addresses the core issue raised by the case: whether the syndicalism act is "repugnant to the due process clause as a restraint of the rights of free speech, assembly, and association." Sanford makes the Court's position clear by stating that the California Syndicalism Act, and those like it in other states, is not an infringement on the First Amendment right of free speech, for the purpose of such acts is to restrain speech that is "inimical," or harmful, to the public welfare. Sanford concludes: "We find no repugnancy in the Syndicalism Act as applied in this case to either the due process or equal protection clauses of the Fourteenth Amendment on any of the grounds upon which its validity has been here challenged." The Fourteenth Amendment, it should be noted, states that "No State shall make or enforce any law which shall abridge the privileges or immunities of citizens of the United States; nor shall any State deprive any person of life, liberty, or property, without due process of law; nor deny to any person within its jurisdiction the equal protection of the laws."

Brandeis Concurrence

The Court reached a unanimous decision, so Justice Louis Brandeis of course concurred. However, he wrote a separate concurrence that legal scholars regard as one of the most eloquent and forceful defenses of the right of free speech in judicial history. He begins by conceding that "although the rights of free speech and assembly are fundamental, they are not, in their nature, absolute." He adds that "their exercise is subject to restriction if the particular restriction proposed is required in order to protect the State from destruction or from serious injury, political, economic, or moral." He clarifies this view: "That the necessity which is essential to a valid restriction does not exist unless speech would produce, or is intended to produce, a clear and imminent danger of some substantive evil which the State constitutionally may seek to prevent has been settled." In referring to "a clear and imminent danger," Brandeis echoes an oft-quoted expression coined by Justice Oliver Wendell Holmes Jr. in *Schenck v. United States* (1919), a case involving a violation of the Espionage Act of 1917: "The question in every case is whether the words used are used in such circumstances and are of such a nature as to create a clear and present danger that they will bring about the substantive evils that the United States Congress has a right to prevent."

Brandeis then offers a stirring defense of free speech that deserves to be quoted in full:

> Those who won our independence believed that the final end of the State was to make men free to develop their faculties, and that, in its government, the deliberative forces should prevail over the arbitrary. . . . They believed that freedom to think as you will and to speak as you think are means indispensable to the discovery and spread of political truth; that, without free speech and assembly, discussion would be futile; that, with them, discussion affords ordinarily adequate protection against the dissemination of noxious doctrine; that the greatest menace to freedom is an inert people; that public discussion is a political duty, and that this should be a fundamental principle of the American government.

He later adds that peech can be restricted only when the state is confronted with a *serious* evil and when the danger is *imminent*—that is, impending or likely to happen soon. "Only an emergency can justify repression," he states. Speech cannot be restricted on the basis of inchoate fears or vague misgivings that something bad *might* happen.

In the end, Brandeis was not concerned with Whitney's speech or her views but with the "conspiracy" to commit crimes by members of the IWW.

Impact

In *Whitney v. California* the Supreme Court upheld a law that a century later would seem to have abridged an individual's freedom of speech. Decided in the context of post-World War I scares regarding Communism, Bolshevism, anarchy, and union agitation, the Court's decision affirmed the right of states to make laws that outlawed "the commission of crime, sabotage, or unlawful acts of force and violence or unlawful methods of terrorism as a means of accomplishing a change in industrial ownership or control, or effecting any political change." Oddly, however, although he voted with the Court majority in a unanimous decision, the opinion is best remembered for Justice Brandeis's concurrence—a spirited defense of freedom of speech, a defense that would influence Court decisions in similar cases for decades to come. Brandeis concurred with the majority, but he did so not because of Whitney's views. Rather, he concurred because he believed a criminal conspiracy was afoot. His view, however, was that untrammeled free speech was vital to a democracy, even when the views being expressed might be repugnant to the majority. Future courts would rely on that concurrence in setting aside statutes written to muzzle people whose views were unpopular.

Questions for Further Study

1. Should speech advocating radical political change be protected by the First Amendment?

2. How can it be determined whether or not speech "disturbs the public peace"?

3. Why were governments, including that of California, so disturbed by speech advocating communism to the point of making it illegal?

Further Reading

Books

Brissenden, Paul F. *The I.W.W.: A Study of American Syndicalism.* 1920. New York: Russell and Russell, 1957.

Dee, Juliet. "Whitney v. California." In *Free Speech on Trial: Communication Perspectives on Landmark Supreme Court Decisions*, edited by Richard A. Parker: 36–51. Tuscaloosa: University of Alabama Press, 2003.

Preston, William, Jr. *Aliens and Dissenters: Federal Suppression of Radicals, 1903–1933*, 2nd ed. Urbana: University of Illinois Press, 1994.

Schultz, David, and John R. Vile, eds. *The Encyclopedia of Civil Liberties in America.* New York: Routledge, 2005.

Stone, Geoffrey R. *Perilous Times: Free Speech in Wartime from the Sedition Act of 1798 to the War on Terrorism.* New York: Norton, 2004.

Strum, Philippa. *Speaking Freely: Whitney v. California and American Speech Law.* Lawrence: University Press of Kansas, 2015.

Articles

Blasi, Vincent. "The First Amendment and the Ideal of Civil Courage: The Brandeis Opinion in *Whitney v. California*." *William and Mary Law Review* 29 (1988): 653–97.

Bobertz, Bradley C. "The Brandeis Gambit: The Making of America's 'First Freedom,' 1909–1931." *William and Mary Law Review* 40 (1999): 557–652.

Collins, Ronald K. L., and David Skover. "Curious Concurrence: Justice Brandeis' Vote in *Whitney v. California*." *Supreme Court Review* (2005): 333–97.

Redish, Martin H. "Advocacy of Unlawful Conduct and the First Amendment: In Defense of Clear and Present Danger." *California Law Review* 70 (1982): 1159–1200.

Rogat, Yosal, and James M. O'Fallon. "Mr. Justice Holmes: A Dissenting Opinion. The Speech Cases." *Stanford Law Review* 36, no. 6 (July 1984): 1349–1406.

Websites

"ACLU History: Early Breakthroughs for Free Speech." ACLU. Accessed February 24, 2023. https://www.aclu.org/other/aclu-history-early-breakthroughs-free-speech.

Hudson, David L., Jr. "Free Speech' Impact of *Whitney v. California*." Freedom Forum Institute. January 8, 2016. https://www.freedomforuminstitute.org/2016/01/08/free-speech-impact-of-whitney-v-california/.

—Commentary by Michael J. O'Neal

WHITNEY V. CALIFORNIA

Document Text

MR. JUSTICE SANFORD delivered the opinion of the Court

By a criminal information filed in the Superior Court of Alameda County, California, the plaintiff in error was charged, in five counts, with violations of the Criminal Syndicalism Act of that State. Statutes, 1919, c. 188, p. 281. She was tried, convicted on the first count, and sentenced to imprisonment. The judgment was affirmed by the District Court of Appeal. 57 Cal. App. 449. Her petition to have the case heard by the Supreme Court was denied. *Ib.,* 453. And the case was brought here on a writ of error which was allowed by the Presiding Justice of the Court of Appeal, the highest court of the State in which a decision could be had. Jud.Code, § 237.

On the first hearing in this Court, the writ of error was dismissed for want of jurisdiction. 269 U.S. 530. Thereafter, a petition for rehearing was granted, *ib.,* 538, and the case was again heard and reargued both as to the jurisdiction and the merits.

The pertinent provisions of the Criminal Syndicalism Act are:

"Section 1. The term 'criminal syndicalism' as used in this act is hereby defined as any doctrine or precept advocating, teaching or aiding and abetting the commission of crime, sabotage (which word is hereby defined as meaning willful and malicious physical damage or injury to physical property), or unlawful acts of force and violence or unlawful methods of terrorism as a means of accomplishing a change in industrial ownership or control, or effecting any political change."

"Sec. 2. Any person who: . . . 4. Organizes or assists in organizing, or is or knowingly becomes a member of, any organization, society, group or assemblage of persons organized or assembled to advocate, teach or aid and abet criminal syndicalism"

"Is guilty of a felony and punishable by imprisonment."

The first count of the information, on which the conviction was had charged that, on or about November 28, 1919, in Alameda County, the defendant, in violation of the Criminal Syndicalism Act,

"did then and there unlawfully, willfully, wrongfully, deliberately and feloniously organize and assist in organizing, and was, is, and knowingly became a member of an organization, society, group and assemblage of persons organized and assembled to advocate, teach, aid and abet criminal syndicalism."

It has long been settled that this Court acquires no jurisdiction to review the judgment of a state court of last resort on a writ of error unless it affirmatively appears on the face of the record that a federal question constituting an appropriate ground for such review was presented in, and expressly or necessarily decided by, such state court. *Crowell v. Randell,* 10 Pet. 368, 35 U. S. 392; *Railroad Co. v. Rock,* 4 Wall, 177, 71 U. S. 180; *California Powder Works v. Davis,* 151 U. S. 389, 151 U. S. 393; *Cincinnati, etc. Railway v. Slade,* 216 U. S. 78, 216 U. S. 83; *Hiawassee Power Co. v. Carolina-Tenn. Co.,* 252 U. S. 341, 252 U. S. 343; *New York v. Kleinert,* 268 U. S. 646, 268 U. S. 650.

Here, the record does not show that the defendant raised, or that the State courts considered or decided, any Federal question whatever, excepting as appears in an order made and entered by the Court of Appeal after it had decided the case and the writ of error had issued and been returned to this Court. A certified copy of that order, brought here as an addition to the record, shows that it was made and entered pursuant to a stipulation of the parties, approved by the court, and that it contains the following statement:

"The question whether the California Criminal Syndicalism Act . . . and its application in this case are repugnant to the provisions of the Fourteenth Amendment to the Constitution of the United States providing that no state shall deprive any person of life, liberty, or property without due process of law, and that all persons shall be accorded the equal protection of the laws, was considered and passed upon by this Court."

In *Cincinnati Packet Co. v. Bay,* 200 U. S. 179, 200 U. S. 182, where it appeared that a federal question had been presented in a petition in error to the State Supreme Court in a case in which the judgment was affirmed without opinion, it was held that the certificate of that court to the effect that it had considered and necessarily decided this question was sufficient to show its existence. *And see Marvin v. Trout,* 199 U. S. 212, 199 U. S. 217, *et seq.; Consolidated Turnpike v. Norfolk, etc. Railway,* 228 U. S. 596, 228 U. S. 599.

So—while the unusual course here taken to show that federal questions were raised and decided below is not to be commended—we shall give effect to the order of the Court of Appeal as would be done if the statement had been made in the opinion of that court when delivered. *See Gross v. United States Mortgage Co.,* 108 U. S. 477, 108 U. S. 484-486; *Philadelphia Fire Association v. New York,* 119 U. S. 110, 119 U. S. 116; *Home for Incurables v. City of New York,* 187 U. S. 155, 187 U. S. 157; *Land & Water Co. v. San Jose Ranch Co.,* 189 U. S. 177, 189 U. S. 179-180; *Rector v. City Deposit Bank,* 200 U. S. 405, 200 U. S. 412; *Haire v. Rice,* 204 U. S. 291, 204 U. S. 299; *Chambers v. Baltimore, etc. Railroad,* 207 U. S. 142, 207 U. S. 148; *Atchison, etc. Railway v. Sowers,* 213 U. S. 55, 213 U. S. 62; *Consolidated Turnpike Co. v. Norfolk, etc. Railway,* 228 U. S. 596, 228 U. S. 599; *Miedrech v. Lauenstein,* 232 U. S. 236, 232 U. S. 242; *North Carolina Railroad v. Zachary,* 232 U. S. 248, 232 U. S. 257; *Chicago, etc. Railway v. Perry,* 259 U. S. 548, 259 U. S. 551.

And here, since it appears from the statement in the order of the Court of Appeal that the question wheth-er the Syndicalism Act and its application in this case was repugnant to the due process and equal protection clauses of the Fourteenth Amendment was considered and passed upon by that court—this being a federal question constituting an appropriate ground for a review of the judgment—we conclude that this Court has acquired jurisdiction under the writ of error. The order dismissing the writ for want of jurisdiction will accordingly be set aside.

We proceed to the determination, upon the merits, of the constitutional question considered and passed upon by the Court of Appeal. Of course, our review is to be confined to that question, since it does not appear, either from the order of the Court of Appeal or from the record otherwise, that any other federal question was presented in and either expressly or necessarily decided by that court. *National Bank v. Commonwealth,* 9 Wall. 353, 76 U. S. 363; *Edwards v. Elliott,* 21 Wall. 532, 88 U. S. 557; *Dewey v. Des Moines,* 173 U. S. 193, 173 U. S. 200; *Keokuk & Hamilton Bridge Co. v. Illinois,* 175 U. S. 626, 175 U. S. 633; *Capital City Dairy Co. v. Ohio,* 183 U. S. 238, 183 U. S. 248; *Haire v. Rice,* 204 U. S. 291, 204 U. S. 301; *Selover, Bates & Co. v. Walsh,* 226 U. S. 112, 226 U. S. 126. *Missouri Pacific Railway v. Coal Co.,* 256 U. S. 134, 256 U. S. 135. It is not enough that there may be somewhere hidden in the record a question which, if it had been raised, would have been of a federal nature. *Dewey v. Des Moines, supra,* 173 U. S. 199; *Keokuk & Hamilton Bridge Co. v. Illinois, supra,* 175 U. S. 634. And this necessarily excludes from our consideration a question sought to be raised for the first time by the assignments of error here—not presented in or passed upon by the Court of Appeal—whether apart from the constitutionality of the Syndicalism Act, the judgment of the Superior Court, by reason of the rulings of that court on questions of pleading, evidence and the like, operated as a denial to the defendant of due process of law. *See Oxley Stave Co. v. Butler County,* 166 U. S. 648, 166 U. S. 660; *Capital City Dairy Co. v. Ohio, supra,* 183 U. S. 248; *Manhattan Life Ins. Co. v. Cohen,* 234 U. S. 123, 234 U. S. 134; *Bass, etc. Ltd. v. Tax Commission,* 266 U. S. 271, 266 U. S. 283.

The following facts, among many others, were established on the trial by undisputed evidence: the defendant, a resident of Oakland, in Alameda County, California, had been a member of the Local Oakland branch of the Socialist Party. This Local sent delegates to the national convention of the Socialist Party held in Chicago in 1919, which resulted in a split between the "radical" group and the old-wing Socialists. The "radicals"—to whom the Oakland delegates adhered—being ejected, went to another hall, and formed the Communist Labor Party of America. Its Constitution provided for the membership of persons subscribing to the principles of the Party and pledging themselves to be guided by its Platform, and for the formation of state organizations conforming to its Platform as the supreme declaration of the Party. In its "Platform and Program," the Party declared that it was in full harmony with "the revolutionary working class parties of all countries," and adhered to the principles of Communism laid down in the Manifesto of the Third International at Moscow, and that its purpose was "to create a unified revolutionary working class movement in America," organizing the workers as a class in a revolutionary class struggle to conquer the capitalist state for the overthrow of capitalist rule, the conquest of political power and the establishment of a working class government, the Dictatorship of the Proletariat, in place of the state machinery of the capitalists, which should make and enforce the laws, reorganize society on the basis of Communism, and bring about the Communist Commonwealth—advocated, as the most important means of capturing state power, the action of the masses, proceeding from the shops and factories, the use of the political machinery of the capitalist state being only secondary; the organization of the workers into "revolutionary industrial unions"; propaganda pointing out their revolutionary nature and possibilities, and great industrial battles showing the value of the strike as a political weapon—commended the propaganda and example of the Industrial Workers of the World and their struggles and sacrifices in the class war—pledged support and cooperation to "the revolutionary industrial proletariat of America" in their struggles against the capitalist class—cited the Seattle and Winnipeg strikes and the numerous strikes all over the country "proceeding without the authority of the old reactionary Trade Union officials," as manifestations of the new tendency—and recommended that strikes of national importance be supported and given a political character, and that propagandists and organizers be mobilized "who cannot only teach, but actually help to put in practice the principles of revolutionary industrial unionism and Communism."

Shortly thereafter, the Local Oakland withdrew from the Socialist Party and sent accredited delegates, in-

cluding the defendant, to a convention held in Oakland in November, 1919, for the purpose of organizing a California branch of the Communist Labor Party. The defendant, after taking out a temporary membership in the Communist Labor Party, attended this convention as a delegate and took an active part in its proceedings. She was elected a member of the Credentials Committee, and, as its chairman, made a report to the convention upon which the delegates were seated. She was also appointed a member of the Resolutions Committee, and, as such, signed the following resolution in reference to political action, among others proposed by the Committee:

"The C.L.P. of California fully recognizes the value of political action as a means of spreading communist propaganda; it insists that, in proportion to the development of the economic strength of the working class, it, the working class, must also develop its political power. The C.L.P. of California proclaims and insists that the capture of political power, locally or nationally by the revolutionary working class, can be of tremendous assistance to the workers in their struggle of emancipation. Therefore, we again urge the workers who are possessed of the right of franchise to cast their votes for the party which represents their immediate and final interest—the C.L.P.—at all elections, being fully convinced of the utter futility of obtaining any real measure of justice or freedom under officials elected by parties owned and controlled by the capitalist class."

The minutes show that this resolution, with the others proposed by the committee, was read by its chairman to the convention before the Committee on the Constitution had submitted its report. According to the recollection of the defendant, however, she herself read this resolution. Thereafter, before the report of the Committee on the Constitution had been acted upon, the defendant was elected an alternate member of the State Executive Committee. The Constitution, as finally read, was then adopted. This provided that the organization should be named the Communist Labor Party of California; that it should be "affiliated with" the Communist Labor Party of America, and subscribe to its Program, Platform and Constitution, and, "through this affiliation," be "joined with the Communist International of Moscow;" and that the qualifications for membership should be those prescribed in the National Constitution. The proposed resolutions were later taken, up and all adopted except that on political action, which caused a lengthy debate, resulting in its defeat and the acceptance of the National Program in its place. After this action, the defendant, without, so far as appears, making any protest, remained in the convention until it adjourned. She later attended as an alternate member one or two meetings of the State Executive Committee in San Jose and San Francisco, and stated, on the trial, that she was then a member of the Communist Labor Party. She also testified that it was not her intention that the Communist Labor Party of California should be an instrument of terrorism or violence, and that it was not her purpose or that of the Convention to violate any known law.

In the light of this preliminary statement, we now take up, insofar as they require specific consideration, the various grounds upon which it is here contended that the Syndicalism Act and its application in this case is repugnant to the due process and equal protection clauses of the Fourteenth Amendment.

1. While it is not denied that the evidence warranted the jury in finding that the defendant became a member of and assisted in organizing the Communist Labor Party of California, and that this was organized to advocate, teach, aid or abet criminal syndicalism as defined by the Act, it is urged that the Act, as here construed and applied, deprived the defendant of her liberty without due process of law in that it has made her action in attending the Oakland convention unlawful by reason of "a subsequent event brought about against her will by the agency of others," with no showing of a specific intent on her part to join in the forbidden purpose of the association, and merely because, by reason of a lack of "prophetic" understanding, she failed to foresee the quality that others would give to the convention. The argument is, in effect, that the character of the state organization could not be forecast when she attended the convention; that she had no purpose of helping to create an instrument of terrorism and violence; that she

"took part in formulating and presenting to the convention a resolution which, if adopted, would have committed the new organization to a legitimate policy of political reform by the use of the ballot;"

that it was not until after the majority of the convention turned out to be "contrary-minded, and other less temperate policies prevailed," that the convention could

have taken on the character of criminal syndicalism, and that, as this was done over her protest, her mere presence in the convention, however violent the opinions expressed therein, could not thereby become a crime. This contention, while advanced in the form of a constitutional objection to the Act, is in effect nothing more than an effort to review the weight of the evidence for the purpose of showing that the defendant did not join and assist in organizing the Communist Labor Party of California with a knowledge of its unlawful character and purpose. This question, which is foreclosed by the verdict of the jury—sustained by the Court of Appeal over the specific objection that it was not supported by the evidence—is one of fact merely, which is not open to review in this Court, involving, as it does, no constitutional question whatever. And we may add that the argument entirely disregards the facts: that the defendant had previously taken out a membership card in the National Party, that the resolution which she supported did not advocate the use of the ballot to the exclusion of violent and unlawful means of bringing about the desired changes in industrial and political conditions, and that, after the constitution of the California Party had been adopted, and this resolution had been voted down and the National Program accepted, she not only remained in the convention, without protest, until its close, but subsequently manifested her acquiescence by attending as an alternate member of the State Executive Committee and continuing as member of the Communist Labor Party.

2. It is clear that the Syndicalism Act is not repugnant to the due process clause by reason of vagueness and uncertainty of definition. It has no substantial resemblance to the statutes held void for uncertainty under the Fourteenth and Fifth Amendments in *International Harvester Co. v. Kentucky*, 234 U. S. 216, 234 U. S. 221, and *United States v. Cohen Grocery*, 255 U. S. 81, 255 U. S. 89, because not fixing an ascertainable standard of guilt. The language of § 2, subd. 4, of the Act, under which the plaintiff in error was convicted, is clear, the definition of "criminal syndicalism "specific.

The Act, plainly, meets the essential requirement of due process that a penal statute be "sufficiently explicit to inform those who are subject to it, what conduct on their part will render them liable to its penalties," and be couched in terms that are not "so vague that men of common intelligence must necessarily guess at its meaning and differ as to its application." *Connally v.*

General Construction Co., 269 U. S. 385, 269 U. S. 391. *And see United States v. Brewer,* 139 U. S. 278, 139 U. S. 288; *Chicago, etc., Railway v. Dey,* (C.C.) 35 Fed. 866, 876; *Tozer v. United States,* (C.C.) 52 Fed. 917, 919. In *Omaechevarria v. Idaho,* 246 U. S. 343, 246 U. S. 348, in which it was held that a criminal statute prohibiting the grazing of sheep on any "range" previously occupied by cattle "in the usual and customary use" thereof, was not void for indefiniteness because it failed to provide for the ascertainment of the boundaries of a "range" or to determine the length of time necessary to constitute a prior occupation a "usual" one, this Court said:

"Men familiar with range conditions and desirous of observing the law will have little difficulty in determining what is prohibited by it. Similar expressions are common in the criminal statutes of other States. This statute presents no greater uncertainty or difficulty, in application to necessarily varying facts, than has been repeatedly sanctioned by this court. *Nash v. United States,* 229 U. S. 373, 229 U. S. 377; *Miller v. Strahl,* 239 U. S. 426, 239 U. S. 434."

So, as applied here, the Syndicalism Act required of the defendant no "prophetic" understanding of its meaning.

And similar Criminal Syndicalism statutes of other States, some less specific in their definitions, have been held by the State courts not to be void for indefiniteness. *State v. Hennessy,* 114 Wash. 351, 364; *State v. Laundy,* 103 Ore. 443, 460; *People v. Ruthenberg,* 229 Mich. 31, 325. *And see Fox v. Washington,* 236 U. S. 273, 236 U. S. 277; *People v. Steelik,* 187 Cal. 361, 372; *People v. Lloyd,* 304 Ill. 23, 34.

3. Neither is the Syndicalism Act repugnant to the equal protection clause on the ground that, as its penalties are confined to those who advocate a resort to violent and unlawful methods as a means of changing industrial and political conditions, it arbitrarily discriminates between such persons and those who may advocate a resort to these methods as a means of maintaining such conditions.

It is, settled by repeated decisions of this Court that the equal protection clause does not take from a State the power to classify in the adoption of police laws, but admits of the exercise of a wide scope of discretion, and avoids what is done only when it is without any reasonable basis, and therefore is purely arbitrary,

and that one who assails the classification must carry the burden of showing that it does not rest upon any reasonable basic, but is essentially arbitrary. *Lindsley v. National Cabonic Gas Co.,* 220 U. S. 61, 220 U. S. 78, and case cited.

A statute does not violate the equal protection clause merely because it is not all-embracing; *Zucht v. King,* 260 U. S. 174, 260 U. S. 177; *James-Dickinson Farm Mortgage Co. v. Harry,* 273 U. S. 119. A State may properly direct its legislation against what it deems an existing evil without covering the whole field of possible abuses. *Patsone v. Pennsylvania,* 232 U. S. 138, 232 U. S. 144; *Farmers Bank v. Federal Reserve Bank,* 262 U. S. 649, 262 U. S. 661; *James-Dickinson Mortgage Co. v. Harry, supra.* The statute must be presumed to be aimed at an evil where experience shows it to be most felt, and to be deemed by the legislature coextensive with the practical need, and is not to be overthrown merely because other instances may be suggested to which also it might have been applied, that being a matter for the legislature to determine unless the case is very clear. *Keokee Coke Co. v Taylor,* 234 U. S. 224, 234 U. S. 227. And it is not open to objection unless the classification is so lacking in any adequate or reasonable basis as to preclude the assumption that it was made in the exercise of the legislative judgment and discretion. *Stebbins v. Riley,* 268 U. S. 137, 268 U. S. 143; *Graves v. Minnesota,* 272 U. S. 425; *Swiss Oil Corporation v. Shanks,* 273 U. S. 407.

The Syndicalism Act is not class legislation; it affects all alike, no matter what their business associations or callings, who come within its terms and do the things prohibited. *See State v. Hennessy, supra,* 361; *State v. Laundy, supra,* 460. And there is no substantial basis for the contention that the legislature has arbitrarily or unreasonably limited its application to those advocating the use of violent and unlawful methods to effect changes in industrial and political conditions, there being nothing indicating any ground to apprehend that those desiring to maintain existing industrial and political conditions did or would advocate such methods. That there is a widespread conviction of the necessity for legislation of this character is indicated by the adoption of similar statutes in several other States.

4. Nor is the Syndicalism Act, as applied in this case, repugnant to the due process clause as a restraint of the rights of free speech, assembly, and association.

That the freedom of speech which is secured by the Constitution does not confer an absolute right to speak, without responsibility, whatever one may choose, or an unrestricted and unbridled license giving immunity for every possible use of language and preventing the punishment of those who abuse this freedom, and that a State in the exercise of its police power may punish those who abuse this freedom by utterances inimical to the public welfare, tending to incite to crime, disturb the public peace, or endanger the foundations of organized government and threaten its overthrow by unlawful means, is not open to question. *Gitlow v. New York,* 268 U. S. 652, 268 U. S. 666-668, and cases cited.

By enacting the provisions of the Syndicalism Act, the State has declared, through its legislative body, that to knowingly be or become a member of or assist in organizing an association to advocate, teach or aid and abet the commission of crimes or unlawful acts of force, violence or terrorism as a means of accomplishing industrial or political changes involves such danger to the public peace and the security of the State, that these acts should be penalized in the exercise of its police power. That determination must be given great weight. Every presumption is to be indulged in favor of the validity of the statute, *Mugler v. Kansas,* 123 U. S. 623, 123 U. S. 661, and it may not be declared unconstitutional unless it is an arbitrary or unreasonable attempt to exercise the authority vested in the State in the public interest. *Great Northern Railway v. Clara City,* 246 U. S. 434, 246 U. S. 439.

The essence of the offense denounced by the Act is the combining with others in an association for the accomplishment of the desired ends through the advocacy and use of criminal and unlawful methods. It partakes of the nature of a criminal conspiracy. *See People v. Steelik, supra,* 376. That such united and joint action involves even greater danger to the public peace and security than the isolated utterances and acts of individuals is clear. We cannot hold that, as here applied, the Act is an unreasonable or arbitrary exercise of the police power of the State, unwarrantably infringing any right of free speech, assembly or association, or that those persons are protected from punishment by the due process clause who abuse such rights by joining and furthering an organization thus menacing the peace and welfare of the State.

We find no repugnancy in the Syndicalism Act as applied in this case to either the due process or equal protection clauses of the Fourteenth Amendment on any of the grounds upon which its validity has been here challenged.

The order dismissing the writ of error will be vacated and set aside, and the judgment of the Court of Appeal Affirmed.

Glossary

due process: the constitutional requirement that when the federal government acts in such a way that denies a citizen of a life, liberty, or property interest, the person must be given notice, the opportunity to be heard, and a decision by a neutral decision-maker

manifesto: a statement of political aims and goals, often, but not always, by a radical group

repugnant to: in legal contexts, opposed to or in violation of; often used to refer to laws or policies that violate the Constitution, especially the Bill of Rights

syndicalism: a movement that advocates direct action by the working class to abolish the capitalist order, including the state, and replace it with a social order based on workers organized into production units

OLMSTEAD V. UNITED STATES

DATE 1928	**CITATION** 277 U.S. 438
AUTHOR William Howard Taft	**SIGNIFICANCE** Held that evidence obtained by a wiretap placed outside the petitioner's premises was not a violation of the petitioner's Fourth or Fifth Amendment rights
VOTE 5–4	

Overview

During the Prohibition period, the government suspected that Roy Olmstead was a bootlegger running a large illegal liquor operation. Without approval from the judiciary, federal agents wiretapped his premises and nearby streets. With the evidence obtained from the wiretaps, Olmstead and his accomplices were convicted for conspiracy to violate the National Prohibition Enforcement Act, which made it against the law to import, possess, or sell liquor. The U.S. Supreme Court sustained his conviction, holding that neither Olmstead's Fourth nor his Fifth Amendment rights under the Constitution had been violated. His Fourth Amendment rights were not violated because the wiretaps were not an illegal search and seizure, and his Fifth Amendment rights were not violated because the wiretapped conversations did not constitute self-incrimination.

Context

Federal agents suspected that Roy Olmstead was directing an illegal $2 million-a-year liquor distribution operation out of an office building and various homes in Seattle, Washington, but they needed evidence. To gather evidence, they tapped the phone lines to Olmstead's home and office and other places where they believed Olmstead's accomplices were conducting the business. They did not trespass on his property but rather carried out the investigation from nearby streets and in the basement of a building where he rented office space. Over the course of several months, the agents gathered evidence tending to prove that Olmstead directed a criminal liquor distribution enterprise that stretched from British Columbia through Washington State. In his employ were at least fifty people, including managers, sales representatives, dispatchers, deliverymen, scouts, bookkeepers, collectors, and even an attorney. The enterprise maintained storage facilities at various locations and used boats and other seagoing vessels to transport the liquor.

Indictments were handed down. About seventy-five people were charged with violating the National Prohibition Enforcement Act or related crimes. Olmstead was convicted of conspiracy when the lower courts rejected his argument that the wiretap evidence should not have been used against him because it was illegally

Roy Olmstead
(Seattle Post-Intelligencer)

obtained and violated the Fourth Amendment prohibition against unreasonable searches and seizures and the Fifth Amendment privilege against compulsory self-incrimination. He also argued that wiretapping was illegal in Washington.

Two major matters were relevant to the context of *Olmstead v. United States*. The first was Prohibition. The temperance movement against the consumption of alcohol, which led to the enactment of Prohibition, began in the nineteenth century, when reformers urged people to give up drinking; in other words, they attacked drinking from the *demand* side. At the turn of the twentieth century, these reformers altered their tactics and attacked liquor consumption from the *supply* side by backing state laws that restricted the sale of alcohol and shut down bars and taverns. By 1914, fourteen states—so-called dry states—had adopted some form of prohibition, and that number had risen to twenty-six by 1919. During the First World War, the Anti-Saloon League was able to get various federal laws against alcohol passed; the purpose was to preserve the morals of servicemen and to conserve grain for food. By this time, the number of congressional representatives from dry states outnumbered those from "wet" states.

It was in this environment that the Eighteenth Amendment to the Constitution—the "Prohibition amendment"—was ratified in 1919. The amendment placed a national ban on the "manufacture, sale, or transportation of intoxicating liquors," although, perhaps oddly, it did not ban the purchase or consumption of liquor. The federal legislation necessary to enforce the amendment came in the form of the National Prohibition Enforcement Act, often called the Volstead Act, passed by Congress on October 28, 1919. President Woodrow Wilson vetoed the bill, but Congress overrode the veto. The ink, though, was barely dry on the amendment when calls for its repeal began. It was the Roaring Twenties. Illegal liquor was commonplace, especially in the cities. Many Americans were arriving at the viewpoint that the federal government had no business regulating personal habits. They became cynical about inconsistent and arbitrary efforts to enforce the law. In 1933, the Twenty-First Amendment was ratified, repealing the Eighteenth. Liquor laws were now back in the hands of the states.

The other major matter relevant to the *Olmstead* case was the Fourth Amendment to the Constitution, which states:

> The right of the people to be secure in their persons, houses, papers, and effects, against unreasonable searches and seizures, shall not be violated, and no Warrants shall issue, but upon probable cause, supported by Oath or affirmation, and particularly describing the place to be searched, and the persons or things to be seized.

In simple terms, the police cannot just storm into a person's house and seize evidence because they think that maybe he has committed a crime. Every person who watches cop shows on television knows that the Fourth Amendment requires the police to obtain a warrant from a judge to search a person's home and seize the suspect's personal property. The warrant has to be based not on mere suspicion but on "probable cause" that evidence of a crime will be found. The warrant has to be particular about the property being searched and the person or property to be seized; the police do not have unfettered authority to act on mere suspicion.

In a 1961 case, *Silverman v. United States*, Justice Potter Stewart articulated the matter clearly. In a case involving gambling offenses, the trial court relied on evidence gathered by means of an electronic listening device pushed through the wall of an adjoining house. In overturning the defendant's conviction, Stewart wrote: "We need not here contemplate the Fourth Amendment implications of . . . frightening paraphernalia which the vaunted marvels of an electronic age may visit upon human society." In 1928, telephones and wiretaps might very well have been considered "frightening paraphernalia." Stewart added: "The Fourth Amendment, and the personal rights which it secures, have a long history. At the very core stands the right of a man to retreat into his own home and there be free from unreasonable governmental intrusion."

In 1967, in *Katz v. United States*, the Court overturned *Olmstead v. United States* in a case that had to do with an electronic listening device attached outside of a phone booth used by the petitioner. Again Justice Stewart wrote for the Court: "Indeed, we have expressly held that the Fourth Amendment governs not only the seizure of tangible items, but extends as well to the recording of oral statements, overheard without any 'technical trespass under . . . local property law.'" Stewart went on to write: "The Government's activities in electronically listening to and recording the petitioner's words violated the privacy upon which he justifiably relied while using the telephone booth, and thus constituted a 'search and seizure' within the meaning of the Fourth Amendment."

At the time the Constitution was written, the Framers could not have anticipated the existence of telephones and electronic listening devices, along with GPS trackers, drones, and other devices. For them, incriminating evidence would most likely have been in the form of "papers." Accordingly, the question before the Taft court was whether electronic impulses "seized" by means of a wiretap are in any sense analogous to the "papers" the Framers contemplated. The Taft court concluded that they were not and that therefore the evidence was admissible.

About the Author

William Howard Taft was the only person in U.S. history to serve as both president of the United States and as chief justice of the Supreme Court. Taft was born in Cincinnati, Ohio, on September 15, 1857. He inherited from his ancestors a desire for public service. His

Chief Justice William Howard Taft delivered the Opinion.
(Harris & Ewing)

grandfather had been a judge, and his father served on the Ohio Supreme Court, as President Ulysses S. Grant's attorney general, and as an ambassador under President Chester A. Arthur. In 1878 Taft graduated second in his class from Yale University. After he graduated from the Cincinnati Law School in 1880, he worked as a prosecuting attorney and became active in Republican Party politics.

Taft's political career, launched in large part at the urging of his wife, began in 1887 when he was appointed to the superior court of Ohio and won election in his own right in 1888. In 1890 President Benjamin Harrison named him solicitor general. Two years later he was appointed to the U.S. District Court for the Sixth Circuit, which included Ohio. At the same time, he taught law and served as the dean of the Cincinnati Law School. In 1901 President William McKinley appointed him governor general of the Philippines, a protectorate the United States acquired as a result of the Spanish American War. In 1904, he became President Theodore Roosevelt's secretary of war. He also worked as a roving ambassador in Cuba, Asia, and elsewhere, and he supervised the construction of the Panama Canal.

In 1908, Taft secured the Republican Party's nomination for president. He won, defeating William Jennings Bryan. He continued many of the reforms of the Roosevelt administration, including bringing antitrust suits against monopolies. Roosevelt and Taft, however, began to part ways: Roosevelt was progressive who expanded executive power; Taft, in contrast, was a conservative and believed that the Constitution restricted presidential powers. When Taft ran for reelection in 1912, Roosevelt mounted a third-party candidacy as head of the Bull Moose Party. Because the Republican vote was split, Democrat Woodrow Wilson was elected.

In the years following his defeat, Taft stayed busy. He taught law at Yale. He served as president of the American Bar Association. He was joint chair of the National War Labor Board. He campaigned for U.S. entry into the League of Nations. But he always wanted to serve as chief justice of the Supreme Court. When Warren G. Harding, a Republican, was elected president in 1920, he had his chance. Harding appointed him to fill the seat left vacant by the death of Edward D. White. The Senate confirmed him on June 30, 1921, and he went on to serve as chief justice for nine years.

Taft inherited a badly divided Court with a large backlog of cases. He introduced reforms that improved not only the Court's efficiency but also the entire federal judicial system. Taft, however, came of age during a time of great popular unrest marked by strikes, boycotts, the growing influence of socialist candidates, the communist revolution in Russia, the "red scares" in the United States, and the formation of the Progressive and Populist parties. It was against this backdrop that he formed his essentially conservative views. He was hesitant to restrict property rights in favor of social experimentation or allow the taxing power of the federal government to be used to correct a social ill. Some of his rulings, however, were relatively more progressive. In *Stafford v. Wallace* (1922), for example, he upheld the Packers and Stockyards Act of 1921, expanding both the definition of interstate commerce and the power of the federal government to regulate it. Similarly, he dissented in *Adkins v. Children's Hospital* (1923) when the Court invalidated a congressional act that set minimum wage standards for women and minor workers in the District of Columbia, writing: "It is not the function of this court to hold congressional acts invalid simply because they are passed to carry out economic views which the court believes to be unwise or unsound."

Taft had another distinction: at 325 pounds, he was the nation's heaviest president. His health began to fail in 1930, forcing him to resign on February 3. He died in Washington, D.C., on March 8, 1930.

Explanation and Analysis of the Document

The Majority Opinion

Chief Justice Taft begins with a thorough examination of the procedural history of the case, the facts surrounding Olmstead's liquor distribution conspiracy, and the way the evidence against the petitioner was gathered. He then turns to a discussion of the Fourth and Fifth Amendments; the relevant portion of the Fifth Amendment states that "No person . . . shall be compelled, in any criminal case, to be a witness against himself." He then examines a number of previous Court cases bearing on these issues. One was *Boyd v. United States* (1886), in which the Court held that an 1874 law requiring a man to turn over private papers was "repugnant to the Fourth and Fifth Amendments." Another was *Weeks v. United States* (1914), in which the Court overturned a conviction for use of the mail to transmit coupons or tickets in an illegal lottery enterprise. Taft notes that the Court in the *Weeks* case found that "the Fourth Amendment, as a principle of protection, was applicable to sealed letters and packages in the mail, and that, consistently with it, such matter could only be opened and examined upon warrants issued on oath or affirmation particularly describing the thing to be seized." In a third case, *Silverthorne Lumber Company v. United States* (1920), the Court held that the seizure of papers from the petitioner's office while he was in custody was illegal and amounted to a "performance" by government officials. Taft examines other cases that reached similar conclusions.

Taft then mentions the invention of the telephone, which had taken place some fifty years earlier. The telephone had the purpose of extending communications, but the language of the Fourth Amendment cannot, he says, be extended to include all the telephone wires extending from a person's home or office: "The intervening wires are not part of his house or office any more than are the highways along which they are stretched."

Taft concludes this part of the opinion by stating that none of the cases he has cited "hold the Fourth Amendment to have been violated as against a defendant unless there has been an official search and seizure of his person, or such a seizure of his papers or his tangible material effects, or an actual physical invasion of his house 'or curtilage' for the purpose of making a seizure." ("Curtilage" refers to an area of land attached to a house and forming one enclosure with it.) Accordingly, the Court majority makes its key pronouncement: that "the wiretapping here disclosed did not amount to a search or seizure within the meaning of the Fourth Amendment."

Taft turns to the issue of whether evidence obtained by intercepting telephone messages was inadmissible because the "mode" of obtaining it was unethical and a misdemeanor under Washington law. He begins by noting that English common law prevailed in Washington, so the rules of evidence are those of common law. The common law rule is "that the admissibility of evidence, is not affected by the illegality of the means by which it was obtained." He then cites legal scholars and case law that supported this principle, concluding that "our general experience shows that much evidence has always been receivable although not obtained by conformity to the highest ethics." He adds that "the history of criminal trials shows numerous cases of prosecutions of oath-bound conspiracies for murder, robbery, and other crimes where officers of the law have disguised themselves and joined the organizations, taken the oaths and given themselves every appearance of active members engaged in the promotion of crime, for the purpose of securing evidence. Evidence secured by such means has always been received." He goes on to state that "whether the State of Washington may prosecute and punish federal officers violating this law and those whose messages were intercepted may sue them civilly is not before us. But clearly a statute, passed twenty years after the admission of the State into the Union cannot affect the rules of evidence applicable in courts of the United States in criminal cases."

On the basis of this reasoning, the Court majority affirms Olmstead's conviction.

The Dissenting Opinion

Justices Oliver Wendell Holmes, Pierce Butler, and Harlan F. Stone dissented from the majority opinion, but it is the dissent written by Justice Louis D. Brandeis that was most exhaustive, and perhaps eloquent, and the one with which the other three dissenters agreed.

Brandeis begins by a further examination of the facts of the case, noting that the transcribed notes of the conversations held by the petitioner amounted to 775 typewritten pages. He notes that with regard to the Fourth Amendment, the majority "claims that the protection given thereby cannot properly be held to include a telephone conversation." Brandis then cites extensive case law in which "this Court has repeatedly sustained the exercise of power by Congress, under various clauses of that instrument, over objects of which the Fathers could not have dreamed," meaning that for Brandeis, the majority's "claims" are not valid. Further, he writes, the Court has held that "general limitations on the powers of Government, like those embodied in the due process clauses of the Fifth and Fourteenth Amendments, do not forbid the United States or the States from meeting modern conditions by regulations which, 'a century ago, or even half a century ago, probably would have been rejected as arbitrary and oppressive.'" He quotes the Court in an earlier case:

> Legislation, both statutory and constitutional, is enacted, it is true, from an experience of evils, but its general language should not, therefore, be necessarily confined to the form that evil had theretofore taken. Time works changes, brings into existence new conditions and purposes. Therefore, a principle, to be vital, must be capable of wider application than the mischief which gave it birth.

The Constitution, in other words, is pliable and must be adapted to changing conditions, of whatever type. He adds that "discovery and invention have made it possible for the Government, by means far more effective than stretching upon the rack [i.e., torture], to obtain disclosure in court of what is whispered in the closet."

Brandeis shows himself to be prescient:

> The progress of science in furnishing the Government with means of espionage is not likely to stop with wiretapping. Ways may

someday be developed by which the Government, without removing papers from secret drawers, can reproduce them in court, and by which it will be enabled to expose to a jury the most intimate occurrences of the home. Advances in the psychic and related sciences may bring means of exploring unexpressed beliefs, thoughts and emotions.

He asks: "Can it be that the Constitution affords no protection against such invasions of individual security?"

Brandeis goes on to cite further case law and legal authority as they pertained to the Fourth and Fifth Amendments, leading him to the conclusion that "the evil incident to invasion of the privacy of the telephone is far greater than that involved in tampering with the mails. Whenever a telephone line is tapped, the privacy of the persons at both ends of the line is invaded and all conversations between them upon any subject, and, although proper, confidential and privileged, may be overheard."

Brandeis then turns philosophical in examining the broad scope of the Bill of Rights:

> The makers of our Constitution undertook to secure conditions favorable to the pursuit of happiness. They recognized the significance of man's spiritual nature, of his feelings, and

of his intellect. They knew that only a part of the pain, pleasure and satisfactions of life are to be found in material things. They sought to protect Americans in their beliefs, their thoughts, their emotions and their sensations. They conferred, as against the Government, the right to be let alone—the most comprehensive of rights, and the right most valued by civilized men. To protect that right, every unjustifiable intrusion by the Government upon the privacy of the individual, whatever the means employed, must be deemed a violation of the Fourth Amendment.

Brandeis concludes that "decency, security and liberty alike demand that government officials shall be subjected to the same rules of conduct that are commands to the citizen. In a government of laws, existence of the government will be imperiled if it fails to observe the law scrupulously." He continues by calling the government a "potent" and "omnipresent teacher." He adds that "if the Government becomes a lawbreaker, it breeds contempt for law; it invites every man to become a law unto himself; it invites anarchy." Brandeis ends with a clarion call: "To declare that, in the administration of the criminal law, the end justifies the means—to declare that the Government may commit crimes in order to secure the conviction of a private criminal—would bring terrible retribution. Against that pernicious doctrine this Court should resolutely set its face."

Questions for Further Study

1. On what basis did the Taft court sustain the conviction of Olmstead?

2. How have technological developments (drones, cell phones, GPS trackers) impacted the issue of "unreasonable searches and seizures" in criminal cases?

3. How might Justice Taft have ruled on a case such as this in light of various high-tech listening devices, such as laser microphones (which can reconstruct audio from a laser beam shot into a room or through a window) or devices that can reconstruct audio from video of thin objects that can pick up sound vibrations, such as houseplants or bags of potato chips?

4. Based on a reading of this case, would the search of a trash can by police be reasonable or not?

Further Reading

Books

Black, Forrest Revere. *Ill-Starred Prohibition Cases: A Study in Judicial Pathology*. Boston: R.G. Badger, 1931.

Hubbart, Phillip. *Making Sense of Search and Seizure Law: A Fourth Amendment Handbook*, 2nd ed. Durham, NC: Carolina Academic Press, 2015.

Murphy, Walter F. *Wiretapping on Trial: A Case Study in the Judicial Process*. New York: Random House, 1966.

Vile, John R., and David L. Hudson Jr., eds. *Encyclopedia of the Fourth Amendment*. Washington, DC: CQ Press, 2013.

Articles

Karabian, Walter. "The Case against Wiretapping." *Pacific Law Journal* 1 (January 1970): 133–45.

Ohm, Paul. "The Olmsteadian Seizure Clause: The Fourth Amendment and the Seizure of Intangible Property." *Stanford Technology Law Review*, 2008: 2–59.

Ryan, Edward. F. "The United States Electronic Eavesdrop Cases." *University of Toronto Law Journal* 19, no. 1 (Winter 1969): 68–76. https://www.jstor.org/stable/i233973.

Steiker, Carol S. "Brandeis in *Olmstead*: Our Government Is the Potent, the Omnipresent Teacher." *Mississippi Law Journal* 79 (Fall 2009): 149–78. https://olemiss.edu/depts/ncjrl/pdf/2009%20Steiker.79.1.pdf.

Websites

Hamm, Richard F. "*Olmstead v. United States*: The Constitutional Challenges of Prohibition Enforcement." Federal Judicial Center, Federal Judicial History Office. 2010. Accessed March 13, 2023, https://constitutionallawreporter.com/wp-content/uploads/2015/06/Olmstead-v.-United-States.pdf.

National Constitution Center staff. "Olmstead Case Was a Watershed for Supreme Court." National Constitution Center. June 4, 2022. Accessed March 13, 2023, https://constitutioncenter.org/blog/olmstead-case-was-a-watershed-for-supreme-court.

—Commentary by Michael J. O'Neal

OLMSTEAD V. UNITED STATES

Document Text

MR. CHIEF JUSTICE TAFT delivered the opinion of the Court

These cases are here by certiorari from the Circuit Court of Appeals for the Ninth Circuit. 19 F.2d 842 and 850. The petition in No. 493 was filed August 30, 1927; in Nos. 532 and 533, September 9, 1927. They were granted with the distinct limitation that the hearing should be confined to the single question whether the use of evidence of private telephone conversations between the defendants and others, intercepted by means of wiretapping amounted to a violation of the Fourth and Fifth Amendments.

The petitioners were convicted in the District Court for the Western District of Washington of a conspiracy to violate the National Prohibition Act by unlawfully possessing, transporting and importing intoxicating liquors and maintaining nuisances, and by selling intoxicating liquors. Seventy-two others in addition to the petitioners were indicted. Some were not apprehended, some were acquitted, and others pleaded guilty.

The evidence in the records discloses a conspiracy of amazing magnitude to import, possess and sell liquor unlawfully.

It involved the employment of not less than fifty persons, of two seagoing vessels for the transportation of liquor to British Columbia, of smaller vessels for coastwise transportation to the State of Washington, the purchase and use of a ranch beyond the suburban limits of Seattle, with a large underground cache for storage and a number of smaller caches in that city,

the maintenance of a central office manned with operators, the employment of executives, salesmen, deliverymen, dispatchers, scouts, bookkeepers, collectors and an attorney. In a bad month, sales amounted to $176,000; the aggregate for a year must have exceeded two millions of dollars.

Olmstead was the leading conspirator and the general manager of the business. He made a contribution of $10,000 to the capital; eleven others contributed $1,000 each. The profits were divided one-half to Olmstead and the remainder to the other eleven. Of the several offices in Seattle, the chief one was in a large office building. In this there were three telephones on three different lines. There were telephones in an office of the manager in his own home, at the homes of his associates, and at other places in the city. Communication was had frequently with Vancouver, British Columbia. Times were fixed for the deliveries of the "stuff," to places along Puget Sound near Seattle, and from there the liquor was removed and deposited in the caches already referred to One of the chief men was always on duty at the main office to receive orders by telephones and to direct their filling by a corps of men stationed in another room—the "bull pen." The call numbers of the telephones were given to those known to be likely customers. At times, the sales amounted to 200 cases of liquor per day.

The information which led to the discovery of the conspiracy and its nature and extent was largely obtained by intercepting messages on the telephones of the conspirators by four federal prohibition officers. Small wires were inserted along the ordinary telephone wires from the residences of four of the petitioners and those leading from the chief office. The insertions were made without trespass upon any property of the defendants. They were made in the basement of the large office building. The taps from house lines were made in the streets near the houses.

The gathering of evidence continued for many months. Conversations of the conspirators, of which refreshing stenographic notes were currently made, were testified to by the government witnesses. They revealed the large business transactions of the partners and their subordinates. Men at the wires heard the orders given for liquor by customers and the acceptances; they became auditors of the conversations between the partners. All this disclosed the conspiracy charged in the indictment. Many of the intercepted conversations were not merely reports, but parts of the criminal acts. The evidence also disclosed the difficulties to which the conspirators were subjected, the reported news of the capture of vessels, the arrest of their men and the seizure of cases of liquor in garages and other places. It showed the dealing by Olmstead, the chief conspirator, with members of the Seattle police, the messages to them which secured the release of arrested members of the conspiracy, and also direct promises to officers of payments as soon as opportunity offered.

The Fourth Amendment provides—

"The right of the people to be secure in their persons, houses, papers, and effects against unreasonable searches and seizures shall not be violated, and no warrants shall issue but upon probable cause, supported by oath or affirmation and particularly describing the place to be searched and the persons or things to be seized."

And the Fifth: "No person . . . shall be compelled, in any criminal case, to be a witness against himself."

It will be helpful to consider the chief cases in this Court which bear upon the construction of these Amendments.

Boyd v. United States, 116 U. S. 616, was an information filed by the District Attorney in the federal court in a cause of seizure and forfeiture against thirty-five cases of plate glass, which charged that the owner and importer, with intent to defraud the revenue, made an entry of the imported merchandise by means of a fraudulent or false invoice. It became important

to show the quantity and value of glass contained in twenty-nine cases previously imported. The fifth section of the Act of June 22, 1874, provided that, in cases not criminal under the revenue laws, the United States Attorney, whenever he thought an invoice belonging to the defendant would tend to prove any allegation made by the United States, might, by a written motion describing the invoice and setting forth the allegation which he expected to prove, secure a notice from the court to the defendant to produce the invoice, and, if the defendant refused to produce it, the allegations stated in the motion should be taken as confessed, but if produced, the United States Attorney should be permitted, under the direction of the court, to make an examination of the invoice, and might offer the same in evidence. This Act had succeeded the Act of 1867, which provided that, in such cases, the District Judge, on affidavit of any person interested, might issue a warrant to the marshal to enter the premises where the invoice was and take possession of it and hold it subject to the order of the judge. This had been preceded by the Act of 1863 of a similar tenor, except that it directed the warrant to the collector, instead of the marshal. The United States Attorney followed the Act of 1874 and compelled the production of the invoice.

The court held the Act of 1874 repugnant to the Fourth and Fifth Amendments. As to the Fourth Amendment, Justice Bradley said (page 116 U. S. 621):

"But, in regard to the Fourth Amendment, it is contended that, whatever might have been alleged against the constitutionality of the acts of 1863 and 1867, that of 1874, under which the order in the present case was made, is free from constitutional objection because it does not authorize the search and seizure of books and papers, but only requires the defendant or claimant to produce them. That is so; but it declares that, if he does not produce them, the allegations which it is affirmed they will prove shall be taken as confessed. This is tantamount to compelling their production, for the prosecuting attorney will always be sure to state the evidence expected to be derived from them as strongly as the case will admit of. It is true that certain aggravating incidents of actual search and seizure, such as forcible entry into a man's house and searching amongst his papers, are wanting, and, to this extent, the proceeding under the Act of 1874 is a mitigation of that which was authorized by the former acts; but it accomplishes the substantial object of those acts in forcing from a party evidence against himself. It is our opinion, therefore, that a compulsory production of a man's private papers to establish a criminal charge against him, or to forfeit his property, is within the scope of the Fourth Amendment to the Constitution in all cases in which a search and seizure would be, because it is a material ingredient, and effects the sole object and purpose of search and seizure."

Concurring, Mr. Justice Miller and Chief Justice Waite said that they did not think the machinery used to get this evidence amounted to a search and seizure, but they agreed that the Fifth Amendment had been violated.

The statute provided an official demand for the production of a paper or document by the defendant for official search and use as evidence on penalty that, by refusal, he should be conclusively held to admit the incriminating character of the document as charged. It was certainly no straining of the language to construe the search and seizure under the Fourth Amendment to include such official procedure.

The next case, and perhaps the most important, is *Weeks v. United States,* 232 U. S. 383—a conviction for using the mails to transmit coupons or tickets in a lottery enterprise. The defendant was arrested by a police officer without a warrant. After his arrest, other police officers and the United States marshal went to his house, got the key from a neighbor, entered the defendant's room and searched it, and took possession of various papers and articles. Neither the marshal nor the police officers had a search warrant. The defendant filed a petition in court asking the return of all his property. The court ordered the return of everything not pertinent to the charge, but denied return of relevant evidence. After the jury was sworn, the defendant again made objection, and, on introduction of the papers, contended that the search without warrant was a violation of the Fourth and Fifth Amendments, and they were therefore inadmissible. This court held that such taking of papers by an official of the United States, acting under color of his office, was in violation of the constitutional rights of the defendant, and, upon making seasonable application, he was entitled to have them restored, and that, by permitting their use upon the trial, the trial court erred.

The opinion cited with approval language of Mr. Justice Field in *Ex parte Jackson,* 96 U. S. 727, 96 U. S. 733, say-

ing that the Fourth Amendment, as a principle of protection, was applicable to sealed letters and packages in the mail, and that, consistently with it, such matter could only be opened and examined upon warrants issued on oath or affirmation particularly describing the thing to be seized.

In *Silverthorne Lumber Company v. United States,* 251 U. S. 385, the defendants were arrested at their homes and detained in custody. While so detained, representatives of the Government, without authority, went to the office of their company and seized all the books, papers and documents found there. An application for return of the things was opposed by the District Attorney, who produced a subpoena for certain documents relating to the charge in the indictment then on file. The court said:

"Thus, the case is not that of knowledge acquired through the wrongful act of a stranger, but it must be assumed that the Government planned, or at all events ratified, the whole performance."

And it held that the illegal character of the original seizure characterized the entire proceeding, and, under the *Weeks* case, the seized papers must be restored.

In *Amos v. United States,* 255 U. S. 313, the defendant was convicted of concealing whiskey on which the tax had not been paid. At the trial, he presented a petition asking that private property seized in a search of his house and store "within his curtilage" without warrant should be returned. This was denied. A woman who claimed to be his wife was told by the revenue officers that they had come to search the premises for violation of the revenue law. She opened the door; they entered, and found whiskey. Further searches in the house disclosed more. It was held that this action constituted a violation of the Fourth Amendment, and that the denial of the motion to restore the whiskey and to exclude the testimony was error.

In *Gouled v. The United States,* 255 U. S. 298, the facts were these: Gouled and two others were charged with conspiracy to defraud the United States. One pleaded guilty, and another was acquitted. Gouled prosecuted error. The matter was presented here on questions propounded by the lower court. The first related to the admission in evidence of a paper surreptitiously taken from the office of the defendant by one acting under the direction of an officer of the Intelligence Department of the Army of the United States. Gouled was suspected of the crime. A private in the U.S. Army, pretending to make a friendly call on him, gained admission to his office and, in his absence, without warrant of any character, seized and carried away several documents. One of these belonging to Gouled, was delivered to the United States Attorney, and by him introduced in evidence. When produced, it was a surprise to the defendant. He had had no opportunity to make a previous motion to secure a return of it. The paper had no pecuniary value, but was relevant to the issue made on the trial. Admission of the paper was considered a violation of the Fourth Amendment.

Agnello v. United States, 269 U. S. 20, held that the Fourth and Fifth Amendments were violated by admission in evidence of contraband narcotics found in defendant's house, several blocks distant from the place of arrest, after his arrest, and seized there without a warrant. Under such circumstances, the seizure could not be justified as incidental to the arrest.

There is no room in the present case for applying the Fifth Amendment unless the Fourth Amendment was first violated. There was no evidence of compulsion to induce the defendants to talk over their many telephones, They were continually and voluntarily transacting business without knowledge of the interception. Our consideration must be confined to the Fourth Amendment.

The striking outcome of the *Weeks* case and those which followed it was the sweeping declaration that the Fourth Amendment, although not referring to or limiting the use of evidence in courts, really forbade its introduction if obtained by government officers through a violation of the Amendment. Theretofore, many had supposed that, under the ordinary common law rules, if the tendered evidence was pertinent, the method of obtaining it was unimportant. This was held by the Supreme Judicial Court of Massachusetts in *Commonwealth v. Dana,* 2 Metcalf, 329, 337. There it was ruled that the only remedy open to a defendant whose rights under a state constitutional equivalent of the Fourth Amendment had been invaded was by suit and judgment for damages, as Lord Camden held in *Entick v. Carrington,* 19 Howell State Trials, 1029. Mr. Justice Bradley made effective use of this case in *Boyd v. United States.* But in the *Weeks* case, and those which

followed, this Court decided with great emphasis, and established as the law for the federal courts, that the protection of the Fourth Amendment would be much impaired unless it was held that not only was the official violator of the rights under the Amendment subject to action at the suit of the injured defendant, but also that the evidence thereby obtained could not be received.

The well known historical purpose of the Fourth Amendment, directed against general warrants and writs of assistance, was to prevent the use of governmental force to search a man's house, his person, his papers and his effects, and to prevent their seizure against his will. This phase of the misuse of governmental power of compulsion is the emphasis of the opinion of the Court in the *Boyd* case. This appears too in the *Weeks* case, in the *Silverthorne* case, and in the *Amos* case.

Gouled v. United States carried the inhibition against unreasonable searches and seizures to the extreme limit. Its authority is not to be enlarged by implication, and must be confined to the precise state of facts disclosed by the record. A representative of the Intelligence Department of the Army, having by stealth obtained admission to the defendant's office, seized and carried away certain private papers valuable for evidential purposes. This was held an unreasonable search and seizure within the Fourth Amendment. A stealthy entrance in such circumstances became the equivalent to an entry by force. There was actual entrance into the private quarters of defendant, and the taking away of something tangible. Here we have testimony only of voluntary conversations secretly overheard.

The Amendment itself shows that the search is to be of material things—the person, the house, his papers, or his effects. The description of the warrant necessary to make the proceeding lawful is that it must specify the place to be searched and the person or *things* to be seized.

It is urged that the language of Mr. Justice Field in *Ex parte Jackson,* already quoted, offers an analogy to the interpretation of the Fourth Amendment in respect of wiretapping. But the analogy fails. The Fourth Amendment may have proper application to a sealed letter in the mail because of the constitutional provision for the Post Office Department and the relations between the Government and those who pay to secure protection of their sealed letters. *See* Revised Statutes, §§ 3978 to 3988, whereby Congress monopolizes the carriage of letters and excludes from that business everyone else, and § 3929, which forbids any postmaster or other person to open any letter not addressed to himself. It is plainly within the words of the Amendment to say that the unlawful rifling by a government agent of a sealed letter is a search and seizure of the sender's papers or effects. The letter is a paper, an effect, and in the custody of a Government that forbids carriage except under its protection.

The United States takes no such care of telegraph or telephone messages as of mailed sealed letters. The Amendment does not forbid what was done here. There was no searching. There was no seizure. The evidence was secured by the use of the sense of hearing, and that only. There was no entry of the houses or offices of the defendants.

By the invention of the telephone fifty years ago and its application for the purpose of extending communications, one can talk with another at a far distant place. The language of the Amendment cannot be extended and expanded to include telephone wires reaching to the whole world from the defendant's house or office. The intervening wires are not part of his house or office any more than are the highways along which they are stretched.

This Court, in *Carroll v. United States*, 267 U. S. 132, 267 U. S. 149, declared:

"The Fourth Amendment is to be construed in the light of what was deemed an unreasonable search and seizure when it was adopted and in a manner which will conserve public interests as well as the interests and rights of individual citizens."

Justice Bradley, in the *Boyd* case, and Justice Clark in the *Gouled* case, said that the Fifth Amendment and the Fourth Amendment were to be liberally construed to effect the purpose of the framers of the Constitution in the interest of liberty. But that cannot justify enlargement of the language employed beyond the possible practical meaning of houses, persons, papers, and effects, or so to apply the words search and seizure as to forbid hearing or sight.

Hester v. United States, 265 U. S. 57, held that the testimony of two officers of the law who trespassed on the defendant's land, concealed themselves one hundred yards away from his house, and saw him come out and hand a bottle of whiskey to another was not inadmissible. While there was a trespass, there was no search of person, house, papers or effects. *United States v. Lee*, 274 U. S. 559, 274 U. S. 563; *Eversole v. State*, 106 Tex.Cr. 567.

Congress may, of course, protect the secrecy of telephone messages by making them, when intercepted, inadmissible in evidence in federal criminal trials by direct legislation, and thus depart from the common law of evidence. But the courts may not adopt such a policy by attributing an enlarged and unusual meaning to the Fourth Amendment. The reasonable view is that one who installs in his house a telephone instrument with connecting wires intends to project his voice to those quite outside, and that the wires beyond his house and messages while passing over them are not within the protection of the Fourth Amendment. Here, those who intercepted the projected voices were not in the house of either party to the conversation.

Neither the cases we have cited nor any of the many federal decisions brought to our attention hold the Fourth Amendment to have been violated as against a defendant unless there has been an official search and seizure of his person, or such a seizure of his papers or his tangible material effects, or an actual physical invasion of his house "or curtilage" for the purpose of making a seizure.

We think, therefore, that the wiretapping here disclosed did not amount to a search or seizure within the meaning of the Fourth Amendment.

What has been said disposes of the only question that comes within the terms of our order granting certiorari in these cases. But some of our number, departing from that order, have concluded that there is merit in the two-fold objection overruled in both courts below—that evidence obtained through intercepting of telephone messages by government agents was inadmissible because the mode of obtaining it was unethical, and a misdemeanor under the law of Washington. To avoid any misapprehension of our views of that objection, we shall deal with it in both of its phases.

While a Territory, the English common law prevailed in Washington, and thus continued after her admission in 1889. The rules of evidence in criminal cases in courts of the United States sitting there, consequently, are those of the common law. United States v. Reid, 12 How. 361, 53 U. S. 363, 53 U. S. 366; *Logan v. United States,* 144 U. S. 263, 144 U. S. 301; *Rosen v. United States,* 245 U. S. 467; *Withaup v. United States,* 127 Fed. 530, 534; *Robinson v. United States,* 292 Fed. 683, 685.

The common law rule is that the admissibility of evidence, is not affected by the illegality of the means by which it was obtained. Professor Greenleaf, in his work on evidence, vol. 1, 12th ed., by Redfield, § 254(a) says:

"It may be mentioned in this place, that though papers and other subjects of evidence may have been *illegally taken* from the possession of the party against whom they are offered, or otherwise unlawfully obtained, this is no valid objection to their admissibility, if they are pertinent to the issue. The court will not take notice how they were obtained, whether lawfully or unlawfully, nor will it form an issue, to determine that question."

Mr. Jones, in his work on the same subject, refers to Mr. Greenleaf's statement and says:

"Where there is no violation of a constitutional guaranty, the verity of the above statement is absolute."

Vol. 5, § 2075, note 3.

The rule is supported by many English and American cases cited by Jones in vol. 5, 2075, note 3, and § 2076, note 6, and by Wigmore, vol. 4, § 2183. It is recognized by this Court, in *Adams v. New York,* 192 U. S. 585. The *Weeks* case announced an exception to the common law rule by excluding all evidence in the procuring of which government officials took part by methods forbidden by the Fourth and Fifth Amendments. Many state courts do not follow the *Weeks* case. *People v. Defore,* 242 N.Y. 13. But those who do treat it as an exception to the general common law rule, and required by constitutional limitations. *Hughes v. State,* 145 Tenn. 544, 551, 566; *State v. Wills,* 91 W.Va. 659, 677; *State v. Slamon,* 73 Vt. 212, 214, 215; *Gindrat v. People,* 138 Ill. 103, 111; *People v. Castree,* 311 Ill. 392, 396, 397; *State v. Gardner,* 77 Mont. 8, 21; *State v. Fahn,* 53 N.Dak. 203, 210. The common law rule must apply in the case at bar. Nor can we, without the sanction of congressional enactment, subscribe to the suggestion that the courts have a discretion to exclude evidence the admission

of which is not unconstitutional because unethically secured. This would be at variance with the common law doctrine generally supported by authority. There is no case that sustains, nor any recognized text book that gives color to, such a view. Our general experience shows that much evidence has always been receivable although not obtained by conformity to the highest ethics. The history of criminal trials shows numerous cases of prosecutions of oath-bound conspiracies for murder, robbery, and other crimes where officers of the law have disguised themselves and joined the organizations, taken the oaths and given themselves every appearance of active members engaged in the promotion of crime, for the purpose of securing evidence. Evidence secured by such means has always been received.

A standard which would forbid the reception of evidence if obtained by other than nice ethical conduct by government officials would make society suffer and give criminals greater immunity than has been known heretofore. In the absence of controlling legislation by Congress, those who realize the difficulties in bringing offenders to justice may well deem it wise that the exclusion of evidence should be confined to cases where rights under the Constitution would be violated by admitting it.

The statute of Washington, adopted in 1909, provides (Remington Compiled Statutes, 1922, § 26518) that:

"Every person . . . who shall intercept, read or in any manner interrupt or delay the sending of a message over any telegraph or telephone line . . . shall be guilty of a misdemeanor

"This statute does not declare that evidence obtained by such interception shall be inadmissible, and, by the common law already referred to, it would not be. *People v. McDonald,* 177 App.Div. (N.Y.) 806. Whether the State of Washington may prosecute and punish federal officers violating this law and those whose messages were intercepted may sue them civilly is not before us. But clearly a statute, passed twenty years after the admission of the State into the Union cannot affect the rules of evidence applicable in courts of the United States in criminal cases. Chief Justice Taney, in United States v. Reid, 12 How. 361, 53 U. S. 363, construing the 34th section of the Judiciary Act, said:

"But it could not be supposed, without very plain words to show it, that Congress intended to give the states the power of prescribing the rules of evidence in trials for offenses against the United States. For this construction would place the criminal jurisprudence of one sovereignty under the control of another."

See also *Withaup v. United States,* 127 Fed. 530, 534.

The judgments of the Circuit Court of Appeals are affirmed. The mandates will go down forthwith under Rule 31.

Affirmed.

MR. JUSTICE BRANDEIS, dissenting

The defendants were convicted of conspiring to violate the National Prohibition Act. Before any of the persons now charged had been arrested or indicted, the telephones by means of which they habitually communicated with one another and with others had been tapped by federal officers. To this end, a lineman of long experience in wiretapping was employed on behalf of the Government and at its expense. He tapped eight telephones, some in the homes of the persons charged, some in their offices. Acting on behalf of the Government and in their official capacity, at least six other prohibition agents listened over the tapped wires and reported the messages taken. Their operations extended over a period of nearly five months. The typewritten record of the notes of conversations overheard occupies 775 typewritten pages. By objections seasonably made and persistently renewed, the defendants objected to the admission of the evidence obtained by wiretapping on the ground that the Government's wiretapping constituted an unreasonable search and seizure in violation of the Fourth Amendment, and that the use as evidence of the conversations overheard compelled the defendants to be witnesses against themselves in violation of the Fifth Amendment.

The Government makes no attempt to defend the methods employed by its officers. Indeed, it concedes that, if wiretapping can be deemed a search and seizure within the Fourth Amendment, such wiretapping as was practiced in the case at bar was an unreasonable search and seizure, and that the evidence thus obtained was inadmissible. But it relies on the language of the Amendment, and it claims that the protection given thereby cannot properly be held to include a telephone conversation.

"We must never forget," said Mr. Chief Justice Marshall in McCulloch v. Maryland, 4 Wheat. 316, 17 U. S. 407, "that it is a constitution we are expounding." Since then, this Court has repeatedly sustained the exercise of power by Congress, under various clauses of that instrument, over objects of which the Fathers could not have dreamed. *See Pensacola Telegraph Co. v. Western Union Telegraph Co.,* 96 U. S. 1, 96 U. S. 9; *Northern Pacific Ry. Co. v. North Dakota,* 250 U. S. 135; *Dakota Central Telephone Co. v. South Dakota,* 250 U. S. 163; *Brooks v. United States,* 267 U. S. 432. We have likewise held that general limitations on the powers of Government, like those embodied in the due process clauses of the Fifth and Fourteenth Amendments, do not forbid the United States or the States from meeting modern conditions by regulations which, "a century ago, or even half a century ago, probably would have been rejected as arbitrary and oppressive." *Village of Euclid v. Ambler Realty Co.,* 272 U. S. 365, 272 U. S. 387; *Buck v. Bell,* 274 U. S. 200. Clauses guaranteeing to the individual protection against specific abuses of power must have a similar capacity of adaptation to a changing world. It was with reference to such a clause that this Court said, in *Weems v. United States,* 217 U. S. 349, 217 U. S. 373:

"Legislation, both statutory and constitutional, is enacted, it is true, from an experience of evils, but its general language should not, therefore, be necessarily confined to the form that evil had theretofore taken. Time works changes, brings into existence new conditions and purposes. Therefore, a principle, to be vital, must be capable of wider application than the mischief which gave it birth. This is peculiarly true of constitutions. They are not ephemeral enactments, designed to meet passing occasions. They are, to use the words of Chief Justice Marshall 'designed to approach immortality as nearly as human institutions can approach it.' The future is their care, and provision for events of good and bad tendencies of which no prophecy can be made. In the application of a constitution, therefore, our contemplation cannot be only of what has been, but of what may be. Under any other rule, a constitution would indeed be as easy of application as it would be deficient in efficacy and power. Its general principles would have little value, and be converted by precedent into impotent and lifeless formulas. Rights declared in words might be lost in reality."

When the Fourth and Fifth Amendments were adopted, "the form that evil had theretofore taken" had been necessarily simple. Force and violence were then the only means known to man by which a Government could directly effect self-incrimination. It could compel the individual to testify—a compulsion effected, if need be, by torture. It could secure possession of his papers and other articles incident to his private life—a seizure effected, if need be, by breaking and entry. Protection against such invasion of "the sanctities of a man's home and the privacies of life" was provided in the Fourth and Fifth Amendments by specific language. *Boyd v. United States,* 116 U. S. 616, 116 U. S. 630. But "time works changes, brings into existence new conditions and purposes." Subtler and more far-reaching means of invading privacy have become available to the Government. Discovery and invention have made it possible for the Government, by means far more effective than stretching upon the rack, to obtain disclosure in court of what is whispered in the closet.

Moreover, "in the application of a constitution, our contemplation cannot be only of what has, been but of what may be." The progress of science in furnishing the Government with means of espionage is not likely to stop with wiretapping. Ways may someday be developed by which the Government, without removing papers from secret drawers, can reproduce them in court, and by which it will be enabled to expose to a jury the most intimate occurrences of the home. Advances in the psychic and related sciences may bring means of exploring unexpressed beliefs, thoughts and emotions. "That places the liberty of every man in the hands of every petty officer" was said by James Otis of much lesser intrusions than these. To Lord Camden, a far slighter intrusion seemed "subversive of all the comforts of society." Can it be that the Constitution affords no protection against such invasions of individual security?

A sufficient answer is found in *Boyd v. United States,* 116 U. S. 616, 116 U. S. 627-630, a case that will be remembered as long as civil liberty lives in the United States. This Court there reviewed the history that lay behind the Fourth and Fifth Amendments. We said with reference to Lord Camden's judgment in *Entick v. Carrington,* 19 Howell's State Trials 1030:

"The principles laid down in this opinion affect the very essence of constitutional liberty and security. They reach farther than the concrete form of the case there before the court, with its adventitious circumstances; they apply to all invasions on the part of the Government and its employes of the sanctities of a man's home and the privacies of life. It is not the breaking of his doors, and the rummaging of his drawers, that constitutes the essence of the offence; but it is the invasion of his indefeasible right of personal security, personal liberty and private property, where that right has never been forfeited by his conviction of some public offence—it is the invasion of this sacred right which underlies and constitutes the essence of Lord Camden's judgment. Breaking into a house and opening boxes and drawers are circumstances of aggravation; but any forcible and compulsory extortion of a man's own testimony or of his private papers to be used as evidence of a crime or to forfeit his goods is within the condemnation of that judgment. In this regard, the Fourth and Fifth Amendments run almost into each other."

In *Ex parte Jackson,* 96 U. S. 727, it was held that a sealed letter entrusted to the mail is protected by the Amendments. The mail is a public service furnished by the Government. The telephone is a public service furnished by its authority. There is, in essence, no difference between the sealed letter and the private telephone message. As Judge Rudkin said below:

"True, the one is visible, the other invisible; the one is tangible, the other intangible; the one is sealed, and the other unsealed, but these are distinctions without a difference."

The evil incident to invasion of the privacy of the telephone is far greater than that involved in tampering with the mails. Whenever a telephone line is tapped, the privacy of the persons at both ends of the line is invaded and all conversations between them upon any subject, and, although proper, confidential and privileged, may be overheard. Moreover, the tapping of one man's telephone line involves the tapping of the telephone of every other person whom he may call or who may call him. As a means of espionage, writs of assistance and general warrants are but puny instruments of tyranny and oppression when compared with wiretapping.

Time and again, this Court in giving effect to the principle underlying the Fourth Amendment, has refused to place an unduly literal construction upon it. This was notably illustrated in the *Boyd* case itself. Taking language in its ordinary meaning, there is no "search" or "seizure" when a defendant is required to produce a document in the orderly process of a court's procedure. "The right of the people to be secure in their persons, houses, papers, and effects, against unreasonable searches and seizures" would not be violated, under any ordinary construction of language, by compelling obedience to a subpoena. But this Court holds the evidence inadmissible simply because the information leading to the issue of the subpoena has been unlawfully secured. *Silverthorne Lumber Co. v. United States,* 251 U. S. 385. Literally, there is no "search" or "seizure" when a friendly visitor abstracts papers from an office; yet we held in *Gouled v. United States,* 255 U. S. 298, that evidence so obtained could not be used. No court which looked at the words of the Amendment, rather than at its underlying purpose, would hold, as this Court did in *Ex parte Jackson,* 96 U. S. 727, 96 U. S. 733, that its protection extended to letters in the mails. The provision against self-incrimination in the Fifth Amendment has been given an equally broad construction. The language is: "No person shall be compelled in any criminal case to be a witness against himself." Yet we have held not only that the protection of the Amendment extends to a witness before a grand jury, although he has not been charged with crime, *Counselman v. Hitchcock,* 142 U. S. 547, 142 U. S. 562, 586, but that:

"[i]t applies alike to civil and criminal proceedings, wherever the answer might tend to subject to criminal responsibility him who gives it. The privilege protects a mere witness as fully as it does one who is also a party defendant."

McCarthy v. Arndsten, 266 U. S. 34, 266 U. S. 40. The narrow language of the Amendment has been consistently construed in the light of its object,

"to insure that a person should not be compelled, when acting as a witness in any investigation, to give testimony which might tend to show that he himself had committed a crime. The privilege is limited to criminal matters, but it is as broad as the mischief against which it seeks to guard."

Counselman v. Hitchcock, supra, p. 142 U. S. 562.

Decisions of this Court applying the principle of the *Boyd* case have settled these things. Unjustified search and seizure violates the Fourth Amendment, whatever the character of the paper; whether the

paper when taken by the federal officers was in the home, in an office, or elsewhere; whether the taking was effected by force, by fraud, or in the orderly process of a court's procedure. From these decisions, it follows necessarily that the Amendment is violated by the officer's reading the paper without a physical seizure, without his even touching it, and that use, in any criminal proceeding, of the contents of the paper so examined—as where they are testified to by a federal officer who thus saw the document, or where, through knowledge so obtained, a copy has been procured elsewhere—any such use constitutes a violation of the Fifth Amendment.

The protection guaranteed by the Amendments is much broader in scope. The makers of our Constitution undertook to secure conditions favorable to the pursuit of happiness. They recognized the significance of man's spiritual nature, of his feelings, and of his intellect. They knew that only a part of the pain, pleasure and satisfactions of life are to be found in material things. They sought to protect Americans in their beliefs, their thoughts, their emotions and their sensations. They conferred, as against the Government, the right to be let alone—the most comprehensive of rights, and the right most valued by civilized men. To protect that right, every unjustifiable intrusion by the Government upon the privacy of the individual, whatever the means employed, must be deemed a violation of the Fourth Amendment. And the use, as evidence in a criminal proceeding, of facts ascertained by such intrusion must be deemed a violation of the Fifth.

Applying to the Fourth and Fifth Amendments the established rule of construction, the defendants' objections to the evidence obtained by wiretapping must, in my opinion, be sustained. It is, of course, immaterial where the physical connection with the telephone wires leading into the defendants' premises was made. And it is also immaterial that the intrusion was in aid of law enforcement. Experience should teach us to be most on our guard to protect liberty when the Government's purposes are beneficent. Men born to freedom are naturally alert to repel invasion of their liberty by evil-minded rulers. The greatest dangers to liberty lurk in insidious encroachment by men of zeal, well meaning but without understanding. Independently of the constitutional question, I am of opinion that the judgment should be reversed. By the laws of Washington, wiretapping is a crime. Pierce's Code, 1921, § 8976(18). To prove its case, the Government was obliged to lay bare the crimes committed by its officers on its behalf. A federal court should not permit such a prosecution to continue. *Compare Harkin v. Brundage,* 276 U. S. 36, *id.,* 604.

The situation in the case at bar differs widely from that presented in *Burdeau v. McDowell,* 256 U. S. 465. There, only a single lot of papers was involved. They had been obtained by a private detective while acting on behalf of a private party; without the knowledge of any federal official; long before anyone had thought of instituting a federal prosecution. Here, the evidence obtained by crime was obtained at the Government's expense, by its officers, while acting on its behalf; the officers who committed these crimes are the same officers who were charged with the enforcement of the Prohibition Act; the crimes of these officers were committed for the purpose of securing evidence with which to obtain an indictment and to secure a conviction. The evidence so obtained constitutes the warp and woof of the Government's case. The aggregate of the Government evidence occupies 306 pages of the printed record. More than 210 of them are filled by recitals of the details of the wiretapping and of facts ascertained thereby. There is literally no other evidence of guilt on the part of some of the defendants except that illegally obtained by these officers. As to nearly all the defendants (except those who admitted guilt), the evidence relied upon to secure a conviction consisted mainly of that which these officers had so obtained by violating the state law.

As Judge Rudkin said below:

"Here we are concerned with neither eavesdroppers nor thieves. Nor are we concerned with the acts of private individuals. . . . We are concerned only with the acts of federal agents whose powers are limited and controlled by the Constitution of the United States."

The Eighteenth Amendment has not, in terms, empowered Congress to authorize anyone to violate the criminal laws of a State. And Congress has never purported to do so. *Compare Maryland v. Soper,* 270 U. S. 9. The terms of appointment of federal prohibition agents do not purport to confer upon them authority to violate any criminal law. Their superior officer, the Secretary of the Treasury, has not instructed them to commit crime on behalf of the United States. It may be assumed that the Attorney General of the United States did not give any such instruction.

When these unlawful acts were committed, they were crimes only of the officers individually. The Government was innocent, in legal contemplation, for no federal official is authorized to commit a crime on its behalf. When the Government, having full knowledge, sought, through the Department of Justice, to avail itself of the fruits of these acts in order to accomplish its own ends, it assumed moral responsibility for the officers' crimes. *Compare The Paquete Habana,* 189 U. S. 453, 189 U. S. 465; *O'Reilly deCamara v. Brooke,* 209 U. S. 45, 209 U. S. 52; *Dodge v. United States,* 272 U. S. 530, 272 U. S. 532; *Gambino v. United States,* 275 U. S. 310. And if this Court should permit the Government, by means of its officers' crimes, to effect its purpose of punishing the defendants, there would seem to be present all the elements of a ratification. If so, the Government itself would become a lawbreaker.

Will this Court, by sustaining the judgment below, sanction such conduct on the part of the Executive? The governing principle has long been settled. It is that a court will not redress a wrong when he who invokes its aid has unclean hands. The maxim of unclean hands comes from courts of equity. But the principle prevails also in courts of law. Its common application is in civil actions between private parties. Where the Government is the actor, the reasons for applying it are even more persuasive. Where the remedies invoked are those of the criminal law, the reasons are compelling.

The door of a court is not barred because the plaintiff has committed a crime. The confirmed criminal is as much entitled to redress as his most virtuous fellow citizen; no record of crime, however long, makes one an outlaw. The court's aid is denied only when he who seeks it has violated the law in connection with the very transaction as to which he seeks legal redress. Then aid is denied despite the defendant's wrong. It is denied in order to maintain respect for law; in order to promote confidence in the administration of justice; in order to preserve the judicial process from contamination. The rule is one, not of action, but of inaction. It is sometimes spoken of as a rule of substantive law. But it extends to matters of procedure, as well. A defense may be waived. It is waived when not pleaded. But the objection that the plaintiff comes with unclean hands will be taken by the court itself. It will be taken despite the wish to the contrary of all the parties to the litigation. The court protects itself.

Decency, security and liberty alike demand that government officials shall be subjected to the same rules of conduct that are commands to the citizen. In a government of laws, existence of the government will be imperiled if it fails to observe the law scrupulously. Our Government is the potent, the omnipresent teacher. For good or for ill, it teaches the whole people by its example. Crime is contagious. If the Government becomes a lawbreaker, it breeds contempt for law; it invites every man to become a law unto himself; it invites anarchy. To declare that, in the administration of the criminal law, the end justifies the means—to declare that the Government may commit crimes in order to secure the conviction of a private criminal—would bring terrible retribution. Against that pernicious doctrine this Court should resolutely set its face.

Glossary

common law: the part of English law that is derived from custom and judicial precedent rather than statutes; usually distinguished from "statutory law"

petitioner: the party that appeals to the Supreme Court, often the defendant in a criminal case

ratification: the process by which the U.S. states approve an amendment to the Constitution

repugnant to: in legal contexts, opposed to or in violation of

POWELL V. ALABAMA

DATE
1932

AUTHOR
George Sutherland

VOTE
7–2

CITATION
287 U.S. 45

SIGNIFICANCE
Ruled that the right to full legal counsel of defendants under the Sixth Amendment in criminal cases cannot be abridged by states and that any curtailment of it would further violate the due process clause of the Fourteenth Amendment

Overview

Argued on October 10, 1932, and decided on November 7, 1932, *Ozie Powell, Willie Roberson, Andy Wright, and Olen Montgomery v. the State of Alabama*, known as *Powell v. Alabama*, was the first case to follow from the Scottsboro Nine trials of 1931. As such, it clarified questions of criminal law regarding the rights of the accused and proper pre-trial procedure. The main issue centered on the extent to which a legal level playing field, referring to adequate, if not equal, attorney representation, was required under the Constitution.

The rapidity with which the trials were conducted and concluded, the harshness of the sentences, and concerns that the defendants' access to adequate legal counsel had been severely compromised piqued the interest of the NAACP and the International Labor Defense arm of the American Communist Party. The trial results were appealed to the Alabama Supreme Court on June 22, 1931, and on March 24, 1932, the Court rejected the appeal. The case then went to the U.S. Supreme Court, which agreed to hear the case on May 27, 1932. The primary significance of the Supreme Court ruling was to emphasize the need for constitutionally mandated defendant safeguards to be maintained and for due process to be followed. In overturning the verdicts and convictions of the Scottsboro defendants, the majority on the Court argued that the right of the accused to counsel was absolute and that the state was obliged to provide legal representation to those defendants who could not afford to hire an attorney, and that the same rights to counsel and due process that were enunciated in the Sixth and Fourteenth Amendments necessarily applied to any state court. *Powell v. Alabama* was the first in a series of cases decided during the 1930s that called into question or reversed long-standing criminal court practices, particularly in southern states.

Context

The period from the late nineteenth through the early twentieth centuries in the United States is generally considered by historian as the point during which the rights of non-white citizens were at their lowest ebb and when legalized white supremacy was at its strongest. Throughout the South, and particularly in the deep southern states of Alabama, Mississippi,

The Scottsboro Boys in 1936
(National Portrait Gallery)

Georgia, Louisiana, and Florida, strict legal codes of racial segregation, voter suppression, and racial discrimination were in full rigor. Even in upper-southern states like Virginia, the Racial Integrity Act of 1924 (which included anti-miscegenation provisions) and the Virginia Sterilization Law of 1924 (which codified eugenics) legalized a rigid racial agenda. This was the so-called Jim Crow system, and one of its pillars was its enforcement by both the state and local courts and law officers. African American defendants were inevitably at a disadvantage. All-white juries and deficient legal representation, together with every sort of intimidation imaginable, reinforced the systemic inequality that by the 1930s had become an engrained way of life. Lynchings of Black men and women occurred on multiple occasions each year. The Ku Klux Klan, long moribund, had experienced a revival in 1916, spurred on by the blockbuster Hollywood film *Birth of a Nation*, which, in a distortion of historical fact, depicted Klansmen as heroic freedom fighters. The resurgent Klan would claim up to five million members during the 1920s. The decade from 1919 to 1929 proved to be

especially horrific: among the significant events were the Red Summer white-supremacist terrorist acts of 1919; the virtual demolition in 1921 of the formerly prosperous African American Greenwood District in Tulsa, Oklahoma; and the Massacre of 1923 in Rosewood, Florida, that claimed some 150 lives. At the same time, ironically, millions of Black Americans left the South to settle in northern urban areas where a cultural outpouring took place that was collectively labeled the Harlem Renaissance, after its best-known center in Harlem, New York. In these urban centers, too, African Americans began to feel more empowered and politically conscious, and the gradual shift from adherence to the Republican Party toward the Democratic Party (the "great switchover")—which became evident in 1932—was well underway.

The stock market crash of 1929 and the subsequent Great Depression proved to be devastating to millions of individuals of all races, particularly for the youth. One of the Depression-engendered phenomena was the rise a sizeable class of itinerant, casual workers known as hobos. Hobos had existed since at least the end of the Civil War, but the massive unemployment initiated by the Depression caused the numbers of such individuals to explode dramatically. An estimated two million hobos are said to have been traveling the country during the 1930s. The stark reality was that to find work, many—particularly the young, unskilled, and impoverished—had to journey far afield to find even seasonal occupations. This could involve traveling thousands of miles, even across the width of the United States. If it was too far to walk and one could not afford a car (as was most often the case), the option was traveling the railroads. Again, since many did not have money for fares, the vast majority opted for "riding the rails" by illegally hopping on freight cars, which was a very risky proposition. Hobo life was rough: many had to sleep in improvised "hobo camps" in open country, beg for food, and dodge law enforcement officers and hired toughs known as "bulls" who were employed by railroad companies to evict hobos from trains. A far smaller number of women rode the hobo trains, though estimates range as high as 8,000, some of whom resorted to prostitution.

It was on March 25, 1931, that a train was passing through northern Alabama on a route from Chattanooga to Memphis, Tennessee, when a scuffle broke out between Black and white hobos. A group of young white hobos began taunting a group of seven Black teenagers, yelling at them to get off because it was a "white man's train." One of the Black teens, Haywood Patterson, was attacked, and the six others came to his assistance, eventually getting the better of the whites, who, having been ejected from the train, ran to the sheriff at nearby Paint Rock, Alabama, claiming they had been attacked. The sheriff and his deputies stopped and boarded the train and arrested the seven Black teens who had been involved in the fight with the white hobos and an additional two who had not been involved but had been unfortunate enough to have been present. Those arrested were Patterson, Charles Norris, Ozie Powell, Eugene Williams, Charlie Weems, Olin Montgomery, Willie Roberson, Andy Wright, and Roy Wright. At this point, two white women who were hoboing and had been hidden up to this point were found by members of the posse. The women, Victoria Price and Ruby Bates, accused the nine Black boys of having raped them. The nine were held at the jail in Scottsboro, Alabama (and hence eventually became

known as the "Scottsboro Nine") and were threatened by a lynch mob. The sheriff phoned for National Guard units, who, under the governor's orders, secured the prison. According to a later account by Bates, who eventually retracted her accusations and confessed to having lied, she and Price had decided on maintaining their false stories to avoid being arrested as vagrants and prostitutes.

The defendants were indicted by a grand jury on March 30, 1931, and first trials were held at Scottsboro Courthouse beginning on April 6. By April 9, eight had been sentenced to death in the electric chair, and the youngest of the defendants, thirteen-year-old Roy Wright, was remanded for retrial as the result of a hung jury. One of the jurors refused to vote for the death penalty in his case and recommended life imprisonment.

About the Author

George Alexander Sutherland was born on March 25, 1862, in the market town of Stony Stratford in Buckinghamshire, England. When Sutherland was a year old, his parents, Alexander George Sutherland and Frances Slater Sutherland, immigrated to Utah as recent converts to the Mormon faith. George, however, apparently never became a Mormon and worshipped in the Episcopalian Church. The family was in a financially straitened situation, with George's father drifting from one odd job to another and, on occasion, even prospecting for gold. George himself worked from 1874 to 1879 for various stores and for Wells Fargo to help support his family until he was able to enter Brigham Young Academy (later University). After a year's hiatus working for the railroad, having graduated from Brigham Young with a bachelor's degree, Sutherland studied law at the University of Michigan before returning to Utah, where he practiced law in Provo (1883–93) and later in Salt Lake City (1893–1901). In 1896 he was elected to the Utah State Senate on the Republican ticket and served till 1900, when he was elected to the U.S. House of Representatives, serving one term (1901–03). In 1904, he successfully ran for one of Utah's U.S. Senate seats and served for two terms, from 1905 to 1917. At first, he supported President Theodore Roosevelt, but by 1912 he was siding with the conservative wing of the Republican Party led by Roosevelt's successor, President William Howard Taft. In 1916 he was defeated in his bid for a third term by the Democratic candidate, William H. King. Setting up a practice in Washington, D.C., Sutherland was nominated to a seat on the Supreme Court by President Warren G. Harding in 1922 and received Senate confirmation without controversy. He would serve as an associate justice under Chief Justices William Howard Taft and (from 1930) Charles Evans Hughes, until his retirement on January 17, 1938. He died on July 18, 1942. Sutherland is generally classified as a judicial conservative: one of the so-called Four Horsemen (a take either on Grantland Rice's famous reference to the Notre Dame football team backfield of 1922–24 or the four horsemen of the biblical Book of Revelation) who would so bedevil President Franklin D. Roosevelt's New Deal programs that he attempted unsuccessfully to increase the Court's membership through the Reform Bill of 1937 (the so-called court-packing plan).

Pierce Butler was born on March 17, 1866, in Northfield, Minnesota, to Irish immigrants Patrick and Mary Ann Butler. He received his education locally, at Carleton College in Northfield, and began practicing law in 1888. After a stint as an elected official (county attorney) from 1892 to 1896, he gravitated mainly toward handling cases involving railroad companies, practicing in both the United States and Canada. As an ardent Republican, he was nominated to the Supreme Court by President Warren G. Harding on December 5, 1922. Butler's was a contentious nomination: liberals saw him as being too conservative and pro-business, and his Catholic faith elicited opposition, notably from the Ku Klux Klan and other far-right groups. As it transpired, however, he was handily confirmed in the U.S. Senate by a 61–8 vote on December 21, 1922. Butler and Sutherland, along with Justices James Clark McReynolds and Willis Van Devanter, constituted the conservative judicial Four Horsemen. Butler served on the Court until his death on November 16, 1939.

Explanation and Analysis of the Document

Associate Justice Sutherland first refers to the sequence of events from the nine defendants' arrest to their arraignment and "not guilty" pleas, and he notes that despite a "further recital" (official statement) to the contrary, they had not yet been provided with legal counsel. He further observes that no mention in the record exists as to when and under what circumstances defense counsel had been provided, except for a vague statement by the presiding trial judge, Alfred E. Hawkins, that he had charged all members of the bar with finding an attorney and expected that "the members of the bar would continue to help the defendants if no counsel appeared."

Justice Sutherland notes that the nine defendants were tried in three groups, in three separate trials, all of which "were completed in a single day." The Supreme Court therefore decided to bundle the appeals from the three cases together under the sobriquet of *Powell v. Alabama* (the other two cases were *Patterson v. Alabama* and *Weems v. Alabama*). Southerland goes on to summarize the appeals process and particularly notes the dissent of Alabama Chief Justice John C. Anderson in the Alabama Supreme Court decision upholding the trials and sentencing, where he asserts that a fair trial and due process had been denied the defendants (Anderson was the only dissenter in this decision). The hostility of the crowd and the use of the military in safeguarding the defendants and court room are touched upon. In clauses four and five, Sutherland summarizes the arguments and lays out the Court's approach: the defense counsels argued, first, that their clients were not accorded a fair and impartial trial; second, that they were not accorded legal counsel nor had sufficient time allotted to plan and mount an effective defense; and third, that "they were tried by juries from which members of their own race were systematically excluded." Rather than wade into the more incendiary questions of trial procedure and the all-white jury system, Sutherland and the Court majority focus in only on the second item: the issue of legal representation.

It is noted that the nine young men were particularly vulnerable because they were illiterate or undereducated, were from out of state (Chattanooga, Tennessee) and did not have timely recourse to relatives and friends; and did not have legal counsel when they were arraigned and pleaded "not guilty." In clauses 12–37 of the Court's majority opinion, Sutherland quotes the trial record to demonstrate that "such designation of counsel as was attempted was either so indefinite or so close upon the trial as to amount to a denial of effective aid." On the day the trial opened, no one answered immediately for the defense. Then, a real estate attorney from Chattanooga named Stephen R. Roddy approached the bench to tell Judge Hawkins that he was appearing only because he had been asked by a group of local people to render what assistance he could for the nine accused. During a rather confused back-and-forth between Judge Hawkins, Roddy, and members of the bar who were present, it was ascertained that Roddy was not qualified to practice in Alabama and was there only to assist in whatever way he could, though he was self-admittedly unfamiliar with Alabama procedure and had had no time to prepare a case for defense. (In fact, he had spent only half an hour, at most, talking to the defendants.) An Alabama attorney named Milo Moody then offered to help Mr. Roddy. It transpired that Moody was sixty-nine years old and had not pleaded a case in a good many years. Notwithstanding, Judge Hawkins approved this impromptu arrangement, and the trials went ahead. Sutherland describes the trial situation as regards legal representation as "casual" and as a "dubious understanding" and again makes note of the defendants being "hurried to trial"—coupling both the instances of inadequate access to counsel and the haste with which procedures in a capital case were carried out as being grounds for overturning the verdicts and ordering a retrial.

The Due Process Clause

Justice Sutherland then deals with the question of whether the due process clause of the Fourteenth Amendment had been violated. In setting the stage for his conclusion, Sutherland refers to a paradoxical situation in English common law where a defendant is permitted access to legal counsel in civil and misdemeanor cases but not when capital and lesser felony charges were concerned. Praising the fact that the newly formed United States had rejected what he saw as "a perversion of all sense of proportion," he cites in some detail the relevant clause in the state constitutions of twelve of the original states asserting and protecting the right to legal counsel (Virginia is the only state not to receive a mention).

Sutherland concludes the majority opinion by stating that the combination of circumstances encompassing the atmosphere of hostility; the haste with which trial proceedings were conducted; the use of the military; the seriousness of the charges and the potential penalty; the defendants' youth and lack of education; and

above all the denial of adequate counsel amounted to contravention of the due process clause. The cases were then remanded back to Alabama state courts for retrial.

Justice Butler's dissent, joined by Justice James Clark McReynolds, takes the stance that, contrary to the majority opinion, denial of legal representation was unproven and there was an actual "inference" in the record of interchange and contact between defense counsels and their clients. Further, Justice Butler sees no evidence of fear or intimidation impacting on the defense counsels and offer the opinion that if proceedings moved too rapidly or provided inadequate time to mount a defense, the defense lawyers had the option to petition for a postponement, but they did not do so. At the heart of the dissenting opinion, however, is Justice Butler's contention that invoking the due process clause of the Fourteenth Amendment in this instance is an assumption by the federal government of a right that was reserved to the states.

Impact

The *Powell v. Alabama* decision reinforced the principle of access to counsel and fair legal representation as being applicable to state courts and indeed mandatory in trials involving capital offenses. While it mentioned, but explicitly refused to address, the issues of racially exclusive juries, the groundwork was laid for future rulings touching upon them—if only by the sheer fact that they were accorded mention. The Scottsboro Affair would not then recede into the background; quite the contrary: on April 1, 1935, following another series of trials and convictions, the Supreme Court ruled in *Norris v. Alabama* that the all-white jury system violated the Fourteenth Amendment's equal protection clause, and therefore the Scottsboro verdicts were again overturned and remanded to the state courts for retrial.

The *Powell v. Alabama* decision, too, went much further than asserting right to counsel. It recognized it as a right that was essential to secure due process and mandated the court to provide such representation, regardless of whether it was requested. In the longer-range scheme, Justice Sutherland's emphasis of the due process clause of the Fourteenth Amendment foreshadowed its future utilization during the NAACP's legal campaign under Charles Hamilton Houston and Thurgood Marshall to dismantle collegiate and school segregation, culminating in the

Brown v. Board (1954) decision, and in subsequent criminal cases where the right to attorney representation had been compromised, notably *Miranda v. Arizona* (1966). The clause was even employed in the landmark interracial marriage case of *Loving v. Virginia* (1967), which overturned the Virginia Racial Integrity Act of 1924.

Though none of the members of the Scottsboro Nine was executed, their cases dragged on for years, and they served varying terms of imprisonment. Clarence Norris was the last survivor of the nine, having escaped while on parole in 1946. He reemerged in Brooklyn, New York, and in 1976 received a pardon from Alabama governor George C. Wallace.

Questions for Further Study

1. What obstacles did African Americans have to confront by 1931, and how did these affect the Scottsboro case?

2. How was the concept of "right of counsel" interpreted and utilized in both Justice Sutherland's brief and in Justice Butler's dissent?

3. To what extent was the Supreme Court's ruling in the *Powell* case groundbreaking and radical? To what degree could it be described as cautious or conservative?

Further Reading

Books

Acker, James R. *Scottsboro and Its Legacy: The Cases That Challenged American Legal and Social Justice.* Westport, CT: Praeger, 2007.

Arkes, Hadley. *The Return of George Sutherland: Restoring a Jurisprudence of Natural Rights.* Princeton, NJ: Princeton University Press, 1994.

Carter, Dan T. *Scottsboro: A Tragedy of the American South.* Baton Rouge: Louisiana State University Press, 2007

Goodman, James. *Stories of Scottsboro: The Rape Case That Shocked 1930s America and Revived the Struggle for Equality.* New York: Pantheon Books, 1994.

Haskins, James. *The Scottsboro Boys.* New York: Holt, 1994.

Horne, Gerald. *Powell v. Alabama: The Scottsboro Boys and American Justice.* New York: Franklin Watts, 1997.

Kinshasa, Kwando M., ed. *The Scottsboro Boys in Their Own Words: Selected Letters, 1931–1950.* Jefferson, NC: McFarland, 2014.

Miller, James A. *Remembering Scottsboro: The Legacy of an Infamous Trial.* Princeton, NJ: Princeton University Press, 2009.

Norris, Clarence, and Sybil D. Washington. *The Last of the Scottsboro Boys: An Autobiography.* New York: Putnam, 1979.

Films/Recordings

Scottsboro: An American Tragedy. Public Broadcasting Service (PBS), The American Experience, 2001.

Websites

"George Sutherland, 1922–1938." Supreme Court Historical Society. Accessed February 23, 2023, https://supremecourthistory.org/associate-justices/george-sutherland-1922-1938/.

"Powell et al. v. State of Alabama. Patterson v. Same. Weems et al. v. Same." Legal Information Institute, Cornell Law School. Accessed February 23, 2023, https://www.law.cornell.edu/supremecourt/text/287/45.

"The Scottsboro Affair." Facing History and Ourselves. Last updated April 29, 2022. Accessed February 23, 2023, https://www.facinghistory.org/resource-library/scottsboro-affair.

—Commentary by Raymond Pierre Hylton

POWELL V. ALABAMA

Document Text

MR. JUSTICE SUTHERLAND delivered the opinion of the Court

These cases were argued together and submitted for decision as one case.

The petitioners, hereinafter referred to as defendants, are negroes charged with the crime of rape, committed upon the persons of two white girls. The crime is said to have been committed on March 25, 1931. The indictment was returned in a state court of first instance on March 31, and the record recites that, on the same day, the defendants were arraigned and entered pleas of not guilty. There is a further recital to the effect that, upon the arraignment, they were represented by counsel. But no counsel had been employed, and aside from a statement made by the trial judge several days later during a colloquy immediately preceding the trial, the record does not disclose when, or under what circumstances, an appointment of counsel was made, or who was appointed. During the colloquy referred to, the trial judge, in response to a question, said that he had appointed all the members of the bar for the purpose of arraigning the defendants, and then, of course, anticipated that the members of the bar would continue to help the defendants if no counsel appeared. Upon the argument here, both sides accepted that as a correct statement of the facts concerning the matter.

There was a severance upon the request of the state, and the defendants were tried in three several groups, as indicated above. As each of the three cases was called for trial, each defendant was arraigned, and, having the indictment read to him, entered a plea of not guilty. Whether the original arraignment and pleas were regarded as ineffective is not shown. Each of the three trials was completed within a single day. Under the Alabama statute, the punishment for rape is to be fixed by the jury, and, in its discretion, may be from ten years' imprisonment to death. The juries found defendants guilty and imposed the death penalty upon all. The trial court overruled motions for new trials and sentenced the defendants in accordance with the verdicts. The judgments were affirmed by the state supreme court. Chief Justice Anderson thought the defendants had not been accorded a fair trial, and strongly dissented. 224 Ala. 524; *id.*, 531; *id.*, 540, 141 So. 215, 195, 201.

In this court, the judgments are assailed upon the grounds that the defendants, and each of them, were denied due process of law and the equal protection of the laws in contravention of the Fourteenth Amendment, specifically as follows: (1) they were not given a fair, impartial and deliberate trial; (2) they were denied the right of counsel, with the accustomed incidents of consultation and opportunity of preparation for trial, and (3) they were tried before juries from which qualified members of their own race were systematically excluded. These questions were properly raised and saved in the courts below.

The only one of the assignments which we shall consider is the second, in respect of the denial of counsel, and it becomes unnecessary to discuss the facts of the case or the circumstances surrounding the prosecution except insofar as they reflect light upon that question.

The record shows that, on the day when the offense is said to have been committed, these defendants, together with a number of other negroes, were upon a freight train on its way through Alabama. On the same train were seven white boys and the two white girls. A fight took place between the negroes and the white boys in the course of which the white boys, with the exception of one named Gilley, were thrown off the train. A message was sent ahead, reporting the fight and asking that every negro be gotten off the train. The participants in the fight, and the two girls, were in an open gondola car. The two girls testified that each of them was assaulted by six different negroes in turn, and they identified the seven defendants as having been among the number. None of the white boys was called to testify, with the exception of Gilley, who was called in rebuttal.

Before the train reached Scottsboro, Alabama, a sheriff's posse seized the defendants and two other negroes. Both girls and the negroes then were taken to Scottsboro, the county seat. Word of their coming and of the alleged assault had preceded them, and they were met at Scottsboro by a large crowd. It does not sufficiently appear that the defendants were seriously threatened with, or that they were actually in danger of, mob violence, but it does appear that the attitude of the community was one of great hostility. The sheriff thought it necessary to call for the militia to assist in safeguarding the prisoners. Chief Justice Anderson pointed out in his opinion that every step taken from the arrest and arraignment to the sentence was accompanied by the military. Soldiers took the defendants to Gadsden for safekeeping, brought them back to Scottsboro for arraignment, returned them to Gadsden for safekeeping while awaiting trial, escorted them to Scottsboro for trial a few days later, and guarded the courthouse and grounds at every stage of the proceedings. It is perfectly apparent that the proceedings, from beginning to end, took place in an atmosphere of tense, hostile and excited public sentiment. During the entire time, the defendants were closely confined or were under military guard. The record does not disclose their ages, except that one of them was nineteen; but the record clearly indicates that most, if not all, of them were youthful, and they are constantly referred to as "the boys." They were ignorant and illiterate. All of them were residents of other states, where alone members of their families or friends resided.

However guilty defendants, upon due inquiry, might prove to have been, they were, until convicted, presumed to be innocent. It was the duty of the court having their cases in charge to see that they were denied no necessary incident of a fair trial. With any error of the state court involving alleged contravention of the state statutes or constitution we, of course, have nothing to do. The sole inquiry which we are permitted to make is whether the federal Constitution was contravened (*Rogers v. Peck*, 199 U. S. 425, 199 U. S. 434; *Hebert v. Louisiana*, 272 U. S. 312, 272 U. S. 316), and as to that, we confine ourselves, as already suggested, to the inquiry whether the defendants were in substance denied the right of counsel, and, if so, whether such denial infringes the due process clause of the Fourteenth Amendment.

First. The record shows that, immediately upon the return of the indictment, defendants were arraigned, and pleaded not guilty. Apparently they were not asked whether they had, or were able to, employ counsel, or wished to have counsel appointed, or whether they had friends or relatives who might assist in that regard if communicated with. That it would not have been an idle ceremony to have given the defendants reasonable opportunity to communicate with their families and endeavor to obtain counsel is demonstrated by the fact that, very soon after conviction, able counsel appeared in their behalf. This was pointed out by Chief Justice Anderson in the course of his dissenting opinion. "They were nonresidents," he said,

"and had little time or opportunity to get in touch with their families and friends who were scattered throughout two other states, and time has demonstrated that they could or would have been represented by able counsel had a better opportunity been given by a reasonable delay in the trial of the cases, judging from the number and activity of counsel that appeared immediately or shortly after their conviction."

224 Ala. at pp. 554-555, 141 So. 201.

It is hardly necessary to say that, the right to counsel being conceded, a defendant should be afforded a fair opportunity to secure counsel of his own choice. Not only was that not done here, but such designation of counsel as was attempted was either so indefinite or so close upon the trial as to amount to a denial of effective and substantial aid in that regard. This will be amply demonstrated by a brief review of the record.

April 6, six days after indictment, the trials began. When the first case was called, the court inquired whether the parties were ready for trial. The state's attorney replied that he was ready to proceed. No one answered for the defendants or appeared to represent or defend them. Mr. Roddy, a Tennessee lawyer not a member of the local bar, addressed the court, saying that he had not been employed, but that people who were interested had spoken to him about the case. He was asked by the court whether he intended to appear for the defendants, and answered that he would like to appear along with counsel that the court might appoint. The record then proceeds:

"The Court: If you appear for these defendants, then I will not appoint counsel; if local counsel are willing to appear and assist you under the circumstances, all right, but I will not appoint them."

"Mr. Roddy: Your Honor has appointed counsel, is that correct?"

"The Court: I appointed all the members of the bar for the purpose of arraigning the defendants, and then, of course, I anticipated them to continue to help them if no counsel appears. "

"Mr Roddy: Then I don't appear then as counsel, but I do want to stay in, and not be ruled out in this case."

"The Court: Of course, I would not do that --"

"Mr. Roddy: I just appear here through the courtesy of Your Honor."

"The Court: Of course, I give you that right; . . ."

And then, apparently addressing all the lawyers present, the court inquired:

". . . well, are you all willing to assist?"

"Mr. Moody: Your Honor appointed us all, and we have been proceeding along every line we know about it under Your Honor's appointment."

"The Court: The only thing I am trying to do is, if counsel appears for these defendants, I don't want to impose on you all, but if you feel like counsel from Chattanooga --"

"Mr. Moody: I see his situation, of course, and I have not run out of anything yet. Of course, if Your Honor

purposes to appoint us, Mr. Parks, I am willing to go on with it. Most of the bar have been down and conferred with these defendants in this case; they did not know what else to do."

"The Court: The thing, I did not want to impose on the members of the bar if counsel unqualifiedly appears; if you all feel like Mr. Roddy is only interested in a limited way to assist, then I don't care to appoint—"

"Mr. Parks: Your Honor, I don't feel like you ought to impose on any member of the local bar if the defendants are represented by counsel."

"The Court: That is what I was trying to ascertain, Mr. Parks."

"Mr. Parks: Of course, if they have counsel, I don't see the necessity of the Court appointing anybody; if they haven't counsel, of course, I think it is up to the Court to appoint counsel to represent them. "

"The Court: I think you are right about it, Mr. Parks, and that is the reason I was trying to get an expression from Mr. Roddy."

"Mr. Roddy: I think Mr. Parks is entirely right about it, if I was paid down here and employed, it would be a different thing, but I have not prepared this case for trial, and have only been called into it by people who are interested in these boys from Chattanooga. Now, they have not given me an opportunity to prepare the case, and I am not familiar with the procedure in Alabama, but I merely came down here as a friend of the people who are interested, and not as paid counsel, and certainly I haven't any money to pay them, and nobody I am interested in had me to come down here has put up any fund of money to come down here and pay counsel. If they should do it, I would be glad to turn it over—a counsel but I am merely here at the solicitation of people who have become interested in this case without any payment of fee and without any preparation for trial, and I think the boys would be better off if I step entirely out of the case according to my way of looking at it and according to my lack of preparation of it and not being familiar with the procedure in Alabama, . . ."

Mr. Roddy later observed:

"If there is anything I can do to be of help to them, I will be glad to do it; I am interested to that extent."

"The Court: Well gentlemen, if Mr. Roddy only appears as assistant that way, I think it is proper that I appoint members of this bar to represent them, I expect that is right. If Mr. Roddy will appear, I wouldn't of course, I would not appoint anybody. I don't see, Mr. Roddy, how I can make a qualified appointment or a limited appointment. Of course, I don't mean to cut off your assistance in any way—Well gentlemen, I think you understand it. "

"Mr. Moody: I am willing to go ahead and help Mr. Roddy in anything I can do about it, under the circumstances."

"The Court: All right, all the lawyers that will; of course, I would not require a lawyer to appear if—"

"Mr. Moody: I am willing to do that for him as a member of the bar; I will go ahead and help do anything I can do."

"The Court: All right."

And in this casual fashion, the matter of counsel in a capital case was disposed of.

It thus will be seen that, until the very morning of the trial, no lawyer had been named or definitely designated to represent the defendants. Prior to that time, the trial judge had "appointed all the members of the bar" for the limited "purpose of arraigning the defendants." Whether they would represent the defendants thereafter if no counsel appeared in their behalf was a matter of speculation only, or, as the judge indicated, of mere anticipation on the part of the court. Such a designation, even if made for all purposes, would, in our opinion, have fallen far short of meeting, in any proper sense, a requirement for the appointment of counsel. How many lawyers were members of the bar does not appear, but, in the very nature of things, whether many or few, they would not, thus collectively named, have been given that clear appreciation of responsibility or impressed with that individual sense of duty which should and naturally would accompany the appointment of a selected member of the bar, specifically named and assigned.

That this action of the trial judge in respect of appointment of counsel was little more than an expansive gesture, imposing no substantial or definite obligation upon any one, is borne out by the fact that, prior to the calling of the case for trial on April 6, a leading member of the local bar accepted employment on the side of the prosecution and actively participated in the trial. It is true that he said that, before doing so, he had understood Mr. Roddy would be employed as counsel for the defendants. This the lawyer in question, of his own accord, frankly stated to the court, and no doubt he acted with the utmost good faith. Probably other members of the bar had a like understanding. In any event, the circumstance lends emphasis to the conclusion that, during perhaps the most critical period of the proceedings against these defendants, that is to say, from the time of their arraignment until the beginning of their trial, when consultation, thoroughgoing investigation and preparation were vitally important, the defendants did not have the aid of counsel in any real sense, although they were as much entitled to such aid during that period as at the trial itself. *People ex rel. Burgess v. Risley,* 66 How.Pr. (N.Y.) 67; *Batchelor v. State,* 189 Ind. 69, 76, 125 N.E. 773.

Nor do we think the situation was helped by what occurred on the morning of the trial. At that time, as appears from the colloquy printed above, Mr. Roddy stated to the court that he did not appear as counsel, but that he would like to appear along with counsel that the court might appoint; that he had not been given an opportunity to prepare the case; that he was not familiar with the procedure in Alabama, but merely came down as a friend of the people who were interested; that he thought the boys would be better off if he should step entirely out of the case. Mr. Moody, a member of the local bar, expressed a willingness to help Mr. Roddy in anything he could do under the circumstances. To this, the court responded, "All right, all the lawyers that will; of course, I would not require a lawyer to appear if—." And Mr. Moody continued, "I am willing to do that for him as a member of the bar; I will go ahead and help do anything I can do." With this dubious understanding, the trials immediately proceeded. The defendants, young, ignorant, illiterate, surrounded by hostile sentiment, haled back and forth under guard of soldiers, charged with an atrocious crime regarded with especial horror in the community where they were to be tried, were thus put in peril of their lives within a few moments after counsel for the first time charged with any degree of responsibility began to represent them.

It is not enough to assume that counsel thus precipitated into the case thought there was no defense, and exercised their best judgment in proceeding to trial without preparation. Neither they nor the court could say what a prompt and thoroughgoing investigation might disclose as to the facts. No attempt was made to investigate. No opportunity to do so was given. Defendants were immediately hurried to trial. Chief Justice Anderson, after disclaiming any intention to criticize harshly counsel who attempted to represent defendants at the trials, said: " . . . the record indicates that the appearance was rather *pro forma* than zealous and active. . . ." Under the circumstances disclosed, we hold that defendants were not accorded the right of counsel in any substantial sense. To decide otherwise would simply be to ignore actualities. This conclusion finds ample support in the reasoning of an overwhelming array of state decisions, among which we cite the following: *Sheppard v. State,* 165 Ga. 460, 464, 141 S.E. 196; *Reliford v. State,* 140 Ga. 777, 79 S.E. 1128; *McArver v. State,* 114 Ga. 514, 40 S.E. 779; *Sanchez v. State,* 199 Ind. 235, 246, 157 N.E. l; *Batchelor v. State,* 189 Ind. 69, 76, 125 N.E. 773; *Mitchell v. Commonwealth,* 225 Ky. 83, 7 S.W. (2d) 823; *Jackson v. Commonwealth,* 215 Ky. 800, 287 S.W. 17; *State v. Collins,* 104 La. 629, 29 So. 180; *State v. Pool,* 50 La.Ann. 449, 23 So. 503; *People ex rel. Burgess v. Risley,* 66 How.Pr.(N.Y.) 67; *State ex rel. Tucker v. Davis,* 9 Okla.Cr. 94, 130 Pac. 962; *Commonwealth v. O'Keefe,* 298 Pa. 169, 148 Atl. 73; *Shaffer v. Territory,* 14 Ariz. 329, 333, 127 Pac. 746.

It is true that great and inexcusable delay in the enforcement of our criminal law is one of the grave evils of our time. Continuances are frequently granted for unnecessarily long periods of time, and delays incident to the disposition of motions for new trial and hearings upon appeal have come in many cases to be a distinct reproach to the administration of justice. The prompt disposition of criminal cases is to be commended and encouraged. But, in reaching that result, a defendant, charged with a serious crime, must not be stripped of his right to have sufficient time to advise with counsel and prepare his defense. To do that is not to proceed promptly in the calm spirit of regulated justice, but to go forward with the haste of the mob.

As the court said in *Commonwealth v. O'Keefe,* 298 Pa. 169, 173, 148 Atl. 73:

"It is vain to give the accused a day in court with no opportunity to prepare for it, or to guarantee him counsel without giving the latter any opportunity to acquaint himself with the facts or law of the case."

"* * * *"

"A prompt and vigorous administration of the criminal law is commendable, and we have no desire to clog the wheels of justice. What we here decide is that to force a defendant, charged with a serious misdemeanor, to trial within five hours of his arrest is not due process of law, regardless of the merits of the case."

Compare *Reliford v. State,* 140 Ga. 777, 778, 79 S.E. 1128.

Second. The Constitution of Alabama provides that, in all criminal prosecutions the accused shall enjoy the right to have the assistance of counsel, and a state statute requires the court in a capital case where the defendant is unable to employ counsel to appoint counsel for him. The state supreme court held that these provisions had not been infringed, and with that holding we are powerless to interfere. The question, however, which it is our duty, and within our power, to decide is whether the denial of the assistance of counsel contravenes the due process clause of the Fourteenth Amendment to the federal Constitution.

If recognition of the right of a defendant charged with a felony to have the aid of counsel depended upon the existence of a similar right at common law as it existed in England when our Constitution was adopted, there would be great difficulty in maintaining it as necessary to due process. Originally, in England, a person charged with treason or felony was denied the aid of counsel, except in respect of legal questions which the accused himself might suggest. At the same time, parties in civil cases and persons accused of misdemeanors were entitled to the full assistance of counsel. After the revolution of 1688, the rule was abolished as to treason, but was otherwise steadily adhered to until 1836, when, by act of Parliament, the full right was granted in respect of felonies generally. 1 Cooley's Const.Lim., 8th ed., 698, *et seq.,* and notes.

An affirmation of the right to the aid of counsel in petty offenses, and its denial in the case of crimes of the gravest character, where such aid is most needed, is so outrageous and so obviously a perversion of all sense of proportion that the rule was constantly, vigorously, and sometimes passionately assailed by English statesmen and lawyers. As early as 1758, Blackstone, although recognizing that the rule was settled at common law, denounced it as not in keeping with the rest of the humane treatment of prisoners by the English law. "For upon what face of reason," he says, "can that assistance be denied to save the life of a man which yet is allowed him in prosecutions for every petty trespass?" 4 Blackstone 355. One of the grounds upon which Lord Coke defended the rule was that, in felonies, the court itself was counsel for the prisoner. 1 Cooley's Const. Lim., *supra*. But how can a judge, whose functions are purely judicial, effectively discharge the obligations of counsel for the accused? He can and should see to it that, in the proceedings before the court, the accused shall be dealt with justly and fairly. He cannot investigate the facts, advise and direct the defense, or participate in those necessary conferences between counsel and accused which sometimes partake of the inviolable character of the confessional.

The rule was rejected by the colonies. Before the adoption of the federal Constitution, the Constitution of Maryland had declared "That, in all criminal prosecutions, every man hath a right . . . to be allowed counsel; . . ." (Art. XIX, Constitution of 1776). The Constitution of Massachusetts, adopted in 1780 (Part the First, Art. XII), the Constitution of New Hampshire, adopted in 1784 (Part I, Art. XV), the Constitution of New York of 1777 (Art. XXXIV), and the Constitution of Pennsylvania of 1776 (Art. IX), had also declared to the same effect. And, in the case of Pennsylvania, as early as 1701, the Penn Charter (Art. V) declared that "all Criminals shall have the same Privileges of Witnesses and Council as their Prosecutors", and there was also a provision in the Pennsylvania statute of May 31, 1718 (Dallas, Laws of Pennsylvania, 1700-1781, Vol. 1, p. 134) that, in capital cases, learned counsel should be assigned to the prisoners.

In Delaware, the Constitution of 1776 (Art. 25), adopted the common law of England, but expressly excepted such parts as were repugnant to the rights and privileges contained in the Declaration of Rights, and the Declaration of Rights, which was adopted on September 11, 1776, provided (Art. 14) "That in all Prosecutions for criminal Offences, every Man hath a Right . . . to be allowed Counsel, . . ." In addition, Penn's Charter, already referred to, was applicable in Delaware. The original Constitution of New Jersey of 1776 (Art. XVI) contained a provision like that of the Penn Charter, to the effect that all criminals should be admitted to the same privileges of counsel as their prosecutors. The original Constitution of North Carolina (1776) did not contain the guarantee, but c. 115, § 85, Sess.Laws, N.Car., 1777 (N. Car.Rev.Laws, 1715-1796, Vol. 1, 316), provided

". . . That every person accused of any crime or misdemeanor whatsoever shall be entitled to council in all matters which may be necessary for his defence, as well to facts as to law; . . ."

Similarly, in South Carolina, the original Constitution of 1776 did not contain the provision as to counsel, but it was provided as early as 1731 (Act of August 20, 1731, § XLIII, Grimke, S.Car.Pub.Laws, 1682-1790, p. 130) that every person charged with treason, murder, felony, or other capital offense should be admitted to make full defense by counsel learned in the law. In Virginia, there was no constitutional provision on the subject, but, as early as August, 1734 (c. VII, § III, Laws of Va. 8th Geo. II, Hening's Stat. at Large, Vol. 4, p. 404), there was an act declaring that, in all trials for capital offenses, the prisoner, upon his petition to the court, should be allowed counsel.

The original Constitution of Connecticut (Art. I, § 9) contained a provision that, "In all criminal prosecutions, the accused shall have the right to be heard by himself and by counsel"; but this constitution was not adopted until 1818. However, it appears that the English common law rule had been rejected in practice long prior to 1796. *See* Zephaniah Swift's "A System of the Laws of the State of Connecticut," printed at Windham by John Byrne, 1795-1796, Vol. II, Bk. 5, "Of Crimes and Punishments," c. XXIV, "Of Trials," pp. 398-399. *

The original Constitution of Georgia (1777) did not contain a guarantee in respect of counsel, but the Constitution of 1798 (Art. III, § 8) provided that

". . . no person shall be debarred from advocating or defending his cause before any court or tribunal, either by himself or counsel, or both."

What the practice was prior to 1798 we are unable to discover. The first constitution adopted by Rhode Island was in 1842, and this constitution contained the usual guarantee in respect of the assistance of counsel in criminal prosecutions. As early as 1798, it was provided by statute, in the very language of the Sixth Amendment to the Federal Constitution, that, "In all criminal prosecutions, the accused shall enjoy the right . . . to have the assistance of counsel for his defence; . . ."

An Act Declaratory of certain Rights of the People of this State, § 6, Rev.Pub.Laws, Rhode Island and Providence Plantations, 1798. Furthermore, while the statute itself is not available, it is recorded as a matter of history that, in 1668 or 1669, the colonial assembly enacted that any person who was indicted might employ an attorney to plead in his behalf. 1 Arnold, History of Rhode Island, 336.

It thus appears that, in at least twelve of the thirteen colonies, the rule of the English common law, in the respect now under consideration, had been definitely rejected, and the right to counsel fully recognized in all criminal prosecutions, save that, in one or two instances, the right was limited to capital offenses or to the more serious crimes, and this court seems to have been of the opinion that this was true in all the colonies. In *Holden v. Hardy,* 169 U. S. 366, 169 U. S. 386, Mr. Justice Brown, writing for the court, said:

"The earlier practice of the common law, which denied the benefit of witnesses to a person accused of felony, had been abolished by statute, though, so far as it deprived him of the assistance of counsel and compulsory process for the attendance of his witnesses, it had not been changed in England. But to the credit of her American colonies, let it be said that so oppressive a doctrine had never obtained a foothold there."

One test which has been applied to determine whether due process of law has been accorded in given instances is to ascertain what were the settled usages and modes of proceeding under the common and statute law of England before the Declaration of Independence, subject, however, to the qualification that they be shown not to have been unsuited to the civil and political conditions of our ancestors by having been followed in this country after it became a nation. *Lowe v. Kansas,* 163 U. S. 81, 163 U. S. 85. *Compare 59 U. S. Hoboken Land & Improvement Co.,* 18 How. 272, 59 U. S. 276-277; *Twining v. New Jersey,* 211 U. S. 78, 211 U. S. 100-101. Plainly, as appears from the foregoing, this test, as thus qualified, has not been met in the present case.

We do not overlook the case of *Hurtado v. California,* 110 U. S. 516, where this court determined that due process of law does not require an indictment by a grand jury as a prerequisite to prosecution by a state for murder. In support of that conclusion the court (pp. 110 U. S. 534-535) referred to the fact that

the Fifth Amendment, in addition to containing the due process of law clause, provides in explicit terms that "No person shall be held to answer for a capital, or otherwise infamous crime, unless on a presentment or indictment of a grand jury, . . . ", and said that, since no part of this important amendment could be regarded as superfluous, the obvious inference is that, in the sense of the Constitution, due process of law was not intended to include, *ex vi termini,* the institution and procedure of a grand jury in any case, and that the same phrase, employed in the Fourteenth Amendment to restrain the action of the states, was to be interpreted as having been used in the same sense and with no greater extent, and that, if it had been the purpose of that Amendment to perpetuate the institution of the grand jury in the states, it would have embodied, as did the Fifth Amendment, an express declaration to that effect.

The Sixth Amendment, in terms, provides that, in all criminal prosecutions, the accused shall enjoy the right "to have the assistance of counsel for his defense." In the face of the reasoning of the *Hurtado* case, if it stood alone, it would be difficult to justify the conclusion that the right to counsel, being thus specifically granted by the Sixth Amendment, was also within the intendment of the due process of law clause. But the *Hurtado* case does not stand alone. In the later case of *Chicago, Burlington & Quincy R. Co. v. Chicago,* 166 U. S. 226, 166 U. S. 241, this court held that a judgment of a state court, even though authorized by statute, by which private property was taken for public use without just compensation, was in violation of the due process of law required by the Fourteenth Amendment notwithstanding that the Fifth Amendment explicitly declares that private property shall not be taken for public use without just compensation. This holding was followed in *Norwood v. Baker,* 172 U. S. 269, 172 U. S. 277; *Smyth v. Ames,* 169 U. S. 466, 169 U. S. 524, and *San Diego Land Co. v. National City,* 174 U. S. 739, 174 U. S. 754.

Likewise, this court has considered that freedom of speech and of the press are rights protected by the due process clause of the Fourteenth Amendment, although in the First Amendment, Congress is prohibited in specific terms from abridging the right. *Gitlow v. New York,* 268 U. S. 652, 268 U. S. 666; *Stromberg v. California,* 283 U. S. 359, 283 U. S. 368; *Near v. Minnesota,* 283 U. S. 697, 283 U. S. 707.

These later cases establish that, notwithstanding the sweeping character of the language in the *Hurtado* case, the rule laid down is not without exceptions. The rule is an aid to construction, and in some instances may be conclusive, but it must yield to more compelling considerations whenever such considerations exist. The fact that the right involved is of such a character that it cannot be denied without violating those "fundamental principles of liberty and justice which lie at the base of all our civil and political institutions" (*Hebert v. Louisiana*, 272 U. S. 312, 272 U. S. 316), is obviously one of those compelling considerations which must prevail in determining whether it is embraced within the due process clause of the Fourteenth Amendment, although it be specifically dealt with in another part of the federal Constitution. Evidently this court, in the later cases enumerated, regarded the rights there under consideration as of this fundamental character. That some such distinction must be observed is foreshadowed in *Twining v. New Jersey*, 211 U. S. 78, 211 U. S. 99, where Mr. Justice Moody, speaking for the court, said that

". . . it is possible that some of the personal rights safeguarded by the first eight Amendments against National action may also be safeguarded against state action, because a denial of them would be a denial of due process of law. *Chicago, Burlington & Quincy R. Co. v. Chicago*, 166 U. S. 226. If this is so, it is not because those rights are enumerated in the first eight Amendments, but because they are of such a nature that they are included in the conception of due process of law."

While the question has never been categorically determined by this court, a consideration of the nature of the right and a review of the expressions of this and other courts, makes it clear that the right to the aid of counsel is of this fundamental character.

It never has been doubted by this court, or any other, so far as we know, that notice and hearing are preliminary steps essential to the passing of an enforceable judgment, and that they, together with a legally competent tribunal having jurisdiction of the case, constitute basic elements of the constitutional requirement of due process of law. The words of Webster, so often quoted, that, by "the law of the land" is intended "a law which hears before it condemns" have been repeated in varying forms of expression in a multitude of decisions. In *Holden v. Hardy*, 169 U. S. 366, 169 U.

S. 389, the necessity of due notice and an opportunity of being heard is described as among the "immutable principles of justice which inhere in the very idea of free government which no member of the Union may disregard." And Mr. Justice Field, in an earlier case, *Galpin v. Page*, 18 Wall. 350, 85 U. S. 368-369, said that the rule that no one shall be personally bound until he has had his day in court was as old as the law, and it meant that he must be cited to appear and afforded an opportunity to be heard.

"Judgment without such citation and opportunity wants all the attributes of a judicial determination; it is judicial usurpation and oppression, and never can be upheld where justice is justly administered."

Citations to the same effect might be indefinitely multiplied, but there is no occasion for doing so.

What, then, does a hearing include? Historically and in practice, in our own country, at least, it has always included the right to the aid of counsel when desired and provided by the party asserting the right. The right to be heard would be, in many cases, of little avail if it did not comprehend the right to be heard by counsel. Even the intelligent and educated layman has small and sometimes no skill in the science of law. If charged with crime, he is incapable, generally, of determining for himself whether the indictment is good or bad. He is unfamiliar with the rules of evidence. Left without the aid of counsel, he may be put on trial without a proper charge, and convicted upon incompetent evidence, or evidence irrelevant to the issue or otherwise inadmissible. He lacks both the skill and knowledge adequately to prepare his defense, even though he have a perfect one. He requires the guiding hand of counsel at every step in the proceedings against him. Without it, though he be not guilty, he faces the danger of conviction because he does not know how to establish his innocence. If that be true of men of intelligence, how much more true is it of the ignorant and illiterate, or those of feeble intellect. If in any case, civil or criminal, a state or federal court were arbitrarily to refuse to hear a party by counsel, employed by and appearing for him, it reasonably may not be doubted that such a refusal would be a denial of a hearing, and, therefore, of due process in the constitutional sense.

The decisions all point to that conclusion. In *Cooke v. United States*, 267 U. S. 517, 267 U. S. 537, it was held that, where a contempt was not in open court, due process of law required charges and a reasonable opportunity to defend or explain. The court added, "We think this includes the assistance of counsel, if requested, . . ." In numerous other cases, the court, in determining that due process was accorded, has frequently stressed the fact that the defendant had the aid of counsel. *See, for example, Felts v. Murphy,* 201 U. S. 123, 201 U. S. 129; *Frank v. Mangum,* 237 U. S. 309, 237 U. S. 344; *Kelley v. Oregon,* 273 U. S. 589, 273 U. S. 591. In *Ex parte Hidekuni Iwata,* 219 Fed. 610, 611, the federal district judge enumerated among the elements necessary to due process of law in a deportation case the opportunity at some stage of the hearing to secure and have the advice and assistance of counsel. In *Ex parte Chin Loy You,* 223 Fed. 833, also a deportation case, the district judge held that, under the particular circumstances of the case, the prisoner, having seasonably made demand, was entitled to confer with and have the aid of counsel. Pointing to the fact that the right to counsel as secured by the Sixth Amendment relates only to criminal prosecutions, the judge said,

". . . but it is equally true that that provision was inserted in the Constitution because the assistance of counsel was recognized as essential to any fair trial of a case against a prisoner."

In *Ex parte Riggins,* 134 Fed. 404, 418, a case involving the due process clause of the Fourteenth Amendment, the court said, by way of illustration, that, if the state should deprive a person of the benefit of counsel, it would not be due process of law. Judge Cooley refers to the right of a person accused of crime to have counsel as perhaps his most important privilege, and, after discussing the development of the English law upon that subject, says: "With us, it is a universal principle of constitutional law that the prisoner shall be allowed a defense by counsel." 1 Cooley's Const.Lim., 8th ed., 700. The same author, as appears from a chapter which he added to his edition of Story on the Constitution, regarded the right of the accused to the presence, advice and assistance of counsel a necessarily included in due process of law. 2 Story on the Constitution, 4th ed., § 1949, p. 668. The state decisions which refer to the matter invariably recognize the right to the aid of counsel as fundamental in character. *E.g., People v. Napthaly,* 105 Cal. 641, 644, 39 Pac. 29; *Cutts v. State,* 54 la. 21, 23, 45 So. 491; *Martin v. State,* 51 Ga. 567, 568; *Sheppard v. State,* 165 Ga. 460, 464, 141 S.E.

196; *State v. Moore,* 61 Kan. 732, 734, 60 Pac. 748; *State v. Ferris,* 16 La.Ann. 424; *State v. Simson,* 38 La.Ann. 23, 24; *State v. Briggs,* 58 W.Va. 291, 292, 52 S.E. 218.

In the light of the facts outlined in the forepart of this opinion—the ignorance and illiteracy of the defendants, their youth, the circumstances of public hostility, the imprisonment and the close surveillance of the defendants by the military forces, the fact that their friends and families were all in other states and communication with them necessarily difficult, and, above all, that they stood in deadly peril of their lives—we think the failure of the trial court to give them reasonable time and opportunity to secure counsel was a clear denial of due process.

But passing that, and assuming their inability, even if opportunity had been given, to employ counsel, as the trial court evidently did assume, we are of opinion that, under the circumstances just stated, the necessity of counsel was so vital and imperative that the failure of the trial court to make an effective appointment of counsel was likewise a denial of due process within the meaning of the Fourteenth Amendment. Whether this would be so in other criminal prosecutions, or under other circumstances, we need not determine. All that it is necessary now to decide, as we do decide, is that, in a capital case, where the defendant is unable to employ counsel and is incapable adequately of making his own defense because of ignorance, feeble mindedness, illiteracy, or the like, it is the duty of the court, whether requested or not, to assign counsel for him as a necessary requisite of due process of law, and that duty is not discharged by an assignment at such a time or under such circumstances as to preclude the giving of effective aid in the preparation and trial of the case. To hold otherwise would be to ignore the fundamental postulate, already adverted to,

"that there are certain immutable principles of justice which inhere in the very idea of free government which no member of the Union may disregard."

Holden v. Hardy, supra. In a case such as this, whatever may be the rule in other cases, the right to have counsel appointed, when necessary, is a logical corollary from the constitutional right to be heard by counsel. *Compare Carpenter & Sprague v. Dane County,* 9 Wis. 274; *Dane County v. Smith,* 13 Wis. 585, 586. *Hendryx v. State,* 130 Ind. 265, 268-269, 29 N.E.

1131; *Cutts v. State,* 54 Fla. 21, 23, 45 So. 491; *People v. Goldenson,* 76 Cal. 328, 344, 19 Pac. 161; *Delk v. State,* 99 Ga. 667, 669-670, 26 S.E. 752.

In *Hendryx v. State, supra,* there was no statute authorizing the assignment of an attorney to defend an indigent person accused of crime, but the court held that such an assignment was necessary to accomplish the ends of public justice, and that the court possessed the inherent power to make it. "Where a prisoner," the court said (p. 269),

"without legal knowledge, is confined in jail, absent from his friends, without the aid of legal advice or the means of investigating the charge against him, it is impossible to conceive of a fair trial where he is compelled to conduct his cause in court, without the aid of counsel. . . . Such a trial is not far removed from an *ex parte* proceeding."

Let us suppose the extreme case of a prisoner charged with a capital offense who is deaf and dumb, illiterate and feeble minded, unable to employ counsel, with the whole power of the state arrayed against him, prosecuted by counsel for the state without assignment of counsel for his defense, tried, convicted and sentenced to death. Such a result, which, if carried into execution, would be little short of judicial murder, it cannot be doubted would be a gross violation of the guarantee of due process of law, and we venture to think that no appellate court, state or federal, would hesitate so to decide. *See Stephenson v. State,* 4

Ohio App. 128; Williams v. State, *163 Ark. 623, 628, 260 S.W. 721;* Grogan v. Commonwealth, *222 Ky. 484, 485, 1 S.W.2d 779; Mullen v. State,* 28 Okla.Cr. 218, 230, 230 Pac. 285; *Williams v. Commonwealth,* (Ky.), 110 S.W. 339, 340. The duty of the trial court to appoint counsel under such circumstances is clear, as it is clear under circumstances such as are disclosed by the record here, and its power to do so, even in the absence of a statute, cannot be questioned. Attorneys are officers of the court, and are bound to render service when required by such an appointment. *See* Cooley, Const. Lim., *supra,* 700 and note.

The United States, by statute, and every state in the Union, by express provision of law or by the determination of its courts, make it the duty of the trial judge, where the accused is unable to employ counsel, to appoint counsel for him. In most states, the rule applies broadly to all criminal prosecutions; in others, it is limited to the more serious crimes; and in a very limited number, to capital cases. A rule adopted with such unanimous accord reflects, if it does not establish, the inherent right to have counsel appointed, at least in cases like the present, and lends convincing support to the conclusion we have reached as to the fundamental nature of that right.

The judgments must be reversed, and the causes remanded for further proceedings not inconsistent with this opinion.

Judgments reversed.

Glossary

counsel: a lawyer hired or appointed to represent the accused in court

due process clause: a clause in the Fourteenth Amendment, which states, in part: "nor shall any State deprive any person of life, liberty, or property, without due process of law"

recital: official statement

right of counsel: the right to qualified legal assistance; one of the rights outlined in the Sixth Amendment, which states, part, that "the accused shall . . . have the Assistance of Counsel for his defence"

systematic exclusion: the exclusion of a class of people (for example, of African Americans from jury duty) in a planned manner or to a degree greater than would happen by chance

A.L.A. SCHECHTER POULTRY CORPORATION V. UNITED STATES

DATE
1935

AUTHOR
Charles E. Hughes

VOTE
9–0

CITATION
295 U.S. 495

SIGNIFICANCE
Effectively nullified parts of New Deal legislation that delegated congressional authority to the president as a violation of the Constitution's commerce clause

Overview

Argued May 2–3, 1935, and decided on May 27, 1935, the case of *A.L.A. Schechter Poultry Corporation v. United States* effectively nullified Title I of the National Industrial Recovery Act of 1933 (NIRA), a key piece of President Franklin D. Roosevelt's New Deal legislation. Title I of the NIRA was aimed at stabilizing and encouraging an expansion of American industry during the global economic collapse of the Great Depression. Within Title I was the Live Poultry Code, which, in addition to other items, banned certain methods of unfair competition, outlined animal selection criteria, and imposed meat quality standards on the poultry industry. The NIRA also provided significant protections for workers and unintentionally promoted monopolies, resulting in considerable labor unrest and loss of commercial and industrial support for the policy. The government had argued that the national economic emergency required special consideration by the judiciary as a necessary practicality. The Schechter Poultry Corporation, a Kosher butcher in New York, was charged with violating the Live Poultry Code for selling uninspected chickens selected individually by custom-

ers. The Court's decision held that the NIRA was an unconstitutional delegation of legislative authority under the commerce clause and that Congress had failed to create rules or methods of regulation to avoid the inherent vagueness of terms such as "fair competition" to allow the federal government to regulate minutia such as individual slaughter selection under interstate commerce. The Court concluded that the country's dire economic circumstances did not justify the NIRA's overly broad delegation or overreach.

Context

The American experience with the Great Depression started on October 29, 1929. Although President Herbert Hoover was concerned with the nation's significant economic issues, his belief that the individuality and self-reliance that characterized the American people would be destroyed by government support did little to mitigate the situation. Voluntary measures by businesses and local governments, along with federal support for public works construction programs and low-interest business loans, were publicly applauded by President Hoover, but they had minimal impact on the continued economic decline of the nation. By 1933, nearly 25 percent of the American labor force was unemployed, productivity had dropped to less than 33 percent of its pre-Depression levels, millions had lost their homes, and many farms were foreclosed. The resulting frustration resulted in a landslide election of Franklin Delano Roosevelt, the former governor of New York, who had promised a "New Deal" for the American people if elected.

In Roosevelt's first hundred days in office, the president pushed through a comprehensive program of legislation through Congress designed to mitigate and reverse the economic conditions affecting the nation. These "First New Deal" programs were necessarily diverse and experimental, as no such effort had previously been attempted. While many were successful and have become part of modern American society—such as the Social Security Administration, the Securities and Exchange Commission, and the Federal Housing Commission—many others were unsuccessful, and still others were exceptionally controversial. One of the more controversial elements of the "First New Deal" was the National Industrial Recovery Act (NIRA). The NIRA was signed into law on June 16, 1933, and was aimed at bringing together labor, business, and government to "encourage national industrial recovery, to foster fair competition, and to provide for the construction of certain useful public works and for other purposes." Because of the experimental nature of the NIRA, the authorities conveyed in the NIRA were set to expire in June 1935.

Despite the vague outlines of its intent, the NIRA fundamentally consisted of two titles, or elements. Title I was one of the most controversial pieces of New Deal legislation, which soon drew much negative response from businesses. Title I effectively placed legislative authority to codify private associations' codes of fair-trade conduct as federal law in the hands of the president. It also provided the president with the power to enforce such laws and provided exemption from existing federal antitrust laws. Title I provided worker security by authorizing the formation of trade unions, banning employers' restrictions on hiring union employees, and establishing maximum hours of labor, minimum rates of pay, and working conditions. Title I also provided for stiff penalties, such as the private forfeiture and nationalization of specific industries,

Chief Justice Charles Evans Hughes wrote the majority opinion.
(Thomas C. Corner)

for violation of the NIRA. To enforce and oversee such efforts, Title I established the National Recovery Administration, which held broad powers to set consumer goods and housing prices to stabilize the economy through coordinating business, labor, and government. Title II established the Public Works Administration (PWA), one of the most successful programs of the New Deal era. Not only did the PWA provide grants or loans to local governments for programs designed to rapidly reduce unemployment locally, but it also had the authority to seize unproductive land or materials for the construction of public works such as roads, bridges, parks, and transportation networks.

In April 1934, President Roosevelt approved a fair-trade code for live poultry butchery and sale, which an association of New York City butchers had advocated. The "Code of Fair Competition for the Live Poultry Industry of the Metropolitan Area in and about the City of New York" aimed to ensure that kosher slaughterhouses provided wholesome and inspected meat to consumers. The association believed that kosher butchers had a reputation for falsifying their sales records and failing to follow local "straight killing" practices. These practices required that birds be butchered and sold based on a "first bird slaughtered, first bird sold" basis. The individual selection process allowed by Schechter, according to the company's defense, argued that many customers believed the personal selection made it easier to attain rabbinical kosher certification for their meat. Within days of the approval, the Schechter Poultry Corporation was indicted and convicted by a federal district court of many counts, including the sale of diseased chickens, falsifying sales records, violation of straight killing, sale of poultry to unlicensed purchasers, and conspiracy to avoid government inspection. The circuit court upheld the conviction, leading Schechter to seek an appeal to the U.S. Supreme Court as a violation of the doctrine of non-delegation of powers within the Constitution of the United States. The government had argued that the national economic emergency required special consideration by the judiciary as a necessary expediency.

About the Author

Charles Evans Hughes was born April 11, 1862, in rural upstate New York to Mary Connelly and David Hughes, a local Baptist minister. Hughes was an exceptionally bright child who began attending Madison College at the age of fourteen. After graduating from Brown University, he briefly took a teaching position before his acceptance to Columbia Law School. He attained a nearly perfect score when he underwent the New York Bar Exam at twenty-two. While practicing private law, he made a national name by bringing charges against the insurance industry for widespread conspiracy to set illegal rates and consumer fraud.

Hughes successfully ran, with backing from Franklin Roosevelt, for governor of New York in 1906. In 1910, Hughes was nominated by President Taft as an associate justice and was quickly confirmed by Senate. In 1916, Hughes resigned his seat and narrowly lost to Woodrow Wilson for the presidency. After this loss, Hughes returned to private law until being appointed as secretary of state for the Harding and Coolidge administrations. Hughes was instrumental in negotiating the post–World War Washington Naval Treaty aimed to prevent a global naval arms race and was generally successful in these voluntary arms-limiting efforts until the mid-1930s.

Hughes returned again to private law in 1925 before being appointed in 1928 as a deputy judge to the Per-

manent Court of International Justice, an international court formed under the League of Nations. Hughes held this seat until being nominated by President Hoover in 1930 to succeed former President Taft as chief justice of the U.S. Supreme Court. Hughes would hold the position until retiring in 1941. The Hughes court was one of balance, with Hughes himself often viewed as an influential swing vote. The Hughes Court sought to root out injustices while mitigating progressive or aggressive excesses. Hughes himself authored twice as many constitutional opinions as any other member of his court. His opinions are widely considered to be not only accessible but succinct, making his opinions a metric for many others to measure their written opinions.

Explanation and Analysis of the Document

Chief Justice Hughes begins his decision by directly addressing the government's defense that the extraordinary conditions created by the Great Depression necessitated special consideration by the Court. Hughes begins bluntly, "Extraordinary conditions, such as an economic crisis, may call for extraordinary remedies, but they cannot create or enlarge constitutional power." With this simple phrase, Hughes begins to outline three key questions with the NIRA. Was the subject matter in question within the legal right of Congress to regulate? Had Congress properly delegated its power to the president? And did the NIRA violate the immunities and privileges extended to every citizen under the Fifth Amendment's takings and due process clauses?

First, Hughes argues that the commerce and labor that the act was attempting to regulate were outside of Congress's constitutional prerogatives and duties. Under the Court's interpretation, "[The] Defendants were engaged in the business of slaughtering chickens and selling them to retailers. They bought their fowls from commission men in a market where most of the supply was shipped in from other States, transported them to their slaughterhouses, and there held them for slaughter and local sale to retail dealers and butchers, who in turn sold directly to consumers. . . . When the poultry had reached the defendants' slaughterhouses, the interstate commerce had ended, and subsequent transactions in their business, including the matters charged in the indictment, were transactions in intrastate commerce." Thus, any commerce issue within a state solely for use or consumption within that state is outside federal regulation.

Second, the NIRA had effectively delegated the legislative authority of Congress to the president to create laws regulating commerce. Hughes reprimands the Legislature for its effort to "abdicate, or transfer to others, [its] essential legislative functions" by failing to "lay down the policies and establish standards" for the executive branch to enforce. Pointedly, Hughes underlines the crux of the issue at hand that "Congress cannot delegate legislative power to the President to exercise an unfettered discretion to make whatever laws he thinks may be needed or advisable for the rehabilitation and expansion of trade and industry."

This, argues Hughes, extends to federal preview for regulation of labor in terms of wages or hours to be worked for businesses or industries concerned entirely with intrastate commerce. "No justification for such regulation is to be found in the fact that wages and hours affect costs and prices, and so indirectly affect interstate commerce, nor in the fact that failure of some States to regulate wages and hours diverts commerce from the States that do regulate them."

Here Hughes argues that all matters of commerce "where goods come to rest within a State temporarily and are later to go forward in intrastate commerce" have only an indirect subjection to federal regulation. Where the line between federal and state law lies as preeminent "can only be drawn as individual cases arise," but the NIRA, he states, is clearly overreaching. According to Hughes's opinion, if language such as that included in the NIRA were to be accepted, then "the federal authority would embrace practically all the activities of the people, and the authority of the State over its domestic concerns would exist only by sufferance of the Federal Government." Clearly, this was not in keeping with the demonstrated heritage of American law and structure of governance.

Finally, Hughes's reading of the Fifth Amendment invalidates the penalties included in the NIRA. Under the takings clause, the seizure of private property for public use without due process of the law (i.e., nationalizing a utility) requires just compensation. The due process clause of the Fifth Amendment was under-

stood to consist of two separate processes, procedural and substantive. As written, the NIRA ignored both as it failed to observe a fair procedure under the law before depriving an individual of life, liberty, or property and failed to observe fundamental rights of the individual from federal interference. This observance of substantive due process extends to prohibiting vague laws, a sentiment echoed and reinforced in the Fourteenth Amendment's equal protection clause.

Thus, according to Hughes, the NIRA upon which the charges against Schechter Poultry Corporation are based is an unconstitutional law. Hughes closes with a concise indictment of the government case—"The provisions of the code which are alleged to have been violated in this case are not a valid exercise of federal power"—and reverses all charges against Schechter Poultry Company.

Impact

Though the NIRA was set to expire in June 1935, the May 1935 opinion was the beginning of the end for the Roosevelt administration's centralization of business efforts. The case marked the beginning of several controversial concepts within the administration—such as the so-called court-packing scheme that would have expanded the Supreme Court through the addition of justices who were ideologically aligned with Roosevelt—and the end of the "First New Deal." After so much public pushback from citizens and businesses, the "Second New Deal" programs were presented with language that focused on building governmental "safety nets" for all citizens and reduced punitive efforts while solidifying the rights of labor. While not strictly identified within *A.L.A. Schechter Poultry Corporation v. United States*, many of the rights and protections afforded under Title I of the NIRA were seen as precarious. This led to the passage of the National Labor Relations Act of 1935 to secure the rights of unionization and arbitration. Additionally, in the observance of false statements in the Schechter case, Congress amended the False Claims Act of 1863 to include not only fraudulent acts levied against the federal government but fraudulent acts "in any matter within the jurisdiction of any department or agency of the United States or of any corporation in which the United States of America is a stockholder."

Questions for Further Study

1. If you were a justice writing an opinion in the Hughes Court, would you have considered the Schechter defense of their actions as a practice of religious freedoms for observant Jews in your opinion? Why or why not?

2. What were some possible motivations for the butcher's association to present their practices for consideration to President Roosevelt? Was one of these motivations more influential in the decision, or were they balanced? Why do you think so?

3. Given what you now know of Chief Justice Hughes, how would he have reacted to the news that FDR wanted to pack the Court? How would you have responded in such a situation?

4. Why do you think Congress was so eager to give its authority to the president? What does this suggest about what was happening in American society at the time?

5. The *Schechter* case argues that a very high threshold must be met before Congress should contemplate abdicating its legislative role to the president. What kind of a situation do you believe would meet this test?

Further Reading

Books

Bernstein, Irving. *The Turbulent Years: A History of the American Worker, 1933–1941*. Chicago: Haymarket Books, 1987.

Ross, William G. *The Chief Justiceship of Charles Evans Hughes, 1930–1941*. Columbia: University of South Carolina Press, 2007.

Schaffer, Butler D. *In Restraint of Trade: The Business Campaign against Competition, 1918–1938*. Lewisburg, PA: Bucknell University Press, 1997.

Skocpol, Theda. "Political Response to Capitalist Crisis: Neo-Marxist Theories of the State and the Case of the New Deal." In *Power: Critical Concepts*, edited by John Scott. Vol. 3. New York: Routledge, 1994.

Weinstien, Michael. *Recovery and Redistribution under the NIRA*. New York: North-Holland Publishing, 1980.

Websites

McBride, Alex. "Schechter v. U.S. (1935)." Supreme Court History: Capitalism and Conflict. December 2006. Accessed February 27, 2023, http://www.thirteen.org/wnet/supremecourt/capitalism/landmark_schechter.html.

"National Recovery Administration (NRA) and the New Deal: A Resource Guide." Library of Congress Research Guides. Accessed February 27, 2023, http://guides.loc.gov/national-recovery-administration.

NCC Staff. "How FDR Lost His Brief War on the Supreme Court." National Constitution Center. Accessed February 5, 2023, http://constitutioncenter.org/blog/how-fdr-lost-his-brief-war-on-the-supreme-court-2.

—Commentary by Bryant Macfarlane

A.L.A. SCHECHTER POULTRY CORPORATION V. UNITED STATES

Document Text

MR. CHIEF JUSTICE HUGHES delivered the opinion of the Court

Petitioners in No. 854 were convicted in the District Court of the United States for the Eastern District of New York on eighteen count of an indictment charging violations of what is known a the "Live Poultry Code," and on an additional count for conspiracy to commit such violations. By demurrer to the indictment and appropriate motions on the trial, the defendants contended (1) that the Code had been adopted pursuant to an unconstitutional delegation by Congress of legislative power; (2) that it attempted to regulate intrastate transactions which lay outside the authority of Congress, and (3) that, in certain provisions, it was repugnant to the due process clause of the Fifth Amendment.

The Circuit Court of Appeals sustained the conviction on the conspiracy count and on sixteen counts for violation of the Code, but reversed the conviction on two counts which charged violation of requirements as to minimum wages and maximum hours of labor, as these were not deemed to be within the congressional power of regulation. On the respective applications of the defendants (No. 854) and of the Government (No. 864), this Court granted writs of certiorari, April 15, 1935.

New York City is the largest live poultry market in the United States. Ninety-six percent. of the live poultry there marketed comes from other States. Three-fourths of this amount arrives by rail and is consigned to commission men or receivers. Most of these freight shipments (about 75 percent) come in at the Manhattan Terminal of the New York Central Railroad, and the remainder at one of the four terminals in New Jersey serving New York City. The commission men transact by far the greater part of the business on a commission basis, representing the shippers as agents and remitting to them the proceeds of sale, less commissions, freight and handling charges. Otherwise, they buy for their own account. They sell to slaughterhouse operators, who are also called marketmen.

The defendants are slaughterhouse operators of the latter class. A.L.A. Schechter Poultry Corporation and Schechter Live Poultry Market are corporations conducting wholesale poultry slaughterhouse markets in Brooklyn, New York City. Joseph Schechter operated the latter corporation and also guaranteed the credits of the former corporation which was operated by Martin, Alex and Aaron Schechter. Defendants ordinarily purchase their live poultry from commission men at the West Washington Market in New York City or at the railroad terminals serving the City, but occasionally they purchase from commission men in Philadelphia. They buy the poultry for slaughter and resale. After the poultry is trucked to their slaughterhouse markets in Brooklyn, it is there sold, usually within twenty-four hours, to retail poultry dealers and butchers who sell directly to consumers. The poultry purchased from defendants is immediately slaughtered, prior to delivery, by *schochtim* in defendants' employ. Defendants do not sell poultry in interstate commerce.

The "Live Poultry Code" was promulgated under § 3 of the National Industrial Recovery Act. That section—the pertinent provisions of which are set forth in the margin—authorizes the President to approve "codes of fair competition." Such a code may be approved for a trade or industry, upon application by one or more trade or industrial associations or groups, if the President finds (1) that such associations or groups "impose no inequitable restrictions on admission to membership therein and are truly representative," and (2) that such codes are not designed

"to promote monopolies or to eliminate or oppress small enterprises and will not operate to discriminate against them, and will tend to effectuate the policy"

of Title I of the Act. Such codes "shall not permit monopolies or monopolistic practices." As a condition of his approval, the President may

"impose such conditions (including requirements for the making of reports and the keeping of accounts) for the protection of consumers, competitors, employees, and others, and in furtherance of the public interest, and may provide such exceptions to and exemptions from the provisions of such code, as the President in his discretion deems necessary to effectuate the policy herein declared."

Where such a code has not been approved, the President may prescribe one, either on his own motion or on complaint. Violation of any provision of a code (so approved or prescribed) "in any transaction in or affecting interstate or foreign commerce" is made a misdemeanor punishable by a fine of not more than $500 for each offense, and each day the violation continues is to be deemed a separate offense.

The "Live Poultry Code" was approved by the President on April 13, 1934. Its divisions indicate its nature and scope. The Code has eight articles entitled (1) purposes, (2) definitions, (3) hours, (4) wages, (5) general labor provisions, (6) administration, (7) trade practice provisions, and (8) general.

The declared purpose is "To effect the policies of title I of the National Industrial Recovery Act." The Code is established as "a code of fair competition for the live poultry industry of the metropolitan area in and about the City of New York." That area is described as embracing the five boroughs of New York City, the counties of Rockland, Westchester, Nassau and Suffolk in the State of New York, the counties of Hudson and Bergen in the State of New Jersey, and the county of Fairfield in the State of Connecticut.

The "industry" is defined as including

"every person engaged in the business of selling, purchasing for resale, transporting, or handling and/or slaughtering live poultry, from the time such poultry comes into the New York metropolitan area to the time it is first sold in slaughtered form,"

and such "related branches "as may from time to time be included by amendment. Employers are styled "members of the industry," and the term employee is defined to embrace "any and all persons engaged in the industry, however compensated," except "members."

The Code fixes the number of hours for workdays. It provides that no employee, with certain exceptions, shall be permitted to work in excess of forty (40) hours in any one week, and that no employee, save as stated, "shall be paid in any pay period less than at the rate of fifty (50) cents per hour." The article containing "general labor provisions" prohibits the employment of any person under sixteen years of age, and declares that employees shall have the right of "collective bargaining," and freedom of choice with respect to labor organizations, in the terms of § 7(a) of the Act. The minimum number of employees who shall be employed by slaughterhouse operators is fixed, the number being graduated according to the average volume of weekly sales.

Provision is made for administration through an "industry advisory committee," to be selected by trade associations and members of the industry, and a "code supervisor," to be appointed, with the approval of the committee, by agreement between the Secretary of Agriculture and the Administrator for Industrial Recovery. The expenses of administration are to be borne by the members of the industry proportionately upon the basis of volume of business, or such other factors as the advisory committee may deem equitable, "subject to the disapproval of the Secretary and/or Administrator."

The seventh article, containing "trade practice provisions," prohibits various practices which are said to constitute "unfair methods of competition." The final article provides for verified reports, such as the Secretary or Administrator may require,

"(1) for the protection of consumers, competitors, employees, and others, and in furtherance of the public interest, and (2) for the determination by the Secretary or Administrator of the extent to which the declared policy of the act is being effectuated by this code."

The members of the industry are also required to keep books and records which "will clearly reflect all financial transactions of their respective business and the financial condition thereof," and to submit weekly reports showing the range of daily prices and volume of sales for each kind of produce.

The President approved the Code by an executive order in which he found that the application for his approval had been duly made in accordance with the provisions of Title I of the National Industrial Recovery Act, that there had been due notice and hearings, that the Code constituted "a code of fair competition" as contemplated by the Act, and complied with its pertinent provisions, including clauses (1) and (2) of subsection (a) of § 3 of Title I, and that the Code would tend "to effectuate the policy of Congress as declared in section 1 of Title I."

The executive order also recited that Secretary of Agriculture and the Administrator of the National Industrial Recovery Act had rendered separate reports as to the provisions within their respective jurisdictions. The Secretary of Agriculture reported that the provisions of the Code

"establishing standards of fair competition (a) are regulations of transactions in or affecting the current of interstate and/or foreign commerce and (b) are reasonable,"

and also that the Code would tend to effectuate the policy declared in Title I of the Act, as set forth in § 1. The report of the Administrator for Industrial Recovery dealt with wages, ours of labor and other labor provisions.

Of the eighteen counts of the indictment upon which the defendants were indicted, aside from the count for conspiracy, two counts charged violation of the minimum wage and maximum hour provisions of the Code, and ten counts were for violation of the requirement (found in the "trade practice provisions") of "straight killing." This requirement was really one of "straight" selling. The term "straight killing" was defined in the Code as

"the practice of requiring persons purchasing poultry for resale to accept the run of any half coop, coop, or coops, as purchased by slaughterhouse operators, except for culls."

The charges in the ten counts, respectively, were that the defendants, in selling to retail dealers and butchers, had permitted "selections of individual chickens taken from particular coops and half-coops."

Of the other six counts, one charged the sale to a butcher of an unfit chicken; two counts charged the making of sales without having the poultry inspected or approved in accordance with regulations or ordinances of the City of New York; two counts charged the making of false reports or the failure to make report relating to the range of daily prices and volume of sales for certain periods, and the remaining count was for sales to slaughterers or dealers who were without licenses required by the ordinances and regulations of the City of New York.

First. Two preliminary points are stressed by the Government with respect to the appropriate approach to the important questions presented. We are told that the provision of the statute authorizing the adoption of codes must be viewed in the light of the grave national crisis with which Congress was confronted. Undoubtedly, the conditions to which power is addressed are always to be considered when the exercise of power is challenged. Extraordinary conditions may call for extraordinary remedies. But the argument necessarily stops short of an attempt to justify action which lies outside the sphere of constitutional authority. Extraordinary conditions do not create or enlarge constitutional power. The Constitution established a national government with powers deemed to be adequate, as they have proved to be both in war and peace, but these powers of the national government are limited by the constitutional grants. Those who act under these grants are not at liberty to transcend the imposed limits because they believe that more or different power is necessary. Such assertions of extraconstitutional authority were anticipated and precluded by the explicit terms of the Tenth Amendment—

"The powers not delegated to the United States by the Constitution, nor prohibited by it to the States, are reserved to the States respectively, or to the people."

The further point is urged that the national crisis demanded a broad and intensive cooperative effort by those engaged in trade and industry, and that this necessary cooperation was sought to be fostered by permitting them to initiate the adoption of codes. But the statutory plan is not simply one for voluntary effort. It does not seek merely to endow voluntary trade or industrial associations or groups with privileges or immunities. It involves the coercive exercise of the lawmaking power. The codes of fair competition which the state attempts to authorize are codes of laws. If valid, they place all persons within their reach under the obligation of positive law, binding equally those who assent and those who do not assent. Violations of the provisions of the codes are punishable as crimes.

Second. The question of the delegation of legislative power. We recently had occasion to review the pertinent decisions and the general principles which govern the determination of this question. *Panama Refining Co. v. Ryan,* 293 U. S. 388. The Constitution provides that

"All legislative powers herein granted shall be vested in a Congress of the United States, which shall consist of a Senate and House of Representatives."

Art I, § 1. And the Congress is authorized "To make all laws which shall be necessary and proper for carrying into execution" its general powers. Art. I, 8, par. 18. The Congress is not permitted to abdicate or to transfer to others the essential legislative functions with which it is thus vested. We have repeatedly recognized the necessity of adapting legislation to complex conditions involving a host of details with which the national legislature cannot deal directly. We pointed out in the *Panama Company* case that the Constitution has never been regarded as denying to Congress the necessary resources of flexibility and practicality which will enable it to perform its function in laying down policies and establishing standards while leaving to selected instrumentalities the making of subordinate rules within prescribed limits, and the determination of facts to which the policy, as declared by the legislature, is to apply. But we said that the constant recognition of the necessity and validity of such provisions, and the wide range of administrative authority which has been developed by means of them, cannot be allowed to obscure the limitations of the authority to delegate, if our constitutional system is to be maintained. *Id.,* p. 298 U. S. 421.

Accordingly, we look to the statute to see whether Congress has overstepped these limitations—whether Congress, in authorizing "codes of fair competition," has itself established the standards of legal obligation,

thus performing its essential legislative function, or, by the failure to enact such standards, has attempted to transfer that function to others.

The aspect in which the question is now presented is distinct from that which was before us in the case of the *Panama Company.* There, the subject of the statutory prohibition was defined. National Industrial Recovery Act, § 9(c). That subject was the transportation in interstate and foreign commerce of petroleum and petroleum products which are produced or withdrawn from storage in excess of the amount permitted by State authority. The question was with respect to the range of discretion given to the President in prohibiting that transportation. *Id.* pp. 293 U. S. 414, 293 U. S. 415, 293 U. S. 430. As to the "codes of fair competition," under § 3 of the Act, the question is more fundamental. It is whether there is any adequate definition of the subject to which the codes are to be addressed.

What is meant by "fair competition" as the term is used in the Act? Does it refer to a category established in the law, and is the authority to make codes limited accordingly? Or is it used as a convenient designation for whatever set of laws the formulators of a code for a particular trade or industry may propose and the President may approve (subject to certain restrictions), or the President may himself prescribe, as being wise and beneficent provisions for the government of the trade or industry in order to accomplish the broad purposes of rehabilitation, correction and expansion which are stated in the first section of Title I?

The Act does not define "fair competition." "Unfair competition," as known to the common law, is a limited concept. Primarily, and strictly, it relates to the palming off of one's goods as those of a rival trader. *Goodyear Manufacturing Co. v. Goodyear Rubber Co.,* 128 U. S. 598, 128 U. S. 604; *Howe Scale Co. v. Wyckoff, Seaman & Benedict,* 198 U. S. 118, 198 U. S. 140; *Hanover Milling Co. v. Metcalf,* 240 U. S. 403, 240 U. S. 413. In recent years, its scope has been extended. It has been held to apply to misappropriation as well as misrepresentation, to the selling of another's goods as one's own—to misappropriation of what equitably belongs to a competitor. *International News Service v. Associated Press,* 248 U. S. 215, 248 U. S. 241, 248 U. S. 242. Unfairness in competition has been predicated of acts which lie outside the ordinary course of business and are tainted by fraud, or coercion, or conduct otherwise prohibited by law. *Id.,* p. 248 U. S. 258. But it is evident that, in its widest range, "unfair competition," as it has been understood in the law, does not reach the objectives of the codes which are authorized by the National Industrial Recovery Act. The codes may, indeed, cover conduct which existing law condemns, but they are not limited to conduct of that sort. The Government does not contend that the Act contemplates such a limitation. It would be opposed both to the declared purposes of the Act and to its administrative construction.

The Federal Trade Commission Act (§ 5) introduced the expression "unfair methods of competition," which were declared to be unlawful. That was an expression new in the law. Debate apparently convinced the sponsors of the legislation that the words "unfair competition," in the light of their meaning at common law, were too narrow. We have sad that the substituted phrase has a broader meaning, that it does not admit of precise definition, its scope being left to judicial determination as controversies arise. *Federal Trade Comm'n v. Raladam Co.,* 283 U. S. 643, 283 U. S. 648, 283 U. S. 649; *Federal Trade Comm'n v. Keppel & Bro.,* 291 U. S. 304, 291 U. S. 310-312. What are "unfair methods of competition" are thus to be determined in particular instances, upon evidence, in the light of particular competitive conditions and of what is found to be a specific and substantial public interest. *Federal Trade Comm'n v. Beech-Nut Packing Co.,* 257 U. S. 441, 257 U. S. 453; *Federal Trade Comm'n v. Klesner,* 280 U. S. 19, 280 U. S. 27, 280 U. S. 28; *Federal Trade Comm'n v. Raladam Co., supra; Federal Trade Comm'n v. Keppel & Bro., supra; Federal Trade Comm'n v. Algoma Lumber Co.,* 291 U. S. 67, 291 U. S. 73. To make this possible, Congress set up a special procedure. A Commission, a *quasi*-judicial body, was created. Provision was made formal complaint, for notice and hearing, for appropriate findings of fact supported by adequate evidence, and for judicial review to give assurance that the action of the Commission is taken within its statutory authority. *Federal Trade Comm'n v. Raladam Co., supra; Federal Trade Comm'n v. Klesner, supra.*

In providing for codes, the National Industrial Recovery Act dispenses with this administrative procedure and with any administrative procedure of an analogous character. But the difference been the code plan of the Recovery Act and the scheme of the Federal Trade Commission Act lies not only in procedure, but in subject matter. We cannot regard the "fair competition" of the codes as antithetical to the "unfair methods of competition" of the Federal Trade Commission Act. The "fair competition" of the codes has a much broader range, and a new significance. The Recovery Act provides that it shall not be construed to impair the powers of the Federal Trade Commission, but, when a code is approved, its provisions are to be the "standards of fair competition" for the trade or industry concerned, and any violation of such standards in any transaction in or affecting interstate or foreign commerce is to be deemed "an unfair method of competition" within the meaning of the Federal Trade Commission Act. § 3(b).

For a statement of the authorized objectives and content of the "codes of fair competition," we are referred repeatedly to the "Declaration of Policy" in section one of Title I of the Recovery Act. Thus, the approval of a code by the President is conditioned on his finding that it "will tend to effectuate the policy of this title." § 3(a). The President is authorized to impose such conditions

"for the protection of consumers, competitors, employees, and others, and in furtherance of the public interest, and may provide such exceptions to and exemptions from the provisions of such code as the President in his discretion deems necessary to effectuate the policy herein declared."

Id. The "policy herein declared" is manifestly that set forth in section one. That declaration embraces a broad range of objectives. Among them we find the elimination of "unfair competitive practices." But even if this clause were to be taken to relate to practices which fall under the ban of existing law, either common law or statute, it is still only one of the authorized aims described in section one. It is there declared to be "the policy of Congress"—"to remove obstructions to the free flow of interstate and foreign commerce which tend to diminish the amount thereof, and to provide for the general welfare by promoting the organization of industry for the purpose of cooperative action among trade groups, to induce and maintain united action of labor and management under adequate governmental sanctions and supervision, to eliminate unfair competitive practices, to promote the fullest possible utilization of the present productive capacity of industries, to avoid undue restriction of production (except as may be temporarily required), to increase the consumption of industrial and agricultural products by increasing purchasing power, to reduce and relieve unemployment, to improve standards of labor, and otherwise to rehabilitate industry and to conserve natural resources. "

Under § 3, whatever "may tend to effectuate" these general purposes may be included in the "codes of fair competition." We think the conclusion is inescapable that the authority sought to be conferred by § 3 was not merely to deal with "unfair competitive practices "which offend against existing law, and could be the subject of judicial condemnation without further legislation, or to create administrative machinery for the application of established principles of law to particular instances of violation. Rather, the purpose is clearly disclosed to authorize new and controlling prohibitions through codes of laws which would embrace what the formulators would propose, and what the President would approve, or prescribe, as wise and beneficient measures for the government of trades and industries in order to bring about their rehabilitation, correction and development, according to the general declaration of policy in section one. Codes of laws of this sort are styled "codes of fair competition."

We find no real controversy upon this point, and we must determine the validity of the Code in question in this aspect. As the Government candidly says in its brief:

"The words 'policy of this title' clearly refer to the 'policy' which Congress declared in the section entitled 'Declaration of Policy'—§ 1. All of the policies there set forth point toward a single goal—the rehabilitation of industry and the industrial recovery which unquestionably was the major policy of Congress in adopting the National Industrial Recovery Act."

And that this is the controlling purpose of the Code now before us appears both from its repeated declarations to that effect and from the scope of its requirements. It will be observed that its provisions as to the hours and wages of employees and its "general labor provisions" were placed in separate articles, and these were not included in the article on "trade practice provisions" declaring what should be deemed to constitute "unfair methods of competition." The Secretary of Agriculture thus stated the objectives of the Live Poultry Code in his report to the President, which was recited in the executive order of approval:

"That said code will tend to effectuate the declared policy of title I of the National Industrial Recovery Act as set forth in section 1 of said act in that the terms and provisions of such code tend to: (a) remove obstructions to the free flow of interstate and foreign commerce which tend to diminish the amount thereof; (b) to provide for the general welfare by promoting the organization of industry for the purpose of cooperative action among trade groups; (c) to eliminate unfair competitive practices; (d) to promote the fullest possible utilization of the present productive capacity of industries; (e) to avoid undue restriction of production (except a may be temporarily required); (f) to increase the consumption of industrial and agricultural products by increasing purchasing power, and (g) otherwise to rehabilitate industry, and to conserve natural resources. "

The Government urges that the codes will

"consist of rules of competition deemed fair for each industry by representative members of that industry— by the persons most vitally concerned and most familiar with its problems."

Instances are cited in which Congress has availed itself of such assistance; as, *e.g.,* in the exercise of its authority over the public domain with respect to the recognition of local customs or rules of miners as to mining claims, or, in matters of a more or less technical nature, as in designating the standard height of drawbar. But would it be seriously contended that Congress could delegate its legislative authority to trade or industrial associations or groups so as to empower them to enact the laws they deem to be wise and beneficent for the rehabilitation and expansion of their trade or industries? Could trade or industrial associations or groups be constituted legislative bodies for that purpose because such associations or groups are familiar with the problems of their enterprises? And, could an effort of that sort be made valid by such a preface of generalities as to permissible aims as we find in section 1 of title I? The answer is obvious. Such a delegation of legislative power is unknown to our law, and is utterly consistent with the constitutional prerogatives and duties of Congress.

The question, then, turns upon the authority which § 3 of the Recovery Act vests in the President to approve or prescribe. If the codes have standing as penal statutes, this must be due to the effect of the executive action. But Congress cannot delegate legislative power to the President to exercise an unfettered discretion to make whatever laws he thinks may be needed or advisable for the rehabilitation and expansion of trade or industry. *See Panama Refining Co. v. Ryan, supra,* and cases there reviewed.

Accordingly, we turn to the Recovery Act to ascertain what limits have been set to the exercise of the President's discretion. *First,* the President, as a condition of approval, is required to find that the trade or industrial associations or groups which propose a code, "impose no inequitable restrictions on admission to membership," and are "truly representative." That condition, however, relates only to the status of the initiators of the new laws, and not to the permissible scope of such laws. *Second,* the President is required to find that the code is not "designed to promote monopolies or to eliminate or oppress small enterprises, and will not operate to discriminate against them." And to this is added a proviso that the code "shall not permit monopolies or monopolistic practices." But these restrictions leave virtually untouched the field of policy envisaged by section one, and, in that wide field of legislative possibilities, the proponents of a code, refraining from monopolistic designs, may roam at will, and the President may approve or disapprove their proposals as he may see fit. That is the precise effect of the further finding that the President is to make—that the code "will tend to effectuate the policy of this title." While this is called a finding, it is really but a statement of an opinion as to the general effect upon the promotion of trade or industry of a scheme of laws. These are the only findings which Congress has made essential in order to put into operation a legislative code having the aims described in the "Declaration of Policy."

Nor is the breadth of the President's discretion left to the necessary implication of this limited requirement as to his findings. As already noted, the President, in approving a code, may impose his own conditions, adding to or taking from what is proposed as, "in his discretion," he thinks necessary "to effectuate the policy" declared by the Act. Of course, he has no less liberty when he prescribes a code on his own motion or on complaint, and he is free to prescribe one if a code has not been approved. The Act provides for the creation by the President of administrative agencies to assist him, but the action or reports of such agencies, or of his other assistants—their recommendations and findings in relation to the making of codes—have no sanction beyond the will of the President, who may accept, modify, or reject them as he pleases. Such recommendations or findings in no way limit the authority which § 3 undertakes to vest in the President with no other conditions than those there specified. And this authority relates to a host of different trades and industries, thus extending the President's discretion to all the varieties of laws which he may deem to be beneficial in dealing with the vast array of commercial and industrial activities throughout the country.

Such a sweeping delegation of legislative power finds no support in the decisions upon which the Government especially relies. By the Interstate Commerce Act, Congress has itself provided a code of laws regulating the activities of the common carriers subject to the Act in order to assure the performance of their services upon just and reasonable terms, with adequate facilities and without unjust discrimination. Congress, from time to time, has elaborated its requirements as needs have been disclosed. To facilitate the application of the standards prescribed by the Act, Congress has provided an expert body. That administrative agency, in dealing with particular cases, is required to act upon notice and hearing, and its orders must be supported by findings of fact which, in turn, are sustained by evidence. *Interstate Commerce Comm'n v. Louisville & Nashville R. Co.,* 227 U. S. 88; *Florida v. United States,* 282 U. S. 194; *United States v. Baltimore & Ohio R. Co.,* 293 U. S. 454. When the Commission is authorized to issue, for the construction, extension or abandonment of lines, a certificate of "public convenience and necessity," or to permit the acquisition by one carrier of the control of another, if that is found to be "in the public interest," we have pointed out that these provisions are not left without standards to guide determination. The authority conferred has direct relation to the standards prescribed for the service of common carriers, and can be exercised only upon findings, based upon evidence, with respect to particular conditions of transportation. *New York Central Securities Co. v. United States,* 287 U. S. 12, 287 U. S. 24, 298 U. S. 25; *Texas & Pacific Railway Co. v. Gulf, Colorado & Santa Fe Ry. Co.,* 270 U. S. 266, 270 U. S. 273; *Chesapeake & Ohio Ry. Co. v. United States,* 283 U. S. 35, 283 U. S. 42.

Similarly, we have held that the Radio Act of 1927 established standards to govern radio communications, and, in view of the limited number of available broadcasting frequencies, Congress authorized allocation and licenses. The Federal Radio Commission was created as the licensing authority in order to secure a reasonable equality of opportunity in radio transmission and reception. The authority of the Commission to grant licenses "as public convenience, interest or necessity requires" was limited by the nature of radio communications and by the scope, character, and quality of the services to be rendered and the relative advantages to be derived through distribution of facilities. These standards established by Congress were to be enforced upon hearing, and evidence, by an administrative body acting under statutory restrictions adapted to the particular activity. *Federal Radio Comm'n v. Nelson Brothers Co.* In *Hampton & Co. v. United States,* 276 U. S. 394, the question related to the "flexible tariff provision" of the Tariff Act of 1922. We held that Congress had described its plan

"to secure by law the imposition of customs duties on articles of imported merchandise which should equal the difference between the cost of producing in a foreign country the articles in question and laying them down for sale in the United States, and the cost of producing and selling like or similar articles in the United States."

As the differences cost might vary from time to time, provision was for the investigation and determination of these differences by the executive branch, so as to make "the adjustments necessary to conform the duties to the standard underlying that policy and plan." *Id.* pp. 276 U. S. 404, 276 U. S. 405. The Court found the same principle to be applicable in fixing customs duties as that which permitted Congress to exercise its ratemaking power in interstate commerce, "by declaring the rule which shall prevail in the legislative fixing of rates" and then remitting "the fixing of such rates" in accordance with its provisions "to a ratemaking body." *Id.,* p. 276 U. S. 409. The Court fully recognized the limitations upon the delegation of legislative power. *Id.* pp. 276 U. S. 408-411.

To summarize and conclude upon this point: Section 3 of the Recovery Act is without precedent. It supplies no standards for any trade, industry or activity. It does not undertake to prescribe rules of conduct to be applied to particular states of fact determined by appropriate administrative procedure. Instead of prescribing rules of conduct, it authorizes the making of codes to prescribe them. For that legislative undertaking, § 3

sets up no standards, aside from the statement of the general aims of rehabilitation, correction and expansion described in section one. In view of the scope of that broad declaration, and of the nature of the few restrictions that are imposed, the discretion of the President in approving or prescribing codes, and thus enacting laws for the government of trade and industry throughout the country, is virtually unfettered. We think that the code-making authority this conferred is an unconstitutional delegation of legislative power.

Third. The question of the application of the provisions of the Live Poultry Code to intrastate transactions. Although the validity of the codes (apart from the question of delegation) rests upon the commerce clause of the Constitution, § 3(a) is not, in terms, limited to interstate and foreign commerce. From the generality of its terms, and from the argument of the Government at the bar, it would appear that § 3(a) was designed to authorize codes without that limitation. But, under § 3(f), penalties are confined to violations of a code provision "in any transaction in or affecting interstate or foreign commerce." This aspect of the case presents the question whether the particular provisions of the Live Poultry Code, which the defendants were convicted for violating and for having conspired to violate, were within the regulating power of Congress.

These provisions relate to the hours and wages of those employed by defendants in their slaughterhouses in Brooklyn, and to the sales there made to retail dealers and butchers.

(1) Were these transactions "*in*" interstate commerce? Much is made of the fact that almost all the poultry coming to New York is sent there from other States. But the code provisions, as here applied, do not concern the transportation of the poultry from other States to New York, or the transactions of the commission men or others to whom it is consigned, or the sales made by such consignees to defendants. When defendants had made their purchases, whether at the West Washington Market in New York City or at the railroad terminals serving the City, or elsewhere, the poultry was trucked to their slaugterhouses in Brooklyn for local disposition. The interstate transactions in relation to that poultry then ended. Defendants held the poultry at their slaughterhouse markets for slaughter and local sale to retail dealers and butchers who, in turn, sold directly to consumers. Neither the

slaughtering nor the sales by defendants were transactions in interstate commerce. *Brown v. Houston,* 114 U. S. 622, 114 U. S. 632, 114 U. S. 633; *Public Utilities Comm'n v. Landon,* 249 U. S. 236, 249 U. S. 245; *Industrial Association v. States,* 268 U. S. 64, 268 U. S. 78, 268 U. S. 79; *Atlantic Coast Line v. Standard Oil Co.,* 275 U. S. 257, 275 U. S. 267.

The undisputed facts thus afford no warrant for the argument that the poultry handled by defendants at their slaughterhouse markets was in a *"current"* or *"flow"* of interstate commerce, and was thus subject to congressional regulation. The mere fact that there may be a constant flow of commodities into a State does not mean that the flow continues after the property has arrived, and has become commingled with the mass of property within the State, and is there held solely for local disposition and use. So far as the poultry here in question is concerned, the flow in interstate commerce had ceased. The poultry had come to a permanent rest within the State. It was not held, used, or sold by defendants in relation to any further transactions in interstate commerce, and was not destined for transportation to other States. Hence, decisions which deal with a stream of interstate commerce—where goods come to rest within a State temporarily and are later to go forward in interstate commerce—and with the regulations of transactions involved in that practical continuity of movement, are not applicable here. *See Swift & Co. v. United States,* 196 U. S. 375, 387, 388 [argument of counsel omitted in electronic version]; *Lemke v. Farmers Grain Co.,* 258 U. S. 50, 258 U. S. 55; *Stafford v. Wallace,* 258 U. S. 495, 258 U. S. 519; *Chicago Board of Trade v. Olsen,* 262 U.S. l, 262 U. S. 35; *Tagg Bros. & Moorhead v. United States,* 280 U. S. 420, 280 U. S. 439.

(2) Did the defendants' transactions directly *"affect"* interstate commerce, so as to be subject to federal regulation? The power of Congress extends not only to the regulation of transactions which are part of interstate commerce, but to the protection of that commerce from injury. It matters not that the injury may be due to the conduct of those engaged in intrastate operations. Thus, Congress may protect the safety of those employed in interstate transportation "no matter what may be the source of the dangers which threaten it." *Southern Ry. Co. v. United States,* 222 U. S. 20, 222 U. S. 27. We said in *Second Employers' Liability Cases,* 223 U. S. 1, 223 U. S. 51, that it is the "effect upon interstate commerce," not "the source of the injury," which is "the

criterion of congressional power." We have held that, in dealing with common carriers engaged in both interstate and intrastate commerce, the dominant authority of Congress necessarily embraces the right to control their intrastate operations in all matters having such a close and substantial relation to interstate traffic that the control is essential or appropriate to secure the freedom of that traffic from interference or unjust discrimination and to promote the efficiency of the interstate service. *The Shreveport Case,* 234 U. S. 342, 234 U. S. 351, 234 U. S. 352; *Wisconsin Railroad Comm'n v. Chicago, B. & Q. R. Co.,* 257 U. S. 563, 257 U. S. 588. And combinations and conspiracies to restrain interstate commerce, or to monopolize any part of it, are nonetheless within the reach of the Anti-Trust Act because the conspirators seek to attain their end by means of intrastate activities. *Coronado Coal Co. v. United Mine Workers,* 268 U. S. 295, 268 U. S. 310; *Bedford Cut Stone Co. v. Stone Cutters Assn.,* 274 U. S. 37, 274 U.S. 46.

We recently had occasion, in *Local 677 v. United States,* 291 U. S. 293, to apply this principle in connection with the live poultry industry. That was a suit to enjoin a conspiracy to restrain and monopolize interstate commerce in violation of the Anti-Trust Act. It was shown that marketmen, teamsters and slaughterers (*shochtim*) had conspired to burden the free movement of live poultry into the metropolitan area in and about New York City. Marketmen had organized an association, had allocated retailers among themselves, and had agreed to increase prices. To accomplish their objects, large amounts of money were raised by levies upon poultry sold, men were hired to obstruct the business dealers who resisted, wholesalers and retailers were spied upon, and, by violence and other forms of intimidation, were prevented from freely purchasing live poultry. Teamsters refused to handle poultry for recalcitrant marketmen, and members of the *shochtim* union refused to slaughter. In view of the proof of that conspiracy, we said that it was unnecessary to decide when interstate commerce ended and when intrastate commerce began. We found that the proved interference by the conspirators "with the unloading, the transportation, the sales by marketmen to retailers, the prices charged, and the amount of profits exacted" operated "substantially and directly to restrain and burden the untrammeled shipment and movement of the poultry" while unquestionably it was in interstate commerce. The intrastate acts of the conspirators were included in the injunction because that was found to be necessary for the protection of interstate commerce against the attempted and illegal restraint. *Id.* pp. 291 U. S. 297, 291 U. S. 299, 291 U. S. 300.

The instant case is not of that sort. This is not a prosecution for a conspiracy to restrain or monopolize interstate commerce in violation of the Anti-Trust Act. Defendants have been convicted not upon direct charges of injury to interstate commerce or of interference with persons engaged in that commerce, but of violations of certain provisions of the Live Poultry Code and of conspiracy to commit these violations. Interstate commerce is brought in only upon the charge that violations of these provisions—as to hours and wages of employees and local sales - "*affected*" interstate commerce.

In determining how far the federal government may go in controlling intrastate transactions upon the ground that they "affect" interstate commerce, there is a necessary and well established distinction between direct and indirect effects. The precise line can be drawn only as individual cases arise, but the distinction is clear in principle. Direct effects are illustrated by the railroad cases we have cited, as, *e.g.,* the effect of failure to use prescribed safety appliances on railroads which are the highways of both interstate and intrastate commerce, injury to an employee engaged in interstate transportation by the negligence of an employee engaged in an intrastate movement, the fixing of rates for intrastate transportation which unjustly discriminate against interstate commerce. But where the effect of intrastate transactions upon interstate commerce is merely indirect, such transactions remain within the domain of state power. If the commerce clause were construed to reach all enterprise and transactions which could be said to have an indirect effect upon interstate commerce, the federal authority would embrace practically all the activities of the people, and the authority of the State over its domestic concerns would exist only by sufferance of the federal government. Indeed, on such a theory, even the development of the State's commercial facilities would be subject to federal control. As we said in the *Minnesota Rate Cases,* 230 U. S. 352, 230 U. S. 410:

"In the intimacy of commercial relations, much that is done in the superintendence of local matters may have an indirect bearing upon interstate commerce. The development of local resources and the extension of local facilities may have a very important effect upon communities less favored, and, to an appreciable degree, alter the course of trade. The freedom of local trade may stimulate interstate commerce, while restrictive measures within the police power of the State enacted exclusively with respect to internal business, as distinguished from interstate traffic, may, in their reflex or indirect influence, diminish the latter and reduce the volume of articles transported into or out of the State."

See also Kidd v. Pearson, 128 U. S. 1, 128 U. S. 21; *Heisler v. Thomas Collier Co.,* 260 U. S. 245, 260 U. S. 259, 260 U. S. 260.

The distinction between direct and indirect effects has been clearly recognized in the application of the Anti-Trust Act. Where a combination or conspiracy is formed, with the intent to restrain interstate commerce or to monopolize any part of it, the violation of the statute is clear. *Coronado Coal Co. v. United Mine Workers,* 268 U. S. 295, 268 U. S. 310. But where that intent is absent, and the objectives are limited to intrastate activities, the fact that there may be an indirect effect upon interstate commerce does not subject the parties to the federal statute, notwithstanding its broad provisions. This principle has frequently been applied in litigation growing out of labor disputes. *United Mine Workers v. Coronado Coal Co.,* 259 U. S. 344, 259 U. S. 410, 259 U. S. 411; *United Leather Workers v. Herkert & Meisel Trunk Co.,* 265 U. S. 457, 265 U. S. 464-467; *Industrial Association v. United States,* 268 U. S. 64, 268 U. S. 82; *Levering & Garrigues Co. v. Morrin,* 289 U. S. 103, 289 U. S. 107, 289 U. S. 108. In the case last cited, we quoted with approval the rule that had been stated and applied in *Industrial Association v. United States, supra,* after review of the decisions, as follows:

"The alleged conspiracy and the acts here complained of spent their intended and direct force upon a local situation—for building is as essentially local as mining, manufacturing or growing crops—and if, by a resulting diminution of the commercial demand, interstate trade was curtailed either generally or in specific instances, that was a fortuitous consequence so remote and indirect as plainly to cause it to fall outside the reach of the Sherman Act."

While these decisions related to the application of the federal statute, and not to its constitutional validity, the distinction between direct and indirect effects of intrastate transactions upon interstate commerce must be recognized as a fundamental one, essential to the maintenance of our constitutional system. Otherwise, as we have said, there would be virtually no limit to the federal power, and, for all practical purposes, we should have a completely centralized government. We must consider the provisions here in question in the light of this distinction.

The question of chief importance relates to the provisions of the Code as to the hours and wages of those employed in defendants' slaughterhouse markets. It is plain that these requirements are imposed in order to govern the details of defendants' management of their local business. The persons employed in slaughtering and selling in local trade are not employed in interstate commerce. Their hours and wages have no direct relation to interstate commerce. The question of how many hours these employees should work and what they should be paid differs in no essential respect from similar questions in other local businesses which handle commodities brought into a State and there dealt in as a part of its internal commerce. This appears from an examination of the considerations urged by the Government with respect to conditions in the poultry trade. Thus, the Government argues that hours and wages affect prices; that slaughterhouse men sell at a small margin above operating costs; that labor represents 50 to 60 percent of these costs; that a slaughterhouse operator paying lower wages or reducing his cost by exacting long hours of work translates his saving into lower prices; that this results in demands for a cheaper grade of goods, and that the cutting of prices brings about a demoralization of the price structure. Similar conditions may be adduced in relation to other businesses. The argument of the Government proves too much. If the federal government may determine the wages and hours of employees in the internal commerce of a State, because of their relation to cost and prices and their indirect effect upon interstate commerce, it would seem that a similar control might be exerted over other elements of cost also affecting prices, such as the number of employees, rents, advertising, methods of doing business, etc. All the processes of production and distribution that enter into cost could likewise be controlled. If the cost of doing an intrastate business is, in itself, the permitted object of federal control, the extent of the regulation of cost would be a question of discretion, and not of power.

The Government also makes the point that efforts to enact state legislation establishing high labor standards have been impeded by the belief that, unless similar action is taken generally, commerce will be diverted from the States adopting such standards, and that this fear of diversion has led to demands for federal legislation on the subject of wages and hours. The apparent implication is that the federal authority under the commerce clause should be deemed to extend to the establishment of rules to govern wages and hours in intrastate trade and industry generally throughout the country, thus overriding the authority of the States to deal with domestic problems arising from labor conditions in their internal commerce.

It is not the province of the Court to consider the economic advantages or disadvantage of such a centralized system. It is sufficient to say that the Federal Constitution does not provide for it. Our growth and development have called for wide use of the commerce power of the federal government in its control over the expanded activities of interstate commerce, and in protecting that commerce from burdens, interferences, and conspiracies to restrain and monopolize it. But the authority of the federal government may not be pushed to such an extreme as to destroy the distinction, which the commerce clause itself establishes, between commerce "among the several States" and the internal concerns of a State. The same answer must be made to the contention that is based upon the serious economic situation which led to the passage of the Recovery Act—the fall in prices, the decline in wages and employment, and the curtailment of the market for commodities. Stress is laid upon the great importance of maintaining wage distributions which would provide the necessary stimulus in starting "the cumulative forces making for expanding commercial activity." Without in any way disparaging this motive, it is enough to say that the recuperative efforts of the federal government must be made in a manner consistent with the authority granted by the Constitution.

We are of the opinion that the attempt, through the provisions of the Code, to fix the hours and wages of employees of defendants in their intrastate business was not a valid exercise of federal power.

The other violations for which defendants were convicted related to the making of local sales. Ten counts, for violation of the provision as to "straight killing" were for permitting customers to make "selections of individual chickens taken from particular coops and half coops." Whether or not this practice is good or bad for the local trade, its effect, if any, upon interstate commerce was only indirect. The same may be said of violations of the Code by intrastate transactions consisting of the sale "of an unfit chicken" and of sales which were not in accord with the ordinances of the City of New York. The requirement of report as to prices and volumes of defendants' sales was incident to the effort to control their intrastate business.

In view of these conclusions, we find it unnecessary to discuss other questions which have been raised as to the validity of certain provisions of the Code under the due process clause of the Fifth Amendment.

On both the grounds we have discussed, the attempted delegation of legislative power, and the attempted regulation of intrastate transaction which affect interstate commerce only indirectly, we hold he code provisions here in question to be invalid and that the judgment of conviction must be reversed.

No. 864—reversed. No. 86—affirmed.

Glossary

commerce clause: a section of the Constitution (Article 1, Section 8, Clause 3) that grants Congress the power to regulate interstate business and trade

due process clause: a clause in the Fifth and Fourteenth Amendments that says that no person shall be "deprived of life, liberty, or property, without due process of law"

Live Poultry Code: a part of the New Deal's National Industrial Recovery Act that included regulations concerning animal selection, meat quality standards, worker protections, and fair competition

promulgated: enacted

takings clause: a clause in the Fifth Amendment that says that private property shall not "be taken for public use, without just compensation"

"unconstitutional delegation of legislative power": the granting of congressional powers to the president, in violation of the separation of powers delineated in the Constitution

UNITED STATES V. CURTISS-WRIGHT

DATE 1936	**CITATION** 299 U.S. 304
AUTHOR George Sutherland	**SIGNIFICANCE** Ruled that the president has significant powers over foreign affairs, a dramatic departure from the Court's previous foreign-affairs rulings, which had cast Congress and the president as partners in the formulation of the nation's foreign policy
VOTE 7–1	

Overview

 The U.S. Supreme Court's pathbreaking opinion in *United States v. Curtiss-Wright Export Corporation* in 1936 remains the most frequently cited case in the annals of the nation's foreign-affairs jurisprudence and is one of the principal pillars of presidential domination of American foreign policy. The issue in the case was whether Congress, in passing a joint resolution in May of 1934 to grant the president power to place an embargo on the export of munitions or arms under certain conditions, had delegated, or transferred, too much of its legislative authority to the president. The Court upheld the statute against the claim that it was an unconstitutional delegation of legislative power. But in his opinion for the Court, Justice George Sutherland soared beyond the narrow issue and unleashed an expansive interpretation of executive power.

Sutherland articulated a theory of broad and inherent executive power derived not from the Constitution but from other sources. Sutherland characterized the president as the "sole organ" of American foreign policy, a phrase that is frequently used in discussions and debates about the scope of presidential power. Presidents, Justice Department lawyers, and administration officials have so frequently invoked the sole organ doctrine to justify foreign-relations actions and policies that it has become known as the "Curtiss-Wright, so I'm right cite."

The *Curtiss-Wright* opinion represented a dramatic departure from the Court's previous foreign-affairs rulings, which had cast Congress and the president as partners in the formulation of the nation's foreign policy and, on numerous occasions, had viewed Congress as the senior partner. But *Curtiss-Wright* abandoned that prescription and championed executive unilateralism. Its influence may be glimpsed in presidential claims of authority to initiate war, order covert military activities, terminate and suspend treaties, negotiate executive agreements, establish military tribunals, order domestic surveillance and extraordinary rendition (the transfer of a person to a foreign nation outside the legal process and often by the use of force), and, generally, to formulate and manage American foreign relations.

Context

The immediate context of the *Curtiss-Wright* case involved a joint resolution that authorized the president, Franklin D. Roosevelt, to halt the sale of arms to Bolivia and Paraguay, then engaged in armed conflict in the Chaco region of Paraguay, if it would help restore peace between the countries. The resolution, an exercise in contingent delegation—a congressional grant of authority to the president that could be implemented upon presidential findings of fact, as required by the statute—reflected a worldwide effort, first undertaken by the League of Nations, to curb violence and war. It was relatively easy for Roosevelt to determine that invoking the statute would help to restore peace, because the Curtiss-Wright Export Corporation was the principal arms supplier for both nations.

The issue was viewed within the context of delegation cases that had established standards and guidelines to govern the exercise of delegated authority. Sutherland's opinion for the Supreme Court reflected his long-standing interest in the constitutional governance of foreign policy. As a U.S. senator, Sutherland had delivered speeches and written articles on the subject. After he left the Senate, he gave a series of lectures on the scope and exercise of presidential power in foreign relations, and they were subsequently published as a book. Sutherland thus wrote about a subject in which he had been deeply immersed. Sutherland's reference to the president as the sole organ of foreign affairs drew upon a speech delivered in 1800 to the House of Representatives by then congressman (and later chief justice) John Marshall, in which he referred to the president as the sole organ of the nation in its foreign relations.

Finally, the question of congressional authority to delegate to the president its power to regulate interstate commerce stood at the center of the lawsuit brought by the Curtiss-Wright Corporation, which was angered by President Roosevelt's order to impose an embargo on its sales of war weapons to Paraguay and Bolivia. Sutherland's opinion, upholding Roosevelt's order based on the statutory authority delegated to him, would have excited little interest. But his opinion, a broad dissertation on the president's power over foreign affairs, has become a focal point of interest since then, as Americans have debated the relative powers of the legislative and executive branches.

About the Author

George Sutherland, one of only four justices of the Supreme Court of foreign birth, was born to British parents in 1862 in Buckinghamshire, England. The Sutherlands, who embraced the faith of the Church of Jesus Christ of Latter-day Saints, immigrated to Springville, Utah, in 1863. Within a few years, the elder Sutherland renounced his faith in the Mormon Church and moved his family to Montana. By 1869, however, they had returned to Utah, where young George Sutherland was educated.

In 1879 Sutherland was enrolled in the newly established Brigham Young Academy in Provo. That school, later renamed Brigham Young University, was sponsored by the Mormon Church and exerted considerable influence on Sutherland. Among other lessons, he took to heart the teaching of Section 101 of the *Doctrine and Covenants*, the official doctrine of the church, that the Constitution was a divinely inspired instrument. Church doctrine, moreover, provided that at some distant point, the Constitution would be hanging by a thread and that church faithful would save it.

Following his education in Utah, Sutherland in 1882 enrolled in law school at the University of Michigan. While at Michigan, he studied under the celebrated chief justice of the Michigan Supreme Court, James Valentine Campbell, from whom he learned the basic outline of his opinion in the *Curtiss-Wright* case. He also was a student of the renowned judge and legal scholar Thomas M. Cooley, a disciple of the philosopher Herbert Spencer, whose advocacy of laissez-faire capitalism, liberty, and individual responsibility greatly influenced Sutherland's conservative philosophy, which emphasized a sharply limited government and discouraged governmental roles in social programs.

Sutherland did not earn a degree at Michigan. He stayed there for a year, married a woman from Utah in 1883, and returned to Provo to practice law with his father. In 1893 he moved to Salt Lake City and joined a leading law firm, which brought greater opportunities and wealth. In 1894, he was one of the principal organizers of the Utah State Bar Association, and the next year he delivered at its annual meeting an address that outlined the role of the judiciary in protecting individuals against society, including its duty to ignore views and sentiments of the majority, a widely held view in America at that time.

Sutherland's prominence in legal and political circles earned for him in 1896 election to Utah's first state legislature. As chair of the Senate Judiciary Committee, he played a key role in advancing legislation that imposed an eight-hour workday limit for miners. The surprisingly progressive stance reflected an independent political streak that enabled him to support the presidential campaign of Democrat William Jennings Bryan. His support of Bryan, he explained, lay in Bryan's advocacy of the free coinage of silver, a mining interest of great importance to Utah.

In 1900, at the age of thirty-eight, Sutherland was elected to the U.S. House of Representatives. He served a single term in Congress before repairing to Utah to broaden his political base in the Utah legislature, which, before the passage of the Seventeenth Amendment (calling for two senators to be elected from each state), would select one U.S. senator. In 1905, Sutherland was elected to the Senate for the first of two terms. His bid for a third term in the 1916 election, the first held under the Seventeenth Amendment, was rejected by Utah voters.

While he was in the Senate, Sutherland became a national figure. He exhibited an abiding interest in the nation's foreign policy. As a member of the Senate Foreign Relations Committee, he became an outspoken critic of President Woodrow Wilson's cautious and, occasionally, pacifistic approach. Nevertheless, he advocated broad, unilateral presidential power in foreign affairs, an approach for which he became well known when he authored the Court's opinion in *United States v. Curtiss-Wright*.

After Sutherland left the Senate, he practiced law in Washington, D.C., and served a term as president of the American Bar Association. In 1922, President Warren G. Harding appointed him to the Court. He was regarded as the leader of the so-called Four Horsemen, a bloc of conservative justices who, for a period of fifteen years, prevailed on many issues before the Court and defeated important New Deal programs. He advanced a robust view of judicial power, which, he believed, was necessary to check governmental encroachments and majoritarian impulses. Much of Sutherland's judicial record has been relegated to the realm of obsolescence, since more of his opinions have been overturned than any other member of the Supreme Court in American history.

George Sutherland's opinion promoted a theory of broad and inherent executive power.
(Library of Congress)

Still, some of Sutherland's work enjoys lasting status. His opinion in 1932 in *Powell v. Alabama* was the first to recognize the right to counsel as an attribute of due process of law. His most significant contribution to American constitutional law, however, is to be found in his opinions reflecting an expansive view of presidential power in foreign relations. Sutherland retired from the Court in 1938 and died in 1942.

Explanation and Analysis of the Document

Curtiss-Wright brought a lawsuit in which it asserted that Congress had violated the Constitution by delegating its legislative power to the president in the joint resolution granting the president power to stop the sale of arms and munitions. The previous year, the Supreme Court had struck down the delegation of legislative power to the president, and Curtiss-Wright claimed that those precedents should be used to hold unconstitutional the delegation of power in this case.

A federal district court agreed with Curtiss-Wright that the measure represented an unconstitutional delegation of legislative power. It did acknowledge the "traditional practice of Congress in reposing the widest discretion in the Executive Department of the government in the conduct of the delicate and nicely posed issues of international relations" (14 F. Supp. 230 [S.D.N.Y. 1936]), but that recognition did not save the statute.

The district court decision was appealed directly to the Supreme Court, where both parties addressed the issue of delegation. The Justice Department defended the delegation by asserting that Congress may delegate to the president authority to investigate, make findings of fact, and implement the legislation in accordance with congressional purpose. In short, the delegation was a valid exercise in contingent delegation; the president had implemented the embargo, since he had determined that it would help restore peace in South America. Government attorneys maintained that previous delegation rulings provided more than adequate support to uphold this act of delegation. Curtiss-Wright argued that the delegation was invalid since it did not provide adequate standards to guide the president. Thus the president was exercising the lawmaking power of Congress in violation of the Constitution's separation of powers.

Sutherland's Opinion

In his opinion for the Supreme Court, Justice Sutherland reversed the district court and upheld the delegation of legislative power to the president to impose an embargo on the sale of arms and munitions to the Chaco region. Sutherland observed that though "we find it unnecessary to determine" whether or not the resolution "had related solely to internal affairs," it would be open to the charge of unlawful delegation. The "whole aim of the resolution is to affect a situation entirely external to the United States, and falling within the category of foreign affairs." Sutherland declared that the two categories of external and internal affairs are different "both in respect of their origin and nature." The principle that the federal government is limited to either enumerated or implied powers "is categorically true only in respect of our internal affairs." The purpose, he wrote, was "to carve from the general mass of legislative powers then possessed by the states such portions as it was thought desirable to vest in the federal government, leaving those not included in the enumeration still in the states." However, that doctrine "applies only to powers which the states had . . . since the states severally never possessed international powers."

The transfer of foreign-affairs powers, Sutherland explained, occurred as a result of the colonies' separation from Great Britain. After the Declaration of Independence, "the powers of external sovereignty passed from the Crown not to the colonies severally, but to the colonies in their collective and corporate capacity as the United States of America." Accordingly, the "external sovereignty of Great Britain . . . passed to the Union." The foreign-affairs powers of the nation were extraconstitutional, that is, independent of the Constitution. "The powers to declare and wage war, to conclude peace, to make treaties, to maintain diplomatic relations with other sovereignties, if they had never been mentioned in the Constitution," Sutherland noted, "would have vested in the federal government as necessary concomitants of nationality."

Sutherland's theory of extraconstitutional power in the realm of external sovereignty creates a virtually unlimited foreign-affairs power for the president:

> In this vast external realm, with its important, complicated, delicate and manifold problems, the President alone has the power to speak or listen as a representative of the nation. He makes treaties with the advice and consent of the Senate; but he alone negotiates. Into the field of negotiation the Senate cannot intrude; and Congress itself is powerless to invade it.

The president's power, Sutherland explains, is not dependent on authority from Congress:

> It is important to bear in mind that we are here dealing not alone with an authority vested in the President by an exertion of legislative power, but with such an authority plus the very delicate, plenary and exclusive power of the President as the sole organ of the federal government in the field of international relations—a power which does not require as a basis for its exercise an act of Congress, but which, of course, like every other governmental power, must be exercised in subordination to the applicable provisions of the Constitution. It is quite apparent that if, in the maintenance of our international relations, embarrassment—perhaps serious embarrassment—is to be avoided and success for

our aims achieved, congressional legislation which is to be made effective through negotiation and inquiry within the international field must often accord to the President a degree of discretion and freedom from statutory restriction which would not be admissible were domestic affairs alone involved.

Sutherland's assertion of vast and sweeping inherent presidential power in foreign affairs, essentially the exercise of the nation's external sovereignty, is vulnerable to historical scrutiny. First, external sovereignty did not circumvent the colonies and the independent states and pass directly to the national government. When Great Britain entered into a peace treaty with America, the so-called preliminary articles of peace of November 30, 1782, these articles were not with a national government. Rather, "His Brittanic Majesty acknowledges the said United States, viz. New Hampshire, Massachusetts-Bay, Rhode-Island and Providence Plantations, Connecticut, New-York, New-Jersey, Pennsylvania, Delaware, Maryland, Virginia, North-Carolina, South Carolina, and Georgia," and referred to them as "free, sovereign and independent States." The colonies formed a Continental Congress in 1774, and it provided a form of national government until the passage of the Articles of Confederation, ratified in 1781, and the drafting of the U.S. Constitution. In 1776 states were acting as sovereign entities. Proof may be found in the Articles of Confederation. Article II of that document stated: "Each State retains its Sovereignty, freedom and independence, and every power ... which is not ... expressly delegated to the United States, in Congress assembled." Further, in Article III, it was provided that "the said states hereby severally enter into a firm league of friendship with each other, for their common defense." Finally, Article IX stated: "The United States in Congress assembled, shall have the sole and exclusive right and power of determining on peace and war ... [and of] entering into treaties and alliances." The decision by the states to delegate to the Continental Congress power over war and treaties demonstrates the error in Sutherland's premise that these powers were derived from "some other source" than the several states (http://www.yale.edu/lawweb/avalon/artconf.htm).

Even if it were to be assumed that the power of external sovereignty had been by some method transferred directly from the British Crown to the Union, it remains to be explained why that power would be vested in the president.

As Justice Felix Frankfurter stated in *Youngstown Sheet and Tube Co. v. Sawyer*, "The fact that power exists in the Government does not vest it in the President" (343 U.S. 579, 604 [1952]). Indeed, the Supreme Court has ruled on several occasions that sovereign power in foreign affairs is held by Congress. At any rate, there is nothing in Sutherland's theory that would explain the location of this power in the presidency. It may be added that Sutherland's assertion of extraconstitutional foreign-affairs powers is undermined by James Madison's statement in Federalist Paper number 45 that "the powers delegated by the proposed Constitution are few and defined.... [They] will be exercised principally on external objects, as war, peace, negotiation, and foreign commerce" (http://www.foundingfathers.info/federalistpapers/fed45.htm). Finally, the Court, since *Curtiss-Wright*, has consistently taken the position that powers are tethered to the Constitution. In 1957, in *Reid v. Covert*, Justice Hugo Black, writing the opinion for the Court, stated: "The United States is entirely a creature of the Constitution. Its powers and authority have no other source. It can act only in accordance with all the limitations imposed by the Constitution" (354 U.S. 1, 16–17 [1957]).

The Sole Organ Doctrine

Sutherland's treatment of foreign-relations powers as essentially executive in nature found clear expression in his reference to the president "as the sole organ of the federal government in the field of international relations—a power which does not require as a basis for its exercise an act of Congress." In that capacity, the president's powers are "plenary and exclusive." Sutherland's depiction of the president as "sole organ" drew upon a speech delivered in 1800 in the House of Representatives by then Congressman (and later chief justice) John Marshall, who stated: "The President is the sole organ of the nation in its external relations. . . . Of consequence, the demand of a foreign nation can only be made on him" (U.S. Congress, vol. 10, pp. 613–614).

Marshall was defending the decision of President John Adams to surrender a British deserter, Jonathan Robbins, in accordance with the Jay Treaty. According to Marshall, the Robbins affair involved a demand upon the United States, and it required a response from the president on behalf of the American people. In the course of his speech, Marshall never asserted that the president's well-established role as sole organ of communication implies authority to make policy. The president, moreover, was fulfilling his duty to implement the extradition provisions of the treaty. Article II of the Constitution provides that it is the president's duty to "take Care that the Laws be faithfully executed." Article VI states that all treaties made "shall be the supreme law of the land." The president, in the performance of his constitutional role, was implementing, not making, a treaty. It is worth noting that Marshall, in his thirty-four years on the Supreme Court, never wrote an opinion in which he embraced Sutherland's characterization of the president as the sole organ of American foreign policy. On the contrary, he wrote numerous opinions in which he asserted the primacy of Congress in matters of war and peace and of national security and foreign affairs.

In drawing upon Marshall's speech, Sutherland infused a purely communicative role with a substantive policy-making role. As a consequence, Sutherland transformed Marshall's depiction of that narrow duty into a vast and sweeping power that exalted presidential domination of American foreign policy. In fact, seeing of the president as the "sole" organ of the nation's foreign policy is at odds with the textual assignment of foreign-relations powers to both the president and Congress. Article I grants to Congress broad powers, including the authority to regulate foreign commerce; raise armies; declare war; grant letters of marque and reprisal (the authority to order military hostilities short of war); make rules governing immigration and naturalization; make regulations governing land and naval forces; define and punish acts of piracy; define offenses against the law of nations; organize, arm, and discipline the militia; and make rules for calling for the militia, among others. The president is vested with only two exclusive foreign-affairs powers. He is commander in chief, but he acts in this capacity by and under the authority of Congress. He also has the power to receive ambassadors. Hamilton, Madison, and Jefferson, among others, agreed that this clerklike function was ceremonial in character. Of course, the president shares with the Senate the authority to make treaties and to appoint ambassadors. The textual grant of authority to the president pales in comparison to that allocated to Congress. The framers of the Constitution did not make the president the sole organ of American foreign policy either by definition or substance.

Indeed, most foreign-relations powers are vested in Congress.

Impact

It is difficult to overestimate the impact of the *Curtiss-Wright* opinion on the scope of executive power. It has been invoked and embraced by presidents and judges, and, as a consequence, it has become a principal pillar of presidential domination of American foreign affairs. For their part, presidents have cited the sole organ doctrine to justify unilateral executive war making, domestic surveillance, the termination and suspension of treaties, extraordinary rendition, the creation of military tribunals, covert acts, the detention of enemy combatants, and executive agreements, as well as a general authority to formulate, manage, and conduct the nation's foreign relations. Courts, moreover, have endorsed the sole organ doctrine, principally as a means of justifying deference to the executive in the conduct of foreign policy.

The sole organ doctrine was invoked by President Roosevelt and embraced by the Supreme Court shortly after it was announced. In 1937, in *United States v. Belmont*, and in 1942, in *United States v. Pink*, the Court cited the doctrine to uphold executive agreements with the Soviet Union. Sutherland himself wrote the opinion in *Belmont*. In recent years, the courts have cited the Sutherland opinion for the proposition that Congress might delegate its power more freely in the area of foreign affairs than in domestic affairs. In other cases, the courts have invoked *Curtiss-Wright* to justify traditional deference to executive judgment in the realm of foreign relations. The Bush administration has drawn upon the opinion to advance broad presidential powers in the conduct of the war in Iraq and in the war on terror.

The opinion has its critics. Scholars have denounced Sutherland's claims of extraconstitutional and inherent powers, his historical theory about the flow of external sovereignty, and the sole organ doctrine itself. To critics, the sole organ doctrine is irreconcilable with the text of the Constitution. The assertion of inherent executive power, moreover, is difficult to square with the framers' conception of executive power and their design of the presidency. In the landmark case *Youngstown Sheet and Tube Co. v. Sawyer* (1952), Justice Robert H. Jackson dismissed much of Sutherland's opinion as "dictum."

The issue in the case, it should be recalled, involved the authority of Congress to delegate its legislative power to the president to impose an arms embargo. The issue, then, involved legislative and not executive power. Sutherland's long discourse on executive power was irrelevant to the issue at hand and thus viewed as dictum.

Questions for Further Study

1. The Court's opinion in *United States v. Curtiss-Wright* has become a principal pillar of presidential domination of American foreign policy. How do Justice Sutherland's assertions of "extraconstitutional" power square with the Founders' conception of the Constitution and presidential power?

2. Justice Sutherland described the president as the "sole organ" of American foreign policy. Does that description reflect the constitutional allocation of foreign-affairs powers? Does that characterization of presidential power find support in the discussions and debates of the Constitutional Convention? What, if anything, do the Federalist Papers have to say about presidential power in foreign affairs?

3. In the *Curtiss-Wright* case, Justice Sutherland characterized the president as the "sole organ" of American foreign policy. In drawing this conclusion he relied on John Marshall's speech in 1800 in which he referred to the president as the "sole organ" of the nation's foreign relations. In your view, was Sutherland's understanding of the president as "sole organ" consistent with Marshall's? If not, what were the substantive differences between the two? Compare and contrast the two views.

4. How has Justice Sutherland's opinion been understood and utilized by presidents and courts over the years? Provide a critique of judicial citations to the *Curtiss-Wright* opinion and presidential invocation of Sutherland's reasoning.

5. Describe and discuss critical evaluations of Justice Sutherland's opinion. Do you agree with criticisms? Why or why not? Explain your position.

6. Compare and contrast Justice Sutherland's description of presidential power with the opinions of the justices in *Youngstown Sheet and Tube. Co. v. Sawyer* (1952).

Further Reading

Books

Arkes, Hadley. *The Return of George Sutherland: Restoring a Jurisprudence of Natural Rights.* Princeton, NJ: Princeton University Press, 1994.

Bruff, Harold. H. *Untrodden Ground: How Presidents Interpret the Constitution.* Chicago: University of Chicago Press, 2015.

Fisher, Louis. *Supreme Court Expansion of Presidential Power: Unconstitutional Leanings.* Lawrence: University Press of Kansas, 2017.

Fisher, Louis. "How Supreme Court Deceptions Inflate Presidential Power." In *The Palgrave Handbook of Deceptive Communication,* edited by Tony Docan-Morgan. Cham, Switzerland: Palgrave Macmillan, 2019: 937–51.

Further Reading

Books

Paschal, Joel Francis. *Mr. Justice Sutherland: A Man against the State.* Princeton, NJ: Princeton University Press, 1951.

Sutherland, George. *Constitutional Power and World Affairs.* New York: Columbia University Press, 1919.

U.S. Congress. Annals o*f the Congress of the United States, 1789–1824.* 42 vols. Washington, DC, 1834–1856.

Articles

Fisher, Louis. "The Staying Power of Erroneous Dicta: From Curtiss-Wright to Zivotofsky." *Constitutional Commentary* 31 (2016): 149–219.

Garner, James W. "Executive Discretion in the Conduct of Foreign Relations." *American Journal of International Law* 31, no. 2 (1937): 289–293.

Gobel, Jr., Julius. "Constitutional History and Constitutional Law." *Columbia Law Review* 38, no. 4 (1938): 555–577.

Levitan, David M. "The Foreign Relations Power: An Analysis of Mr. Justice Sutherland's Theory." *Yale Law Journal* 55, no. 3 (1946): 467–497.

Lofgren, Charles. "*United States v. Curtiss-Wright Export Corporation*: An Historical Reassessment." *Yale Law Journal* 83, no. 1 (1973): 1–32.

Patterson, C. Perry. "*In Re The United States v. The Curtiss-Wright Corporation.*" *Texas Law Review* 22 (1944): 286–308.

Quarles, James. "The Federal Government: As to Foreign Affairs, Are Its Powers Inherent as Distinguished from Delegated?" *Georgetown Law Journal* 32 (1944): 375–383.

Websites

"Articles of Confederation." The Avalon Project at Yale Law School website. Accessed March 29, 2023. https://avalon.law.yale.edu/18th_century/artconf.asp.

"Federalist No. 45." Founding Fathers website. Accessed March 29, 2023. http://www.foundingfathers.info/federalistpapers/fed45.htm.

"Preliminary Articles of Peace: November 30, 1782." The Avalon Project at Yale Law School website. Accessed March 29, 2023. https://avalon.law.yale.edu/18th_century/prel1782.asp.

"United States v. Curtiss-Wright Export Corporation, 299 U.S. 304 (1936)." FindLaw website. Accessed March 29, 2023. http://caselaw.lp.findlaw.com/cgi-bin/getcase.pl?court=us&vol=299&invol=304.

—Commentary by David Gray Adler

UNITED STATES V. CURTISS-WRIGHT

Document Text

Mr. Justice Sutherland Delivered the Opinion of the Court

On January 27, 1936, an indictment was returned in the court below, the first count of which charges that appellees, beginning with the 29th day of May, 1934, conspired to sell in the United States certain arms of war, namely, fifteen machine guns, to Bolivia, a country then engaged in armed conflict in the Chaco, in violation of the Joint Resolution of Congress approved May 28, 1934, and the provisions of a proclamation issued on the same day by the President of the United States pursuant to authority conferred by section 1 of the resolution. In pursuance of the conspiracy, the commission of certain overt acts was alleged, details of which need not be stated. The Joint Resolution (chapter 365, 48 Stat. 811) follows: "Resolved by the Senate and House of Representatives of the United States of America in Congress assembled, That if the President finds that the prohibition of the sale of arms and munitions of war in the United States to those countries now engaged in armed conflict in the Chaco may contribute to the reestablishment of peace between those countries, and if after consultation with the governments of other American Republics and with their cooperation, as well as that of such other governments as he may deem necessary, he makes proclamation to that effect, it shall be unlawful to sell, except under such limitations and exceptions as the President prescribes, any arms or munitions of war in any place in the United States to the countries now engaged in that armed conflict, or to any person, company, or association acting in the interest of either country, until oth-

erwise ordered by the President or by Congress. Sec. 2. Whoever sells any arms or munitions of war in violation of section 1 shall, on conviction, be punished by a fine not exceeding $10,000 or by imprisonment not exceeding two years, or both."

The President's proclamation (48 Stat. 1744, No. 2087), after reciting the terms of the Joint Resolution, declares:

"Now, Therefore, I, Franklin D. Roosevelt, President of the United States of America, acting under and by virtue of the authority conferred in me by the said joint resolution of Congress, do hereby declare and proclaim that I have found that the prohibition of the sale of arms and munitions of war in the United States to those countries now engaged in armed conflict in the Chaco may contribute to the reestablishment of peace between those countries, and that I have consulted with the governments of other American Republics and have been assured of the cooperation of such governments as I have deemed necessary as contemplated by the said joint resolution; and I do hereby admonish all citizens of the United States and every person to abstain from every violation of the provisions of the joint resolution above set forth, hereby made applicable to Bolivia and Paraguay, and I do hereby warn them that all violations of such provisions will be rigorously prosecuted.

And I do hereby enjoin upon all officers of the United States charged with the execution of the laws thereof, the utmost diligence in preventing violations of the said joint resolution and this my proclamation issued thereunder, and in bringing to trial and punishment any offenders against the same.

And I do hereby delegate to the Secretary of State the power of prescribing exceptions and limitations to the application of the said joint resolution of May 28, 1934, as made effective by this my proclamation issued thereunder."

On November 14, 1935, this proclamation was revoked (49 Stat. 3480), in the following terms:

"Now, therefore, I, Franklin D. Roosevelt, President of the United States of America, do hereby declare and proclaim that I have found that the prohibition of the sale of arms and munitions of war in the United States to Bolivia or Paraguay will no longer be necessary as a contribution to the reestablishment of peace between those countries, and the above-mentioned Proclamation of May 28, 1934, is hereby revoked as to the sale of arms and munitions of war to Bolivia or Paraguay from and after November 29, 1935, provided, however, that this action shall not have the effect of releasing or extinguishing any penalty, forfeiture or liability incurred under the aforesaid Proclamation of May 28, 1934, or the Joint Resolution of Congress approved by the President on the same date; and that the said Proclamation and Joint Resolution shall be treated as remaining in force for the purpose of sustaining any proper action or prosecution for the enforcement of such penalty, forfeiture or liability."

Appellees severally demurred to the first count of the indictment on the grounds (1) that it did not charge facts sufficient to show the commission by appellees of any offense against any law of the United States; (2) that this court of the indictment charges a conspiracy to violate the Joint Resolution and the Presidential proclamation, both of which had expired according to the terms of the Joint Resolution by reason of the revocation contained in the Presidential proclamation of November 14, 1935, and were not in force at the time when the indictment was found. The points urged in support of the demurrers were, first, that the Joint Resolution effects an invalid delegation of legislative power to the executive; second, that the Joint Resolution never became effective because of the failure of the President to find essential jurisdictional facts; and, third, that the second proclamation operated to put an end to the alleged liability under the Joint Resolution.

The court below sustained the demurrers upon the first point, but overruled them on the second and third points. (D.C.) 14 F.Supp. 230. The government appealed to this court under the provisions of the Criminal Appeals Act of March 2, 1907, 34 Stat. 1246, as amended, U.S.C., title 18, 682 (18 U.S.C.A. 682). That act authorizes the United States to appeal from a district court direct to this court in criminal cases where, among other things, the decision sustaining a demurrer to the indictment or any count thereof is based upon the invalidity or construction of the statute upon which the indictment is founded.

First. It is contended that by the Joint Resolution the going into effect and continued operation of the resolution was conditioned (a) upon the President's judgment as to its beneficial effect upon the re-establishment of peace between the countries engaged in armed conflict in the Chaco; (b) upon the making of a proclamation, which was left to his unfettered discretion, thus constituting an attempted substitution of the President's will for that of Congress; (c) upon the making of a proclamation putting an end to the operation of the resolution, which again was left to the President's unfettered discretion; and (d) further, that the extent of its operation in particular cases was subject to limitation and exception by the President, controlled by no standard. In each of these particulars, appellees urge that Congress abdicated its essential functions and delegated them to the Executive.

Whether, if the Joint Resolution had related solely to internal affairs, it would be open to the challenge that it constituted an unlawful delegation of legislative power to the Executive, we find it unnecessary to determine. The whole aim of the resolution is to affect a situation entirely external to the United States, and falling within the category of foreign affairs. The determination which we are called to make, therefore, is whether the Joint Resolution, as applied to that situation, is vulnerable to attack under the rule that forbids a delegation of the lawmaking power. In other words, assuming (but not deciding) that the challenged delegation, if it were confined to internal affairs, would be invalid, may it nevertheless be sustained on the ground that its exclusive aim is to afford a remedy for a hurtful condition within foreign territory?

It will contribute to the elucidation of the question if we first consider the differences between the powers of the federal government in respect of foreign or external affairs and those in respect of domestic or internal affairs. That there are differences between them, and that these differences are fundamental, may not be doubted.

The two classes of powers are different, both in respect of their origin and their nature. The broad statement that the federal government can exercise no powers except those specifically enumerated in the Constitution, and such implied powers as are necessary and proper to carry into effect the enumerated powers, is categorically true only in respect of our internal affairs. In that field, the primary purpose of the Constitution was to carve from the general mass of legislative powers then possessed by the states such portions as it was thought desirable to vest in the federal government, leaving those not included in the enumeration still in the states. *Carter v. Carter Coal Co.*, 298 U.S. 238, 294, 56 S.Ct. 855, 865. That this doctrine applies only to powers which the states had is self-evident. And since the states severally never possessed international powers, such powers could not have been carved from the mass of state powers but obviously were transmitted to the United States from some other source. During the Colonial period, those powers were possessed exclusively by and were entirely under the control of the Crown. By the Declaration of Independence, "the Representatives of the United States of America" declared the United (not the several) Colonies to be free and independent states, and as such to have "full Power to levy War, conclude Peace, contract Alliances, establish Commerce and to do all other Acts and Things which Independent States may of right do."

As a result of the separation from Great Britain by the colonies, acting as a unit, the powers of external sovereignty passed from the Crown not to the colonies severally, but to the colonies in their collective and corporate capacity as the United States of America. Even before the Declaration, the colonies were a unit in foreign affairs, acting through a common agency—namely, the Continental Congress, composed of delegates from the thirteen colonies. That agency exercised the powers of war and peace, raised an army, created a navy, and finally adopted the Declaration of Independence. Rulers come and go; governments end and forms of government change; but sovereignty survives. A political society cannot endure without a supreme will somewhere. Sovereignty is never held in suspense. When, therefore, the external sovereignty of Great Britain in respect of the colonies ceased, it immediately passed to the Union. See *Penhallow v. Doane*, 3 Dall. 54, 80, 81, Fed. Cas. No. 10925. That fact was given practical application almost at once. The treaty of peace, made on September 3, 1783, was concluded between his Brittanic Majesty and the "United States of America."

The Union existed before the Constitution, which was ordained and established among other things to form "a more perfect Union." Prior to that event, it is clear that the Union, declared by the Articles of Confederation to be "perpetual," was the sole possessor of external sovereignty, and in the Union it remained without change save in so far as the Constitution in express terms qualified its exercise. The Framers' Convention was called and exerted its powers upon the irrefutable postulate that though the states were several their people in respect of foreign affairs were one. Compare The Chinese Exclusion Case, 130 U.S. 581, 604, 606 S., 9 S.Ct. 623. In that convention, the entire absence of state power to deal with those affairs was thus forcefully stated by Rufus King:

> "The states were not 'sovereigns' in the sense contended for by some. They did not possess the peculiar features of sovereignty,—they could not make war, nor peace, nor alliances, nor treaties. Considering them as political beings, they were dumb, for they could not speak to any foreign sovereign whatever. They were deaf, for they could not hear any propositions from such sovereign. They had not even the organs or faculties of defence or offence, for they could not of themselves raise troops, or equip vessels, for war."
> 5 Elliot's Debates, 212.1.

It results that the investment of the federal government with the powers of external sovereignty did not depend upon the affirmative grants of the Constitution. The powers to declare and wage war, to conclude peace, to make treaties, to maintain diplomatic relations with other sovereignties, if they had never been mentioned in the Constitution, would have vested in the federal government as necessary concomitants of nationality. Neither the Constitution nor the laws passed in pursuance of it have any force in foreign territory unless in respect of our own citizens (see *American Banana Co. v. United Fruit Co.*, 213 U.S. 347, 356, 29 S.Ct. 511, 16 Ann.Cas. 1047); and operations of the nation in such territory must be governed by treaties, international understandings and compacts, and the principles of international law. As a member of the family of nations, the right and power of the United States in that field are equal to the right and power of the other members of the international family. Otherwise, the United States is not completely sovereign. The power to acquire territory by discovery and occupation (*Jones v. United States*, 137 U.S. 202, 212, 11 S.Ct. 80), the power to expel undesirable aliens (*Fong Yue Ting v. United States*, 149 U.S. 698, 705 et seq., 13 S.Ct. 1016), the power to make such international agreements as do not constitute treaties in the constitutional sense (*Altman & Co. v. United States*, 224 U.S. 583, 600, 601 S., 32 S.Ct. 593; Crandall, Treaties, Their Making and Enforcement (2d Ed.) p. 102 and note 1), none of which is expressly affirmed by the Constitution, nevertheless exist as inherently inseparable from the conception of nationality. This the court recognized, and in each of the cases cited found the warrant for its conclusions not in the provisions of the Constitution, but in the law of nations.

In *Burnet v. Brooks*, 288 U.S. 378, 396, 53 S.Ct. 457, 461, 86 A.L.R. 747, we said, "As a nation with all the attributes of sovereignty, the United States is vested with all the powers of government necessary to maintain an effective control of international relations." Cf. *Carter v. Carter Coal Co.*, supra, 298 U.S. 238, at page 295, 56 S.Ct. 855, 865. Not only, as we have shown, is the federal power over external affairs in origin and essential character different from that over internal affairs, but participation in the exercise of the power is significantly limited. In this vast external realm, with its important, complicated, delicate and manifold problems, the President alone has the power to speak or listen as a representative of the nation. He makes treaties with the advice and consent of the Senate; but he alone negotiates. Into the field of negotiation the Senate cannot intrude; and Congress itself is powerless to invade it. As Marshall said in his great argument

of March 7, 1800, in the House of Representatives, "The President is the sole organ of the nation in its external relations, and its sole representative with foreign nations." Annals, 6th Cong., col. 613. The Senate Committee on Foreign Relations at a very early day in our history (February 15, 1816), reported to the Senate, among other things, as follows:

> "The President is the constitutional representative of the United States with regard to foreign nations. He manages our concerns with foreign nations and must necessarily be most competent to determine when, how, and upon what subjects negotiation may be urged with the greatest prospect of success. For his conduct he is responsible to the Constitution. The committee considers this responsibility the surest pledge for the faithful discharge of his duty. They think the interference of the Senate in the direction of foreign negotiations calculated to diminish that responsibility and thereby to impair the best security for the national safety. The nature of transactions with foreign nations, moreover, requires caution and unity of design, and their success frequently depends on secrecy and dispatch."

It is important to bear in mind that we are here dealing not alone with an authority vested in the President by an exertion of legislative power, but with such an authority plus the very delicate, plenary and exclusive power of the President as the sole organ of the federal government in the field of international relations—a power which does not require as a basis for its exercise an act of Congress, but which, of course, like every other governmental power, must be exercised in subordination to the applicable provisions of the Constitution. It is quite apparent that if, in the maintenance of our international relations, embarrassment—perhaps serious embarrassment—is to be avoided and success for our aims achieved, congressional legislation which is to be made effective through negotiation and inquiry within the international field must often accord to the President a degree of discretion and freedom from statutory restriction which would not be admissible were domestic affairs alone involved. Moreover, he, not Congress, has the better opportunity of knowing the conditions which prevail in foreign countries, and especially is this true in time of war. He has his confidential sources of information. He has his agents in the form of diplomatic, consular and other officials. Secrecy in respect of information gathered by them may be highly necessary, and the premature disclosure of it productive of harmful results. Indeed, so clearly is this true that the first President refused to accede to a request to lay before the House of Representatives the instructions, correspondence and documents relating to the negotiation of the Jay Treaty—a refusal the wisdom of which was recognized by the House itself and has never since been doubted. In his reply to the request, President Washington said:

> "The nature of foreign negotiations requires caution, and their success must often depend on secrecy; and even when brought to a conclusion a full disclosure of all the measures, demands, or eventual concessions which may have been proposed or contemplated would be extremely impolitic; for this might have a pernicious influence on future negotiations, or produce immediate inconveniences, perhaps danger and mischief, in relation to other powers. The necessity of such caution and secrecy was one cogent reason for vesting the power of making treaties in the President, with the advice and consent of the Senate, the principle on which that body was formed confining it to a small number of members. To admit, then, a right in the House of Representatives to demand and to have as a matter of course all the papers respecting a negotiation with a foreign power would be to establish a dangerous precedent."

The marked difference between foreign affairs and domestic affairs in this respect is recognized by both houses of Congress in the very form of their requisitions for information from the executive departments. In the case of every department except the Department of State, the resolution directs the official to furnish the information. In the case of the State Department, dealing with foreign affairs, the President is requested to furnish the information "if not incompatible with the public interest." A statement that to furnish the information is not compatible with the public interest rarely, if ever, is questioned.

When the President is to be authorized by legislation to act in respect of a matter intended to affect a situation in foreign territory, the legislator properly bears in mind the important consideration that the form of the President's action—or, indeed, whether he shall act at all—may well depend, among other things, upon the nature of the confidential information which he has or may thereafter receive, or upon the effect which his action may have upon our foreign relations. This consideration, in connection with what we have already said on the subject discloses the unwisdom of requiring Congress in this field of governmental power to lay down narrowly definite standards by which the President is to be governed. As this court said in *Mackenzie v. Hare*, 239 U.S. 299, 311, 36 S.Ct. 106, 108, Ann. Cas.1916E, 645, "As a government, the United States is invested with all the attributes of sovereignty. As it has the character of nationality it has the powers of nationality, especially those which concern its relations and intercourse with other countries. We should hesitate long before limiting or embarrassing such powers."

In the light of the foregoing observations, it is evident that this court should not be in haste to apply a general rule which will have the effect of condemning legislation like that under review as constituting an unlawful delegation of legislative power. The principles which justify such legislation find overwhelming support in the unbroken legislative practice which has prevailed almost from the inception of the national government to the present day.

Let us examine, in chronological order, the acts of legislation which warrant this conclusion:

The Act of June 4, 1794, authorized the President to lay, regulate and revoke embargoes. He was "authorized" "whenever, in his opinion, the public safety shall so require," to lay the embargo upon all ships and vessels in the ports of the United States, including those of foreign nations, "under such regulations as the circumstances of the case may require, and to continue or revoke the same, whenever he shall think proper." C. 41, 1 Stat. 372. A prior joint resolution of May 7, 1794, (1 Stat. 401), had conferred unqualified power on the President to grant clearances, notwithstanding an existing embargo, to ships or vessels belonging to citizens of the United States bound to any port beyond the Cape of Good Hope.

The Act of March 3, 1795 (c. 53, 1 Stat. 444), gave the President authority to permit the exportation of arms, cannon and military stores, the law prohibiting such exports to the contrary notwithstanding, the only pre-scribed guide for his action being that such exports should be in "cases connected with the security of the commercial interest of the United States, and for public purposes only."

By the Act of June 13, 1798 (c. 53, 5, 1 Stat. 566), it was provided that if the government of France "shall clearly disavow, and shall be found to refrain from the aggressions, depredations and hostilities" there-tofore maintained against vessels and property of the citizens of the United States, "in violation of the faith of treaties, and the laws of nations, and shall thereby acknowledge the just claims of the United States to be considered as in all respects neutral, ... it shall be law-ful for the President of the United States, being well ascertained of the premises, to remit and discontinue the prohibitions and restraints hereby enacted and declared; and he shall be, and is hereby authorized to make proclamation thereof accordingly."

By section 4 of the Act of February 9, 1799 (c. 2, 1 Stat. 615), it was made "lawful" for the President, "if he shall deem it expedient and consistent with the interest of the United States," by order to remit certain restraints and prohibitions imposed by the act with respect to the French Republic, and also to revoke any such order "whenever, in his opinion, the interest of the United States shall require."

Similar authority, qualified in the same way was con-ferred by section 6 of the Act of February 7, 1800, c. 10, 2 Stat. 9.

Section 5 of the Act of March 3, 1805 (c. 41, 2 Stat. 341), made it lawful for the President, whenever an armed vessel entering the harbors or waters within the ju-risdiction of the United States and required to depart therefrom should fail to do so, not only to employ the land and naval forces to compel obedience, but, "if he shall think it proper, it shall be lawful for him to forbid, by proclamation, all intercourse with such vessel, and with every armed vessel of the same nation, and the officers and crew thereof; to prohibit all supplies and aid from being furnished them" and to do various oth-er things connected therewith. Violation of the Presi-dent's proclamation was penalized.

On February 28, 1806, an act was passed (c. 9, 2 Stat. 351) to suspend commercial intercourse between the United States and certain parts of the Island of St. Domingo. A penalty was prescribed for its viola-tion. Notwithstanding the positive provisions of the act, it was by section 5 (2 Stat. 352) made "lawful" for the President to remit and discontinue the restraints and prohibitions imposed by the act at any time "if he shall deem it expedient and consistent with the interests of the United States" to do so. Likewise in respect of the Non-intercourse Act of March 1, 1809 (c. 24, 2 Stat. 528); the President was "authorized" (section 11, p. 530), in case either of the countries af-fected should so revoke or modify her edicts "as that they shall cease to violate the neutral commerce of the United States," to proclaim the fact, after which the suspended trade might be renewed with the na-tion so doing.

Practically every volume of the United States Statutes contains one or more acts or joint resolutions of Con-gress authorizing action by the President in respect of subjects affecting foreign relations, which either leave the exercise of the power to his unrestricted judg-ment, or provide a standard far more general than that which has always been considered requisite with re-gard to domestic affairs. Many, though not all, of these acts are designated in the footnote. It well may be as-sumed that these legislative precedents were in mind when Congress passed the joint resolutions of April 22, 1898, 30 Stat. 739; March 14, 1912, 37 Stat. 630 (22 U.S.C.A. 236 and note); and January 31, 1922, 42 Stat. 361 (22 U.S.C.A. 236), to prohibit the export of coal or other war material. The resolution of 1898 authorized the President "in his discretion, and with such limita-tion and exceptions as shall seem to him expedient" to prohibit such exportations. The striking identity of language found in the second resolution mentioned above and in the one now under review will be seen upon comparison. The resolution of March 14, 1912 (see 22 U.S.C.A. 236 and note) provides:

"That whenever the President shall find that in any American country conditions of domestic violence ex-ist which are promoted by the use of arms or munitions of war procured from the United States, and shall make proclamation thereof, it shall be unlawful to export ex-cept under such limitations and exceptions as the Pres-ident shall prescribe any arms or munitions of war from any place in the United States to such country until oth-erwise ordered by the President or by Congress.

Sec. 2. That any shipment of material hereby declared unlawful after such a proclamation shall be punishable by fine not exceeding ten thousand dollars, or imprisonment not exceeding two years, or both."

The third resolution is in substantially the same terms, but extends to any country in which the United States exercises extraterritorial jurisdiction, and provides for the President's action not only when conditions of domestic violence exist which are promoted, but also when such conditions may be promoted, by the use of such arms or munitions of war.

We had occasion to review these embargo and kindred acts in connection with an exhaustive discussion of the general subject of delegation of legislative power in a recent case, *Panama Refining Co. v. Ryan*, 293 U.S. 388, 421, 422 S., 55 S.Ct. 241, 249, and, in justifying such acts, pointed out that they confided to the President "an authority which was cognate to the conduct by him of the foreign relations of the government."

The result of holding that the joint resolution here under attack is void and unenforceable as constituting an unlawful delegation of legislative power would be to stamp this multitude of comparable acts and resolutions as likewise invalid. And while this court may not, and should not, hesitate to declare acts of Congress, however many times repeated, to be unconstitutional if beyond all rational doubt it finds them to be so, an impressive array of legislation such as we have just set forth, enacted by nearly every Congress from the beginning of our national existence to the present day, must be given unusual weight in the process of reaching a correct determination of the problem. A legislative practice such as we have here, evidenced not by only occasional instances, but marked by the movement of a steady stream for a century and a half of time, goes a long way in the direction of proving the presence of unassailable ground for the constitutionality of the practice, to be found in the origin and history of the power involved, or in its nature, or in both combined.

In *The Laura*, 114 U.S. 411, 416, 5 S.Ct. 881, 883, this court answered a challenge to the constitutionality of a statute authorizing the Secretary of the Treasury to remit or mitigate fines and penalties in certain cases, by repeating the language of a very early case (*Stuart v. Laird*, 1 Cranch 299, 309) that the long practice and acquiescence under the statute was a "practical exposition . .

. too strong and obstinate to be shaken or controlled. Of course, the question is at rest, and ought not now to be disturbed." In *Burrow-Giles Lithographic Co. v. Sarony*, 111 U.S. 53, 57, 4 S.Ct. 279, 281, the constitutionality of R.S. 4952, conferring upon the author, inventor, designer or proprietor of a photograph certain rights, was involved. Mr. Justice Miller, speaking for the court, disposed of the point by saying: "The construction placed upon the constitution by the first act of 1790 and the act of 1802, by the men who were contemporary with its formation, many of whom were members of the convention which framed it, is of itself entitled to very great weight, and when it is remembered that the rights thus established have not been disputed during a period of nearly a century, it is almost conclusive."

In *Field v. Clark*, 143 U.S. 649, 691, 12 S.Ct. 495, 504, this court declared that "the practical construction of the constitution, as given by so many acts of congress, and embracing almost the entire period of our national existence, should not be overruled, unless upon a conviction that such legislation was clearly incompatible with the supreme law of the land." The rule is one which has been stated and applied many times by this court. As examples, see *Ames v. Kansas*, 111 U.S. 449, 469, 4 S.Ct. 437; *McCulloch v. Maryland*, 4 Wheat. 316, 401; *Downes v. Bidwell*, 182 U.S. 244, 286, 21 S.Ct. 770.

The uniform, long-continued and undisputed legislative practice just disclosed rests upon an admissible view of the Constitution which, even if the practice found far less support in principle than we think it does, we should not feel at liberty at this late day to disturb.

We deem it unnecessary to consider, seriatim, the several clauses which are said to evidence the unconstitutionality of the Joint Resolution as involving an unlawful delegation of legislative power. It is enough to summarize by saying that, both upon principle and in accordance with precedent, we conclude there is sufficient warrant for the broad discretion vested in the President to determine whether the enforcement of the statute will have a beneficial effect upon the re-establishment of peace in the affected countries; whether he shall make proclamation to bring the resolution into operation; whether and when the resolution shall cease to operate and to make proclamation accordingly; and to prescribe limitations and exceptions to which the enforcement of the resolution shall be subject.

Second. The second point raised by the demurrer was that the Joint Resolution never became effective because the President failed to find essential jurisdictional facts; and the third point was that the second proclamation of the President operated to put an end to the alleged liability of appellees under the Joint Resolution. In respect of both points, the court below overruled the demurrer, and thus far sustained the government.

The government contends that, upon an appeal by the United States under the Criminal Appeals Act from a decision holding an indictment bad, the jurisdiction of the court does not extend to questions decided in favor of the United States, but that such questions may only be reviewed in the usual way after conviction. We find nothing in the words of the statute or in its purposes which justify this conclusion. The demurrer in the present case challenges the validity of the statute upon three separate and distinct grounds. If the court below had sustained the demurrer without more, an appeal by the government necessarily would have brought here for our determination all of these grounds, since in that case the record would not have disclosed whether the court considered the statute invalid upon one particular ground or upon all of the grounds alleged. The judgment of the lower court is that the statute is invalid. Having held that this judgment cannot be sustained upon the particular ground which that court assigned, it is now open to this court to inquire whether or not the judgment can be sustained upon the rejected grounds which also challenge the validity of the statute and, therefore, constitute a proper subject of review by this court under the Criminal Appeals Act (18 U.S.C.A. 682). *United States v. Hastings*, 296 U.S. 188, 192, 56 S.Ct. 218, 219.

In *Langnes v. Green*, 282 U.S. 531, 51 S.Ct. 243, where the decree of a District Court (32 F.(2d) 284) had been assailed upon two grounds and the Circuit Court of Appeals (35 F(2d) 447) had sustained the attack upon one of such grounds only, we held that a respondent in certiorari might nevertheless urge in this court in support of the decree the ground which the intermediate appellate court had rejected. That principle is applicable here.

We proceed, then, to a consideration of the second and third grounds of the demurrers which, as we have said, the court below rejected.

1. The Executive proclamation recites, "I have found that the prohibition of the sale of arms and munitions of war in the United States to those countries now engaged in armed conflict in the Chaco may contribute to the reestablishment of peace between those countries, and that I have consulted with the governments of other American Republics and have been assured of the cooperation of such governments as I have deemed necessary as contemplated by the said joint resolution." This finding satisfies every requirement of the Joint Resolution. There is no suggestion that the resolution is fatally uncertain or indefinite; and a finding which follows its language, as this finding does, cannot well be challenged as insufficient.

But appellees, referring to the words which we have italicized above, contend that the finding is insufficient because the President does not declare that the cooperation of such governments as he deemed necessary included any American republic, and, therefore, the recital contains no affirmative showing of compliance in this respect with the Joint Resolution. The criticism seems to us wholly wanting in substance. The President recites that he has consulted with the governments of other American republics, and that he has been assured of the co-operation of such governments as he deemed necessary as contemplated by the joint resolution. These recitals, construed together, fairly include within their meaning American republics.

2. The second proclamation of the President, revoking the first proclamation, it is urged, had the effect of putting an end to the Joint Resolution, and in accordance with a well-settled rule no penalty could be enforced or punishment inflicted thereafter for an offense committed during the life of the Joint Resolution in the absence of a provision in the resolution to that effect. There is no doubt as to the general rule or as to the absence of a saving clause in the Joint Resolution. But is the case presented one which makes the rule applicable?

It was not within the power of the President to repeal the Joint Resolution; and his second proclamation did not purport to do so. It "revoked" the first proclamation; and the question is, did the revocation of the proclamation have the effect of abrogating the resolution or of precluding its enforcement in so far as that involved the prosecution and punishment of offenses committed during the life of the first proclamation? We are of opinion that it did not.

Prior to the first proclamation, the Joint Resolution was an existing law, but dormant, awaiting the creation of a particular situation to render it active. No action or lack of action on the part of the President could destroy its potentiality. Congress alone could do that. The happening of the designated events—namely, the finding of certain conditions and the proclamation by the President—did not call the law into being. It created the occasion for it to function. The second proclamation did not put an end to the law or affect what had been done in violation of the law. The effect of the proclamation was simply to remove for the future a condition of affairs which admitted of its exercise.

We should have had a different case if the Joint Resolution had expired by its own terms upon the issue of the second proclamation. Its operative force, it is true, was limited to the period of time covered by the first proclamation. And when the second proclamation was issued. the resolution ceased to be a rule for the future. It did not cease to be the law for the antecedent period of time. The distinction is clearly pointed out by the Superior Court of Judicature of New Hampshire in *Stevens v. Dimond*, 6 N.H. 330, 332, 333. There, a town by-law provided that, if certain animals should be found going at large between the first day of April and the last day of October, etc., the owner would incur a prescribed penalty. The trial court directed the jury that the by-law, being in force for a year only, had expired so that the defendant could not be called upon to answer for a violation which occurred during the designated period. The state appellate court reversed, saying that when laws "expire by their own limitation, or are repealed, they cease to be the law in relation to past, as well as the future, and can no longer be enforced in any case. No case is, however, to be found in which it was ever held before that they thus ceased to be law, unless they expired by express limitation in themselves, or were repealed. It has never been decided that they cease to be law, merely because the time they were intended to regulate had expired. . . . A very little consideration of the subject will convince any one that a limitation of the time to which a statute is to apply, is a very different thing from the limitation of the time a statute is to continue in force."

The first proclamation of the President was in force from the 28th day of May, 1934, to the 14th day of November, 1935. If the Joint Resolution had in no way depended upon Presidential action, but had provided explicitly that, at any time between May 28, 1934, and November 14, 1935, it should be unlawful to sell arms or munitions of war to the countries engaged in armed conflict in the Chaco, it certainly could not be successfully contended that the law would expire with the passing of the time fixed in respect of offenses committed during the period.

The judgment of the court below must be reversed and the cause remanded for further proceedings in accordance with the foregoing opinion.

It is so ordered.

Glossary

delegation: congressional grant or transfer of power to the president

manifold: of many and varied kinds; having many forms

plenary: complete, unlimited

seriatim: separately, or severally

sovereignty: supreme power over a subject, a government or a nation; ultimate authority or dominion

unfettered: unlimited or unrestricted

NATIONAL LABOR RELATIONS BOARD V. JONES & LAUGHLIN STEEL CORPORATION

DATE 1937	**CITATION** 301 U.S. 1
AUTHOR Charles Evans Hughes	**SIGNIFICANCE** Drastically expanded Congress's power to regulate commerce by approving the National Labor Relations Act (NLRA), which required Congress to recognize the effect of labor conditions on commerce
VOTE 5–4	

Overview

The National Labor Relations Act (NLRA) of 1935 had been a cornerstone of President Franklin D. Roosevelt's New Deal. While the Supreme Court had invalidated other New Deal legislation because it required too broad a reading of the Constitution's commerce clause, here Chief Justice Charles Evans Hughes took a more expansive view despite those earlier precedents. The main constitutional issue here was whether Congress could regulate economic factors that only had an indirect effect on commerce, and Hughes accepted that justification. Doing so opened up many other possible areas for federal economic regulation under the commerce clause.

Hughes also called the right of workers to organize into unions "fundamental." He directly equated that right with the right of businesses to organize themselves and choose their own agents. While business interests denounced the NLRA as biased, Hughes reaffirmed a connection between the intention of the law to promote labor peace and the continued flow of interstate commerce. By making this connection, he laid the groundwork for all subsequent federal labor legislation in the United States.

James McReynolds, in his dissent (joined by Willis Van Devanter, George Sutherland, and Pierce Butler, emphasized the indirect relationship between labor practices at one facility and the stream of interstate commerce, arguing that to draw that connection out was an overreach on the part of Congress.

Context

Earlier precedents from the Supreme Court, most notably *Carter v. Carter Coal* (1936), suggested that the Supreme Court would never approve an expanded interpretation of the commerce clause. While *West Coast Hotel v. Parrish* (1937) marked the beginning of a new liberal majority, this case carried greater importance because of the major role that the NLRA played in President Roosevelt's New Deal and his program to bring about economic recovery. Courts had once treated trade unions as illegal conspiracies. The NLRA wrote protections for them into law for the first time and forced the federal government to remain neutral in disputes between managers and workers. While that might not sound noteworthy, it marked a huge

The Hughes Court in 1937
(Erich Salomon)

change from much of American history, when governments at all levels actively supported management. The NLRA created the National Labor Relations Board (NLRB) to help the two sides work out their differences without the need for a strike, which would have drastically affected interstate commerce.

The NLRB enforced the framework of the NLRA that regulated the practices of managers and workers when organizing and recognizing trade unions. By doing so, it prohibited unfair labor practices by both employers and workers. Because managers had more power in unorganized workplaces, they were more likely to try to evade these restrictions than unions were. They did so by firing union organizers or by setting up so-called company unions, which they could then dominate. As a result, its passage and approval by the Supreme Court was a huge win for organized labor and a stinging defeat for many anti-union companies. While the NLRA could not guarantee that workers would win the representation elections that the NLRB oversaw, just the possibility of having an election marked a new era for organized labor.

There had been a huge increase in labor organizing since the start of the Great Depression. Even though jobs were scarce, many workers demanded better wages and working conditions because simply having a job was not enough to guarantee their economic survival. The Roosevelt administration had offered some encouragement to trade unions in its National Industrial Recovery Act but had not recognized the right of workers to organize until the passage of the NLRA in 1935. Many of these workers were inspired by the new Roosevelt administration and its early attempts to promote collective bargaining. On the other hand, many large corporations fought the organization of their workers for both economic and philosophical reasons. The American steel industry, which had been essentially nonunion since the 1890s, fought trade unions particularly hard.

This test of the NLRA began when Jones & Laughlin, the fourth-largest steel producer in the United States, fired ten union organizers at its plant in Aliquippa, Pennsylvania. An NLRB investigation found that the workers had been fired illegally and ordered them reinstated. Jones

& Laughlin sued the NLRB, arguing that the NLRA itself was unconstitutional. This case attracted considerable attention because many anti-union employers had been unwilling to follow the NLRA until its constitutionality had been tested in the U.S. Supreme Court. Despite this resistance, many unions used the passage of the NLRA as inspiration to organize even if their employers had refused to follow the act. During the twenty-one months between the passage of the NLRA and its approval in the *Jones & Laughlin* decision, union representation in American workplaces grew from 3,317,000 to 8,200,000 members. After the Supreme Court approved the NLRA in this case, the number of the NLRB staff grew significantly. This made it possible to enforce the act in many more workplaces than before.

Although unions, as well as the percentage of workers represented by unions in the American workforce, have declined in recent years, the federal protection given to them by the NLRA has never been challenged.

About the Author

Charles Evans Hughes was the son of a Baptist minister and a native of New York State. He had an extensive career in politics off the bench. He was governor of New York before he became an associate justice. He resigned that position to become the Republican Party's nominee for president of the United States in 1916. He lost to incumbent Woodrow Wilson by such a small margin that it is said that he went to bed on election night thinking he would be president. He served as U.S. secretary of state between 1921 and 1925, until Herbert Hoover appointed him chief justice in 1930.

In his first stint as a Supreme Court justice, Hughes cultivated a reputation as moderate. Even though he was a Wall Street banker before entering politics, his early record on the Court reflects middle-ground views on the role of the federal government in the American economy. After being appointed chief justice by Republican Herbert Hoover, he tended to favor the economic reforms of Franklin Roosevelt's New Deal. Some of this may reflect the political sensibilities he developed during his career in government. Hughes resigned from the Court in 1941.

James Clark McReynolds was a Kentucky lawyer who was best known as an antitrust attorney before entering government as President Woodrow Wilson's

attorney general in 1913. Wilson appointed him an associate justice of the Supreme Court in 1914. He served until 1941. McReynolds was best known on the Court for his persistent conservatism and opposition to Franklin Roosevelt's New Deal. In his private life, he was a bigot, a misogynist, and an anti-Semite.

Explanation and Analysis of the Document

Summary of the Law

Chief Justice Hughes begins with a summary of the law because the circumstances of the case are not in doubt. The NLRB investigated Jones & Laughlin and then challenged the constitutionality of the law creating the board rather than question the facts. Because the National Labor Relations Act is long and complicated, Hughes does not try to summarize the whole thing. Instead, he notes that its constitutionality turns on the Court's interpretation of the commerce clause, specifically the nature of the relations between what Congress wants to regulate and commerce itself.

The Scope of the Act

Although the steel company argued that the situation here was the same as in *A.L.A. Schechter Poultry Corp. v. United States* (1935), Hughes is willing to interpret congressional intent in a way that would save the act. Since the act says that labor practices that "affect commerce" are subject to the act, Hughes thinks that relationship is enough to justify the regulation. He also notes that this definition is limited enough that it does not affect all industry, and even if it did, the act does not require anyone to join or recognize a union; it only lets the workers decided for themselves what to do.

With respect to unfair labor practices, Hughes notes that the right to organize is a "fundamental right" and that condemning the failure to recognize that right is within the proper scope of legislative authority. While many earlier Court decisions had recognized counterweights to union organization like the freedom of contract, Hughes is acknowledging the legislative protection of the right to organize as a worthy counterweight to that protection.

Production vs. Commerce

The *Schechter* decision from 1935 hinged on this distinction. The correct use of the commerce clause, the Court had argued, depended upon the distinction between activities relating to commerce and production. The first was acceptable, but the second was not. The government here argued that the two were indistinguishable, and this time Hughes accepts that argument because just getting the ingredients needed to make steel (iron ore, coal, limestone, and so on) was so dependent on interstate commerce.

Hughes also eliminates an argument about "the flow" of commerce that had been an essential part of the *Schechter* case. Congress, he suggests, cannot only stop burdens and obstructions to commerce but can also use its power to promote commerce. Labor peace promotes commerce, and keeping labor disputes from turning into strikes keeps that commerce flowing. He notes that the power to regulate commerce is not unlimited but finds the relationship here to be clear and reasonable, so therefore the legislation is constitutional.

Employer Rights

Jones & Laughlin cited many arguments inspired by cases from previous cases related to its rights to operate its business the way it saw fit, but Hughes refuses to operate in what he calls "an intellectual vacuum." The relationship between strikes and interstate commerce was clear enough to him to justify this kind of reasonable interference with those rights in the public interest. Employers had been so used to getting their way in the courts that Hughes felt the need to offer a short history of labor in America to establish this relationship, even though their loud protests over any kind of union signaled tacit recognition that they knew this relationship was true.

While Hughes notes that the act had been criticized for being pro-labor, Hughes underscores its neutrality and basic reasonableness near the end of his opinion. Both sides receive administrative due process under the NLRA. Reinstating union members fired for that membership, which is what happened at Jones & Laughlin, was a reasonable way to resolve the dispute. The same was true of forcing the company to pay back wages.

McReynolds's Dissent

In his dissent, McReynolds takes the same limited view of the government's powers that was done in earlier cases involving New Deal legislation. He makes particular note that two smaller companies are involved in cases grouped in with this one, where the relationship to interstate commerce is much more indirect than with Jones & Laughlin. That makes the Court's majority opinion to be a much greater destruction of existing precedent.

McReynolds would have invalidated the law on the grounds that it violated liberty of contract, a nineteenth-century idea that, among its many uses, made labor unions appear much more threatening than they actually were. To McReynolds, the right of employers to pick who works for them is more fundamental than any workers' right to organize. Both the argument over commerce and the freedom of contract would come up again in subsequent tests of New Deal legislation, and because of the changing political circumstances in the country and on the Court, McReynolds' ideas would remain in the minority for the rest of the New Deal and most of the rest of the twentieth century.

Impact

The National Labor Relations Act was the most important law with respect to labor in the history of the United States. A huge wave of strikes accompanied its passage because anti-union employers refused to recognize their employees' organization. In short, failure to abide by the law greatly affected interstate commerce. This proved particularly true for the steel industry, which provided raw materials for so many different heavy industries in the United States. Therefore, the Court's acceptance of the NLRA in this case had an immediate economic impact that quickly spread through the American economy.

After the decision in this case, it was unclear whether the reasoning here would extend to legal tests of other New Deal legislation. But then Justice Willis Van Devanter retired, giving Roosevelt the opportunity to appoint the first Supreme Court justice of his presidency. Because Van Devanter had voted with the conservative bloc on the Court, this solidified the new liberal majority and assured the survival of all subsequent New Deal legislation tested before the Court. By the early 1940s, all the dissenters in this case had left the Court, and Hughes's new, expansive view of the commerce clause would persist for many decades.

Hughes's acceptance of a broad interpretation of the commerce clause set the stage for the Court to approve other kinds of New Deal interventions in the American economy, such as a federal minimum wage. By doing this, the president's infamous court packing plan (which would have added a justice to the Supreme Court for every existing justice over seventy years of age) became politically unnecessary. The famous "switch in time that saved nine" refers to Justice Owen Roberts changing his vote on a line of freedom of contract cases, but a continued line of 5–4 cases that recognized this expanded commerce clause was equally important. Later cases involving the commerce clause showed this same expansive view of congressional power.

The continued existence of the NLRA marks one of the primary legacies of the New Deal. Every later federal labor law amends this one in some way, and even though some of those laws have limited its scope, the NLRA persists to this day. Had the Supreme Court ruled differently in this case, Franklin D. Roosevelt's impact on the present-day United States would have been very different.

Questions for Further Study

1. Where would you draw the limit on Congress's power to regulate interstate commerce? Should it include labor rights, or does recognizing labor rights make Congress's power under the commerce clause essentially unlimited?

2. Hughes and his colleagues on the majority seemed more willing to accept a broad interpretation of the commerce clause because of the economic emergency caused by the Depression. Should the interpretation of the Constitution depend upon economic circumstances?

3. Historians believe that President Roosevelt's overwhelming reelection in 1936 influenced the decision in this and other cases from the 1937 Supreme Court term. Should the interpretation of the Constitution depend upon political circumstances?

Further Reading

Books

Hiltzik, Michael. *The New Deal: A Modern History*. New York: Free Press, 2011.

Kennedy, David M. *Freedom from Fear: The American People in Depression and War, 1929–1945*. New York: Oxford University Press, 1999.

Morris, Charles J. *The Blue Eagle at Work: Reclaiming Democratic Rights in the American Workplace*. Ithaca: ILR Press, 2005.

Witt, Elder, ed. *The Supreme Court and Its Work*. Washington, D.C.: Congressional Quarterly, Inc., 1981.

Articles

Cortner, Richard C. "National Labor Relations Board v. Jones & Laughlin Steel Corp." In *The Oxford Companion to the Supreme Court*, 572–73. New York: Oxford University Press, 1992.

—Commentary by Jonathan Rees

NATIONAL LABOR RELATIONS BOARD V. JONES & LAUGHLIN STEEL CORPORATION

Document Text

MR. CHIEF JUSTICE HUGHES delivered the opinion of the Court

In a proceeding under the National Labor Relations Act of 1935, the National Labor Relations Board found that the respondent, Jones & Laughlin Steel Corporation, had violated the Act by engaging in unfair labor practices affecting commerce. The proceeding was instituted by the Beaver Valley Lodge No. 200, affiliated with the Amalgamated Association of Iron, Steel and Tin Workers of America, a labor organization. The unfair labor practices charged were that the corporation was discriminating against members of the union with regard to hire and tenure of employment, and was coercing and intimidating its employees in order to interfere with their self-organization. The discriminatory and coercive action alleged was the discharge of certain employees.

The National Labor Relations Board, sustaining the charge, ordered the corporation to cease and desist from such discrimination and coercion, to offer reinstatement to ten of the employees named, to make good their losses in pay, and to post for thirty days notices that the corporation would not discharge or discriminate against members, or those desiring to become members, of the labor union. As the corporation failed to comply, the Board petitioned the Circuit Court of Appeals to enforce the order. The court denied the petition, holding that the order lay beyond the range of federal power. 83 F.2d 998. We granted certiorari.

The scheme of the National Labor Relations Act— which is too long to be quoted in full—may be briefly stated. The first section sets forth findings with respect to the injury to commerce resulting from the denial by employers of the right of employees to organize and from the refusal of employers to accept the procedure of collective bargaining. There follows a declaration that it is the policy of the United States to eliminate these causes of obstruction to the free flow of commerce. The Act then defines the terms it uses, including the terms "commerce" and "affecting commerce." § 2. It creates the National Labor Relations Board, and prescribes its organization. §§ 6. It sets forth the right of employees to self-organization and to bargain collectively through representatives of their own choosing. § 7. It defines "unfair labor practices." § 8. It lays down rules as to the representation of employees for the purpose of collective bargaining. § 9. The Board is empowered to prevent the described unfair labor practices affecting commerce and the Act prescribes the procedure to that end. The Board is authorized to petition designated courts to secure the enforcement of its orders. The findings of the Board as to the facts, if supported by evidence, are to be conclusive. If either party, on application to the court, shows that additional evidence is material and that there were reasonable grounds for the failure to adduce such evidence in the hearings before the Board, the court may order the additional evidence to be taken. Any person aggrieved by a final order of the Board may obtain a review in the designated courts with the same procedure as in the case of an application by the Board for the enforcement of its order. § 10. The Board has broad powers of investigation. § 11. Interference with members of the Board or its agents in the performance of their duties is punishable by fine and imprisonment. § 12. Nothing in the Act is to be construed, to interfere with the right to strike. § 13. There is a separability clause to the effect that, if any provision of the Act or its application to any person or circumstances shall be held invalid, the remainder of the Act or its application to other persons or circumstances shall not be affected. § 15. The particular provisions which are involved in the instant case will be considered more in detail in the course of the discussion. The procedure in the instant case followed the statute. The labor union filed with the Board its verified charge.

The Board thereupon issued its complaint against the respondent alleging that its action in discharging the employees in question constituted unfair labor practices affecting commerce within the meaning of § 8, subdivisions (1) and (3), and § 2, subdivisions (6) and (7) of the Act. Respondent, appearing specially for the purpose of objecting to the jurisdiction of the Board, filed its answer. Respondent admitted the discharges, but alleged that they were made because of inefficiency or violation of rule or for other good reasons, and were not ascribable to union membership or activities. As an affirmative defense, respondent challenged the constitutional validity of the statute and its applicability in the instant case. Notice of hearing was given, and respondent appeared by counsel. The Board first took up the issue of jurisdiction, and evidence was presented by both the Board and the respondent. Respondent then moved to dismiss the complaint for lack of jurisdiction, and, on denial of that motion, respondent, in accordance with its special appearance, withdrew from further participation in the hearing. The Board received evidence upon the merits, and, at its close, made its findings and order.

Contesting the ruling of the Board, the respondent argues (1) that the Act is in reality a regulation of labor relations, and not of interstate commerce; (2) that the Act can have no application to the respondent's relations with its production employees, because they are not subject to regulation by the federal government, and (3) that the provisions of the Act violate § 2 of Article III and the Fifth and Seventh Amendments of the Constitution of the United States.

The facts as to the nature and scope of the business of the Jones & Laughlin Steel Corporation have been found by the Labor Board, and, so far as they are essen-

tial to the determination of this controversy, they are not in dispute. The Labor Board has found: the corporation is organized under the laws of Pennsylvania and has its principal office at Pittsburgh. It is engaged in the business of manufacturing iron and steel in plants situated in Pittsburgh and nearby Aliquippa, Pennsylvania. It manufactures and distributes a widely diversified line of steel and pig iron, being the fourth largest producer of steel in the United States. With its subsidiaries—nineteen in number—it is a completely integrated enterprise, owning and operating ore, coal and limestone properties, lake and river transportation facilities, and terminal railroads located at its manufacturing plants. It owns or controls mines in Michigan and Minnesota. It operates four ore steamships on the Great Lakes, used in the transportation of ore to its factories. It owns coal mines in Pennsylvania. It operates towboats and steam barges used in carrying coal to its factories. It owns limestone properties in various places in Pennsylvania and West Virginia. It owns the Monongahela connecting railroad which connects the plants of the Pittsburgh works and forms an interconnection with the Pennsylvania, New York Central, and Baltimore and Ohio Railroad systems. It owns the Aliquippa and Southern Railroad Company, which connects the Aliquippa works with the Pittsburgh and Lake Erie, part of the New York Central system. Much of its product is shipped to its warehouses in Chicago, Detroit, Cincinnati and Memphis—to the last two places by means of its own barges and transportation equipment. In Long Island City, New York, and in New Orleans, it operates structural steel fabricating shops in connection with the warehousing of semi-finished materials sent from its works. Through one of its wholly owned subsidiaries, it owns, leases and operates stores, warehouses and yards for the distribution of equipment and supplies for drilling and operating oil and gas wells and for pipelines, refineries, and pumping stations. It has sales offices in twenty cities in the United States and a wholly owned subsidiary which is devoted exclusively to distributing its product in Canada. Approximately 75 percent. of its product is shipped out of Pennsylvania.

Summarizing these operations, the Labor Board concluded that the works in Pittsburgh and Aliquippa

"might be likened to the heart of a self-contained, highly integrated body. They draw in the raw materials from Michigan, Minnesota, West Virginia, Pennsylvania, in part through arteries and by means controlled by the respondent; they transform the materials and then pump them out to all parts of the nation through the vast mechanism which the respondent has elaborated."

To carry on the activities of the entire steel industry, 33,000 men mine ore, 44,000 men mine coal, 4,000 men quarry limestone, 16,000 men manufacture coke, 343,000 men manufacture steel, and 83,000 men transport its product. Respondent has about 10,000 employees in its Aliquippa plant, which is located in a community of about 30,000 persons.

Respondent points to evidence that the Aliquippa plant, in which the discharged men were employed, contains complete facilities for the production of finished and semi-finished iron and steel products from raw materials; that its works consist primarily of a by-product coke plant for the production of coke; blast furnaces for the production of pig iron; open hearth furnaces and Bessemer converters for the production of steel; blooming mills for the reduction of steel ingots into smaller shapes, and a number of finishing mills such as structural mills, rod mills, wire mills, and the like. In addition, there are other buildings, structures and equipment, storage yards, docks and an intra-plant storage system. Respondent's operations at these works are carried on in two distinct stages, the first being the conversion of raw materials into pig iron and the second being the manufacture of semi-finished and finished iron and steel products, and, in both cases, the operations result in substantially changing the character, utility and value of the materials wrought upon, which is apparent from the nature and extent of the processes to which they are subjected and which respondent fully describes. Respondent also directs attention to the fact that the iron ore which is procured from mines in Minnesota and Michigan and transported to respondent's plant is stored in stockpiles for future use, the amount of ore in storage varying with the season, but usually being enough to maintain operations from nine to ten months; that the coal which is procured from the mines of a subsidiary located in Pennsylvania and taken to the plant at Aliquippa is there, like ore, stored for future use, approximately two to three months' supply of coal being always on hand, and that the limestone which is obtained in Pennsylvania and West Virginia is also stored in amounts usually adequate to run the blast furnaces for a few weeks. Various details of operation, transportation, and distribution are also mentioned which, for the present purpose, it is not necessary to detail.

Practically all the factual evidence in the case, except that which dealt with the nature of respondent's business, concerned its relations with the employees in the Aliquippa plant whose discharge was the subject of the complaint. These employees were active leaders in the labor union. Several were officers, and others were leaders of particular groups. Two of the employees were motor inspectors; one was a tractor driver; three were crane operators; one was a washer in the coke plant, and three were laborers. Three other employees were mentioned in the complaint, but it was withdrawn as to one of them and no evidence was heard on the action taken with respect to the other two.

While respondent criticizes the evidence and the attitude of the Board, which is described as being hostile toward employers and particularly toward those who insisted upon their constitutional rights, respondent did not take advantage of its opportunity to present evidence to refute that which was offered to show discrimination and coercion. In this situation, the record presents no ground for setting aside the order of the Board so far as the facts pertaining to the circumstances and purpose of the discharge of the employees are concerned. Upon that point, it is sufficient to say that the evidence supports the findings of the Board that respondent discharged these men "because of their union activity and for the purpose of discouraging membership in the union." We turn to the questions of law which respondent urges in contesting the validity and application of the Act.

First. The scope of the Act.—The Act is challenged in its entirety as an attempt to regulate all industry, thus invading the reserved powers of the States over their local concerns. It is asserted that the references in the Act to interstate and foreign commerce are colorable, at best; that the Act is not a true regulation of such commerce or of matters which directly affect it, but, on the contrary, has the fundamental object of placing under the compulsory supervision of the federal government all industrial labor relations within the nation. The argument seeks support in the broad words of the preamble (section one) and in the sweep of the provisions of the Act, and it is further insisted that its legislative history shows an essential universal purpose in the light of which its scope cannot be limited by either construction or by the application of the separability clause.

If this conception of terms, intent, and consequent inseparability were sound, the Act would necessarily fall by reason of the limitation upon the federal power which inheres in the constitutional grant, as well as because of the explicit reservation of the Tenth Amendment. *Schechter Corp. v. United States,* 295 U. S. 495, 295 U. S. 549, 295 U. S. 550, 295 U. S. 554. The authority of the federal government may not be pushed to such an extreme as to destroy the distinction, which the commerce clause itself establishes, between commerce "among the several States" and the internal concerns of a State. That distinction between what is national and what is local in the activities of commerce is vital to the maintenance of our federal system. *Id.*

But we are not at liberty to deny effect to specific provisions, which Congress has constitutional power to enact, by superimposing upon them inferences from general legislative declarations of an ambiguous character, even if found in the same statute. The cardinal principle of statutory construction is to save, and not to destroy. We have repeatedly held that, as between two possible interpretations of a statute, by one of which it would be unconstitutional and by the other valid, our plain duty is to adopt that which will save the act. Even to avoid a serious doubt, the rule is the same. *Federal Trade Comm'n v. American Tobacco Co.,* 264 U. S. 298 307; *Panama R. Co. v. Johnson,* 264 U. S. 375, 264 U. S. 390; *Missouri Pacific R. Co. v. Boone,* 270 U. S. 466, 270 U. S. 472; *Blodgett v. Holden,* 275 U. S. 142, 275 U. S. 148; *Richmond Screw Anchor Co. v. United States,* 275 U. S. 331, 275 U. S. 346.

We think it clear that the National Labor Relations Act may be construed so as to operate within the sphere of constitutional authority. The jurisdiction conferred upon the Board, and invoked in this instance, is found in § 10(a), which provides:

"SEC. 10(a). The Board is empowered, as hereinafter provided, to prevent any person from engaging in any unfair labor practice (listed in section 8) affecting commerce. "

The critical words of this provision, prescribing the limits of the Board's authority in dealing with he labor practices, are "affecting commerce." The Act specifically defines the "commerce" to which it refers (§ 2(6)):

"The term 'commerce' means trade, traffic, commerce, transportation, or communication among the several States, or between the District of Columbia or any Territory of the United States and any State or other Territory, or between any foreign country and any State, Territory, or the District of Columbia, or within the District of Columbia or any Territory, or between points in the same State but through any other State or any Territory or the District of Columbia or any foreign country."

There can be no question that the commerce thus contemplated by the Act (aside from that within a Territory or the District of Columbia) is interstate and foreign commerce in the constitutional sense. The Act also defines the term "affecting commerce" (§ 2(7)):

"The term 'affecting commerce' means in commerce, or burdening or obstructing commerce or the free flow of commerce, or having led or tending to lead to a labor dispute burdening or obstructing commerce or the free flow of commerce."

This definition is one of exclusion as well as inclusion. The grant of authority to the Board does not purport to extend to the relationship between all industrial employees and employers. Its terms do not impose collective bargaining upon all industry regardless of effects upon interstate or foreign commerce. It purports to reach only what may be deemed to burden or obstruct that commerce, and, thus qualified, it must be construed as contemplating the exercise of control within constitutional bounds. It is a familiar principle that acts which directly burden or obstruct interstate or foreign commerce, or its free flow, are within the reach of the congressional power. Acts having that effect are not rendered immune because they grow out of labor disputes. *See Texas & N.O. R . Co. v. Railway Clerks,* 281 U. S. 548, 281 U. S. 570; *Schechter Corp. v. United States, supra,* pp. 295 U. S. 544, 295 U. S. 545; *Virginian Railway v. System Federation, No. 40,* 300 U. S. 515. It is the effect upon commerce, not the source of the injury, which is the criterion. *Second Employers' Liability Cases,* 223 U. S. 1, 223 U. S. 51. Whether or not particular action does affect commerce in such a close and intimate fashion as to be subject to federal control, and hence to lie within the authority conferred upon the Board, is left by the statute to be determined as individual cases arise. We are thus to inquire whether, in the instant case, the constitutional boundary has been passed.

Second. The fair labor practices in question.—The unfair labor practices found by the Board are those defined in § 8, subdivisions (1) and (3). These provide:

"Sec. 8. It shall be an unfair labor practice for an employer --"

"(1) To interfere with, restrain, or coerce employees in the exercise of the rights guaranteed in section 7."

"(3) By discrimination in regard to hire or tenure of employment or any term or condition of employment to encourage or discourage membership in any labor organization.... "

Section 8, subdivision (1), refers to § 7, which is as follows:

"Sec. 7. Employees shall have the right to self-organization, to form, join, or assist labor organizations, to bargain collectively through representatives of their own choosing, and to engage in concerted activities, for the purpose of collective bargaining or other mutual aid or protection."

Thus, in its present application, the statute goes no further than to safeguard the right of employees to self-organization and to select representatives of their own choosing for collective bargaining or other mutual protection without restraint or coercion by their employer.

That is a fundamental right. Employees have as clear a right to organize and select their representatives for lawful purposes as the respondent has to organize its business and select its own officers and agents. Discrimination and coercion to prevent the free exercise of the right of employees to self-organization and representation is a proper subject for condemnation by competent legislative authority. Long ago we stated the reason for labor organizations. We said that they were organized out of the necessities of the situation; that a single employee was helpless in dealing with an employer; that he was dependent ordinarily on his daily wage for the maintenance of himself and family; that, if the employer refused to pay him the wages that he thought fair, he was nevertheless unable to leave the employ and resist arbitrary and unfair treatment; that union was essential to give laborers opportunity to deal on an equality with their employer. *American Steel Foundries v. Tri-City Central Trades Council,* 257 U. S. 184, 257 U. S. 209. We reiterated these views when we had under consideration the Railway Labor Act of 1926. Fully recognizing the legality of collective action on the part of employees in order to safeguard their proper interests, we said that Congress was not required to ignore this right, but could

safeguard it. Congress could seek to make appropriate collective action of employees an instrument of peace, rather than of strife. We said that such collective action would be a mockery if representation were made futile by interference with freedom of choice. Hence, the prohibition by Congress of interference with the selection of representatives for the purpose of negotiation and conference between employers and employees, "instead of being an invasion of the constitutional right of either, was based on the recognition of the rights of both." *Texas & N.O. R. Co. v. Railway Clerks, supra.* We have reasserted the same principle in sustaining the application of the Railway Labor Act as amended in 1934. *Virginian Railway Co. v. System Federation, No. 40, supra.*

Third. The application of the Act to employees engaged in production.—The principle involved.—Respondent says that whatever may be said of employees engaged in interstate commerce, the industrial relations and activities in the manufacturing department of respondent's enterprise are not subject to federal regulation. The argument rests upon the proposition that manufacturing, in itself, is not commerce. *Kidd v. Pearson,* 128 U. S. 1, 128 U. S. 20, 21; *United Mine Workers v. Coronado Coal Co.,* 259 U. S. 344, 259 U. S. 407, 259 U. S. 408; *Oliver Iron Co. v. Lord,* 262 U. S. 172, 262 U. S. 178; *United Leather Workers v. Herkert & Meisel Trunk Co.,* 265 U. S. 457, 265 U. S. 465; *Industrial Association v. United States,* 268 U. S. 64, 268 U. S. 82; *Coronado Coal Co. v. United Mine Workers,* 268 U. S. 295, 268 U. S. 310; *Schechter Corp. v. United States, supra,* p. 295 U. S. 547; *Carter v. Carter Coal Co.,* 298 U. S. 238, 298 U. S. 304, 298 U. S. 317, 298 U. S. 327.

The Government distinguishes these cases. The various parts of respondent's enterprise are described as interdependent and as thus involving "a great movement of iron ore, coal and limestone along well defined paths to the steel mills, thence through them, and thence in the form of steel products into the consuming centers of the country—a definite and well understood course of business." It is urged that these activities constitute a "stream" or "flow" of commerce, of which the Aliquippa manufacturing plant is the focal point, and that industrial strife at that point would cripple the entire movement. Reference is made to our decision sustaining the Packers and Stockyards Act. *Stafford v. Wallace,* 258 U. S. 495. The Court found that the stockyards were but a "throat" through which the current of Commerce flowed and the transactions which there occurred could not be separated from that movement.

Hence, the sales at the stockyards were not regarded as merely local transactions, for, while they created "a local change of title," they did not "stop the flow," but merely changed the private interests in the subject of the current. Distinguishing the cases which upheld the power of the State to impose a nondiscriminatory tax upon property which the owner intended to transport to another State, but which was not in actual transit and was held within the State subject to the disposition of the owner, the Court remarked:

"The question, it should be observed, is not with respect to the extent of the power of Congress to regulate interstate commerce, but whether a particular exercise of state power in view of its nature and operation must be deemed to be in conflict with this paramount authority."

Id., p. 258 U. S. 526. *See Minnesota v. Blasius,* 290 U. S. 1, 290 U. S. 8. Applying the doctrine of *Stafford v. Wallace, supra,* the Court sustained the Grain Futures Act of 1922 with respect to transactions on the Chicago Board of Trade, although these transactions were "not in and of themselves interstate commerce." Congress had found that they had become "a constantly recurring burden and obstruction to that commerce." *Chicago Board of Trade v. Olsen,* 262 U. S. 1, 262 U. S. 32; *compare Hill v. Wallace,* 259 U. S. 44, 259 U. S. 69. *See also Tagg Bros. & Moorhead v. United States,* 280 U. S. 420.

Respondent contends that the instant case presents material distinctions. Respondent says that the Aliquippa plant is extensive in size and represents a large investment in buildings, machinery and equipment. The raw materials which are brought to the plant are delayed for long periods and, after being subjected to manufacturing processes, "are changed substantially as to character, utility and value." The finished products which emerge

"are to a large extent manufactured without reference to preexisting orders and contracts, and are entirely different from the raw materials which enter at the other end."

Hence, respondent argues that,

"If importation and exportation in interstate commerce do not singly transfer purely local activities into the field of congressional regulation, it should follow that their combination would not alter the local situation."

Arkadelphia Milling Co. v. St. Louis Southwestern Ry. Co., 249 U. S. 134, 249 U. S. 151; *Oliver Iron Co. v. Lord, supra.*

We do not find it necessary to determine whether these features of defendant's business dispose of the asserted analogy to the "stream of commerce" cases. The instances in which that metaphor has been used are but particular, and not exclusive, illustrations of the protective power which the Government invokes in support of the present Act. The congressional authority to protect interstate commerce from burdens and obstructions is not limited to transactions which can be deemed to be an essential part of a "flow" of interstate or foreign commerce. Burdens and obstructions may be due to injurious action springing from other sources. The fundamental principle is that the power to regulate commerce is the power to enact "all appropriate legislation" for "its protection and advancement" (*The Daniel Ball,* 10 Wall. 557, 77 U. S. 564); to adopt measures "to promote its growth and insure its safety" (*Mobile County v. Kimball,* 102 U. S. 691, 102 U. S. 696, 102 U. S. 697); "to foster, protect, control and restrain." *Second Employers' Liability Cases, supra,* p. 223 U. S. 47. *See Texas & N.O. R. Co. v. Railway Clerks, supra.* That power is plenary, and may be exerted to protect interstate commerce "no matter what the source of the dangers which threaten it." *Second Employers' Liability Cases,* p. 223 U. S. 51; *Schechter Corp. v. United States, supra.* Although activities may be intrastate in character when separately considered, if they have such a close and substantial relation to interstate commerce that their control is essential or appropriate to protect that commerce from burdens and obstructions, Congress cannot be denied the power to exercise that control. *Schechter Corp. v. United States, supra.* Undoubtedly the scope of this power must be considered in the light of our dual system of government, and may not be extended so as to embrace effects upon interstate commerce so indirect and remote that to embrace them, in view of our complex society, would effectually obliterate the distinction between what is national and what is local and create a completely centralized government. *Id.* The question is necessarily one of degree. As the Court said in *Chicago Board of Trade v. Olsen, supra,* p. 262 U. S. 37, repeating what had been said in *Stafford v. Wallace, supra:*

"Whatever amounts to more or less constant practice, and threatens to obstruct or unduly to burden the freedom of interstate commerce is within the regulatory power of Congress under the commerce clause and it is primarily for Congress to consider and decide the fact of the danger and meet it."

That intrastate activities, by reason of close and intimate relation to interstate commerce, may fall within federal control is demonstrated in the case of carriers who are engaged in both interstate and intrastate transportation. There federal control has been found essential to secure the freedom of interstate traffic from interference or unjust discrimination and to promote the efficiency of the interstate service. *Shreveport Case,* 234 U. S. 342, 234 U. S. 351, 234 U. S. 352; *Wisconsin Railroad Comm'n v. Chicago, B. & Q. R. Co.,* 257 U. S. 563, 257 U. S. 588. It is manifest that intrastate rates deal primarily with a local activity. But, in ratemaking, they bear such a close relation to interstate rates that effective control of the one must embrace some control over the other. *Id.* Under the Transportation Act, 1920, Congress went so far as to authorize the Interstate Commerce Commission to establish a statewide level of intrastate rates in order to prevent an unjust discrimination against interstate commerce. *Wisconsin Railroad Comm'n v. Chicago, B. & Q. R. Co., supra; Florida v. United States,* 282 U. S. 194, 282 U. S. 210, 282 U. S. 211. Other illustrations are found in the broad requirements of the Safety Appliance Act and the Hours of Service Act. *Southern Railway Co. v. United States,* 222 U. S. 20; *Baltimore & Ohio R. Co. v. Interstate Commerce Comm'n,* 221 U. S. 612. It is said that this exercise of federal power has relation to the maintenance of adequate instrumentalities of interstate commerce. But the agency is not superior to the commerce which uses it. The protective power extends to the former because it exists as to the latter.

The close and intimate effect which brings the subject within the reach of federal power may be due to activities in relation to productive industry although the industry, when separately viewed, is local. This has been abundantly illustrated in the application of the federal Anti-Trust Act. In the *Standard Oil* and *American Tobacco* cases, 221 U. S. 221 U.S. 1, 221 U. S. 106, that statute was applied to combinations of employers engaged in productive industry.

Counsel for the offending corporations strongly urged that the Sherman Act had no application because the acts complained of were not acts of interstate or foreign commerce, nor direct and immediate in their effect on interstate or foreign commerce, but primarily affected manufacturing and not commerce. 221 U.S. pp. 5, 125 [argument of counsel omitted in electronic version]. Counsel relied upon the decision in *United States v. Knight Co.,* 156 U. S. 1. The Court stated their contention as follows:

"That the act, even if the averments of the bill be true, cannot be constitutionally applied, because to do so would extend the power of Congress to subjects *dehors* the reach of its authority to regulate commerce, by enabling that body to deal with mere questions of production of commodities within the States."

And the Court summarily dismissed the contention in these words:

"But all the structure upon which this argument proceeds is based upon the decision in *United States v. E. C. Knight Co.,* 156 U. S. 1. The view, however, which the argument takes of that case and the arguments based upon that view have been so repeatedly pressed upon this court in connection with the interpretation and enforcement of the Anti-trust Act, and have been so necessarily and expressly decided to be unsound as to cause the contentions to be plainly foreclosed and to require no express notice"

(citing cases). 221 U.S. pp. 221 U. S. 68, 221 U. S. 69.

Upon the same principle, the Anti-Trust Act has been applied to the conduct of employees engaged in production. *Loewe v. Lawlor,* 208 U. S. 274; *Coronado Coal Co. v. United Mine Workers, supra; Bedford Cut Stone Co. v. Stone Cutters' Assn.,* 274 U. S. 37. *See also Local 16 v. United States,* 291 U. S. 293, 291 U. S. 397; *Schechter Corp. v. United States, supra.* The decisions dealing with the question of that application illustrate both the principle and its limitation. Thus, in the first *Coronado* case, the Court held that mining was not interstate commerce, that the power of Congress did not extend to its regulation as such, and that it had not been shown that the activities there involved—a local strike—brought them within the provisions of the Anti-Trust Act, notwithstanding the broad terms of that statute. A similar conclusion was reached in *United Leather Workers v. Herkert & Meisel Trunk Co., supra, Industrial Association v. United States, supra, and Levering & Garrigues Co. v. Morrin,* 289 U. S. 103, 289 U. S. 107. But, in the first *Coronado* case, the Court also said that "if Congress deems certain recurring practices, though not really part of interstate commerce, likely to obstruct, restrain or burden it, it has the power to subject them to national supervision and restraint."

259 U.S. p. 259 U. S. 408. And, in the second *Coronado* case, the Court ruled that, while the mere reduction in the supply of an article to be shipped in interstate commerce by the illegal or tortious prevention of its manufacture or production is ordinarily an indirect and remote obstruction to that commerce, nevertheless when the

"intent of those unlawfully preventing the manufacture or production is shown to be to restrain or control the supply entering and moving in interstate commerce, or the price of it in interstate markets, their action is a direct violation of the Anti-Trust Act."

268 U.S. p. 268 U. S. 310. And the existence of that intent may be a necessary inference from proof of the direct and substantial effect produced by the employees' conduct. *Industrial Association v. United States,* 268 U.S. p. 268 U. S. 81. What was absent from the evidence in the first *Coronado* case appeared in the second, and the Act was accordingly applied to the mining employees.

It is thus apparent that the fact that the employees here concerned were engaged in production is not determinative. The question remains as to the effect upon interstate commerce of the labor practice involved. In the *Schechter case, supra,* we found that the effect there was so remote as to be beyond the federal power. To find "immediacy or directness" there was to find it "almost everywhere," a result inconsistent with the maintenance of our federal system. In the *Carter* case, *supra,* the Court was of the opinion that the provisions of the statute relating to production were invalid upon several grounds—that there was improper delegation of legislative power, and that the requirements not only went beyond any sustainable measure of protection of interstate commerce, but were also inconsistent with due process. These cases are not controlling here.

Fourth. Effects of the unfair labor practice in respondent's enterprise.—Giving full weight to respondent's contention with respect to a break in the complete continuity of the "stream of commerce" by reason of respondent's manufacturing operations, the fact remains that the stoppage of those operations by industrial strife would have a most serious effect upon interstate commerce. In view of respondent's far-flung activities, it is idle to say that the effect would be indirect or remote. It is obvious that it would be immediate, and might be catastrophic. We are asked to shut our eyes to the plainest facts of our national life, and to deal with the question of direct and indirect effects in an intellectual vacuum. Because there may be but indirect and remote effects upon interstate commerce in connection with a host of local enterprises throughout the country, it does not follow that other industrial activities do not have such a close and intimate relation to interstate commerce as to make the presence of industrial strife a matter of the most urgent national concern. When industries organize themselves on a national scale, making their relation to interstate commerce the dominant factor in their activities, how can it be maintained that their industrial labor relations constitute a forbidden field into which Congress may not enter when it is necessary to protect interstate commerce from the paralyzing consequences of industrial war? We have often said that interstate commerce itself is a practical conception. It is equally true that interferences with that commerce must be appraised by a judgment that does not ignore actual experience.

Experience has abundantly demonstrated that the recognition of the right of employees to self-organization and to have representatives of their own choosing for the purpose of collective bargaining is often an essential condition of industrial peace. Refusal to confer and negotiate has been one of the most prolific causes of strife. This is such an outstanding fact in the history of labor disturbances that it is a proper subject of judicial notice, and requires no citation of instances. The opinion in the case of *Virginian Railway Co. v. System Federation, No. 40, supra,* points out that, in the case of carriers, experience has shown that, before the amendment of 1934 of the Railway Labor Act,

"when there was no dispute as to the organizations authorized to represent the employees and when there was a willingness of the employer to meet such representative for a discussion of their grievances, amicable adjustment of differences had generally followed, and strikes had been avoided."

That, on the other hand,

"a prolific source of dispute had been the maintenance by the railroad of company unions and the denial by railway management of the authority of representatives chosen by their employees."

The opinion in that case also points to the large measure of success of the labor policy embodied in the Railway Labor Act. But, with respect to the appropriateness of the recognition of self-organization and representation in the promotion of peace, the question is not essentially different in the case of employees in industries of such a character that interstate commerce is put in jeopardy from the case of employees of transportation companies. And of what avail is it to protect the facility of transportation if interstate commerce is throttled with respect to the commodities to be transported!

These questions have frequently engaged the attention of Congress, and have been the subject of many inquiries. The steel industry is one of the great basic industries of the United States, with ramifying activities affecting interstate commerce at every point. The Government aptly refers to the steel strike of 1919-1920, with its far-reaching consequences. The fact that there appears to have been no major disturbance in that industry in the more recent period did not dispose of the possibilities of future and like dangers to interstate commerce which Congress was entitled to foresee and to exercise its protective power to forestall. It is not necessary again to detail the facts as to respondent's enterprise. Instead of being beyond the pale, we think that it presents in a most striking way the close and intimate relation which a manufacturing industry may have to interstate commerce, and we have no doubt that Congress had constitutional authority to safeguard the right of respondent's employees to self-organization and freedom in the choice of representatives for collective bargaining.

Fifth. The means which the Act employs.—Questions under the due process clause and other constitutional restrictions.—Respondent asserts its right to conduct its business in an orderly manner without being subjected to arbitrary restraints. What we have said points to the fallacy in the argument. Employees have their correlative right to organize for the purpose of securing the redress of grievances and to promote agreements with employers relating to rates of pay and conditions of work. *Texas & N.O. R. Co. v. Railway Clerks, supra; Virginian Railway Co. v. System Federation, No. 40.* Restraint for the purpose of preventing an unjust interference with that right cannot be considered arbitrary

or capricious. The provision of § 9(a) that representatives, for the purpose of collective bargaining, of the majority of the employees in an appropriate unit shall be the exclusive representatives of all the employees in that unit imposes upon the respondent only the duty of conferring and negotiating with the authorized representatives of its employees for the purpose of settling a labor dispute. This provision has its analogue in § 2, Ninth, of the Railway Labor Act, which was under consideration in *Virginian Railway Co. v. System Federation, No. 40, supra.* The decree which we affirmed in that case required the Railway Company to treat with the representative chosen by the employees and also to refrain from entering into collective labor agreements with anyone other than their true representative as ascertained in accordance with the provisions of the Act. We said that the obligation to treat with the true representative was exclusive, and hence imposed the negative duty to treat with no other. We also pointed out that, as conceded by the Government, the injunction against the Company's entering into any contract concerning rules, rates of pay and working conditions except with a chosen representative was "designed only to prevent collective bargaining with anyone purporting to represent employees" other than the representative they had selected. It was taken "to prohibit the negotiation of labor contracts generally applicable to employees" in the described unit with any other representative than the one so chosen, "but not as precluding such individual contracts" as the Company might "elect to make directly with individual employees." We think this construction also applies to § 9(a) of the National Labor Relations Act.

The Act does not compel agreements between employers and employees. It does not compel any agreement whatever. It does not prevent the employer "from refusing to make a collective contract and hiring individuals on whatever terms" the employer "may by unilateral action determine." The Act expressly provides in § 9(a) that any individual employee or a group of employees shall have the right at any time to present grievances to their employer. The theory of the Act is that free opportunity for negotiation with accredited representatives of employees is likely to promote industrial peace, and may bring about the adjustments and agreements which the Act, in itself, does not attempt to compel. As we said in *Texas & N.O. R. Co. v. Railway Clerks, supra,* and repeated in *Virginian Rail-*

way Co. v. System Federation, No. 40, supra, the cases of *Adair v. United States,* 208 U. S. 161, and *Coppage v. Kansas,* 236 U. S. 1, are inapplicable to legislation of this character. The Act does not interfere with the normal exercise of the right of the employer to select its employees or to discharge them. The employer may not, under cover of that right, intimidate or coerce its employees with respect to their self-organization and representation, and, on the other hand, the Board is not entitled to make its authority a pretext for interference with the right of discharge when that right is exercised for other reasons than such intimidation and coercion. The true purpose is the subject of investigation with full opportunity to show the facts. It would seem that, when employers freely recognize the right of their employees to their own organizations and their unrestricted right of representation, there will be much less occasion for controversy in respect to the free and appropriate exercise of the right of selection and discharge.

The Act has been criticized as one-sided in its application; that it subjects the employer to supervision and restraint and leaves untouched the abuses for which employees may be responsible; that it fails to provide a more comprehensive plan—with better assurances of fairness to both sides and with increased chances of success in bringing about, if not compelling, equitable solutions of industrial disputes affecting interstate commerce. But we are dealing with the power of Congress, not with a particular policy or with the extent to which policy should go. We have frequently said that the legislative authority, exerted within its proper field, need not embrace all the evils within its reach. The Constitution does not forbid "cautious advance, step by step," in dealing with the evils which are exhibited in activities within the range of legislative power. *Carroll v. Greenwich Insurance Co.,* 199 U. S. 401, 199 U. S. 411; *Keokee Coke Co. v. Taylor,* 234 U. S. 224, 234 U. S. 227; *Miller v. Wilson,* 236 U. S. 373, 236 U. S. 384; *Sproles v. Binford,* 286 U. S. 374, 286 U. S. 396. The question in such cases is whether the legislature, in what it does prescribe, has gone beyond constitutional limits.

The procedural provisions of the Act are assailed. But these provisions, as we construe them, do not offend against the constitutional requirements governing the creation and action of administrative bodies. *See Interstate Commerce Comm'n v. Louisville & Nashville R. Co.,* 227 U. S. 88, 227 U. S. 91. The Act establishes standards to which the Board must conform. There must be complaint, notice and hearing. The Board must receive evidence and make findings. The findings as to the facts are to be conclusive, but only if supported by evidence. The order of the Board is subject to review by the designated court, and only when sustained by the court may the order be enforced. Upon that review, all questions of the jurisdiction of the Board and the regularity of its proceedings, all questions of constitutional right or statutory authority, are open to examination by the court. We construe the procedural provisions as affording adequate opportunity to secure judicial protection against arbitrary action in accordance with the well settled rules applicable to administrative agencies set up by Congress to aid in the enforcement of valid legislation. It is not necessary to repeat these rules which have frequently been declared. None of them appears to have been transgressed in the instant case. Respondent was notified and heard. It had opportunity to meet the charge of unfair labor practices upon the merits, and, by withdrawing from the hearing, it declined to avail itself of that opportunity. The facts found by the Board support its order, and the evidence supports the findings. Respondent has no just ground for complaint on this score.

The order of the Board required the reinstatement of the employees who were found to have been discharged because of their "union activity" and for the purpose of "discouraging membership in the union." That requirement was authorized by the Act. § 10(c). In *Texas & N.O. R. Co. v. Railway Clerks, supra,* a similar order for restoration to service was made by the court in contempt proceedings for the violation of an injunction issued by the court to restrain an interference with the right of employees as guaranteed by the Railway Labor Act of 1926. The requirement of restoration to service of employees discharged in violation of the provisions of that Act was thus a sanction imposed in the enforcement of a judicial decree. We do not doubt that Congress could impose a like sanction for the enforcement of its valid regulation. The fact that, in the one case, it was a judicial sanction, and, in the other, a legislative one, is not an essential difference in determining its propriety.

Respondent complains that the Board not only ordered reinstatement but directed the payment of wages for the time lost by the discharge, less amounts earned by the employee during that period. This part of the order was also authorized by the Act. § 10(c). It is argued that the requirement is equivalent to a money judgment and hence contravenes the Seventh Amendment with respect to trial by jury. The Seventh Amendment provides that, "In suits at common law, where the value in controversy shall exceed twenty dollars, the right of trial by jury shall be preserved." The Amendment thus preserves the right which existed under the common law when the Amendment was adopted. *Shields v. Thomas,* 18 How. 253, 59 U. S. 262; *In re Wood,* 210 U. S. 246, 210 U. S. 258; *Dimick v. Schiedt,* 293 U. S. 474, 293 U. S. 476; *Baltimore & Carolina Line v. Redman,* 295 U. S. 654, 295 U. S. 657. Thus, it has no application to cases where recovery of money damages is an incident to equitable relief even though damages might have been recovered in an action at law. *Clark v. Wooster,* 119 U. S. 322, 119 U. S. 325; *Pease v. Rathbun-Jones Engineering Co.,* 243 U. S. 273, 243 U. S. 279. It does not apply where the proceeding is not in the nature of a suit at common law. *Guthrie National Bank v. Guthrie,* 173 U. S. 528, 173 U. S. 537.

The instant case is not a suit at common law or in the nature of such a suit. The proceeding is one unknown to the common law. It is a statutory proceeding. Reinstatement of the employee and payment for time lost are requirements imposed for violation of the statute, and are remedies appropriate to its enforcement. The contention under the Seventh Amendment is without merit.

Our conclusion is that the order of the Board was within its competency, and that the Act is valid as here applied. The judgment of the Circuit Court of Appeals is reversed, and the cause is remanded for further proceedings in conformity with this opinion.

Reversed.

MR. JUSTICE McREYNOLDS delivered the following dissenting opinion

MR. JUSTICE VAN DEVANTER, MR. JUSTICE SUTHERLAND, MR. JUSTICE BUTLER, and I are unable to agree with the decisions just announced.

We conclude that these causes were rightly decided by the three Circuit Courts of Appeals, and that their judgments should be affirmed. The opinions there given without dissent are terse, well considered, and sound. They disclose the meaning ascribed by experienced judges to what this Court has often declared, and are set out below in full.

Considering the far-reaching import of these decisions, the departure from what we understand has been consistently ruled here, and the extraordinary power confirmed to a Board of three, the obligation to present our views becomes plain.

The Court, as we think, departs from well established principles followed in *Schechter Poultry Corp. v. United States,* 295 U. S. 495 (May, 1935), and *Carter v. Carter Coal Co.,* 298 U. S. 238 (May, 1936). Upon the authority of those decisions, the Circuit Courts of Appeals of the Fifth, Sixth, and Second Circuits in the causes now before us have held the power of Congress under the commerce clause does not extend to relations between employers and their employees engaged in manufacture, and therefore the Act conferred upon the National Labor Relations Board no authority in respect of matters covered by the questioned orders. In *Foster Bros. Mfg. Co. v. Labor Board,* 85 F.2d 984, the Circuit Court of Appeals, Fourth Circuit, held the act inapplicable to manufacture, and expressed the view that, if so extended, it would be invalid. Six District Courts, on the authority of *Schechter's* and *Carter's* cases, have held that the Board has no authority to regulate relations between employers and employees engaged in local production. No decision or judicial opinion to the contrary has been cited, and we find none. Every consideration brought forward to uphold the act before us was applicable to support the acts held unconstitutional in causes decided within two years. And the lower courts rightly deemed them controlling.

By its terms, the Labor Act extends to employers, large and small, unless excluded by definition, and declares that if one of these interferes with, restrains, or coerces any employee regarding his labor affiliations, etc., this shall be regarded as unfair labor practice. And a "labor organization" means any organization of any kind or any agency or employee representation committee or plan which exists for the purpose in whole or in part of dealing with employers concerning grievances, labor disputes, wages, rates of pay, hours of employment, or conditions of work.

The three respondents happen to be manufacturing concerns—one large, two relatively small. The act is now applied to each upon grounds common to all. Obviously what is determined as to these concerns may gravely affect a multitude of employers who engage in a great variety of private enterprises—mercantile, manufacturing, publishing, stock-raising, mining, etc. It puts into the hands of a Board power of control over purely local industry beyond anything heretofore deemed permissible.

II

[No. 419] Circuit Court of Appeals (Fifth Circuit)

Opinion June 15, 1936, 83 F.2d 998

Before Foster, Sibley, and Hutcheson, Circuit Judges.

"Per Curiam."

"The National Labor Relations Board has petitioned us to enforce an order made by it, which requires Jones & Laughlin Steel Corporation, organized under the laws of Pennsylvania, to reinstate certain discharged employees in its steel plant in Aliquippa, Pa. and to do other things in that connection."

"The petition must be denied, because, under the facts found by the Board and shown by the evidence, the Board has no jurisdiction over a labor dispute between employer and employees touching the discharge of laborers in a steel plant, who were engaged only in manufacture. The Constitution does not vest in the Federal Government the power to regulate the relation as such of employer and employee in production or manufacture."

"One who produces or manufactures a commodity, subsequently sold and shipped by him in interstate commerce, whether such sale and shipment were originally intended or not, has engaged in two distinct and separate activities. So far as he produces or manufactures a commodity, his business is purely local. So far as he sells and ships, or contracts to sell and ship, the commodity to customers in another state, he engages in interstate commerce. In respect of the former, he is subject only to regulation by the state; in respect of the latter, to regulation only by the federal government. *Utah Power & L. Co. v. Pfost,* 286 U. S. 165, 286 U. S. 182. Production is not commerce, but a step in preparation for commerce. *Chassaniol v. Greenwood,* 291 U. S. 584, 291 U. S. 587."

"We have seen that the word 'commerce' is the equivalent of the phrase 'intercourse for the purposes of trade.'

Plainly, the incidents leading up to and culminating in the mining of coal do not constitute such intercourse. The employment of men, the fixing of their wages, hours of labor, and working conditions, the bargaining in respect of these things, whether carried on separately or collectively, each and all constitute intercourse for the purposes of production, not of trade. The latter is a thing apart from the relation of employer and employee, which, in all producing occupations, is purely local in character. Extraction of coal from the mine is the aim and the completed result of local activities. Commerce in the coal mined is not brought into being by force of these activities, but by negotiations, agreements, and circumstances entirely apart from production. Mining brings the subject matter of commerce into existence. Commerce disposes of it."

"*Carter v. Carter Coal Company,* 298 U. S. 238, decided May 18, 1936."

"That the employer has a very large business, the interruption of which by a strike of employees which might happen, and that, in consequence of such strike, production might be stopped and interstate commerce in the products affected, does not make the regulation of the relation justified under the commerce power of Congress, because the possible effect on interstate commerce is too remote to warrant Federal invasion of the state's right to regulate the employer-employee relation. Nor is it important that the employer imports part of his raw materials in interstate commerce and sells and exports a large part of his product in interstate commerce, which imports and exports would possibly be stopped by a possible strike. The employers' entire business thus connected together does not, as respects federal power, make a case different from that in which importation of materials, manufacture of them, and sale and export of the product are conducted by three persons. The employer here, by doing all three things, does not alter the respective constitutional spheres of the federal and state governments. The making and fabrication of steel by Jones & Laughlin Steel Corporation is production regulable by the state of Pennsylvania, notwithstanding the corporation also engages in interstate commerce regulable by Congress in bringing in its raw materials, and again in selling and delivering its products. No specific present intent appears to impede or destroy interstate commerce by means of a strike in a manufacturing plant, or other like direct obstruction to or burden on interstate commerce. The order we are asked to enforce is not shown to be one authorized to be made under the authority of Congress. *Carter v. Carter Coal Co., supra.*"

"The petition is denied."

III

[Nos. 420-421] Circuit Court of Appeals (Sixth Circuit)

Opinion June 30, 1936, 85 F.2d 391

Before Moorman, Hicks, and Simons, Circuit Judges

"Per Curiam."

"The National Labor Relations Board has filed a petition in this Court to enforce an order issued by it in proceedings which it instituted against the Fruehauf Trailer Company. The order directs the Trailer Company to cease and desist from discharging or threatening to discharge any of its employees because of their activities in connection with the United Automobile Workers Federal Labor Union No. 19,375 to cease discouraging its employees from becoming members of that union, to offer to certain of its former employees immediate and full reinstatement in their former positions without prejudice to their seniority rights, to make such employees whole for any losses of pay that they have suffered by reason of their discharge by paying them what they would have earned as wages from the dates of their discharges, and to post notices throughout its Detroit plant, in conspicuous places, stating that it has ceased and desisted from discharging or threatening to discharge its employees for joining the United Automobile Workers Federal Labor Union No.19,375. The Fruehauf Trailer Company has filed its petition seeking a review of the order and praying that the court set it aside. The record of the proceeding before the Labor Board has been filed, and the two petitions have been heard together in this court."

"The Fruehauf Trailer Company is a corporation organized and existing under the laws of the state of Michigan, and is engaged in the manufacture, assembly, and sale of automobile trailers at its plant in Detroit, Mich. The material and parts used in the manufacture and production of the trailers are shipped to the plant. After the trailers are manufactured, many of them are shipped to other states for sale and use. The order in question undertakes to regulate and control the Trailer Company's relations and dealings with its employees engaged in the production and manufacture of trailers at the company's plant in Detroit, and does not directly affect any of the activities of the Trailer Company in the purchasing and transporting to its plant of materials and parts for the manufacture and production of trailers or in the shipping or selling of such trailers after they are manufactured. It was issued under the authority of the Act of Congress of July 5, 1935, known as the National Labor Relations Act. The authority for the act is claimed under the commerce clause of the Constitution. Since the order is directed to the control and regulation of the relations between the Trailer Company and its employees in respect to their activities in the manufacture and production of trailers, and does not directly affect any phase of any interstate commerce in which the Trailer Company may be engaged, and since, under the ruling of *Carter v. Carter Coal Company,* 298 U. S. 238, the Congress has no authority or power to regulate or control such relations between the Trailer Company and its employees, the National Labor Relations Board was without authority to issue the order. *See Labor Board v. Jones & Laughlin Steel Corporation,* 83 F.2d 998, decided June 15, 1936."

"The petition of the Board is accordingly dismissed, and the order is set aside."

IV

[Nos. 422-423] Circuit Court of Appeals (Second Circuit)

Opinion July 13, 1936, 85 F.2d 1

Before Manton, Swan, and A.N. Hand, Circuit Judges.

"Per Curiam."

"The respondent, a Virginia corporation, is a manufacturer of men's clothing with its principal office and its factory in Richmond, Va. Practically all the raw materials used are brought from other states into Virginia, where respondent manufactures them into men's clothing. About 83 percent of the manufactured products are sold f.o.b. Richmond, to customers located in states other than Virginia."

"Two sets of charges were filed with petitioner's local regional director by the Amalgamated Clothing Workers of America, a labor union of workers in the men's clothing industry, in which it was alleged that the respondent violated the National Labor Relations Act by discharging from its employ, and discriminating against 29 out of 800 of its employees, because they had engaged in union activities. The Board filed complaints under § 10(b) of the Act, and, after a hearing, respondent was found to have violated the act and was ordered to cease and desist from the unfair labor practices."

"Petitioner's theory is that the respondent is engaged in interstate commerce because of the shipment of raw materials to it from other states and the shipment of its finished products to other states, and, in addition, that the flow of commerce doctrine, as exemplified in *Swift & Co. v. United States,* 196 U. S. 375, brings this manufacturer within the federal power to regulate commerce. Respondent contends that the National Labor Relations Act, as applied to it, is unconstitutional and therefore invalid, and that the attempt to enforce its provisions against it is illegal."

"It is shown that the alleged unfair labor practices complained of occurred in the manufacture of clothing in Richmond, Va. None of the workers involved had to do with the transportation of the clothing after its manufacture. They were engaged in various operations in the Richmond factory."

"The relations between the employer and its employees in this manufacturing industry were merely incidents of production. In its manufacturing, respondent was in no way engaged in interstate commerce, nor did its labor practices so directly affect interstate commerce as to come within the federal commerce power. *Carter v. Carter Coal Co.,* 298 U. S. 238; *Schechter Poultry Corp. v. United States,* 295 U. S. 495. No authority warrants the conclusion that the powers of the Federal Government permit the regulation of the dealings between employers or employees when engaged in the purely local business of manufacture."

"Therefore, the orders to cease and desist may not be enforced."

"Petitions denied."

V

In each cause, the Labor Board formulated and then sustained a charge of unfair labor practices towards persons employed only in production. It ordered restoration of discharged employees to former positions with payment for losses sustained. These orders were declared invalid below upon the ground that respondents, while carrying on production operations, were not thereby engaging in interstate commerce; that labor practices in the course of such operations did not directly affect interstate commerce; consequently respondents' actions did not come within congressional power.

Respondent in No. 419 is a large, integrated manufacturer of iron and steel products, the fourth largest in the United States. It has two production plants in Pennsylvania where raw materials brought from points outside the state are converted into finished products, which are thereafter distributed in interstate commerce throughout many states. The Corporation has assets amounting to $180,000,000, gross income $47,000,000, and employs 22,000 people, 10,000 in the Aliquippa plant, where the complaining employees worked. So far as they relate to essential principles presently important, the activities of this Corporation, while large, do not differ materially from those of the other respondents and very many small producers and distributors. It has attained great size; occupies an important place in business; owns and operates mines of ore, coal, and limestone outside Pennsylvania, the output of which, with other raw material, moves to the production plants. At the plants, this movement ends. Having come to rest, this material remains in warehouses, storage yards, etc., often for months, until the process of manufacture begins. After this has been completed, the finished products go into interstate commerce. The discharged employees labored only in the manufacturing department. They took no part in the transportation to or away from the plant, nor did they participate in any activity which preceded or followed manufacture.

Our concern is with those activities which are common to the three enterprises. Such circumstances as are merely fortuitous—size, character of products, etc., may be put on one side. The wide sweep of the statute will more readily appear if consideration be given to the Board's proceedings against the smallest and relatively least important, the Clothing Company. If the act applies to the relations of that Company to employees in production, of course, it applies to the larger respondents with like business elements, although the affairs of the latter may present other characteristics. Though differing in some respects, all respondents procure raw materials outside the state where they manufacture, fabricate within, and then ship beyond, the state.

In Nos. 420, 421, the respondent, Michigan corporation, manufactures commercial trailers for automobiles from raw materials brought from outside that state, and thereafter sells these in many states. It has a single manufacturing plant at Detroit and annual receipts around $3,000,000; 900 people are employed.

In Nos. 422, 423, the respondent is a Virginia corporation engaged in manufacturing and distributing men's clothing. It has a single plant and chief office at Richmond, annual business amounting perhaps to $2,000,000, employs 800, brings in almost all raw material from other states and ships the output in interstate commerce. There are some 3,300 similar plants for manufacturing clothing in the United States, which together employ 150,000 persons and annually put out products worth $800,000,000.

VI

The Clothing Company is a typical small manufacturing concern which produces less than one-half of one percent of the men's clothing produced in the United States and employs 800 of the 150,000 workmen engaged therein. If closed today, the ultimate effect on commerce in clothing obviously would be negligible. It stands alone, is not seeking to acquire a monopoly or to restrain trade. There is no evidence of a strike by its employees at any time or that one is now threatened, and nothing to indicate the probable result if one should occur.

Some account of the Labor Board's proceedings against this Company will indicate the ambit of the act as presently construed.

September 28, 1935, the Amalgamated Clothing Workers of America, purporting to act under § 10(b) of the National Labor Relations Act, filed with the Board a

"Charge," stating that the Clothing Company had engaged in unfair labor practices within the meaning of the act—§ 8(1)(3)—in that it had, on stated days in August and September, 1935, unjustifiably discharged, demoted or discriminated against some 20 named members of that union and, in other ways, had restrained, interfered with, and coerced employees in the exercise of their right of free choice of representatives for collective bargaining. And further "that said labor practices are unfair labor practices affecting commerce within the meaning of said Act."

This "Charge" contained no description of the Company's business, no word concerning any strike against it past, present or threatened. The number of persons employed or how many of these had joined the union is not disclosed.

Thereupon, the Board issued a "Complaint" which recited the particulars of the "Charge," alleged incorporation of the Company in Virginia, and ownership of a plant at Richmond where it is continuously engaged in the "production, sale and distribution of men's clothing;" that material is brought from other states and manufactured into clothing, which is sold and shipped to many states, etc., "all of aforesaid constituting a continuous flow of commerce among the several states." Also that, while operating the Richmond plant, the Clothing Company discharged, demoted, laid off or discriminated against some 20 persons

"employed in production at the said plant . . . for the reason that all of the said employees, and each of them, joined and assisted a labor organization known as the Amalgamated Clothing Workers of America, and engaged in concerted activities with other employees for the purpose of collective bargaining and other mutual aid and protection,"

etc. Further, that the Company circulated among its employees and undertook to coerce them to sign a writing expressing satisfaction with conditions; induced some members of the union to withdraw; did other similar things, etc.—all of which amounted to unfair labor practices affecting commerce within the meaning of § 8(1)(3)(4) and § 2(6)(7) of the Labor Act.

"The aforesaid unfair labor practices occur in commerce among the several states, and on the basis of experience in the aforesaid plant and others in the same and other industries, burden and obstruct such commerce and the free flow thereof and have led and tend to lead to labor disputes burdening and obstructing such commerce and the free flow thereof."

The complaint says nothing concerning any strike against the Clothing Company past, present, or threatened; there is no allegation concerning the number of persons employed, how many joined the union, or the value of the output.

The respondent filed a special appearance objecting to the Board's jurisdiction, which was overruled; also an answer admitting the discharge of certain employees, but otherwise it generally denied the allegations of the "Complaint."

Thereupon, the Board demanded access to the Company's private records of accounts, disclosure of the amount of capital invested by its private owners, the names of all of its employees, its payrolls, the amounts and character of all purchases and from whom made, the amounts of sales and to whom made, including the number and kind of units, the number of employees in the plant during eight years, the names and addresses of the directors and officers of the Company, the names and addresses of its salesmen, the stock ownership of the Company, the affiliation, if any, with other companies, and the former occupations and businesses of its stockholders.

During hearings held at Richmond and Washington, unfettered by rules of evidence, it received a mass of testimony, largely irrelevant. Much related to the character of respondent's business, general methods used in the men's clothing industry, the numbers employed and the general effect of strikes therein. The circumstances attending the discharge or demotion of the specified employees were brought out.

Following this the Board found—

The men's clothing industry of the United States ranks sixteenth in the number of wage earners employed, with more than 3,000 firms and 150,000 workers engaged. The steps in the typical process of manufacture are described. Raw material is brought in from many states, and, after fabrication, the garments are sold and delivered through canvassers and retailers.

"The men's clothing industry is thus an industry which is nearly entirely dependent in its operations upon purchases and sales in interstate commerce and upon interstate transportation."

The Amalgamated Clothing Workers of America is a labor organization composed of over 125,000 men and women employed in making clothing. Members are organized in local unions. Before recognition of this union by employers, long and bitter strikes occurred, some of which are described. The union has striven consistently to improve the general economic and social conditions of members. Benefits that flow from recognizing and cooperating with it are realized by manufacturers.

Description is given of the Clothing Company's operations, the sources of its raw material (nearly all outside Virginia), and the method used to dispose of its output. Eighty-two percent is sold to customers beyond Virginia. It is among the fifty largest firms in the industry, and among the ten of that group paying the lowest average wage.

In the summer of 1935, the employees at the Richmond plant formed a local of the Amalgamated Clothing Workers and solicited memberships. The management at once indicated opposition, and declared it would not permit employees to join. Hostile acts and the circumstances of the discharge or demotion of complaining employees are described. It is said all were discharged or demoted because of union membership. And further that

"Interference by employers in the men's clothing industry with the activities of employees in joining and assisting labor organizations and their refusal to accept the procedure of collective bargaining has led and tends to lead to strikes and other labor disputes that burden and obstruct commerce and the free flow thereof. In those cases, where the employees have been permitted to organize freely and the employers have been willing to bargain collectively, strikes and industrial unrest have gradually disappeared, as shown in Finding 19. But where the employer has taken the contrary position, strikes have ensued that have resulted in substantial or total cessation of production in the factories involved and obstruction to and burden upon the flow of raw materials and finished garments in interstate commerce."

The number of employees who joined the union does not appear; the general attitude of employees towards the union or the Company is not disclosed; the terms of employment are not stated—whether at will, by the day, or by the month. What the local chapter was especially seeking at the time we do not know.

It does not appear that, either prior or subsequent to the "Complaint," there has been any strike, disorder, or industrial strife at respondent's factory, or any interference with or stoppage of production or shipment of its merchandise. Nor that alleged unfair labor practices at its plant had materially affected manufacture, sale, or distribution; or materially affected, burdened or obstructed the flow of products; or affected, burdened or obstructed the flow of interstate commerce, or tended to do so.

The Board concluded that the Clothing Company had discriminated in respect to tenure and employment, and thereby had discouraged membership in the union; that it had interfered with, restrained, and coerced its employees in violation of rights guaranteed by § 7 of the National Labor Relations Act; that these acts occurred in the course and conduct of commerce among the states, immediately affect employees engaged in the course and conduct of interstate commerce, and tend to lead to labor disputes burdening and obstructing such commerce and the free flow thereof.

An order followed, March 28, 1936, which commanded immediate reinstatement of eight discharged employees and payment of their losses; also that the Company should cease and desist from discharging or discriminating against employees because of connections with the union, should post notices, etc. On the same day, the Board filed a petition asking enforcement of the order in the United States Circuit Court of Appeals (Second Circuit) at New York, which was denied July 13, 1936. *Labor Board v. Friedman-Harry Marks Clothing Co.,* 85 F.2d 1.

VII

The precise question for us to determine is whether, in the circumstances disclosed, Congress has power to authorize what the Labor Board commanded the respondent to do. Stated otherwise, in the circumstances here existing, could Congress, by statute, direct what the Board has ordered? General disquisitions concerning the enactment are of minor, if any, importance. Circumstances not treated as essential to the exercise of power by the Board may, of course, be disregarded. The record in Nos. 422, 423, a typical case, plainly presents these essentials, and we may properly base further discussion upon the circumstances there disclosed.

A relatively small concern caused raw material to be shipped to its plant at Richmond, Virginia, converted this into clothing, and thereafter shipped the product to points outside the State. A labor union sought members among the employees at the plant, and obtained some. The Company's management opposed this effort, and, in order to discourage it, discharged eight who had become members. The business of the Company is so small that to close its factory would have no direct

or material effect upon the volume of interstate commerce in clothing. The number of operatives who joined the union is not disclosed; the wishes of other employees is not shown; probability of a strike is not found.

The argument in support of the Board affirms:

"Thus, the validity of any specific application of the preventive measures of this Act depends upon whether industrial strife resulting from the practices in the particular enterprise under consideration would be of the character which Federal power could control if it occurred. If strife in that enterprise could be controlled, certainly it could be prevented."

Manifestly that view of congressional power would extend it into almost every field of human industry. With striking lucidity, fifty years ago, *Kidd v. Pearson,* 128 U. S. 1, 128 U. S. 21, declared:

"If it be held that the term [commerce with foreign nations and among the several states] includes the regulation of all such manufactures as are intended to be the subject of commercial transactions in the future, it is impossible to deny that it would also include all productive industries that contemplate the same thing. The result would be that congress would be invested, to the exclusion of the states, with the power to regulate not only manufacture, but also agriculture, horticulture, stock-raising, domestic fisheries, mining—in short, every branch of human industry."

This doctrine found full approval in *United States v. E. C. Knight Co.,* 156 U. S. 1, 156 U. S. 12-13; *Schechter Poultry Corp. v. United States, supra,* and *Carter v. Carter Coal Co., supra,* where the authorities are collected and principles applicable here are discussed.

In *Knight's* case, Chief Justice Fuller, speaking for the Court, said:

"Doubtless the power to control the manufacture of a given thing involves, in a certain sense, the control of its disposition, but this is a secondary, and not the primary, sense; and, although the exercise of that power may result in bringing the operation of commerce into play, it does not control it, and affects it only incidentally and indirectly. Commerce succeeds to manufacture, and is not a part of it. . . . It is vital that the independence of the commercial power and of the police power, and the delimitation between them, however sometimes perplexing, should always be recognized and observed, for, while the one furnishes the strongest bond of union, the other is essential to the preservation of the autonomy of the states as required by our dual form of government, and acknowledged evils, however grave and urgent they may appear to be, had better be borne than the risk be run, in the effort to suppress them, of more serious consequences by resort to expedients of even doubtful constitutionality."

In *Schechter's* case, we said:

"In determining how far the federal government may go in controlling intrastate transactions upon the ground that they 'affect' interstate commerce, there is a necessary and well established distinction between direct and indirect effects. The precise line can be drawn only as individual cases arise, but the distinction is clear in principle. . . . But where the effect of intrastate transactions upon interstate commerce is merely indirect, such transactions remain within the domain of state power. If the commerce clause were construed to reach all enterprises and transactions which could be said to have an indirect effect upon interstate commerce, the federal authority would embrace practically all the activities of the people, and the authority of the state over its domestic concerns would exist only by sufferance of the federal government. Indeed, on such a theory, even the development of the state's commercial facilities would be subject to federal control."

Carter's case declared:

"Whether the effect of a given activity or condition is direct or indirect is not always easy to determine. The word 'direct' implies that the activity or condition invoked or blamed shall operate proximately, not mediately, remotely, or collaterally, to produce the effect. It connotes the absence of an efficient intervening agency or condition. And the extent of the effect bears no logical relation to its character. The distinction between a direct and an indirect effect turns not upon the magnitude of either the cause or the effect, but entirely upon the manner in which the effect has been brought about. If the production by one man of a single ton of coal intended for interstate sale and shipment, and actually so sold and shipped, affects interstate commerce indirectly, the effect does not become direct by multiplying the tonnage, or increasing the

number of men employed, or adding to the expense or complexities of the business, or by all combined."

Any effect on interstate commerce by the discharge of employees shown here would be indirect and remote in the highest degree, as consideration of the facts will show. In No. 419, ten men out of ten thousand were discharged; in the other cases, only a few. The immediate effect in the factor may be to create discontent among all those employed, and a strike may follow which, in turn, may result in reducing production, which ultimately may reduce the volume of goods moving in interstate commerce. By this chain of indirect and progressively remote events, we finally reach the evil with which it is said the legislation under consideration undertakes to deal. A more remote and indirect interference with interstate commerce or a more definite invasion of the powers reserved to the states is difficult, if not impossible, to imagine.

The Constitution still recognizes the existence of states with indestructible powers; the Tenth Amendment was supposed to put them beyond controversy.

We are told that Congress may protect the "stream of commerce," and that one who buys raw material without the state, manufactures it therein, and ships the output to another state is in that stream. Therefore it is said he may be prevented from doing anything which may interfere with its flow.

This, too, goes beyond the constitutional limitations heretofore enforced. If a man raises cattle and regularly delivers them to a carrier for interstate shipment, may Congress prescribe the conditions under which he may employ or discharge helpers on the ranch? The products of a mine pass daily into interstate commerce; many things are brought to it from other states. Are the owners and the miners within the power of Congress in respect of the latter's tenure and discharge? May a mill owner be prohibited from closing his factory or discontinuing his business because so to do would stop the flow of products to and from his plant in interstate commerce?

May employees in a factory be restrained from quitting work in a body because this will close the factory and thereby stop the flow of commerce? May arson of a factory be made a federal offense whenever this would interfere with such flow? If the business cannot continue with the existing wage scale, may Congress command a reduction? If the ruling of the Court just announced is adhered to, these questions suggest some of the problems certain to arise.

And if this theory of a continuous "stream of commerce" as now defined is correct, will it become the duty of the federal government hereafter to suppress every strike which by possibility it may cause a blockade in that stream? *In re Debs,* 158 U. S. 564. Moreover, since Congress has intervened, are labor relations between most manufacturers and their employees removed from all control by the state? *Oregon-Washington R. Co. v. Washington,* 270 U. S. 87.

To this argument, *Arkadelphia Milling Co. v. St. Louis Southwestern R. Co.,* 249 U. S. 134, 249 U. S. 150, affords an adequate reply. No such continuous stream is shown by these records as that which counsel assume.

There is no ground on which reasonably to hold that refusal by a manufacturer, whose raw materials come from states other than that of his factory and whose products are regularly carried to other states, to bargain collectively with employees in his manufacturing plant directly affects interstate commerce. In such business, there is not one, but two, distinct movements or streams in interstate transportation. The first brings in raw material, and there ends. Then follows manufacture, a separate and local activity. Upon completion of this, and not before, the second distinct movement or stream in interstate commerce begins, and the products go to other states. Such is the common course for small as well as large industries. It is unreasonable and unprecedented to say the commerce clause confers upon Congress power to govern relations between employers and employees in these local activities. *Stout v. Pratt,* 12 F. Supp. 864. In *Schechter's* case, we condemned as unauthorized by the commerce clause assertion of federal power in respect of commodities which had come to rest after interstate transportation. And, in *Carter's* case, we held Congress lacked power to regulate labor relations in respect of commodities before interstate commerce has begun.

It is gravely stated that experience teaches that, if an employer discourages membership in "any organization of any kind"

"in which employees participate, and which exists for the purpose in whole or in part of dealing with employers concerning grievances, labor disputes, wages, rates of pay, hours of employment or conditions of work,"

discontent may follow, and this in turn may lead to a strike, and as the outcome of the strike there may be a block in the stream of interstate commerce. Therefore, Congress may inhibit the discharge! Whatever effect any cause of discontent may ultimately have upon commerce is far too indirect to justify congressional regulation. Almost anything—marriage, birth, death—may in some fashion affect commerce.

VIII

That Congress has power by appropriate means, not prohibited by the Constitution, to prevent direct and material interference with the conduct of interstate commerce is settled doctrine. But the interference struck at must be direct and material, not some mere possibility contingent on wholly uncertain events, and there must be no impairment of rights guaranteed. A state by taxation on property may indirectly but seriously affect the cost of transportation; it may not lay a direct tax upon the receipts from interstate transportation. The first is an indirect effect, the other direct.

This power to protect interstate commerce was invoked in *Standard Oil Co. v. United States,* 221 U. S. 1, and *United States v. American Tobacco Co.,* 221 U. S. 106. In each of those cases, a combination sought to monopolize and restrain interstate commerce through purchase and consequent control of many large competing concerns engaged both in manufacture and interstate commerce. The combination was sufficiently powerful, and action by it so persistent, that success became a dangerous probability. Here, there is no such situation, and the cases are inapplicable in the circumstances. There is no conspiracy to interfere with commerce unless it can be said to exist among the employees who became members of the union. There is a single plant operated by its own management, whose only offense, as alleged, was the discharge of a few employees in the production department because they belonged to a union, coming within the broad definition of "labor organization" prescribed by § 2(5) of the Act. That definition includes any organization in which employees participate and which exists for the purpose in whole or in part of dealing with employers concerning grievances, wages, &c.

Section 13 of the Labor Act provides: "Nothing in this Act shall be construed so as to interfere with or impede or diminish in any way the right to strike." And yet it is ruled that to discharge an employee in a factory because he is a member of a labor organization (any kind) may create discontent which may lead to a strike and this may cause a block in the "stream of commerce;" consequently, the discharge may be inhibited. Thus, the act exempts from its ambit the very evil which counsel insist may result from discontent caused by a discharge of an association member, but permits coercion of a nonmember to join one.

The things inhibited by the Labor Act relate to the management of a manufacturing plant—something distinct from commerce and subject to the authority of the state. And this may not be abridged because of some vague possibility of distant interference with commerce.

IX

Texas & New Orleans R. Co. v. Brotherhood of Railway & Steamship Clerks, 281 U. S. 548, is not controlling. There, the Court, while considering an act definitely limited to common carriers engaged in interstate transportation over whose affairs Congress admittedly has wide power, declared:

"The petitioners invoke the principle declared in *Adair v. United States,* 208 U. S. 161, and *Coppage v. Kansas,* 236 U. S. 1, but these decisions are inapplicable. The Railway Labor Act of 1926 does not interfere with the normal exercise of the right of the carrier to select its employees or to discharge them. The statute is not aimed at this right of the employers, but at the interference with the right of employees to have representatives of their own choosing. As the carriers subject to the act have no constitutional right to interfere with the freedom of the employees in making their selections, they cannot complain of the statute on constitutional grounds."

Adair's case, *supra,* presented the question:

"May Congress make it a criminal offense against the United States, as, by the tenth section of the act of 1898 it does, for an agent or officer of an interstate carrier, having full authority in the premises from the carrier, to discharge an employee from service simply because of his membership in a labor organization?"

The answer was no.

"While, as already suggested, the right of liberty and property guaranteed by the Constitution against deprivation without due process of law is subject to such reasonable restraints as the common good or the general welfare may require, it is not within the functions of government—at least, in the absence of contract between the parties—to compel any person, in the course of his business and against his will, to accept or retain the personal services of another, or to compel any person, against his will, to perform personal services for another. The right of a person to sell his labor upon such terms as he deems proper is, in its essence, the same as the right of the purchaser of labor or prescribe the conditions upon which he will accept such labor from the person offering to sell it. So the right of the employee to quit the service of the employer, for whatever reason, is the same as the right of the employer, for whatever reason, to dispense with the services of such employee. It was the legal right of the defendant Adair—however unwise such a course might have been—to discharge Coppage because of his being a member of a labor organization as it was the legal right of Coppage, if he saw fit to do so, however unwise such course on his part might have been, to quit the service in which he was engaged because the defendant employed some persons who were not members of a labor organization. In all such particulars, the employer and the employee have equality of right, and any legislation that disturbs that equality is an arbitrary interference with the liberty of contract which no government can legally justify in a free land. . . . The provision of the statute under which the defendant was convicted must be held to be repugnant to the Fifth Amendment, and as not embraced by nor within the power of Congress to regulate interstate commerce, but, under the guise of regulating interstate commerce, and as applied to this case, it arbitrarily sanctions an illegal invasion of the personal liberty as well as the right of property of the defendant Adair."

Coppage v. Kansas, following the *Adair* case, held that a state statute declaring it a misdemeanor to require an employee to agree not to become a member of a labor organization during the time of his employment was repugnant to the due process clause of the Fourteenth Amendment.

The right to contract is fundamental, and includes the privilege of selecting those with whom one is willing to assume contractual relations. This right is unduly abridged by the act now upheld. A private owner is deprived of power to manage his own property by freely selecting those to whom his manufacturing operations are to be entrusted. We think this cannot lawfully be done in circumstances like those here disclosed.

It seems clear to us that Congress has transcended the powers granted.

Glossary

commerce: the buying and selling of goods, especially on a large scale or involving transportation

commerce clause: Article I, Section 8, Clause 3 of the U.S. Constitution, which states that Congress has the power "to regulate commerce with foreign nations, and among the several states, and with the Indian tribes"

dual system of government: referring to the system wherein the federal and state governments have separate and clearly defined jurisdictions

---

WEST COAST HOTEL V. PARRISH

DATE 1937	**CITATION** 300 U.S. 379
AUTHOR Charles Evans Hughes	**SIGNIFICANCE** By upholding a Washington State minimum wage law, allowed states to use their police powers to impinge on the freedom of contract for the first time since before the Lochner decision in 1905
VOTE 5–4	

Overview

West Coast Hotel has both a legal and a political significance. On the legal side, it marked a sharp turn away from *Morehead v. New York ex rel. Tipaldo* (1936), which saw the Court invalidate an almost identical state minimum wage law the previous year. It also represented an overwhelming counterweight to the idea of substantive due process, essentially using the protections of the Fourteenth Amendment to assert new rights, at least in economic matters. From this point on, the justices would no longer be as deferential to ideas that limited the ability of governments to regulate economic activity, like the freedom of contract.

Thanks to changing political circumstances, a new liberal era on the Court began with this opinion. *West Coast Hotel* marked the beginning of what became known as the "switch in time that saved nine." It was the first case in a string of cases in which the Supreme Court, which had once overturned New Deal legislation by a 5–4 majority, started approving it by the same margin. While sometimes credited to President Roosevelt's near-simultaneous campaign to add additional justices to the Supreme Court, Justice Owen Roberts's

switch from the conservative to liberal faction on the Supreme Court predated that so-called Court-packing plan and was more closely tied to the huge size of Roosevelt's reelection victory in November 1936.

Context

The U.S. Supreme Court had been the greatest impediment on the implementation of New Deal legislation during Franklin Roosevelt's first term in office. After winning that first election, Roosevelt had encouraged Congress to break new ground with respect to the federal government regulating the economy, whether that meant the incentives for farmers contained in the Agricultural Adjustment Act or the development of detailed regulations for entire industries with the National Industrial Recovery Act. The Court found both of those laws unconstitutional, in *Schechter Poultry Corporation v. United States* in 1935 and *United States v. Butler* in 1936.

In November 1936, Roosevelt beat the Republican governor of Kansas, Alf Landon, by the greatest electoral majority in the history of the United States. He saw that victory not only as a vindication of his policies but as a justification for him to take on the Supreme Court itself. Soon after the election he proposed his Court-packing plan, which would have increased the size of the Court by one justice for each existing justice over the age of seventy. While this plan ultimately failed to pass Congress, Roosevelt's decision to even propose it symbolized the pressure on the Supreme Court to develop a friendlier attitude toward economic regulation by the federal government. Justice Owen Roberts, who had been voting against New Deal legislation that came before the Court, joined the liberal justices for the first time in this case. Notably, he did this before Roosevelt introduced his Court-packing plan. Whether or not Roberts knew the plan was coming is impossible to tell. Nonetheless, Roberts certainly knew about the election results and adjusted his legal philosophy apparently in response to the wishes of a large majority of American voters.

By doing so, Roberts and his colleagues overturned an enormous amount of legal precedent regarding the freedom of contract. That precedent stemmed from *Lochner v. New York* (1905). The case, which limited the hours worked by employees in that state's baking industry on the grounds of freedom of contract, had led to findings against many other state attempts to regulate employment relationships on the same grounds. *Adkins v. Children's Hospital* (1923) relied on this same idea of freedom of contract to invalidate a board that was supposed to set minimum wages for women workers in the District of Columbia. *Morehead v. New York ex rel. Tipaldo* (1936) used the same principle to invalidate a minimum wage law in New York.

The Washington Supreme Court had upheld a minimum wage law many times before the *Tipaldo* case. It did so again for a law approved in *West Coast Hotel* that affected only workers who were women and children despite the recent U.S. Supreme Court precedent. These laws were a legacy of the Progressive Era, where many states passed similar laws on the grounds of paternalism. Some of those laws, despite impinging upon freedom of contract, actually met the approval of the Supreme Court. See, for example, *Muller v. Oregon* (1908). Many feminists actually opposed those laws because they were so paternalistic, yet these precedents would serve as a foundation for the eventual approval of labor laws that improved the circumstances of all workers

Owen J. Roberts's shift to join the majority was dubbed "The switch in time that saved nine" by humorist Cal Tinney.
(Library of Congress)

during the New Deal Era, after Roberts made his switch between the *Tipaldo* and *West Coast Hotel* cases.

While the *Tipaldo* decision had ample precedent, that precedent proved extremely unpopular in the context of the Great Depression. Even the Republican Party opposed that decision in its 1936 platform. That unpopularity explains why Justice Owen Roberts switched his vote from the conservative faction to the liberal one when very similar legislation came before the Court during its next term. That one vote was enough to essentially invalidate all this precedent. More importantly, the willingness of the Court to ignore the freedom of contract in cases that involved state legislation signaled that it might be willing to do so for federal legislation as well. The court did precisely that when the National Labor Relations Act of 1935 (NLRA) came before it in *National Labor Relations Board v. Jones & Laughlin Steel Company* later in 1937.

About the Author

Charles Evans Hughes was the son of a Baptist minister and a native of New York State. He had an extensive career in politics off the bench. He was governor of New York before he became an associate justice. He resigned that position to become the Republican Party's nominee for president of the United States in 1916. He lost to incumbent Woodrow Wilson by such a small margin that it is said that he went to bed on election night thinking he would be president. He served as U.S. secretary of state between 1921 and 1925, until Herbert Hoover appointed him chief justice in 1930.

In his first stint as a Supreme Court justice, Hughes cultivated a reputation as moderate. Even though he was a Wall Street banker before entering politics, his early record on the Court reflects middle-ground views on the role of the federal government in the American economy. After being appointed chief justice by Republican Herbert Hoover, he tended to favor the economic reforms of Franklin Roosevelt's New Deal. Some of this may reflect the political sensibilities he developed during his career in government. Hughes resigned from the Court in 1941.

Justice George Sutherland emigrated from England at a young age to the Utah frontier by his Mormon parents. While the family soon soured on Mormonism, they stayed in the territory. Sutherland served as an associate justice on the Supreme Court from 1922 to 1938. Before joining the Court, Sutherland was a Utah lawyer who served in the territorial legislature, the U.S. House of Representatives, and two terms in the U.S. Senate. On the Court, Sutherland was a fierce proponent of freedom of contract, but his politics were not always traditionally conservative. Sutherland resigned from the Supreme Court after what was called the "switch in time that saved nine" because his judicial philosophy had become unpopular.

Explanation and Analysis of the Document

Circumstances

Hughes begins by summarizing the law at issue in the case. In that summary, he makes special note of the public mission that the Washington legislature assumed in setting wages for women and minors to assure that they could support themselves and stay healthy while doing so. He then notes the circumstances leading to the case. Elsie Parrish, a hotel maid, sued her employer, West Coast Hotel, demanding the difference between the wages she was actually paid and the minimum wage set by the state. The hotel argued that the statute in question violated the Fourteenth Amendment because it did not respect freedom of contract.

Precedent

Hughes notes that the precedents of both *Adkins v. Children's Hospital* (1923) and *Tipaldo* (1936) are relevant to this case because all the statutes involved are similar. Hughes suggests that *Adkins* was not challenged under the *Tipaldo* decision since the opinion of the Washington Supreme Court uses police power to uphold the Washington law, but he had to revisit the precedent here. Hughes argues that the popularity of state laws regulating the economy and the onset of the Depression since the *Adkins* decision justified a reexamination.

Hughes then goes on to directly attack the freedom of contract, noting that it is nowhere mentioned in the Constitution. Hughes recognizes that liberty does appear, but constitutional liberty can be restricted when it is subjected to the restraint of due process. Reasonable regulation in the interest of the community, in Hughes's conception, is due process. Hughes then goes on to cite many Supreme Court cases in which the freedom of contract has been restricted by other interests, such as worker safety. Hughes's decision places the regulation of wages in this line of cases rather than allow the freedom of contract to trump any regulation of wages at all, as was the case in *Adkins*.

The Value of Labor

In his opinion, Hughes notes that the argument against the law in question is that it eliminates the value of the services rendered as the basis of the wages that will get paid. The *Adkins* case involved a minimum wage law, and the Court objected to it on the grounds that it violated the principles of a free market since there would be no chance for supply and demand to set the fair value of the labor of the employees. While the attorneys for the hotel offer the same reasoning as in *Adkins*, Hughes suggests otherwise. Even though this is a minimum wage, Hughes argues, citing earlier dissents, that the minimum wage law does not set a wage. It only offers a floor that no employer can go below.

More importantly, Hughes cites the disparate power between women and children and their employers as a justification for the State of Washington to exercise its police power in this way. These groups have no power in no small part precisely because they are generally underpaid. Improving their wages will improve their bargaining position, which will, in turn, improve their health and safety. Since the solution is a logical way to address precisely the problem of their powerlessness, this is a reasonable use of the state's police power and therefore a reasonable infringement upon the liberty of free enterprise.

The Cost of Exploitation

Hughes concludes his opinion with an argument that is obviously inspired by the Great Depression. Quite logically, he notes that workers who do not hold enough bargaining power to obtain a living wage will likely become the responsibility of the state. Many people during the Depression, including people who still held jobs, found themselves in this position during this dark time. Therefore, the state and the community that supported it held a very clear interest in making sure that employees made wages that were high enough to allow them to support themselves.

This law only applied to women and children, but these are the groups in society that held the very least power when bargaining wages with their employer. Just because the state legislature had not yet extended the same protection to men did not mean they could not do so. Indeed, many states had used women as a starting point for protective labor legislation that was later extended to men. Later federal legislation, the Fair Labor Standards Act (FLSA), extended the minimum wage to all workers, no matter their gender.

Sutherland's Dissent

Justice George Sutherland had been the author of the majority opinion in the *Adkins v. Children's Hospital* case, so it is no surprise that he did not change his mind about the issues involved during the intervening fourteen years. With respect to the decision to revisit *Adkins* in light of the Depression, Sutherland argues that the principles behind the Constitution do not change with changing economic circumstances. He also denounces the idea that the Constitution is a living document that must be interpreted in light of the present. He accuses the majority in this case of amending the Constitution through interpretation. In short, he accuses the justices of playing politics.

Sutherland restates the same rationale he used in *Adkins* in his dissenting opinion here. He notes the long history of freedom of contract cases that the Court has decided, and he notes the similarity between the statute that was overturned in *Adkins* but upheld here. While the Court recognized in *Adkins* that there were restrictions on the freedom of contract, Sutherland notes that it was supposed to have been the fallback position when determining the constitutionality of state legislation, and that means that the case precedent should have been respected. Because the businesses that were being regulated were not charged with a public interest, in his view and as the Court decided in earlier cases, freedom of contract should have trumped the police power of the state in this instance. Sutherland also believed it was unconstitutional to treat women and men differently, as the State of Washington did with this law.

Sutherland was joined in his dissent by Willis Van Devanter, James McReynolds, and Pierce Butler.

Impact

Franklin Roosevelt's New Deal is often divided between its first and second phases. While much of the First New Deal's legislation was invalidated by a Supreme Court with a conservative majority, after *West Coast Hotel*, the opposite would be true for the Second New Deal, which included major reforms such as the NLRA and the Fair Labor Standards Act of 1938. It is no coincidence that the Court upheld two different New Deal statutes, albeit minor ones, the same day that it announced this decision. It approved more major decisions in the following months and years.

The principles established in this case made that change possible. These labor laws have proven to be one of the most lasting legacies of the New Deal. Without the Court taking the initial step of negating substantive due process in *Parrish*, later decisions approving those laws never could have been written. As years passed and Franklin Roosevelt got to appoint an increasing number of Supreme Court justices, this new liberal majority became enshrined. By 1940, justices nominated by President Roosevelt formed a majority on the Supreme Court. This is the root of the popular notion amongst historians that Franklin Roosevelt lost the battle over his Court-packing plan but ultimately won the war.

Substantive due process, although sometimes thought to have been destroyed by Hughes's decision, has continued in noneconomic matters despite the decision in this case. The right to privacy and the now very limited right of women to have an abortion are two examples that still depend upon that doctrine. Substantive due process in economic matters has even made something of a comeback in conservative legal circles in recent years. The extremely conservative majority on the Supreme Court in the 2020s might soon resuscitate this idea to prevent many kinds of government regulation, thereby making Justice Sutherland's warning about the Court playing politics relevant once more.

Questions for Further Study

1. How far should the government be able to go to protect its citizens and promote the common good? What other kinds of contracts besides the terms and conditions of employment should the government be able to regulate?

2. If freedom of contract is never mentioned in the Constitution, is that a right that deserves to be respected?

3. Should the Constitution be read as a living document that depends upon present circumstances for interpreting its principles, or should the conditions laid down at the time of its passage be permanent?

Further Reading

Books

Hiltzik, Michael. *The New Deal: A Modern History*. New York: Free Press, 2011.

Kennedy, David M. *Freedom from Fear: The American People in Depression and War, 1929–1945*. New York: Oxford University Press, 1999.

Witt, Elder, ed. *The Supreme Court and Its Work*. Washington, D.C.: Congressional Quarterly, Inc., 1981.

Articles

Dudziak, Mary L. "West Coast Hotel v. Parrish." In *The Oxford Companion to the Supreme Court*, 924. New York: Oxford University Press, 1992.

—Commentary by Jonathan Rees

WEST COAST HOTEL V. PARRISH

Document Text

MR. CHIEF JUSTICE HUGHES delivered the opinion of the Court

This case presents the question of the constitutional validity of the minimum wage law of the State of Washington.

The Act, entitled "Minimum Wages for Women," authorizes the fixing of minimum wages for women and minors. Laws of 1913 (Washington) chap. 174; Remington's Rev.Stat. (1932), § 7623 *et seq.* It provides:

"SECTION 1. The welfare of the State of Washington demands that women and minors be protected from conditions of labor which have a pernicious effect on their health and morals. The State of Washington, therefore, exercising herein its police and sovereign power declares that inadequate wages and unsanitary conditions of labor exert such pernicious effect."

"SEC. 2. It shall be unlawful to employ women or minors in any industry or occupation within the State of Washington under conditions of labor detrimental to their health or morals, and it shall be unlawful to employ women workers in any industry within the State of Washington at wages which are not adequate for their maintenance."

"SEC. 3. There is hereby created a commission to be known as the 'Industrial Welfare Commission' for the State of Washington, to establish such standards of wages and conditions of labor for women and minors employed within the State of Washington as shall be held hereunder to be reasonable and not detrimental to health and morals, and which shall be sufficient for the decent maintenance of women."

Further provisions required the Commission to ascertain the wages and conditions of labor of women and minors within the State. Public hearings were to be held. If, after investigation, the Commission found that, in any occupation, trade or industry, the wages paid to women were "inadequate to supply them necessary cost of living and to maintain the workers in health," the Commission was empowered to call a conference of representatives of employers and employees together with disinterested persons representing the public. The conference was to recommend to the Commission, on its request, an estimate of a minimum wage adequate for the purpose above stated, and, on the approval of such a recommendation, it became the duty of the Commission to issue an obligatory order fixing minimum wages. Any such order might be reopened, and the question reconsidered with the aid of the former conference or a new one. Special licenses were authorized for the employment of women who were "physically defective or crippled by age or otherwise," and also for apprentices, at less than the prescribed minimum wage.

By a later Act, the Industrial Welfare Commission was abolished, and its duties were assigned to the Industrial Welfare Committee, consisting of the Director of Labor and Industries, the Supervisor of Industrial Insurance, the Supervisor of Industrial Relations, the Industrial Statistician, and the Supervisor of Women in Industry. Laws of 1921 (Washington) c. 7; Remington's Rev.Stat. (1932), §§ 10840, 10893.

The appellant conducts a hotel. The appellee, Elsie Parrish, was employed as a chambermaid and (with her husband) brought this suit to recover the difference between the wages paid her and the minimum wage fixed pursuant to the state law. The minimum wage was $14.50 per week of 48 hours. The appellant challenged the act as repugnant to the due process clause of the Fourteenth Amendment of the Constitution of the United States. The Supreme Court of the State, reversing the trial court, sustained the statute and directed judgment for the plaintiffs. *Parrish v. West Coast Hotel Co.,* 185 Wash. 581, 55 P.2d 1083. The case is here on appeal.

The appellant relies upon the decision of this Court in *Adkins v. Children's Hospital,* 261 U. S. 525, which held invalid the District of Columbia Minimum Wage Act, which was attacked under the due process clause of the Fifth Amendment. On the argument at bar, counsel for the appellees attempted to distinguish the *Adkins* case upon the ground that the appellee was employed in a hotel, and that the business of an innkeeper was affected with a public interest. That effort at distinction is obviously futile, as it appears that, in one of the cases ruled by the *Adkins* opinion, the employee was a woman employed as an elevator operator in a hotel. *Adkins v. Lyons,* 261 U. S. 525, at p. 261 U. S. 542.

The recent case of *Morehead v. New York ex rel. Tipaldo,* 298 U. S. 587, came here on certiorari to the New York court, which had held the New York minimum wage act for women to be invalid. A minority of this Court thought that the New York statute was distinguishable in a material feature from that involved in the *Adkins* case, and, that for that and other reasons, the New York statute should be sustained. But the Court of Appeals of New York had said that it found no material difference between the two statutes, and this Court held that the "meaning of the statute" as fixed by the decision of the state court "must be accepted here as if the meaning had been specifically expressed in the enactment." *Id.,* p. 298 U. S. 609. That view led the affirmance by this Court of the judgment in the *Morehead* case, as the Court considered that the only question before it was whether the *Adkins* case was distinguishable, and that reconsideration of that decision had not been sought. Upon that point, the Court said:

"The petition for the writ sought review upon the ground that this case [*Morehead*] is distinguishable from that one [*Adkins*]. No application has been made for reconsideration of the constitutional question there decided. The validity of the principles upon which that decision rests is not challenged. This court confines itself to the ground upon which the writ was asked or granted. . . . Here, the review granted was no broader than that sought by the petitioner. . . . He is not entitled, and does not ask, to be heard upon the question whether the *Adkins* case should be overruled. He maintains that it may be distinguished on the ground that the statutes are vitally dissimilar."

We think that the question which was not deemed to be open in the *Morehead* case is open and is necessarily presented here. The Supreme Court of Washington has upheld the minimum wage statute of that State. It has decided that the statute is a reasonable exercise of the police power of the State. In reaching that conclusion, the state court has invoked principles long established by this Court in the application of the Fourteenth Amendment. The state court has refused to regard the decision in the *Adkins* case as determinative, and has pointed to our decisions both before and since that case as justifying its position. We are of the opinion that this ruling of the state court demands on our part a reexamination of the *Adkins* case. The importance of the question, in which many States having similar laws are concerned, the close division by which the decision in the *Adkins* case was reached, and the economic conditions which have supervened, and in the light of which the reasonableness of the exercise of the protective power of the State must be considered, make it not only appropriate, but we think imperative, that, in deciding the present case, the subject should receive fresh consideration.

The history of the litigation of this question may be briefly stated. The minimum wage statute of Washington was enacted over twenty-three years ago. Prior to the decision in the instant case, it had twice been held valid by the Supreme Court of the State. *Larsen v. Rice,* 100 Wash. 642, 171 Pac. 1037; *Spokane Hotel Co. v. Younger,* 113 Wash. 359, 194 Pac. 595. The Washington statute is essentially the same as that enacted in Oregon in the same year. Laws of 1913 (Oregon) chap. 62. The validity of the latter act was sustained by the Supreme Court of Oregon in *Stettler v. O'Hara,* 69 Ore. 519, 139 Pac. 743, and *Simpson v. O'Hara,* 70 Ore. 261, 141 Pac. 158. These cases, after reargument, were affirmed here by an equally divided court, in 1917. 243 U.S. 629. The law of Oregon thus continued in effect. The District of Columbia Minimum Wage Law (40 Stat.

960) was enacted in 1918. The statute was sustained by the Supreme Court of the District in the *Adkins* case. Upon appeal, the Court of Appeals of the District first affirmed that ruling, but, on rehearing, reversed it, and the case came before this Court in 1923. The judgment of the Court of Appeals holding the Act invalid was affirmed, but with Chief Justice Taft, Mr. Justice Holmes and Mr. Justice Sanford dissenting, and Mr. Justice Brandeis taking no part. The dissenting opinions took the ground that the decision was at variance with the principles which this Court had frequently announced and applied. In 1925 and 1927, the similar minimum wage statutes of Arizona and Arkansas were held invalid upon the authority of the *Adkins* case. The Justices who had dissented in that case bowed to the ruling, and Mr. Justice Brandeis dissented. *Murphy v. Sardell*, 269 U.S. 530; *Donham v. West-Nelson Co.*, 273 U.S. 657. The question did not come before us again until the last term in the *Morehead* case, as already noted. In that case, briefs supporting the New York statute were submitted by the States of Ohio, Connecticut, Illinois, Massachusetts, New Hampshire, New Jersey and Rhode Island. 298 U.S. p. 604, note. Throughout this entire period, the Washington statute now under consideration has been in force.

The principle which must control our decision is not in doubt. The constitutional provision invoked is the due process clause of the Fourteenth Amendment, governing the States, as the due process clause invoked in the *Adkins* case governed Congress. In each case, the violation alleged by those attacking minimum wage regulation for women is deprivation of freedom of contract. What is this freedom? The Constitution does not speak of freedom of contract. It speaks of liberty and prohibits the deprivation of liberty without due process of law. In prohibiting that deprivation, the Constitution does not recognize an absolute and uncontrollable liberty. Liberty in each of its phases has its history and connotation. But the liberty safeguarded is liberty in a social organization which requires the protection of law against the evils which menace the health, safety, morals and welfare of the people. Liberty under the Constitution is thus necessarily subject to the restraints of due process, and regulation which is reasonable in relation to its subject and is adopted in the interests of the community is due process.

This essential limitation of liberty in general governs freedom of contract in particular. More than twen-

ty-five years ago, we set forth the applicable principle in these words, after referring to the cases where the liberty guaranteed by the Fourteenth Amendment had been broadly described:

"But it was recognized in the cases cited, as in many others, that freedom of contract is a qualified, and not an absolute, right. There is no absolute freedom to do as one wills or to contract as one chooses. The guaranty of liberty does not withdraw from legislative supervision that wide department of activity which consists of the making of contracts, or deny to government the power to provide restrictive safeguards. Liberty implies the absence of arbitrary restraint, not immunity from reasonable regulations and prohibitions imposed in the interests of the community."

Chicago, B. & Q. R. Co. v. McGuire, 219 U.S. 549, 219 U.S. 567.

This power under the Constitution to restrict freedom of contract has had many illustrations. That it may be exercised in the public interest with respect to contracts between employer and employee is undeniable. Thus, statutes have been sustained limiting employment in underground mines and smelters to eight hours a day (*Holden v. Hardy*, 169 U.S. 366); in requiring redemption in cash of store orders or other evidences of indebtedness issued in the payment of wages (*Knoxville Iron Co. v. Harbison*, 183 U.S. 13); in forbidding the payment of seamen's wages in advance (*Patterson v. Bark Eudora*, 190 U.S. 169); in making it unlawful to contract to pay miners employed at quantity rates upon the basis of screened coal instead of the weight of the coal as originally produced in the mine (*McLean v. Arkansas*, 211 U.S. 539); in prohibiting contracts limiting liability for injuries to employees (*Chicago, B. & Q. R. Co. v. McGuire, supra*); in limiting hours of work of employees in manufacturing establishments (*Bunting v. Oregon*, 243 U.S. 426), and in maintaining workmen's compensation laws (*New York Central R. Co. v. White*, 243 U.S. 188; *Mountain Timber Co. v. Washington*, 243 U.S. 219). In dealing with the relation of employer and employed, the legislature has necessarily a wide field of discretion in order that there may be suitable protection of health and safety, and that peace and good order may be promoted through regulations designed to insure wholesome conditions of work and freedom from oppression. *Chicago, B. & Q. R. Co. v. McGuire, supra*, p. 219 U.S. 570.

The point that has been strongly stressed that adult employees should be deemed competent to make their own contracts was decisively met nearly forty years ago in *Holden v. Hardy, supra,* where we pointed out the inequality in the footing of the parties. We said (*Id.* 169 U. S. 397):

"The legislature has also recognized the fact, which the experience of legislators in many States has corroborated, that the proprietors of these establishments and their operatives do not stand upon an equality, and that their interests are, to a certain extent, conflicting. The former naturally desire to obtain as much labor as possible from their employes, while the latter are often induced by the fear of discharge to conform to regulations which their judgment, fairly exercised, would pronounce to be detrimental to their health or strength. In other words, the proprietors lay down the rules and the laborers are practically constrained to obey them. In such cases, self-interest is often an unsafe guide, and the legislature may properly interpose its authority."

And we added that the fact

"that both parties are of full age and competent to contract does not necessarily deprive the State of the power to interfere where the parties do not stand upon an equality, or where the public health demands that one party to the contract shall be protected against himself."

"The State still retains an interest in his welfare, however reckless he may be. The whole is no greater than the sum of all the parts, and when the individual health, safety and welfare are sacrificed or neglected, the State must suffer."

It is manifest that this established principle is peculiarly applicable in relation to the employment of women, in whose protection the State has a special interest. That phase of the subject received elaborate consideration in *Muller v. Oregon* (1908), 208 U. S. 412, where the constitutional authority of the State to limit the working hours of women was sustained. We emphasized the consideration that "woman's physical structure and the performance of maternal functions place her at a disadvantage in the struggle for subsistence," and that her physical wellbeing "becomes an object of public interest and care in order to preserve the strength and vigor of the race." We emphasized the need of protecting women against oppression despite her possession of contractual rights. We said that,

"though limitations upon personal and contractual rights may be removed by legislation, there is that in her disposition and habits of life which will operate against a full assertion of those rights. She will still be where some legislation to protect her seems necessary to secure a real equality of right."

Hence, she was

"properly placed in a class by herself, and legislation designed for her protection may be sustained even when like legislation is not necessary for men and could not be sustained."

We concluded that the limitations which the statute there in question "placed upon her contractual powers, upon her right to agree with her employer as to the time she shall labor," were "not imposed solely for her benefit, but also largely for the benefit of all." Again, in *Quong Wing v. Kirkendall,* 223 U. S. 59, 223 U. S. 63, in referring to a differentiation with respect to the employment of women, we said that the Fourteenth Amendment did not interfere with state power by creating a "fictitious equality." We referred to recognized classifications on the basis of sex with regard to hours of work and in other matters, and we observed that the particular points at which that difference shall be enforced by legislation were largely in the power of the State. In later rulings, this Court sustained the regulation of hours of work of women employees in *Riley v. Massachusetts,* 232 U. S. 671 (factories), *Miller v. Wilson,* 236 U. S. 373 (hotels), and *Bosley v. McLaughlin,* 236 U. S. 385 (hospitals).

This array of precedents and the principles they applied were thought by the dissenting Justices in the *Adkins* case to demand that the minimum wage statute be sustained. The validity of the distinction made by the Court between a minimum wage and a maximum of hours in limiting liberty of contract was especially challenged. 261 U.S. p. 261 U. S. 564. That challenge persists, and is without any satisfactory answer. As Chief Justice Taft observed:

"In absolute freedom of contract, the one term is as important as the other, for both enter equally into the consideration given and received, a restriction as to the one is not greater, in essence, than the other, and is of the same kind. One is the multiplier, and the other the multiplicand."

And Mr. Justice Holmes, while recognizing that "the distinctions of the law are distinctions of degree," could

"perceive no difference in the kind or degree of interference with liberty, the only matter with which we have any concern, between the one case and the other. The bargain is equally affected whichever half you regulate."

One of the points which was pressed by the Court in supporting its ruling in the *Adkins* case was that the standard set up by the District of Columbia Act did not take appropriate account of the value of the services rendered. In the *Morehead* case, the minority thought that the New York statute had met that point in its definition of a "fair wage," and that it accordingly presented a distinguishable feature which the Court could recognize within the limits which the *Morehead* petition for certiorari was deemed to present. The Court, however, did not take that view, and the New York Act was held to be essentially the same as that for the District of Columbia. The statute now before us is like the latter, but we are unable to conclude that, in its minimum wage requirement, the State has passed beyond the boundary of its broad protective power.

The minimum wage to be paid under the Washington statute is fixed after full consideration by representatives of employers, employees and the public. It may be assumed that the minimum wage is fixed in consideration of the services that are performed in the particular occupations under normal conditions. Provision is made for special licenses at less wages in the case of women who are incapable of full service. The statement of Mr. Justice Holmes in the *Adkins* case is pertinent:

"This statute does not compel anybody to pay anything. It simply forbids employment at rates below those fixed as the minimum requirement of health and right living. It is safe to assume that women will not be employed at even the lowest wages allowed unless they earn them, or unless the employer's business can sustain the burden. In short the law, in its character and operation, is like hundreds of so-called police laws that have been upheld."

And Chief Justice Taft forcibly pointed out the consideration which is basic in a statute of this character:

"Legislatures which adopt a requirement of maximum hours or minimum wages may be presumed to believe that, when sweating employers are prevented from paying unduly low wages by positive law, they will continue their business, abating that part of their profits which were wrung from the necessities of their employees, and will concede the better terms required by the law, and that, while in individual cases hardship may result, the restriction will enure to the benefit of the general class of employees in whose interest the law is passed, and so to that of the community at large."

We think that the views thus expressed are sound, and that the decision in the *Adkins* case was a departure from the true application of the principles governing the regulation by the State of the relation of employer and employed. Those principles have been reenforced by our subsequent decisions. Thus, in *Radice v. New York,* 264 U. S. 292, we sustained the New York statute which restricted the employment of women in restaurants at night. In *O'Gorman & Young v. Hartford Fire Insurance Co.,* 282 U. S. 251, which upheld an act regulating the commissions of insurance agents, we pointed to the presumption of the constitutionality of a statute dealing with a subject within the scope of the police power and to the absence of any factual foundation of record for deciding that the limits of power had been transcended. In *Nebbia v. New York,* 291 U. S. 502, dealing with the New York statute providing for minimum prices for milk, the general subject of the regulation of the use of private property and of the making of private contracts received an exhaustive examination, and we again declared that, if such laws

"have a reasonable relation to a proper legislative purpose, and are neither arbitrary nor discriminatory, the requirements of due process are satisfied;"

that

"with the wisdom of the policy adopted, with the adequacy or practicability of the law enacted to forward it, the courts are both incompetent and unauthorized to deal;"

that

"times without number, we have said that the legislature is primarily the judge of the necessity of such an enactment, that every possible presumption is in favor of its validity, and that, though the court may hold views inconsistent with the wisdom of the law, it may not be annulled unless palpably in excess of legislative power."

With full recognition of the earnestness and vigor which characterize the prevailing opinion in the *Adkins* case, we find it impossible to reconcile that ruling with these well considered declarations. What can be closer to the public interest than the health of women and their protection from unscrupulous and overreaching employers? And if the protection of women is a legitimate end of the exercise of state power, how can it be said that the requirement of the payment of a minimum wage fairly fixed in order to meet the very necessities of existence is not an admissible means to that end? The legislature of the State was clearly entitled to consider the situation of women in employment, the fact that they are in the class receiving the least pay, that their bargaining power is relatively weak, and that they are the ready victims of those who would take advantage of their necessitous circumstances. The legislature was entitled to adopt measures to reduce the evils of the "sweating system," the exploiting of workers at wages so low as to be insufficient to meet the bare cost of living, thus making their very helplessness the occasion of a most injurious competition. The legislature had the right to consider that its minimum wage requirements would be an important aid in carrying out its policy of protection. The adoption of similar requirements by many States evidences a deep-seated conviction both as to the presence of the evil and as to the means adapted to check it. Legislative response to that conviction cannot be regarded as arbitrary or capricious, and that is all we have to decide. Even if the wisdom of the policy be regarded as debatable and its effects uncertain, still the legislature is entitled to its judgment.

There is an additional and compelling consideration which recent economic experience has brought into a strong light. The exploitation of a class of workers who are in an unequal position with respect to bargaining power, and are thus relatively defenceless against the denial of a living wage, is not only detrimental to their health and wellbeing, but casts a direct burden for their support upon the community. What these workers lose in wages, the taxpayers are called upon to pay. The bare cost of living must be met. We may take judicial notice of the unparalleled demands for relief which arose during the recent period of depression and still continue to an alarming extent despite the degree of economic recovery which has been achieved. It is unnecessary to cite offi-

cial statistics to establish what is of common knowledge through the length and breadth of the land. While, in the instant case, no factual brief has been presented, there is no reason to doubt that the State of Washington has encountered the same social problem that is present elsewhere. The community is not bound to provide what is, in effect, a subsidy for unconscionable employers. The community may direct its lawmaking power to correct the abuse which springs from their selfish disregard of the public interest. The argument that the legislation in question constitutes an arbitrary discrimination, because it does not extend to men, is unavailing. This Court has frequently held that the legislative authority, acting within its proper field, is not bound to extend its regulation to all cases which it might possibly reach. The legislature "is free to recognize degrees of harm and it may confine its restrictions to those classes of cases where the need is deemed to be clearest." If

"the law presumably hits the evil where it is most felt, it is not to be overthrown because there are other instances to which it might have been applied."

There is no "doctrinaire requirement" that the legislation should be couched in all embracing terms. *Carroll v. Greenwich Insurance Co.,* 199 U. S. 401, 199 U. S. 411; *Patsone v. Pennsylvania,* 232 U. S. 138, 232 U. S. 144; *Keokee Coke Co. v. Taylor,* 234 U. S. 224, 234 U. S. 227; *Sproles v. Binford,* 286 U. S. 374, 286 U. S. 396; *Semler v. Oregon Board,* 294 U. S. 608, 294 U. S. 610, 294 U. S. 611. This familiar principle has repeatedly been applied to legislation which singles out women, and particular classes of women, in the exercise of the State's protective power. *Miller v. Wilson, supra,* p. 236 U. S. 384; *Bosley v. McLaughlin, supra,* pp. 236 U. S. 394, 236 U. S. 395; *Radice v. New York, supra,* pp. 264 U. S. 295-298. Their relative need in the presence of the evil, no less than the existence of the evil itself, is a matter for the legislative judgment.

Our conclusion is that the case of *Adkins v. Children's Hospital, supra,* should be, and it is, overruled. The judgment of the Supreme Court of the State of Washington is

Affirmed.

MR. JUSTICE SUTHERLAND, dissenting

MR. JUSTICE VAN DEVANTER, MR. JUSTICE MCREYNOLDS, MR. JUSTICE BUTLER and I think the judgment of the court below should be reversed.

The principles and authorities relied upon to sustain the judgment were considered in *Adkins v. Children's Hospital,* 261 U. S. 525, and *Morehead v. New York ex rel. Tipaldo,* 298 U. S. 587, and their lack of application to cases like the one in hand was pointed out. A sufficient answer to all that is now said will be found in the opinions of the court in those cases. Nevertheless, in the circumstances, it seems well to restate our reasons and conclusions.

Under our form of government, where the written Constitution, by its own terms, is the supreme law, some agency, of necessity, must have the power to say the final word as to the validity of a statute assailed as unconstitutional. The Constitution makes it clear that the power has been intrusted to this court when the question arises in a controversy within its jurisdiction, and, so long as the power remains there, its exercise cannot be avoided without betrayal of the trust.

It has been pointed out many times, as in the *Adkins* case, that this judicial duty is one of gravity and delicacy, and that rational doubts must be resolved in favor of the constitutionality of the statute. But whose doubts, and by whom resolved? Undoubtedly it is the duty of a member of the court, in the process of reaching a right conclusion, to give due weight to the opposing views of his associates; but, in the end, the question which he must answer is not whether such views seem sound to those who entertain them, but whether they convince him that the statute is constitutional or engender in his mind a rational doubt upon that issue. The oath which he takes as a judge is not a composite oath, but an individual one. And, in passing upon the validity of a statute, he discharges a duty imposed upon *him,* which cannot be consummated justly by an automatic acceptance of the views of others which have neither convinced, nor created a reasonable doubt in, his mind. If upon a question so important he thus surrender his deliberate judgment, he stands forsworn. He cannot subordinate his convictions to that extent and keep faith with his oath or retain his judicial and moral independence.

The suggestion that the only check upon the exercise of the judicial power, when properly invoked to declare a constitutional right superior to an unconstitutional statute, is the judge's own faculty of self-restraint is both ill-considered and mischievous. Self-restraint belongs in the domain of will, and not of judgment. The check

upon the judge is that imposed by his oath of office, by the Constitution, and by his own conscientious and informed convictions, and since he has the duty to make up his own mind and adjudge accordingly, it is hard to see how there could be any other restraint. This court acts as a unit. It cannot act in any other way, and the majority (whether a bare majority or a majority of all but one of its members) therefore establishes the controlling rule as the decision of the court, binding, so long as it remains unchanged, equally upon those who disagree and upon those who subscribe to it. Otherwise, orderly administration of justice would cease. But it is the right of those in the minority to disagree, and sometimes, in matters of grave importance, their imperative duty to voice their disagreement at such length as the occasion demands—always, of course, in terms which, however forceful, do not offend the proprieties or impugn the good faith of those who think otherwise.

It is urged that the question involved should now receive fresh consideration, among other reasons, because of "the economic conditions which have supervened"; but the meaning of the Constitution does not change with the ebb and flow of economic events. We frequently are told in more general words that the Constitution must be construed in the light of the present. If by that it is meant that the Constitution is made up of living words that apply to every new condition which they include, the statement is quite true. But to say, if that be intended, that the words of the Constitution mean today what they did not mean when written—that is, that they do not apply to a situation now to which they would have applied then—is to rob that instrument of the essential element which continues it in force as the people have made it until they, and not their official agents, have made it otherwise.

The words of Judge Campbell in *Twitchell v. Blodgett,* 13 Mich. 127, 139-140, apply with peculiar force. "But it may easily happen," he said,

"that specific provisions may, in unforeseen emergencies, turn out to have been inexpedient. This does not make these provisions any less binding. Constitutions cannot be changed by events alone. They remain binding as the acts of the people in their sovereign capacity, as the framers of Government, until they are amended or abrogated by the action prescribed by the authority which created them. It is not competent for any department of the Government to change a constitution, or declare it changed, simply because it appears ill-adapted to a new state of things."

"... Restrictions have, it is true, been found more likely than grants to be unsuited to unforeseen circumstances ... But, where evils arise from the application of such regulations, their force cannot be denied or evaded, and the remedy consists in repeal or amendment, and not in false construction."

The principle is reflected in many decisions of this court. *See South Carolina v. United States,* 199 U. S. 437, 199 U. S. 448-449; *Lake County v. Rollins,* 130 U. S. 662, 130 U. S. 670; *Knowlton v. Moore,* 178 U. S. 41, 178 U. S. 95; *Rhode Island v. Massachusetts,* 12 Pet. 657, 37 U. S. 723; *Craig v. Missouri,* 4 Pet. 410, 431-432; *Ex parte Bain,* 121 U. S. 1, 121 U. S. 12; *Maxwell v. Dow,* 176 U. S. 581, 176 U. S. 602; *Jarrolt v. Moberly,* 103 U. S. 580, 103 U. S. 586.

The judicial function is that of interpretation; it does not include the power of amendment under the guise of interpretation. To miss the point of difference between the two is to miss all that the phrase "supreme law of the land" stands for, and to convert what was intended as inescapable and enduring mandates into mere moral reflections.

If the Constitution, intelligently and reasonably construed in the light of these principles, stands in the way of desirable legislation, the blame must rest upon that instrument, and not upon the court for enforcing it according to its terms. The remedy in that situation—and the only true remedy—is to amend the Constitution. Judge Cooley, in the first volume of his Constitutional Limitations (8th ed.), p. 124, very clearly pointed out that much of the benefit expected from written constitutions would be lost if their provisions were to be bent to circumstances or modified by public opinion. He pointed out that the common law, unlike a constitution, was subject to modification by public sentiment and action which the courts might recognize, but that

"a court or legislature which should allow a change in public sentiment to influence it in giving to a written constitution a construction not warranted by the intention of its founders would be justly chargeable with reckless disregard of official oath and public duty, and if its course could become a precedent, these instruments would be of little avail. ... What a court is to do,

therefore, is *to declare the law as written,* leaving it to the people themselves to make such changes as new circumstances may require. The meaning of the constitution is fixed when it is adopted, and it is not different at any subsequent time when a court has occasion to pass upon it."

The *Adkins* case dealt with an act of Congress which had passed the scrutiny both of the legislative and executive branches of the government. We recognized that thereby these departments had affirmed the validity of the statute, and properly declared that their determination must be given great weight, but we then concluded, after thorough consideration, that their view could not be sustained. We think it not inappropriate now to add a word on that subject before coming to the question immediately under review.

The people, by their Constitution, created three separate, distinct, independent and coequal departments of government. The governmental structure rests, and was intended to rest, not upon any one or upon any two, but upon all three of these fundamental pillars. It seems unnecessary to repeat what so often has been said, that the powers of these departments are different, and are to be exercised independently. The differences clearly and definitely appear in the Constitution. Each of the departments is an agent of its creator, and one department is not and cannot be the agent of another. Each is answerable to its creator for what it does, and not to another agent. The view, therefore, of the Executive and of Congress that an act is constitutional is persuasive in a high degree; but it is not controlling.

Coming, then, to a consideration of the Washington statute, it first is to be observed that it is in every substantial respect identical with the statute involved in the *Adkins* case. Such vices as existed in the latter are present in the former. And if the *Adkins* case was properly decided, as we who join in this opinion think it was, it necessarily follows that the Washington statute is invalid.

In support of minimum wage legislation it has been urged, on the one hand, that great benefits will result in favor of underpaid labor, and, on the other hand, that the danger of such legislation is that the minimum will tend to become the maximum, and thus bring down the earnings of the more efficient toward the level of the less efficient employees. But with these speculations we have nothing to do. We are concerned only with the question of constitutionality.

That the clause of the Fourteenth Amendment which forbids a state to deprive any person of life, liberty or property without due process of law includes freedom of contract is so well settled as to be no longer open to question. Nor reasonably can it be disputed that contracts of employment of labor are included in the rule. *Adair v. United States,* 208 U. S. 161, 208 U. S. 174-175; *Coppage v. Kansas,* 236 U. S. 1, 236 U. S. 10, 236 U. S. 14. In the first of these cases, Mr. Justice Harlan, speaking for the court, said,

"The right of a person to sell his labor upon such terms as he deems proper is, in its essence, the same as the right of the purchaser of labor to prescribe the conditions upon which he will accept such labor from the person offering to sell. . . . In all such particulars, the employer and employee have equality of right, and any legislation that disturbs that equality is an arbitrary interference with the liberty of contract which no government can legally justify in a free land."

In the *Adkins* case, we referred to this language, and said that, while there was no such thing as absolute freedom of contract, but that it was subject to a great variety of restraints, nevertheless, freedom of contract was the general rule, and restraint the exception, and that the power to abridge that freedom could only be justified by the existence of exceptional circumstances. This statement of the rule has been many times affirmed, and we do not understand that it is questioned by the present decision.

We further pointed out four distinct classes of cases in which this court from time to time had upheld statutory interferences with the liberty of contract. They were, in brief, (1) statutes fixing rates and charges to be exacted by businesses impressed with a public interest; (2) statutes relating to contracts for the performance of public work; (3) statutes prescribing the character, methods and time for payment of wages, and (4) statutes fixing hours of labor. It is the last class that has been most relied upon as affording support for minimum wage legislation, and much of the opinion in the *Adkins* case (261 U.S. 261 U. S. 547-553) is devoted to pointing out the essential distinction between fixing hours of labor and fixing wages. What is there said need not be repeated. It is enough for present purposes to say that statutes of the former class deal with an incident of the employment having no necessary effect upon wages. The parties are left free to contract about wages, and thereby equalize such additional burdens as may be imposed upon the employer as a result of the restrictions as to hours by an adjustment in respect of the amount of wages. This court, wherever the question is adverted to, has been careful to disclaim any purpose to uphold such legislation as fixing wages, and has recognized an essential difference between the two. *E.g., Bunting v. Oregon,* 243 U. S. 426; *Wilson v. New,* 243 U. S. 332, 243 U. S. 345-346, 243 U. S. 353-354, *and see* Freund, Police Power, § 318.

We then pointed out that minimum wage legislation such as that here involved does not deal with any business charged with a public interest, or with public work, or with a temporary emergency, or with the character, methods or periods of wage payments, or with hours of labor, or with the protection of persons under legal disability, or with the prevention of fraud. It is, simply and exclusively, a law fixing wages for adult women who are legally as capable of contracting for themselves as men, and cannot be sustained unless upon principles apart from those involved in cases already decided by the court.

Two cases were involved in the *Adkins* decision. In one of them, it appeared that a woman 21 years of age, who brought the suit, was employed as an elevator operator at a fixed salary. Her services were satisfactory, and she was anxious to retain her position, and her employer, while willing to retain her, was obliged to dispense with her services on account of the penalties prescribed by the act. The wages received by her were the best she was able to obtain for any work she was capable of performing, and the enforcement of the order deprived her, as she alleged, not only of that employment, but left her unable to secure any position at which she could make a living with as good physical and moral surroundings and as good wages as she was receiving and was willing to take. The Washington statute, of course, admits of the same situation and result, and, for aught that appears to the contrary, the situation in the present case may have been the same as that just described. Certainly, to the extent that the statute applies to such cases, it cannot be justified as a reasonable restraint upon the freedom of contract. On the contrary, it is essentially arbitrary.

Neither the statute involved in the *Adkins* case nor the Washington statute, so far as it is involved here, has the slightest relation to the capacity or earning power of the employee, to the number of hours which constitute the day's work, the character of the place where the work is to be done, or the circumstances or surroundings of ,he employment. The sole basis upon which the question of validity rests is the assumption that the employee is entitled to receive a sum of money sufficient to provide a living for her, keep her in health, and preserve her morals. And, as we pointed out at some length in that case (pp. 261 U. S. 555-557), the question thus presented for the determination of the board cannot be solved by any general formula prescribed by a statutory bureau, since it is not a composite, but an individual, question to be answered for each individual, considered by herself.

What we said further in that case (pp. 261 U. S. 557-559), is equally applicable here:

"The law takes account of the necessities of only one party to the contract. It ignores the necessities of the employer by compelling him to pay not less than a certain sum not only whether the employee is capable of earning it, but irrespective of the ability of his business to sustain the burden, generously leaving him, of course, the privilege of abandoning his business as an alternative for going on at a loss. Within the limits of the minimum sum, he is precluded, under penalty of fine and imprisonment, from adjusting compensation to the differing merits of his employees. It compels him to pay at least the sum fixed in any event, because the employee needs it, but requires no service of equivalent value from the employee. It therefore undertakes to solve but one-half of the problem. The other half is the establishment of a corresponding standard of efficiency, and this forms no part of the policy of the legislation, although in practice the former half without the latter must lead to ultimate failure, in accordance with the inexorable law that no one can continue indefinitely to take out more than he puts in without ultimately exhausting the supply. The law is not confined to the great and powerful employers, but embraces those whose bargaining power may be as weak as that of the employee. It takes no account of periods of stress and business depression, of crippling losses which may leave the employer himself without adequate means of livelihood. To the extent that the sum fixed exceeds the fair value of the services rendered, it amounts to a compulsory exaction from the employer for the support of a partially indigent person, for whose condition there rests upon him no peculiar responsibility, and therefore, in effect, arbitrarily shifts to his shoulders a burden which, if it belongs to anybody, belongs to society as a whole."

"The feature of this statute which, perhaps more than any other, puts upon it the stamp of invalidity is that it exacts from the employer an arbitrary payment for a purpose and upon a basis having no causal connection with his business, or the contract, or the work the employee engages to do. The declared basis, as already pointed out, is not the value of the service rendered, but the extraneous circumstance that the employee needs to get a prescribed sum of money to insure her subsistence, health and morals. The ethical right of every worker, man or woman, to a living wage may be conceded. One of the declared and important purposes of trade organizations is to secure it. And with that principle and with every legitimate effort to realize it, in fact, no one can quarrel; but the fallacy of the proposed method of attaining it is that it assumes that every employer is bound at all events to furnish it. The moral requirement implicit in every contract of employment, *viz.*, that the amount to be paid and the service to be rendered shall bear to each other some relation of just equivalence, is completely ignored. The necessities of the employee are alone considered, and these arise outside of the employment, are the same when there is no employment, and as great in one occupation as in another. Certainly the employer, by paying a fair equivalent for the service rendered, though not sufficient to support the employee, has neither caused nor contributed to her poverty. On the contrary, to the extent of what he pays, he has relieved it. In principle, there can be no difference between the case of selling labor and the case of selling goods. If one goes to the butcher, the baker or grocer to buy food, he is morally entitled to obtain the worth of his money, but he is not entitled to more. If what he gets is worth what he pays, he is not justified in demanding more simply because he needs more, and the shopkeeper, having dealt fairly and honestly in that transaction, is not concerned in any peculiar sense with the question of his customer's necessities. Should a statute undertake to vest in a commission power to determine the quantity of food necessary for individual support and require the shopkeeper, if he sell to the individual at all, to furnish that quantity at not more than a fixed maximum, it would undoubtedly fall before the constitutional test. The fallacy of any argument in support of the validity of such a statute would be quickly exposed. The argument in support of that now being considered is equally fallacious, though the weakness of it may not be so plain. A statute requiring an employer to pay in money, to pay at prescribed and regular intervals, to pay the value of the services rendered, even to pay with fair relation to the extent of the benefit obtained from the service, would be understandable. But a statute which prescribes payment without regard to any of these things, and solely with relation to circumstances apart from the contract of employment, the business affected by it and the work done under it, is so clearly the product of a naked, arbitrary exercise of power that it cannot be allowed to stand under the Constitution of the United States."

Whether this would be equally or at all true in respect of the statutes of some of the states we are not called upon to say. They are not now before us, and it is enough that it applies in every particular to the Washington statute now under consideration.

The Washington statute, like the one for the District of Columbia, fixes minimum wages for adult women. Adult men and their employers are left free to bargain as they please, and it is a significant and an important fact that all state statutes to which our attention has been called are of like character. The common law rules restricting the power of women to make contracts have, under our system, long since practically disappeared. Women today stand upon a legal and political equality with men. There is no longer any reason why they should be put in different classes in respect of their legal right to make contracts; nor should they be denied, in effect, the right to compete with men for work paying lower wages which men may be willing to accept. And it is an arbitrary exercise of the legislative power to do so. In the *Tipaldo* case, 298 U. S. 587, 298 U. S. 615, it appeared that the New York legislature had passed two minimum wage measures—one dealing with women alone, the other with both men and women. The act which included men was vetoed by the governor. The other, applying to women alone, was approved. The "factual background" in respect of both measures was substantially the same. In pointing out the arbitrary discrimination which resulted (pp. 298 U. S. 615-617) we said:

"These legislative declarations, in form of findings or recitals of fact, serve well to illustrate why any measure that deprives employers and adult women of freedom to agree upon wages, leaving employers and men employees free so to do, is necessarily arbitrary. Much, if not all, that in them is said in justification of the regulations that the Act imposes in respect of women's wages applies with equal force in support of the same regulation of men's wages. While men are left free to fix their wages by agreement with employers, it would be fanciful to suppose that the regulation of women's wages would be useful to prevent or lessen the evils listed in the first section of the Act. Men in need of work are as likely as women to accept the low wages offered by unscrupulous employers. Men in greater number than women support themselves and dependents, and, because of need, will work for whatever wages they can get, and that without regard to the value of the service, and even though the pay is less than minima prescribed in accordance with this Act. It is plain that, under circumstances such as those portrayed in the 'Factual background,' prescribing of minimum wages for women alone would unreasonably restrain them in competition with men and tend arbitrarily to deprive them of employment and a fair chance to find work."

An appeal to the principle that the legislature is free to recognize degrees of harm, and confine its restrictions accordingly, is but to beg the question, which is, since the contractual rights of men and women are the same, does the legislation here involved, by restricting only the rights of women to make contracts as to wages, create an arbitrary discrimination? We think it does. Difference of sex affords no reasonable ground for making a restriction applicable to the wage contracts of all working women from which like contracts of all working men are left free. Certainly a suggestion that the bargaining ability of the average woman is not equal to that of the average man would lack substance. The ability to make a fair bargain, as everyone knows, does not depend upon sex.

If, in the light of the facts, the state legislation, without reason or for reasons of mere expediency, excluded men from the provisions of the legislation, the power was exercised arbitrarily. On the other hand, if such legislation in respect of men was properly omitted on the ground that it would be unconstitutional, the same conclusion of unconstitutionality is inescapable in respect of similar legislative restraint in the case of women, 261 U.S. 261 U. S. 553.

Finally, it may be said that a statute absolutely fixing wages in the various industries at definite sums and forbidding employers and employees from contracting for any other than those designated would probably not be thought to be constitutional. It is hard to see why the power to fix minimum wages does not con-note a like power in respect of maximum wages. And yet, if both powers be exercised in such a way that the minimum and the maximum so nearly approach each other as to become substantially the same, the right to make any contract in respect of wages will have been completely abrogated.

A more complete discussion may be found in the *Adkins* and *Tipaldo* cases cited *supra.*

Glossary

due process clause: Section 1, sentence 2 of the Fourteenth Amendment, which states, in part: "nor shall any State deprive any person of life, liberty, or property, without due process of law"

police power: includes not only the government's power to protect the safety of private property and the safety of its citizens, but also the ways that any government can regulate the economy and other aspects of society for the promotion of the common good

substantive due process: the idea that rights not explicitly mentioned in the Constitution are still protected by the Constitution because of the due process clause of the Fourteenth Amendment; many economic rights were recognized under this doctrine during the late nineteenth and early twentieth centuries

---

CANTWELL V. CONNECTICUT

DATE	CITATION
1940	310 U.S. 296

AUTHOR	SIGNIFICANCE
Owen J. Roberts	Ruled that even though religious speech and religious solicitation may be offensive, such speech is protected under the First and Fourteenth Amendments provided it does not threaten bodily harm.

VOTE	
9–0	

Overview

Argued on March 29, 1940, and decided on May 20, 1940, the case of *Cantwell v. Connecticut* solidified the legal definition of protected speech in relation to religion. Before the opinion, it was not definitively clear what constitutional limits existed on speech of a religious nature. Though federal protections were primarily agreed upon, there was little concurrence regarding how far these protections went at local or state levels. The case came before the court after three Jehovah's Witnesses, all men of the Cantwell family, were arrested for traveling door-to-door selling materials proselytizing against the Catholic religion in a predominately Catholic neighborhood of New Haven, Connecticut. The Cantwells' proselytizing effort offended two men to the point that the men reacted angrily. The Cantwells were arrested under a Connecticut law requiring solicitors to apply for and obtain a certificate before soliciting funds from the public and for inciting a breach of the peace. The Cantwells appealed to the Connecticut Supreme Court claiming a violation of their civil rights. The Connecticut Supreme Court's opinion upheld the state law as a legal effort to protect the public from fraud but dismissed charges of breaching the peace against two of

the Cantwells. The Cantwells sought an appeal through the U.S. Supreme Court. The Hughes Court reversed the lower court's decision entirely and, in so doing, legally defined the omnipresent protections for the freedom of religious speech. The case ushered in an era of increased demonstration of religious liberties in American society.

Context

The American experience with the Great Depression from 1929 to 1941 not only brought about economic and industrial unrest; it also forced American society to contemplate suffering in ways not considered since the Civil War and Reconstruction era. Individual and collective domestic suffering was contrasted with questions about international pacifism, social and racial justice, and persecution. Many turned to religious communities for comfort, commiseration, or material aid, and they did so at the very time when these organizations could least support charitable outreach. The New Deal that came about in 1933 brought about new questions about the "proper" roles of church and state, which were under significant flux considering the

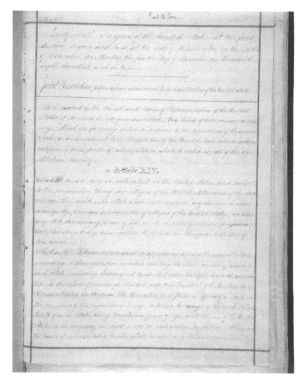

The Fourteenth Amendment. The case held that the First Amendment's free exercise clause is incorporated against the states by the Fourteenth Amendment.
(National Archives)

large transitory population of nearly 13 million Americans. This transitory population tore down some theological communities while it forged new ones largely motivated by international and domestic activism and engagement. While many of these were reputable charitable organizations, others preyed on people to defraud them of money or property. Connecticut was one of several states that responded to these conditions by creating a law requiring anyone soliciting for charitable or religious purposes to have a permit issued by a state official. Before issuing the permit, the official was required to determine if the purpose of the collection was legitimate and if the effort conformed "to reasonable standards of efficiency and integrity."

Though founded nearly fifty years before the Great Depression, the Jehovah's Witnesses had reorganized in 1931. They began proselytizing both the Great Apostasy—the notion that mainstream Christian denominations had moved away from the authentic Christian faith—and the imminent approach of the Second Coming of Christ. Like many other Christian sects, Jehovah's Witnesses believe that proselytization is an obligation of faith.

On April 26, 1938, devout Jehovah's Witnesses Newton Cantwell and his adult sons Jesse and Russell were traveling door-to-door along Cassius Street in New Haven, Connecticut, a predominately Roman Catholic neighborhood. The Cantwells had religious materials, including pamphlets, books, a portable record player, and a record entitled "Enemies" that preached a robust anti-Catholic message. While making their way down Cassius Street, the Cantwells came across two men who agreed to listen to the recording but got irate when hearing the message the Cantwells were spreading. The men said they were significantly tempted to physically strike Jesse Cantwell, who held the record player. However, they restrained themselves to verbal insults and threats to motivate the Cantwells to leave. After the Cantwells left, the men called the police, who shortly after that arrested Newton, Jesse, and Russell Cantwell for solicitation without a permit and inciting a breach of the peace.

The Cantwells argued that they practiced a demonstration of faith protected by the Constitution. As such, they did not believe that the Connecticut law was constitutional. Instead, they argued that the law was simply a way to prevent their effort to spread their message. Furthermore, their actions were in no way an effort to incite any breach of the peace. When appealed to the Connecticut Supreme Court, the court upheld the State's position on the permit issue. Still, it remanded the charges of inciting a breach of the peace against Newton and Russell Cantwell to a new trial. The Connecticut Supreme Court upheld Jesse Cantwell's conviction, arguing that his playing the record ultimately caused the altercation to erupt. The Cantwells sought an appeal to the U.S. Supreme Court.

About the Author

Owen Roberts was born May 2, 1875, in Germantown, Pennsylvania, to Emily Laferty and Josephus Roberts, a local businessman. Roberts graduated with honors from the University of Pennsylvania Law School in 1898. He opened a private practice in Philadelphia in 1898. After cofounding a thriving practice in 1912, Roberts was appointed by President Calvin Coolidge to investigate the Teapot Dome scandal, which ultimately led to the downfall of the sitting secretary of interior, Albert Fall, and other government officials for bribery.

Roberts was nominated by President Herbert Hoover as an associate justice in 1930 after Hoover's first nomination was rejected for confirmation by Senate. Roberts, alongside Chief Justice Charles E. Hughes, would serve as a crucial swing vote on the Court. While an important member of the Court, Roberts was not a prolific voice on the bench but was influential in many other ways. Appointed by Roosevelt as a primary investigator into the Pearl Harbor attack of December 7, 1941, Roberts was highly critical of the military preparation and actions leading to the attack. Roberts led a wartime commission beginning in 1943 to help identify and protect monuments, art, and archives in war zones. This commission, named after Roberts, was also responsible for investigating, documenting, and prosecuting the plunder of art and artifacts by Nazis across Europe until 1946, when the effort was absorbed into the State Department.

Despite these important services, by 1945, Roberts's relationship with the rest of the Court had become so strained that he retired and burned his entire collection of legal and judicial papers. Roberts would serve on the General Convention of the Episcopal Church, become a key member of the Dublin Convention that sought to alter the United Nations from a general assembly into a global legislature, and serve as dean of the University of Pennsylvania Law School until 1951. Roberts retired from public life in 1951 and passed away after a prolonged illness in 1955.

Explanation and Analysis of the Document

Justice Roberts begins his opinion by outlining the charges against the Cantwells, then taking each charge as an individual point. First, Roberts examines all three Cantwells' verdicts of guilt of solicitation without a permit. Here the Cantwells argued that under the Fourteenth Amendment, such a requirement "denied them freedom of speech and prohibited their free exercise of religion." Furthermore, one had to agree that the first charge was valid to charge any of them for breaking the peace. Speaking for the Court, Roberts opines that such a law "deprives them of their liberty without due process of law in contravention of the Fourteenth Amendment. The fundamental concept of liberty embodied in that Amendment embraces the liberties guaranteed by the First Amendment."

Roberts expounds upon this by interpreting the holistic definition of religious freedom under the Constitution as a reinforcing duality. "The constitutional inhibition of legislation on the subject of religion has a double aspect," he writes. "On the one hand, it forestalls compulsion by law of the acceptance of any creed or the practice of any form of worship.... On the other hand, it safeguards the free exercise of the chosen form of religion. Thus, the Amendment embraces two concepts—freedom to believe and freedom to act." Having solidified the freedom of religion as a duality of practice, Roberts then confirms that states definitively have the right to regulate the "times, the places, and the manner of soliciting upon its streets, and of holding meetings thereon, and may in other respects safeguard the peace, good order, and comfort of the community without unconstitutionally invading the liberties protected by the Fourteenth Amendment." However, the requirement to attain approval from the state before religiously related action "amounts to a prior restraint on the exercise of their religion within the meaning of the Constitution."

More important, the ability of the state to determine the validity of a religious intent is, according to Roberts, "censorship of religion" in denial of liberty as protected by both the First and Fourteenth Amendments. And such arguments that the judiciary would correct any wrongful denial after a trial is, in Roberts's words, "is as obnoxious to the Constitution as one providing for like restraint by administrative action."

Having established that the Cantwells were conducting themselves well within their constitutionally protected rights, Roberts turns to the charge of breaking the peace. Here Roberts acknowledges the ideological tightrope that must be walked in understanding the legal issue at hand. "The fundamental law declares the interest of the United States that the free exercise of religion be not prohibited and that freedom to communicate information and opinion be not abridged.... The offense known as breach of the peace embraces a great variety of conduct destroying or menacing public order and tranquility. It includes not only violent acts, but acts and words likely to produce violence in others." But without such overwhelming evidence or demonstration of forthcoming violence, "a State may not unduly suppress free communication of views, religious or other, under the guise of conserving desirable conditions."

Roberts then states that Jesse Cantwell was rightfully on a public thoroughfare; he had asked and was granted permission by passersby to play his message; this message was not disruptive enough to have been heard by anyone outside of those individuals who had given permission; and the message played was indeed offensive not only to Roman Catholics but to "all others who respect the honestly held religious faith of their fellows." Despite the offense that such a message had caused, the Court found that the Cantwells were not in any way attempting to breach the peace but were only attempting to "persuade a willing listener to buy a book or to contribute money in the interest of what Cantwell, however misguided others may think him, conceived to be true religion." Roberts then underlines this opinion by stating that despite its excesses or vilification, such communications and their resulting discussions are "essential to enlightened opinion and right conduct on the part of the citizens of a democracy"—especially a democracy composed of "many races and many creeds."

Roberts is clear that this liberty was not a free-for-all but had discernable limits. "The danger in these times from the coercive activities of those who in the delusion of racial or religious conceit would incite violence and breaches of the peace in order to deprive others of their equal right to the exercise of their liberties, is emphasized by events familiar to all. These and other transgressions of those limits the States appropriately may punish." Clearly, the requirement for punishment for such speech must require a "clear and present menace to public peace." The convictions were reversed as the case presented met none of these tests.

Impact

The most significant impact of the Cantwell decision was that religious expression rose, even if religiosity within American society remained relatively stable. Such religious freedoms aided and hindered social and civil progress in the ensuing years but demonstrated the importance of the individual practice of religion as paramount in American society. In preceding decades, it would not be uncommon for individuals to proclaim a duty to protect the freedom of speech of all, even if the aim of the speech was objectionable to the individual. In understanding the overall impact of the Cantwell decision, it must be understood that a healthy democracy is built from all members' freely expressed support or opposition before a majority opinion is reached. *Cantwell v. Connecticut* is important to a healthy democracy because of its overarching theme that a balance must be struck between the individual and the state so that neither federal nor state government can unjustifiably infringe upon the individual right to exercise religious practice freely without a compelling state interest.

Questions for Further Study

1. Was Jesse Cantwell intending to incite a reaction that would break the peace by playing the record? Explain your reasoning.

2. Was the opinion issued in *Cantwell v. Connecticut* shaped by international persecution of Jews? Why do you believe this?

3. Could the opinion rendered in *Cantwell v. Connecticut* have been the same without the protections of the Fourteenth Amendment? Why or why not?

4. If you were a justice hearing this case, what would you require to hear in the government's claim to support an intentional breach of peace case against the Cantwells?

5. What can we learn from the *Cantwell* case when considering draft legislation to protect citizens?

Further Reading

Books

Alley, Robert S. *The Constitution & Religion: Leading Supreme Court Cases on Church and State*. Amherst, NY: Prometheus Books, 1999.

Hare, Ivan, and James Weinstein. *Extreme Speech and Democracy*. New York: Oxford University Press, 2009.

Hunter, James Davidson, and Os Guinness, eds. *Articles of Faith, Articles of Peace: The Religious Liberty Clauses and the American Public Philosophy*. Washington, DC: Brookings Institute Press, 2010.

Sehat, David. *The Myth of American Religious Freedom*. New York: Oxford University Press, 2010.

Articles

"Religion: Freedom of Faith." *Time*, April 8, 1940.

Websites

Batlan, Katharine M. "Offense at Your Door: Roman Catholics, Jehovah's Witnesses, Judicial Review, and Cantwell v. Connecticut, 1938–1940." Master's thesis. University of Texas at Austin, May 2014. Accessed February 27, 2023. http://repositories.lib.utexas.edu/handle/2152/32466.

"Laws Neutral to Religious Practice during the 1940s and 1950s." Constitution Annotated. Accessed February 27, 2023, http://constitution.congress.gov/browse/essay/amdt1-4-3-1/ALDE_00013223/.

"'Let Our People Be': The 'Sacred Sacrament' and Freedom of Religion." Podcast. Center for C-SPAN Scholarship & Engagement, Brian Lamb School of Communication, Purdue University. Accessed February 27, 2023, http://www.cla.purdue.edu/academic/communication/cspan/ccse/civics-literacy-initiative/10-let-our-people-be.html.

—Commentary by Bryant Macfarlane

CANTWELL V. CONNECTICUT

Document Text

MR. JUSTICE ROBERTS delivered the opinion of the Cour

Newton Cantwell and his two sons, Jesse and Russell, members of a group known as Jehovah's Witnesses and claiming to be ordained ministers, were arrested in New Haven, Connecticut, and each was charged by information in five counts, with statutory and common law offenses. After trial in the Court of Common Pleas of New Haven County, each of them was convicted on the third count, which charged a violation of § 294 of the General Statutes of Connecticut, and on the fifth count, which charged commission of the common law offense of inciting a breach of the peace. On appeal to the Supreme Court, the conviction of all three on the third count was affirmed. The conviction of Jesse Cantwell on the fifth count was also affirmed, but the conviction of Newton and Russell on that count was reversed, and a new trial ordered as to them.

By demurrers to the information, by requests for rulings of law at the trial, and by their assignments of error in the State Supreme Court, the appellants pressed the contention that the statute under which the third count was drawn was offensive to the due process clause of the Fourteenth Amendment because, on its face and as construed and applied, it denied them freedom of speech and prohibited their free exercise of religion. In like manner, they made the point that they could not be found guilty on the fifth count without violation of the Amendment.

We have jurisdiction on appeal from the judgments on the third count, as there was drawn in question the validity of a state statute under the Federal Constitution and the decision was in favor of validity. Since the conviction on the fifth count was not based upon a statute, but presents a substantial question under the Federal Constitution, we granted the writ of certiorari in respect of it.

The facts adduced to sustain the convictions on the third count follow. On the day of their arrest, the appellants were engaged in going singly from house to house on Cassius Street in New Haven. They were individually equipped with a bag containing books and pamphlets on religious subjects, a portable phonograph, and a set of records, each of which, when played, introduced, and was a description of, one of the books. Each appellant asked the person who responded to his call for permission to play one of the records. If permission was granted, he asked the person to buy the book described, and, upon refusal, he solicited such contribution towards the publication of the pamphlets as the listener was willing to make. If a contribution was received, a pamphlet was delivered upon condition that it would be read.

Cassius Street is in a thickly populated neighborhood where about ninety percent of the residents are Roman Catholics. A phonograph record, describing a book entitled "Enemies," included an attack on the Catholic religion. None of the persons interviewed were members of Jehovah's Witnesses.

The statute under which the appellants were charged provides:

No person shall solicit money, services, subscriptions or any valuable thing for any alleged religious, charitable or philanthropic cause, from other than a member of the organization for whose benefit such person is soliciting or within the county in which such person or organization is located unless such cause shall have been approved by the secretary of the public welfare council. Upon application of any person in behalf of such cause, the secretary shall determine whether such cause is a religious one or is a bona fide object of charity or philanthropy and conforms to reasonable standards of efficiency and integrity, and, if he shall so find, shall approve the same and issue to the authority in charge a certificate to that effect. Such certificate may be revoked at any time. Any person violating any provision of this section shall be fined not more than one hundred dollars or imprisoned not more than thirty days or both.

The appellants claimed that their activities were not within the statute, but consisted only of distribution of books, pamphlets, and periodicals. The State Supreme Court construed the finding of the trial court to be that,

> in addition to the sale of the books and the distribution of the pamphlets, the defendants were also soliciting contributions or donations of money for an alleged religious cause, and thereby came within the purview of the statute.

It overruled the contention that the Act, as applied to the appellants, offends the due process clause of the Fourteenth Amendment because it abridges or denies religious freedom and liberty of speech and press. The court stated that it was the solicitation that brought the appellants within the sweep of the Act, and not their other activities in the dissemination of literature. It declared the legislation constitutional as an effort by the State to protect the public against fraud and imposition in the solicitation of funds for what purported to be religious, charitable, or philanthropic causes.

The facts which were held to support the conviction of Jesse Cantwell on the fifth count were that he stopped two men in the street, asked, and received, permission to play a phonograph record, and played the record

"Enemies," which attacked the religion and church of the two men, who were Catholics. Both were incensed by the contents of the record, and were tempted to strike Cantwell unless he went away. On being told to be on his way, he left their presence. There was no evidence that he was personally offensive or entered into any argument with those he interviewed.

The court held that the charge was not assault or breach of the peace or threats on Cantwell's part, but invoking or inciting others to breach of the peace, and that the facts supported the conviction of that offense.

First. We hold that the statute, a construed and applied to the appellants, deprives them of their liberty without due process of law in contravention of the Fourteenth Amendment. The fundamental concept of liberty embodied in that Amendment embraces the liberties guaranteed by the First Amendment. The First Amendment declares that Congress shall make no law respecting an establishment of religion or prohibiting the free exercise thereof. The Fourteenth Amendment has rendered the legislatures of the states as incompetent as Congress to enact such laws. The constitutional inhibition of legislation on the subject of religion has a double aspect. On the one hand, it forestalls compulsion by law of the acceptance of any creed or the practice of any form of worship. Freedom of conscience and freedom to adhere to such religious organization or form of worship as the individual may choose cannot be restricted by law. On the other hand, it safeguards the free exercise of the chosen form of religion. Thus, the Amendment embraces two concepts—freedom to believe and freedom to act. The first is absolute, but, in the nature of things, the second cannot be. Conduct remains subject to regulation for the protection of society. The freedom to act must have appropriate definition to preserve the enforcement of that protection. In every case, the power to regulate must be so exercised as not, in attaining a permissible end, unduly to infringe the protected freedom. No one would contest the proposition that a State may not, by statute, wholly deny the right to preach or to disseminate religious views. Plainly, such a previous and absolute restraint would violate the terms of the guarantee. It is equally clear that a State may, by general and nondiscriminatory legislation, regulate the times, the places, and the manner of soliciting upon its streets, and of holding meetings thereon, and may in other respects safeguard the peace, good order, and comfort of the community without unconstitutionally invading the liberties protected by the Fourteenth Amendment. The appellants are right in their insistence that the Act in question is not such a regulation. If a certificate is procured, solicitation is permitted without restraint, but, in the absence of a certificate, solicitation is altogether prohibited.

The appellants urge that to require them to obtain a certificate as a condition of soliciting support for their views amounts to a prior restraint on the exercise of their religion within the meaning of the Constitution. The State insists that the Act, as construed by the Supreme Court of Connecticut, imposes no previous restraint upon the dissemination of religious views or teaching, but merely safeguards against the perpetration of frauds under the cloak of religion. Conceding that this is so, the question remains whether the method adopted by Connecticut to that end transgresses the liberty safeguarded by the Constitution.

The general regulation, in the public interest, of solicitation, which does not involve any religious test and does not unreasonably obstruct or delay the collection of funds is not open to any constitutional objection, even though the collection be for a religious purpose. Such regulation would not constitute a prohibited previous restraint on the free exercise of religion or interpose an inadmissible obstacle to its exercise.

It will be noted, however, that the Act requires an application to the secretary of the public welfare council of the State; that he is empowered to determine whether the cause is a religious one, and that the issue of a certificate depends upon his affirmative action. If he finds that the cause is not that of religion, to solicit for it becomes a crime. He is not to issue a certificate as a matter of course. His decision to issue or refuse it involves appraisal of facts, the exercise of judgment, and the formation of an opinion. He is authorized to withhold his approval if he determines that the cause is not a religious one. Such a censorship of religion as the means of determining its right to survive is a denial of liberty protected by the First Amendment and included in the liberty which is within the protection of the Fourteenth.

The State asserts that, if the licensing officer acts arbitrarily, capriciously, or corruptly, his action is subject to judicial correction. Counsel refer to the rule prevailing in Connecticut that the decision of a commission or an administrative official will be reviewed upon a claim that

> it works material damage to individual or corporate rights, or invades or threatens such rights, or is so unreasonable as to justify judicial intervention, or is not consonant with justice, or that a legal duty has not been performed.

It is suggested that the statute is to be read as requiring the officer to issue a certificate unless the cause in question is clearly not a religious one, and that, if he violates his duty, his action will be corrected by a court.

To this suggestion there are several sufficient answers. The line between a discretionary and a ministerial act is not always easy to mark, and the statute has not been construed by the state court to impose a mere ministerial duty on the secretary of the welfare council. Upon his decision as to the nature of the cause the right to solicit depends. Moreover, the availability of a judicial remedy for abuses in the system of licensing still leaves that system one of previous restraint which, in the field of free speech and press, we have held inadmissible. A statute authorizing previous restraint upon the exercise of the guaranteed freedom by judicial decision after trial is as obnoxious to the Constitution as one providing for like restraint by administrative action.

Nothing we have said is intended even remotely to imply that, under the cloak of religion, persons may, with impunity, commit frauds upon the public. Certainly penal laws are available to punish such conduct. Even the exercise of religion may be at some slight inconvenience in order that the State may protect its citizens from injury. Without doubt, a State may protect its citizens from fraudulent solicitation by requiring a stranger in the community, before permitting him publicly to solicit funds for any purpose, to establish his identity and his authority to act for the cause which he purports to represent. The State is likewise free to regulate the time and manner of solicitation generally, in the interest of public safety, peace, comfort or convenience. But to condition the solicitation of aid for the perpetuation of religious views or systems upon a license, the grant of which rests in the exercise of a determination by state authority as to what is a religious cause, is to lay a forbidden burden upon the exercise of liberty protected by the Constitution.

Second. We hold that, in the circumstances disclosed, the conviction of Jesse Cantwell on the fifth count must be set aside. Decision as to the lawfulness of the conviction demands the weighing of two conflicting interests. The fundamental law declares the interest of the United States that the free exercise of religion be not prohibited and that freedom to communicate information and opinion be not abridged. The State of Connecticut has an obvious interest in the preservation and protection of peace and good order within her borders. We must determine whether the alleged protection of the State's interest, means to which end would, in the absence of limitation by the Federal Constitution, lie wholly within the State's discretion, has been pressed, in this instance, to a point where it has come into fatal collision with the overriding interest protected by the federal compact.

Conviction on the fifth count was not pursuant to a statute evincing a legislative judgment that street discussion of religious affairs, because of its tendency to provoke disorder, should be regulated, or a judgment that the playing of a phonograph on the streets should in the interest of comfort or privacy be limited or prevented. Violation of an Act exhibiting such a legislative judgment and narrowly drawn to prevent the supposed evil would pose a question differing from that we must here answer. Such a declaration of the State's policy would weigh heavily in any challenge of the law as infringing constitutional limitations. Here, however, the judgment is based on a common law concept of the most general and undefined nature. The court below has held that the petitioner's conduct constituted the commission of an offense under the state law, and we accept its decision as binding upon us to that extent.

The offense known as breach of the peace embraces a great variety of conduct destroying or menacing public order and tranquility. It includes not only violent acts, but acts and words likely to produce violence in others. No one would have the hardihood to suggest that the principle of freedom of speech sanctions incitement to riot, or that religious liberty connotes the privilege to exhort others to physical attack upon those belonging to another sect. When clear and present danger of riot, disorder, interference with traffic upon the public streets, or other immediate threat to public safety, peace, or order appears, the power of the State to prevent or punish is obvious. Equally obvious is it that a State may not unduly suppress free communication of views, religious or other, under the guise of conserving desirable conditions. Here we have a situation analogous to a conviction under a statute sweeping in a great variety of conduct under a general and indefinite characterization, and leaving to the executive and judicial branches too wide a discretion in its application.

Having these considerations in mind, we note that Jesse Cantwell, on April 26, 1938, was upon a public street, where he had a right to be and where he had a right peacefully to impart his views to others. There is no showing that his deportment was noisy, truculent, overbearing or offensive. He requested of two pedestrians permission to play to them a phonograph record. The permission was granted. It is not claimed that he intended to insult or affront the hearers by playing the record. It is plain that he wished only to interest them in his propaganda. The sound of the phonograph is not shown to have disturbed residents of the street, to have drawn a crowd, or to have impeded traffic. Thus far, he had invaded no right or interest of the public, or of the men accosted.

The record played by Cantwell embodies a general attack on all organized religious systems as instruments of Satan and injurious to man; it then singles out the Roman Catholic Church for strictures couched in terms which naturally would offend not only persons of that persuasion, but all others who respect the honestly held religious faith of their fellows. The hearers were, in fact, highly offended. One of them said he felt like hitting Cantwell, and the other that he was tempted to throw Cantwell off the street. The one who testified he felt like hitting Cantwell said, in answer to the question "Did you do anything else or have any other reaction?" "No, sir, because he said he would take the victrola, and he went." The other witness testified that he told Cantwell he had better get off the street before something happened to him, and that was the end of the matter, as Cantwell picked up his books and walked up the street.

Cantwell's conduct, in the view of the court below, considered apart from the effect of his communication upon his hearers, did not amount to a breach of the peace. One may, however, be guilty of the offense if he commit acts or make statements likely to provoke violence and disturbance of good order, even though no such eventuality be intended. Decisions to this effect are many, but examination discloses that, in practically all, the provocative language which was held to amount to a breach of the peace consisted of profane, indecent, or abusive remarks directed to the person of the hearer. Resort to epithets or personal abuse is not in any proper sense communication of information or opinion safeguarded by the Constitution, and its punishment as a criminal act would raise no question under that instrument.

We find in the instant case no assault or threatening of bodily harm, no truculent bearing, no intentional discourtesy, no personal abuse. On the contrary, we find only an effort to persuade a willing listener to buy a book or to contribute money in the interest of what Cantwell, however misguided others may think him, conceived to be true religion.

In the realm of religious faith, and in that of political belief, sharp differences arise. In both fields the tenets of one man may seem the rankest error to his neighbor. To persuade others to his own point of view, the pleader, as we know, at times resorts to exaggeration, to vilification of men who have been, or are, prominent in church or state, and even to false statement. But the people of this nation have ordained, in the light of history, that, in spite of the probability of excesses and abuses, these liberties are, in the long view, essential to enlightened opinion and right conduct on the part of the citizens of a democracy.

The essential characteristic of these liberties is that, under their shield, many types of life, character, opinion and belief can develop unmolested and unobstructed. Nowhere is this shield more necessary than in our own country, for a people composed of many races and of many creeds. There are limits to the exercise of these liberties. The danger in these times from the coercive activities of those who in the delusion of racial or religious conceit would incite violence and breaches of the peace in order to deprive others of their equal right to the exercise of their liberties, is emphasized by events familiar to all. These and other transgressions of those limits the States appropriately may punish.

Although the contents of the record not unnaturally aroused animosity, we think that, in the absence of a statute narrowly drawn to define and punish specific conduct as constituting a clear and present danger to a substantial interest of the State, the petitioner's communication, considered in the light of the constitutional guarantees, raised no such clear and present menace to public peace and order as to render him liable to conviction of the common law offense in question.

The judgment affirming the convictions on the third and fifth counts is reversed, and the cause is remanded for further proceedings not inconsistent with this opinion.

Reversed.

Glossary

appellants: persons bringing a case on appeal to the Supreme Court

capricious: unpredictable; impulsive

due process clause: a portion of the Fourteenth Amendment that states that a person must not be deprived of "life, liberty, or property, without due process of law"

free exercise clause: the portion of the First Amendment that protects citizens' right to practice their religion as they please

---

WICKARD V. FILBURN

DATE 1942	**CITATION** 317 U.S. 111
AUTHOR Robert H. Jackson	**SIGNIFICANCE** Significantly expanded the authority of Congress to regulate economic activity by reinterpreting the commerce clause to include minor intrastate economic activity
VOTE 8–0	

Overview

The Supreme Court ruling in *Wickard v. Filburn* overturned more than a century of precedents by dramatically increasing the power of Congress to regulate the economy. The case was argued on May 4, 1942, and reargued on October 13, with a ruling issued on November 9. In 1938, the Agricultural Adjustment Act (AAA) established quotas on certain crops, ranging from peanuts to cotton to wheat, as part of an effort to keep prices stable. The appellee, Roscoe C. Filburn, was a small farmer in Ohio who was charged with overproduction of wheat in 1941. Filburn admitted to growing more wheat than he was allowed under the government's allotment system, but he argued that the additional crops were used to feed the animals on his farm. The farmer did not sell the extra wheat; therefore, he contended, it was exempt from the AAA.

A district court ruled in Filburn's favor, but the government appealed to the Supreme Court. In its decision, the Court rejected the appellee's argument. Writing for the unanimous court, Associate Justice Robert H. Jackson noted that if the Ohio farmer had not grown his own wheat, he would have had to purchase the crop. If other farmers followed Filburn's example, the combined result would have a major impact on the price of wheat. Consequently, Congress did have a right under the commerce clause to prohibit Filburn's extra production. The ruling ran counter to past Supreme Court decisions, which differentiated between interstate commerce (economic activity that involved multiple states) and intrastate commerce (economic activity within a state, especially minor activities).

Context

The Great Depression (1929–39) devastated the U.S. economy. Economic output declined by more than 15 percent, and unemployment rose to 25 percent. One of the causes of the Great Depression was agricultural overproduction. U.S. farms grew so many crops that the prices of commodities such as corn and wheat fell by more than two-thirds. Furthermore, as the economies of other countries collapsed, they stopped or reduced their purchase of U.S.-grown crops. The result was that many farmers lost their lands since they were unable to make enough money to pay back loans or

Robert H. Jackson wrote the unanimous opinion.
(Library of Congress)

mortgages. This created more unemployment and strained banks and financial institutions, which had to foreclose on the properties.

In an effort to help farmers and stabilize the economy, Congress enacted the Agricultural Adjustment Act (AAA) of 1933. The law was one of a series of measures that were collectively known as the New Deal and were the result of efforts by the administration of Franklin D. Roosevelt to reduce the worst consequences of the Great Depression. The New Deal measures dramatically expanded the authority of the federal government to regulate commerce and agricultural production. The New Deal was deeply opposed by conservatives, who contended that its actions violated the Constitution by creating a government that was too powerful and intrusive.

Under the 1933 law, the government bought excess crops and livestock from farmers and paid subsidies for planters to refrain from growing some crops. To pay for the subsidies, the government enacted new taxes on agricultural processing companies. To oversee the programs, the Agricultural Adjustment Administration was created. However, in 1936, the Supreme Court in *United States v. Butler* ruled 6–3 that Congress had exceeded its

authority in the way the tax and subsidy system was created. The decision also argued that oversight of farms was a function of the states, not the federal government.

U.S. v. Butler was one of a series of Supreme Court cases that were decided by a conservative majority led by Chief Justice Charles Evans Hughes, a former Republican governor of New York. The Court overturned many of the initial New Deal initiatives. However, beginning in 1937, President Roosevelt had been able to appoint a growing number of liberal justices to the court following the retirement or deaths of their predecessors. By 1942, Roosevelt had appointed seven of the Court's justices. Meanwhile, Harlan F. Stone had replaced Hughes as chief justice in July 1941. These changes dramatically altered the approach of the Court to New Deal legislation. Beginning in 1937, the Court increasingly upheld Roosevelt's programs.

In response to *U.S. v. Butler*, Congress enacted a revised version of the AAA in 1938. This measure established limits on how much individual farms could grow through a quota system: the farms could only produce a certain amount of a crop, based on their size. The revised program still paid subsidies, but it was funded by general revenues instead of a specific tax on one group (the food processors). To participate in the new AAA, farm groups had to vote in a referendum on whether to accept the government's terms. There were different votes for each of the major crops, such that cotton growers voted in one initiative, for example, while wheat famers voted in another, and so forth. The 1938 bill also established a system of insurance, the Federal Crop Insurance Corporation, or FCIC, so farmers could protect themselves from crop failures or poor harvests.

The new quota system was effective but unpopular. The number of acres that were planted with wheat dropped from 81 million in 1937 to 62 million the next year. Harvests of other commodities also dropped. The AAA had the added benefit of prompting farmers to diversify and plant other crops since they could not use all of their fields for one product.

Some farmers opposed the new AAA because they did not like the idea of fields being uncultivated. Others opposed the degree of control the law gave to the government. Opponents of the AAA formed groups such as the Corn Belt Liberty League, which sought to convince Congress to repeal the measure. In 1940, Filburn decided to plant more than his allotted quota in a direct challenge to the AAA.

Under the AAA allotment, Filburn was permitted to plant wheat on 11.1 acres in 1941. Instead, he planted 23 acres. The additional acres yielded 239 bushels of wheat above his quota. The farmer did not sell the extra wheat but used it around his farm to feed his animals and make flour for his family's use. He was fined $117.11 for the overproduction, and a lien was placed on his regular crop until he paid. When Filburn went to trial, the district court ruled in his favor. The court argued that a radio address by the secretary of agriculture had unduly influenced the 1941 referendum, in which what farmers had approved the quota system on a vote of 81 percent in favor and 19 percent opposed. The government appealed the district court's ruling to the Supreme Court.

About the Author

Robert F. Jackson was born on February 13, 1892, in Spring Creek, Pennsylvania, but grew up in the small town of Frewsburg in southwestern New York. After he graduated from high school, he served as an apprentice at his uncle's law firm and then attended Albany Law School. Jackson became a lawyer in 1913 and quickly earned a reputation as having a keen legal mind.

Jackson was a lifelong Democrat and an early protégé of future president Franklin D. Roosevelt. In 1934, Roosevelt appointed Jackson to a post with the agency that would become the Internal Revenue Service. Two years later, Jackson was named an assistant attorney general for the United States. Then in 1938, Roosevelt appointed the lawyer to be the solicitor general, in which capacity he argued cases before the Supreme Court. After two years, Jackson was appointed as the U.S. attorney general.

Jackson's tenure was brief as Roosevelt named him to the Supreme Court in June 1941 after Hughes retired and Stone became chief justice. Jackson served on the Court until October 1954 and was involved in some of the most influential cases of the 1900s. Throughout his tenure, Jackson was noted a proponent of civil liberties but generally regarded as a moderate on most other issues. He dissented in the 1944 case *Korematsu v. United States*, in which the Court ruled that it was constitutional for the government to place Japanese Americans and others in internment camps during World War II. Jackson also participated in the 1954 decision in *Brown v. Board*, which ended segregation in public schools.

From 1945 to 1946, Jackson took a leave of absence to serve as the lead prosecutor for the United States at the Nuremberg trials of the surviving Nazi leaders from World War II.

Jackson died of a heart attack on October 9, 1954.

Explanation and Analysis of the Document

The Supreme Court reversed the district court's decision in favor of Filburn and instead ruled for the government in a unanimous verdict (one justice, James F. Byrnes, resigned in the midst of the case to become the director of the Office of Economic Stabilization). Jackson begins his opinion with a succinct overview of the facts of the case, including background on Filburn's farm, his specific violations of the 1938 AAA, and the government's response. He also outlines Filburn's basic argument that the AAA violates the Fifth Amendment of the Constitution. This provision prohibits the government from taking property from individuals to be used for the broader population unless the property owner receives recompense. Furthermore, the farmer argued that the AAA was not compatible with Article 1, Section 8, Clause 3 of the Constitution (the commerce clause), which gives the government the authority to regulate interstate business and financial transactions, including the movement of goods.

The justice then provides a synopsis of the AAA. He concentrates on those aspects of the law that relate to the production of wheat. Jackson notes that the intent of the AAA was to prevent large surpluses or shortages of the crop by regulating how much is grown. When it appeared that the production of wheat would exceed the nation's average annual use, including exports, by 35 percent or more, the secretary of agriculture could impose quotas.

Jackson next deconstructs the ruling of the district court. While doing so, he begins to build the foundation for the Supreme Court's decision. The justice dismisses the lower court's concerns over the radio address by the secretary of agriculture. Jackson questions whether there is any evidence that the speech had any impact on the vote and contends that the court gave too much weight to the address.

At the core of Jackson's opinion is a reinterpretation of the scope of the commerce clause. Past court decisions had generally agreed that the legislature's authority to control interstate commerce was confined to activities that involved multiple states or that crossed state lines. Indeed, Filburn contended that his activities were local and confined to his own farm. They were therefore outside of the scope of the commerce clause.

Jackson refutes the appellee's argument by detailing the evolution of the Court's interpretation of the commerce clause. He argues that in its early days, the Supreme Court interpreted the commerce clause very broadly in decisions such as *Gibbons v. Ogden*. In the 1824 case, the Court affirmed the authority of Congress to control interstate commerce and overrule state laws that conflicted with federal regulations.

He writes that Congress did not begin to utilize the clause in any significant way until the passage of the Interstate Commerce Act in 1887. This law gave the government the authority to regulate railroads. That industry became the first to have guidelines put in place by the government over how it could operate. Since that law went into effect, Congress gradually expanded its ability to oversee other aspects of the economy. Jackson cites the 1890 Sherman Antitrust Act as an example. The act was the first enacted at the federal level to prevent monopolies and was followed by a succession of other laws. One significant feature of these new measures was that they necessitated a greater role for the Supreme Court in defining the boundaries of the legislature's power.

Jackson acknowledges that the Court often acted as a brake on the expansion of federal power, especially in the 1930s. This reluctance was abandoned by 1937, and Jackson summarizes a succession of cases that confirm the legislature's power to regulate commerce to protect Americans and maintain the economy. In the case of wheat production, the justice explains that at the time, thirty-two of the forty-eight states did not produce enough wheat to meet their needs. Instead, they depended on the surplus production of sixteen states that grew more of the crop than they used. In

addition, wheat exports were mainly provided by these same sixteen. Jackson asserts that Congress had to control the wheat market because of the possibility that it might collapse if the price fell too low.

Filburn claimed that his production of wheat for use on his farms was so small that it did not affect the broader market for the crop. Jackson acknowledges that Filburn's extra wheat would not make much of an impact. However, he notes that the additional wheat used by Jackson would otherwise have to have been purchased. If a large number of farmers stopped buying wheat for home use, it would have a significant influence on wheat prices. Prices would likely continue to fall, forcing more farmers out of business. Consequently, Congress did have both the authority and the need to regulate the wheat sector.

Jackson also rejects Filburn's Fifth Amendment arguments. He writes that to control the total supply of a product, Congress had to be able to control the supply at an individual level. Therefore, Congress had to impose penalties if people violated the law. Those who obeyed were essentially guaranteed a minimum profit, but the system only worked if everyone participated. Jackson concludes by affirming the Court's belief that the fine and the resultant lien were justified. He discusses Filburn's decision and the need for structures to be in place to prevent future violations of the law. Jackson also argues that even with the fine, Filburn still benefited from the law because it had stabilized prices and ensured access to future markets.

Jackson adopts an activist approach in his interpretation of the commerce clause. He argues for expanded powers for both the legislature and the courts. In doing so, he is endorsing the idea of a living Constitution, one that can be updated as times change through reinterpretation. In contrast, many of his predecessors had embraced judicial restraint—a legal approach that emphasizes the original text of the Constitution and accepts broad limits on judicial and legislative power.

Impact

The ruling in the case dramatically expanded the scope and power of Congress to regulate commerce. After decades of skepticism toward congressional efforts to exert more authority over the economy, *Wickard v.*

Filburn ushered in an era during which the Court reversed its course. By the 2000s, there were few aspects of the U.S. economy that were not regulated by the government. There are strict rules on the manufacture and sale of products ranging from foods to automobiles to electronics. For example, automobiles must have certain safety features, such as seatbelts and airbags, and meet minimum mileage standards. An April 2022 rule mandated that car manufacturers in the United States achieve an average of 49 miles per gallon across all of the automobiles and light trucks are produced by the year 2026. Restaurants, businesses, and even recreational sites are subject to laws on worker and consumer safety. The federal Occupational Safety and Health Administration requires that employees use safety glasses when working in professions where there might be flying debris. The Food and Drug Administration (FDA) performs tests and studies on new medicines or drugs before they can be offered to the public. For instance, the FDA had to approve the various COVID-19 vaccines in 2020 before they became available for common use.

Until the 1970s, the government steadily increased its oversight of economic activities, with the executive branch taking on a greater role. In 1946, the Administrative Procedure Act granted federal agencies the authority to make rules that had the force of law without direct congressional approval to carry out functions that Congress had assigned to those bureaucracies. This authority under the commerce clause has increasingly been challenged by critics who argue that the power to make rules should only be held by Congress. For instance, the Environmental Protection Agency (EPA) has the authority to develop rules that have the same weight as laws passed by Congress. However, the Supreme Court in the 2022 case *West Virginia v. Environmental Protection Agency* ruled that the EPA did not have the right to limit carbon emissions from individual states. That authority resided only with Congress, according to the Court.

Wickard v. Filburn changed an important distinction in the legal definition of interstate commerce. Before the ruling, the courts had generally held that economic activity that was local in nature (limited in geographic scope and monetary amount) was the domain of the states. The federal government was limited to exercising control over larger, multistate enterprises that impacted large numbers of people. By broadening the scope of activity that could be considered interstate commerce (or that affected interstate commerce), Jackson's opinion set the stage for the dramatic expansion of government regulation and oversight of everyday life.

Questions for Further Study

1. Why did some farmers oppose the Agricultural Adjustment Act of 1938? Did the law generally help or hurt farmers?

2. Why did the district court rule in Filburn's favor? What was the court's main rationale for its decision? How did Justice Jackson refute the arguments of the district court?

3. How did the ruling in *Wickard v. Filburn* expand the economic authority of Congress? What were Jackson's main justifications for the new power?

Further Reading

Books

Albertson, Dean. *Roosevelt's Farmer: Claude R. Wickard in the New Deal*. New York: Columbia University Press, 1961.

Choate, Jean. *Disputed Ground: Farm Groups That Opposed the New Deal Agricultural Program*. Jefferson, NC: McFarland, 2002.

Conant, Michael. *The Constitution and Economic Regulation: The Commerce Clause and the Fourteenth Amendment*. New York: Routledge, 2008.

Conkin, Paul. *A Revolution Down on the Farm: The Transformation of American Agriculture Since 1929*. Lexington: University of Kentucky Press, 2008.

Gerhart, Eugene. *Robert H. Jackson: Country Lawyer, Supreme Court Justice, America's Advocate*. Getzville, NY: William S. Hein, 2003.

Hiltzik, Michael. *The New Deal: A Modern History*. New York: Free Press, 2011.

Hockett, Jeffrey D. *New Deal Justice: The Constitutional Jurisprudence of Hugo L. Black, Felix Frankfurter, and Robert H. Jackson*. Lanham, MD: Rowman & Littlefield, 1996.

Shubert, Glendon. *Dispassionate Justice: A Synthesis of the Judicial Opinions of Robert H. Jackson*. Indianapolis, IN: Bobbs-Merrill, 1969.

Websites

"Great Depression Facts." Franklin D. Roosevelt Presidential Library and Museum website. Accessed January 10, 2023, https://www.fdrlibrary.org/great-depression-facts.

"Wickard v. Filburn (1942)." National Constitution Center website. Accessed January 10, 2023, https://constitutioncenter.org/the-constitution/supreme-court-case-library/wickard-v-filburn.

—Commentary by Tom Lansford

WICKARD V. FILBURN

Document Text

MR. JUSTICE JACKSON delivered the opinion of the Court

The appellee filed his complaint against the Secretary of Agriculture of the United States, three members of the County Agricultural Conservation Committee for Montgomery County, Ohio, and a member of the State Agricultural Conservation Committee for Ohio. He sought to enjoin enforcement against himself of the marketing penalty imposed by the amendment of May 26, 1941 to the Agricultural Adjustment Act of 1938, upon that part of his 1941 wheat crop which was available for marketing in excess of the marketing quota established for his farm. He also sought a declaratory judgment that the wheat marketing quota provisions of the Act, as amended and applicable to him, were unconstitutional because not sustainable under the Commerce Clause or consistent with the Due Process Clause of the Fifth Amendment.

The Secretary moved to dismiss the action against him for improper venue, but later waived his objection and filed an answer. The other appellants moved to dismiss on the ground that they had no power or authority to enforce the wheat marketing quota provisions of the Act, and, after their motion was denied, they answered, reserving exceptions to the ruling on their motion to dismiss. The case was submitted for decision on the pleadings and upon a stipulation of facts.

The appellee for many years past has owned and operated a small farm in Montgomery County, Ohio, maintaining a herd of dairy cattle, selling milk, raising poultry, and selling poultry and eggs. It has been his practice to raise a small acreage of winter wheat, sown in the Fall and harvested in the following July; to sell a portion of the crop; to feed part to poultry and livestock on the farm, some of which is sold; to use some in making flour for home consumption, and to keep the rest for the following seeding. The intended disposition of the crop here involved has not been expressly stated.

In July of 1940, pursuant to the Agricultural Adjustment Act of 1938, as then amended, there were established for the appellee's 1941 crop a wheat acreage allotment of 11.1 acres and a normal yield of 20.1 bushels of wheat an acre. He was given notice of such allotment in July of 1940, before the Fall planting of his 1941 crop of wheat, and again in July of 1941, before it was harvested. He sowed, however, 23 acres, and harvested from his 11.9 acres of excess acreage 239 bushels, which, under the terms of the Act as amended on May 26, 1941, constituted farm marketing excess, subject to a penalty of 49 cents a bushel, or $117.11 in all. The appellee has not paid the penalty, and he has not postponed or avoided it by storing the excess under regulations of the Secretary of Agriculture, or by delivering it up to the Secretary. The Committee, therefore, refused him a marketing card, which was, under the terms of Regulations promulgated by the Secretary, necessary to protect a buyer from liability to the penalty and upon its protecting lien.

The general scheme of the Agricultural Adjustment Act of 1938 as related to wheat is to control the volume moving in interstate and foreign commerce in order to avoid surpluses and shortages and the consequent abnormally low or high wheat prices and obstructions to commerce. Within prescribed limits and by prescribed standards, the Secretary of Agriculture is directed to ascertain and proclaim each year a national acreage allotment for the next crop of wheat, which is then apportioned to the states and their counties, and is eventually broken up into allotments for individual farms. Loans and payments to wheat farmers are authorized in stated circumstances.

The Act further provides that, whenever it appears that the total supply of wheat as of the beginning of any marketing year, beginning July 1, will exceed a normal year's domestic consumption and export by more than 35 percent, the Secretary shall so proclaim not later than May 15 prior to the beginning of such marketing year, and that, during the marketing year, a compulsory national marketing quota shall be in effect with respect to the marketing of wheat. Between the issuance of the proclamation and June 10, the Secretary must, however, conduct a referendum of farmers who will be subject to the quota, to determine whether they favor or oppose it; and, if more than one-third of the farmers voting in the referendum do oppose, the Secretary must, prior to the effective date of the quota, by proclamation suspend its operation.

On May 19, 1941, the Secretary of Agriculture made a radio address to the wheat farmers of the United States in which he advocated approval of the quotas and called attention to the pendency of the amendment of May 26, 1941, which had at the time been sent by Congress to the White House, and pointed out its provision for an increase in the loans on wheat to 85 percent of parity. He made no mention of the fact that it also increased the penalty from 15 cents a bushel to one-half of the parity loan rate of about 98 cents, but stated that,

"Because of the uncertain world situation, we deliberately planted several million extra acres of wheat. . . . Farmers should not be penalized because they have provided insurance against shortages of food."

Pursuant to the Act, the referendum of wheat growers was held on May 31, 1941. According to the required published statement of the Secretary of Agriculture, 81 percent of those voting favored the marketing quota, with 19 percent opposed.

The court below held, with one judge dissenting, that the speech of the Secretary invalidated the referendum, and that the amendment of May 26, 1941,

"insofar as it increased the penalty for the farm marketing excess over the fifteen cents per bushel prevailing at the time of planting and subjected the entire crop to a lien for the payment thereof,"

should not be applied to the appellee because, as so applied, it was retroactive, and in violation of the Fifth Amendment, and, alternatively, because the equities of the case so required. 43 F. Supp. 1017. Its Judgment permanently enjoined appellants from collecting a marketing penalty of more than 15 cents a bushel on the farm marketing excess of appellee's 1941 wheat crop, from subjecting appellee's entire 1941 crop to a lien for the payment of the penalty, and from collecting a 15-cent penalty except in accordance with the provisions of § 339 of the Act as that section stood prior to the amendment of May 26, 1941. The Secretary and his codefendants have appealed.

I

The holding of the court below that the Secretary's speech invalidated the referendum is manifest error. Read as a whole and in the context of world events that constituted his principal theme, the penalties of which he spoke were more likely those in the form of ruinously low prices resulting from the excess supply, rather than the penalties prescribed in the Act. But, under any interpretation, the speech cannot be given the effect of invalidating the referendum. There is no evidence that any voter put upon the Secretary's words the interpretation that impressed the court below or was in any way misled. There is no showing that the speech influenced the outcome of the referendum. The record, in fact, does not show that any, and does not suggest a basis for even a guess as to how many, of the voting farmers dropped work to listen to "Wheat Farmers and the Battle for Democracy" at 11:30 in the morning of May 19th, which was a busy hour in one of the busiest of seasons. If this discourse intended reference to this legislation at all, it was, of course, a public Act, whose terms were readily available, and the speech did not purport to be an exposition of its provisions.

To hold that a speech by a Cabinet officer, which failed to meet judicial ideals of clarity, precision, and exhaustiveness, may defeat a policy embodied in an Act of

Congress would invest communication between administrators and the people with perils heretofore unsuspected. Moreover, we should have to conclude that such an officer is able to do by accident what he has no power to do by design. Appellee's complaint, insofar as it is based on this speech, is frivolous, and the injunction, insofar as it rests on this ground, is unwarranted. *United States v. Rock Royal Cooperative,* 307 U. S. 533.

II

It is urged that, under the Commerce Clause of the Constitution, Article I, § 8, clause 3, Congress does not possess the power it has in this instance sought to exercise. The question would merit little consideration, since our decision in *United States v. Darby,* 312 U. S. 100, sustaining the federal power to regulate production of goods for commerce, except for the fact that this Act extends federal regulation to production not intended in any part for commerce, but wholly for consumption on the farm. The Act includes a definition of "market" and its derivatives, so that, as related to wheat, in addition to its conventional meaning, it also means to dispose of

"by feeding (in any form) to poultry or livestock which, or the products of which, are sold, bartered, or exchanged, or to be so disposed of."

Hence, marketing quotas not only embrace all that may be sold without penalty, but also what may be consumed on the premises. Wheat produced on excess acreage is designated as "available for marketing" as so defined, and the penalty is imposed thereon. Penalties do not depend upon whether any part of the wheat, either within or without the quota, is sold or intended to be sold. The sum of this is that the Federal Government fixes a quota including all that the farmer may harvest for sale or for his own farm needs, and declares that wheat produced on excess acreage may neither be disposed of nor used except upon payment of the penalty, or except it is stored as required by the Act or delivered to the Secretary of Agriculture.

Appellee says that this is a regulation of production and consumption of wheat. Such activities are, he urges, beyond the reach of Congressional power under the Commerce Clause, since they are local in character, and their effects upon interstate commerce are, at most, "indirect." In answer, the Government argues that the statute regulates neither production nor consumption, but only marketing, and, in the alternative, that, if the Act does go beyond the regulation of marketing, it is sustainable as a "necessary and proper" implementation of the power of Congress over interstate commerce.

The Government's concern lest the Act be held to be a regulation of production or consumption, rather than of marketing, is attributable to a few dicta and decisions of this Court which might be understood to lay it down that activities such as "production," "manufacturing," and "mining" are strictly "local" and, except in special circumstances which are not present here, cannot be regulated under the commerce power because their effects upon interstate commerce are, as matter of law, only "indirect." Even today, when this power has been held to have great latitude, there is no decision of this Court that such activities may be regulated where no part of the product is intended for interstate commerce or intermingled with the subjects thereof. We believe that a review of the course of decision under the Commerce Clause will make plain, however, that questions of the power of Congress are not to be decided by reference to any formula which would give controlling force to nomenclature such as "production" and "indirect" and foreclose consideration of the actual effects of the activity in question upon interstate commerce.

At the beginning, Chief Justice Marshall described the federal commerce power with a breadth never yet exceeded. *Gibbons v. Ogden,* 9 Wheat. 1, 22 U. S. 194-195. He made emphatic the embracing and penetrating nature of this power by warning that effective restraints on its exercise must proceed from political, rather than from judicial, processes. *Id.* at 22 U. S. 197.

For nearly a century, however, decisions of this Court under the Commerce Clause dealt rarely with questions of what Congress might do in the exercise of its granted power under the Clause, and almost entirely with the permissibility of state activity which it was claimed discriminated against or burdened interstate commerce. During this period, there was perhaps little occasion for the affirmative exercise of the commerce power, and the influence of the Clause on American life and law was a negative one, resulting almost wholly from its operation as a restraint upon the powers of the states. In discussion and decision, the point of reference, instead of being what was "necessary and proper" to the exercise by Congress of its granted power, was often some concept of sovereignty thought to be implicit in the status of statehood. Certain activities such as "production," "manufacturing," and "mining" were occasionally said to be within the province of state governments and beyond the power of Congress under the Commerce Clause.

It was not until 1887, with the enactment of the Interstate Commerce Act, that the interstate commerce power began to exert positive influence in American law and life. This first important federal resort to the commerce power was followed in 1890 by the Sherman Anti-Trust Act and, thereafter, mainly after 1903, by many others. These statutes ushered in new phases of adjudication, which required the Court to approach the interpretation of the Commerce Clause in the light of an actual exercise by Congress of its power thereunder.

When it first dealt with this new legislation, the Court adhered to its earlier pronouncements, and allowed but little scope to the power of Congress. *United States v. Knight Co.,* 156 U. S. 1. These earlier pronouncements also played an important part in several.of the five cases in which this Court later held that Acts of Congress under the Commerce Clause were in excess of its power.

Even while important opinions in this line of restrictive authority were being written, however, other cases called forth broader interpretations of the Commerce Clause destined to supersede the earlier ones, and to bring about a return to the principles first enunciated by Chief Justice Marshall in *Gibbons v. Ogden, supra.*

Not long after the decision of *United States v. Knight Co., supra,* Mr. Justice Holmes, in sustaining the exercise of national power over intrastate activity, stated for the Court that "commerce among the States is not a technical legal conception, but a practical one, drawn from the course of business." *Swift & Co. v. United States,* 196 U. S. 375, 196 U. S. 398. It was soon demonstrated that the effects of many kinds of intrastate activity upon interstate commerce were such as to make them a proper subject of federal regulation. In some cases sustaining the exercise of federal power over intrastate matters, the term "direct" was used for the purpose of stating, rather than of reaching, a result; in others, it was treated as synonymous with "substantial" or "material"; and in others it was not used at all. Of late, its use has been abandoned in cases dealing with questions of federal power under the Commerce Clause.

In the *Shreveport Rate Cases,* 234 U. S. 342, the Court held that railroad rates of an admittedly intrastate character and fixed by authority of the state might, nevertheless, be revised by the Federal Government because of the economic effects which they had upon interstate commerce. The opinion of Mr. Justice Hughes found federal intervention constitutionally authorized because of

"matters having such a close and substantial relation to interstate traffic that the control is essential or appropriate to the security of that traffic, to the efficiency of the interstate service, and to the maintenance of conditions under which interstate commerce may be conducted upon fair terms and without molestation or hindrance."

Id. at 234 U. S. 351.

The Court's recognition of the relevance of the economic effects in the application of the Commerce Clause, exemplified by this statement, has made the mechanical application of legal formulas no longer feasible. Once an economic measure of the reach of the power granted to Congress in the Commerce Clause is accepted, questions of federal power cannot be decided simply by finding the activity in question to be "production," nor can consideration of its economic effects be foreclosed by calling them "indirect." The present Chief Justice has said in summary of the present state of the law:

"The commerce power is not confined in its exercise to the regulation of commerce among the states. It extends to those activities intrastate which so affect interstate commerce, or the exertion of the power of Congress over it, as to make regulation of them appropriate means to the attainment of a legitimate end, the effective execution of the granted power to regulate interstate commerce. . . . The power of Congress over interstate commerce is plenary and complete in itself, may be exercised to its utmost extent, and acknowledges no limitations other than are prescribed in the Constitution. . . . It follows that no form of state activity can constitutionally thwart the regulatory power granted by the commerce clause to Congress. Hence, the reach of that power extends to those intrastate activities which in a substantial way interfere with or obstruct the exercise of the granted power."

United States v. Wrightwood Dairy Co., 315 U. S. 110, 315 U. S. 119.

Whether the subject of the regulation in question was "production," "consumption," or "marketing" is, therefore, not material for purposes of deciding the question of federal power before us. That an activity is of local character may help in a doubtful case to determine whether Congress intended to reach it. The same consideration might help in determining whether, in the absence of Congressional action, it would be permissible for the state to exert its power on the subject matter, even though, in so doing, it to some degree affected interstate commerce. But even if appellee's activity be local, and though it may not be regarded as commerce, it may still, whatever its nature, be reached by Congress if it exerts a substantial economic effect on interstate commerce, and this irrespective of whether such effect is what might at some earlier time have been defined as "direct" or "indirect."

The parties have stipulated a summary of the economics of the wheat industry. Commerce among the states in wheat is large and important. Although wheat is raised in every state but one, production in most states is not equal to consumption. Sixteen states, on average, have had a surplus of wheat above their own requirements for feed, seed, and food. Thirty-two states and the District of Columbia, where production has been below consumption, have looked to these surplus-producing states for their supply, as well as for wheat for export and carry-over.

The wheat industry has been a problem industry for some years. Largely as a result of increased foreign production and import restrictions, annual exports of wheat and flour from the United States during the ten-year period ending in 1940 averaged less than 10 percent of total production, while, during the 1920's, they averaged more than 25 percent. The decline in the export trade has left a large surplus in production which, in connection with an abnormally large supply of wheat and other grains in recent years, caused congestion in a number of markets; tied up railroad cars, and caused elevators in some instances to turn away grains, and railroads to institute embargoes to prevent further congestion.

Many countries, both importing and exporting, have sought to modify the impact of the world market conditions on their own economy. Importing countries have taken measures to stimulate production and self-sufficiency. The four large exporting countries of Argentina, Australia, Canada, and the United States have all undertaken various programs for the relief of growers. Such measures have been designed, in part at least, to protect the domestic price received by producers. Such plans have generally evolved towards control by the central government.

In the absence of regulation, the price of wheat in the United States would be much affected by world conditions. During 1941, producers who cooperated with the Agricultural Adjustment program received an average price on the farm of about $1.16 a bushel, as compared with the world market price of 40 cents a bushel.

Differences in farming conditions, however, make these benefits mean different things to different wheat growers. There are several large areas of specialization in wheat, and the concentration on this crop reaches 27 percent of the crop land, and the average harvest runs as high as 155 acres. Except for some use of wheat as stock feed and for seed, the practice is to sell the crop for cash. Wheat from such areas constitutes the bulk of the interstate commerce therein.

On the other hand, in some New England states, less than one percent of the crop land is devoted to wheat, and the average harvest is less than five acres per farm. In 1940, the average percentage of the total wheat production that was sold in each state, as measured by value ranged from 29 percent thereof in Wisconsin to 90 percent in Washington. Except in regions of large-scale production, wheat is usually grown in rotation with other crops; for a nurse crop for grass seeding, and as a cover crop to prevent soil erosion and leaching. Some is sold, some kept for seed, and a percentage of the total production much larger than in areas of specialization is consumed on the farm and grown for such purpose. Such farmers, while growing some wheat, may even find the balance of their interest on the consumer's side.

The effect of consumption of home-grown wheat on interstate commerce is due to the fact that it constitutes the most variable factor in the disappearance of the wheat crop. Consumption on the farm where grown appears to vary in an amount greater than 20 percent of average production. The total amount of wheat consumed as food varies but relatively little, and use as seed is relatively constant.

The maintenance by government regulation of a price for wheat undoubtedly can be accomplished as effectively by sustaining or increasing the demand as by limiting the supply. The effect of the statute before us is to restrict the amount which may be produced for market and the extent, as well, to which one may forestall resort to the market by producing to meet his own needs. That appellee's own contribution to the demand for wheat may be trivial by itself is not enough to remove him from the scope of federal regulation where, as here, his contribution, taken together with that of many others similarly situated, is far from trivial. *Labor Board v. Fairblatt,* 306 U. S. 601, 306 U. S. 606 *et seq.; United States v. Darby supra* at 312 U. S. 123.

It is well established by decisions of this Court that the power to regulate commerce includes the power to regulate the prices at which commodities in that commerce are dealt in and practices affecting such prices. One of the primary purposes of the Act in question was to increase the market price of wheat, and, to that end, to limit the volume thereof that could affect the market. It can hardly be denied that a factor of such volume and variability as home-consumed wheat would have a substantial influence on price and market conditions. This may arise because being in marketable condition such wheat overhangs the market, and, if induced by rising prices, tends to flow into the market and check price increases. But if we assume that it is never marketed, it supplies a need of the man who grew it which would otherwise be reflected by purchases in the open market. Home-grown wheat in this sense competes with wheat in commerce. The stimulation of commerce is a use of the regulatory function quite as definitely as prohibitions or restrictions thereon. This record leaves us in no doubt that Congress may properly have considered that wheat consumed on the farm where grown, if wholly outside the scheme of regulation, would have a substantial effect in defeating and obstructing its purpose to stimulate trade therein at increased prices.

It is said, however, that this Act, forcing some farmers into the market to buy what they could provide for themselves, is an unfair promotion of the markets and prices of specializing wheat growers. It is of the essence of regulation that it lays a restraining hand on the self-interest of the regulated, and that advantages from the regulation commonly fall to others. The conflicts of economic interest between the regulated and those who advantage by it are wisely left under our system to resolution by the Congress under its more flexible and responsible legislative process. Such conflicts rarely lend themselves to judicial determination. And with the wisdom, workability, or fairness, of the plan of regulation, we have nothing to do.

III

The statute is also challenged as a deprivation of property without due process of law contrary to the Fifth Amendment, both because of its regulatory effect on the appellee and because of its alleged retroactive effect. The court below sustained the plea on the ground of forbidden retroactivity, "or, in the alternative, that the equities of the case as shown by the record favor the plaintiff." 43 F. Supp. 1017, 1019. An Act of Congress is not to be refused application by the courts as arbitrary and capricious and forbidden by the Due Process Clause merely because it is deemed in a particular case to work an inequitable result.

Appellee's claim that the Act works a deprivation of due process even apart from its allegedly retroactive effect is not persuasive. Control of total supply, upon which the whole statutory plan is based, depends upon control of individual supply. Appellee's claim is not that his quota represented less than a fair share of the national quota, but that the Fifth Amendment requires that he be free from penalty for planting wheat and disposing of his crop as he sees fit.

We do not agree. In its effort to control total supply, the Government gave the farmer a choice which was, of course, designed to encourage cooperation and discourage noncooperation. The farmer who planted within his allotment was, in effect, guaranteed a minimum return much above what his wheat would have brought if sold on a world market basis. Exemption from the applicability of quotas was made in favor of small producers. The farmer who produced in excess of his quota might escape penalty by delivering his wheat to the Secretary, or by storing it with the privilege of sale without penalty in a later year to fill out his quota, or irrespective of quotas if they are no longer in effect, and he could obtain a loan of 60 percent of the rate for cooperators, or about 59 cents a bushel, on so much of his wheat as would be subject to penalty if marketed. Finally, he might make other disposition of his wheat, subject to the penalty. It is agreed that, as the result of the wheat programs, he is able to market his wheat at a price "far above any world price based on the natural reaction of supply and demand." We can hardly find a denial of due process in these circumstances, particularly since it is even doubtful that appellee's burdens under the program outweigh his benefits. It is hardly lack of due process for the Government to regulate that which it subsidizes.

The amendment of May 26, 1941, is said to be invalidly retroactive in two respects: first, in that it increased the penalty from 15 cents to 49 cents a bushel; secondly, in that, by the new definition of "farm marketing excess," it subjected to the penalty wheat which had theretofore been subject to no penalty at all, *i.e.*, wheat not "marketed" as defined in the Act.

It is not to be denied that, between seed time and harvest, important changes were made in the Act which affected the desirability and advantage of planting the excess acreage. The law, as it stood when the appellee planted his crop, made the quota for his farm the normal or the actual production of the acreage allotment, whichever was greater, plus any carry-over wheat that he could have marketed without penalty in the preceding marketing year. The Act also provided that the farmer who, while quotas were in effect, marketed wheat in excess of the quota for the farm on which it was produced should be subject to a penalty of 15 cents a bushel on the excess so marketed. Marketing of wheat was defined as including disposition "by feeding (in any form) to poultry or livestock which, or the products of which, are sold, bartered, or exchanged, . . ." The amendment of May 26, 1941, made before the appellee had harvested the growing crop, changed the quota and penalty provisions. The quota for each farm became the actual production of acreage planted to wheat, less the normal or the actual production, whichever was smaller, of any excess acreage. Wheat in excess of this quota,

known as the "farm marketing excess" and declared by the amendment to be "regarded as available for marketing," was subjected to a penalty fixed at 50 percent of the basic loan rate for cooperators, or 49 cents, instead of the penalty of 15 cents which obtained at the time of planting. At the same time, there was authorized an increase in the amount of the loan which might be made to noncooperators such as the appellee upon wheat which "would be subject to penalty if marketed" from about 34 cents per bushel to about 59 cents. The entire crop was subjected by the amendment to a lien for the payment of the penalty.

The penalty provided by the amendment can be postponed or avoided only by storing the farm marketing excess according to regulations promulgated by the Secretary or by delivering it to him without compensation; and the penalty is incurred and becomes due on threshing. Thus, the penalty was contingent upon an act which appellee committed not before, but after, the enactment of the statute, and, had he chosen to cut his excess and cure it or feed it as hay, or to reap and feed it with the head and straw together, no penalty would have been demanded. Such manner of consumption is not uncommon. Only when he threshed, and thereby made it a part of the bulk of wheat overhanging the market, did he become subject to penalty. He has made no effort to show that the value of his excess wheat consumed without threshing was less than it would have been had it been threshed while subject to the statutory provisions in force at the time of planting. Concurrently with the increase in the amount of the penalty, Congress authorized a substantial increase in the amount of the loan which might be made to cooperators upon stored farm marketing excess wheat. That appellee is the worse off for the aggregate of this legislation does not appear; it only appears that, if he could get all that the Government gives and do nothing that the Government asks, he would be better off than this law allows. To deny him this is not to deny him due process of law. *Cf. Mulford v. Smith*, 307 U. S. 38.

Reversed.

Glossary

commerce clause: a section of the Constitution (Article 1, Section 8, Clause 3) that grants Congress the power to regulate interstate business and trade

interstate commerce: trading or transporting goods, services, or money across state borders

intrastate activity: commerce or transportation within a state

lien: the legal right to seize property as payment for a debt

WEST VIRGINIA STATE BOARD OF EDUCATION V. BARNETTE

DATE	CITATION
1943	319 U.S. 624

AUTHOR	SIGNIFICANCE
Robert H. Jackson	Held that the free speech clause of the First Amendment prohibits public schools from compelling students to salute the American flag or say the Pledge of Allegiance

VOTE	
6–3	

Overview

West Virginia State Board of Education v. Barnette was a landmark decision holding that the free speech rights guaranteed by the First Amendment to the Constitution protect public school students from being compelled to salute the American flag or to recite the Pledge of Allegiance. The Court's decision is celebrated as one of the Court's most forceful defenses of free speech rights, calling them "beyond the reach of majorities and officials." *Barnette* overruled a decision on the same issue, *Minersville School District v. Gobitis*, issued just three years earlier, in 1940. The decision was a victory for the Jehovah's Witnesses, whose religious beliefs forbade them from pledging or saluting symbols such as the flag. Felix Frankfurter, Owen Roberts, and Stanley F. Reed dissented.

It should be noted that the correct spelling of the family name is Barnett. A court clerk misspelled the name as "Barnette" in filing court papers.

Context

Barnette arose in the context of World War II. The Nazi regime in Germany was arresting thousands of Jehovah's Witnesses who refused to salute the Nazi flag based on their interpretation of verses 4 and 5 of the biblical book of Exodus, chapter 20, which states: "Thou shalt not make unto thee any graven image, or any likeness of anything that is in heaven above, or that is in the earth beneath, or that is in the water under the earth; thou shalt not bow down thyself to them nor serve them." According to the Jehovah's Witnesses, a flag is a "graven image," and accordingly they refused to salute it. In the United States, children of Jehovah's Witnesses had been expelled from school because they refused to salute the American flag; some officials even threatened to send them to reformatories for juvenile delinquents, and parents of these children were prosecuted for fostering delinquency.

In this climate, the U.S. Supreme Court ruled, in *Minersville School District v. Gobitis* (1940), that Pledge of Allegiance requirements did not violate the First Amendment as it pertained to freedom of religion. In response, the legislature of West Virginia amended its laws to require the state's schools to provide instruction in history, civics, and in the constitutions of the United States and of the state "for the purpose of teaching, fostering and perpetuating the ideals, principles and spirit of Americanism." The state board of

Students pledging allegiance to the flag
(Library of Congress)

education was directed to "prescribe the courses of study covering these subjects" for public schools. Further, the board adopted a resolution requiring that teachers and pupils "shall be required to participate in the salute honoring the Nation represented by the Flag; provided, however, that refusal to salute the Flag be regarded as an Act of insubordination, and shall be dealt with accordingly."

The Barnett children, who were Jehovah's Witnesses, were instructed by their father not to salute the flag or recite the Pledge of Allegiance. After they were expelled, the parents brought suit in district court to enjoin enforcement of the regulations. The district court ruled in the Barnetts' favor, but the school district appealed to the U.S. Supreme Court, which issued its decision, perhaps ironically, on Flag Day, June 14, 1943.

About the Author

Robert Houghwout Jackson was born in Spring Creek, Pennsylvania, in 1892. The son of William Eldred and Angelina Houghwout Jackson, he grew up in Frewsburg, New York. The last person to serve as associate justice on the Supreme Court without obtaining a law degree, Jackson passed his bar exam after two years apprenticing for a law firm in nearby Jamestown, New York, and taking a year of course work at Albany Law School in Albany, New York. Following a successful career in private practice, Jackson in 1931 accepted a nomination from then governor Franklin D. Roosevelt to serve on the New York State Commission to Investigate the Administration of Justice. This was to prove formative for his career, much of which focused on the problems inherent in the criminal justice system, such as equality before the law and the pursuit of justice and truth rather than simply pursuit of convictions.

Jackson carried this approach with him into federal service, where he served in the Department of Internal Revenue and as assistant attorney general in the Tax Division and the Antitrust Division, before being named solicitor general in 1938 and then U.S attorney general in 1940. His reputation for pursuing truth and justice as fairly and objectively as possible earned him high renown among his peers, and he brought that same resolve to the Supreme Court, to which he was appointed in 1941. Although Jackson was a staunch defender of individual liberties, he nevertheless strove in his opinions to delineate both individual rights and liberties and the constitutional powers of the state and federal governments, leaving behind a nuanced intellectual legacy.

Jackson's chief legacy, however, rests on the Nuremberg war crimes tribunals, which he was instrumental in creating and seeing through. In the closing days of World War II, one of President Harry Truman's first actions in office was to ask Jackson to represent the United States in the creation of a postwar criminal tribunal to bring the deposed heads of the Nazi state to justice. The Allies had agreed in principle to such proceedings earlier in the war, and Jackson worked throughout the summer of 1945 to turn that agreement into a working tribunal. His efforts paid off, and on August 8, 1945, the Allies signed the London Charter, outlining the aims and methods of the war crimes tribunal, which began in the fall of 1945. Jackson, selected to serve as U.S. chief of counsel during the proceedings, delivered the opening and closing statements for the first trial, speeches that rank among the most eloquent and important of his career. With the trials in Germany over, Jackson returned to the bench in 1946. On October 9, 1954, Jackson suffered a fatal heart attack and was buried in Frewsburg, New York.

Explanation and Analysis of the Document

In 1940 the Supreme Court decided *Minersville School District v. Gobitis*, which held that school districts could compel students to salute the flag despite any religious objections they might have. The Jehovah's Witnesses had brought the case before the court, arguing that saluting the flag amounted to idolatry according to their beliefs and thus that they had a First Amendment right not to be forced to violate their religious conscience. The Court disagreed, ruling against them. Shortly, however, public opinion turned against the *Gobitis* decision, provoked by reports of physical violence committed against Jehovah's Witnesses who refused to salute the flag and by several prominent patriotic organizations calling for legislation to make flag observance voluntary.

Given the change in public opinion, Walter Barnett and several other Jehovah's Witnesses brought suit against the West Virginia State Board of Education, again arguing that they had a right not to be compelled to violate their religious beliefs by participating in actions that they believed were contrary to those beliefs. This time the Jehovah's Witnesses were successful, and the Supreme Court struck down West Virginia's law, voiding the idea that students could be compelled to salute the flag.

The *Gobitis* opinion rested on four foundations, each of which Jackson dismantles in his opinion in *Barnette*. First, *Gobitis* claimed that when faced with the dilemma of choosing between a weak government and one strong enough to threaten the liberties of the people, the latter should be preferred. In *Barnette*, Jackson dismisses this argument as incorrect and beside the point. Carried to its conclusion, he notes, there would be no foundation for individual liberties. Further, that government which does not threaten the people's liberties is not necessarily weak; indeed, Jackson cites preservation of individual freedom as the mark of a strong government.

Second, *Gobitis* held that striking down school board requirements would entangle the Supreme Court too deeply in local affairs, making the Court, in effect, a national school board. Again, Jackson says that this claim is false, noting that the Fourteenth Amendment protects the citizen from the states and their offices, including local school boards. Third, *Gobitis* held that the Court was ill equipped to interfere in matters such as local school board policy. Because the Court was not competent to rewrite the rules, *Gobitis* states, the legislatures are the proper venue for dictating policy changes. Not so, counters Jackson. The Court is certainly competent to adjudge whether freedoms protected by the Bill of Rights are being infringed upon, and in cases where fundamental rights are in question, such as the right to conscience or free speech, then the Court can and must intervene.

Last, *Gobitis* found that because national unity forms the basis for national security, measures promoting this unity should not be hindered. Jackson does not take exception to this idea itself but rather the means by which it is to be achieved. As always, he defers to persuasion and force of argument rather than validating compulsion. Where persuasion fails, he notes, conflict follows, leading inevitably to persecution. This being the case, Jackson's opinion concludes that coercing unity of expression by enforcing the flag salute is an unconstitutional abridgment of free speech, and thus he overturns *Gobitis*.

The *Barnette* decision is remarkable in three ways. First, it is unusual for a case to be overturned so swiftly after being decided, as *Gobitis* was. Second, in the midst of World War II, the decision protected the rights of a religious minority in the face of laws designed to enforce national unity. Last, the *Barnette* decision was a major victory for religious minorities and their right to practice their faith, but the fact that it was decided on freedom of speech grounds also marked a major turning point in constitutional jurisprudence. For the remainder of the century, religious freedom cases came more and more to be argued and won on free speech grounds and not on the basis of freedom of religion.

Impact

Jackson's opinion in *Barnette* is regarded by legal historians as one of the Supreme Court's most eloquent, sweeping, forceful statements regarding fundamental freedoms guaranteed by the Bill of Rights. After *Barnette*, the Court abandoned the doctrine established in *Reynolds v. United States* (1878), which held that a religious duty was not a defense to a criminal charge. In its place, the Court with *Barnette* created a religious exemption for members of different religions. Thus, for example, in *Sherbert v. Verner* (1963), the Court upheld the claim of a Seventh-day Adventist for unemployment benefits despite her refusal to work on Saturday, the religion's Sabbath. In *Wisconsin v. Yoder* (1872), the Court sustained the right of Amish parents to withhold their children from public schools past the eighth grade. In *Masterpiece Cakeshop, Ltd. v. Colorado Civil Rights Commission* (2018), the Court held that requiring a bakeshop owner, a devout Christian, to create a wedding cake for a same-sex couple would violate his First Amendment free exercise of religion rights.

Questions for Further Study

1. What is the central question presented in the *Barnette* case?

2. Which clauses in the First Amendment protect religious freedom, and how does either or both apply to the *Barnette* case?

3. Imagine that a court is hearing a case in which religious values or beliefs are in conflict with the law. How should the court go about resolving the conflict?

4. Which case did *Barnette* overturn, and why?

Further Reading

Books

Alley, Robert S. *The Constitution and Religion: Leading Supreme Court Cases on Church and State.* Amherst, NY: Prometheus Books, 1999: 428–436.

Peters, Shawn. *Judging Jehovah's Witnesses: Religious Persecution and the Dawn of the Rights Revolution.* Lawrence: University Press of Kansas, 2000.

Sandmann, Warren. "West Virginia State Board of Education v. Barnette." In *Free Speech on Trial: Communication Perspectives on Landmark Supreme Court Decisions*, edited by Richard A. Parker: 100–15. Tuscaloosa: University of Alabama Press, 2003.

Articles

Gey, Stephen G. "'Under God,' the Pledge of Allegiance, and Other Religious Trivia." *North Carolina Law Review* 81 (2003): 1865–1925.

Klass, Gregory. "The Very Idea of a First Amendment Right Against Compelled Subsidization." *University of California at Davis Law Review* 38 (2005): 1087–1139.

Laycock, Douglas. "Theology Scholarships, the Pledge of Allegiance, and Religious Liberty: Avoiding the Extremes but Missing the Liberty." *Harvard Law Review* 118 (2004): 155–246. https://www.jstor.org/stable/4093279.

Mazzotta, Symone. "*West Virginia v. Barnette*: The Freedom to Not Pledge Allegiance." National Constitution Center, June 14, 2017. https://constitutioncenter.org/blog/west-virginia-v.-barnette-the-freedom-to-not-pledge-allegiance.

Peterson, Gregory L., et al. "Recollections of *West Virginia State Board of Education v. Barnette*." *St. John's Law Review* 81, no. 4 (Fall 2007): 755–96. https://scholarship.law.stjohns.edu/cgi/viewcontent.cgi?article=1191&context=lawreview.

—Commentary by Anthony Santoro and Michael J. O'Neal

WEST VIRGINIA STATE BOARD OF EDUCATION V. BARNETTE

Document Text

***MR. JUSTICE JACKSON** delivered the opinion of the Court*

Following the decision by this Court on June 3, 1940, in *Minersville School District v. Gobitis,* 310 U. S. 586, the West Virginia legislature amended its statutes to require all schools therein to conduct courses of instruction in history, civics, and in the Constitutions of the United States and of the State

"for the purpose of teaching, fostering and perpetuating the ideals, principles and spirit of Americanism, and increasing the knowledge of the organization and machinery of the government."

Appellant Board of Education was directed, with advice of the State Superintendent of Schools, to "prescribe the courses of study covering these subjects" for public schools. The Act made it the duty of private, parochial and denominational schools to prescribe courses of study "similar to those required for the public schools."

The Board of Education on January 9, 1942, adopted a resolution containing recitals taken largely from the Court's *Gobitis* opinion and ordering that the salute to the flag become "a regular part of the program of activities in the public schools," that all teachers and pupils

"shall be required to participate in the salute honoring the Nation represented by the Flag; provided, however, that refusal to salute the Flag be regarded as an act of insubordination, and shall be dealt with accordingly."

The resolution originally required the "commonly accepted salute to the Flag," which it defined. Objections to the salute as "being too much like Hitler's" were raised by the Parent and Teachers Association, the Boy and Girl Scouts, the Red Cross, and the Federation of Women's Clubs. Some modification appears to have been made in deference to these objections, but no concession was made to Jehovah's Witnesses. What is now required is the "stiff-arm" salute, the saluter to keep the right hand raised with palm turned up while the following is repeated:

"I pledge allegiance to the Flag of the United States of America and to the Republic for which it stands; one Nation, indivisible, with liberty and justice for all."

Failure to conform is "insubordination," dealt with by expulsion. Readmission is denied by statute until compliance. Meanwhile, the expelled child is "unlawfully absent," and may be proceeded against as a delinquent. His parents or guardians are liable to prosecution, and, if convicted, are subject to fine not exceeding $50 and Jail term not exceeding thirty days. Appellees, citizens of the United States and of West Virginia, brought suit in the United States District Court for themselves and others similarly situated asking its injunction to restrain enforcement of these laws and regulations against Jehovah's Witnesses. The Witnesses are an unincorporated body teaching that the obligation imposed by law of God is superior to that of laws enacted by temporal government. Their religious beliefs include a literal version of Exodus, Chapter 20, verses 4 and 5, which says:

"Thou shalt not make unto thee any graven image, or any likeness of anything that is in heaven above, or that is in the earth beneath, or that is in the water under the earth; thou shalt not bow down thyself to them nor serve them."

They consider that the flag is an "image" within this command. For this reason, they refuse to salute it.

Children of this faith have been expelled from school and are threatened with exclusion for no other cause. Officials threaten to send them to reformatories maintained for criminally inclined juveniles. Parents of such children have been prosecuted, and are threatened with prosecutions for causing delinquency.

The Board of Education moved to dismiss the complaint, setting forth these facts and alleging that the law and regulations are an unconstitutional denial of religious freedom, and of freedom of speech, and are invalid under the "due process" and "equal protection" clauses of the Fourteenth Amendment to the Federal Constitution. The cause was submitted on the pleadings to a District Court of three judges. It restrained enforcement as to the plaintiffs and those of that class. The Board of Education brought the case here by direct appeal.

This case calls upon us to reconsider a precedent decision, as the Court, throughout its history, often has been required to do. Before turning to the *Gobitis* case, however, it is desirable to notice certain characteristics by which this controversy is distinguished.

The freedom asserted by these appellees does not bring them into collision with rights asserted by any other individual. It is such conflicts which most frequently require intervention of the State to determine where the rights of one end and those of another begin. But the refusal of these persons to participate in the ceremony does not interfere with or deny rights of others to do so. Nor is there any question in this case that their behavior is peaceable and orderly. The sole conflict is between authority and rights of the individual. The State asserts power to condition access to public education on making a prescribed sign and profession and at the same time to coerce attendance by punishing both parent and child. The latter stand on a right of self-determination in matters that touch individual opinion and personal attitude.

As the present CHIEF JUSTICE said in dissent in the *Gobitis* case, the State may

"require teaching by instruction and study of all in our history and in the structure and organization of our government, including the guaranties of civil liberty, which tend to inspire patriotism and love of country."

310 U.S. at 310 U. S. 604. Here, however, we are dealing with a compulsion of students to declare a belief. They are not merely made acquainted with the flag salute so that they may be informed as to what it is or even what it means. The issue here is whether this slow and easily neglected route to aroused loyalties constitutionally may be short-cut by substituting a compulsory salute and slogan. This issue is not prejudiced by the Court's previous holding that, where a State, without compelling attendance, extends college facilities to pupils who voluntarily enroll, it may prescribe military training as part of the course without offense to the Constitution. It was held that those who take advantage of its opportunities may not, on ground of conscience, refuse compliance with such conditions. *Hamilton v. Regents,* 293 U. S. 245. In the present case, attendance is not optional. That case is also to be distinguished from the present one, because, independently of college privileges or requirements, the State has power to raise militia and impose the duties of service therein upon its citizens.

There is no doubt that, in connection with the pledges, the flag salute is a form of utterance. Symbolism is a primitive but effective way of communicating ideas. The use of an emblem or flag to symbolize some system, idea, institution, or personality is a short-cut from mind to mind. Causes and nations, political parties, lodges, and ecclesiastical groups seek to knit the loyalty of their followings to a flag or banner, a color or design. The State announces rank, function, and authority through crowns and maces, uniforms and black robes; the church speaks through the Cross, the Crucifix, the altar and shrine, and clerical raiment. Symbols of State often convey political ideas, just as religious symbols come to convey theological ones. Associated with many of these symbols are appropriate gestures of acceptance or respect: a salute, a bowed or bared head, a bended knee. A person gets from a symbol the meaning he puts into it, and what is one man's comfort and inspiration is another's jest and scorn.

Over a decade ago, Chief Justice Hughes led this Court in holding that the display of a red flag as a symbol of opposition by peaceful and legal means to organized government was protected by the free speech guaranties of the Constitution. *Stromberg v. California,* 283 U. S. 359. Here, it is the State that employs a flag as a symbol of adherence to government as presently organized. It requires the individual to communicate by word and sign his acceptance of the political ideas it thus bespeaks. Objection to this form of communication, when coerced, is an old one, well known to the framers of the Bill of Rights.

It is also to be noted that the compulsory flag salute and pledge requires affirmation of a belief and an attitude of mind. It is not clear whether the regulation contemplates that pupils forego any contrary convictions of their own and become unwilling converts to the prescribed ceremony, or whether it will be acceptable if they simulate assent by words without belief, and by a gesture barren of meaning. It is now a commonplace that censorship or suppression of expression of opinion is tolerated by our Constitution only when the expression presents a clear and present danger of action of a kind the State is empowered to prevent and punish. It would seem that involuntary affirmation could be commanded only on even more immediate and urgent grounds than silence. But here, the power of compulsion is invoked without any allegation that remaining passive during a flag salute ritual creates a clear and present danger that would justify an effort even to muffle expression. To sustain the compulsory flag salute, we are required to say that a Bill of Rights which guards the individual's right to speak his own mind left it open to public authorities to compel him to utter what is not in his mind.

Whether the First Amendment to the Constitution will permit officials to order observance of ritual of this nature does not depend upon whether as a voluntary exercise we would think it to be good, bad or merely innocuous. Any credo of nationalism is likely to include what some disapprove or to omit what others think essential, and to give off different overtones as it takes on different accents or interpretations. If official power exists to coerce acceptance of any patriotic creed, what it shall contain cannot be decided by courts, but must be largely discretionary with the ordaining authority, whose power to prescribe would no doubt include power to amend. Hence, validity of the asserted power to force an American citizen publicly to profess any statement of belief, or to engage in any ceremony of assent to one, presents questions of power that must be considered independently of any idea we may have as to the utility of the ceremony in question.

Nor does the issue, as we see it, turn on one's possession of particular religious views or the sincerity with which they are held. . . . It is not necessary to inquire whether nonconformist beliefs will exempt from the duty to salute unless we first find power to make the salute a legal duty. . . .

Government of limited power need not be anemic government. Assurance that rights are secure tends to diminish fear and jealousy of strong government, and, by making us feel safe to live under it, makes for its better support. Without promise of a limiting Bill of Rights, it is doubtful if our Constitution could have mustered enough strength to enable its ratification. To enforce those rights today is not to choose weak government over strong government. It is only to adhere as a means of strength to individual freedom of mind in preference to officially disciplined uniformity for which history indicates a disappointing and disastrous end. . . .

It was also considered in the *Gobitis* case that functions of educational officers in States, counties and school districts were such that to interfere with their authority "would in effect make us the school board for the country."

The Fourteenth Amendment, as now applied to the States, protects the citizen against the State itself and all of its creatures—Boards of Education not excepted. These have, of course, important, delicate, and highly discretionary functions, but none that they may not perform within the limits of the Bill of Rights. That they are educating the young for citizenship is reason for scrupulous protection of Constitutional freedoms of the individual, if we are not to strangle the free mind at its source and teach youth to discount important principles of our government as mere platitudes. . . .

The *Gobitis* opinion reasoned that this is a field "where courts possess no marked, and certainly no controlling, competence," that it is committed to the legislatures, as well as the courts, to guard cherished liberties, and that it is constitutionally appropriate to "fight out the wise use of legislative authority in the forum of public opinion and before legislative assemblies, rather than to transfer such a contest to the judicial arena," since all the "effective means of inducing political changes are left free."

The very purpose of a Bill of Rights was to withdraw certain subjects from the vicissitudes of political controversy, to place them beyond the reach of majorities and officials, and to establish them as legal principles to be applied by the courts. One's right to life, liberty, and property, to free speech, a free press, freedom of worship and assembly, and other fundamental rights may not be submitted to vote; they depend on the outcome of no elections. . . .

Nor does our duty to apply the Bill of Rights to assertions of official authority depend upon our possession of marked competence in the field where the invasion of rights occurs.... We act in these matters not by authority of our competence, but by force of our commissions. We cannot, because of modest estimates of our competence in such specialties as public education, withhold the judgment that history authenticates as the function of this Court when liberty is infringed.

Lastly, and this is the very heart of the *Gobitis* opinion, it reasons that "National unity is the basis of national security," that the authorities have "the right to select appropriate means for its attainment," and hence reaches the conclusion that such compulsory measures toward "national unity" are constitutional. Upon the verity of this assumption depends our answer in this case.

National unity, as an end which officials may foster by persuasion and example, is not in question. The problem is whether, under our Constitution, compulsion as here employed is a permissible means for its achievement....

As governmental pressure toward unity becomes greater, so strife becomes more bitter as to whose unity it shall be. Probably no deeper division of our people could proceed from any provocation than from finding it necessary to choose what doctrine and whose program public educational officials shall compel youth to unite in embracing. Ultimate futility of such attempts to compel coherence is the lesson of every such effort from the Roman drive to stamp out Christianity as a disturber of its pagan unity, the Inquisition, as a means to religious and dynastic unity, the Siberian exiles as a means to Russian unity, down to the fast failing efforts of our present totalitarian enemies. Those who begin coercive elimination of dissent soon find themselves exterminating dissenters. Compulsory unification of opinion achieves only the unanimity of the graveyard.

It seems trite but necessary to say that the First Amendment to our Constitution was designed to avoid these ends by avoiding these beginnings....

The case is made difficult not because the principles of its decision are obscure, but because the flag involved is our own. Nevertheless, we apply the limitations of the Constitution with no fear that freedom to be intellectually and spiritually diverse or even contrary will disintegrate the social organization. To believe that patriotism will not flourish if patriotic ceremonies are voluntary and spontaneous, instead of a compulsory routine, is to make an unflattering estimate of the appeal of our institutions to free minds.... But freedom to differ is not limited to things that do not matter much. That would be a mere shadow of freedom. The test of its substance is the right to differ as to things that touch the heart of the existing order.

If there is any fixed star in our constitutional constellation, it is that no official, high or petty, can prescribe what shall be orthodox in politics, nationalism, religion, or other matters of opinion, or force citizens to confess by word or act their faith therein. If there are any circumstances which permit an exception, they do not now occur to us.

Glossary

anemic: weak, lacking energy

***Gobitis* case:** a 1940 case, *Minersville School District v. Gobitis*, about a student who was expelled from school for refusing to salute the American flag

innocuous: harmless

Inquisition: beginning in the twelfth century, tribunals and commissions established by the Roman Catholic Church to stamp out heresy

vicissitudes: changes

KOREMATSU V. UNITED STATES

<table>
<tr><td>DATE
1944</td><td>CITATION
323 U.S. 214</td></tr>
<tr><td>AUTHOR
Hugo Black</td><td>SIGNIFICANCE
Ruled that President Franklin D. Roosevelt's Executive Order 9066, which ordered Japanese Americans to be held in internment camps during World War II, was constitutional</td></tr>
<tr><td>VOTE
6–3</td><td></td></tr>
</table>

Overview

Korematsu v. United States was a landmark Supreme Court case concerning the constitutionality of President Franklin D. Roosevelt's Executive Order 9066, which ordered Japanese Americans to be held in internment camps during World War II. In a 6–3 decision made on December 14, 1944, the Court came down on the side of the government, ruling that the order was constitutional in an opinion written by Associate Justice Hugo Black. The ruling reflected a long-standing precedent that the president and Congress could take extraordinary actions to protect the nation during times of crisis, especially wartime.

The executive order followed the surprise Japanese attack on the U.S. naval base at Pearl Harbor in Hawaii on December 7, 1941, which brought the United States into World War II. The attack devastated the U.S. Pacific Fleet. It also unleashed a wave of anti-Japanese sentiment and paranoia across the country. Some government officials and everyday Americans were convinced that the attack could not have occurred without action by spies and saboteurs. The order was officially designed to prevent any future espionage or sabotage by creating exclusion zones around military areas. In the aftermath of the executive order, on May 19, 1942, authorities began to forcibly relocate Japanese Americans to camps.

The *Korematsu* decision is universally considered one of the Court's worst moments. While Black upheld the internment of Fred Korematsu on the ground that the need to protect the American people outweighs the need to protect the rights of any individual or any racial group, his pronouncement that "all legal restrictions which curtail the rights of a single racial group are immediately suspect" contains the seeds of a vital aspect of the Court's increasing emphasis on civil rights, the "strict scrutiny" test developed to assess when government action violates equal protection. Meanwhile, in a dissenting opinion, Associate Justice Robert H. Jackson argued that the executive order violated the Constitution by allowing the government to discriminate along racial lines.

Context

World War II began when Germany invaded Poland on September 1, 1939. Great Britain and France de-

Civil rights activist Fred Korematsu (second from right) and his family
(Wikimedia Commons)

clared war on Germany in response, and the conflict quickly escalated. While the U.S. government began to prepare for war, most Americans wanted the nation to remain neutral in the global conflict. Japan was an ally of Germany. Tensions between the United States and Japan had escalated significantly in the late 1930s over the latter country's invasion of China. The incursion into China prompted the Roosevelt administration to impose an oil embargo on Japan. As relations deteriorated between the two countries, Japan launched a surprise aerial and submarine attack on the U.S. Pacific Fleet at Pearl Harbor, Hawaii, on December 7, 1941, without formally declaring war.

The Japanese attack killed 2,403 U.S. service members and civilians and shattered the U.S. Pacific Fleet, sinking four battleships and sinking or damaging fifteen other vessels. Japanese losses were light, with twenty-nine aircraft destroyed, along with four small "midget" submarines. In total, sixty-four Japanese sailors and pilots were killed. The following day, Japan and the United States declared war on each other; on December 11, Japan's allies, Germany and Italy, also declared war on the United States. Japanese forces were soon engaged in offensives against U.S. and Allied positions throughout the Pacific, capturing the U.S. territories of Guam, Wake Island, and the Philippines.

The success of the Japanese attacks prompted fears of further attacks on Hawaii and the U.S. Pacific Coast. It also unleashed a wave of patriotism and a desire for revenge. Millions of Americans joined, or tried to join, the military. People rushed to purchase savings bonds, which helped finance the war. There were also campaigns to collect materials such as household pots and pans to be melted down and converted for use in the war effort. Americans were expected to make sacrifices and go to extraordinary lengths to support the war effort. Food, gas, and other consumer products were rationed.

The first major U.S. victory against the Japanese was the Battle of Midway on June 4–7, 1942, during which U.S. naval forces defeated a larger Japanese armada and prevented the invasion of Midway Island, whose capture was seen as a stepping stone for the conquest of Hawaii by Japan. Following the battle, the war in the Pacific continued for three more years. During the fighting, more than 111,600 Americans died, with more than 253,000 wounded.

Throughout the war, the Supreme Court generally granted wide deference to the executive branch on security issues. This reflected longstanding trends in U.S. constitutional law. During times of national emergency, the courts typically deferred to the government when claims about national security were raised. This was true for several reasons. The Constitution made the president commander in chief of the military and gave the chief executive broad powers to protect the country. The president was also given broad powers to conduct U.S. foreign policy and diplomacy. The framers of the Constitution recognized that there were times when military or strategic decisions had to be made by a single person; consequently, although Congress alone had the power to declare war, the president was mainly responsible for the conduct of any war and for protecting the United States.

For example, when eight German saboteurs were captured in June 1942, Roosevelt ordered, in Executive Proclamation 2561, that they and future spies be tried by military tribunals. Opponents of the military tribunals challenged their legality. However, the Supreme Court decided in *Ex parte Quirin* (July 31, 1942) that the tribunals were constitutional because a distinction existed between enemy combatants in uniform, who were entitled to protections granted prisoners of war under international law, and spies or enemy agents caught out of uniform. The *Ex parte Quirin* decision and the subsequent *Korematsu* case reflected the willingness of the Court to allow the government to implement policies during wartime that would generally be prohibited during peace.

About the Author

Hugo Lafayette Black was a son of the South, born in 1886 in rural Harlan, Alabama, and raised in the town of Ashland, Alabama. His early legal career gave little indication of promise before politics afforded him a means of raising himself in the world. After holding a few local offices, Black decided to run for the U.S. Senate. The tactics he employed to get there were both practical and opportunistic. As a means of widening his base of support, Black used a populist orientation to appeal to organized labor, an alliance that led to his being called a "Bolshevik." During this same period, when acting as defense counsel during a notorious murder trial, Black appealed to racial and religious bias to win his client's acquittal. In 1923 he joined the Ku Klux Klan because, as he said later, most Alabama jurors were Klansmen. It was a decision he came to regret, and he resigned from the Klan two years later. Still, Black's election to the Senate in 1926 was clearly aided by Klan support.

In the Senate, Black pursued a populist agenda, vigorously investigating improper ties between government and business and pushing for a thirty-hour workweek. His ardent support for the New Deal—and, in particular, for Franklin Roosevelt's plan to pack the Supreme Court with devotees as a means of ousting the old guard—attracted the president's attention. In 1937 Black himself became one of Roosevelt's Court nominees. Black's nomination was approved handily, but it was followed almost immediately by public revelation of his history with the Klan. Black confronted the issue head on by making a public confession over the radio, declaring that he had had no connection with the Klan for more than a dozen years and that he had no intention of having any further association with the organization.

Soon Roosevelt had appointed enough justices to make a "second," more liberal Court than the one Chief Justice Charles Evans Hughes had led since 1930. Joined by such like-minded individuals as William O. Douglas and Frank Murphy, Black began his ascent as one of the Court's leading liberal thinkers by voting with a new coalition that upheld important New Deal legislation and emphasized individual rights, as in *Johnson v. Zerbst* (1938), a Sixth Amendment right-to-counsel case for which Black wrote the opinion of the Court. Black went on to lead the Court's so-called due process revolution, although one of the most significant cases for which he is remembered gave civil libertarians fresh reason to doubt his liberal credentials: he wrote the opinion of the Court in *Korematsu v. United States* (1944), the case upholding the internment of Japanese Americans during World War II.

Black was one of the most vivid and controversial personalities ever to occupy a seat on the Supreme Court bench. As a onetime Ku Klux Klan member, Black would seem an unlikely defender of the First Amendment, and yet he became the very embodiment of a black letter, literalist jurist, with his commitment to the rights established in the first eight amendments to the Constitution making him into one of the Court's intellectual leaders. He carried a dog-eared copy of the Constitution around in his right coat pocket and referred to it often. "That Constitution is my legal bible," he would declare. "I cherish every word of it from the first to the last." No part of the Constitution was more sacred to Black than the First Amendment, which, as he frequently—and pointedly—noted, begins with the words "Congress shall make no law." For Black the framers of the Constitution meant what they wrote, and he demanded proof that laws being scrutinized by the Court were not in violation of any of the prohibitions that follow these words.

Black's commitment to individual rights was an almost inevitable consequence of his fealty to the Bill of Rights. When his customary literalist approach to constitutional interpretation proved inapposite to certain aspects of his agenda, he turned instead to what the historical record could tell him about original intent. In *Adamson v. California* (1947), for example, Black famously argued in dissent that his reading of the Fourteenth Amendment's adoption indicated that the framers intended to incorporate the Bill of Rights, thus making these protections binding at the state as well as the federal level. Conversely, Black refused to support rights others read into the Constitution without literal, written evidence to support their position. He was, for example, ardently opposed to the majority's extension of a broad right of marital privacy in *Griswold v. Connecticut* (1965).

Although he did support the right of the *New York Times* to publish the Pentagon Papers in *New York Times Co. v. United States* (1971), other opinions dating from the later period of his career reflect the same restraint and conservatism one detects in Black's vigorous *Griswold*

dissent. Black always maintained that his was a consistent, disciplined approach to constitutional analysis. By the mid-1960s, Black had no stomach for the increasingly expansive reading of equal protection by the Court as headed by Earl Warren. The revolution he had set in motion seemed to have taken on a life of its own and passed him by. Black nonetheless hung on almost to the end. When he retired in 1971 after thirty-four years, he did so as one of the longest-serving justices the Court has ever known.

Explanation and Analysis of the Document

After the Japanese attack on the U.S. Pacific Fleet at Pearl Harbor, sentiment against the Japanese—even against Japanese Americans—ran high. Despite the ongoing war in Europe and tensions with Japan, most Americans were shocked by the attack. Many could not believe that the Japanese were able to launch such a successful strike without warning, and some government officials and military leaders argued that Japan must have used spies and saboteurs to plan the attack. The combination of surprise and resentment toward Japan added to existing levels of intolerance and racism against Japanese Americans. In 1900, there were only about twenty-five thousand Japanese living in the United States, mostly in Hawaii and along the Pacific Coast. However, over the next two decades, more than one hundred thousand Japanese immigrants came to the mainland United States. Anti-immigrant sentiment toward new arrivals led to the 1924 Immigration Act, which banned people from non-European nations from moving to the United States. Nonetheless, the second-generation Japanese Americans, known as Nisei, and third-generation, or Sansei, had prospered as farmers, entrepreneurs, and professionals in the United States. They were U.S. citizens and generally considered themselves as American as their neighbors and fellow citizens.

On February 19, 1942, President Roosevelt issued Executive Order 9066, permitting parts of the country to be declared military areas from which anyone could be excluded. As a result, authorities began to forcibly relocate people of Japanese, German, and Italian ancestry or citizenship (these three countries being the main U.S. enemies in the war). Approximately eleven thousand Germans and three thousand Italians had to move away from the Pacific Coast. However, Japanese Americans made up the largest number of those forced to relocate. Eventually some 112,000 Japanese Americans—both native born and immigrants, were put into internment camps. An estimated 70 percent of those interned were U.S. citizens.

Those covered by the order were sent to one of ten internment camps in Arizona, Arkansas, California, Colorado, Idaho, Utah, and Wyoming. The camps were in remote, often desolate areas, with few amenities or services. There were shortages of fuel and other commodities. The internees ran the day-to-day operations of the facilities, serving as cooks, service workers, and teachers. Those who worked were paid between $12 and $19 per month, at a time when the average wage in the United States was about $95 per month. The camps were guarded by units of the U.S. Army.

One of those affected by the order was Fred Korematsu, an American-born descendant of Japanese immigrants who had grown up and lived in the San Francisco Bay Area. Health issues resulted in Korematsu's rejection from military service, but he was working in the defense industry when he became subject to the internment order. Because he did not want to be indefinitely separated from his Italian American girlfriend, Korematsu moved to a nearby town, changed his name, and underwent minor facial surgery in an effort to disguise himself as Mexican American. He was eventually arrested, convicted, paroled, and sent to a relocation camp in Utah.

Korematsu challenged his conviction, arguing that the exclusion order was unconstitutional because it authorized powers beyond those granted to Congress, the president, or the military and because it was applied on a racially discriminatory basis. He argued that the measure violated the due process clause of the Fifth Amendment. The clause forbids the government to deny citizens "life, liberty, or property, without due process of law." The government countered that the exclusion zones and the internment policy were necessary to prevent and counteract espionage and sabotage in a time of war. The government won in the lower courts, whereupon Korematsu appealed to the Supreme Court.

Korematsu v. United States, argued in October 1944, was one of a number of cases concerning Japanese internment that came before the Court after the enactment of Executive Order 9066. The Court had handed down its opinion in *Hirabayashi v. United States* on June 21 of the previous year, citing the demands of wartime as reasons for upholding the appellant's conviction for violating a curfew and failing to report to a detention center. Racial discrimination resulting from wartime legislation might be a necessary consequence of the need for national security. Faced with a similar set of facts in *Korematsu*, Black addresses the discrimination issue directly, stating unqualifiedly that all legal restrictions negatively affecting the rights of a racial group are inherently suspect and must be subject to "the most rigid scrutiny." Having said as much, Black goes on to uphold Korematsu's conviction for the same reason put forth by the Court in *Hirabayashi*: the need to protect the American people outweighs the need to protect the rights of any individual or any racial group. Thus, since some Japanese Americans refused to swear loyalty to the United States, the military, which was charged with enforcing the intent of Executive Order 9066 but was unable to expediently segregate the loyal from the disloyal, was obliged to apply exclusion regulations to the whole group. Korematsu was excluded from the off-limits military area not because of his race, Black asserts, but because of the nation's being at war with the Japanese Empire. This argument exemplified the willingness of the Court to defer to the government on security matters.

The dissenting justices based their arguments on the racial implications of Executive Order 9066. The Fourteenth Amendment to the Constitution, ratified in 1868, requires that all citizens receive "equal protection" under the law. In other words, all citizens should be treated equally unless there is a compelling reason not to do so. Such reasons could be determined only through due process, and Justice Jackson argued that race or ethnic background was not a compelling reason to deny equal protection.

Korematsu is the only case in the history of the Supreme Court in which a restrictive law subjected to the "rigid scrutiny" test was deemed constitutional. It would be challenged in the future but remained in place throughout the twentieth century.

Impact

Roosevelt's executive order and the subsequent *Korematsu* decision were devastating to the Japanese American community on the West Coast. Like other Americans during the war, they were already subject to hardships and sacrifices, but they also were forced to leave their homes and businesses to be put in camps, where they were often treated like the enemy. Meanwhile, propaganda campaigns that aimed to bolster the morale of civilians and increase support for the war often utilized racist and xenophobic portrayals of the Japanese. This made it more difficult for the Nisei and Sensei and translated into an unfortunate degree of public support for the internment camps.

Japanese Americans in Hawaii fared better than their counterparts on the Pacific Coast and Alaska. Only about two thousand were taken into custody or relocated. This was because the military and the civilian government of the territory argued that the Nisei were critical to the war effort and local economy.

Even while they were in internment camps Japanese American males were subject to military conscription, and more than twenty thousand served in the U.S. military during the war, while approximately one hundred women joined the voluntary Women's Army Corps, and several hundred volunteered as military nurses. The U.S. Army's 442nd Regimental Combat Team was made up of Japanese Americans, and eventually more than fourteen thousand Nisei and Sensei served in the unit. It was the most decorated infantry unit in the history of the U.S. Army, winning more than eighteen thousand awards over a two-year period, including twenty-one Medals of Honor, the highest award for bravery in the U.S. military. Many members of the unit would later attribute its success to efforts by the soldiers to prove their loyalty to the United States. The 442nd Regimental Combat Team and other Japanese American units served only in Europe, not in the Pacific.

Roosevelt rescinded Executive Order 9066 in December 1944 as it became clear that the United States and its allies were winning the war. The internees were allowed to return home, although many had lost their businesses or dwellings. All of the camps were dismantled within a year of the end of the war.

In 1980 Fred Korematsu once again challenged his conviction in court. In 1984 the U.S. District Court for the Northern District of California overturned Korematsu's earlier conviction on the ground that the government had willingly suppressed evidence concerning the military necessity for interning Japanese Americans during the war. The second *Korematsu* case, however, merely addressed its particular facts, leaving the law of the 1944 case in place. In 1988 Congress authorized payments of $20,000 each to 82,219 survivors of the internment camps after the government issued an official apology, but *Korematsu v. United States* remained on the books as "good law."

On September 24, 2017, President Donald J. Trump issued Executive Proclamation 9645, which restricted the entry into the United States of citizens from eight countries for security reasons. The prohibition was challenged in court, and in the case *Hawaii v. Trump,* on June 26, 2018, the Supreme Court allowed the policy to go into effect. However, in the 5–4 decision, written by Chief Justice John Roberts, the Court repudiated the *Korematsu* decision. The opinion asserted that history had determined that the decision was flawed and that it was time to recognize the injustice of *Korematsu.*

Questions for Further Study

1. What three actions were Japanese Americans required to take as a result of Executive Order 9066?

2. What were Korematsu's main claims in challenging the executive order? How did Black respond to those contentions?

3. What were the most significant points from the case *Hirabayashi v. United States* that served as a precedent for the *Korematsu* decision?

4. What were the main arguments that Justice Black made in justifying the use of internment camps?

Further Reading

Books

Bannai, Lorraine K. *Enduring Conviction: Fred Korematsu and His Quest for Justice.* Seattle: University of Washington Press, 2015.

Burton, Jeffery F., Mary M. Farrell, Florence B. Lord, and Richard W. Lord, eds. *Confinement and Ethnicity: An Overview of World War II Japanese American Relocation Sites.* Seattle: University of Washington Press, 2002.

Daniels, Roger. *The Japanese American Cases: The Rule of Law in Time of War.* Lawrence: University of Kansas Press, 2013.

Irons, Peter, ed. *Justice Delayed: The Record of the Japanese American Internment Cases.* Middletown, CT: Wesleyan University Press, 1989.

Schwartz, Bernard. *A History of the Supreme Court.* New York: Oxford University Press, 1993.

Websites

Korematsu v. United States (1944). Landmark Cases of the U.S. Supreme Court. Accessed March 29, 2023. https://www.landmarkcases.org/cases/korematsu-v-united-states.

Korematsu v. United States. Legal Information Institute. Cornell Law School. Accessed March 29, 2023. https://www.law.cornell.edu/supremecourt/text/323/214.

—Commentary by Tom Lansford

KOREMATSU V. UNITED STATES

Document Text

MR. JUSTICE BLACK delivered the opinion of the Court

The petitioner, an American citizen of Japanese descent, was convicted in a federal district court for remaining in San Leandro, California, a "Military Area," contrary to Civilian Exclusion Order No. 34 of the Commanding General of the Western Command, U.S. Army, which directed that, after May 9, 1942, all persons of Japanese ancestry should be excluded from that area. No question was raised as to petitioner's loyalty to the United States. The Circuit Court of Appeals affirmed, and the importance of the constitutional question involved caused us to grant certiorari.

It should be noted, to begin with, that all legal restrictions which curtail the civil rights of a single racial group are immediately suspect. That is not to say that all such restrictions are unconstitutional. It is to say that courts must subject them to the most rigid scrutiny. Pressing public necessity may sometimes justify the existence of such restrictions; racial antagonism never can. . . .

In the light of the principles we announced in the *Hirabayashi* case, we are unable to conclude that it was beyond the war power of Congress and the Executive to exclude those of Japanese ancestry from the West Coast war area at the time they did. True, exclusion from the area in which one's home is located is a far greater deprivation than constant confinement to the home from 8 p.m. to 6 a.m. Nothing short of apprehension by the proper military authorities of the gravest imminent danger to the public safety can constitutionally justify either. But exclusion from a threatened area, no less than curfew, has a definite and close relationship to the prevention of espionage and sabotage. The military authorities, charged with the primary responsibility of defending our shores, concluded that curfew provided inadequate protection and ordered exclusion. They did so, as pointed out in our *Hirabayashi* opinion, in accordance with Congressional authority to the military to say who should, and who should not, remain in the threatened areas.

In this case the petitioner challenges the assumptions upon which we rested our conclusions in the *Hirabayashi* case. He also urges that by May 1942, when Order No. 34 was promulgated, all danger of Japanese invasion of the West Coast had disappeared. After careful consideration of these contentions we are compelled to reject them.

Here, as in the *Hirabayashi* case, . . . "we cannot reject as unfounded the judgment of the military authorities and of Congress that there were disloyal members of that population, whose number and strength could not be precisely and quickly ascertained. We cannot say that the war-making branches of the Government did not have ground for believing that in a critical hour such persons could not readily be isolated and separately dealt with, and constituted a menace to the national defense and safety, which demanded that prompt and adequate measures be taken to guard against it."

Like curfew, exclusion of those of Japanese origin was deemed necessary because of the presence of an unascertained number of disloyal members of the group, most of whom we have no doubt were loyal to this country. It was because we could not reject the finding of the military authorities that it was impossible to bring about an immediate segregation of the disloyal from the loyal that we sustained the validity of the curfew order as applying to the whole group. In the instant case, temporary exclusion of the entire group was rested by the military on the same ground. The judgment that exclusion of the whole group was for the same reason a military imperative answers the contention that the exclusion was in the nature of group punishment based on antagonism to those of Japanese origin. That there were members of the group who retained loyalties to Japan has been confirmed by investigations made subsequent to the exclusion. Approximately five thousand American citizens of Japanese ancestry refused to swear unqualified allegiance to the United States and to renounce allegiance to the Japanese Emperor, and several thousand evacuees requested repatriation to Japan.

We uphold the exclusion order as of the time it was made and when the petitioner violated it. . . . In doing so, we are not unmindful of the hardships imposed by it upon a large group of American citizens. But hardships are part of war, and war is an aggregation of hardships. All citizens alike, both in and out of uniform, feel the impact of war in greater or lesser measure. Citizenship has its responsibilities as well as its privileges, and in time of war the burden is always heavier. Compulsory exclusion of large groups of citizens from their homes, except under circumstances of direst emergency and peril, is inconsistent with our basic governmental institutions. But when under conditions of modern warfare our shores are threatened by hostile forces, the power to protect must be commensurate with the threatened danger. . . .

We are thus being asked to pass at this time upon the whole subsequent detention program in both assembly and relocation centers, although the only issues framed at the trial related to petitioner's remaining in the prohibited area in violation of the exclusion order. Had petitioner here left the prohibited area and gone to an assembly center we cannot say either as a matter of fact or law that his presence in that center would have resulted in his detention in a relocation center. Some who did report to the assembly center were not sent to relocation centers, but were released upon condition that they remain outside the prohibited zone until the military orders were modified or lifted. This

illustrates that they pose different problems and may be governed by different principles. The lawfulness of one does not necessarily determine the lawfulness of the others. This is made clear when we analyze the requirements of the separate provisions of the separate orders. These separate requirements were that those of Japanese ancestry (1) depart from the area; (2) report to and temporarily remain in an assembly center; (3) go under military control to a relocation center there to remain for an indeterminate period until released conditionally or unconditionally by the military authorities. Each of these requirements, it will be noted, imposed distinct duties in connection with the separate steps in a complete evacuation program. Had Congress directly incorporated into one Act the language of these separate orders, and provided sanctions for their violations, disobedience of any one would have constituted a separate offense. . . .

Since the petitioner has not been convicted of failing to report or to remain in an assembly or relocation center, we cannot in this case determine the validity of those separate provisions of the order. It is sufficient here for us to pass upon the order which petitioner violated. To do more would be to go beyond the issues raised, and to decide momentous questions not contained within the framework of the pleadings or the evidence in this case. It will be time enough to decide the serious constitutional issues which petitioner seeks to raise when an assembly or relocation order is applied or is certain to be applied to him, and we have its terms before us. . . .

It is said that we are dealing here with the case of imprisonment of a citizen in a concentration camp solely because of his ancestry, without evidence or inquiry concerning his loyalty and good disposition towards the United States. Our task would be simple, our duty clear, were this a case involving the imprisonment of a loyal citizen in a concentration camp because of racial prejudice. Regardless of the true nature of the assembly and relocation centers—and we deem it unjustifiable to call them concentration camps with all the ugly connotations that term implies—we are dealing specifically with nothing but an exclusion order. To cast this case into outlines of racial prejudice, without reference to the real military dangers which were presented, merely confuses the issue. Korematsu was not excluded from the Military Area because of hostility to him or his race. He was excluded because we are at war with the Japanese Empire, because the properly constituted military authorities feared an invasion of our West Coast and felt constrained to take proper security measures, because they decided that the military urgency of the situation demanded that all citizens of Japanese ancestry be segregated from the West Coast temporarily, and finally, because Congress, reposing its confidence in this time of war in our military leaders—as inevitably it must—determined that they should have the power to do just this. There was evidence of disloyalty on the part of some, the military authorities considered that the need for action was great, and time was short. We cannot—by availing ourselves of the calm perspective of hindsight—now say that at that time these actions were unjustified.

Glossary

concentration camp: a detention center in which a group of people are gathered together or "concentrated," usually characterized by extremely harsh treatment of prisoners

dissenting opinion: a response to a legal decision in which justices on the same court express disagreement with their colleagues

exclusion order: Executive Order 9066, issued by President Franklin Roosevelt on February 19, 1942, whereby persons considered to be a military threat could be excluded from certain areas

Hirabayashi case: *Hirabayashi v. United States*, in which the Supreme Court upheld the constitutionality of the exclusion order

instant: present

imperative: requirement

pass: judge or rule

petitioner: one who brings a case before a court

precedent: legal ruling that serves as the basis or model for future cases

reposing: resting

sanctions: punishments

SWEATT V. PAINTER

DATE 1950 **AUTHOR** Fred M. Vinson **VOTE** 9–0	**CITATION** 339 U.S. 629 **SIGNIFICANCE** Challenged the doctrine of "separate but equal" *Plessy v. Ferguson* established in 1896 by ruling that Texas's prohibition of integrated education resulted in unequal treatment when Heman Marion Sweatt was refused admission to the University of Texas's law school

Overview

 On June 5, 1950, the U.S. Supreme Court rendered its decision in the case *Sweatt v. Painter*. In 1946 an African American, Heman Marion Sweatt, applied for admission to the law school at the University of Texas in Austin; at the time, the president of the university was Theophilus Painter. The Texas constitution, however, prohibited integrated education; therefore, Sweatt was denied admission because of his race. He filed suit, but a Texas trial court delayed the case for six months to give the state time to establish a "separate but equal" law school for Blacks in Houston; that law school would eventually evolve into Texas Southern University. Sweatt challenged this step in the Texas Court of Civil Appeals, which affirmed thes trial court's ruling.

After the Texas Supreme Court refused to hear the case on appeal, Sweatt, represented by William J. Durham and Thurgood Marshall (the future U.S. Supreme Court justice), appealed to the U.S. Supreme Court. The fundamental legal question the case presented was whether the University of Texas admissions policy violated the equal protection clause of the Fourteenth

Amendment to the U.S. Constitution. The Court unanimously held that it did and ruled that Sweatt be admitted to the University of Texas Law School. In its ruling, written by Chief Justice Frederick Moore (Fred M.) Vinson, the Court stated that the law school for "Negroes," which had begun operation in 1947, was not equal to the University of Texas Law School in such matters as course selection, faculty, the library, and prestige. Further, the Court found that the proposed law school's separation from the University of Texas Law School would make it difficult for its graduates to compete in the legal profession.

Context

The backdrop for *Sweatt v. Painter* was the landmark case *Plessy v. Ferguson*, on which the U.S. Supreme Court ruled in 1896. After the Civil War, the Thirteenth Amendment to the Constitution outlawed slavery in the United States. The Fourteenth Amendment was adopted on July 9, 1868, in large part to secure the civil liberties of newly freed slaves. The key section of the Fourteenth Amendment is Section 1, which states:

The Travis County Courthouse, where Sweatt's court case took place, was renamed the Heman Marion Sweatt Travis County Courthouse in 2005.
(Larry D. Moore)

All persons born or naturalized in the United States and subject to the jurisdiction thereof, are citizens of the United States and of the State wherein they reside. No State shall make or enforce any law which shall abridge the privileges or immunities of citizens of the United States; nor shall any State deprive any person of life, liberty, or property, without due process of law; nor deny to any person within its jurisdiction the equal protection of the laws.

Thus, the Fourteenth Amendment extends "equal protection of the laws" to all citizens.

In 1883 the Supreme Court heard a set of cases that had been consolidated into what are called the Civil Rights Cases. The Court's ruling in the Civil Rights Cases was a setback for African Americans, for it held that the Fourteenth Amendment applied only to the actions of government. Thus, segregation on the part of government was unconstitutional, but segregation on the part of private parties, including businesses, was

not. Worse, the Court ruled that the Civil Rights Act of 1875 was unconstitutional. That act had said that

all persons within the jurisdiction of the United States shall be entitled to the full and equal enjoyment of the accommodations, advantages, facilities, and privileges of inns, public conveyances on land or water, theaters, and other places of public amusement; subject only to the conditions and limitations established by law, and applicable alike to citizens of every race and color, regardless of any previous condition of servitude.

In the wake of the Civil Rights Cases decision, numerous states and municipalities, particularly (but not exclusively) in the South, passed so-called Jim Crow laws that segregated African Americans and kept them in subservient positions. One well-known law was Act 111, also known as the Separate Car Act, which the state of Louisiana passed in 1890 and required separate accommodations for Blacks and whites on railroad cars. To challenge the law, the Citizens' Committee to Test the Separate Car Act enlisted Homer Plessy, who was one-eighth Black (and thus Black according to Louisiana law), to ride in a railroad car reserved for whites. While he was on the train, Plessy announced that he was Black and submitted to arrest for violating the act. The committee had ensured that a detective was in the car to make the arrest.

Plessy's case wound its way to the Supreme Court, which in an eight-to-one decision held that the separate accommodations called for in the Louisiana law did not violate the equal protection clause of the Fourteenth Amendment. Writing for the majority, Justice Henry Billings Brown stated:

> We consider the underlying fallacy of the plaintiff's argument to consist in the assumption that the enforced separation of the two races stamps the colored race with a badge of inferiority. If this be so, it is not by reason of anything found in the act, but solely because the colored race chooses to put that construction upon it.

The lone dissenter was Justice John Marshall Harlan, who famously wrote:

> But in view of the Constitution, in the eye of the law, there is in this country no superior, dominant, ruling class of citizens. There is no caste here. Our Constitution is color-blind, and neither knows nor tolerates classes among citizens. In respect of civil rights, all citizens are equal before the law.

Harlan's view would ultimately gain acceptance, but for the next half century the Court's decision in *Plessy v. Ferguson* upheld the doctrine of "separate but equal." Determined to attack it was the National Association for the Advancement of Colored People (NAACP) and its Legal Defense and Education Fund. Under the leadership of Charles Hamilton Houston and, later, Thurgood Marshall, the NAACP made the decision to launch an assault on Jim Crow in the courts by focusing on education.

One of the first cracks in the separate-but-equal doctrine appeared in the mid-1930s with the *Murray v. Maryland* case (sometimes referred to as *Pearson et al. v. Murray*). It was argued by Marshall, who himself had been denied admission to the University of Maryland Law School because he was Black. Marshall's argument before the Baltimore City Circuit Court was that because the "white" and "Black" law schools in Maryland were unequal, the only remedy was to allow the plaintiff, Donald Gaines Murray, to enroll in the University of Maryland Law School. The Maryland Court of Appeals agreed, ruling in January 1936 that "the state has undertaken the function of education in the law, but has omitted students of one race from the only adequate provision made for it, and omitted them solely because of their color," and Murray was admitted.

The crack widened in 1938 with the Supreme Court's decision in *Missouri ex rel. Gaines v. Canada.* (*Ex rel.* is an abbreviation of *ex relatione*, a Latin expression used in the law to mean "on behalf of.") The Court ruled that states with a school for white students must provide in-state education to Blacks, either by allowing Blacks and whites to attend the same school or by creating a second school for Blacks. The problem with this ruling, of course, was that any such educational institution hurriedly thrown together solely for Blacks was unlikely to be equal to all-white institutions in facilities, faculty, and prestige, but at least the Court was beginning to chip away at the denial of higher education to African Americans by all-white institutions.

During World War II, issues involving national security preoccupied the Court. After the war, however, civil rights began to dominate the Court's docket, and wider fissures opened in the separate-but-equal doctrine. The time for change was ripe. During the war, President Franklin Roosevelt had desegregated the defense industries and federal government hiring. After the war, the public was growing more aware of the atrocities that had been committed by Nazi Germany, including the wholesale denial of civil rights to Jews and other groups. On July 26, 1948, President Harry S. Truman issued Executive Order 9981, desegregating the military, and that year the United Nations passed the Universal Declaration of Human Rights.

In this climate, other key Supreme Court cases challenged the separate-but-equal doctrine. In 1948 the Court ruled in *Sipuel v. Board of Regents of the University of Oklahoma* that Oklahoma was required to admit qualified African Americans to the previously all-white University of Oklahoma Law School. This was only a partial victory, for when Ada Lois Sipuel was finally admitted, she was compelled to sit in a raised chair apart from other students behind a sign that read "colored." She was also required to use a separate entrance to the law school and eat alone in the cafeteria. Later that year, the Court struck down restrictive racial covenants in housing in *Shelley v. Kraemer*. (A covenant is an agreement, in this case an agreement by a property owner not to sell his or her property to non-Caucasians.) On the same day that the Court issued its decision in *Sweatt v. Painter*, it also issued its decision in *McLaurin v. Oklahoma State Regents*, ruling that African Americans admitted to a state university had to be granted full access to the school's facilities.

Heman Sweatt was born in 1912 in Houston, Texas. He graduated from college in 1934 and worked as a schoolteacher before entering the University of Michigan Medical School. He soon returned to Houston, however, and found work as a postal clerk. In the 1940s he became active in the civil rights movement; he attended meetings of the Houston branch of the NAACP and worked on voter-registration drives. During his efforts to end discrimination among postal workers, he became interested in the law and decided to pursue a law degree. His suit against the University of Texas Law School was a test case. The Houston NAACP had wanted to find an African American who would apply to the law school and, after that person inevitably had been rejected because of race, file suit. Sweatt volunteered to assume that role. As the case wound its way through the court system, Sweatt gave public presentations at NAACP fund-raising events; he was also subjected to threats and harassment. Finally, the Supreme Court heard oral arguments on the case on April 4, 1950, and issued its decision on June 5.

About the Author

Frederick Moore Vinson was the only member of the Supreme Court to have served in all three branches of government. He was born in Louisa, Kentucky, on January 22, 1890, and from an early age displayed a remarkable intellect, graduating at the top of his class from Kentucky Normal College in 1908. In 1911 he graduated from Centre College Law School with the highest scores in the school's history. A talented baseball player, he played semiprofessional ball in the Ken-

tucky Blue Grass League and tried out for the Cincinnati Reds. But he returned to Louisa, where he became a small-town lawyer. He won his first elective office in 1921 as commonwealth attorney for the Thirty-second Judicial District of Kentucky. Three years later, Vinson won a special election to complete an unexpired term in the U.S. House of Representatives, where he served until 1938, except for the years from 1929 to 1931. For his support of New Deal programs, President Franklin Roosevelt appointed him to the U.S. Court of Appeals for the District of Columbia, where he took his seat on the bench in 1938.

Vinson's service in the executive branch of government began in 1943, when he resigned from the court and became director of the Office of Economic Stabilization. There his chief task was controlling inflation during the war by fighting off requests from businesses for price increases and from organized labor for wage increases. Other posts in the executive branch soon followed. In March 1945 he became administrator of the Federal Loan Agency. One month later, he was appointed director of the Office of War Mobilization and Reconversion, the purpose of which was to ensure the smooth conversion from a wartime to a peacetime economy. President Truman recognized Vinson's skills as a fiscal manager and in July 1945 appointed him secretary of the Treasury. In this post he played a major role in creating the International Bank for Reconstruction and Development and the International Monetary Fund.

In April 1946, Chief Justice Harlan Fiske Stone died. To replace him, Truman turned to Vinson, who took his seat on the High Court as chief justice on June 24, 1946, a position he held until his death. His tenure as chief justice coincided with the early years of the cold war and the nation's fear of Communism. Vinson supported the right of the federal government to legislate against groups that advocated the overthrow of the American system. Throughout his judicial career, he was deferential to executive and legislative authority. He upheld, for example, President Truman's emergency seizure of the coal mines following a nationwide strike in 1946, and in 1952 he dissented from a Court ruling that Truman had exceeded his authority by interceding in the steelworkers' strike during the Korean War and forcing a labor settlement, claiming wartime executive power. Truman held Vinson in high regard and mentioned his name as a possible successor as president. Vinson died of a heart attack in his apartment in Washington, D.C., on September 8, 1953. He had devoted nearly his entire career to public service and left behind an estate worth less than $1,000.

Explanation and Analysis of the Document

The written decision in *Sweatt v. Painter* begins with a number of legalities typically found in a Supreme Court written decision. Usually, these introductory remarks are prepared by the justice's clerk (often a recent law school graduate who does research for the justice). The opening paragraph, called the syllabus, is a brief description of the case. It identifies the petitioner (Sweatt) and the respondent (nominally Painter but in reality the University of Texas Law School) and summarizes the basis of the Court's ruling and the ruling itself. A person can read the syllabus and get the essence of the case without having to read the entire decision. The word *Reversed* indicates that the Court has reversed the decision of the lower court, in this instance the Texas Court of Civic Appeals. What follows is a brief description of the case's history, noting that it had begun in a Texas trial court, was appealed to the Texas Court of Civic Appeals, was returned to the trial court, and then was appealed to the Texas Supreme Court. The document states that the trial court "denied mandamus to compel [Sweatt's] admission to the University of Texas Law School." *Mandamus* is Latin for "we command" and is commonly used in law to refer to a court order requiring a lower court or a government official to perform a duty or to refrain from doing something. In this instance, the trial court refused to require the university law school to admit Sweatt, thus giving the state of Texas time to cobble together a law school for African Americans.

Further legalities follow. The document identifies the attorneys who argued the case for both the petitioner and the respondent. It then notes that amici curiae briefs were filed for both the plaintiff and the defendant. *Amici curiae* is a Latin expression meaning "friends of the court" and refers to briefs submitted by outside parties in support of one position or the other. In complex litigation, particularly a case with broad implications, it is common for individuals and organizations to attempt to sway the Court with analyses

of the case and additional information that the Court might find useful. Typically, in a brief filed by one who appeals a case, in this instance Sweatt, the emphasis must be on legal errors that the lower courts made; the brief does not reargue the facts of the case or anything outside of the law. Amici curiae briefs often range widely in discussing the broader implications of the issues at hand.

With preliminaries disposed of, Vinson outlines the Court's decision. In the first paragraph, he presents the legal question the case raises: "To what extent does the Equal Protection Clause of the Fourteenth Amendment limit the power of a state to distinguish between students of different races in professional and graduate education in a state university?" He goes on to note that "broader issues have been urged for our consideration," likely a reference to the content of the amici curiae briefs, but Vinson indicates that he is going to rule on the case strictly in conformity with the law as he sees it. This is an indication that the Court was not going to reexamine *Plessy v. Ferguson.*

Paragraphs 2 and 3 summarize the facts of the case and refer again to its history, from the trial court through the Texas Supreme Court. Vinson notes that mandamus was denied, which gave the state time to establish a law school for African Americans. Sweatt, though, refused to enroll in the new law school. The Texas Court of Civic Appeals then returned the case to the trial court "without prejudice," meaning that none of the rights or privileges of the persons involved was waived or lost. In other words, the court said that essentially the case was to begin again. In paragraph 4, Vinson notes that when the case was remanded, or sent back to the trial court, the court ruled that the new law school for African Americans was "substantially equivalent" to the University of Texas Law School. The Texas Court of Civic Appeals affirmed the ruling of the trial court, and the Texas Supreme Court refused to hear Sweatt's appeal of this ruling. Accordingly, Sweatt appealed to the U.S. Supreme Court, which "granted certiorari," a legal term that means the Court has required the lower court to turn over the trial records; it also indicates that the Court has agreed to hear the case.

With paragraphs 5 and 6, Vinson begins his analysis of the case. He notes that the facilities at the two institutions were markedly different. At the University of Texas, the faculty was larger, and the law library contained considerably more materials. In contrast, the law school for African Americans was not accredited, though Vinson points out in paragraph 7 that the school, three years after its formation, was on its way toward accreditation. He also mentions that the new law school lacked the prestige of the University of Texas; for example, the new law school did not have an Order of the Coif, a prestigious national scholastic society whose members have an inside track to the best jobs as attorneys. In paragraph 8, Vinson concludes that the University of Texas Law School was clearly superior in the opportunities it afforded students. He also notes that the University of Texas was superior in intangible features: "reputation of the faculty, experience of the administration, position and influence of the alumni, standing in the community, traditions and prestige." Paragraph 10 goes on to point out another disadvantage that the African American students would face at a separate law school: They would be isolated from the 85 percent of the state's population, including judges, other attorneys, officials, and others who were part of the environment in which a person would practice law.

Paragraph 10 responds to the state's claim that excluding Blacks from the University of Texas would be no different from excluding whites from the new law school. Vinson dismisses this argument by saying that as a practical matter, no University of Texas student would want to attend the new law school, given its obvious inferiority. Notice that Vinson cites *Shelley v. Kraemer*: "Equal protection of the laws is not achieved through indiscriminate imposition of inequalities." In paragraph 11, Vinson cites other precedents, including *Sipuel v. Board of Regents of the University of Oklahoma* and *Missouri ex rel. Gaines v. Canada*, to emphasize that the equal protection clause of the Fourteenth Amendment requires states to provide equal opportunities in legal education for their citizens. Bowing to these precedents, Vinson concludes in paragraph 12 that the "petitioner may claim his full constitutional right: legal education equivalent to that offered by the State to students of other races." Vinson rejects the view that *Plessy v. Ferguson* allowed the state to provide a pretense of equivalency. At the same time, he rejects the view that the Court should reexamine *Plessy*. Paragraph 13 concludes the decision: "We hold that the Equal Protection Clause of the Fourteenth Amendment requires that petitioner be admitted to the University of Texas Law School."

Impact

One specific impact of the case was the establishment of what is today Texas Southern University in Houston, with an enrollment of more than nine thousand undergraduates and more than two thousand graduate students. The university was established on March 3, 1947, in response to Sweatt's lawsuit. At the time, the Houston College for Negroes was part of the Houston public school district. The state assumed control of the college, which then formed the core of what was originally called Texas State University for Negroes. The law school is now called the Thurgood Marshall School of Law.

The chief goal of the NAACP in the 1930s and 1940s was to overturn *Plessy v. Ferguson*. Thurgood Marshall and the NAACP had hoped that *Sweatt v. Painter* would have given the Supreme Court that opportunity. They were disappointed. The Court, under the leadership of Chief Justice Vinson, was essentially conservative, and Vinson himself was reluctant to overturn earlier Supreme Court decisions. He said as much in his decision in this case when he wrote: "Because of this traditional reluctance to extend constitutional interpretations to situations or facts which are not before the Court, much of the excellent research and detailed argument presented in these cases is unnecessary to their disposition." Near the end of his decision he stated explicitly that *Plessy* would not be reexamined. Put simply, the Court declined specifically to overturn *Plessy v. Ferguson*.

Matters did not end there, however. Civil rights advocates in 1950 recognized that *Sweatt v. Painter*, along with *McLaurin v. Oklahoma State Regents* and earlier cases with a bearing on equal protection in the realm of higher education, had undermined the separate-but-equal doctrine and that it was only a matter of time before the doctrine would collapse. That time arrived four years later with the watershed case *Brown v. Board of Education*, which Marshall argued before the Court. In a unanimous decision, the Court, under Chief Justice Earl Warren, held that "separate educational facilities are inherently unequal" and that racial segregation in public schools—then mandated by law in the District of Columbia and seventeen states in the South and Midwest—violated the equal protection clause of the Fourteenth Amendment. (It should be noted that sixteen states in the Northeast, Midwest, and West specifically outlawed racial segregation in schools, and another eleven states had no laws on the matter.) This decision finally drove a stake through the heart of the separate-but-equal doctrine.

Sweatt enrolled at the University of Texas Law School in 1950. The case had taken a toll on his physical and emotional health, however, and he withdrew from the school in 1952. He then received a scholarship from the School of Social Work at Atlanta University and completed a master's degree there in 1954. In the ensuing years he worked for the NAACP in Cleveland, Ohio; returned to Atlanta as the assistant director of the city's chapter of the Urban League; and taught at Atlanta University. In 1987 the University of Texas Law School inaugurated the annual Heman Sweatt Symposium in Civil Rights and offers an annual scholarship in his name.

Questions for Further Study

1. What was the "separate-but-equal" doctrine? Where and how did it originate? What impact did the doctrine have on African Americans?

2. Read this document in conjunction with Charles Hamilton Houston's "Educational Inequalities Must Go!" (1935). How was *Sweatt v. Painter* part of an overall strategy designed to challenge the separate-but-equal doctrine?

3. What other developments in the 1940s perhaps contributed to a climate of opinion that led to the Court's ruling in *Sweatt v. Painter*?

4. How did *Sweatt v. Painter* (and other Court cases) pave the way for the Court's landmark ruling in *Brown v. Board of Education*?

5. What is the meaning of the equal protection clause of the Fourteenth Amendment? Why was this clause at the center of the Court's ruling in *Sweatt v. Painter* and other cases?

Further Reading

Books

Browne-Marshall, Gloria J. *Race, Law, and American Society: 1607–Present*. New York: Routledge, 2007.

Davis, Abraham L., and Barbara Luck Graham. *The Supreme Court, Race, and Civil Rights: From Marshall to Rehnquist*. Thousand Oaks, Calif.: Sage Publications, 1995.

Greenberg, Jack. *Crusaders in the Courts: How a Dedicated Band of Lawyers Fought for the Civil Rights Revolution*. New York: Basic Books, 1994.

Harrison, Maureen, and Steve Gilbert, eds. *Civil Rights Decisions of the U.S. Supreme Court: 20th Century*. San Diego, Calif.: Excellent Books, 1994.

Howard, John R. *The Shifting Wind: The Supreme Court and Civil Rights from Reconstruction to Brown*. Albany: State University of New York Press, 1999.

Klarman, Michael J. *From Jim Crow to Civil Rights: The Supreme Court and the Struggle for Racial Equality*. New York: Oxford University Press, 2004.

Lavergne, Gary M. *Before Brown: Heman Marion Sweatt, Thurgood Marshall, and the Long Road to Justice*. Austin: University of Texas Press, 2010.

Tsesis, Alexander. *We Shall Overcome: A History of Civil Rights and the Law*. New Haven, Conn.: Yale University Press, 2008.

Woodward, C. Vann. *The Strange Career of Jim Crow*, 3rd rev. ed. New York: Oxford University Press, 1974.

Articles

Kirk, W. Aston, and John T. Q. King. "Desegregation of Higher Education in Texas." *Journal of Negro Education* 27, no. 3 (Summer 1958): 318–323.

Levy, David W. "Before Brown: The Racial Integration of American Higher Education." *Journal of Supreme Court History* 24, no. 3 (1999): 298–313.

Miller, Adam Scott. "Whatever Means Necessary: Uncovering the Case of *Sweatt v. Painter* and Its Legal Importance." *History in the Making* 4, no. 6 (2011).

Websites

Burns, Richard Allen. "Heman Marion Sweatt." Handbook of Texas Online. Accessed March 2, 2023, http://www.tshaonline.org/handbook/online//articles/SS/fsw23.html.

—Commentary by Michael J. O'Neal

SWEATT V. PAINTER

Document Text

Mr. Chief Justice Vinson delivered the opinion of the Court

This case and *McLaurin v. Oklahoma State Regents*, post, present different aspects of this general question: To what extent does the Equal Protection Clause of the Fourteenth Amendment limit the power of a state to distinguish between students of different races in professional and graduate education in a state university? Broader issues have been urged for our consideration, but we adhere to the principle of deciding constitutional questions only in the context of the particular case before the Court. We have frequently reiterated that this Court will decide constitutional questions only when necessary to the disposition of the case at hand, and that such decisions will be drawn as narrowly as possible. *Rescue Army v. Municipal Court*, . . . (1947), and cases cited therein. Because of this traditional reluctance to extend constitutional interpretations to situations or facts which are not before the Court, much of the excellent research and detailed argument presented in these cases is unnecessary to their disposition.

In the instant case, petitioner filed an application for admission to the University of Texas Law School for the February, 1946 term. His application was rejected solely because he is a Negro. Petitioner thereupon brought this suit for mandamus against the appropriate school officials, respondents here, to compel his admission. At that time, there was no law school in Texas which admitted Negroes.

The state trial court recognized that the action of the State in denying petitioner the opportunity to gain a legal education while granting it to others deprived him of the equal protection of the laws guaranteed by the Fourteenth Amendment. The court did not grant the relief requested, however, but continued the case for six months to allow the State to supply substantially equal facilities. At the expiration of the six months, in December, 1946, the court denied the writ on the showing that the authorized university officials had adopted an order calling for the opening of a law school for Negroes the following February. While petitioner's appeal was pending, such a school was made available, but petitioner refused to register therein. The Texas Court of Civil Appeals set aside the trial court's judgment and ordered the cause "remanded generally to the trial court for further proceedings without prejudice to the rights of any party to this suit."

On remand, a hearing was held on the issue of the equality of the educational facilities at the newly established school as compared with the University of Texas Law School. Finding that the new school offered petitioner "privileges, advantages, and opportunities for the study of law substantially equivalent to those offered by the State to white students at the University of Texas," the trial court denied mandamus. The Court of Civil Appeals affirmed . . . (1948). Petitioner's application for a writ of error was denied by the Texas Supreme Court. We granted certiorari . . . (1949), because of the manifest importance of the constitutional issues involved.

The University of Texas Law School, from which petitioner was excluded, was staffed by a faculty of sixteen full-time and three part-time professors, some of whom are nationally recognized authorities in their field. Its student body numbered 850. The library contained over 65,000 volumes. Among the other facilities available to the students were a law review, moot court facilities, . . . scholarship funds, and Order of the Coif affiliation. The school's alumni occupy the most distinguished positions in the private practice of the law and in the public life of the State. It may properly be considered one of the nation's ranking law schools.

The law school for Negroes which was to have opened in February, 1947, would have had no independent faculty or library. The teaching was to be carried on by four members of the University of Texas Law School faculty, who were to maintain their offices at the University of Texas while teaching at both institutions. Few of the 10,000 volumes ordered for the library had arrived; nor was there any full-time librarian. The school lacked accreditation.

Since the trial of this case, respondents report the opening of a law school at the Texas State University for Negroes. It is apparently on the road to full accreditation. It has a faculty of five full-time professors; a student body of 23; a library of some 16,500 volumes serviced by a full-time staff; a practice court and legal aid association; and one alumnus who has become a member of the Texas Bar.

Whether the University of Texas Law School is compared with the original or the new law school for Negroes, we cannot find substantial equality in the educational opportunities offered white and Negro law students by the State. In terms of number of the faculty, variety of courses and opportunity for specialization, size of the student body, scope of the library, availability of law . . . review and similar activities, the University of Texas Law School is superior. What is more important, the University of Texas Law School possesses to a far greater degree those qualities which are incapable of objective measurement but which make for greatness in a law school. Such qualities, to name but a few, include reputation of the faculty, experience of the administration, position and influence of the alumni, standing in the community, traditions and prestige. It is difficult to believe that one who had a free choice between these law schools would consider the question close.

Moreover, although the law is a highly learned profession, we are well aware that it is an intensely practi-

cal one. The law school, the proving ground for legal learning and practice, cannot be effective in isolation from the individuals and institutions with which the law interacts. Few students and no one who has practiced law would choose to study in an academic vacuum, removed from the interplay of ideas and the exchange of views with which the law is concerned. The law school to which Texas is willing to admit petitioner excludes from its student body members of the racial groups which number 85% of the population of the State and include most of the lawyers, witnesses, jurors, judges and other officials with whom petitioner will inevitably be dealing when he becomes a member of the Texas Bar. With such a substantial and significant segment of society excluded, we cannot conclude that the education offered petitioner is substantially equal to that which he would receive if admitted to the University of Texas Law School.

It may be argued that excluding petitioner from that school is no different from excluding white students from the new law school. This contention overlooks realities. It is unlikely that a member of a group so decisively in the majority, attending a school with rich traditions . . . prestige which only a history of consistently maintained excellence could command, would claim that the opportunities afforded him for legal education were unequal to those held open to petitioner. That such a claim, if made, would be dishonored by the State, is no answer. "Equal protection of the laws is not achieved through indiscriminate imposition of inequalities." *Shelley v. Kraemer . . .* (1948).

It is fundamental that these cases concern rights which are personal and present. This Court has stated unanimously that "The State must provide [legal education] for [petitioner] in conformity with the equal protection clause of the Fourteenth Amendment and provide it as soon as it does for applicants of any other group." *Sipuel v. Board of Regents . . .* (1948). That case "did not present the issue whether a state might not satisfy the equal protection clause of the Fourteenth Amendment by establishing a separate law school for Negroes." *Fisher v. Hurst . . .* (1948). In *Missouri ex rel. Gaines v. Canada . . .* (1938), the Court, speaking through Chief Justice Hughes, declared that "petitioner's right was a personal one. It was as an individual that he was entitled to the equal protection of the laws, and the State was bound to furnish him within its borders facilities for legal education substantially equal to those which the State there afforded for persons of the white race, whether or not other negroes sought the same opportunity." These are the only cases in this Court which present the issue of the constitutional validity of race distinctions in state-supported graduate and professional education.

In accordance with these cases, petitioner may claim his full constitutional right: legal education equivalent to that offered by the State to students of other races. Such education is not available to him in a separate law school as offered by the State. We cannot, therefore, . . . agree with respondents that the doctrine of *Plessy v. Ferguson* . . . (1896), requires affirmance of the judgment below. Nor need we reach petitioner's contention that *Plessy v. Ferguson* should be reexamined in the light of contemporary knowledge respecting the purposes of the Fourteenth Amendment and the effects of racial segregation. . . .

We hold that the Equal Protection Clause of the Fourteenth Amendment requires that petitioner be admitted to the University of Texas Law School. The judgment is reversed and the cause is remanded for proceedings not inconsistent with this opinion.

Reversed.

Glossary

Amici curiae: Latin for "friends of the court," referring to outside parties who submit briefs to the court in support of one position or the other

certiorari: a writ by an appeals court commanding a lower court to produce the records of a case; "granting certiorari" means that the higher court has agreed to hear the case.

Chief Justice Hughes: Charles Evans Hughes, whose tenure as chief justice coincided with the years of the Great Depression

ex relatione: a Latin expression used in the law to mean "on behalf of"

mandamus: Latin for "we command," used in law to refer to a court order requiring a lower court or a government official to perform a duty or to refrain from doing something

Order of the Coif: a prestigious national scholastic society for law students

remand: the act of a higher court sending a case back to a lower court for action

Reversed: an indication that a higher court has reversed the ruling of a lower court in the case at hand

writ of error: a judicial writ from an appellate court ordering the court of record to produce the records of trial; an appeal

DENNIS V. UNITED STATES

DATE	CITATION
1951	341 U.S. 494
AUTHOR	**SIGNIFICANCE**
Fred M. Vinson	Upheld the constitutionality of the 1940 Smith Act, which made it a crime to advocate for the overthrow of the U.S. government, thereby permitting the government to censor speech and expression
VOTE	
6–2	

Overview

Dennis v. United States was a decision that affirmed the authority of the U.S. government to use prior restraint against dissidents. The case was argued on December 4, 1950, and the Court's decision was announced on June 4, 1951. Eugene Dennis and ten other members of the U.S. Communist Party had been arrested for plotting to overthrow the U.S. government. The accused claimed their actions were protected by the First Amendment. The defendants had been charged under the 1940 Smith Act, which had been passed on the eve of the U.S. entry into World War II (1941) to be used against subversives who might support the Nazis or other potential U.S. enemies. The case was heard at the beginning of the Cold War, when the United States was in the midst of the Korean War (1950–53) and a concurrent wave of anti-communism.

The majority of the justices voted to uphold the convictions of the eleven communists. Chief Justice Fred M. Vinson wrote the plurality opinion, representing his views and those of three other justices, while Felix Frankfurter and Robert Jackson authored separate, concurring opinions. Central to Vinson's argument was the

idea that Dennis and the others had presented "a clear and probable danger" to the United States by teaching communism. Hugo Black and William O. Douglas dissented from their colleagues and argued that the appellants were protected by the First Amendment.

Context

After the end of World War II in 1945, the United States found itself in another global struggle. The Cold War between the United States and the Soviet Union lasted from 1947 to 1991 and was marked by competition over global power and influence. The struggle was known as the Cold War because the two superpowers avoided outright war and instead fought a series of proxy conflicts around the world. The conflict was an ideological contest between the democracy and free market capitalism of the United States and the authoritarianism and communism of the Soviet Union.

After World War II, the Soviet Union aggressively supported communist uprisings and takeovers of non-communist states. For instance, the Soviets installed communist regimes throughout Eastern Europe and backed uprisings in countries such as Greece. In 1949, communists took over China. The following year, North Korea, an ally of the Soviet Union and China, invaded South Korea, an ally of the United States.

The Korean War heightened concerns in the United States over subversion or treason by communists in the country. A U.S. senator from Wisconsin, Joseph McCarthy, claimed to have evidence that a number of communists had infiltrated the federal government. His claims led to a period of investigations and persecution of suspected communists known as McCarthyism or the "Red Scare" (communists were derisively known as "reds"). There was a widespread, though unfounded, fear that communists would undermine support for democracy and the U.S. government and launch a revolution to install a pro-Soviet regime. Many Americans suffered various forms of repression during this period. Some lost their jobs or occupations because of suspicions that they were communists or communist sympathizers.

In the midst of the McCarthy era, eleven members of the Communist Party in the United States, including the group's secretary general, Eugene Dennis, were arrested and charged with plotting to overthrow the U.S. government. During the 1949 trial, the prosecution did not contend that the defendants had a specific plan to seize control of the country. Instead, the prosecutor argued that Dennis and his compatriots' belief system was based on the replacement of the existing U.S. government with a communist regime. Furthermore, books, pamphlets, and other communist literature called for uprisings by the working class to destroy the existing economic and political system.

Dennis and his colleagues were found guilty under the Smith Act on October 14, 1949. This law forbade people from calling for the violent overthrow of the U.S. government. It was enacted in 1940 to be used against those who might undermine U.S. efforts to prepare for the nation's entry into World War II. After World War II, the Smith Act was used to prosecute communists during the early years of the Cold War.

Critics of the Smith Act argued that it violated the First Amendment, which guaranteed that Americans had the right to free speech and freedom of expression. However, in the aftermath of World War I, the Court created two doctrines to assess whether criticism of

the government could be banned. For instance, in 1919, in the case *Schenck v. United States*, the Court created the "clear and present danger" doctrine. This approach protected speech unless that expression created a clear and present danger to the United States. Under the doctrine, speech that was constitutional in peacetime might be considered dangerous in wartime. Therefore, criticism of the government might be acceptable during peacetime but could be deemed as treason in wartime. The Court also used the "bad tendency" test, which held that speech could be censored if its main intent or "tendency" was to produce a result that Congress had declared illegal. The debate over free speech versus national security would continue for years and remain a source of contention into the twenty-first century.

Dennis and his codefendants appealed their conviction, but a court of appeals upheld the conviction. The eleven Communist Party members then again appealed, this time to the Supreme Court.

About the Author

Fred M. Vinson was born in the small, rural town of Louisa, Kentucky, on January 22, 1890. He attended Centre College in Danville, Kentucky, where he earned a law degree in 1911. Vinson served in U.S. Army during World War I and was elected as commonwealth's attorney (an official who prosecutes cases for local or state government). In 1924, the young prosecutor was elected to the U.S. House of Representatives as a Democrat. While in Congress, he became friends with future President Harry S. Truman.

In 1937, Vinson was appointed a federal judge on the Court of Appeals for the District of Columbia. The future Supreme Court justice resigned as a judge in 1943, in the midst of World War II, to accept a new position as the director of the Office of Economic Stabilization. Truman named Vinson secretary of the treasury in 1945, but the following year the president nominated him to be chief justice of the Supreme Court. He was sworn in to that post on June 24, 1946.

Vinson's tenure as chief justice was marked by strong internal divisions in the Court. Vinson was a moderate on most issues but developed a reputation as a staunch supporter of expanded powers for the federal government. For instance, in 1952 he dissented, along with two of his colleagues, in the case *Youngstown Sheet and Tube Co. v. Sawyer*, when the majority ruled that President Truman did not have the constitutional authority to take control of steel mills in an effort to forestall a strike that would have reduced production during the Korean War.

In two major cases, the chief justice backed enhanced security authority for the national government. In the 1950 case *American Communications Association v. Douds*, Vinson wrote the 5–1 majority opinion that confirmed the power of the government to require union officials to sign statements that they were not communists. In *Dennis v. United States* in 1951, Vinson again wrote the majority opinion, which upheld the conviction of eleven members of the Communist Party for advocating the overthrow of the U.S. government.

Vinson died of a heart attack while still in office on September 8, 1953.

Explanation and Analysis of the Document

The ruling in the Dennis case was complicated and produced five opinions: the majority opinion written by Vinson and joined by three other justices; two concurring opinions that backed the chief justice; and two separate dissenting views that opposed the decision. Chief Justice Vinson's opinion highlighted the perceived danger of communism to the U.S. political system and defended the constitutionality of the Smith Act.

Vinson includes the text of the Smith Act in his decision and provides a summary of the conviction of Dennis and his ten codefendants. The communists were charged with creating an organization whose goal was the violent overthrow of the U.S. government. The chief justice notes that the Supreme Court was not retrying the original case. Indeed, there was ample evidence that the eleven were members of the Communist Party and that they advocated the replacement of the current U.S. political system with one based on communism. Instead, the Court had to decide whether the government had the authority to suppress organizations such as the Communist Party or whether political groups had a First Amendment right to promote regime change in the United States. Here Vinson draws a distinction between "advocacy" and "discussion." He

Eugene Dennis in a 1948 mugshot
(Library of Congress)

contends that the Smith Act did not ban hypothetical discussions about alternative forms of government. People could debate or argue the merits of communism. It was healthy for a free society to publicly examine various ideas and concepts, including those that might be opposed by the majority of citizens. However, there were limits to speech. Vinson writes that there are times when First Amendment rights have to be evaluated against larger societal concerns.

Clear and Probable Danger Test

To clarify when speech could be banned, Vinson cites the *Schenck* decision and the clear and present danger test. The chief justice cites other cases that bolster his argument, including *American Communications Association v. Douds*, which he had authored a year earlier. Vinson also incorporates the main argument of the court that had ruled on the appeal of Dennis and his colleagues. In that decision, the chief justice of the Court of Appeals for the Second Circuit, Learned Hand, modified the clear and present danger doctrine to that of "clear and probable danger." This lowered the threshold by which courts assessed the potential danger of speech. Hand's opinion argued that speech did not have to present an immediate threat (a "present" danger) but could be a likely hazard. In adopting the clear and probable doctrine, Vinson notes that the communists do not need to be in the midst of an actual plot to overthrow the government. A conspiracy to foster the subversive scheme would be enough for a conviction under the Smith Act. This was because government could not necessarily wait for an uprising to occur; it needed the authority to intervene and stop the conspiracy before it was acted upon. This was especially true in the case of Dennis and his comrades in that the evidence indicated that they wanted a speedy takeover of the government through force.

Vinson acknowledges that his opinion could be criticized because of the vague nature of what types of speech could pose a clear and probable threat. He accepts that the Smith Act could be interpreted too broadly. However, the chief justice argues that future cases will be decided on an individual basis. The line between acceptable speech and expression and that which may be banned may be unclear. This would especially be true in instances where defendants may not realize that their speech poses an imminent danger. Vinson expresses his faith that future justices will be able to review cases and recognize those distinctions in an appropriate manner. He also asserts that his clear and probable danger test is not an exact formula but one open to interpretation.

The Concurrences and Dissents

Justices Frankfurter and Jackson concurred with Vinson's opinion. Frankfurter's opinion emphasizes the right of any government to defend itself from threats, including internal dangers. However, the justice notes that even that duty can be limited by the First Amendment. Frankfurther's main difference with Vinson is over the clear and probable danger test. He instead argues that there is not a need for a new standard. Existing cases and legal principles can be used to confirm the guilty verdict in the Dennis case. Jackson also argues that there is no need for a new standard because existing precedent can be used to justify the guilty convictions. For instance, he notes that there already exist measures that criminalize conspiracies that are meant to break laws.

In his dissent, Justice Hugo Black argues strongly that Dennis and his codefendants were protected by the First Amendment. He further contends that parts of the Smith Act are unconstitutional. Central to his ar-

gument is the fact that the communists did not take any direct action to overthrow the government. They merely discussed and advocated in favor of a new governmental system. Black's dissent emerged as a celebrated defense of free speech and expression.

William O. Douglas accepts that there are limits to free speech in his dissent. However, those limits exist only in the most extenuating circumstances. He disputes the reasoning of the Court's majority that the eleven communists exceeded those boundaries. Douglas dwells on the distinction between action and advocacy. According to his dissent, there is a difference between instructing people on how to commit violent acts, such as killing the president, and arguing in favor of the overthrow of the government. Douglas warns the Court not to equate speech and action. One is protected; the other is not. The justice also cautions the Court and the nation as a whole against overreactions during times of threat. The result could be a loss of liberty that would only weaken the nation by eroding its core principles.

Impact

The Dennis decision coincided with the widespread wave of anti-communist sentiment in the United States in the 1950s. The decision was issued in the midst of the McCarthy era, when many Americans believed that communist groups across the United States were actively trying to topple the government. Vinson's opinion in the case reflected the general feeling that the government needed expanded powers to fight communism both at home and abroad. The decision was also in line with past cases such as *Schenck v. United States*, in which the Supreme Court deferred to government efforts to increase security authority during times of national crisis. The Court had historically permitted some infringements on civil liberties when public officials argued that the restrictions were necessary to protect U.S. citizens.

By affirming the constitutionality of the Smith Act, the Court's ruling opened the door for additional prosecutions for sedition. More than fifty suspected communists or members of supposed anti-government groups were arrested across the nation over the next year. However, by the mid-1950s, many people had become tired of McCarthyism and its excesses. The Korean War had ended in 1953, and although the Cold War continued, the fear of a communist takeover of the government had declined significantly.

In addition, the composition of the Supreme Court changed dramatically. Vinson died in office and was replaced by former California governor Earl Warren in 1954. Warren, a moderate Republican, was much more skeptical of enhanced security powers for the government. Besides Warren, by 1957 there were three other new justices on the Court.

In 1957, in *Yates v. United States*, the Court overturned the convictions of fourteen members of the Communist Party who had been found guilty under the Smith Act. In the 6–1 decision, the Court created a distinction between advocating the overthrow of the government and teaching specific steps to take to topple it. In other words, it was permissible to discuss the overthrow of the government in an abstract manner as long as there were no specific plans to take action. The ruling dramatically weakened the Smith Act.

The 1969 case *Brandenburg v. Ohio* went further and prohibited the government from suppressing speech unless it called for imminent violence or insurrection or was likely to lead to such lawlessness. *Brandenburg* effectively overturned a series of cases, including *Schenck* and *Dennis*, and ended the use of the clear and present danger test. With *Dennis* overturned, the Supreme Court ushered in an era of expanded free speech rights.

Questions for Further Study

1. Why did many Americans fear communism in the late 1940s and 1950s? Were their concerns justified?

2. What is the clear and present danger test? How did the Court use this doctrine to limit free speech? Is the test an appropriate way to judge whether speech or expression should be banned?

3. Should the Supreme Court grant the government expanded national security powers during crises or national emergencies? Which is more important, security or personal freedom?

Further Reading

Books

Belknap, Michal R. *Cold War Political Justice: The Smith Act, the Communist Party, and American Civil Liberties.* Westport, CT: Greenwood Press, 1977.

O'Brien, David M. *Congress Shall Make No Law: The First Amendment, Unprotected Expression, and the Supreme Court.* Lanham, MD: Rowman & Littlefield, 2010.

Snyder, Brad. *Democratic Justice: Felix Frankenfurter, the Supreme Court and the Making of the Liberal Establishment.* New York: Norton, 2022.

St. Clair, James E., and Linda C. Gugin. *Chief Justice Fred M. Vinson of Kentucky: A Political Biography.* Lexington: University Press of Kentucky, 2021.

Urofsky, Melvin I. *Dissent and the Supreme Court: Its Role in the Court's History and the Nation's Constitutional Dialogue.* New York: Vintage, 2017.

Articles

Belknap, Michal R. "Why Dennis?" *Marquette Law Review* 96, no. 4 (2013).

Gorfinkel, John A., and Julian W. Mack II. "*Dennis v. United States* and the Clear and Present Danger Rule." *California Law Review* 39, no. 4 (December 1951).

Wiecek, William M. "The Legal Foundation of Domestic Anticommunism: The Background of Dennis v. United States." *Supreme Court Review*, 2001.

Websites

"*Dennis v. United States*." *Global Freedom of Expression*, Columbia University website. Accessed January 12, 2023, https://globalfreedomofexpression.columbia.edu/cases/dennis-v-united-states/.

Walker, James L. "*Dennis v. United States* (1951)." *The First Amendment Encyclopedia*, Middle Tennessee State University website, 2009. Accessed January 12, 2023, https://www.mtsu.edu/first-amendment/article/190/dennis-v-united-states.

—Commentary by Tom Lansford

DENNIS V. UNITED STATES

Document Text

MR. CHIEF JUSTICE VINSON announced the judgment of the Court

Petitioners were indicted in July, 1948, for violation of the conspiracy provisions of the Smith Act, 54 Stat. 671, 18 U.S.C. (1946 ed.) § 11, during the period of April, 1945, to July, 1948. The pretrial motion to quash the indictment on the grounds, *inter alia,* that the statute was unconstitutional was denied, *United States v. Foster,* 80 F. Supp. 479, and the case was set for trial on January 17, 1949. A verdict of guilty as to all the petitioners was returned by the jury on October 14, 1949. The Court of Appeals affirmed the convictions. 183 F.2d 201. We granted certiorari, 340 U.S. 863, limited to the following two questions: (1) Whether either § 2 or § 3 of the Smith Act, inherently or as construed and applied in the instant case, violates the First Amendment and other provisions of the Bill of Rights; (2) whether either § 2 or § 3 of the Act, inherently or as construed and applied in the instant case, violates the First and Fifth Amendments because of indefiniteness.

Sections 2 and 3 of the Smith Act, 54 Stat. 671, 18 U.S.C. (1946 ed.) §§ 10, 11 (*see* present 18 U.S.C. § 2385), provide as follows:

"SEC. 2.(a) It shall be unlawful for any person—"

"(1) to knowingly or willfully advocate, abet, advise, or teach the duty, necessity, desirability, or propriety of overthrowing or destroying any government in the United States by force or violence, or by the assassination of any officer of any such government;"

"(2) with intent to cause the overthrow or destruction of any government in the United States, to print, publish, edit, issue, circulate, sell, distribute, or publicly display any written or printed matter advocating, advising, or teaching the duty, necessity, desirability, or propriety of overthrowing or destroying any government in the United States by force or violence;"

"(3) to organize or help to organize any society, group, or assembly of persons who teach, advocate, or encourage the overthrow or destruction of any government in the United States by force or violence; or to be or become a member of, or affiliate with, any such society, group, or assembly of persons, knowing the purposes thereof."

"(b) For the purposes of this section, the term 'government in the United States' means the Government of the United States, the government of any State, Territory, or possession of the United States, the government of the District of Columbia, or the government of any political subdivision of any of them."

"SEC. 3. It shall be unlawful for any person to attempt to commit, or to conspire to commit, any of the acts prohibited by the provisions of this title."

The indictment charged the petitioners with willfully and knowingly conspiring (1) to organize as the Communist Party of the United States of America a society, group and assembly of persons who teach and advocate the overthrow and destruction of the Government of the United States by force and violence, and (2) knowingly and willfully to advocate and teach the duty and necessity of overthrowing and destroying the Government of the United States by force and violence. The indictment further alleged that § 2 of the Smith Act proscribes these acts and that any conspiracy to take such action is a violation of § 3 of the Act.

The trial of the case extended over nine months, six of which were devoted to the taking of evidence, resulting in a record of 16,000 pages. Our limited grant of the writ of certiorari has removed from our consideration any question as to the sufficiency of the evidence to support the jury's determination that petitioners are guilty of the offense charged. Whether, on this record, petitioners did, in fact, advocate the overthrow of the Government by force and violence is not before us, and we must base any discussion of this point upon the conclusions stated in the opinion of the Court of Appeals, which treated the issue in great detail. That court held that the record in this case amply supports the necessary finding of the jury that petitioners, the leaders of the Communist Party in this country, were unwilling to work within our framework of democracy, but intended to initiate a violent revolution whenever the propitious occasion appeared. Petitioners dispute the meaning to be drawn from the evidence, contending that the Marxist-Leninist doctrine they advocated taught that force and violence to achieve a Communist form of government in an existing democratic state would be necessary only because the ruling classes of that state would never permit the transformation to be accomplished peacefully, but would use force and violence to defeat any peaceful political and economic gain the Communists could achieve. But the Court of Appeals held that the record supports the following broad conclusions: by virtue of their control over the political apparatus of the Communist Political Association, petitioners were able to transform that organization into the Communist Party; that the policies of the Association were changed from peaceful cooperation with the United States and its economic and political structure to a policy which had existed before the United States and the Soviet Union were fighting a common enemy, namely, a policy which worked for the overthrow of the Government by force and violence; that the Communist Party is a highly disciplined organization, adept at infiltration into strategic positions, use of aliases, and double meaning language; that the Party is rigidly controlled; that Communists, unlike other political parties, tolerate no dissension from the policy laid down by the guiding forces, but that the approved program is slavishly followed by the members of the Party; that the literature of the Party and the statements and activities of its leaders, petitioners here, advocate, and the general goal of the Party was, during the period in question, to achieve a successful overthrow of the existing order by force and violence.

I

It will be helpful in clarifying the issues to treat next the contention that the trial judge improperly interpreted the statute by charging that the statute required an unlawful intent before the jury could convict. More specifically, he charged that the jury could not find the petitioners guilty under the indictment unless they found that petitioners had the intent to "overthrow . . . the Government of the United States by force and violence as speedily as circumstances would permit."

Section 2(a)(1) makes it unlawful

"to knowingly or willfully advocate, . . . or teach the duty, necessity, desirability, or propriety of overthrowing or destroying any government in the United States by force or violence. . . . ;"

Section 2(a)(3), "to organize or help to organize any society, group, or assembly of persons who teach, advocate, or encourage the overthrow. . . ." Because of the fact that § 2(a)(2) expressly requires a specific intent to overthrow the Government, and because of the absence of precise language in the foregoing subsections, it is claimed that Congress deliberately omitted any such requirement. We do not agree. It would require a far greater indication of congressional desire that intent not be made an element of the crime than the use of the disjunctive "knowingly or willfully" in § 2(a)(1), or the omission of exact language in § 2(a)(3). The structure and purpose of the statute demand the inclusion of intent as an element of the crime. Congress was concerned with those who advocate and organize for the overthrow of the Government. Certainly those who recruit and combine for the purpose of advocating overthrow intend to bring about that overthrow. We hold that the statute requires as an essential element of the crime proof of the intent of those who are charged with its violation to overthrow the Government by force and violence. *See Williams v. United States*, 341 U. S. 97, 341 U. S. 101-102 (1951); *Screws v. United States*, 325 U. S. 91, 325 U. S. 101-105 (1945); *Cramer v. United States*, 325 U. S. 1, 325 U. S. 31 (1945).

Nor does the fact that there must be an investigation of a state of mind under this interpretation afford any basis for rejection of that meaning. A survey of Title 18 of the U.S. Code indicates that the vast majority of the crimes designated by that Title require, by express language, proof of the existence of a certain mental state, in words such as "knowingly," "maliciously," "willfully," "with the purpose of," "with intent to," or combinations or permutations of these and synonymous terms. The existence of a *mens rea* is the rule of, rather than the exception to, the principles of Anglo-American criminal jurisprudence. *See American Communications Assn. v. Douds,* 339 U. S. 382, 339 U. S. 411 (1950).

It has been suggested that the presence of intent makes a difference in the law when an "act otherwise excusable or carrying minor penalties" is accompanied by such an evil intent. Yet the existence of such an intent made the killing condemned in *Screws, supra,* and the beating in *Williams, supra,* both clearly and severely punishable under state law, offenses constitutionally punishable by the Federal Government. In those cases, the Court required the Government to prove that the defendants intended to deprive the victim of a constitutional right. If that precise mental state may be an essential element of a crime, surely an intent to overthrow the Government of the United States by advocacy thereof is equally susceptible of proof.

II

The obvious purpose of the statute is to protect existing Government not from change by peaceable, lawful and constitutional means, but from change by violence, revolution and terrorism. That it is within the power of the Congress to protect the Government of the United States from armed rebellion is a proposition which requires little discussion. Whatever theoretical merit there may be to the argument that there is a "right" to rebellion against dictatorial governments is without force where the existing structure of the government provides for peaceful and orderly change. We reject any principle of governmental helplessness in the face of preparation for revolution, which principle, carried to its logical conclusion, must lead to anarchy. No one could conceive that it is not within the power of Congress to prohibit acts intended to overthrow the Government by force and violence. The question with which we are concerned here is not whether Congress

has such power, but whether the means which it has employed conflict with the First and Fifth Amendments to the Constitution.

One of the bases for the contention that the means which Congress has employed are invalid takes the form of an attack on the face of the statute on the grounds that, by its terms, it prohibits academic discussion of the merits of Marxism-Leninism, that it stifles ideas and is contrary to all concepts of a free speech and a free press. Although we do not agree that the language itself has that significance, we must bear in mind that it is the duty of the federal courts to interpret federal legislation in a manner not inconsistent with the demands of the Constitution. *American Communications Assn. v. Douds,* 339 U. S. 382, 339 U. S. 407 (1950). We are not here confronted with cases similar to *Thornhill v. Alabama,* 310 U. S. 88 (1940); *Herndon v. Lowry,* 301 U. S. 242 (1937), and *De Jonge v. Oregon,* 299 U. S. 353 (1937), where a state court had given a meaning to a state statute which was inconsistent with the Federal Constitution. This is a federal statute which we must interpret as well as judge. Herein lies the fallacy of reliance upon the manner in which this Court has treated judgments of state courts. Where the statute as construed by the state court transgressed the First Amendment, we could not but invalidate the judgments of conviction.

The very language of the Smith Act negates the interpretation which petitioners would have us impose on that Act. It is directed at advocacy, not discussion. Thus, the trial judge properly charged the jury that they could not convict if they found that petitioners did "no more than pursue peaceful studies and discussions or teaching and advocacy in the realm of ideas." He further charged that it was not unlawful

"to conduct in an American college or university a course explaining the philosophical theories set forth in the books which have been placed in evidence."

Such a charge is in strict accord with the statutory language, and illustrates the meaning to be placed on those words. Congress did not intend to eradicate the free discussion of political theories, to destroy the traditional rights of Americans to discuss and evaluate ideas without fear of governmental sanction. Rather Congress was concerned with the very kind of activity in which the evidence showed these petitioners engaged.

III

But although the statute is not directed at the hypothetical cases which petitioners have conjured, its application in this case has resulted in convictions for the teaching and advocacy of the overthrow of the Government by force and violence, which, even though coupled with the intent to accomplish that overthrow, contains an element of speech. For this reason, we must pay special heed to the demands of the First Amendment marking out the boundaries of speech.

We pointed out in *Douds, supra,* that the basis of the First Amendment is the hypothesis that speech can rebut speech, propaganda will answer propaganda, free debate of ideas will result in the wisest governmental policies. It is for this reason that this Court has recognized the inherent value of free discourse. An analysis of the leading cases in this Court which have involved direct limitations on speech, however, will demonstrate that both the majority of the Court and the dissenters in particular cases have recognized that this is not an unlimited, unqualified right, but that the societal value of speech must, on occasion, be subordinated to other values and considerations.

No important case involving free speech was decided by this Court prior to *Schenck v. United States,* 249 U. S. 47 (1919). Indeed, the summary treatment accorded an argument based upon an individual's claim that the First Amendment protected certain utterances indicates that the Court at earlier dates placed no unique emphasis upon that right. It was not until the classic dictum of Justice Holmes in the *Schenck* case that speech *per se* received that emphasis in a majority opinion. That case involved a conviction under the Criminal Espionage Act, 40 Stat. 217. The question the Court faced was whether the evidence was sufficient to sustain the conviction. Writing for a unanimous Court, Justice Holmes stated that the

"question in every case is whether the words used are used in such circumstances and are of such a nature as to create a clear and present danger that they will bring about the substantive evils that Congress has a right to prevent."

249 U.S. at 249 U. S. 52. But the force of even this expression is considerably weakened by the reference at the end of the opinion to *Goldman v. United States,* 245 U. S. 474 (1918), a prosecution under the same statute. Said Justice Holmes,

"Indeed, [*Goldman*] might be said to dispose of the present contention if the precedent covers all *media concludendi.* But as the right to free speech was not referred to specially, we have thought fit to add a few words."

249 U.S. at 249 U. S. 52. The fact is inescapable, too, that the phrase bore no connotation that the danger was to be any threat to the safety of the Republic. The charge was causing and attempting to cause insubordination in the military forces and obstruct recruiting. The objectionable document denounced conscription and its most inciting sentence was, "You must do your share to maintain, support and uphold the rights of the people of this country." 249 U.S. at 249 U. S. 51. Fifteen thousand copies were printed, and some circulated. This insubstantial gesture toward insubordination in 1917 during war was held to be a clear and present danger of bringing about the evil of military insubordination.

In several later cases involving convictions under the Criminal Espionage Act, the nub of the evidence the Court held sufficient to meet the "clear and present danger" test enunciated in *Schenck* was as follows: *Frohwerk v. United States,* 249 U. S. 204 (1919)—publication of twelve newspaper articles attacking the war; *Debs v. United States,* 249 U. S. 211 (1919)—one speech attacking United States' participation in the war; *Abrams v. United States,* 250 U. S. 616 (1919)—circulation of copies of two different socialist circulars attacking the war; *Schaefer v. United States,* 251 U. S. 466 (1920)—publication of a German language newspaper with allegedly false articles, critical of capitalism and the war; *Pierce v. United States,* 252 U. S. 239 (1920)—circulation of copies of a four-page pamphlet written by a clergyman, attacking the purposes of the war and United States' participation therein. Justice Holmes wrote the opinions for a unanimous Court in *Schenck, Frohwerk* and *Debs.* He and Justice Brandeis dissented in *Abrams, Schaefer* and *Pierce.* The basis of these dissents was that, because of the protection which the First Amendment gives to speech, the evidence in each case was insufficient to show that the defendants had created the requisite danger under *Schenck.* But these dissents did not mark a change of principle. The dissenters doubted only the probable effectiveness of the puny efforts toward subversion. In *Abrams,* they wrote,

"I do not doubt for a moment that, by the same reasoning that would justify punishing persuasion to murder, the United States constitutionally may punish speech that produces or is intended to produce a clear and imminent danger that it will bring about forthwith certain substantive evils that the United States constitutionally may seek to prevent."

250 U.S. at 250 U. S. 627. And in *Schaefer* the test was said to be one of "degree," 251 U.S. at 251 U. S. 482, although it is not clear whether "degree" refers to clear and present danger or evil. Perhaps both were meant.

The rule we deduce from these cases is that, where an offense is specified by a statute in nonspeech or nonpress terms, a conviction relying upon speech or press as evidence of violation may be sustained only when the speech or publication created a "clear and present danger" of attempting or accomplishing the prohibited crime, *e.g.,* interference with enlistment. The dissents, we repeat, in emphasizing the value of speech, were addressed to the argument of the sufficiency of the evidence.

The next important case before the Court in which free speech was the crux of the conflict was *Gitlow v. New York,* 268 U. S. 652 (1925). There, New York had made it a crime to advocate "the necessity or propriety of overthrowing ... organized government by force. . . ." The evidence of violation of the statute was that the defendant had published a Manifesto attacking the Government and capitalism. The convictions were sustained, Justices Holmes and Brandeis dissenting. The majority refused to apply the "clear and present danger" test to the specific utterance. Its reasoning was as follows: the "clear and present danger" test was applied to the utterance itself in *Schenck* because the question was merely one of sufficiency of evidence under an admittedly constitutional statute. *Gitlow* however, presented a different question. There a legislature had found that a certain kind of speech was, itself, harmful and unlawful. The constitutionality of such a state statute had to be adjudged by this Court just as it determined the constitutionality of any state statute, namely, whether the statute was "reasonable." Since it was entirely reasonable for a state to attempt to protect itself from violent overthrow, the statute was perforce reasonable. The only question remaining in the case became whether there was evidence to support the conviction, a question which gave the majority no

difficulty. Justices Holmes and Brandeis refused to accept this approach, but insisted that, wherever speech was the evidence of the violation, it was necessary to show that the speech created the "clear and present danger" of the substantive evil which the legislature had the right to prevent. Justices Holmes and Brandeis, then, made no distinction between a federal statute which made certain acts unlawful, the evidence to support the conviction being speech, and a statute which made speech itself the crime. This approach was emphasized in *Whitney v. California,* 274 U. S. 357 (1927), where the Court was confronted with a conviction under the California Criminal Syndicalist statute. The Court sustained the conviction, Justices Brandeis and Holmes concurring in the result. In their concurrence they repeated that, even though the legislature had designated certain speech as criminal, this could not prevent the defendant from showing that there was no danger that the substantive evil would be brought about.

Although no case subsequent to *Whitney* and *Gitlow* has expressly overruled the majority opinions in those cases, there is little doubt that subsequent opinions have inclined toward the Holmes-Brandeis rationale. And in *American Communications Assn. v. Douds, supra,* we were called upon to decide the validity of § 9(h) of the Labor Management Relations Act of 1947. That section required officials of unions which desired to avail themselves of the facilities of the National Labor Relations Board to take oaths that they did not belong to the Communist Party and that they did not believe in the overthrow of the Government by force and violence. We pointed out that Congress did not intend to punish belief, but rather intended to regulate the conduct of union affairs. We therefore held that any indirect sanction on speech which might arise from the oath requirement did not present a proper case for the "clear and present danger" test, for the regulation was aimed at conduct, rather than speech. In discussing the proper measure of evaluation of this kind of legislation, we suggested that the Homes-Brandeis philosophy insisted that, where there was a direct restriction upon speech, a "clear and present danger" that the substantive evil would be caused was necessary before the statute in question could be constitutionally applied. And we stated,

"[The First] Amendment requires that one be permitted to believe what he will. It requires that one be permitted to advocate what he will unless there is a clear and present danger that a substantial public evil will result therefrom."

339 U.S. at 339 U. S. 412. But we further suggested that neither Justice Holmes nor Justice Brandeis ever envisioned that a shorthand phrase should be crystallized into a rigid rule to be applied inflexibly without regard to the circumstances of each case. Speech is not an absolute, above and beyond control by the legislature when its judgment, subject to review here, is that certain kinds of speech are so undesirable as to warrant criminal sanction. Nothing is more certain in modern society than the principle that there are no absolutes, that a name, a phrase, a standard has meaning only when associated with the considerations which gave birth to the nomenclature. *See American Communications Assn. v. Douds,* 339 U.S. at 339 U. S. 397. To those who would paralyze our Government in the face of impending threat by encasing it in a semantic straitjacket we must reply that all concepts are relative.

In this case, we are squarely presented with the application of the "clear and present danger" test, and must decide what that phrase imports. We first note that many of the cases in which this Court has reversed convictions by use of this or similar tests have been based on the fact that the interest which the State was attempting to protect was itself too insubstantial to warrant restriction of speech. In this category we may put such cases as *Schneider v. State,* 308 U. S. 147 (1939); *Cantwell v. Connecticut,* 310 U. S. 296 (1940); *Martin v. Struthers,* 319 U. S. 141 (1943); *West Virginia Board of Education v. Barnette,* 319 U. S. 624 (1943); *Thomas v. Collins,* 323 U. S. 516 (1945); *Marsh v. Alabama,* 326 U. S. 501 (1946); *but cf. Prince v. Massachusetts,* 321 U. S. 158 (1944); *Cox v. New Hampshire,* 312 U. S. 569 (1941). Overthrow of the Government by force and violence is certainly a substantial enough interest for the Government to limit speech. Indeed, this is the ultimate value of any society, for if a society cannot protect its very structure from armed internal attack, it must follow that no subordinate value can be protected. If, then, this interest may be protected, the literal problem which is presented is what has been meant by the use of the phrase "clear and present danger" of the utterances bringing about the evil within the power of Congress to punish.

Obviously, the words cannot mean that, before the Government may act, it must wait until the putsch is about to be executed, the plans have been laid and the signal is awaited. If Government is aware that a group aiming at its overthrow is attempting to indoctrinate its members and to commit them to a course whereby they will strike when the leaders feel the circumstances permit, action by the Government is required. The argument that there is no need for Government to concern itself, for Government is strong, it possesses ample powers to put down a rebellion, it may defeat the revolution with ease needs no answer. For that is not the question. Certainly an attempt to overthrow the Government by force, even though doomed from the outset because of inadequate numbers or power of the revolutionists, is a sufficient evil for Congress to prevent. The damage which such attempts create both physically and politically to a nation makes it impossible to measure the validity in terms of the probability of success, or the immediacy of a successful attempt. In the instant case, the trial judge charged the jury that they could not convict unless they found that petitioners intended to overthrow the Government "as speedily as circumstances would permit." This does not mean, and could not properly mean, that they would not strike until there was certainty of success. What was meant was that the revolutionists would strike when they thought the time was ripe. We must therefore reject the contention that success or probability of success is the criterion.

The situation with which Justices Holmes and Brandeis were concerned in *Gitlow* was a comparatively isolated event, bearing little relation in their minds to any substantial threat to the safety of the community. Such also is true of cases like *Fiske v. Kansas,* 274 U. S. 380 (1927), and *De Jonge v. Oregon,* 299 U. S. 353 (1937); *but cf. Lazar v. Pennsylvania,* 286 U.S. 532 (1932). They were not confronted with any situation comparable to the instant one—the development of an apparatus designed and dedicated to the overthrow of the Government, in the context of world crisis after crisis.

Chief Judge Learned Hand, writing for the majority below, interpreted the phrase as follows:

"In each case, [courts] must ask whether the gravity of the 'evil,' discounted by its improbability, justifies such invasion of free speech as is necessary to avoid the danger."

183 F.2d at 212. We adopt this statement of the rule. As articulated by Chief Judge Hand, it is as succinct and inclusive as any other we might devise at this time. It takes into consideration those factors which we deem relevant, and relates their significances. More we cannot expect from words.

Likewise, we are in accord with the court below, which affirmed the trial court's finding that the requisite danger existed. The mere fact that, from the period 1945 to 1948, petitioners' activities did not result in an attempt to overthrow the Government by force and violence is, of course, no answer to the fact that there was a group that was ready to make the attempt. The formation by petitioners of such a highly organized conspiracy, with rigidly disciplined members subject to call when the leaders, these petitioners, felt that the time had come for action, coupled with the inflammable nature of world conditions, similar uprisings in other countries, and the touch-and-go nature of our relations with countries with whom petitioners were in the very least ideologically attuned, convince us that their convictions were justified on this score. And this analysis disposes of the contention that a conspiracy to advocate, as distinguished from the advocacy itself, cannot be constitutionally restrained, because it comprises only the preparation. It is the existence of the conspiracy which creates the danger. *Cf. Pinkerton v. United States,* 328 U. S. 640 (1946); *Goldman v. United States,* 245 U. S. 474 (1918); *United States v. Rabinowich,* 238 U. S. 78 (1915). If the ingredients of the reaction are present, we cannot bind the Government to wait until the catalyst is added.

IV

Although we have concluded that the finding that there was a sufficient danger to warrant the application of the statute was justified on the merits, there remains the problem of whether the trial judge's treatment of the issue was correct. He charged the jury, in relevant part, as follows:

"In further construction and interpretation of the statute, I charge you that it is not the abstract doctrine of overthrowing or destroying organized government by unlawful means which is denounced by this law, but the teaching and advocacy of action for the accomplishment of that purpose, by language reasonably and ordinarily calculated to incite persons to such action.

Accordingly, you cannot find the defendants or any of them guilty of the crime charged unless you are satisfied beyond a reasonable doubt that they conspired to organize a society, group and assembly of persons who teach and advocate the overthrow or destruction of the Government of the United States by force and violence and to advocate and teach the duty and necessity of overthrowing or destroying the Government of the United States by force and violence, with the intent that such teaching and advocacy be of a rule or principle of action and by language reasonably and ordinarily calculated to incite persons to such action, all with the intent to cause the overthrow or destruction of the Government of the United States by force and violence as speedily as circumstances would permit."

"* * * *"

"If you are satisfied that the evidence establishes beyond a reasonable doubt that the defendants, or any of them, are guilty of a violation of the statute, as I have interpreted it to you, I find as matter of law that there is sufficient danger of a substantive evil that the Congress has a right to prevent to justify the application of the statute under the First Amendment of the Constitution."

"This is matter of law about which you have no concern. It is a finding on a matter of law which I deem essential to support my ruling that the case should be submitted to you to pass upon the guilt or innocence of the defendants...."

It is thus clear that he reserved the question of the existence of the danger for his own determination, and the question becomes whether the issue is of such a nature that it should have been submitted to the jury.

The first paragraph of the quoted instructions calls for the jury to find the facts essential to establish the substantive crime, violation of §§ 2(a)(1) and 2(a)(3) of the Smith Act, involved in the conspiracy charge. There can be no doubt that, if the jury found those facts against the petitioners, violation of the Act would be established. The argument that the action of the trial court is erroneous in declaring as a matter of law that such violation shows sufficient danger to justify the punishment despite the First Amendment rests on the theory that a jury must decide a question of the application of the First Amendment. We do not agree.

When facts are found that establish the violation of a statute, the protection against conviction afforded by the First Amendment is a matter of law. The doctrine that there must be a clear and present danger of a substantive evil that Congress has a right to prevent is a judicial rule to be applied as a matter of law by the courts. The guilt is established by proof of facts. Whether the First Amendment protects the activity which constitutes the violation of the statute must depend upon a judicial determination of the scope of the First Amendment applied to the circumstances of the case.

Petitioners' reliance upon Justice Brandeis' language in his concurrence in *Whitney, supra,* is misplaced. In that case, Justice Brandeis pointed out that the defendant could have made the existence of the requisite danger the important issue at her trial, but that she had not done so. In discussing this failure, he stated that the defendant could have had the issue determined by the court or the jury. No realistic construction of this disjunctive language could arrive at the conclusion that he intended to state that the question was only determinable by a jury. Nor is the incidental statement of the majority in *Pierce, supra,* of any more persuasive effect. There, the issue of the probable effect of the publication had been submitted to the jury, and the majority was apparently addressing its remarks to the contention of the dissenters that the jury could not reasonably have returned a verdict of guilty on the evidence. Indeed, in the very case in which the phrase was born, *Schenck,* this Court itself examined the record to find whether the requisite danger appeared, and the issue was not submitted to a jury. And in every later case in which the Court has measured the validity of a statute by the "clear and present danger" test, that determination has been by the court, the question of the danger not being submitted to the jury.

The question in this case is whether the statute which the legislature has enacted may be constitutionally applied. In other words, the Court must examine judicially the application of the statute to the particular situation, to ascertain if the Constitution prohibits the conviction. We hold that the statute may be applied where there is a "clear and present danger" of the substantive evil which the legislature had the right to prevent. Bearing, as it does, the marks of a "question of law," the issue is properly one for the judge to decide.

V

There remains to be discussed the question of vagueness—whether the statute as we have interpreted it is too vague, not sufficiently advising those who would speak of the limitations upon their activity. It is urged that such vagueness contravenes the First and Fifth Amendments. This argument is particularly nonpersuasive when presented by petitioners, who, the jury found, intended to overthrow the Government as speedily as circumstances would permit. *See Abrams v. United States,* 250 U. S. 616, 250 U. S. 627-629 (1919) (dissenting opinion); *Whitney v. California,* 274 U. S. 357, 274 U. S. 373 (1927) (concurring opinion); *Taylor v. Mississippi,* 319 U. S. 583, 319 U. S. 589 (1943). A claim of guilelessness ill becomes those with evil intent. *Williams v. United States,* 341 U. S. 97, 341 U. S. 101-102 (1951); *Jordan v. De George,* 341 U. S. 223, 341 U. S. 230-232 (1951); *American Communications Assn. v. Douds,* 339 U.S. at 339 U. S. 413; *Screws v. United States,* 325 U. S. 91, 325 U. S. 101 (1945).

We agree that the standard as defined is not a neat, mathematical formulary. Like all verbalizations it is subject to criticism on the score of indefiniteness. But petitioners themselves contend that the verbalization "clear and present danger" is the proper standard. We see no difference, from the standpoint of vagueness, whether the standard of "clear and present danger" is one contained *in haec verba* within the statute, or whether it is the judicial measure of constitutional applicability. We have shown the indeterminate standard the phrase necessarily connotes. We do not think we have rendered that standard any more indefinite by our attempt to sum up the factors which are included within its scope. We think it well serves to indicate to those who would advocate constitutionally prohibited conduct that there is a line beyond which they may not go—a line which they, in full knowledge of what they intend and the circumstances in which their activity takes place, will well appreciate and understand. *Williams, supra,* at 341 U. S. 101-102; *Jordan, supra,* at 341 U. S. 230-232; *United States v. Petrillo,* 332 U. S. 1, 332 U. S. 7 (1948); *United States v. Wurzbach,* 280 U. S. 396, 280 U. S. 399 (1930); *Nash v. United States,* 229 U. S. 373, 229 U. S. 376-377 (1913). Where there is doubt as to the intent of the defendants, the nature of their activities, or their power to bring about the evil, this Court will review the convictions with the scrupulous care demanded by our Constitution. But we are not convinced that, because there may be borderline cases at some time in the future, these convictions should be reversed because of the argument that these petitioners could not know that their activities were constitutionally proscribed by the statute.

We have not discussed many of the questions which could be extracted from the record, although they were treated in detail by the court below. Our limited grant of the writ of certiorari has withdrawn from our consideration at this date those questions, which include, *inter alia,* sufficiency of the evidence, composition of jury, and conduct of the trial.

We hold that §§ 2(a)(1), 2(a)(3) and 3 of the Smith Act do not inherently, or as construed or applied in the instant case, violate the First Amendment and other provisions of the Bill of Rights, or the First and Fifth Amendments because of indefiniteness. Petitioners intended to overthrow the Government of the United States as speedily as the circumstances would permit. Their conspiracy to organize the Communist Party and to teach and advocate the overthrow of the Government of the United States by force and violence created a "clear and present danger" of an attempt to overthrow the Government by force and violence. They were properly and constitutionally convicted for violation of the Smith Act. The judgments of conviction are

Affirmed.

MR. JUSTICE BLACK, *dissenting*

Here again, as in *Breard v. Alexandria, post,* p. 341 U. S. 622, decided this day, my basic disagreement with the Court is not as to how we should explain or reconcile what was said in prior decisions, but springs from a fundamental difference in constitutional approach. Consequently, it would serve no useful purpose to state my position at length.

At the outset, I want to emphasize what the crime involved in this case is, and what it is not. These petitioners were not charged with an attempt to overthrow the Government. They were not charged with overt acts of any kind designed to overthrow the Government. They were not even charged with saying anything or writing anything designed to overthrow the Government. The charge was that they agreed to assemble and to talk and publish certain ideas at a later date: the indict-

ment is that they conspired to organize the Communist Party and to use speech or newspapers and other publications in the future to teach and advocate the forcible overthrow of the Government. No matter how it is worded, this is a virulent form of prior censorship of speech and press, which I believe the First Amendment forbids. I would hold § 3 of the Smith Act authorizing this prior restraint unconstitutional on its face and as applied.

But let us assume, contrary to all constitutional ideas of fair criminal procedure, that petitioners, although not indicted for the crime of actual advocacy, may be punished for it. Even on this radical assumption, the other opinions in this case show that the only way to affirm these convictions is to repudiate directly or indirectly the established "clear and present danger" rule. This the Court does in a way which greatly restricts the protections afforded by the First Amendment. The opinions for affirmance indicate that the chief reason for jettisoning the rule is the expressed fear that advocacy of Communist doctrine endangers the safety of the Republic. Undoubtedly a governmental policy of unfettered communication of ideas does entail dangers. To the Founders of this Nation, however, the benefits derived from free expression were worth the risk. They embodied this philosophy in the First Amendment's command that "Congress shall make no law . . . abridging the freedom of speech, or of the press. . . ." I have always believed that the First Amendment is the keystone of our Government, that the freedoms it guarantees provide the best insurance against destruction of all freedom. At least as to speech in the realm of public matters, I believe that the "clear and present danger" test does not "mark the furthermost constitutional boundaries of protected expression," but does "no more than recognize a minimum compulsion of the Bill of Rights." *Bridges v. California,* 314 U. S. 252, 314 U. S. 263.

So long as this Court exercises the power of judicial review of legislation, I cannot agree that the First Amendment permits us to sustain laws suppressing freedom of speech and press on the basis of Congress' or our own notions of mere "reasonableness." Such a doctrine waters down the First Amendment so that it amounts to little more than an admonition to Congress. The Amendment as so construed is not likely to protect any but those "safe" or orthodox views which rarely need its protection. I must also express my objection to the holding because, as MR. JUSTICE DOUGLAS dissent shows, it sanctions the determination of a crucial issue of fact by the judge, rather than by the jury. Nor can I let this opportunity pass without expressing my objection to the severely limited grant of certiorari in this case which precluded consideration here of at least two other reasons for reversing these convictions: (1) the record shows a discriminatory selection of the jury panel which prevented trial before a representative cross-section of the community; (2) the record shows that one member of the trial jury was violently hostile to petitioners before and during the trial.

Public opinion being what it now is, few will protest the conviction of these Communist petitioners. There is hope, however, that, in calmer times, when present pressures, passions and fears subside, this or some later Court will restore the First Amendment liberties to the high preferred place where they belong in a free society.

MR. JUSTICE DOUGLAS, dissenting

If this were a case where those who claimed protection under the First Amendment were teaching the techniques of sabotage, the assassination of the President, the filching of documents from public files, the planting of bombs, the art of street warfare, and the like, I would have no doubts. The freedom to speak is not absolute; the teaching of methods of terror and other seditious conduct should be beyond the pale along with obscenity and immorality. This case was argued as if those were the facts. The argument imported much seditious conduct into the record. That is easy, and it has popular appeal, for the activities of Communists in plotting and scheming against the free world are common knowledge. But the fact is that no such evidence was introduced at the trial. There is a statute which makes a seditious conspiracy unlawful. Petitioners, however, were not charged with a "conspiracy to overthrow" the Government. They were charged with a conspiracy to form a party and groups and assemblies of people who teach and advocate the overthrow of our Government by force or violence and with a conspiracy to advocate and teach its overthrow by force and violence. It may well be that indoctrination in the techniques of terror to destroy the Government would be indictable under either statute. But the teaching which is condemned here is of a different character.

So far as the present record is concerned, what petitioners did was to organize people to teach and themselves teach the Marxist-Leninist doctrine contained chiefly in four books: Stalin, Foundations of Leninism (1924); Marx and Engels, Manifesto of the Communist Party (1848); Lenin, The State and Revolution (1917); History of the Communist Party of the Soviet Union (B.) (1939).

Those books are to Soviet Communism what Mein Kampf was to Nazism. If they are understood, the ugliness of Communism is revealed, its deceit and cunning are exposed, the nature of its activities becomes apparent, and the chances of its success less likely. That is not, of course, the reason why petitioners chose these books for their classrooms. They are fervent Communists to whom these volumes are gospel. They preached the creed with the hope that some day it would be acted upon.

The opinion of the Court does not outlaw these texts nor condemn them to the fire, as the Communists do literature offensive to their creed. But if the books themselves are not outlawed, if they can lawfully remain on library shelves, by what reasoning does their use in a classroom become a crime? It would not be a crime under the Act to introduce these books to a class, though that would be teaching what the creed of violent overthrow of the Government is. The Act, as construed, requires the element of intent—that those who teach the creed believe in it. The crime then depends not on what is taught, but on who the teacher is. That is to make freedom of speech turn not on *what is said*, but on the intent with which it is said. Once we start down that road, we enter territory dangerous to the liberties of every citizen.

There was a time in England when the concept of constructive treason flourished. Men were punished not for raising a hand against the king, but for thinking murderous thoughts about him. The Framers of the Constitution were alive to that abuse, and took steps to see that the practice would not flourish here. Treason was defined to require overt acts—the evolution of a plot against the country into an actual project. The present case is not one of treason. But the analogy is close when the illegality is made to turn on intent, not on the nature of the act. We then start probing men's minds for motive and purpose; they become entangled in the law not for what they did, but *for what they thought;* they get convicted not for what they said, but for the purpose with which they said it.

Intent, of course, often makes the difference in the law. An act otherwise excusable or carrying minor penalties may grow to an abhorrent thing if the evil intent is present. We deal here, however, not with ordinary acts, but with speech, to which the Constitution has given a special sanction.

The vice of treating speech as the equivalent of overt acts of a treasonable or seditious character is emphasized by a concurring opinion, which, by invoking the law of conspiracy, makes speech do service for deeds which are dangerous to society. The doctrine of conspiracy has served divers and oppressive purposes, and, in its broad reach, can be made to do great evil. But never until today has anyone seriously thought that the ancient law of conspiracy could constitutionally be used to turn speech into seditious conduct. Yet that is precisely what is suggested. I repeat that we deal here with speech alone, not with speech plus acts of sabotage or unlawful conduct. Not a single seditious act is charged in the indictment. To make a lawful speech unlawful because two men conceive it is to raise the law of conspiracy to appalling proportions. That course is to make a radical break with the past and to violate one of the cardinal principles of our constitutional scheme.

Free speech has occupied an exalted position because of the high service it has given our society. Its protection is essential to the very existence of a democracy. The airing of ideas releases pressures which otherwise might become destructive. When ideas compete in the market for acceptance, full and free discussion exposes the false, and they gain few adherents. Full and free discussion even of ideas we hate encourages the testing of our own prejudices and preconceptions. Full and free discussion keeps a society from becoming stagnant and unprepared for the stresses and strains that work to tear all civilizations apart.

Full and free discussion has indeed been the first article of our faith. We have founded our political system on it. It has been the safeguard of every religious, political, philosophical, economic, and racial group amongst us. We have counted on it to keep us from embracing what is cheap and false; we have trusted the common sense of our people to choose the doc-trine true to our genius and to reject the rest. This has been the one single outstanding tenet that has made our institutions the symbol of freedom and equality. We have deemed it more costly to liberty to suppress a despised minority than to let them vent their spleen. We have above all else feared the political censor. We have wanted a land where our people can be exposed to all the diverse creeds and cultures of the world.

There comes a time when even speech loses its constitutional immunity. Speech innocuous one year may at another time fan such destructive flames that it must be halted in the interests of the safety of the Republic. That is the meaning of the clear and present danger test. When conditions are so critical that there will be no time to avoid the evil that the speech threatens, it is time to call a halt. Otherwise, free speech which is the strength of the Nation will be the cause of its destruction.

Yet free speech is the rule, not the exception. The restraint to be constitutional must be based on more than fear, on more than passionate opposition against the speech, on more than a revolted dislike for its contents. There must be some immediate injury to society that is likely if speech is allowed. The classic statement of these conditions was made by Mr. Justice Brandeis in his concurring opinion in *Whitney v. California,* 274 U. S. 357, 274 U. S. 376-377,

"Fear of serious injury cannot alone justify suppression of free speech and assembly. Men feared witches and burnt women. It is the function of speech to free men from the bondage of irrational fears. To justify suppression of free speech, there must be reasonable ground to fear that serious evil will result if free speech is practiced. There must be reasonable ground to believe that the danger apprehended is imminent. There must be reasonable ground to believe that the evil to be prevented is a serious one. Every denunciation of existing law tends in some measure to increase the probability that there will be violation of it. Condonation of a breach enhances the probability. Expressions of approval add to the probability. Propagation of the criminal state of mind by teaching syndicalism increases it. Advocacy of law-breaking heightens it still further. But even advocacy of violation, however reprehensible morally, is not a justification for denying free speech where the advocacy falls short of incitement and there is nothing to indicate that the advocacy would be immediately acted on. The wide difference between advocacy and incitement, between preparation and attempt, between assembling and conspiracy, must be borne in mind. In order to support a finding of clear and present danger, it must be shown either that immediate serious violence was to be expected or was advocated, or that the past conduct furnished reason to believe that such advocacy was then contemplated."

"Those who won our independence by revolution were not cowards. They did not fear political change. They did not exalt order at the cost of liberty. To courageous, self-reliant men, with confidence in the power of free and fearless reasoning applied through the processes of popular government, no danger flowing from speech can be deemed clear and present unless the incidence of the evil apprehended is so imminent that it may befall before there is opportunity for full discussion. *If there be time to expose through discussion the falsehood and fallacies, to avert the evil by the processes of education, the remedy to be applied is more speech, not enforced silence.*"

(Italics added.)

I had assumed that the question of the clear and present danger, being so critical an issue in the case, would be a matter for submission to the jury. It was squarely held in *Pierce v. United States,* 252 U. S. 239, 252 U. S. 244, to be a jury question. Mr. Justice Pitney, speaking for the Court, said,

"Whether the statement contained in the pamphlet had a natural tendency to produce the forbidden consequences, as alleged, was a question to be determined not upon demurrer, but by the jury at the trial."

That is the only time the Court has passed on the issue. None of our other decisions is contrary. Nothing said in any of the nonjury cases has detracted from that ruling. The statement in *Pierce v. United States, supra,* states the law as it has been, and as it should be. The Court, I think, errs when it treats the question as one of law.

Yet, whether the question is one for the Court or the jury, there should be evidence of record on the issue. This record, however, contains no evidence whatsoever showing that the acts charged, *viz.,* the teaching of the Soviet theory of revolution with the hope that it will be realized, have created any clear and present danger to the Nation. The Court, however, rules to the contrary. It says,

"The formation by petitioners of such a highly organized conspiracy, with rigidly disciplined members subject to call when the leaders, these petitioners, felt that the time had come for action, coupled with the inflammable nature of world conditions, similar uprisings in other countries, and the touch-and-go nature of our relations with countries with whom petitioners were in the very least ideologically attuned, convince us that their convictions were justified on this score."

That ruling is, in my view, not responsive to the issue in the case. We might as well say that the speech of petitioners is outlawed because Soviet Russia and her Red Army are a threat to world peace.

The nature of Communism as a force on the world scene would, of course, be relevant to the issue of clear and present danger of petitioners' advocacy within the United States. But the primary consideration is the strength and tactical position of petitioners and their converts in this country. On that, there is no evidence in the record. If we are to take judicial notice of the threat of Communists within the nation, it should not be difficult to conclude that, as a political party, they are of little consequence. Communists in this country have never made a respectable or serious showing in any election. I would doubt that there is a village, let alone a city or county or state, which the Communists could carry. Communism in the world scene is no bogeyman; but Communism as a political faction or party in this country plainly is. Communism has been so thoroughly exposed in this country that it has been crippled as a political force. Free speech has destroyed it as an effective political party. It is inconceivable that those who went up and down this country preaching the doctrine of revolution which petitioners espouse would have any success. In days of trouble and confusion, when bread lines were long, when the unemployed walked the streets, when people were starving, the advocates of a short-cut by revolution might have a chance to gain adherents. But today there are no such conditions. The country is not in despair; the people know Soviet Communism; the doctrine of Soviet revolution is exposed in all of its ugliness, and the American people want none of it.

How it can be said that there is a clear and present danger that this advocacy will succeed is, therefore, a mystery. Some nations less resilient than the United States, where illiteracy is high and where democratic traditions are only budding, might have to take drastic steps and jail these men for merely speaking their creed. But in America, they are miserable merchants of unwanted ideas; their wares remain unsold. The fact that their ideas are abhorrent does not make them powerful.

The political impotence of the Communists in this country does not, of course, dispose of the problem. Their numbers; their positions in industry and government; the extent to which they have, in fact, infiltrated the police, the armed services, transportation, stevedoring, power plants, munitions works, and other critical places—these facts all bear on the likelihood that their advocacy of the Soviet theory of revolution will endanger the Republic. But the record is silent on these facts. If we are to proceed on the basis of judicial notice, it is impossible for me to say that the Communists in this country are so potent or so strategically deployed that they must be suppressed for their speech. I could not so hold unless I were willing to conclude that the activities in recent years of committees of Congress, of the Attorney General, of labor unions, of state legislatures, and of Loyalty Boards were so futile as to leave the country on the edge of grave peril. To believe that petitioners and their following are placed in such critical positions as to endanger the Nation is to believe the incredible. It is safe to say that the followers of the creed of Soviet Communism are known to the FBI; that, in case of war with Russia, they will be picked up overnight, as were all prospective saboteurs at the commencement of World War II; that the invisible army of petitioners is the best known, the most beset, and the least thriving of any fifth column in history. Only those held by fear and panic could think otherwise.

This is my view if we are to act on the basis of judicial notice. But the mere statement of the opposing views indicates how important it is that we know the facts before we act. Neither prejudice nor hate nor senseless fear should be the basis of this solemn act. Free speech—the glory of our system of government—should not be sacrificed on anything less that plain and objective proof of danger that the evil advocated is imminent. On this record, no one can say that petitioners and their converts are in such a strategic position as to have even the slightest chance of achieving their aims.

The First Amendment provides that "Congress shall make no law . . . abridging the freedom of speech." The Constitution provides no exception. This does not mean, however, that the Nation need hold its hand until it is in such weakened condition that there is no time to protect itself from incitement to revolution. Seditious conduct can always be punished. But the command of the First Amendment is so clear that we should not allow Congress to call a halt to free speech except in the extreme case of peril from the speech itself. The First Amendment makes confidence in the common sense of our people and in their maturity of judgment the great postulate of our democracy. Its philosophy is that violence is rarely, if ever, stopped by denying civil liberties to those advocating resort to force. The First Amendment reflects the philosophy of Jefferson

"that it is time enough for the rightful purposes of civil government for its officers to interfere when principles break out into overt acts against peace and good order."

The political censor has no place in our public debates. Unless and until extreme and necessitous circumstances are shown, our aim should be to keep speech unfettered and to allow the processes of law to be invoked only when the provocateurs among us move from speech to action.

Vishinsky wrote in 1938 in The Law of the Soviet State, "In our state, naturally, there is and can be no place for freedom of speech, press, and so on for the foes of socialism."

Our concern should be that we accept no such standard for the United States. Our faith should be that our people will never give support to these advocates of revolution, so long as we remain loyal to the purposes for which our Nation was founded.

Glossary

authoritarian rule: a political system in which the central government holds all or most political power, usually led by a single individual or small group; the opposite of democracy

communism: a far-left political ideology in which there is collective ownership of property and government control of the economy with the objective of a classless society

First Amendment: the first article of the Bill of Rights (the first ten amendments to the U.S. Constitution), which guarantees the rights of speech, religion, assembly, a free press, and the ability to petition the government

prior restraint: the censorship of materials that are deemed harmful by the government before their publication

subversive action: action intended to undermine the political or social systems of a country

YOUNGSTOWN SHEET AND TUBE CO. V. SAWYER

DATE 1952	**CITATION** 343 U.S. 57
AUTHOR Hugo Black	**SIGNIFICANCE** Limited the inherent authority of the president, declaring the president did not have emergency power to seize control of an industry in the midst of a crisis
VOTE 6–3	

Overview

Youngstown Sheet and Tube Co. v. Sawyer, famously known as the Steel Seizure Case, is a landmark decision that belongs in the pantheon of great constitutional law cases. The case generated high political drama, sharp legal conflict, and tides of public opinion, with the U.S. Supreme Court facing issues of surpassing importance for a nation committed to the rule of law. The defining issue in the case—whether the president possesses an inherent or emergency power to seize control of an industry, such as the steel mills, in the midst of a crisis—compelled the Supreme Court to engage in the most penetrating examination of executive power in the country's history.

The case originated in a threatened strike by steelworkers. President Harry S. Truman announced on April 8, 1952, the issue of Executive Order No. 10340, which directed Secretary of Commerce Charles Sawyer to seize the steel industry to avert a nationwide strike that the president feared would jeopardize America's war effort in Korea as well as other foreign policy and national security objectives. In the executive order, President Truman grounded the seizure order in the authority vested in him by "the Constitution and laws of the United States, and as President of the United States and Commander in Chief of the armed forces." The steel companies immediately brought suit to seek a temporary restraining order. In federal court the next day, the assistant attorney general, Holmes Baldridge, asserted that the seizure was based upon the inherent executive powers of the president and not on any statute. The federal judge David A. Pine shocked the nation when he rejected President Truman's assertions and ruled that the action was unconstitutional.

Judge Pine's ruling that nothing in the Constitution supports the assertion of an undefined, unlimited inherent power in the presidency was affirmed by the Supreme Court, by a 6–3 vote. In the majority opinion written by Justice Hugo Black, the Court rejected the claim of such an inherent presidential power. Of the five concurring opinions accompanying Black's opinion, Justice Robert H. Jackson's became the most influential and, like the decision itself, came to cast a lengthy shadow over the development of American constitutional law.

Harry S. Truman
(Frank Gatteri, United States Army Signal Corps)

Context

President Truman was surrounded by controversies and difficulties when he issued the order to seize the steel mills. His approval ratings had plummeted to all-time lows, which deprived him of deference and political stock; indeed, he had little cachet on the eve of the directive. The public's low regard for Truman stemmed from several factors, including anxiety about the Korean War, the considerable economic problems convulsing the nation, the accusations and charges of corruption and incompetence that were hurled at the Truman administration, and the assertions that the administration was soft on communism. In some ways, Truman could not have been more vulnerable to the ill effects of a nationwide strike by steelworkers.

The pressures arising from the Korean War engulfed Truman. The war was one of his own making; on June 27, 1950, Truman ordered land and sea forces to Korea, where they quickly became embroiled in what was increasingly viewed as an unwinnable war. By the time Truman issued the seizure order, the United States had already sustained 128,000 casualties. In addition, there

appeared to be no progress in the conflict and no prospect for progress. Negotiations with North Korea were stalled, and Americans were becoming increasingly embittered by the war.

The characterization of the conflict as "Mr. Truman's War" reflected the fact that he had taken the nation to war without any official declaration of war or authorization from Congress. Critics rightly pointed out that Truman was the first president in U.S. history to claim the unilateral constitutional authority to initiate war. Senator Robert Taft (R-Ohio), for one, furthermore justly asserted that Truman's action was unconstitutional, since the Constitution granted to Congress the sole and exclusive authority to initiate or commence war. The Korean War was also unpopular because Americans had made so many sacrifices during World War II (which had ended only five years earlier) that they were exhausted and not equipped for another conflict. The nation's citizens had willingly shouldered the burdens of World War II because the causes, threats, and goals were so clear. Truman recognized this, and he in fact sought to downplay the range and significance of the Korean War by labeling it a police action. The public relations effort was undercut, however, by the high casualties and the seemingly indefinite nature of the war.

Moreover, the great economic sacrifices that Americans had borne in World War II were starting to seem fruitless, since the nation's economy was in distress at the time of the seizure order. Citizens were chafing under the many controls that had been imposed on the economy—the country was fettered with wage controls, price controls, production controls, and rent controls—and they blamed Truman. Inflationary pressures further rocked the economy, and the toll exacted exacerbated political difficulties for the president.

Truman's political problems stemmed from other sources as well. His administration was racked with charges of corruption, and while Truman himself was never accused of dishonesty, it was said that he was aware of the corruption but chose to ignore it. In addition, he was charged with being soft on Communism, a politically deadly assertion at a time when McCarthyism dominated the political landscape. With low public standing, he had little ammunition to defend himself when Americans decried his seizure of the steel industry. Newspaper editorials accused him of dictatorship, and members of Congress called for his impeachment. President Truman thus found himself being politically bashed from all directions.

About the Author

Hugo Black was born on February 27, 1886, in Clay County, Alabama. He attended public schools and Ashland College in Ashland, Alabama. In 1906 he was graduated from the law department at the University of Alabama, in Tuscaloosa. In that same year he embarked on a law practice, and in 1907 he moved to Birmingham, where he renewed his practice. As a lawyer, Black focused on personal injury suits. Black served in World War I, holding the rank of captain in the Eighty-first Field Artillery and serving as regimental adjutant in the Nineteenth Artillery Brigade from 1917 to 1918. After the war, he returned to Birmingham, where he became a judge on the local police court. He subsequently served as prosecuting attorney for Jefferson County, Alabama.

Black's political career assumed a high trajectory when, in 1926, he was elected as a Democrat to the U.S. Senate. He was reelected in 1932 and served until he resigned his seat on August 19, 1937, after his appointment to the U.S. Supreme Court. While he was in the Senate, Black served as chairman of the Committee on Education and Labor, became known as a skillful investigator, and defended governmental investigations into corporate and business practices. He was an ardent proponent of President Franklin D. Roosevelt's New Deal and an advocate of Roosevelt's ill-fated court-packing plan in 1937, in which Roosevelt sought to increase the size of the Supreme Court so as to neutralize the influence of anti–New Deal justices then sitting on the Court.

Black was rewarded for his hard work and loyalty to the New Deal programs on August 17, 1937, when President Roosevelt nominated him to the Supreme Court. After being confirmed by the Senate, Black took his seat on the Court on October 4, 1937. Following his confirmation, news broke that Black had been a member of the Ku Klux Klan while practicing law in Alabama. Black effectively laid concerns to rest when he explained that many young lawyers in the South had joined the Klan during that time period if they wanted any clients.

By virtually all accounts, Black is regarded as one of the great Supreme Court justices. He was a staunch defender of civil liberties and remained an advocate of an absolutist approach to freedom of speech throughout his career on the high bench. However, he did admit in *Korematsu v. United States* (1944) that in certain circumstances civil rights needed to take a backseat to national security concerns, as he authored the Court's opinion upholding the evacuation order of Japanese Americans from their homes on the West Coast.

Justice Black's jurisprudence was characterized by a high regard for the original design. He believed that it was the duty of the Court to apply the intentions of the framers when discernible. He was renowned, moreover, for his advocacy of the concept of the incorporation of the Bill of Rights. In fact, Black was one of the most forceful proponents of the position that the framers of the Fourteenth Amendment had effectively nationalized the Bill of Rights, making it applicable to the states.

He was widely viewed as a champion of First Amendment freedoms. In the area of free speech, for example, he wrote powerful dissents, as in *Dennis v. United States* (1951), in which he condemned the governmental prosecution and persecution of those who espoused communism. However, he was not willing to extend the protection of free speech as broadly where symbolic speech was concerned, because he drew a distinction between pure speech and its representation in symbols.

Black wrote his last opinion in the landmark case of *New York Times Co. v. United States* (1971), also known as the Pentagon Papers Case. In that acclaimed opinion, he defended the right of the *New York Times* and other newspapers to publish the Pentagon Papers—a voluminous study on American involvement in Vietnam—on the ground that the First Amendment prohibited prior restraint and that the American people had a right to know when they had been deceived by their government. Justice Black served on the Court until his resignation on September 17, 1971, just days before his death on September 25, in Bethesda, Maryland.

Explanation and Analysis of the Document

While President Truman grounded his seizure order on the authority under "the Constitution and laws of the United States, and as President of the United States and Commander in Chief of the armed forces of the United States," the Justice Department later argued in federal district court that the president had acted solely on the basis of inherent executive power, without any statutory authority. The assistant attorney general Holmes Baldridge told Judge Pine that the courts were powerless to control the exercise of presidential power under emergency conditions. Baldridge maintained that the president's emergency power was broad enough to meet any emergency. The only limitations on that power, he explained, were at the ballot box and in Congress's power of impeachment. At a news conference shortly after Baldridge's argument in federal court, President Truman was asked whether, if he could seize the steel mills under his inherent powers, he could "also seize the newspapers and/or radio stations?" Truman answered: "Under similar circumstances the President of the United States has to act for whatever is for the best of the country" (Truman, p. 273).

The Truman administration's assertion of an inherent emergency power was rejected by the federal district judge David Pine in a blistering opinion. In holding Truman's seizure of the steel industry to be unconstitutional, he acknowledged that a nationwide strike could cause extensive damage to the country, but he declared that a strike "would be less injurious to the public than the injury which would flow from a timorous judicial recognition that there is some basis for this claim to unlimited and unrestrained Executive power, which would be implicit in a failure to grant the injunction [to prohibit the seizure]" (103 F. Supp. 569, 577 [D.D.C. 1952]).

The case was framed for the Supreme Court by the Truman administration's claim of an inherent presidential power. On June 2, 1952, the Court, by a divided 6–3 vote, sustained Judge Pine's decision. The majority opinion sharply rejected the president's contention. In addition, five members of the Court—William Douglas, Felix Frankfurter, Robert Jackson, Harold Burton, and Tom Clark—wrote concurring opinions exploring presidential power in an emergency; while they expressed different views, they were united in their denial of an inherent executive power to seize private property when Congress has by statute prohibited it. Of the various opinions, Black's and Jackson's are the most significant.

Justice Hugo Black's Majority Opinion

In the first paragraph of his opinion for the Court, Justice Black lays bare the distinctions between the arguments of the two sides. The owners of the steel mills contend that President Truman's order constitutes

lawmaking, a power vested by the Constitution in Congress and not in the president. As such, the president has acted unconstitutionally. The administration, on the other hand, argues that the president acted to prevent a nationwide strike that would have inflicted great injury upon the country. In meeting the emergency, it is argued, the president is drawing upon the aggregate of his powers, including his inherent power, his authority as commander in chief, and his power as chief executive of the nation.

In paragraphs 2–4, Justice Black reviews the facts of the case, beginning with the dispute between the steel companies and the steelworkers that precipitated the call for a strike. After reviewing the lower court action, Black states in paragraph 5 that two particular issues have come before the Supreme Court. The first issue involves the question of whether the constitutional validity of the president's order should be determined. The second regards whether the president has the power to issue the order.

In paragraph 6 of his opinion, Justice Black assesses the administration's argument that Judge Pine never should have considered the merits of the case. Lawyers for the government contended that injunctive relief should have been denied to the steel companies, since the seizure of their property did not inflict irreparable damages and since even if damages had been suffered, the companies should have sought compensation in the Court of Claims. Black rejects those arguments by explaining that previous cases have cast doubt on the right to recover compensation in the Court of Claims when property has been unlawfully taken by the government for public use, the alleged purpose behind the seizure. In addition, Black believed that incalculable damages would indeed be sustained by the steel industry. As a result, he ruled that the case was ripe for review and that the Court should consider the merits of the issues.

In paragraph 7, Black states, famously, "The President's power, if any, to issue the order must stem either from an act of Congress or from the Constitution itself." Here, Black is expounding a fundamental principle of American constitutionalism. He notes that the Truman administration has not advanced any statutory authority for the seizure order. Black points out in a critical passage that Congress had, in its deliberation over the 1947 Taft-Hartley Act, given consideration to an amendment that would have authorized the presidential seizure of property in an emergency—but Congress refused to vest the president with such authority. As such, as Black and other justices state, Congress effectively prohibited the president from taking property. Given that denial of authority, Black explains, the president's order would be constitutional only if it were grounded in the Constitution.

In paragraph 9, Justice Black makes short shrift of the commander-in-chief argument. While acknowledging that the "theater of war" is an expanding concept, he holds that it is not so expansive as to authorize the presidential seizure of private property within the United States. That power, Black notes, is vested in Congress, since it is a function to be performed by the nation's lawmakers. Black is surely right on this point. If the president possessed the authority to take private property, one would wonder where his authority would stop; the Constitution rejects the concept of unlimited power.

In paragraph 10, moreover, Justice Black rejects the vesting clause as justification for the president's order. In fact, as a matter of definition and enumeration of powers, the president's duty to execute the laws precludes him from making the laws. Here, Black is emphasizing a fundamental principle of the doctrine of separation of powers: Where a power is granted to one branch, it may not be exercised by another. Black points out that the president's role in the lawmaking process extends to the recommendation of legislation and to the veto of bills that he thinks unwise. In all events, Black justly insists, Article I of the Constitution vests the lawmaking power in Congress, not in the president.

Thus, the principal vice of Truman's order, as Black explains in paragraph 11, is that the president is engaging in lawmaking. His seizure order is not executing a policy enacted by Congress; it reflects, rather, a presidential policy that the president alone directs to be executed. In fact, as Black points out, the order assumes the form of a statute: It includes a preamble explaining why the president has adopted the policy, just as statutes set forth the reasoning behind the policy adopted by Congress. Truman's order, moreover, authorizes a governmental official to create additional rules and regulations, an act also reflecting the properties of a statute. According to Black, the fact that previous presidents have ordered the seizure of property is of no moment; most of the seizures had involved the exercise of statutory authority, as Justice Frankfurter notes in his concurring opinion. In any case, as Black states, Congress has not and may not surrender its constitutional power to seize property.

In the closing paragraph of his opinion, Justice Black provides a powerful summation, reminding readers that the framers of the Constitution made the solemn decision to entrust the lawmaking power to Congress—in "good and bad times." A recounting of the familiar historical reasons that led the framers to that crucial decision is not necessary, Black explains. Rather, it should suffice to say that in a republic, the legislature is appointed as the lawmaking branch of government. At the time of the founding of the United States, the precise distinction between a monarchy and a republic was clearly understood to lie in the fact that the republican legislature made the law and the executive was subordinate to the law. Black's opinion rests on a solid historical foundation.

Impact

Youngstown is, without question, one of the great cases in American constitutional law. It has exerted considerable influence on the minds of judges, scholars, elected officials, and the public. The case represents the most penetrating judicial examination of presidential power ever conducted by the Supreme Court and constitutes one of the rare judicial rebukes to the claim of presidential power during wartime; it also demonstrates the capacity of the Court to play a major role in maintaining constitutional balance. Moreover, the case's denial of the assertion of inherent executive power constitutes a landmark rejection of a claim to near limitless power that endangered the principles of constitutionalism and republicanism.

The impact of *Youngstown* may be measured in both its immediate and its long-term effects on the country. When the decision came down, it signaled to Americans a clear, crisp judicial rejection of the broad claims to presidential power asserted by the Truman administration. Newspapers that had condemned Truman's claim to unlimited emergency power embraced and celebrated the Court's courage and constitutional vision. The administration, of course, was dejected. The president had perceived an emergency, had acted in a manner that he sincerely believed to be in the best interests of the nation, and was thoroughly rejected by a Court that included several close friends and colleagues. In fact, Truman had been led to believe by Chief Justice Fred Vinson that his actions would be upheld by the Court. In response to the ruling, the steelworkers immediately implemented their planned strike, which lasted 53 days, from June 2 to July 24.

In some ways, the very willingness of the Court to review and reject presidential assertions of power represents *Youngstown*'s real legacy. The Court's ruling helped to reestablish some measure of balance between the president and Congress. It also reminded the nation that the executive is subordinate to the law, not above it. Furthermore, the denial of the claim of an inherent executive power was critical to the maintenance of the American constitutional government. After all, the claim amounted to an assertion of a presidential power to make law, since it would have permitted the president to act not only in the absence of legislation but also in violation of it. The concept of a presidential power to defy law contradicts not only the oath of office but also the duty of the president to enforce the laws of the nation, as required by the "take care" clause. Thet specter of a president flouting the law, acting arbitrarily, and ignoring the constitutional power of Congress to make law and seize property summons the ghosts of tyrants, dictators, and monarchs.

As a matter of constitutional influence, Justice Robert Jackson's concurring opinion, rather than Justice

Black's majority opinion, has been more frequently cited and invoked by scholars and judges in discussions of *Youngstown*. Critics of Black's opinion have derided it as being overly simple and formalistic as well as unmindful of the nuances and subtleties of the separation of powers. Those criticisms may not be altogether fair. After all, the five concurring opinions joined Black in his declaration that Congress had, in consideration of the Taft-Hartley Act, precluded presidential seizure of property when members vote against a provision that would have vested such authority in the president. Moreover, the concurring justices agreed on the essential point that the president has no inherent authority to violate the law. Nonetheless, Jackson's concurring opinion has been more widely celebrated as a more sophisticated explanation of presidential power.

While Jackson's opinion has won praise from scholars and judges for its fluid approach to presidential power, the overarching impact of Youngstown has been seen in its encouragement to subsequent courts to check presidential power. In the Pentagon Papers Case (*New York Times Co. v. United States*, 1972), the Court rejected President Richard Nixon's claim of an inherent presidential power for the defense of national security broad enough to permit him to seek an injunction to prevent the New York Times from publishing the Pentagon Papers. In *United States v. Nixon* (1974), the Court drew upon *Youngstown* to reject Nixon's claim of an absolute executive privilege. In the annals of American constitutional law, *Youngstown* will forever be regarded as a decision that reinforced constitutionalism and the rule of law.

Questions for Further Study

1. In his opinion for the Court in *Youngstown*, Justice Black denounces President Truman's assertion of an inherent power to confront emergencies. Do you believe that the president has such power? If so, what are its limits? By what method would you draw limits around such a power?

2. Is it possible to reconcile the concept of a presidency created and defined by the Constitution with the concept of an emergency executive power? Explain.

3. Irrespective of the Court's ruling in *Youngstown*, what did the framers of the Constitution think about the concept of an inherent presidential power? Are their views relevant to the modern era?

4. The Black and Jackson opinions use different approaches in considering the separation of powers. Which approach do you find more useful? If a power, such as the lawmaking power, is granted to one branch, should another branch be permitted to exercise it? Explain.

Further Reading

Books

Marcus, Maeva. *Truman and the Steel Seizure Case: The Limits of Presidential Power.* Durham, NC: Duke University Press, 1994.

Truman, Harry S. *Public Papers of the Presidents of the United States: Harry S Truman, 1945–1953.* Washington, DC: U.S. Government Printing Office, 1966.

Westin, Alan F. *The Anatomy of a Constitutional Law Case.* New York: Macmillan, 1958.

Articles

Adler, David Gray. "The Steel Seizure Case and Inherent Presidential Power." *Constitutional Commentary* 19 (2002): 155–213.

Edelson, Chris. "The Law: The Hollowing Out of Youngstown: How Congress and the Courts Can Restore Limits on Presidential Power." *Presidential Studies Quarterly* 47, no. 4 (December 2017): 816–830.

Warber, Adam L., Yu Ouyang, and Richard W. Waterman. "Landmark Executive Orders: Presidential Leadership through Unilateral Action." *Presidential Studies Quarterly* 48, no. 1 (March 2018): 110–126.

Websites

Harry S. Truman Library and Museum. Accessed March 29, 2023. https://www.trumanlibrary.gov/library/executive-orders/10340/executive-order-10340.

—Commentary by David Gray Adler

YOUNGSTOWN SHEET AND TUBE CO. V. SAWYER

Document Text

Mr. Justice Black Delivered the Opinion of the Court

We are asked to decide whether the President was acting within his constitutional power when he issued an order directing the Secretary of Commerce to take possession of and operate most of the Nation's steel mills. The mill owners argue that the President's order amounts to lawmaking, a legislative function which the Constitution has expressly confided to the Congress, and not to the President. The Government's position is that the order was made on findings of the President that his action was necessary to avert a national catastrophe which would inevitably result from a stoppage of steel production, and that, in meeting this grave emergency, the President was acting within the aggregate of his constitutional powers as the Nation's Chief Executive and the Commander in Chief of the Armed Forces of the United States. The issue emerges here from the following series of events:

In the latter part of 1951, a dispute arose between the steel companies and their employees over terms and conditions that should be included in new collective bargaining agreements. Long-continued conferences failed to resolve the dispute. On December 18, 1951, the employees' representative, United Steelworkers of America, CIO, gave notice of an intention to strike when the existing bargaining agreements expired on December 31. The Federal Mediation and Conciliation Service then intervened in an effort to get labor and management to agree. This failing, the President on December 22, 1951, referred the dispute to the Feder-

al Wage Stabilization Board to investigate and make recommendations for fair and equitable terms of settlement. This Board's report resulted in no settlement. On April 4, 1952, the Union gave notice of a nationwide strike called to begin at 12:01 a.m. April 9. The indispensability of steel as a component of substantially all weapons and other war materials led the President to believe that the proposed work stoppage would immediately jeopardize our national defense and that governmental seizure of the steel mills was necessary in order to assure the continued availability of steel. Reciting these considerations for his action, the President, a few hours before the strike was to begin, issued Executive Order 10340, a copy of which is attached as an appendix. The order directed the Secretary of Commerce to take possession of most of the steel mills and keep them running. The Secretary immediately issued his own possessory orders, calling upon the presidents of the various seized companies to serve as operating managers for the United States. They were directed to carry on their activities in accordance with regulations and directions of the Secretary. The next morning the President sent a message to Congress reporting his action. Cong.Rec. April 9, 1952, p. 3962. Twelve days later, he sent a second message. Cong.Rec. April 21, 1952, p. 4192. Congress has taken no action.

Obeying the Secretary's orders under protest, the companies brought proceedings against him in the District Court. Their complaints charged that the seizure was not authorized by an act of Congress or by any constitutional provisions. The District Court was asked to declare the orders of the President and the Secretary invalid and to issue preliminary and permanent injunctions restraining their enforcement. Opposing the motion for preliminary injunction, the United States asserted that a strike disrupting steel production for even a brief period would so endanger the wellbeing and safety of the Nation that the President had "inherent power" to do what he had done—power "supported by the Constitution, by historical precedent, and by court decisions." The Government also contended that, in any event, no preliminary injunction should be issued, because the companies had made no showing that their available legal remedies were inadequate or that their injuries from seizure would be irreparable. Holding against the Government on all points, the District Court, on April 30, issued a preliminary injunction restraining the Secretary from "continuing the seizure and possession of the plants . . . and from acting under the purported authority of Executive Order No. 10340." 103 F.Supp. 569. On the same day, the Court of Appeals stayed the District Court's injunction. 90 U.S.App.D.C., 197 F.2d 582. Deeming it best that the issues raised be promptly decided by this Court, we granted certiorari on May 3 and set the cause for argument on May 12.

Two crucial issues have developed: *First.* Should final determination of the constitutional validity of the President's order be made in this case which has proceeded no further than the preliminary injunction stage? *Second.* If so, is the seizure order within the constitutional power of the President?

It is urged that there were nonconstitutional grounds upon which the District Court could have denied the preliminary injunction, and thus have followed the customary judicial practice of declining to reach and decide constitutional questions until compelled to do so. On this basis, it is argued that equity's extraordinary injunctive relief should have been denied because (a) seizure of the companies' properties did not inflict irreparable damages, and (b) there were available legal remedies adequate to afford compensation for any possible damages which they might suffer. While separately argued by the Government, these two contentions are here closely related, if not identical. Arguments as to both rest in large part on the Government's claim that, should the seizure ultimately be held unlawful, the companies could recover full compensation in the Court of Claims for the unlawful taking. Prior cases in this Court have cast doubt on the

right to recover in the Court of Claims on account of properties unlawfully taken by government officials for public use as these properties were alleged to have been. See e.g., *Hooe v. United States*, 218 U.S. 322, 335-336; *United States v. North American Co.*, 253 U.S. 330, 333. But see *Larson v. Domestic & Foreign Corp.*, 337 U.S. 682, 701-702. Moreover, seizure and governmental operation of these going businesses were bound to result in many present and future damages of such nature as to be difficult, if not incapable, of measurement. Viewing the case this way, and in the light of the facts presented, the District Court saw no reason for delaying decision of the constitutional validity of the orders. We agree with the District Court, and can see no reason why that question was not ripe for determination on the record presented. We shall therefore consider and determine that question now.

II

The President's power, if any, to issue the order must stem either from an act of Congress or from the Constitution itself. There is no statute that expressly authorizes the President to take possession of property as he did here. Nor is there any act of Congress to which our attention has been directed from which such a power can fairly be implied. Indeed, we do not understand the Government to rely on statutory authorization for this seizure. There are two statutes which do authorize the President to take both personal and real property under certain conditions. However, the Government admits that these conditions were not met, and that the President's order was not rooted in either of the statutes. The Government refers to the seizure provisions of one of these statutes (201(b) of the Defense Production Act) as "much too cumbersome, involved, and time-consuming for the crisis which was at hand."

Moreover, the use of the seizure technique to solve labor disputes in order to prevent work stoppages was not only unauthorized by any congressional enactment; prior to this controversy, Congress had refused to adopt that method of settling labor disputes. When the Taft-Hartley Act was under consideration in 1947, Congress rejected an amendment which would have authorized such governmental seizures in cases of emergency. Apparently it was thought that the technique of seizure, like that of compulsory arbitration, would interfere with the process of collective bargaining. Consequently, the plan Congress adopted in that Act did not provide for seizure under any circumstances. Instead, the plan sought to bring about settlements by use of the customary devices of mediation, conciliation, investigation by boards of inquiry, and public reports. In some instances, temporary injunctions were authorized to provide cooling-off periods. All this failing, unions were left free to strike after a secret vote by employees as to whether they wished to accept their employers' final settlement offer.

It is clear that, if the President had authority to issue the order he did, it must be found in some provision of the Constitution. And it is not claimed that express constitutional language grants this power to the President. The contention is that presidential power should be implied from the aggregate of his powers under the Constitution. Particular reliance is placed on provisions in Article II which say that "The executive Power shall be vested in a President . . ."; that "he shall take Care that the Laws be faithfully executed," and that he "shall be Commander in Chief of the Army and Navy of the United States."

The order cannot properly be sustained as an exercise of the President's military power as Commander in Chief of the Armed Forces. The Government attempts to do so by citing a number of cases upholding broad powers in military commanders engaged in day-to-day fighting in a theater of war. Such cases need not concern us here. Even though "theater of war" be an expanding concept, we cannot with faithfulness to our constitutional system hold that the Commander in Chief of the Armed Forces has the ultimate power as such to take possession of private property in order to keep labor disputes from stopping production. This is a job for the Nation's lawmakers, not for its military authorities.

Nor can the seizure order be sustained because of the several constitutional provisions that grant executive power to the President. In the framework of our Constitution, the President's power to see that the laws are faithfully executed refutes the idea that he is to be a lawmaker. The Constitution limits his functions in the lawmaking process to the recommending of laws he thinks wise and the vetoing of laws he thinks bad. And the Constitution is neither silent nor equivocal about who shall make laws which the President is to execute. The first section of the first article says that "All legislative Powers herein granted shall be vested

in a Congress of the United States. . . ." After granting many powers to the Congress, Article I goes on to provide that Congress may

> make all Laws which shall be necessary and proper for carrying into Execution the foregoing Powers, and all other Powers vested by this Constitution in the Government of the United States, or in any Department or Officer thereof.

The President's order does not direct that a congressional policy be executed in a manner prescribed by Congress—it directs that a presidential policy be executed in a manner prescribed by the President. The preamble of the order itself, like that of many statutes, sets out reasons why the President believes certain policies should be adopted, proclaims these policies as rules of conduct to be followed, and again, like a statute, authorizes a government official to promulgate additional rules and regulations consistent with the policy proclaimed and needed to carry that policy into execution. The power of Congress to adopt such public policies as those proclaimed by the order is beyond question. It can authorize the taking of private property for public use. It can make laws regulating the relationships between employers and employees, prescribing rules designed to settle labor disputes, and fixing wages and working conditions in certain fields of our economy. The Constitution does not subject this lawmaking power of Congress to presidential or military supervision or control.

It is said that other Presidents, without congressional authority, have taken possession of private business enterprises in order to settle labor disputes. But even if this be true, Congress has not thereby lost its exclusive constitutional authority to make laws necessary and proper to carry out the powers vested by the Constitution "in the Government of the United States, or any Department or Officer thereof."

The Founders of this Nation entrusted the lawmaking power to the Congress alone in both good and bad times. It would do no good to recall the historical events, the fears of power, and the hopes for freedom that lay behind their choice. Such a review would but confirm our holding that this seizure order cannot stand.

The judgment of the District Court is Affirmed.

Glossary

Court of Appeals: a court having jurisdiction, or power, to review and revise lower court rulings

Executive Order: an order or regulation issued by a president pursuant to constitutional or statutory authority

executive power: power to execute laws; in the United States, the enumerated or implied powers vested in the president by Article II of the Constitution

inherent power: power said to originate in the nature of the office, enumerated or implied powers

injunction: a prohibitive remedy issued by a court forbidding the defendant to do or perform some act

BROWN V.
BOARD OF EDUCATION

DATE 1954	**CITATION** 347 U.S. 483
AUTHOR Earl Warren	**SIGNIFICANCE** Declared that legally mandated segregation in public schools is unconstitutional under the Fourteenth Amendment's equal protection clause
VOTE 9–0	

Overview

Brown v. Board of Education of Topeka was the 1954 Supreme Court decision that declared that legally mandated segregation in public schools is unconstitutional under the Fourteenth Amendment's equal protection clause. The landmark case was actually a combination of five cases that challenged school segregation in Delaware, South Carolina, Virginia, and Topeka, Kansas. In a companion case, *Bolling v. Sharpe*, segregation in the District of Columbia's public schools was declared unconstitutional under the due process clause of the Fifth Amendment. *Brown* was a pivotal case in the history of the Supreme Court. Although *Brown* did not explicitly reverse the Court's earlier ruling in the 1896 case *Plessy v. Ferguson*, which permitted states to provide "separate but equal" facilities for people of different races, it was clearly the beginning of the end of the Supreme Court's willingness to give constitutional sanction to state-sponsored segregation. *Brown* was the first decision authored by the recently appointed Chief Justice Earl Warren and was a harbinger of the new, more activist role that the Court would take in protecting civil rights and civil liberties under his leadership.

Brown should be seen against the broader background of segregation in American history. By the end of the nineteenth century, southern states, and indeed quite a few states outside of the South, were developing an American system of apartheid through what were often called Jim Crow laws. This system of segregation mandated the separation of Blacks and whites in almost every observable facet of public life. Separate water fountains, park benches, railroad cars, and other facilities were common. All of the southern states and a number of border states also maintained separate school facilities for Blacks and whites. Although the Supreme Court's decision in *Plessy* had declared that Blacks could be required to use separate facilities if those facilities were equal to those provided for whites, states that maintained racially separate schools provided schools for African Americans that were usually greatly inferior in resources and programs to those provided for whites. Glaring inequalities in educational facilities prompted the National Association for the Advancement of Colored People (NAACP) to begin a decades-long litigation campaign to challenge segregation in public education. That campaign would eventually result in the decision in *Brown*.

Context

The NAACP began to develop its strategy to attack segregation in state schools in the 1930s. The organization began cautiously enough by attacking segregation in professional schools, principally law schools, of state universities. Law schools were selected because state university systems usually had only one law school each, and it would be relatively easy to make the case that providing a state law school for white students while providing none for Blacks violated the principle that a state had to provide equal facilities. The NAACP also believed that litigation designed to force states to permit Black students to attend state law schools would provoke less adverse political reaction than lawsuits designed to integrate public primary and secondary schools. The architect of the NAACP's litigation strategy, Charles Hamilton Houston, would achieve success before World War II with his victory in the 1938 case *Missouri ex rel. Gaines v. Canada*. In that case, the Supreme Court held that Missouri's exclusion of African Americans from the state's law school was unconstitutional even though Missouri was willing to pay tuition for Black students to attend law school out of state. The NAACP met with success in similar litigation in other states.

Although the NAACP had some success with litigation designed to desegregate professional schools before World War II, the changes in racial attitudes brought about by the war played a key role in paving the way for the decision in *Brown*. In particular, the war brought about a new assertiveness on the part of African Americans as many Blacks left the rural South, along with its the traditional patterns of racial domination, for the armed forces and the industrial cities of the North and West. With new experiences came a new willingness to struggle for equal rights. The fight against Nazi racism also caused many white Americans to question traditional racial attitudes. Furthermore, the social sciences were increasingly calling established racial prejudices into question. The publication in 1944 of the Swedish social scientist Gunnar Myrdal's book *An American Dilemma: The Negro Problem and Modern Democracy* had a significant impact, causing many university-educated people to question the practice of segregation.

The changes in the racial atmosphere in postwar America spurred the NAACP to confront legally mandated segregation. The organization achieved significant

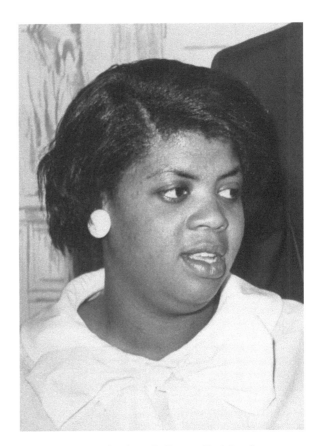

1964 photograph of Linda Brown Smith, whose father, along with several other familes, sued the Board of Education of Topeka, Kansas.
(Library of Congress)

victories in its fight against segregated professional education, and other important victories came in the legal struggle against general discrimination. The 1948 case *Shelley v. Kraemer*, in which the Supreme Court declared that courts could not enforce restrictive covenants barring minorities from buying homes in white neighborhoods, was an indication of the Court's willingness to give the Fourteenth Amendment a broader reading than it had in the past. Following this decision, many in the NAACP believed that the time was right for a frontal assault on segregated education.

Between 1950 and 1952 the NAACP, under the leadership of Thurgood Marshall and his associates, began preparing the cases that would come to be known as *Brown v. Board of Education*. The case by which the litigation is known arose in Topeka, Kansas—a state that, unlike those in the South, did not have statewide segregation. Instead, the state gave localities the option to have segregated schools. The elementary schools in Topeka were indeed segregated, and Oliver Brown, a

NAACP chief counsel Thurgood Mashall
(Library of Congress)

Black resident of the city, filed suit so that his daughter might attend a school reserved for whites. That school was nearer to the Brown home and had better facilities.

In 1952 the Supreme Court consolidated the different desegregation cases. The first set of oral arguments was heard by the Court in December of that year; in June 1953, the Court asked for a second set of oral arguments designed to specifically address the issue of whether the Fourteenth Amendment was intended to mandate school desegregation. As that issue was being researched, Chief Justice Frederick M. Vinson died, in September 1953. He was replaced by Earl Warren. Most observers agree that the new chief justice made a critical difference to the outcome of the case.

About the Author

Earl Warren was born in Los Angeles, California, in 1891. He was a graduate of the University of California at Berkeley and of that university's law school. Warren served in the U.S. Army during World War I as an officer in charge of training troops deploying to France.

Warren began his legal career in California in 1920 as a prosecutor with the Alameda County district attorney's office. In 1925 he was appointed district attorney to fill a vacancy. Elected district attorney in his own right the following year, he would remain in that office until his election as California's attorney general in 1938.

Warren was a product of the California Republican politics of the Progressive Era. As district attorney and as attorney general, he was generally supportive of reforms in the criminal justice system, such as with his willingness to extend due process rights and legal representation to defendants in criminal cases. These were generally not required at the time by the federal courts, which by and large were not applying most of the criminal defendants' rights provisions of the Fourth, Fifth, and Sixth Amendments to the states. Warren was also somewhat ahead of the times in his attitudes toward African Americans. He considered appointing a Black attorney to the attorney general's staff in 1938.

Ironically enough, anti-Asian bias probably helped propel Warren to the national stage. Warren shared the anti-Asian sentiments that were common among whites on the West Coast in the early part of the twentieth century. Near the beginning of his career, he was a member of an anti-Asian group, Native Sons of the Golden West. As attorney general in the winter and spring of 1942, Warren was a leading advocate of Japanese internment, at first advocating internment only for Japanese aliens but later supporting the internment of Japanese Americans as well. His support for Japanese internment doubtless aided Warren in his gaining election as governor of California in 1942. Warren would run for vice president on the Republican ticket with Governor Thomas Dewey of New York in 1948.

Warren was appointed chief justice by President Dwight David Eisenhower in 1953 to replace Chief Justice Frederick M. Vinson, who had died in office. Warren's entire tenure as chief justice was marked by controversy, beginning with the decision in *Brown* and continuing until his retirement from the Supreme Court in 1969. Under Warren, the Court dealt with some of the most contentious issues in postwar American life, including school desegregation, reapportionment, the rights of criminal defendants, birth control, and the right to privacy. Warren's critics charged that he extended the reach of the Court into areas unauthorized and unintended by the Constitution's framers and that he and his allies on the Court often employed dubious legal reasoning. Warren's supporters noted that the Court under his direction was a vital force in making equal protection and the Bill of Rights living principles for millions of Americans. Later on as chief justice, at the direction of Lyndon B. Johnson, Warren would head the President's Commission on the Assassination of President Kennedy, often referred to as the Warren Commission. Warren died in 1974.

Explanation and Analysis of Document

Brown v. Board of Education of Topeka is a Supreme Court case and as such begins with a syllabus presenting basic information about the case. This information includes the parties, the lower court whose decision is being appealed, and the dates that the case was argued before the Supreme Court. The case was taken on appeal from a decision by the District Court for the District of Kansas. An asterisked footnote relates that *Brown* is being consolidated with other school segregation cases from South Carolina, Virginia, and Delaware. The syllabus also gives a summary of the decision and lists the attorneys who made oral arguments before the Court on behalf of the parties in *Brown* and the companion cases. The syllabus also lists briefs filed by amici curiae ("friends of the court," persons or organizations not party to a case who file a brief in support of a party or to inform the court with respect to a legal or policy issue) in *Brown* and the companion cases. Of special interest is the fact that the assistant attorney general J. Lee Rankin argued for the United States in support of desegregation.

The Majority Opinion

Chief Justice Earl Warren begins with a straightforward presentation of the issues. His first paragraph notes that the desegregation cases have come from different states—Kansas, South Carolina, Virginia, and Delaware—and that while each state presents somewhat different issues with respect to local laws and local conditions, the clear principal issue of legal segregation is common to all of the cases.

Stylistically, Warren's opinion makes extensive use of footnotes not only to cite relevant authorities but also to carry the burden of informing the reader of major

legal and factual arguments. As had become common in twentieth-century legal writing, footnotes served to supply a judicial decision with a kind of supplemental narrative, augmenting the main points being made in the body of the opinion. This style of judicial writing was doubtless encouraged, perhaps mandated, by the practice of parties and amici curiae filing extensive briefs in major cases. The increasing use of "Brandeis briefs"— briefs providing wide-ranging amounts of information to the Court from the social and physical sciences, as modeled after that filed by Louis Brandeis in *Muller v. Oregon* (1908)—probably also hastened the development of the lengthy use of footnotes in judicial opinions.

The first footnote here discusses how *Brown* and the companion cases fared in the U.S. district courts. Included in this discussion are the legal and factual findings of these courts. With respect to *Brown*, a three-judge panel of the District Court for the District of Kansas found that segregated public education indeed had a detrimental effect on Black students, but that court nonetheless upheld segregated education because the facilities for Blacks and whites were held to be equal with respect to buildings, transportation, curricula, and the educational qualifications of the teachers. The district court in South Carolina found that the facilities available to Black students were inferior to those of whites, but the court nonetheless upheld segregation on the grounds that South Carolina officials were making efforts to equalize facilities. In Virginia, the district court ordered officials to make efforts to equalize the schools. In Delaware, the state courts had ordered desegregation, and state officials were appealing that order.

Warren moves in the second and third paragraphs to presenting the central claims of the NAACP and of the parents who were bringing suit. He zeroes in on the crux of these claims in the third paragraph, noting, "The plaintiffs contend that segregated public schools are not 'equal' and cannot be made 'equal,' and that hence they are deprived of the equal protection of the laws." Warren's opinion spends relatively little time examining the history of this argument, but it is a claim with a long history, one that antedates *Brown* by at least a century. In particular, the NAACP argued that segregation was inherently stigmatizing, an argument that was older than the Fourteenth Amendment (ratified in 1868) and its equal protection clause, under which *Brown* and the other cases were brought.

This argument made its first judicial appearance in the antebellum Massachusetts school desegregation case *Roberts v. City of Boston* (1850). In that case, African American parents argued that Boston's system of school segregation essentially stigmatized Black children by setting up a caste system dividing Black and white. The Massachusetts Supreme Judicial Court rejected the argument, in effect establishing the "separate but equal" doctrine, a point Warren notes in footnote 6. The argument that segregation stigmatized African Americans and hence violated the Fourteenth Amendment's guarantee of equal protection under the law would later be heard and rejected by the Supreme Court in *Plessy v. Ferguson* (1896), with the Supreme Court making the "separate but equal" doctrine a part of federal constitutional law.

Part of the NAACP's aim in *Brown* was to have segregated schools declared unconstitutional on the grounds that the system of school segregation forced Black children into schools that were vastly inferior to those reserved for white students. The systems of school segregation that prevailed in the southern states usually featured vast inequalities in the levels of education provided to Black and white children. Black schools were usually funded at a fraction of the level of white schools. In many districts, Blacks were confined to one-room schoolhouses in which all grades were to be educated, while whites had separate elementary and secondary schools. Black schools were usually separate and decidedly unequal with respect to the qualifications and pay for Black teachers and the physical facilities in which Black schools were housed. Correcting all of this was part of the NAACP's aim in litigating against school segregation. In addition, the civil rights organization shared the view held by its nineteenth-century predecessors that the very act of segregating, of signaling out Blacks for separate treatment, was inherently stigmatizing and more appropriate to a caste system than to the practices of American democracy. The NAACP advocate Thurgood Marshall, in his oral argument before Earl Warren and other members of the Court on December 8, 1953, presented the issue starkly: "Why, of all the multitudinous groups of people in this country, you have to single out the Negroes and give them this separate treatment?"

This was clearly an issue involving the Fourteenth Amendment's equal protection clause, and in the fourth and fifth paragraphs the new chief justice begins addressing the Fourteenth Amendment and what it mandated in these circumstances. Here, Warren begins moving into territory that would forever make *Brown* an object of controversy among constitutional commentators. He argues that the history of the Fourteenth Amendment is inconclusive regarding what it had to say with respect to school segregation. In fact, Warren frames *Brown* as a case pitting modern realities against inconclusive history. In the fifth paragraph he focuses on the history of public education at the time of the enactment of the Fourteenth Amendment, noting that public education had not yet taken hold in the South and that practically all southern Blacks at the time were illiterate. He juxtaposes that situation with modern circumstances: "Today, in contrast, many Negroes have achieved outstanding success in the arts and sciences, as well as in the business and professional world." Warren uses this contrast between the relative lack of importance of public education at the time of the enactment of the Fourteenth Amendment and its much greater importance at the time of the *Brown* decision to set up what will be his principal argument in paragraphs 8 and 9, namely, that the question of segregated education and its constitutionality under the Fourteenth Amendment had to be considered in light of the importance of public education in modern—that is, post–World War II—American society and not in light of its relative unimportance at the beginning of the Reconstruction era.

In the sixth paragraph Warren takes on the "separate but equal" doctrine, seeking to show that it is less than the solid precedent that its champions claimed. Indeed, the argument for the constitutionality of segregated schools rested on the "separate but equal" precedent provided in *Plessy*. The former solicitor general John W. Davis, representing South Carolina in an oral argument before the Supreme Court, emphasized the importance of *Plessy*, highlighting the fact that the lower federal courts and the Supreme Court had repeatedly reaffirmed the "separate but equal" doctrine and asserting that the Court should follow precedent and apply the doctrine in the case of school segregation. Davis's arguments were echoed by other supporters of school segregation.

Warren notes that the Court's earliest interpretations of the Fourteenth Amendment stressed that the amendment was designed to prohibit state-imposed racial discrimination; the "separate but equal" doctrine did not become part of the Supreme Court's jurisprudence until 1896—more than a generation after the enactment of the amendment. He also notes that *Plessy* involved transportation, not education. Warren further states that since *Plessy*, the Supreme Court had only heard six cases involving the "separate but equal" doctrine, with none reviewing the essential validity of the doctrine. He next cites the decisions involving segregation in graduate and professional schools. Warren's aims in this discussion are clear. While not directly challenging the *Plessy* precedent, he effectively isolates it as a decision that was not consistent with judicial interpretations made close to the enactment of the Fourteenth Amendment. He also gives *Plessy* a narrow reading so that it might be seen as a precedent that at most applies to the field of transportation. That case, according to Warren, was one that had not been thoroughly examined by the Court and in any event was made problematic, particularly in the field of education, by the graduate-school segregation cases.

Paragraphs 7–9 are used to frame the issues before the Court. Warren largely frames these issues in the way that the NAACP and the plaintiffs had presented them. The primary issue is segregation, and it is an issue that goes beyond tangible factors to encompass philosophical ones as well as the subtle reality of stigmatization. In paragraph 7 Warren uses footnote 9 to relate that the district court in Kansas had actually found substantial equality in the Black and white schools. Warren indicates that regardless of this finding, segregation itself and its effect on public education remain of paramount concern.

Paragraph 8 is where Warren stakes out a clear claim as a proponent—indeed, one of the earliest explicit proponents—of the notion of a "living constitution," the idea that jurists should go beyond the concerns and assumptions of the framers of constitutional provisions and instead look at and reevaluate the Constitution in light of modern circumstances. He starts the paragraph, "In approaching this problem, we cannot turn the clock back to 1868, when the Amendment was adopted, or even to 1896, when *Plessy v. Ferguson* was written. We must consider public education in the light of its full development and its present place in American life throughout the Nation." In paragraphs 9–11 Warren goes on to outline the impor-

tance of education in modern American life and to conclude that segregated schools deprive members of minority groups of equal educational opportunities even when the tangible resources are equal.

Paragraph 12 lays a psychological basis for the opinion—one that would leave the *Brown* decision with a lingering controversy that persists to the present day. Warren cites the works of a number of psychologists—including, most prominently, the Black psychologist Kenneth Clark—on the effects of segregation on the self-esteem of Black children. These citations would lead many critics to charge that the chief justice was engaging in sociology rather than jurisprudence. Even many critics sympathetic to the outcome in *Brown* later expressed some discomfort with the use of psychological evidence, claiming that it gave the decision a less firm footing, such that it could potentially be undone by shifts in findings in the social sciences. Clearly, what Warren is doing is examining the plaintiffs' arguments that segregation stigmatized Black students by comparing those claims to the findings of the psychological experts of the day.

Paragraph 14 provides the Court's conclusion that "in the field of public education, the doctrine of 'separate but equal' has no place." Paragraph 15 provides a hint about some of the behind-the-scenes negotiations that Warren and the other justices went through to secure a unanimous decision in *Brown*. Here, Warren calls for the reargument of the cases to allow the Court to consider remedies for school segregation. Warren recognized the importance of establishing the constitutional principle that segregated public schools violated the equal protection clause of the Fourteenth Amendment. As such, he was greatly concerned with getting a unanimous Court to agree to that constitutional principle—an achievement that had been very much in doubt during judicial conferences. Thus, as part of the strategy to obtain a unanimous opinion, Warren agreed to have *Brown* initially decide only the principle that segregated schools were unconstitutional, deferring the question of how the decision would be implemented for another day. Paragraph 14, the last paragraph, lays the groundwork for the second case, commonly known as *Brown II*, which would be heard the following year, and the more than two decades of desegregation litigation that would follow.

Impact

It is probably no exaggeration to say that *Brown* was the most significant case decided by the Supreme Court in its history. While the decision would take decades to implement, *Brown* was critical as a harbinger of the federal government's return to the civil rights arena, an arena from which it had been largely absent since Reconstruction. *Brown* would also provide a tremendous boost to the civil rights movement of the 1950s and 1960s. The knowledge that the Court was now going to interpret the Constitution as prohibiting the kind of caste-like distinctions that had been a feature of Black life in the United States from the very beginning helped encourage a greater assertiveness on the part of African Americans, who proceeded to successfully protest the formal segregation of Jim Crow laws in the South and, later, more subtle forms of discrimination throughout the nation.

Brown's impact in the courts was a little more complicated. The case commonly known as *Brown v. Board of Education* led to a successor case of the same name, known as *Brown II*, in 1955. That case resulted in a ruling that required the desegregation of separate school systems with "all deliberate speed." This order, in turn, led to protracted battles in federal district courts over the precise details and timing of school desegregation plans, which lasted decades. Nonetheless, the decision in *Brown* effectively led to the death of the "separate but equal" doctrine as well as to the negation of the idea that governmental bodies could practice the kind of formal discrimination against members of minority groups that had been common before *Brown*.

Questions for Further Study

1. Compare and contrast Chief Justice Earl Warren's opinion in *Brown* with Justice John Marshall Harlan's dissent in *Plessy v. Ferguson*. Although both opinions argue against the "separate but equal" doctrine, they do so in different ways. Which opinion do you believe is stronger, and why?

2. Many have criticized Warren's opinion for ignoring the original intent of the Fourteenth Amendment. How important should the intentions of the framers be considered in modern constitutional interpretation?

3. In light of the continued existence of de facto school segregation in many communities, should *Brown* be judged a failure?

4. Some critics fault Warren for writing a weak decision that would take very long to implement. Other students of the case argue that if Warren had not written a cautious decision, he would have had difficulty getting a unanimous Court to agree with the decision, which would have brought about more resistance to *Brown*. Which argument do you find more persuasive?

5. Should Warren have included psychological evidence in his decision, or should he have based his decision solely on legal sources?

Further Reading

Books

Cottrol, Robert J., Raymond T. Diamond, and Leland B. Ware. *Brown v. Board of Education: Caste, Culture, and the Constitution.* Lawrence: University Press of Kansas, 2003.

Kluger, Richard. *Simple Justice: The History of Brown v. Board of Education and Black America's Struggle for Equality.* New York: Knopf, 2004.

Martin, Waldo. *Brown v. Board of Education: A Brief History with Documents.* Boston: Bedford/St. Martin's, 2019.

Myrdal, Gunnar. *An American Dilemma: The Negro Problem and Modern Democracy.* New York: Harper & Brothers, 1944.

Patterson, James T. *Brown v. Board of Education: A Civil Rights Milestone and Its Troubled Legacy.* New York: Oxford University Press, 2001.

Tushnet, Mark. *The NAACP's Legal Strategy against Segregated Education, 1925–1950.* Chapel Hill: University of North Carolina Press, 1987.

White, G. Edward. *Earl Warren: A Public Life.* New York: Oxford University Press, 1982.

Whitman, Mark. *Brown v Board of Education.* Princeton, NJ: Markus Wiener Publishers, 2015.

Further Reading

Articles

Bond, Julian. "With All Deliberate Speed: *Brown v. Board of Education.*" *Indiana Law Journal* 90 (2015): 1671+.

López, Gerardo R., and Rebeca Burciago. "The Troublesome Legacy of *Brown v. Board of Education.*" *Educational Administration Quarterly* 50, no. 5 (December 2014): 796–811.

Straus, Ryane McAuliffe, and Scott Lemieux. "The Two Browns: Policy Implementation and the Retrenchment of *Brown v. Board of Education.*" *New Political Science* 38, no. 1 (2016): 44–60.

Terbeek, Calvin. "'Clocks Must Always Be Turned Back': *Brown v. Board of Education* and the Racial Origins of Constitutional Originalism." *American Political Science Review* 115, no. 3 (August 2021): 821–34.

Websites

"Brown v. Board of Education: Digital Archive." University of Michigan Library website. Accessed February 26, 2020. https://www.lib.umich.edu/brown-versus-board-education/.

"Teaching with Documents: Documents Related to *Brown v. Board of Education.*" National Archives: Educators and Students website. Accessed February 26, 2020. https://www.archives.gov/education/lessons/brown-v-board/.

—Commentary by Robert Cottroll and Michael J. O'Neal

BROWN V.
BOARD OF EDUCATION

Document Text

Mr. Chief Justice Warren Delivered the Opinion of the Court

These cases come to us from the States of Kansas, South Carolina, Virginia, and Delaware. They are premised on different facts and different local conditions, but a common legal question justifies their consideration together in this consolidated opinion.

In each of the cases, minors of the Negro race, through their legal representatives, seek the aid of the courts in obtaining admission to the public schools of their community on a nonsegregated basis. In each instance, they had been denied admission to schools attended by white children under laws requiring or permitting segregation according to race. This segregation was alleged to deprive the plaintiffs of the equal protection of the laws under the Fourteenth Amendment. In each of the cases other than the Delaware case, a three-judge federal district court denied relief to the plaintiffs on the so-called "separate but equal" doctrine announced by this Court in *Plessy v. Ferguson*, 163 U.S. 537. Under that doctrine, equality of treatment is accorded when the races are provided substantially equal facilities, even though these facilities be separate. In the Delaware case, the Supreme Court of Delaware adhered to that doctrine, but ordered that the plaintiffs be admitted to the white schools because of their superiority to the Negro schools.

The plaintiffs contend that segregated public schools are not "equal" and cannot be made "equal," and that hence they are deprived of the equal protection of the laws. Because of the obvious importance of the question presented, the Court took jurisdiction. Argument was heard in the 1952 Term, and reargument was heard this Term on certain questions propounded by the Court.

Reargument was largely devoted to the circumstances surrounding the adoption of the Fourteenth Amendment in 1868. It covered exhaustively consideration of the Amendment in Congress, ratification by the states, then-existing practices in racial segregation, and the views of proponents and opponents of the Amendment. This discussion and our own investigation convince us that, although these sources cast some light, it is not enough to resolve the problem with which we are faced. At best, they are inconclusive. The most avid proponents of the post-War Amendments undoubtedly intended them to remove all legal distinctions among "all persons born or naturalized in the United States." Their opponents, just as certainly, were antagonistic to both the letter and the spirit of the Amendments and wished them to have the most limited effect. What others in Congress and the state legislatures had in mind cannot be determined with any degree of certainty.

An additional reason for the inconclusive nature of the Amendment's history with respect to segregated schools is the status of public education at that time. In the South, the movement toward free common schools, supported by general taxation, had not yet taken hold. Education of white children was largely in the hands of private groups. Education of Negroes was almost nonexistent, and practically all of the race were illiterate. In fact, any education of Negroes was forbidden by law in some states. Today, in contrast, many Negroes have achieved outstanding success in the arts and sciences, as well as in the business and professional world. It is true that public school education at the time of the Amendment had advanced further in the North, but the effect of the Amendment on Northern States was generally ignored in the congressional debates. Even in the North, the conditions of public education did not approximate those existing today. The curriculum was usually rudimentary; ungraded schools were common in rural areas; the school term was but three months a year in many states, and compulsory school attendance was virtually unknown. As a consequence, it is not surprising that there should be so little in the history of the Fourteenth Amendment relating to its intended effect on public education.

In the first cases in this Court construing the Fourteenth Amendment, decided shortly after its adoption, the Court interpreted it as proscribing all state-imposed discriminations against the Negro race. The doctrine of "separate but equal" did not make its appearance in this Court until 1896 in the case of *Plessy v. Ferguson*, supra, involving not education but transportation. American courts have since labored with the doctrine for over half a century. In this Court, there have been six cases involving the "separate but equal" doctrine in the field of public education. In *Cumming v. County Board of Education*, 175 U.S. 528, and *Gong Lum v. Rice*, 275 U.S. 78, the validity of the doctrine itself was not challenged.

In more recent cases, all on the graduate school level, inequality was found in that specific benefits enjoyed by white students were denied to Negro students of the same educational qualifications. *Missouri ex rel. Gaines v. Canada*, 305 U.S. 337; *Sipuel v. Oklahoma*, 332 U.S. 631; *Sweatt v. Painter*, 339 U.S. 629; *McLaurin v. Oklahoma State Regents*, 339 U.S. 637. In none of these cases was it necessary to reexamine the doctrine to grant relief to the Negro plaintiff. And in *Sweatt v. Painter*, supra, the Court expressly reserved decision on the question whether *Plessy v. Ferguson* should be held inapplicable to public education.

In the instant cases, that question is directly presented. Here, unlike *Sweatt v. Painter*, there are findings below that the Negro and white schools involved have been equalized, or are being equalized, with respect to buildings, curricula, qualifications and salaries of teachers, and other "tangible" factors. Our decision,

therefore, cannot turn on merely a comparison of these tangible factors in the Negro and white schools involved in each of the cases. We must look instead to the effect of segregation itself on public education.

In approaching this problem, we cannot turn the clock back to 1868, when the Amendment was adopted, or even to 1896, when *Plessy v. Ferguson* was written. We must consider public education in the light of its full development and its present place in American life throughout the Nation. Only in this way can it be determined if segregation in public schools deprives these plaintiffs of the equal protection of the laws.

Today, education is perhaps the most important function of state and local governments. Compulsory school attendance laws and the great expenditures for education both demonstrate our recognition of the importance of education to our democratic society. It is required in the performance of our most basic public responsibilities, even service in the armed forces. It is the very foundation of good citizenship. Today it is a principal instrument in awakening the child to cultural values, in preparing him for later professional training, and in helping him to adjust normally to his environment. In these days, it is doubtful that any child may reasonably be expected to succeed in life if he is denied the opportunity of an education. Such an opportunity, where the state has undertaken to provide it, is a right which must be made available to all on equal terms.

We come then to the question presented: Does segregation of children in public schools solely on the basis of race, even though the physical facilities and other "tangible" factors may be equal, deprive the children of the minority group of equal educational opportunities? We believe that it does.

In *Sweatt v. Painter*, supra, in finding that a segregated law school for Negroes could not provide them equal educational opportunities, this Court relied in large part on "those qualities which are incapable of objective measurement but which make for greatness in a law school." In *McLaurin v. Oklahoma State Regents*, supra, the Court, in requiring that a Negro admitted to a white graduate school be treated like all other students, again resorted to intangible considerations: ". . . his ability to study, to engage in discussions and exchange views with other students, and, in general, to learn his profession." Such considerations apply with added force to children in grade and high schools. To separate them from others of similar age and qualifications solely because of their race generates a feeling of inferiority as to their status in the community that may affect their hearts and minds in a way unlikely ever to be undone. The effect of this separation on their educational opportunities was well stated by a finding in the Kansas case by a court which nevertheless felt compelled to rule against the Negro plaintiffs:

> "Segregation of white and colored children in public schools has a detrimental effect upon the colored children. The impact is greater when it has the sanction of the law, for the policy of separating the races is usually interpreted as denoting the inferiority of the negro group. A sense of inferiority affects the motivation of a child to learn. Segregation with the sanction of law, therefore, has a tendency to [retard] the educational and mental development of negro children and to deprive them of some of the benefits they would receive in a racial[ly] integrated school system."

Whatever may have been the extent of psychological knowledge at the time of *Plessy v. Ferguson*, this finding is amply supported by modern authority. Any language in *Plessy v. Ferguson* contrary to this finding is rejected.

We conclude that, in the field of public education, the doctrine of "separate but equal" has no place. Separate educational facilities are inherently unequal. Therefore, we hold that the plaintiffs and others similarly situated for whom the actions have been brought are, by reason of the segregation complained of, deprived of the equal protection of the laws guaranteed by the Fourteenth Amendment. This disposition makes unnecessary any discussion whether such segregation also violates the Due Process Clause of the Fourteenth Amendment.

Because these are class actions, because of the wide applicability of this decision, and because of the great variety of local conditions, the formulation of decrees in these cases presents problems of considerable complexity. On reargument, the consideration of appropriate relief was necessarily subordinated to the primary question—the constitutionality of segregation in public education. We have now announced that such segregation is a denial of the equal protection of the laws. In order that we may have the full assistance of the parties in formulating decrees, the cases will be restored to the docket, and the parties are requested to present further argument on Questions 4 and 5 previously propounded by the Court for the reargument this Term. The Attorney General of the United States is again invited to participate. The Attorneys General of the states requiring or permitting segregation in public education will also be permitted to appear as amici curiae upon request to do so by September 15, 1954, and submission of briefs by October 1, 1954.

It is so ordered.

Glossary

amici curiae: persons or organizations not party to a case who file a brief in support of a party or to inform the court with respect to a legal or policy issue

class actions: suits where representatives of a class of persons may sue on behalf of themselves and similarly situated individuals

common schools: public schools (as used in the nineteenth century)

disposition: settlement; resolution

sanction: approval

HERNANDEZ V. TEXAS

DATE
1954

AUTHOR
Earl Warren

VOTE
9–0

CITATION
347 U.S. 475

SIGNIFICANCE
Ruled that the exclusion of Mexican Americans from juries because of their ethnicity violated the Fourteenth Amendmente

Overview

In the 1950s, it was common in Texas and other U.S. states to not allow Mexican Americans to serve on juries. In 1951, Pete Hernandez, a Mexican American, was convicted or murder in Jackson County, Texas, by an all-white jury. He was sentenced to life in prison for the crime. Hernandez's lawyers appealed his conviction, arguing that by excluding Mexican Americans from the jury, the state had violated their client's Fourteenth Amendment right to equal protection.

The Texas Court of Criminal Appeals denied Hernandez's appeal. That court ruled that Mexican Americans were classified as white at the time and therefore not one of the special classes that were covered by the Fourteenth Amendment. At that time of the conviction, the amendment was applied only to racial groups (known as special classes), such as African Americans, and not ethnic ancestry.

The Supreme Court reviewed the case and in a unanimous decision overturned the conviction of Hernandez. The Court noted that there was a history of discrimination against Mexican Americans in Texas and evidence that the group was considered separate and distinct from the white community. The Court rejected the narrow interpretation of the Fourteenth Amendment. It ruled that Hernandez had the right to be tried by a jury that included Mexican Americans. The ruling significantly expanded the scope of the amendment. It is considered an important milestone in the civil rights movement.

Context

The Hernandez case took place in the midst of the civil rights movement, a widespread campaign to guarantee rights to groups historically subject to discrimination. The movement began in the 1950s and was a broad effort throughout the United States to gain equality for African Americans and other disadvantaged groups. Civil rights advocates utilized a number of approaches to overturn formal and informal forms of discrimination and repression. For instance, one of the early leaders of the civil rights movement, Dr. Martin Luther King Jr., advocated nonviolent civil disobedience to overcome racism. Other leaders sought to utilize the legal system to overturn laws and official policies that discriminated against people because of their race or ethnicity.

Mexican Americans faced various forms of discrimination and racism in Texas, among other regions, in the 1950s. Many public areas had separate facilities, such as bathrooms, for whites and other races. School segregation of Hispanic students was common until 1948, when the state court case *Delgado v. Bastrop Independent School District* prompted counties to begin integrating Mexican American and white students (integration of African American students would not begin after the 1954 Supreme Court case *Brown v. Board of Education*, which was tried in the same session by the Hernandez case). More than 100 towns in Texas enacted new forms of segregation in the 1950s. Hispanics had long faced problems trying to register to vote. In addition, although the Sixth Amendment guaranteed that all U.S. citizens had the right to a trial by a "jury of their peers," 70 of the 254 counties in Texas prevented Mexican Americans from serving on juries.

An all-white jury convicted Hernandez of the murder of Cayetano "Joe" Espinosa on August 7, 1951. Espinosa had been shot and killed in a bar in Edna, a small town in southeastern Texas. Edna was the capital of Jackson County, which was one of the areas that did not allow Hispanics to serve on juries. Hernandez was twenty-one years old and made a living as a cotton picker at the time of the crime. He was in the bar drinking alcohol when he became unruly. Hernandez was forcibly removed from the bar. He then went home, got a gun, and returned to the bar, where he shot Espinosa.

A group of Mexican American lawyers volunteered to represent Hernandez at his trial. John J. Herrera was Hernandez's initial lawyer; however, his team eventually grew and included Gustavo "Gus" Garcia, Carlos Cadena, and James de Anda, among others. The lawyers hoped to use the case to remove the barriers to Hispanics serving on juries in Texas and did not charge Hernandez for their work. Instead, the litigators relied on individual donations and raised funds from the community. The legal team hoped to replicate the strategy that African Americans were using in the *Brown* case—to use the courts to secure civil rights and thereby override opposition to integration by state legislatures and elected officials.

Hernandez's legal team challenged the jury selection process by asserting that Hernandez had a right to have a jury of his peers, which would include Mexican Americans. This right was guaranteed by the Fourteenth

SUPREME COURT OF THE UNITED STATES

No. 406.—OCTOBER TERM, 1953.

| Pete Hernandez, Petitioner, *v.* The State of Texas. | On Writ of Certiorari to the Court of Criminal Appeals of the State of Texas. |

[May 3, 1954.]

MR. CHIEF JUSTICE WARREN delivered the opinion of the Court.

The petitioner, Pete Hernandez, was indicted for the murder of one Joe Espinosa by a grand jury in Jackson County, Texas. He was convicted and sentenced to life imprisonment. The Texas Court of Criminal Appeals affirmed the judgment of the trial court. —— Tex. Crim. Rep. ——, 251 S. W, 2d 531. Prior to the trial, the petitioner, by his counsel, offered timely motions to quash the indictment and the jury panel. He alleged that persons of Mexican descent were systematically excluded from service as jury commissioners,[1] grand jurors, and petit jurors, although there were such persons fully

---

[1] Texas law provides that at each term of court, the judge shall appoint three to five jury commissioners. The judge instructs these commissioners as to their duties. After taking an oath that they will not knowingly select a grand juror they believe unfit or unqualified, the commissioners retire to a room in the courthouse where they select from the county assessment roll the names of 16 grand jurors from different parts of the county. These names are placed in a sealed envelope and delivered to the clerk. Thirty days before court meets, the clerk delivers a copy of the list to the sheriff who summons the jurors. Vernon's Tex. Code Crim. Proc., 1948, Arts. 333–350.

The general jury panel is also selected by the jury commission. Vernon's Tex. Civ. Stat., 1942, Art. 2107. In capital cases, a special venire may be selected from the list furnished by the commissioners. Vernon's Tex. Code Crim. Proc., 1948, Art. 592.

The decision in **Hernandez v. Texas** *was delivered by Chief Justice Earl Warren.*
(Library of Congress)

Amendment, which required all citizens to be treated equally; the salient part of the amendment was known as the equal protection clause. Garcia's team examined the county's jury rolls and found that no Hispanic had served on a jury in Jackson County in almost three decades despite the fact that Mexican Americans comprised about 14 percent of the population.

The trial court rejected the legal team's claim by countering that Hispanics were considered ethnically white; therefore, an all-white jury was a jury of Hernandez's peers. This argument reflected the official stance by Texas that the Fourteenth Amendment only applied to African Americans at the time. African Americans were considered a special class because of the long history of discrimination and racism directed toward the community. This approach was known as the "two-class theory," which held that the Fourteenth Amendment had been created to help African Americans and consequently did not apply to Hispanics or other groups.

Hernandez was convicted and sentenced to life in prison on August 11, 1951. His legal team appealed the conviction to the Texas Court of Criminal Appeals, but that tribunal confirmed the verdict of the trial court in October 1952. Hernandez's lawyers then asked the Supreme Court to review the case. The Court agreed and heard oral arguments from both sides on January 11, 1954. Garcia and his fellow attorneys became the first Mexican American lawyers to argue a case before the Supreme Court. Garcia was chosen to argue the case before the Court because he was considered the most eloquent speaker. They were able to convince the Court to broaden its interpretation of the Fourteenth Amendment to include Hispanic Americans and other ethnic groups. In a unanimous decision, the Court ordered Texas to giver Hernandez a new trial, this time with a jury that included Mexican Americans. Hernandez pleaded guilty and was sentenced to twenty years in prison.

About the Author

Earl Warren was regarded as one of the most influential chief justices of the Supreme Court. He oversaw a series of cases that dramatically expanded civil rights and civil liberties for all Americans. Warren was born in Los Angeles, California, on March 19, 1891. He decided to become a lawyer at a young age. Warren graduated from the University of California at Berkeley in 1912 and received a law degree from there in 1914. During World War I, he served in the U.S. Army. He became a deputy district attorney in 1920 before being appointed to the vacant position of district attorney for Alameda County in 1925. The future Supreme Court justice was elected to that office in 1926 as a Republican, and he was reelected in 1930 and 1934.

Warren earned a reputation as diligent and honest law enforcement official. In 1938 he was elected attorney general of California, the state's highest legal official. In 1942, Warren was elected governor of California. The moderate Republican was extremely popular and became the only person elected governor of that state on three consecutive occasions.

President Dwight D. Eisenhower named Warren chief justice of the Supreme Court in 1953. His tenure coincided with the beginnings of the modern civil rights movement. Warren worked strenuously to broaden the personal freedoms of all Americans. As chief jus-

tice, he presided over some of the most significant civil rights cases in U.S. history. In 1954, *Brown v. Board of Education* made segregation illegal in public education, while *Gomillion v. Lightfoot* in 1960 banned electoral districts based only on race, and *Mapp v. Ohio* expanded individual protections against unconstitutional searches and the seizure of property by law enforcement. *Miranda v. Arizona* in 1966 required police officers to ensure that suspects were aware of their legal rights (such as the right to "remain silent" during arrests or interrogations). Other cases expanded free speech rights and clarified religious freedoms and freedom from religion.

The former California governor's tenure as chief justice was not without come controversy. Some accused Warren of expanding rights beyond what was intended by the Constitution. They argued that some of the Court's decisions should have been left for Congress or the states to take action on. However, without the Warren Court, efforts to secure civil rights and civil liberties would have faced more difficulties and a more uncertain outcome.

Warren retired from the Court in 1969. He later died in Washington, D.C., on July 9, 1974.

Explanation and Analysis of the Document

Chief Justice Warren authored the unanimous decision. As was his style, the former California governor crafted an opinion that was very straightforward and concise. He presented the arguments of both the petitioner and the respondent and clearly explained the rationale for the Court's decision.

The central issue for the Court was whether Hispanics in Jackson County were treated differently because of their ethnicity. If they were subject to discrimination, the Court might designate them a special class. Warren begins his opinion with a brief overview of the case. The chief justice then notes that the Court has long considered it a violation of the equal protection clause of the Fourteenth Amendment if a person is tried before a jury in which all people of a particular race or ethnicity are deliberately excluded. This doctrine was established in the1880 case *Strauder v. West Virginia*. In that ruling, the Supreme Court held that states could not prevent people from serving on juries because of race or ethnicity. If a large segment of the population is qualified to serve on juries but is regularly prevented from doing so, the Court sees this as proof that the equal protection clause has not been upheld.

Warren acknowledges that the state of Texas has argued that the Fourteenth Amendment was based what was described as a "two-class theory" which only designated two groups: whites and African Americans. African Americans were designated a special class because of the long history of discrimination against them. Texas law recognized Hispanics as white and therefore not entitled to special protections under the Fourteenth Amendment. Warren rejected this line of argument. He instead wrote that the Fourteenth Amendment was not reserved only for African Americans but could be applied to all groups. The chief justice did not go so far as to designate Mexican Americans as a separate minority but argued that they were a distinct group or class that was subject to discrimination.

Warren noted that even courts in Texas recognized that there were special classes that deserved equal protection under the Fourteenth Amendment. For instance, in the 1925 case *Juarez v. State*, the Court of Criminal Appeals of Texas ruled that counties could not prevent Roman Catholics from serving on juries simply because of their religion. Indeed, Texas courts had in some cases already extended the equal protection clause to Mexican Americans. In the 1949 case *Clifton v. Puente*, a court ruled that communities could not enact restrictive covenants that forbade the sale of property to Mexican Americans.

In Texas, juries were selected by a jury commission that numbered between three and five. The jury commissioners were appointed by judges. These commissioners reviewed lists of potential jurors and then picked candidates for grand and petit juries. Warren determined that the Texas method for choosing juries was not itself discriminatory. However, the way the law was implemented resulted in discrimination. The justices reached this determination after the petitioner presented evidence that Hispanics in Jackson County were treated unequally and subject to discrimination.

Warren recounts that Garcia and his fellow attorneys presented a range of proof that Mexican Americans faced discrimination in Jackson County. The chief jus-

tice pointed out that although Hispanics comprised about 14 percent of the county's population, they were underrepresented among businesses or civic groups. In addition, the county court had separate bathrooms for whites and other races and ethnicities (including Hispanics). There was even evidence of segregation in businesses. Warren specifically cites one restaurant that had a sign "No Mexicans Served." Based on the evidence presented, the chief justice concluded that the petitioners had clearly proved a pattern of general discrimination and a clear separation between whites and Mexican Americans. This meant that Hispanics could be considered a special class.

Evidence from Texas confirmed the existence of discrimination. Warren wrote that despite the large number of citizens of Mexican descent in Jackson County, the state of Texas admitted that no Hispanics had served on a grand or petit jury in more than 25 years. Meanwhile, more than 6,000 whites had been called for jury service. The state also acknowledged that many of the county's Hispanic citizens were qualified to serve as jurors. In addition, no Hispanics had been appointed as jury commissioners.

Warren noted that the five commissioners who oversaw the selection of a jury for the Hernandez trial testified that they did not intentionally discriminate. They maintained that they simply tried to choose the most qualified potential jurors. Warren did not formally accuse the commissioners of deceit but expressed the incredulity of the Court that discrimination had not played some role in preventing Hispanics from serving on juries for almost three decades in Jackson County. The chief justice accepted that it was possible that there would be times when a jury might not be diverse. However, it was impossible that random chance had prevented Mexican Americans from being chosen for all of those years.

The chief justice concluded his opinion by rebuffing an argument that a literal interpretation of the Fourteenth Amendment would require proportional representation on juries; in other words, that the composition of all juries would have to reflect the racial and ethnic populations of their respective communities. Warren rejects this contention and instead states that the equal protection clause required that no group be excluded from possible jury service because of its race, ethnicity, or national origin.

Warren's clear arguments in the case left no room for debate or speculation about the intent of the justices. The unanimous decision added weight to the ruling and demonstrated that the justices were all of the same legal opinion. The fact that the decision was authored by the chief justice sent a further signal about the Court's view of the Fourteenth Amendment's equal protection clause.

Impact

Hernandez v. Texas was one of a series of Supreme Court cases that helped shape the modern civil rights movement. The case was instrumental in launching a new effort to ensure the civil rights and civil liberties for Hispanics. The outcome of the case was especially important because it dealt with discrimination in a tacit rather than official manner. There were no specific laws that forbade Mexican Americans from serving on juries, but the result of widespread racism was to disempower Hispanics and deprive them of their constitutional right to a trial by a jury of their peers.

Through most of the history of the United States, Hispanics faced significant challenges. They were subject to various forms of discrimination but classified as white and therefore not afforded the appropriate civil rights protections.

The *Hernandez* decision extended the equal protection clause to all ethnicities and nationalities, including those groups that were considered white. In doing so, the case, along with the landmark *Brown* decision of the same year, began the lengthy process of dismantling segregation.

The civil rights victory in the *Hernandez* case motivated Hispanics to expand efforts to gain full equality. Mexican Americans would take more direct action in the coming decades, with the rise of the Chicano movement in the 1960s along with parallel efforts to increase Hispanic political representation, especially in Congress.

The 1970 case *Cisneros v. Corpus Christi Independent School District* broadened the *Hernandez* decision by recognizing Hispanics as a separate ethnic minority group and entitled to the same civil rights protections as African Americans. De Anda, one of the lawyers from the *Hernandez* case, was the lead attorney in the *Cisneros* decision.

Questions for Further Study

1. What is the equal protection clause of the Fourteenth Amendment? How was it violated in the *Hernandez* case?

2. What were the main arguments that Hernandez's lawyers used to prove that Mexican Americans were discriminated against for jury service in Jackson County, Texas? Were there formal laws that forbade Hispanics from being chosen for juries?

3. According to Warren's legal opinion in the case, what was the status of Mexican Americans in comparison with other racial or ethnic groups? Was Warren correct in his argument? Why or why not?

Further Reading

Books

García, Ignacio M. *White but Not Equal: Mexican Americans, Jury Discrimination, and the Supreme Court.* Tucson: University of Arizona Press, 2009.

Herda, D. J. *Earl Warren: A Life of Truth and Justice.* Guilford, CT: Prometheus Books, 2019.

Newton, Jim. *Justice for All: Earl Warren and the Nation He Made.* New York: Riverhead Books, 2007.

Olivas, Michael A. Ed. *"Colored Men" and "Hombres Aquí": Hernández v. Texas and the Emergence of Mexican-American Lawyering.* Hispanic Civil Rights Series. Houston, TX: Arte Público Press, 2006.

Rosales, F. Arturo. *Chicano! A History of the Mexican American Civil Rights Movement.* Houston: University of Houston/Arte Público Press, 1997.

Soltero, Carlos R. *Latinos and American Law: Landmark Supreme Court Cases.* Austin, TX: University of Texas Press, 2006.

Articles

Bradshaw, Gilbert. "Who's Black, Who's Brown, and Who Cares: A Legal Discussion of Hernandez v. Texas." *Brigham Young University Education and Law Journal* (2007).

Crook, Jamie L. "From Hernandez v. Texas to the Present: Doctrinal Shifts in the Supreme Court's Latina/o Jurisprudence." *Harvard Latino Law Review* 11 (2008).

Websites

"1954: Hernandez v. Texas." *A Latinx Resource Guide: Civil Rights Cases and Events in the United States.* Library of Congress Research Guides. Accessed January 10, 2023. https://guides.loc.gov/latinx-civil-rights/hernandez-v-texas.

—Commentary by Tom Lansford

HERNANDEZ V. TEXAS

Document Text

MR. CHIEF JUSTICE WARREN delivered the opinion of the Court

The petitioner, Pete Hernandez, was indicted for the murder of one Joe Espinosa by a grand jury in Jackson County, Texas. He was convicted and sentenced to life imprisonment. The Texas Court of Criminal Appeals affirmed the judgment of the trial court. 251 S.W.2d 531. Prior to the trial, the petitioner, by his counsel, offered timely motions to quash the indictment and the jury panel. He alleged that persons of Mexican descent were systematically excluded from service as jury commissioners, grand jurors, and petit jurors, although there were such persons fully qualified to serve residing in Jackson County. The petitioner asserted that exclusion of this class deprived him, as a member of the class, of the equal protection of the laws guaranteed by the Fourteenth Amendment of the Constitution. After a hearing, the trial court denied the motions. At the trial, the motions were renewed, further evidence taken, and the motions again denied. An allegation that the trial court erred in denying the motions was the sole basis of petitioner's appeal. In affirming the judgment of the trial court, the Texas Court of Criminal Appeals considered and passed upon the substantial federal question raised by the petitioner. We granted a writ of certiorari to review that decision. 346 U.S. 811.

In numerous decisions, this Court has held that it is a denial of the equal protection of the laws to try a defendant of a particular race or color under an indictment issued by a grand jury, or before a petit jury, from which all persons of his race or color have, solely because of that race or color, been excluded by the State, whether acting through its legislature, its courts, or its executive or administrative officers. Although the Court has had little occasion to rule on the question directly, it has been recognized since *Strauder v. West Virginia,* 100 U. S. 303, that the exclusion of a class of persons from jury service on grounds other than race or color may also deprive a defendant who is a member of that class of the constitutional guarantee of equal protection of the laws. The State of Texas would have us hold that there are only two classes—white and Negro—within the contemplation of the Fourteenth Amendment. The decisions of this Court do not support that view. And, except where the question presented involves the exclusion of persons of Mexican descent from juries, Texas courts have taken a broader view of the scope of the equal protection clause.

Throughout our history, differences in race and color have defined easily identifiable groups which have at times required the aid of the courts in securing equal treatment under the laws. But community prejudices are not static, and, from time to time, other differences from the community norm may define other groups which need the same protection. Whether such a group exists within a community is a question of fact. When the existence of a distinct class is demonstrated, and it is further shown that the laws, as written or as applied, single out that class for different treatment not based on some reasonable classification, the guarantees of the Constitution have been violated. The Fourteenth Amendment is not directed solely against discrimination due to a "two-class theory"—that is, based upon differences between "white" and Negro.

As the petitioner acknowledges, the Texas system of selecting grand and petit jurors by the use of jury commissions is fair on its face and capable of being utilized without discrimination. But, as this Court has held, the system is susceptible to abuse, and can be employed in a discriminatory manner. The exclusion of otherwise eligible persons from jury service solely because of their ancestry or national origin is discrimination prohibited by the Fourteenth Amendment. The Texas statute makes no such discrimination, but the petitioner alleges that those administering the law do.

The petitioner's initial burden in substantiating his charge of group discrimination was to prove that persons of Mexican descent constitute a separate class in Jackson County, distinct from "whites." One method by which this may be demonstrated is by showing the attitude of the community. Here, the testimony of responsible officials and citizens contained the admission that residents of the community distinguished between "white" and "Mexican." The participation of persons of Mexican descent in business and community groups was shown to be slight. Until very recent times, children of Mexican descent were required to attend a segregated school for the first four grades. At least one restaurant in town prominently displayed a sign announcing "No Mexicans Served." On the courthouse grounds at the time of the hearing, there were two men's toilets, one unmarked, and the other marked "Colored Men" and "Hombres Aqui" ("Men Here"). No substantial evidence was offered to rebut the logical inference to be drawn from these facts, and it must be concluded that petitioner succeeded in his proof.

Having established the existence of a class, petitioner was then charged with the burden of proving discrimination. To do so, he relied on the pattern of proof established by *Norris v. Alabama,* 294 U. S. 587. In that case, proof that Negroes constituted a substantial segment of the population of the jurisdiction, that some Negroes were qualified to serve as jurors, and that none had been called for jury service over an extended period of time, was held to constitute *prima facie* proof of the systematic exclusion of Negroes from jury service. This holding, sometimes called the "rule of exclusion," has been applied in other cases, and it is available in supplying proof of discrimination against any delineated class.

The petitioner established that 14% of the population of Jackson County were persons with Mexican or Latin American surnames, and that 11% of the males over 21 bore such names. The County Tax Assessor testified that 6 or 7 percent of the freeholders on the tax rolls of the County were persons of Mexican descent. The State of Texas stipulated that,

"for the last twenty-five years, there is no record of any person with a Mexican or Latin American name having served on a jury commission, grand jury or petit jury in Jackson County."

The parties also stipulated that

"there are some male persons of Mexican or Latin American descent in Jackson County who, by virtue of being citizens, freeholders, and having all other legal prerequisites to jury service, are eligible to serve as members of a jury commission, grand jury and/or petit jury."

The petitioner met the burden of proof imposed in *Norris v. Alabama, supra.* To rebut the strong *prima facie* case of the denial of the equal protection of the laws guaranteed by the Constitution thus established, the State offered the testimony of five jury commissioners that they had no discriminated against persons of Mexican or Latin American descent in selecting jurors. They stated that their only objective had been to select those whom they thought were best qualified. This testimony is not enough to overcome the petitioner's case. As the Court said in *Norris v. Alabama:*

"That showing as to the long-continued exclusion of negroes from jury service, and as to the many negroes qualified for that service, could not be met by mere generalities. If, in the presence of such testimony as defendant adduced, the mere general assertions by officials of their performance of duty were to be accepted as an adequate justification for the complete exclusion of negroes from jury service, the constitutional provision . . . would be but a vain and illusory requirement."

The same reasoning is applicable to these facts.

Circumstances or chance may well dictate that no persons in a certain class will serve on a particular jury or during some particular period. But it taxes our credulity to say that mere chance resulted in their being no members of this class among the over six thousand jurors called in the past 25 years. The result bespeaks discrimination, whether or not it was a conscious decision on the part of any individual jury commissioner. The judgment of conviction must be reversed.

To say that this decision revives the rejected contention that the Fourteenth Amendment requires proportional representation of all the component ethnic groups of the community on every jury ignores the facts. The petitioner did not seek proportional representation, nor did he claim a right to have persons of Mexican descent sit on the particular juries which he faced. His only claim is the right to be indicted and tried by juries from which all members of his class are not systematically excluded—juries selected from among all qualified persons regardless of national origin or descent. To this much he is entitled by the Constitution.

Reversed.

Glossary

appeal: a request that a higher court examine the ruling of a lower court

Fourteenth Amendment: an 1868 amendment to the U.S. Constitution that, among other things, guarantees equal protection for all citizens and requires due process before certain rights may be limited

grand jury: a special jury that determines whether or not there is enough evidence to charge a person with a crime

opinion: a legal decision

petit jury: a panel of citizens that hears evidence in a trial and determines guilt or innocence or fault

petitioner: a person or group seeking an appeal or other action by a court

systematic exclusion: the exclusion of a class of people (for example, of African Americans from jury duty) in a planned manner or to a degree greater than would happen by chance

GOMILLION V. LIGHTFOOT

DATE	CITATION
1960	364 U.S. 339
AUTHOR	SIGNIFICANCE
Felix Frankfurter	Held that a state violates the Fifteenth Amendment when it constructs boundary lines between electoral districts for the purpose of denying equal representation to African Americans
VOTE	
9–0	

Overview

 Felix Frankfurter remains something of an enigma. An activist in early life, after his appointment to the Supreme Court, he came to stand for a restraint that seemed at odds with his past. The opinions he wrote while he was on the Court also often seem to contradict each other. In the case of *Gomillion v. Lightfoot*, Charles G. Gomillion, a Black citizen of Tuskegee, Alabama, sued Phil M. Lightfoot, Tuskegee's mayor, along with other city and county officials over a gerrymandering scheme that changed city boundaries in a way that deprived almost all Tuskegee's registered African American voters of their franchise in municipal elections while not taking the right to vote away from a single white citizen. Here, in one of his last opinions, Frankfurter was willing to sidestep his own carefully formulated prohibition against adjudicating apportionment disputes so that he could strike down a state law that discriminated against Black voters. In his opinion in *Gomillion v. Lightfoot*, he argued that the law was a violation of the Fifteenth Amendment, which prohibits states from denying anyone the right to vote on account of race, color, or previous condition of servitude.

Context

Gomillion v. Lightfoot would lay the foundation for passage of the Voting Rights Act of 1965, which prohibited discriminatory voting practices. The case takes its name from lead plaintiff Charles A. Gomillion, a professor at what at the time was called the Tuskegee Normal and Industrial Institute. Gomillian was the institute's dean of students and chair of the social sciences division and for years had led voter registration drives for African Americans in Tuskegee. In 1957 he learned that a bill was being promoted in the state legislature that would redefine the boundaries of the city to ensure election victories by white voters in 1960. Gomillion and others appealed to the city council and lobbied the state legislature. In spite of their efforts, Local Act No. 140 passed in the state legislature. It redrew the boundaries of the city from a simple square to a twenty-eight-sided figure. The effect of the redrawn boundaries was to disenfranchise all but a small handful of the city's nearly 400 African American voters—but none of its white residents.

In response, Gomillion and the Tuskegee Civic Association launched a boycott of white-owned businesses and took legal action. He and other petitioners argued

The Macon County Courthouse in Tuskegee, Alabama
(Wikimedia Commons)

in court that the act violated the due process and equal protection clauses of the Fourteenth Amendment. Because the act disenfranchised a wildly disproportionate number of Black voters, it clearly had a discriminatory intent. The petitioners also pointed out that the author of the act, State Senator Samuel Engelhardt Jr., was the executive secretary of the White Citizens' Council of Alabama. The goal of Engelhardt and the legislature was to prevent African Americans from registering to vote in the wake of their efforts in the post–World War II era to play a larger part in the civic life of the city.

About the Author

Before Felix Frankfurter came to the U.S. Supreme Court, he had achieved a long and accomplished career as a liberal political activist and academic. Most onlookers assumed that he would continue to function in both roles on the Court but that his liberalism, rather than his academic nature, would predominate.

In fact, it was his academic side that did. Frankfurter's penchant for pedantry combined with his philosophy of deference to legislative and administrative decision making, and the result muted both others' expectations and his own judicial accomplishments. His philosophy of judging, which emphasized process over results, was designed to be a value-neutral method of reaching a decision. This *process jurisprudence*, as it has come to be known, has been championed by some as an admirable form of judicial restraint. To others, Frankfurter's brand of judging more closely resembled abdication of responsibility.

Perhaps ironically, given Frankfurter's avowedly impersonal approach to his job on the Court, more than one Frankfurter observer has associated the justice's uncommonly reverential attitude toward the institutions of American government and their codified roles with his biography. Born in Vienna, Austria, in 1882, Frankfurter immigrated to the United States with his family when he was twelve years old. Like many other European immigrants, the Frankfurters settled on the Lower East Side of Manhattan. Within five years, however, the Frankfurters had moved uptown to the more affluent Yorkville section of New York City. Felix discovered his own route to upward mobility to be in education, entering City College in 1901 and going from there to Harvard Law School, where he graduated first in his class in 1906. At Harvard, Frankfurter was introduced to the case method, an innovative, ostensibly scientific method of studying law.

But Harvard also introduced Frankfurter to the kind of idealism about the law espoused by Louis D. Brandeis, the "people's attorney," who would later become both a Supreme Court justice and one of Frankfurter's closest friends. Frankfurter followed Brandeis's example by choosing a career in public service, beginning with a position in the office of Henry L. Stimson, the U.S. Attorney for New York. Frankfurter had a gift for friendship, and his alliance with Stimson stood him in good stead as he followed the latter to Washington to serve in the administrations of Presidents Theodore Roosevelt and William Howard Taft. Stimson left Washington after the election of Woodrow Wilson, and Frankfurter followed shortly thereafter when he was invited to join the Harvard Law School faculty. Frankfurter had, of course, logged a sterling academic record while at Harvard, but it was a talk he had delivered in 1912 at the twenty-fifth anniversary of the *Harvard Law Re-*

view that seems to have clinched the job. That speech, which emphasized the limited role of courts in interpreting economic regulation, stressed the necessity of permitting legislatures to experiment in order to meet the shifting necessities of a changing world. "The Constitution," Frankfurter intoned prophetically, "was not intended to limit this field of experimentation."

Frankfurter taught at Harvard, focusing on the new field of administrative law, from 1914 until he joined the Supreme Court in 1939, but his commitment to public service and to economic progressivism frequently took him far from Cambridge, Massachusetts. Together with the editors Walter Lippmann and Walter Weyl, he was instrumental in founding the influential political and cultural magazine *New Republic*. Although he had never been an observant Jew, at the urging of Brandeis, Frankfurter helped spearhead the new American Zionist movement. After lobbying in support of Brandeis's ultimately successful Supreme Court nomination, Frankfurter took over his friend's role defending progressive labor legislation for the National Consumers' League.

During World War I, Frankfurter served as secretary and counsel to the Mediation Commission on Labor Problems, established to settle defense industry strikes, and chaired the War Labor Policies Board. These experiences familiarized him with labor politics, and he came to sympathize with those he viewed as underdogs, such as the radical labor leader Thomas Mooney. After the war, Frankfurter helped found the controversial American Civil Liberties Union, and in 1927 he took up the even more controversial cause of the immigrant anarchists Nicola Sacco and Bartolomeo Vanzetti, whom many believed had been framed for murder. The article he published in the prestigious *Atlantic Monthly* focused on the judicial overreaching that marred the Sacco and Vanzetti trial, and it cemented Frankfurter's reputation in some quarters as a radical.

In 1932 Frankfurter turned down a seat on the Massachusetts Supreme Judicial Court and took up the cause of Franklin Delano Roosevelt. When Roosevelt moved into the White House in 1933, Frankfurter became one of the president's staunchest "Brain Trust" lieutenants, supporting New Deal legislation and supplying bright young Harvard Law graduates—who came to be known as Frankfurter's "Happy Hot Dogs"—to staff

the administration. Roosevelt rewarded him first with an offer to become solicitor general (which Frankfurter declined) and then, in 1939, with a nomination to replace Benjamin Cardozo on the Supreme Court. Owing to Frankfurter's activism on behalf of liberal causes and his continuing alliance with Roosevelt, observers expected him to continue along a progressive track once on the Court. A few years earlier, the previously conservative Court had experienced a profound reorientation in response to Roosevelt's ultimately unsuccessful plan to pack it with supporters, and during Frankfurter's tenure this leftward shift intensified. But Frankfurter, who many believed would assume intellectual leadership of the Court, was obliged to take a back seat as his onetime friend, Hugo Black, acted as midwife to the birth of new individual rights. Frankfurter, ideologically opposed to abstract principles and political outcomes, reconciled with his archrival only toward the end of their mutual Court tenures, by which time Black had drifted closer to Frankfurter's judicial conservatism. Frankfurter retired from the Court in 1962 after suffering a debilitating stroke. He died two and a half years later, at the age of eighty-two.

Explanation and Analysis of the Document

Charles G. Gomillion was one of a number of Black citizens of Tuskegee, Alabama, who sued Phil M. Lightfoot, Tuskegee's mayor, as well as other city and county officials over a gerrymandering scheme that changed city boundaries into a "strangely irregular twenty-eight-sided figure" that deprived all but four or five of Tuskegee's registered African American voters of their franchise in municipal elections while not depriving a single white citizen of his or her right to vote. Lawyers for Tuskegee and Macon County repeatedly cited in their briefs and oral arguments the holding of *Colegrove v. Green*, the 1946 redistricting case in which Justice Frankfurter claimed that questions of legislative apportionment were beyond the reach of the judiciary. It was poetic justice that Frankfurter was now obliged to write the opinion of the unanimous *Gomillion* Court.

Frankfurter needed to defend both his earlier opinion and his core value of judicial restraint. He does so by declaring that the Tuskegee law, unlike that addressed in *Colegrove*, was intended to injure only Black voters and was therefore a violation of the Fifteenth Amendment, which prohibits states from denying anyone the right to vote on account of race, color, or previous condition of servitude. As such, the case concerned not a political question but a violation of the Constitution. Furthermore, Frankfurter says, while *Colegrove* concerned legislative inaction over a lengthy period, the law currently before the Court was of recent vintage and plainly reflected legislative intent to deprive Black citizens of Tuskegee of their right to vote. State power—even when employed in a "political" redefinition of municipal boundaries—could not be used in violation of a right conferred by the Constitution.

Frankfurter's analysis contains an inherent contradiction: What is to prevent white citizens suffering disenfranchisement from seeking similar relief? While the intent of the Fifteenth Amendment might have been to ensure African American suffrage, the words of the amendment make it applicable to all "citizens of the United States." In a concurring opinion, Justice Charles Whittaker argues that the equal protection clause of the Fourteenth Amendment offers a clearer basis for disallowing the type of racially discriminatory apportionment under consideration in *Gomillion*. Whittaker would soon be proved right; just days after the *Gomillion* decision was handed down, the Court indicated its intention to hear another reapportionment case, *Baker v. Carr* (1962). Frankfurter urged his fellow justices not to take on *Baker*, which he considered to involve a political question; granting jurisdiction would ne-

cessitate overruling *Colegrove*. Justice William Brennan's opinion for the Court in *Baker* did not explicitly overturn *Colegrove*. Brennan noted, however, that four of the seven justices in *Colegrove* had expressed their belief that the Court did have jurisdiction but that one of the four, fearing a remedy could not be found before the next election for the malapportionment alleged in the case, had voted with Frankfurter not to consider an appeal in *Colegrove*. It was a fine point without much resonance for anyone other than Frankfurter: *Baker* would mark the inauguration of the reapportionment revolution and the end of Frankfurter's Supreme Court career.

Impact

The case demonstrated that state powers were subject to limitations imposed by the U.S. Constitution. Accordingly, states were not insulated from federal judicial review when they placed federally protected rights in jeopardy. In 1961, the results of the decision went into effect; the gerrymandering was reversed and the original map reinstituted. In 1980 the Court modified its ruling in *Gomillion* in *Mobile v. Bolden*, ruling that both racially discriminatory intent and effect would have to be shown for intervention by federal courts for violations of the Voting Rights Act. Two years later, however, Congress amended the Voting Rights Act to return the law to its status before *Bolden*. Under the amended law, it was sufficient to show discriminatory *effect*. It was not necessary to show discriminatory *intent*.

Questions for Further Study

1. How did *Gomillion v. Lightfoot* affect the voting rights of African Americans?

2. What did the Supreme Court decide in *Gomillion v. Lightfoot*?

3. What is "gerrymandering," and what role did it play in this case?

4. What did the petitioners in this case bring a legal complaint against?

Further Reading

Books

Norrell, Robert J. *Reaping the Whirlwind: The Civil Rights Movement in Tuskegee.* New York: Alfred A. Knopf, 1985.

Snyder, Brad. *Democratic Justice: Felix Frankfurter, the Supreme Court, and the Making of the Liberal Establishment.* New York: Norton, 2022.

Taper, Bernard. *Gomillion versus Lightfoot: The Tuskegee Gerrymander Case.* New York: McGraw-Hill, 1962.

Urofsky, Melvin I. *Felix Frankfurter: Judicial Restraint and Individual Liberties.* Boston: Twayne Publishing, 1991.

Articles

Elwood, William A. "An Interview with Charles G. Gomillion." *Callaloo* 40 (Summer 1989): 576–99. https://www.jstor.org/stable/2931304.

Entin, Jonathan L. "Of Squares and Uncouth Twenty-Eight-Sided Figures: Reflections on *Gomillion v. Lightfoot* after Half a Century." *Washburn Law Journal* 50 (2010–11): 133–46.

Gomillion, C. G. "The Negro Voter in the South." *Journal of Negro Education* 26, no. 3 (Summer 1957): 281–86. https://www.jstor.org/stable/i314396.

—Commentary by Lisa Paddock and Michael J. O'Neal

GOMILLION V. LIGHTFOOT

Document Text

At this stage of the litigation we are not concerned with the truth of the allegations, that is, the ability of petitioners to sustain their allegations by proof. The sole question is whether the allegations entitle them to make good on their claim that they are being denied rights under the United States Constitution. The complaint, charging that Act 140 is a device to disenfranchise Negro citizens, alleges the following facts: Prior to Act 140 the City of Tuskegee was square in shape; the Act transformed it into a strangely irregular twenty-eight-sided figure as indicated in the diagram appended to this opinion. The essential inevitable effect of this redefinition of Tuskegee's boundaries is to remove from the city all save only four or five of its 400 Negro voters while not removing a single white voter or resident. The result of the Act is to deprive the Negro petitioners discriminatorily of the benefits of residence in Tuskegee, including, inter alia, the right to vote in municipal elections.

These allegations, if proven, would abundantly establish that Act 140 was not an ordinary geographic redistricting measure even within familiar abuses of gerrymandering. If these allegations upon a trial remained uncontradicted or unqualified, the conclusion would be irresistible, tantamount for all practical purposes to a mathematical demonstration, that the legislation is solely concerned with segregating white and colored voters by fencing Negro citizens out of town so as to deprive them of their pre-existing municipal vote.

It is difficult to appreciate what stands in the way of adjudging a statute having this inevitable effect inval-

id in light of the principles by which this Court must judge, and uniformly has judged, statutes that, howsoever speciously defined, obviously discriminate against colored citizens. "The [Fifteenth] Amendment nullifies sophisticated as well as simple-minded modes of discrimination." ...

The complaint amply alleges a claim of racial discrimination. Against this claim the respondents have never suggested, either in their brief or in oral argument, any countervailing municipal function which Act 140 is designed to serve. The respondents invoke generalities expressing the State's unrestricted power—unlimited, that is, by the United States Constitution—to establish, destroy, or reorganize by contraction or expansion its political subdivisions, to wit, cities, counties, and other local units. We freely recognize the breadth and importance of this aspect of the State's political power. To exalt this power into an absolute is to misconceive the reach and rule of this Court's decisions in the leading case of *Hunter v. Pittsburgh*, and related cases relied upon by respondents. ...

In short, the cases that have come before this Court regarding legislation by States dealing with their political subdivisions fall into two classes: (1) those in which it is claimed that the State, by virtue of the prohibition against impairment of the obligation of contract (Art. I, 10) and of the Due Process Clause of the Fourteenth Amendment, is without power to extinguish, or alter the boundaries of, an existing municipality; and (2) in which it is claimed that the State has no power to change the identity of a municipality whereby citizens of a pre-existing municipality suffer serious economic disadvantage.

Neither of these claims is supported by such a specific limitation upon State power as confines the States under the Fifteenth Amendment. As to the first category, it is obvious that the creation of municipalities—clearly a political act—does not come within the conception of a contract under the Dartmouth College case. As to the second, if one principle clearly emerges from the numerous decisions of this Court dealing with taxation it is that the Due Process Clause affords no immunity against mere inequalities in tax burdens, nor does it afford protection against their increase as an indirect consequence of a State's exercise of its political powers.

Particularly in dealing with claims under broad provisions of the Constitution, which derive content by an interpretive process of inclusion and exclusion, it is imperative that generalizations, based on and qualified by the concrete situations that gave rise to them, must not be applied out of context in disregard of variant controlling facts. Thus, a correct reading of the seemingly unconfined dicta of Hunter and kindred cases is not that the State has plenary power to manipulate in every conceivable way, for every conceivable purpose, the affairs of its municipal corporations, but rather that the State's authority is unrestrained by the particular prohibitions of the Constitution considered in those cases.

The Hunter opinion itself intimates that a state legislature may not be omnipotent even as to the disposition of some types of property owned by municipal corporations. Further, other cases in this Court have refused to allow a State to abolish a municipality, or alter its boundaries, or merge it with another city, without preserving to the creditors of the old city some effective recourse for the collection of debts owed them....

This line of authority conclusively shows that the Court has never acknowledged that the States have power to do as they will with municipal corporations regardless of consequences. Legislative control of municipalities, no less than other state power, lies within the scope of relevant limitations imposed by the United States Constitution. The observation in *Graham v. Folsom* becomes relevant: "The power of the State to alter or destroy its corporations is not greater than the power of

the State to repeal its legislation.'"...

If all this is so in regard to the constitutional protection of contracts, it should be equally true that, to paraphrase, such power, extensive though it is, is met and overcome by the Fifteenth Amendment to the Constitution of the United States, which forbids a State from passing any law which deprives a citizen of his vote because of his race. The opposite conclusion, urged upon us by respondents, would sanction the achievement by a State of any impairment of voting rights whatever so long as it was cloaked in the garb of the realignment of political subdivisions....

The respondents find another barrier to the trial of this case in *Colegrove v. Green*. In that case the Court passed on an Illinois law governing the arrangement of congressional districts within that State. The complaint rested upon the disparity of population between the different districts which rendered the effectiveness of each individual's vote in some districts far less than in others. This disparity came to pass solely through shifts in population between 1901, when Illinois organized its congressional districts, and 1946, when the complaint was lodged. During this entire period elections were held under the districting scheme devised in 1901. The Court affirmed the dismissal of the complaint on the ground that it presented a subject not meet for adjudication. The decisive facts in this case, which at this stage must be taken as proved, are wholly different from the considerations found controlling in *Colegrove*.

That case involved a complaint of discriminatory apportionment of congressional districts. The appellants in *Colegrove* complained only of a dilution of the strength of their votes as a result of legislative inaction over a course of many years. The petitioners here complain that affirmative legislative action deprives them of their votes and the consequent advantages that the ballot affords. When a legislature thus singles out a readily isolated segment of a racial minority for special discriminatory treatment, it violates the Fifteenth Amendment. In no case involving unequal weight in voting distribution that has come before the Court did the decision sanction a differentiation on racial lines whereby approval was given to unequivocal withdrawal of the vote solely from colored citizens. Apart from all else, these considerations lift this controversy out of the so-called "political" arena and into the conventional sphere of constitutional litigation.

In sum, as Mr. Justice Holmes remarked, when dealing with a related situation, in *Nixon v. Herndon*, "Of course the petition concerns political action," but "The objection that the subject matter of the suit is political is little more than a play upon words." A statute which is alleged to have worked unconstitutional deprivations of petitioners' rights is not immune to attack simply because the mechanism employed by the legislature is a redefinition of municipal boundaries. According to the allegations here made, the Alabama Legislature has not merely redrawn the Tuskegee city limits with incidental inconvenience to the petitioners; it is more accurate to say that it has deprived the petitioners of the municipal franchise and consequent rights and to that end it has incidentally changed the city's boundaries. While in form this is merely an act redefining metes and bounds, if the allegations are established, the inescapable human effect of this essay in geometry and geography is to despoil colored citizens, and only colored citizens, of their theretofore enjoyed voting rights. That was not *Colegrove v. Green*.

When a State exercises power wholly within the domain of state interest, it is insulated from federal judicial review. But such insulation is not carried over when state power is used as an instrument for circumventing a federally protected right. This principle has had many applications. It has long been recognized in cases which have prohibited a State from exploiting a power acknowledged to be absolute in an isolated context to justify the imposition of an "unconstitutional condition." What the Court has said in those cases is equally applicable here, viz., that "Acts generally lawful may become unlawful when done to accomplish an unlawful end, . . . and a constitutional power cannot be used by way of condition to attain an unconstitutional result."

Glossary

Act 140: the Tuskegee redistricting ordinance

Due Process Clause: a guarantee, under the Fifth and Fourteenth Amendments, of the individual's right to be formally charged for a crime and granted a fair trial

gerrymandering: political redistricting intended to benefit certain groups at the expense of others

Graham v. Folsom: a 1906 Supreme Court decision concerning "the power of the state to alter or destroy its municipal corporations"

Hunter v. Pittsburgh: a 1907 Supreme Court case involving redistricting

"in disregard of variant controlling facts": without taking into account other significant factors

inter alia: among other things

metes and bounds: a legal description for a piece of real estate, involving markers and directional headings to clearly identify the boundaries of the parcel

Mr. Justice Holmes: Oliver Wendell Holmes Jr. (1841–1935)

municipal corporations: city or town governments

Nixon v. Herndon: a 1927 case in which the Supreme Court struck down a Texas law that prevented Blacks from voting in the Democratic primaries

plenary: planning

respondents: parties against whom a case is brought by the petitioners

sanction: grant approval to

viz.: abbreviation for the Latin *videlicet*, meaning "for example"

MAPP V. OHIO

DATE 1961	**CITATION** 367 U.S. 643
AUTHOR Tom C. Clark	**SIGNIFICANCE** Ruled that evidence illegally seized by law enforcement officials was inadmissible in state courts, thereby extending the scope of the Fourteenth Amendment
VOTE 6–3	

Overview

In the *Mapp v. Ohio* ruling on June 19, 1961, the Supreme Court used the due process clause of the Fourteenth Amendment to expand the scope of the Fourth Amendment, which forbade searches and seizures of property without a warrant. The Court had ruled in the 1914 case *Weeks v. United States* that evidence illicitly collected by law enforcement officers could not be used in federal courts. Known in legal terms as the exclusionary rule, this legal protection was designed to ensure that police officers complied with the Fourth Amendment.

In the *Mapp* case, Cleveland, Ohio, police officers wanted to search Dollree "Dolly" Mapp's house in an effort to find a suspected bomber on May 23, 1957. The suspect was wanted for questioning in a bombing attack on one of Mapp's neighbors. The police targeted Mapp's residence because she had known ties to organized crime.

Mapp refused to allow the law enforcement officers to enter her house without a warrant after speaking to her lawyer by phone. The police eventually forced their way into the home and conducted a search of the premises. They told Mapp that they had a warrant and showed her a piece of paper. Mapp seized the paper, but the police then physically restrained her and took the supposed warrant back. The homeowner later argued that she had grabbed the warrant because she believed it was simply a blank piece of paper. The police did not find the suspect they were after, but they did find a trunk that contained illegal pornographic materials. Mapp was charged with possessing illicit materials. At her trial, no warrant was produced by the prosecution. Nonetheless, Mapp was convicted. She was sentenced to seven years in prison.

Mapp appealed the verdict, arguing that her First Amendment right to free expression been violated and that she had a right to the illicit materials. Her initial appeal was rejected by the Ohio Court of Appeals, and a second appeal was denied by the Ohio Supreme Court, even though both courts accepted that the search had been illegal. Mapp appealed again, and the U.S. Supreme Court agreed to hear her case. Oral arguments before the Court were held on March 29, 1961.

A 6–3 majority on the Court overturned Mapp's conviction. It did not rule on whether the First Amendment gave an individual the right to own pornographic materials. Instead, the Court held that the exclusionary rule applied to the states. The ruling overturned the 1949 case *Wolf v. Colorado*, in which the Court found that only the federal government was bound by the exclusionary rule. The ruling was seen as controversial and produced a plurality decision with three concurrences, while three justices joined in a dissent. The *Mapp* decision has been criticized for allowing guilty parties to go free because of what some have described as a legal "technicality." However, the precedent affirmed an important constitutional protection against excessive search-and-seizure powers for law enforcement.

Context

Legal protections against unlawful searches and the use of evidence obtained illicitly have a long history in English common law. However, it was not until the Fourth Amendment was ratified (1791) that these rights were codified at a national level in the new United States. The Amendment was both an affirmation of the importance of private property and a reaction against British practices during the Revolutionary War, including the use of broad warrants that allowed authorities to search places and seize items without a specific cause.

Meanwhile, the exclusionary rule would evolve slowly from 1791. It was not until the end of the 1800s that the Supreme Court began to rule that evidence could be excluded if it was gained in violation of the Fourth or Fifth Amendments (the Fifth Amendment guaranteed that Americans did not have to provide testimony that could incriminate them). Still, it was not until the *Weeks* decision that the Supreme Court formally adopted the exclusionary rule. After the 1914 decision, evidence that was secured unlawfully could not be used in federal cases. The exclusionary rule was strengthened in the 1920 case *Silverthorne Lumber Company v. United States*. In this ruling, the Court held that even evidence that was obtained indirectly because of an unconstitutional search was the "fruit of a poisonous tree" and could not be used by law enforcement.

Both *Weeks* and *Silverthorne* applied only to federal cases, not the states. Instead, different states adopted different approaches to the exclusionary rule. Some states passed laws to adopt the exclusionary rule, while oth-

The author of the majority opinion, Justice Tom C. Clark
(Supreme Court of the United States)

ers had less-formal protections against unreasonable searches and seizures. The disparity among the states was not limited to the Fourth Amendment. The Bill of Rights (the first ten amendments to the Constitution) affirmed the core civil liberties of the United States, ranging from freedom of religion to the right to trial by jury. However, it was initially only applied to the federal government, not the states. Under the nation's federal system, the framers of the Constitution believed that the individual states should be free to craft their own protections for individual and group rights. Indeed, some states had stronger guarantees for civil liberties than those contained in the Bill of Rights. However, other states did not. The 1833 Supreme Court case *Barron v. City of Baltimore* affirmed that principle that the Bill of Rights was limited to the federal government.

It was not until after the passage of the Fourteenth Amendment (1868) that the basic liberties contained in the Bill of Rights began to be applied to the states. One component of the amendment was the due process clause. This mandated that states could not enact laws that took away a person's basic rights, including "life, liberty, or property," without justification. To justify the loss of these rights, states would have to follow due process, which was interpreted as court action. For instance, a person could not be imprisoned (a loss of liberty) without a trial or other court process.

The Supreme Court began using the due process clause of the Fourteenth Amendment to apply the Bill of Rights to the states in the twentieth century. For example, in 1925, in one of the more famous cases about civil liberties, the Court ruled in *Gitlow v. New York* that the First Amendment right to free speech applied to the states. The use of the Fourteenth Amendment to expand the civil liberties of the Bill of Rights came to be known as the incorporation doctrine. The Court would use this approach throughout the century.

Despite the incorporation doctrine, in 1949 the Supreme Court ruled in *Wolf v. Colorado* that the exclusionary rule did not apply to the states. However, beginning with the appointment of former California governor Earl Warren as chief justice in 1953, the Court began to use the incorporation doctrine far more broadly than in the past. Warren would lead the Supreme Court until his retirement in 1969. During that time, the Court significantly expanded the scope of civil liberties through the Fourteenth Amendment and cases such as *Mapp v. Ohio*.

About the Author

Thomas "Tom" C. Clark was born in Dallas, Texas, on September 23, 1899. He served in the National Guard during World War I and then went to law school at the University of Texas. After he completed his degree in 1922, Clark became an assistant district attorney in 1927. A lifelong Democrat, he later worked as an attorney for the Justice Department during the administration of President Franklin D. Roosevelt. During World War II, Clark became friends with future Supreme Court chief justice Earl Warren and future president Harry S. Truman. In 1945, Truman appointed Clark as attorney general of the United States, a post he held until 1949. Once in office, Clark became noted for his support for civil rights for African Americans. However, he also led efforts by the Truman administration to suppress communism during the early years of the Cold War.

In 1949, Truman named Clark to the Supreme Court. A moderate, Clark sided with the government on a number

of cases. The former attorney general often voted to uphold the authority of federal agencies, especially in cases that involved crimes. He was a close confidant of Chief Justice Fred Vinson. Clark often joined Vinson in his legal decisions. When Vinson died in 1953, he was replaced by Clark's friend Earl Warren. From 1953 onward, Clark became more liberal on cases dealing with civil rights and civil liberties. He authored the Court's decision in *Mapp v. Ohio* and was part of the majority in the 1963 case *Gideon v. Wainwright*, which guaranteed the right to an attorney even if a defendant could not afford one. However, in 1966, Clark dissented from the majority in *Miranda v. Arizona*, the case that required law enforcement to ensure that suspects were aware of their legal rights.

Clark retired from the Supreme Court in 1967 after his son Ramsey Clark was named U.S. attorney general. He died on June 13, 1977.

Explanation and Analysis of the Document

In a lengthy decision, Clark does not dwell on Mapp's argument that she had a constitutional right to own pornographic materials. Indeed, the First Amendment aspect of the appeal was not one of the main factors in the decision, even though that aspect of the case was the central focus of the justices during the oral arguments. Instead, he offers a strong defense of the Fourth Amendment's protections against unreasonable searches and seizures of evidence. The justice is very critical of the actions of the police in the case.

Clark analyzes the arguments used by the Ohio courts in Mapp's trial and her initial appeal. He notes that the Ohio Supreme Court based its decision on previous cases, principally *Weeks* and *Wolf*. The justice then proceeds to deconstruct the Ohio courts' rationale and instead explain the importance of extending the exclusionary rule to include the states.

Clark writes that if state law enforcement officials are allowed to search people's property and seize items without warrants, then the Fourth Amendment is "of no value" and could be removed from the Bill of Rights. He contends that the exclusionary rule is an integral part of the Fourth Amendment. It guarantees that law enforcement officials follow strict protocols. In doing so, they actually develop stronger cases that are more easily prosecuted. It also prevents law enforcement from conducting random searches in the hopes that they will discover some illegal activity or items.

The majority opinion refutes contentions that the exclusionary rule weakens law enforcement. Since the rule had been in force at the federal level since the *Weeks* decision, law enforcement agencies such as the Federal Bureau of Investigation (FBI) had operated under its restraints. Clark pointedly comments that there were no indications that the FBI's ability to investigate and prosecute criminals had been undermined by the exclusionary rule. If the FBI could operate effectively with the rule, so then could state law enforcements agencies. Besides, Clark points out that it would be unfair for those accused of federal crimes to be held to one standard while those accused of state crimes were subject to another. Furthermore, if there were two standards, there might be a temptation for federal prosecutors to turn their cases over to the states if they had violated the exclusionary rule. State prosecutors would be able to use illicit evidence that was otherwise denied to their federal counterparts.

Even the states had begun to recognize the centrality of the exclusionary rule in the aftermath of the *Wolf* case. For example, in the late 1940s, more than two-thirds of the states did not recognize the rule. By the time of the Mapp case, about half of the states that had been opposed to the rule had since incorporated it into state practice. In some instances, this was done by passing new laws; in others, it was accomplished by court action at the state level.

Clark also links the exclusionary rule from the Fourth Amendment with the right to avoid self-incrimination (the right not to testify against oneself) from the Fifth Amendment. The justice sees these two rights as fundamental to the U.S. legal system. They collectively serve to restrain law enforcement agencies from abusing those who do not have the power or resources to defend themselves from the power of the state. Hence, the majority of the court endorsed the decision to overturn Mapp's conviction and to overrule the precedent set in the *Wolf* case by applying the Fourth Amendment and the exclusionary rule to the states.

Justice William J. Brennan joined Clark's opinion, as did chief justice Warren. Justices Hugo Black and William O. Douglas concurred with the majority, although Black argued that the exclusionary rule was based on both the Fourth Amendment and Fifth Amendment (not the Fourth Amendment alone). Justice Potter Stewart also concurred but wrote a separate opinion because he agreed with parts of the dissenting opinion written by Justice John Marshall Harlan. He also did not endorse or oppose Clark's constitutional arguments.

Harlan was joined in his dissent by Justices Felix Frankfurter and Charles Evans Whittaker. In his dissent, Harlan argues in favor of the *Wolf* decision. He contends that states and state courts should be left to determine whether to apply the exclusionary rule. Harlan's dissent is based on the concept of judicial restraint. Judicial restraint emphasizes the importance of past decisions and holds that those rulings should only be overturned if they were an obvious error. Harlan writes that the majority of the Court wanted to extend the exclusionary rule because they believed it was the right thing to do but not because past cases had overtly violated the Constitution.

Harlan did not believe that the Fourth Amendment explicitly called for evidence to be thrown out if the police made a mistake or if there was a procedural error in a search. His dissent would be used by future critics of the exclusionary rule who argued that not all evidence should be discarded in instances of minor errors or blunders by law enforcement. Such mistakes did not always warrant allowing a clearly guilty person to go free because of tainted evidence.

Impact

Mapp v. Ohio was a landmark decision that dramatically changed the criminal justice system of the United States. It expanded the scope of the exclusionary rule, and over time it strengthened the legal protections afforded by the concept. Because of the ruling, police at the national, state, and local levels all had to have a warrant or probable cause before they could search someone's home or other property. That warrant had to be reviewed by a judge or other legal official for accuracy and to make sure that it listed what was being searched and why.

The ruling significantly altered the way law enforcement officials carried out their duties. It required police to be much more thorough and careful in their investigations. Police departments and prosecutors also had to be more diligent in how they handled evidence. This reinforced protections that had long been a part of U.S. legal history.

The decision was controversial. Many of its critics agreed with Justice Harlan that mistakes or minor errors in warrants or the collection of evidence should not be result in allowing guilty people to remain free. Since the *Mapp* decision, the Supreme Court has carved out some exemptions to the exclusionary rule. For instance, in the 1968 case *Terry v. Ohio*, the Court created what became known as the "Terry stop." This doctrine allows police to stop and search individuals if they have a reasonable suspicion that the person is committing a crime or about to engage in criminal activity. However, Terry stops are also controversial because some may abuse this prerogative to target racial or ethnic groups.

The Mapp case was one of a number of decisions from the Court under Chief Justice Warren that expanded civil rights and civil liberties. Taken together, these cases represented a significant shift to a more activist Court and an expanded role for the justices in the broader realm of U.S. politics.

Questions for Further Study

1. What is the exclusionary rule? How does it protect people from overzealous law enforcement officers? What is the main criticism of the rule?

2. What is the incorporation doctrine? How did the Supreme Court use the doctrine to expand civil liberties and civil rights?

3. Why is the Fourth Amendment so important in the *Mapp* case? Explain the relationship between the Fourth and Fifth Amendments according to Justice Clark.

4. What were the main criticisms of the ruling in the *Mapp* case? How did the Supreme Court respond to these criticisms?

Further Reading

Books

Amar, Akhil Reed. *The Bill of Rights: Creation and Reconstruction*. New Haven, CT: Yale University Press, 1998.

Konvitz, Milton. *Fundamental Rights: History of a Constitutional Doctrine*. New York: Routledge, 2017.

Lieberman, Jethro. *A Practical Companion to the Constitution: How the Supreme Court Has Ruled on Abortions from Abortion to Zoning*. Berkeley: University of California Press, 1999.

Long, Carolyn. *Mapp v. Ohio: Guarding against Unreasonable Searches and Seizures*. Lawrence: University Press of Kansas, 2006.

Maclin, Tracey. *The Supreme Court and the Fourth Amendment's Exclusionary Rule*. Oxford: Oxford University Press, 2012.

Stephens, Otis H., Jr., and Richard A. Glenn. *Unreasonable Searches and Seizures: Rights and Liberties under the Law*. Santa Barbara, CA: ABC-CLIO, 2005.

Articles

Pizzi, William T. "The Need to Overrule *Mapp v. Ohio*." *University of Ohio Law Review* 82 (2011).

Wildenthal, Bryan. "The Lost Compromise: Reassessing the Early Understanding in Court and Congress on Incorporation of the Bill of Rights in the Fourteenth Amendment." *Ohio State Law Journal* 61, no. 3 (2000): 1051.

Websites

"Mapp v. Ohio." *Landmark Cases: Historic Supreme Court Cases*. C-SPAN. Accessed January 30, 2023. https://landmarkcases.c-span.org/Case/9/Mapp-v.-Ohio#:~:text=June%2019%2C%201961-,Mapp%20v.,criminal%20trial%20in%20state%20court.

"Mapp v. Ohio (1961)." National Constitution Center. Accessed January 30, 2023. https://constitutioncenter.org/the-constitution/supreme-court-case-library/mapp-v-ohio.

—Commentary by Tom Lansford

MAPP V. OHIO

Document Text

MR. JUSTICE CLARK delivered the opinion of the Court

Appellant stands convicted of knowingly having had in her possession and under her control certain lewd and lascivious books, pictures, and photographs in violation of § 2905.34 of Ohio's Revised Code. As officially stated in the syllabus to its opinion, the Supreme Court of Ohio found that her conviction was valid though "based primarily upon the introduction in evidence of lewd and lascivious books and pictures unlawfully seized during an unlawful search of defendant's home . . . ." 170 Ohio St. 427-428, 166 N.E.2d 387, 388.

On May 23, 1957, three Cleveland police officers arrived at appellant's residence in that city pursuant to information that "a person [was] hiding out in the home, who was wanted for questioning in connection with a recent bombing, and that there was a large amount of policy paraphernalia being hidden in the home." Miss Mapp and her daughter by a former marriage lived on the top floor of the two-family dwelling. Upon their arrival at that house, the officers knocked on the door and demanded entrance, but appellant, after telephoning her attorney, refused to admit them without a search warrant. They advised their headquarters of the situation and undertook a surveillance of the house.

The officers again sought entrance some three hours later when four or more additional officers arrived on the scene. When Miss Mapp did not come to the door immediately, at least one of the several doors to the house was forcibly opened and the policemen gained admittance. Meanwhile Miss Mapp's attorney arrived,

but the officers, having secured their own entry, and continuing in their defiance of the law, would permit him neither to see Miss Mapp nor to enter the house. It appears that Miss Mapp was halfway down the stairs from the upper floor to the front door when the officers, in this highhanded manner, broke into the hall. She demanded to see the search warrant. A paper, claimed to be a warrant, was held up by one of the officers. She grabbed the "warrant" and placed it in her bosom. A struggle ensued in which the officers recovered the piece of paper and as a result of which they handcuffed appellant because she had been "belligerent" in resisting their official rescue of the "warrant" from her person. Running roughshod over appellant, a policeman "grabbed" her, "twisted [her] hand," and she "yelled [and] pleaded with him" because "it was hurting." Appellant, in handcuffs, was then forcibly taken upstairs to her bedroom where the officers searched a dresser, a chest of drawers, a closet and some suitcases. They also looked into a photo album and through personal papers belonging to the appellant. The search spread to the rest of the second floor including the child's bedroom, the living room, the kitchen and a dinette. The basement of the building and a trunk found therein were also searched. The obscene materials for possession of which she was ultimately convicted were discovered in the course of that widespread search.

At the trial, no search warrant was produced by the prosecution, nor was the failure to produce one explained or accounted for. At best, "There is, in the record, considerable doubt as to whether there ever was any warrant for the search of defendant's home."

170 Ohio St. at 430, 166 N.E.2d at 389. The Ohio Supreme Court believed a "reasonable argument" could be made that the conviction should be reversed "because the methods' employed to obtain the [evidence] . . . were such as to 'offend "a sense of justice,"'" "but the court found determinative the fact that the evidence had not been taken "from defendant's person by the use of brutal or offensive physical force against defendant." 170 Ohio St. at 431, 166 N.E.2d at 389-390.

The State says that, even if the search were made without authority, or otherwise unreasonably, it is not prevented from using the unconstitutionally seized evidence at trial, citing *Wolf v. Colorado*, 338 U. S. 25 (1949), in which this Court did indeed hold "that, in a prosecution in a State court for a State crime, the Fourteenth Amendment does not forbid the admission of evidence obtained by an unreasonable search and seizure." On this appeal, of which we have noted probable jurisdiction, 364 U.S. 868, it is urged once again that we review that holding.

I

Seventy-five years ago, in *Boyd v. United States*, 116 U. S. 616, 630 (1886), considering the Fourth and Fifth Amendments as running "almost into each other" on the facts before it, this Court held that the doctrines of those Amendments

"apply to all invasions on the part of the government and its employes of the sanctity of a man's home and the privacies of life. It is not the breaking of his doors, and the rummaging of his drawers, that constitutes the essence of the offence; but it is the invasion of his indefeasible right of personal security, personal liberty and private property. . . . Breaking into a house and opening boxes and drawers are circumstances of aggravation; but any forcible and compulsory extortion of a man's own testimony or of his private papers to be used as evidence to convict him of crime or to forfeit his goods, is within the condemnation . . . [of those Amendments]."

The Court noted that

"constitutional provisions for the security of person and property should be liberally construed. . . . It is the duty of courts to be watchful for the constitutional rights of the citizen, and against any stealthy encroachments thereon."

In this jealous regard for maintaining the integrity of individual rights, the Court gave life to Madison's prediction that "independent tribunals of justice . . . will be naturally led to resist every encroachment upon rights expressly stipulated for in the Constitution by the declaration of rights." I Annals of Cong. 439 (1789). Concluding, the Court specifically referred to the use of the evidence there seized as "unconstitutional." Less than 30 years after *Boyd*, this Court, in *Weeks v. United States*, 232 U. S. 383 (1914), stated that

"the Fourth Amendment . . . put the courts of the United States and Federal officials, in the exercise of their power and authority, under limitations and restraints [and] . . . forever secure[d] the people, their persons, houses, papers and effects against all unreasonable searches and seizures under the guise of law . . . , and the duty of giving to it force and effect is obligatory upon all entrusted under our Federal system with the enforcement of the laws."

Specifically dealing with the use of the evidence unconstitutionally seized, the Court concluded

"If letters and private documents can thus be seized and held and used in evidence against a citizen accused of an offense, the protection of the Fourth Amendment declaring his right to be secure against such searches and seizures is of no value, and, so far as those thus placed are concerned, might as well be stricken from the Constitution. The efforts of the courts and their officials to bring the guilty to punishment, praiseworthy as they are, are not to be aided by the sacrifice of those great principles established by years of endeavor and suffering which have resulted in their embodiment in the fundamental law of the land."

Finally, the Court in that case clearly stated that use of the seized evidence involved "a denial of the constitutional rights of the accused." Thus, in the year 1914, in the *Weeks* case, this Court "for the first time" held that, "in a federal prosecution, the Fourth Amendment barred the use of evidence secured through an illegal search and seizure." *Wolf v. Colorado, supra*, at 28. This Court has ever since required of federal law officers a strict adherence to that command which this Court has held to be a clear, specific, and constitutionally required—even if judicially implied—deterrent safeguard without insistence upon which the Fourth Amendment would have been reduced to "a form of words." Holmes,

J., *Silverthorne Lumber Co. v. United States*, 251 U. S. 385, 392 (1920). It meant, quite simply, that "conviction by means of unlawful seizures and enforced confessions . . . should find no sanction in the judgments of the courts. . . ," *Weeks v. United States, supra*, at 392, and that such evidence "shall not be used at all." *Silverthorne Lumber Co. v. United States, supra*, at 392.

There are in the cases of this Court some passing references to the *Weeks* rule as being one of evidence. But the plain and unequivocal language of *Weeks*—and its later paraphrase in *Wolf*—to the effect that the *Weeks* rule is of constitutional origin, remains entirely undisturbed. In *Byars v. United States*, 273 U. S. 28 (1927), a unanimous Court declared that "the doctrine [cannot] . . . be tolerated *under our constitutional system*, that evidences of crime discovered by a federal officer in making a search without lawful warrant may be used against the victim of the unlawful search where a timely challenge has been interposed." (emphasis added). The Court, in *Olmstead v. United States*, 277 U. S. 438 (1928), in unmistakable language restated the *Weeks* rule:

"The striking outcome of the *Weeks* case and those which followed it was the sweeping declaration that the Fourth Amendment, although not referring to or limiting the use of evidence in courts, really forbade its introduction if obtained by government officers through a violation of the Amendment."

In *McNabb v. United States*, 318 U. S. 332 (1943), we note this statement:

"[A] conviction in the federal courts, the foundation of which is evidence obtained in disregard of liberties deemed fundamental by the Constitution, cannot stand. *Boyd v. United States . . . Weeks v. United States. . . .* And this Court has, on Constitutional grounds, set aside convictions, both in the federal and state courts, which were based upon confessions 'secured by protracted and repeated questioning of ignorant and untutored persons, in whose minds the power of officers was greatly magnified' . . . or 'who have been unlawfully held incommunicado without advice of friends or counsel'. . . ."

Significantly, in *McNabb*, the Court did then pass on to formulate a rule of evidence, saying, "[i]n the view we take of the case, however, it becomes unnecessary to reach the Constitutional issue, [for] . . . [t]he princi-

ples governing the admissibility of evidence in federal criminal trials have not been restricted . . . to those derived solely from the Constitution."

II

In 1949, 35 years after *Weeks* was announced, this Court, in *Wolf v. Colorado, supra*, again for the first time, discussed the effect of the Fourth Amendment upon the States through the operation of the Due Process Clause of the Fourteenth Amendment. It said:

"[W]e have no hesitation in saying that, were a State affirmatively to sanction such police incursion into privacy, it would run counter to the guaranty of the Fourteenth Amendment."

Nevertheless, after declaring that the "security of one's privacy against arbitrary intrusion by the police" is "implicit in the concept of ordered liberty' and, as such, enforceable against the States through the Due Process Clause," *cf. Palko v. Connecticut*, 302 U. S. 319 (1937), and announcing that it "stoutly adhere[d]" to the *Weeks* decision, the Court decided that the *Weeks* exclusionary rule would not then be imposed upon the States as "an essential ingredient of the right." 338 U.S. at 27-29. The Court's reasons for not considering essential to the right to privacy, as a curb imposed upon the States by the Due Process Clause, that which decades before had been posited as part and parcel of the Fourth Amendment's limitation upon federal encroachment of individual privacy, were bottomed on factual considerations.

While they are not basically relevant to a decision that the exclusionary rule is an essential ingredient of the Fourth Amendment as the right it embodies is vouchsafed against the States by the Due Process Clause, we will consider the current validity of the factual grounds upon which *Wolf* was based.

The Court in *Wolf* first stated that "[t]he contrariety of views of the States" on the adoption of the exclusionary rule of *Weeks* was "particularly impressive"; and, in this connection, that it could not "brush aside the experience of States which deem the incidence of such conduct by the police too slight to call for a deterrent remedy . . . by overriding the [States'] relevant rules of evidence." While, in 1949, prior to the *Wolf* case, almost two-thirds of the States were opposed to the use of the exclusionary rule, now, despite the *Wolf* case, more than half of those since passing upon it, by their own legislative or judicial decision, have wholly or partly adopted or adhered to the *Weeks* rule. *See Elkins v. United States*, 364 U. S. 206, Appendix, pp. 224-232 (1960). Significantly, among those now following the rule is California, which, according to its highest court, was "compelled to reach that conclusion because other remedies have completely failed to secure compliance with the constitutional provisions. . . ." *People v. Cahan*, 44 Cal. 2d 434, 445, 282 P.2d 905, 911 (1955). In connection with this California case, we note that the second basis elaborated in *Wolf* in support of its failure to enforce the exclusionary doctrine against the States was that "other means of protection" have been afforded "the right to privacy." 338 U.S. at 30. The experience of California that such other remedies have been worthless and futile is buttressed by the experience of other States. The obvious futility of relegating the Fourth Amendment to the protection of other remedies has, moreover, been recognized by this Court since *Wolf. See Irvine v. California*, 347 U. S. 128, 137 (1954).

Likewise, time has set its face against what *Wolf* called the "weighty testimony" of *People v. Defore*, 242 N.Y. 13, 150 N.E. 585 (1926). There, Justice (then Judge) Cardozo, rejecting adoption of the *Weeks* exclusionary rule in New York, had said that "[t]he Federal rule as it stands is either too strict or too lax." 242 N.Y. at 22, 150 N.E. at 588. However, the force of that reasoning has been largely vitiated by later decisions of this Court. These include the recent discarding of the "silver platter" doctrine which allowed federal judicial use of evidence seized in violation of the Constitution by state agents, *Elkins v. United States, supra;* the relaxation of the formerly strict requirements as to standing to challenge the use of evidence thus seized, so that now the procedure of exclusion, "ultimately referable to constitutional safeguards," is available to anyone even "legitimately on [the] premises" unlawfully searched, *Jones v. United States*, 362 U. S. 257, 266-267 (1960); and, finally, the formulation of a method to prevent state use of evidence unconstitutionally seized by federal agents, *Rea v. United States*, 350 U. S. 214 (1956). Because there can be no fixed formula, we are admittedly met with "recurring questions of the reasonableness of searches," but less is not to be expected when dealing with a Constitution, and, at any rate, "[r]easonableness is in the first instance for the [trial court] . . . to determine." *United States v. Rabinowitz*, 339 U. S. 56, 63 (1950).

It therefore plainly appears that the factual considerations supporting the failure of the *Wolf* Court to include the *Weeks* exclusionary rule when it recognized the enforceability of the right to privacy against the States in 1949, while not basically relevant to the constitutional consideration, could not, in any analysis, now be deemed controlling.

III

Some five years after *Wolf*, in answer to a plea made here Term after Term that we overturn its doctrine on applicability of the *Weeks* exclusionary rule, this Court indicated that such should not be done until the States had "adequate opportunity to adopt or reject the [*Weeks*] rule." *Irvine v. California, supra*, at 134. There again, it was said:

"Never until June of 1949 did this Court hold the basic search and seizure prohibition in any way applicable to the states under the Fourteenth Amendment." *Ibid.*

And only last Term, after again carefully reexamining the *Wolf* doctrine in *Elkins v. United States, supra*, the Court pointed out that "the controlling principles" as to search and seizure and the problem of admissibility "seemed clear" until the announcement in *Wolf* "that the Due Process Clause of the Fourteenth Amendment does not itself require state courts to adopt the exclusionary rule" of the *Weeks* case. At the same time, the Court pointed out, "the underlying constitutional doctrine which *Wolf* established . . . that the Federal Constitution . . . prohibits unreasonable searches and seizures by state officers" had undermined the "foundation upon which the admissibility of state-seized evidence in a federal trial originally rested...." *Ibid.* The Court concluded that it was therefore obliged to hold, although it chose the narrower ground on which to do so, that all evidence obtained by an unconstitutional search and seizure was inadmissible in a federal court regardless of its source. Today we once again examine *Wolf's* constitutional documentation of the right to privacy free from unreasonable state intrusion, and, after its dozen years on our books, are led by it to close the only courtroom door remaining open to evidence secured by official lawlessness in flagrant abuse of that basic right, reserved to all persons as a specific guarantee against that very same unlawful conduct. We hold that all evidence obtained by searches and seizures in violation of the Constitution is, by that same authority, inadmissible in a state court.

IV

Since the Fourth Amendment's right of privacy has been declared enforceable against the States through the Due Process Clause of the Fourteenth, it is enforceable against them by the same sanction of exclusion as is used against the Federal Government. Were it otherwise, then, just as without the *Weeks* rule the assurance against unreasonable federal searches and seizures would be "a form of words," valueless and undeserving of mention in a perpetual charter of inestimable human liberties, so too, without that rule, the freedom from state invasions of privacy would be so ephemeral and so neatly severed from its conceptual nexus with the freedom from all brutish means of coercing evidence as not to merit this Court's high regard as a freedom "implicit in the concept of ordered liberty." At the time that the Court held in *Wolf* that the Amendment was applicable to the States through the Due Process Clause, the cases of this Court, as we have seen, had steadfastly held that as to federal officers the Fourth Amendment included the exclusion of the evidence seized in violation of its provisions. Even *Wolf* "stoutly adhered" to that proposition. The right to privacy, when conceded operatively enforceable against the States, was not susceptible of destruction by avulsion of the sanction upon which its protection and enjoyment had always been deemed dependent under the *Boyd, Weeks* and *Silverthorne* cases. Therefore, in extending the substantive protections of due process to all constitutionally unreasonable searches—state or federal—it was logically and constitutionally necessary that the exclusion doctrine—an essential part of the right to privacy—be also insisted upon as an essential ingredient of the right newly recognized by the *Wolf* case. In short, the admission of the new constitutional right by *Wolf* could not consistently tolerate denial of its most important constitutional privilege, namely, the exclusion of the evidence which an accused had been forced to give by reason of the unlawful seizure. To hold otherwise is to grant the right but, in reality, to withhold its privilege and enjoyment. Only last year, the Court itself recognized that the purpose of the exclusionary rule "is to deter—to compel respect for the constitutional guaranty in the only effectively available way—by removing the incentive to disregard it." *Elkins v. United States, supra*, at 217.

Indeed, we are aware of no restraint, similar to that rejected today, conditioning the enforcement of any other basic constitutional right. The right to privacy, no less important than any other right carefully and particularly reserved to the people, would stand in marked contrast to all other rights declared as "basic to a free society." *Wolf v. Colorado, supra*, at 27. This Court has not hesitated to enforce as strictly against the States as it does against the Federal Government the rights of free speech and of a free press, the rights to notice and to a fair, public trial, including, as it does, the right not to be convicted by use of a coerced confession, however logically relevant it be, and without regard to its reliability. *Rogers v. Richmond*, 365 U. S. 534 (1961). And nothing could be more certain than that, when a coerced confession is involved, "the relevant rules of evidence" are overridden without regard to "the incidence of such conduct by the police," slight or frequent. Why should not the same rule apply to what is tantamount to coerced testimony by way of unconstitutional seizure of goods, papers, effects, documents, etc.? We find that, as to the Federal Government, the Fourth and Fifth Amendments and, as to the States, the freedom from unconscionable invasions of privacy and the freedom from convictions based upon coerced confessions do enjoy an "intimate relation" in their perpetuation of "principles of humanity and civil liberty [secured] . . . only after years of struggle," *Bram v. United States*, 168 U. S. 532, 543-544 (1897). They express "supplementing phases of the same constitutional purpose to maintain inviolate large areas of personal privacy." *Feldman v. United States*, 322 U. S. 487, 489-490 (1944). The philosophy of each Amendment and of each freedom is complementary to, although not dependent upon, that of the other in its sphere of influence—the very least that together they assure in either sphere is that no man is to be convicted on unconstitutional evidence. *Cf. Rochin v. California*, 342 U. S. 165, 173 (1952).

V

Moreover, our holding that the exclusionary rule is an essential part of both the Fourth and Fourteenth Amendments is not only the logical dictate of prior cases, but it also makes very good sense. There is no war between the Constitution and common sense. Presently, a federal prosecutor may make no use of evidence illegally seized, but a State's attorney across the street may, although he supposedly is operating under the enforceable prohibitions of the same Amendment. Thus, the State, by admitting evidence unlawfully seized, serves to encourage disobedience to the Federal Constitution which it is bound to uphold. Moreover, as was said in *Elkins*, "[t]he very essence of a healthy federalism depends upon the avoidance of needless conflict between state and federal courts." 364 U.S. at 221. Such a conflict, hereafter needless, arose this very Term in *Wilson v. Schnettler*, 365 U. S. 381 (1961), in which, and in spite of the promise made by *Rea*, we gave full recognition to our practice in this regard by refusing to restrain a federal officer from testifying in a state court as to evidence unconstitutionally seized by him in the performance of his duties. Yet the double standard recognized until today hardly put such a thesis into practice. In nonexclusionary States, federal officers, being human, were by it invited to, and did, as our cases indicate, step across the street to the State's attorney with their unconstitutionally seized evidence. Prosecution on the basis of that evidence was then had in a state court in utter disregard of the enforceable Fourth Amendment. If the fruits of an unconstitutional search had been inadmissible in both state and federal courts, this inducement to evasion would have been sooner eliminated. There would be no need to reconcile such cases as *Rea* and *Schnettler*, each pointing up the hazardous uncertainties of our heretofore ambivalent approach.

Federal-state cooperation in the solution of crime under constitutional standards will be promoted, if only by recognition of their now mutual obligation to respect the same fundamental criteria in their approaches. "However much in a particular case insistence upon such rules may appear as a technicality that inures to the benefit of a guilty person, the history of the criminal law proves that tolerance of shortcut methods in law enforcement impairs its enduring effectiveness." *Miller v. United States*, 357 U. S. 301, 313 (1958). Denying shortcuts to only one of two cooperating law enforcement agencies tends naturally to breed legitimate suspicion of "working arrangements" whose results are equally tainted. *Byars v. United States*, 273 U. S. 28 (1927); *Lustig v. United States*, 338 U. S. 74 (1949).

There are those who say, as did Justice (then Judge) Cardozo, that, under our constitutional exclusionary doctrine, "[t]he criminal is to go free because the constable has blundered." *People v. Defore*, 242 N.Y. at 21, 150 N.E. at 587. In some cases, this will undoubtedly be the result. But, as was said in *Elkins*, "there is another consideration—the imperative of judicial integrity." 364 U.S. at 222. The criminal goes free, if he must, but it is the law that sets him free. Nothing can destroy a government more quickly than its failure to observe its own laws, or worse, its disregard of the charter of

its own existence. As Mr. Justice Brandeis, dissenting, said in *Olmstead v. United States*, 277 U. S. 438, 485 (1928): "Our Government is the potent, the omnipresent teacher. For good or for ill, it teaches the whole people by its example. . . . If the Government becomes a lawbreaker, it breeds contempt for law; it invites every man to become a law unto himself; it invites anarchy." Nor can it lightly be assumed that, as a practical matter, adoption of the exclusionary rule fetters law enforcement. Only last year, this Court expressly considered that contention and found that "pragmatic evidence of a sort" to the contrary was not wanting. *Elkins v. United States, supra*, at 218. The Court noted that

"The federal courts themselves have operated under the exclusionary rule of *Weeks* for almost half a century; yet it has not been suggested either that the Federal Bureau of Investigation has thereby been rendered ineffective, or that the administration of criminal justice in the federal courts has thereby been disrupted. Moreover, the experience of the states is impressive. . . . The movement towards the rule of exclusion has been halting, but seemingly inexorable." *Id.* at 218-219.

The ignoble shortcut to conviction left open to the State tends to destroy the entire system of constitutional restraints on which the liberties of the people rest. Having once recognized that the right to privacy embodied in the Fourth Amendment is enforceable against the States, and that the right to be secure against rude invasions of privacy by state officers is, therefore, constitutional in origin, we can no longer permit that right to remain an empty promise. Because it is enforceable in the same manner and to like effect as other basic rights secured by the Due Process Clause, we can no longer permit it to be revocable at the whim of any police officer who, in the name of law enforcement itself, chooses to suspend its enjoyment. Our decision, founded on reason and truth, gives to the individual no more than that which the Constitution guarantees him, to the police officer no less than that to which honest law enforcement is entitled, and, to the courts, that judicial integrity so necessary in the true administration of justice.

The judgment of the Supreme Court of Ohio is reversed, and the cause remanded for further proceedings not inconsistent with this opinion.

Reversed and remanded.

Glossary

civil liberties: individual and group protections against the government

district attorney: a government official who oversees investigations and prosecutions of those accused of crimes

Fifth Amendment: a constitutional amendment ratified in 1791 that protects people against being forced to testify against themselves (self-incrimination); guarantees that people cannot be tried twice for the same crime and that they are afforded due process; and requires the government to provide compensation when private property is seized for use by the public

Fourteenth Amendment: a constitutional amendment ratified in 1868 that, among other things, guarantees equal protection for all citizens and requires due process before certain rights may be limited

Fourth Amendment: a constitutional amendment ratified in 1791 that forbids "unreasonable searches and seizures"

oral arguments: the part of a legal proceeding where both sides present their cases orally and respond to questions and comments from judges

BAKER V. CARR

DATE	CITATION
1962	369 U.S. 186

AUTHOR	SIGNIFICANCE
William J. Brennan Jr.	Held that there were no "political questions" to be answered in this case and that legislative apportionment was an issue in which courts could intervene

VOTE	
6–2	

Overview

The pivotal U.S. Supreme Court case *Baker v. Carr* (1962) decided that questions concerning redistricting (attempts to alter the configuration and delineation of voting districts) are not simply political questions but come under the purview of the courts. With this decision, federal courts were allowed to intervene in and decide reapportionment cases. The case was decided on a 6–2 vote, with Felix Frankfurter and John Marshall Harlan II both writing dissents.

The constitution of Tennessee required that legislative districts be redrawn every ten years in accord with the federal census to configure districts of substantially equal population. Charles Baker, a Republican in the county that includes Memphis, brought suit, claiming that no redistricting had been done since 1901. His urban area was thus underrepresented by comparison with neighboring rural areas. The state of Tennessee claimed that if legislative malapportionment existed, the discrepancy had to be resolved through the political process. William J. Brennan, writing for the majority, sided with the plaintiff in stating that the complaint clearly sets forth a case that arises under the Constitution and that therefore the courts unquestionably have jurisdiction.

Context

Baker v. Carr was decided in the context of redistricting in the state of Tennessee. In all the states, boundary lines are drawn around congressional districts for purposes of sending representatives to both the state and the federal legislatures. Generally, the intention is for the population of the districts within a state to be relatively equal so that each district has roughly the same amount of impact on an election. From time to time, states engage in the redistricting process, meaning that lines are shifted in response to shifts in population. Very often, redistricting becomes a political issue as various constituencies strive to ensure that they are adequately represented. Redistricting often becomes a heated issue.

The plaintiff in this case was Charles Baker, a resident of Shelby County, Tennessee, which encompasses Memphis. Baker served as the mayor of the nearby

***Justice William J. Brennan Jr. wrote the majority
opinion.***
(Library of Congress)

town of Millington. According to the state constitution, the legislative districts for the Tennessee General Assembly were to be redrawn every ten years with a view to ensuring that districts have roughly equal populations; the same was to be done for U.S. congressional districts. In his filing, Baker complained that Tennessee had not undergone redistricting since 1901, reflecting the results of the 1900 census.

By the time Baker filed suit, the population of Tennessee had grown substantially, by a factor of five, and had undergone major population shifts. Specifically, he complained that the population of his district in Shelby County—an urban district—was ten times that of many more rural districts. Accordingly, in his view, rural citizens were overrepresented in comparison with urban citizens. He argued that this discrepancy denied him the equal protection of the laws as required by the Fourteenth Amendment to the Constitution. As Justice Brennan put it: "The injury which appellants assert is that this classification disfavors the voters in the counties in which they reside, placing them in a position of

constitutionally unjustifiable inequality vis-a-vis voters in irrationally favored counties." The defendant in the case was Joe Carr, who at the time was serving as Tennessee's secretary of state; Carr was not responsible for drawing district lines, which was the job of the legislature, but he was sued as the official responsible for the way elections in the state were conducted.

Tennessee argued that the makeup of legislative districts was a political question, not a judicial one. In essence, the state argued that the judiciary, including the Supreme Court, had no authority to draw district lines or to intervene in the state's process of doing so. This had been the Court's holding in *Colegrove v. Green* in 1946. In that case, Justice Frankfurter stated that "Courts ought not to enter this political thicket" and maintained that any inadequate apportionment had to be addressed through the political process.

About the Author

William Brennan, U.S. Supreme Court justice, was one of the architects of the constitutional revolution that radically changed American life in the second half of the twentieth century. As Chief Justice Earl Warren's right-hand man, Brennan was responsible for crafting majority opinions such as *Baker v. Carr*, which helped to establish the principle of "one person, one vote" and which Warren always referred to as the most important decision handed down during his momentous tenure on the Court. Brennan, whose politics placed him squarely at the Warren Court's center, was also responsible for crafting majorities for opinions such as the one he wrote in *New York Times Co. v. Sullivan*, which managed to greatly expand the First Amendment while avoiding his more liberal colleagues' wish to make criticism of public officials immune to libel suits. During the Warren years (1953–1969), Brennan was the justice least likely to dissent from the majority's views; but later, during the tenures of Chief Justices Warren Burger and William Rehnquist, he frequently played the role of passionate dissenter, most notably in death penalty cases. Nonetheless, as late as a year before he retired from an increasingly conservative Court, Brennan marshaled a majority in *Texas v. Johnson* and engineered an opinion that expanded the definition of protected speech. It is no accident that Brennan is remembered not only for the law he made but also for his skills as a coalition builder.

Born in Newark, New Jersey, on April 25, 1906, the son of Irish working-class parents, William Joseph Brennan Jr. could be said to have inherited the social activism he later exhibited on the high bench. His father worked as coal stoker at a brewery, hard labor that prompted him to become, first, a leader of the local labor union and, later, a reformer as member of the Newark Board of Commissioners. William Jr. shared many of his father's attitudes, but not—at least not overtly—his father's taste for politics. After graduating with an advanced business degree from the Wharton School at the University of Pennsylvania, Brennan attended Harvard Law School. He practiced law privately for only a short while before commencing a campaign to reform the New Jersey court system. Within a few years, he was sitting on the state supreme court bench, where, seemingly anticipating the role he would later play in connection to Earl Warren, Brennan became New Jersey Chief Justice Arthur Vanderbilt's closest associate.

Brennan arrived at the U.S. Supreme Court on October 16, 1956, appointed by President Dwight D. Eisenhower when Congress was in recess. When the Senate reconvened and voted on Brennan's appointment, only one voice was raised against him: that of Joseph McCarthy, who presumably objected not to Brennan's jurisprudence but to the latter's onetime comparison of McCarthy's Communist-hunting tactics with those employed at the Salem witch trials. Later, Eisenhower would come to regret his choice. Asked if he had made any mistakes as president, he responded, "Yes, two, and they are both sitting on the Supreme Court." Eisenhower grew to dislike Brennan's liberality on the Court almost as much as he disliked Warren's. And, indeed, Warren and Brennan worked together closely throughout Warren's tenure, meeting together privately to discuss strategies for bringing the other justices around to their view of current cases before each weekly judicial conference. Warren valued Brennan not only for his ability to parse and articulate a legal argument but also for his persuasiveness. Achieving unanimity—or, barring that, the clearest majority possible—was of the utmost importance to Warren, who sought to make his Court's precedents stick. Brennan was, in every sense, Warren's ambassador.

During the subsequent tenures of Chief Justices Burger and Rehnquist (respectively, 1969–1986 and 1986–2005), the politics of the Court shifted steadily rightward, and Brennan eventually lost both his leadership role and some of his optimism. Increasingly, he found himself in the minority, and whereas he had written few dissents during the Warren years, after 1969 the number rose steadily. Brennan's closest associate became Thurgood Marshall, one of the few other remaining members of the liberal voting bloc that had been responsible for so many of the Warren Court's momentous decisions. Brennan and Marshall frequently voted together—and they always voted together against imposing the death penalty, which both men believed to be inherently unconstitutional. In later years Brennan was nonetheless still an influential figure, drafting important opinions for the Court on gender discrimination and affirmative action, as well as First Amendment freedoms. He retired on July 20, 1990, having written 1,360 opinions, a number bested only by his fellow Warren Court liberal, William O. Douglas.

Explanation and Analysis of the Document

Although *Baker v. Carr* did not establish the principle of "one person, one vote" (which would come the following year with William O. Douglas's opinion in *Gray v. Sanders*), Brennan's opinion for the Court certainly set the stage for what came to be known as the "reapportionment revolution." Prior to *Baker*, state-mandated legislative districts had continued to favor rural voters, even after populations had shifted to urban areas. In *Baker*, for example, residents of Memphis, Nashville, and Knoxville, Tennessee, sued Joe C. Carr, the Tennessee secretary of state, to force him to redraw the state's existing legislative districts. The boundaries of these districts had remained unchanged since 1901. As a result, the votes of those inhabiting rural districts carried more weight, individually and collectively, than did those of their more numerous urban counterparts.

The plaintiffs, believing that only a federal forum could bring redress, brought their suit in federal district court, asking that the Tennessee apportionment act, which required reapportionment of the state's ninety-five counties only every ten years (a directive that had plainly been disregarded) be declared unconstitutional and that state officials be enjoined from conducting further elections under the existing act. The district court, citing the principle requiring that so-called legal questions were for legislatures, rather than courts to decide, dismissed the case. The plaintiffs then appealed directly to the U.S. Supreme Court, claiming, as they had in the lower court, that their right to equal protection under the laws, granted by the Fourteenth Amendment, had been violated.

The ostensible issue before the high bench was whether federal courts could mandate equality among legislative districts. At its core, however, *Baker* concerned the scope and power of the Supreme Court itself. Seventeen years earlier, in *Colegrove v. Green* (1946), Justice Felix Frankfurter had written a plurality opinion for a seven-member Court (one justice was absent, and a recent vacancy had not been filled) declaring that the high court had no authority to entertain cases concerning apportionment of state legislatures. Now, in the last opinion he would write before retiring from the Court, Frankfurter—always the advocate for judicial restraint—dissented from the majority, once again warning against the Court's entry into a "political thicket." *Colegrove* had been decided by a vote of three to three to one, with Justice Wiley B. Rutledge concurring in the result but not with Frankfurter's reasoning. Because of the unusual circumstances surrounding its decision, the status of *Colegrove* as precedent had always been shaky. Brennan's opinion for the Court in *Baker* destroyed that status entirely.

The appellants in *Baker* had appealed to the Supreme Court for a writ of certiorari, meaning that Court review was discretionary and requiring the justices to vote first on the issue of hearing the case. When this vote was taken, a bare majority of the justices (five) supported Frankfurter's contention that *Baker* was a political case outside Court jurisdiction. Only four justices are required to grant certiorari, however, and the Court agreed to hear the case. After two days of oral argument, on April 19 and 20, 1961, the Court was still split four to four on the merits of the appeal, with Justice Potter Stewart still undecided. Chief Justice Earl Warren, cognizant of *Baker*'s significance and potential for overturning *Colegrove*, held the case over for reargument in the next Court term. When *Baker* was reargued on October 9, 1961, neither side introduced anything new, and afterward Frankfurter attacked the plaintiffs' case with a sixty-page memorandum written to his colleagues. Only Brennan responded in kind, and his lengthy memo, addressing the injustice of malapportionment but asking only that Tennessee be obliged to defend its apportionment system (and

intending to convince the still recalcitrant Stewart), carried the day. For his part, Warren, too, was convinced by Brennan's argument, and he assigned Brennan to write an opinion for what would eventually be a six-member majority (two justices dissented, and one did not participate) to overturn *Colegrove* and grant the Tennessee plaintiffs their day in court.

Brennan's opinion, though ultimately supporting the appellants' contention that Tennessee had acted unconstitutionally, comes at the matter tangentially. After rehearsing the facts of the case, Brennan addresses more technical matters. The court below had dismissed the case on grounds that federal courts lacked jurisdiction and that *Baker* presented a question that could not be resolved by judicial means. Brennan carefully distinguishes between these two arguments: whereas a case that is nonjusticiable can still be considered by a court up to the point of decision, the court is barred from entertaining a case over which it lacks jurisdiction. In *Baker* the complaint clearly sets forth a case that arises under the Constitution; therefore, the district court unquestionably has jurisdiction. What is more, the appellants have sufficient interest in the value of their votes to be granted standing to sue. Justiciability presents a knottier problem for Brennan, who nonetheless succeeds in distinguishing this case, which concerns a question of federalism, from one raising a political question about the relationship among the three branches of government. The appellants, Brennan concludes, have a cause of action, and he sends their case back to the lower court "for further proceedings consistent with this opinion."

Baker was decided on very narrow grounds, but it was nonetheless hard fought. Justice Charles Whittaker found the pressure put on him by some of his colleagues during the Court's consideration of the case too much to bear. He was hospitalized for exhaustion before *Baker* was decided, and he took no part in its decision. A week after *Baker* was handed down on March 26, 1962, Whittaker resigned from the Court. Frankfurter, embittered by his defeat, suffered a debilitating stroke a few weeks later. On August 28, 1962, he, too, resigned from the Court. For urban residents of Tennessee—and other states—*Baker* had a happier aftermath. Within a year of its decision, thirty-six other states were involved in reapportionment suits. A string of Supreme Court cases that followed effectively declared the apportionment of every state legislature unconstitutional. Soon population equality was required of virtually all electoral districts, and even state senate seats were apportioned on the basis of population.

Impact

Earl Warren often referred to *Baker v. Carr* as the most interesting and important case decided during his tenure on the Court. It was also incredibly thorny, causing Justice Charles E. Whittaker to recuse himself from the case and, it is thought, contributing to his failing health. Because the case succeeded in transferring political power from the largely landowning, largely conservative rural population to the more heterogeneous populace of the cities, *Baker* can be said to have opened the door to the major social realignment America underwent during the Warren era as well as, perhaps, the conservative backlash that took place decades later. Indeed, the case required not just Tennessee but all states to redistrict during the 1960s; often they had to do so several times. By increasing the political power of urban areas, the influence of rural areas was diminished, changing the nation's political landscape.

Questions for Further Study

1. What was the significance of the growing urban versus rural divide in the twentieth century for the political process?

2. On what basis did the Court majority find in favor of Baker?

3. In his dissent, Justice Harlan wrote: "I can find nothing in the Equal Protection Clause or elsewhere in the Federal Constitution which expressly or impliedly supports the view that state legislatures must be so structured as to reflect with approximate equality the voice of every voter." Is this position fair to voters?

4. What impact did the Court's decision in this case have on the social fabric of the United States in ensuing years and decades?

Further Reading

Books

Johnson, John W., ed. *Historic U.S. Court Cases: An Encyclopedia*, Vol. 1, 2nd ed. New York: Routledge, 2003.

Peltason, Jack W. "*Baker v. Carr.*" In *The Oxford Companion to the Supreme Court of the United States*, edited by Kermit L. Hall: 67–70. New York: Oxford University Press, 1992.

Tushnet, Mark. *I Dissent: Great Opposing Opinions in Landmark Supreme Court Cases*. Boston: Beacon Press, 2008.

Articles

Mikva, Abner J. "Justice Brennan and the Political Process: Assessing the Legacy of *Baker v. Carr.*" *University of Illinois Law Review* (1995): 683–98.

Neal, Phil C. "*Baker v. Carr*: Politics in Search of Law." *Supreme Court Review* (1962): 252–327.

—Commentary by Lisa Paddock and Michael J. O'Neal

BAKER V. CARR

Document Text

The District Court was uncertain whether our cases withholding federal judicial relief rested upon a lack of federal jurisdiction or upon the inappropriateness of the subject matter for judicial consideration—what we have designated "nonjusticiability." The distinction between the two grounds is significant. In the instance of nonjusticiability, consideration of the cause is not wholly and immediately foreclosed; rather, the Court's inquiry necessarily proceeds to the point of deciding whether the duty asserted can be judicially identified and its breach judicially determined, and whether protection for the right asserted can be judicially molded. In the instance of lack of jurisdiction the cause either does not "arise under" the Federal Constitution, laws or treaties (or fall within one of the other enumerated categories of Art. III, 2), or is not a "case or controversy" within the meaning of that section; or the cause is not one described by any jurisdictional statute. Our conclusion . . . that this cause presents no nonjusticiable "political question" settles the only possible doubt that it is a case or controversy. . . .

It is clear that the cause of action is one which "arises under" the Federal Constitution. The complaint alleges that the 1901 statute effects an apportionment that deprives the appellants of the equal protection of the laws in violation of the Fourteenth Amendment. Dismissal of the complaint upon the ground of lack of jurisdiction of the subject matter would, therefore, be justified only if that claim were "so attenuated and unsubstantial as to be absolutely devoid of merit." . . . Since the complaint plainly sets forth a case arising under the Constitution, the subject matter is within the federal judicial power defined in Art. III, 2, and so within the power of Congress to assign to the jurisdiction of the District Courts. . . .

The appellees refer to *Colegrove v. Green* . . . as authority that the District Court lacked jurisdiction of the subject matter. Appellees misconceive the holding of that case. The holding was precisely contrary to their reading of it. Seven members of the Court participated in the decision. Unlike many other cases in this field which have assumed without discussion that there was jurisdiction, all three opinions filed in *Colegrove* discussed the question. . . .

We hold that the District Court has jurisdiction of the subject matter of the federal constitutional claim asserted in the complaint. . . .

Have the appellants alleged such a personal stake in the outcome of the controversy as to assure that concrete adverseness which sharpens the presentation of issues upon which the court so largely depends for illumination of difficult constitutional questions? This is the gist of the question of standing. It is, of course, a question of federal law. . . .

We hold that the appellants do have standing to maintain this suit. . . . These appellants seek relief in order to protect or vindicate an interest of their own, and of those similarly situated. Their constitutional claim is, in substance, that the 1901 statute constitutes arbitrary and capricious state action, offensive to the Fourteenth Amendment in its irrational disregard of the standard of apportionment prescribed by the State's Constitution or of any standard, effecting a gross disproportion of representation to voting population. The injury which appellants assert is that this classification disfavors the voters in the counties in which they reside, placing them in a position of constitutionally unjustifiable inequality vis-a-vis voters . . . in irrationally favored counties. A citizen's right to a vote free of arbitrary impairment by state action has been judicially recognized as a right secured by the Constitution....

It would not be necessary to decide whether appellants' allegations of impairment of their votes by the 1901 apportionment will, ultimately, entitle them to any relief, in order to hold that they have standing to seek it. If such impairment does produce a legally cognizable injury, they are among those who have sustained it.... They are entitled to a hearing and to the District Court's decision on their claims....

In holding that the subject matter of this suit was not justiciable, the District Court relied on *Colegrove v. Green*. ... We understand the District Court to have read the cited cases as compelling the conclusion that since the appellants sought to have a legislative apportionment held unconstitutional, their suit presented a "political question" and was therefore nonjusticiable. We hold that this challenge to an apportionment presents no nonjusticiable "political question."...

We come, finally, to the ultimate inquiry whether our precedents as to what constitutes a nonjusticiable "political question" bring the case before us under the umbrella of that doctrine. ... The question here is the consistency of state action with the Federal Constitution. We have no question decided, or to be decided, by a political branch of government coequal with this Court. Nor do we risk embarrassment of our government abroad, or grave disturbance at home if we take issue with Tennessee as to the constitutionality of her action here challenged. Nor need the appellants, in order to succeed in this action, ask the Court to enter upon policy determinations for which judicially manageable standards are lacking. Judicial standards under the Equal Protection Clause are well developed and familiar, and it has been open to courts since the enactment of the Fourteenth Amendment to determine, if on the particular facts they must, that a discrimination reflects no policy, but simply arbitrary and capricious action.

We conclude that the complaint's allegations of a denial of equal protection present a justiciable constitutional cause of action upon which appellants are entitled to a trial and a decision. The right asserted is within the reach of judicial protection under the Fourteenth Amendment.

The judgment of the District Court is reversed and the cause is remanded for further proceedings consistent with this opinion.

Glossary

appellants: persons bringing a case on appeal to the Supreme Court

appellees: persons against whom a case is appealed to the Supreme Court

apportionment: the determination of the proportional number of members each U.S. state sends to the House of Representatives, based on population figures

holding: the Supreme Court's ruling

judicial relief: the means by which a court applies a judicial remedy—that is, a solution to the problem presented to it by a given case

justiciable: subject to trial in a law court

offensive to: in violation of

relief: judicial relief

remanded: sent back to a lower court

standing: legal right to bring a lawsuit, which in the United States requires, among other things, clear proof that the party bringing the suit is directly and materially affected by the issue at hand

ENGEL V. VITALE

DATE 1962	**CITATION** 370 U.S. 421
AUTHOR Hugo L. Black	**SIGNIFICANCE** Clarified the separation of church and state by declaring that official prayers in public schools were unconstitutional under the First Amendment
VOTE 6–1	

Overview

In 1955, New York's State Board of Regents, which oversaw the state's public school system, approved a recommendation for public school students to recite a short prayer before classes. School districts across the state had the option on whether to implement the prayer, which became known as the Regents' prayer. The prayer was Christian but nondenominational. Students were allowed to opt out of saying the prayer if they chose. A school district in Long Island, New York, was one of those that adopted the recommendation. However, in 1962, the district's prayer policy was challenged in court by a group of ten parents that included non-Christian families. The group was supported by atheist organizations and civil liberties groups. The coalition challenging the measures was led by Steven Engel, among others. Engel was Jewish and a member of the American Civil Liberties Union (ACLU), a group that promoted individual and collective freedoms.

The plaintiffs in the case argued that the Regents' prayer violated the establishment clause of the First Amendment, which forbids Congress from establishing a state religion. The amendment also contains the free exercise clause, which prevents Congress from taking action that interferes with a person's ability to practice their religion. Together, the two clauses were the foundation for religious freedom in the United States.

State courts in New York rejected the argument that the prayer violated the establishment clause, prompting the plaintiffs to appeal to the Supreme Court. Oral arguments before the Court were held on April 3, 1962, and the justices announced their decision on June 25, 1962. Written by Justice Hugo L. Black, the ruling declared that New York's school prayer violated the establishment clause of the First Amendment. The six-member majority in the case argued that government cannot promote religion in schools, even if the activity is nondenominational students are allowed to opt out. Justice Potter Stewart dissented in the case. Justice Felix Frankfurter had suffered a stroke and did not participate in the case. Neither did Justice Byron White, who was named to the Court after the oral arguments were held in the case (White replaced Justice Charles Evans Whittaker, who resigned on March 31, 1962).

Engel v. Vitale *challenged school prayer*
(Library of Congress)

The ruling became a precedent for later cases on the separation of church and state. Many Christian denominations criticized the decision as an overreach of the Court. They argued that in trying to keep government from promoting religion, the justices were actually suppressing expressions of faith instead of being neutral. Others accused the Court of inadvertently interfering with the free exercise clause.

Context

In Great Britain's North American colonies in the seventeenth and eighteenth centuries, most of the colonies established a single Christian denomination as their official church. Most of the colonies recognized the Church of England (Anglicanism) as their official religion; some of the northern New England colonies had Congregationalism as their formal denomination. A few colonies, including Delaware and Pennsylvania, did not have offi-

cial churches; Delaware had been founded as a haven for Catholics and Pennsylvania for Quakers, both denominations having faced discrimination in Great Britain, as had the Congregationalists. Those colonies with official churches used taxes to support the denominations. After the Revolutionary War, religious minorities, including Baptists, Methodists, Lutherans, and Quakers, argued that it was unfair for public funds to be used to support religious groups. Prominent leaders such as future presidents Thomas Jefferson and James Madison led efforts to create a "wall of separation" between church and state in Virginia. Virginia's laws on religious freedom inspired the First Amendment's establishment and free exercise clauses. The Amendment was part of the Bill of Rights (the first ten amendments to the Constitution). However, initially the Bill of Rights was only applied to the federal government, not the states.

For most of U.S. history, the establishment clause was generally interpreted to mean that the federal government could not create a state religion. In addition, until the twentieth century, the First Amendment was applied only to the federal government and not the states. By the 1960s, many states had policies in place for mandatory or voluntary prayers. Almost half the states also had some form of religious education or Bible reading. In some states these policies had been in place for decades, while others, such as New York, adopted them in the 1940s and 1950s in an effort to promote good behavior and positive ethics among children.

In 1947, the Supreme Court attempted to clarify the meaning of the establishment clause in the case *Everson v. Board of Education*. The Court ruled in a 5–4 decision that a New Jersey law in which tax funds were used to pay for busing students to schools, including private religious schools, was constitutional. Hugo Black was the author of the decision. He used Jefferson's notion of a "wall of separation" between the government and religion as the core of his opinion, but he wrote that laws needed to balance the establishment clause with the free exercise clause. Black argued that busing was a general service like utilities or police or fire service, and governments could not deny these public works to organizations just because they were religious. To do so would be to discriminate against churches or other religious organizations and therefore violate the free exercise clause. For instance, a city-built sidewalk in front of a church would benefit the house of faith but not violate the establishment clause if the sidewalk also passed in front of other non-religious properties. One of the most important aspects of the *Everson* case was that it also extended the First Amendment's religious protections to include state governments by using the Fourteenth Amendment.

After the *Everson* ruling, a growing number of organizations such as the ACLU began to challenge school prayer policies as a violation of church and state. The trend was part of a broader reaction by non-Christian faiths to ensure that all beliefs were treated equally and that the government did not favor one religion over others. They also did want their children to be forced to participate in religious activities of another faith. In addition, atheists and others who did not believe in formal religion objected to practices that exposed children to religious rituals. Concurrently, the Supreme Court had become more liberal on civil liberties issues with the appointment of former California Governor Earl Warren as chief justice in 1953. The Warren Court significantly expanded civil liber-

ties and civil rights in a series of landmark decisions, including the *Engel* case.

About the Author

Hugo L. Black was one of the most influential and longest-serving members of the Supreme Court. He was born in Harlan, Alabama, on February 27, 1886. The future Supreme Court justice earned a law degree from the University of Alabama in 1906. Black served in the U.S. Army during World War I and was elected to the U.S. Senate in 1926. He was a lifelong Democrat. Black became a member of the Ku Klux Klan (KKK) but resigned in 1925. Although he later repudiated his decision to join the group, Black voted against federal anti-lynching laws in the 1920s and 1930s.

In the Senate, Black developed a reputation as a reformer and a staunch advocate for good government. He was also a close ally of President Franklin D. Roosevelt. In 1937, the president appointed the Alabama senator to the Supreme Court. Black was questioned over his ties to the KKK but was confirmed as a justice on the Court by the Senate on a vote of 63–16.

During his lengthy tenure on the Court, Black had ongoing and bitter feuds with a number of his colleagues, including Felix Frankfurter, Robert H. Jackson, and John Marshall Harlan II. His feud with Jackson was so intense that Black threatened to resign if President Harry S. Truman named the former to be chief justice. Black generally joined a group of justices that formed the liberal wing of the Court, especially during the period that Warren was chief justice. Nonetheless, he also advocated a literal approach to the Constitution and often criticized his colleagues on the Court for judicial decisions that seemed to deviate from the original intent of the document.

Black infamously authored the majority decision in the 1944 case *Korematsu v. United States*, which upheld the constitutionality of relocating Japanese Americans on the Pacific Coast into internment camps during World War II. However, Black would later emerge as a strong supporter of civil liberties, especially those contained in the First Amendment. He rejected efforts to curtail free speech or to censor the press. Black's opinions in the *Everson* and *Engel* cases helped define the Court's approach to religious liberty and the relationship between organized religion and the government. He believed in a firm separation of church and state.

Black resigned from the Supreme Court on September 17, 1971, due to poor health. He subsequently suffered a stroke on died on September 25. He had served on the Supreme Court for thirty-four years.

Explanation and Analysis of the Document

In his opinion for the majority in the *Engel* case, Black wrote of the importance of the separation of church and state. He began his ruling by pointing out that there could be little doubt that the recommended prayer was a religious activity. Therefore, it violated the wall of separation since government officials had written the prayer. Black provided a wealth of historical background. He described how many of the early British migrants to North America sought freedom to worship as they pleased. Many were fleeing from government-imposed religious practices. This background motivated the framers of the Bill of Rights. He specifically cited the importance of Madison and Jefferson in crafting the 1785 Virginia Statute for Religious Freedom to ensure that all religious groups were equal before the law. Madison later wrote the First Amendment.

Although he argued strongly for the necessity of the separation of church and state, Black also made an effort to ensure that people did not read his ruling as an attack on religion. The justice wrote that his opinion should not in any way be read as a demonstration of "hostility toward religion or prayer." He emphasized the importance of faith throughout history and especially in the founding of the United States. However, he asserted that the goal of religious freedom could only be achieved through a separation of church and state. Religion should instead be left to people of faith. The faithful should look to their religious leaders and not the government to guide their faith.

The justice affirmed that the First Amendment's religious protections were applicable to the states, as well as the federal government. Beginning in the twentieth century, the Supreme Court had used the Fourteenth Amendment in a succession of cases to apply the First Amendment to states though what came to be known as the incorporation doctrine.

Black rejected the contentions of the attorneys for New York who tried to dismiss concerns over the recommended prayer because students were not required to recite its lines and were even allowed to leave the room when the prayer was spoken. Black warned that a government did not have to directly force people to participate in a religious activity to violate the First Amendment's establishment clause. Students might nonetheless feel coerced into reciting the prayer. The state's representatives also emphasized the nondenominational nature of the prayer, asserting that it could not promote a state religion when it was general and broad in nature. Black also discounted this argument. Even a nondenominational Christian prayer emphasized the Christian faith as more important than other religions. It excluded other faiths. He quoted Madison, who warned that if government could promote Christianity over other religions, it could also eventually elevate one branch of the faith over others. Black forcefully argued that any time there was a connection between government and religion, both are harmed. He wrote that unions of church and state only "destroy government and degrade religion."

Concurrence

Justice William O. Douglas concurred with Black's ruling, although with a twist. Douglas wrote that there was broad agreement that the state had not forced students to participate in the prayer. He pointed out that before the school year began, each parent and everyone that paid taxes was sent a letter that explained the policy. The letter informed parents that children had the option to participate or excuse themselves from the room without any reprisal. It was possible that in some classrooms, the only person reciting the prayer would be the teacher. However, he did not think that forced participation was the main problem with the activity. Douglas argued that since the teachers were being paid while they led the class in prayer, the state was actually financing a religious activity, something that clearly violated the establishment clause. The justice went on to criticize the *Everson* decision. He wrote that the ruling was "out of line" with the First Amendment. He concluded his concurrence with a passionate declaration that governments must remain free of entanglements with religion and that even the smallest breach of this principle could result in a broad erosion of religious liberty. If schools used public financing for one small activity, they opened a door to eventually begin supporting other religious projects or functions.

Dissent

Justice Stewart disagreed with the Court's majority and penned a dissent. He contended that the New York law did not violate anyone's free exercise of religion since students were allowed to opt out of participating in the activity. Stewart argued that the prayer was so broad that it could not be used as a means to establish a state religion. He noted that both chambers of Congress began each day with a prayer. The Supreme Court itself opened its day with the phrase "God save the United States and this Honorable Court." Furthermore, Stewart reminded his fellow justices that Congress had added the phrase "one nation under God" to the Pledge of Allegiance in 1954, while "In God We Trust" had appeared on U.S. currency since 1865. The justice finished his dissent by gently chiding his colleague Justice Douglas. Stewart pointed out that military chaplains and priests who work for state or federal prisons are paid by various governments. Consequently, the federal government, along with the states, already financed religious activities.

Impact

Engel v. Vitale was a landmark case that altered the relationship between state governments and schools on religious issues. While the earlier *Everson* decision had seemed to strike a balance between the establishment clause and the free exercise clause, *Engel* clearly and significantly broadened the definition of what constituted a violation of church and state. Where the establishment clause had generally been seen as a mainly a prohibition against the creation of a specific government-sponsored church, *Engel* served as the basis for later Supreme Court cases that made the wall of separation more concrete. The following year, the Supreme Court reinforced the *Engel* decision in the case *Abington School District v. Schempp*, which ruled in an 8–1 decision that reciting the Lord's Prayer was unconstitutional, as were school-led Bible readings, including voluntary ones.

The *Engel* decision was met with widespread condemnation. Many Christians and conservative leaders criticized the ruling and predicted that it would lead to government-sponsored efforts to suppress religion. The core of their argument was that the decision upset the balance between the free exercise clause and the establishment clause. The ruling also came at a time when the Court was dominated by a liberal majority that issued a series of rulings that broadened the scope of civil rights and civil liberties but also seemed, to some observers, to go too far in some cases in striking a balance between individual freedoms and the public good.

The decision became part of the broader culture war between conservatives and liberals over traditional aspects of U.S. culture. This included sometimes fierce debates over whether to rename activities such as Christmas concerts to holiday concerts in an effort to make the events more inclusive and welcoming to all peoples. There have also been public arguments and cases over the display of religious symbols, such as the Ten Commandments, or the use of slogans such as "In God We Trust."

The Supreme Court would revisit religion and schools in multiple cases after *Engel* and *Abington*. In 1971, the Court used the *Abington* precedent in the case *Lemon v. Kurtzman*, which established a three-part test to determine whether a law or policy violated the establishment clause. In 2000, the Court ruled in *Santa Fe Independent School District v. Doe* that voluntary, student-led, nondenominational prayer before a football game violated the establishment clause, since the prayer was recited over a loudspeaker. This implied government endorsement of the prayer.

The *Lemon* decision was essentially overturned in 2022 by the case of *Kennedy v. Bremerton School District*. The case centered on a football coach, Joseph Kennedy, who prayed in the center of the field after the games. Sometimes players joined him. The school system fired Kennedy, who sued over what he argued was a violation of his free exercise rights. The majority of the Supreme Court agreed with him in a 6–3 decision. The decision seemed to indicate that the more conservative court of the 2020s might seek to again redefine the balance between the establishment clause and the free exercise clause.

Questions for Further Study

1. What were the origins of the establishment clause of the First Amendment? How did the colonial experiences of the North American colonies lead figures such as Thomas Jefferson and James Madison to seek a "wall of separation" between church and state?

2. What is the main difference between the establishment clause and the free exercise clause of the First Amendment? How can efforts to protect one clause affect the other?

3. Why was there such a negative public reaction to the *Engel* case? What were the main criticisms of the decision?

Further Reading

Books

DelFattore, Joan. *The Fourth R: Conflicts over Religion in America's Public Schools*. New Haven, CT: Yale University Press, 2004.

Dierenfield, Bruce J. *The Battle over School Prayer: How Engel v. Vitale Changed America*. Lawrence: University Press of Kansas, 2007.

Gold, Susan Dudley. *Engel v. Vitale: Prayer in the Schools*. New York: Cavendish Square, 2007.

Muir, William K. *Prayer in the Public Schools*. Chicago: University of Chicago Press, 1967.

Sorauf, Frank J. *The Wall of Separation: The Constitutional Politics of Church and State*. Princeton, NJ: Princeton University Press, 1976.

Articles

Elifson, K. W., and Hadaway, C. K. "Prayer in Public Schools: When Church and State Collide." *Public Opinion Quarterly* 49 (1985).

McGuire, Kevin T. "Public Schools, Religious Establishments, and the US Supreme Court: An Examination of Policy Compliance." *American Politics Research* 37, no. 1 (2009).

Websites

"Engel v. Vitale (1962)." National Constitution Center. Accessed January 30, 2023. https://constitutioncenter.org/the-constitution/supreme-court-case-library/engel-v-vitale.

—Commentary by Tom Lansford

ENGEL V. VITALE

Document Text

MR. JUSTICE BLACK delivered the opinion of the Court

The respondent Board of Education of Union Free School District No. 9, New Hyde Park, New York, acting in its official capacity under state law, directed the School District's principal to cause the following prayer to be said aloud by each class in the presence of a teacher at the beginning of each school day:

"Almighty God, we acknowledge our dependence upon Thee, and we beg Thy blessings upon us, our parents, our teachers and our Country."

This daily procedure was adopted on the recommendation of the State Board of Regents, a governmental agency created by the State Constitution to which the New York Legislature has granted broad supervisory, executive, and legislative powers over the State's public school system. These state officials composed the prayer which they recommended and published as a part of their "Statement on Moral and Spiritual Training in the Schools," saying:

"We believe that this Statement will be subscribed to by all men and women of good will, and we call upon all of them to aid in giving life to our program."

Shortly after the practice of reciting the Regents' prayer was adopted by the School District, the parents of ten pupils brought this action in a New York State Court insisting that use of this official prayer in the public schools was contrary to the beliefs, religions, or religious practices of both themselves and their children. Among other things, these parents challenged the constitutionality of both the state law authorizing the School District to direct the use of prayer in public schools and the School District's regulation ordering the recitation of this particular prayer on the ground that these actions of official governmental agencies violate that part of the First Amendment of the Federal Constitution which commands that "Congress shall make no law respecting an establishment of religion"—a command which was "made applicable to the State of New York by the Fourteenth Amendment of the said Constitution." The New York Court of Appeals, over the dissents of Judges Dye and Fuld, sustained an order of the lower state courts which had upheld the power of New York to use the Regents' prayer as a part of the daily procedures of its public schools so long as the schools did not compel any pupil to join in the prayer over his or his parents' objection.

We granted certiorari to review this important decision involving rights protected by the First and Fourteenth Amendments. We think that, by using its public school system to encourage recitation of the Regents' prayer, the State of New York has adopted a practice wholly inconsistent with the Establishment Clause. There can, of course, be no doubt that New York's program of daily classroom invocation of God's blessings as prescribed in the Regents' prayer is a religious activity. It is a solemn avowal of divine faith and supplication for the blessings of the Almighty. The nature of such a prayer has always been religious, none of the respondents has denied this, and the trial court expressly so found:

"The religious nature of prayer was recognized by Jefferson, and has been concurred in by theological writers, the United States Supreme Court, and State courts and administrative officials, including New York's Commissioner of Education. A committee of the New York Legislature has agreed."

"The Board of Regents as *amicus curiae,* the respondents, and intervenors all concede the religious nature of prayer, but seek to distinguish this prayer because it is based on our spiritual heritage. . . ." The petitioners contend, among other things, that the state laws requiring or permitting use of the Regents' prayer must be struck down as a violation of the Establishment Clause because that prayer was composed by governmental officials as a part of a governmental program to further religious beliefs. For this reason, petitioners argue, the State's use of the Regents' prayer in its public school system breaches the constitutional wall of separation between Church and State. We agree with that contention, since we think that the constitutional prohibition against laws respecting an establishment of religion must at least mean that, in this country, it is no part of the business of government to compose official prayers for any group of the American people to recite as a part of a religious program carried on by government.

It is a matter of history that this very practice of establishing governmentally composed prayers for religious services was one of the reasons which caused many of our early colonists to leave England and seek religious freedom in America. The Book of Common Prayer, which was created under governmental direction and which was approved by Acts of Parliament in 1548 and 1549, set out in minute detail the accepted form and content of prayer and other religious ceremonies to be used in the established, tax supported Church of England. The controversies over the Book and what should be its content repeatedly threatened to disrupt the peace of that country as the accepted forms of prayer in the established church changed with the views of the particular ruler that happened to be in control at the time. Powerful groups representing some of the varying religious views of the people struggled among themselves to impress their particular views upon the Government and obtain amendments of the Book more suitable to their respective notions of how religious services should be conducted in order that the official religious establishment would advance their particular religious beliefs. Other groups, lacking the necessary political power

to influence the Government on the matter, decided to leave England and its established church and seek freedom in America from England's governmentally ordained and supported religion.

It is an unfortunate fact of history that, when some of the very groups which had most strenuously opposed the established Church of England found themselves sufficiently in control of colonial governments in this country to write their own prayers into law, they passed laws making their own religion the official religion of their respective colonies. Indeed, as late as the time of the Revolutionary War, there were established churches in at least eight of the thirteen former colonies and established religions in at least four of the other five. But the successful Revolution against English political domination was shortly followed by intense opposition to the practice of establishing religion by law. This opposition crystallized rapidly into an effective political force in Virginia, where the minority religious groups such as Presbyterians, Lutherans, Quakers and Baptists had gained such strength that the adherents to the established Episcopal Church were actually a minority themselves. In 1785-1786, those opposed to the established Church, led by James Madison and Thomas Jefferson, who, though themselves not members of any of these dissenting religious groups, opposed all religious establishments by law on grounds of principle, obtained the enactment of the famous "Virginia Bill for Religious Liberty" by which all religious groups were placed on an equal footing so far as the State was concerned. Similar though less far-reaching legislation was being considered and passed in other states.

By the time of the adoption of the Constitution, our history shows that there was a widespread awareness among many Americans of the dangers of a union of Church and State. These people knew, some of them from bitter personal experience, that one of the greatest dangers to the freedom of the individual to worship in his own way lay in the Government's placing its official stamp of approval upon one particular kind of prayer or one particular form of religious services. They knew the anguish, hardship and bitter strife that could come when zealous religious groups struggled with one another to obtain the Government's stamp of approval from each King, Queen, or Protector that came to temporary power. The Constitution was intended to avert a part of this danger by leaving the government of this country in the hands of the people, rather than in the hands of any monarch. But this safeguard was not enough. Our Founders were no more willing to let the content of their prayers and their privilege of praying whenever they pleased be influenced by the ballot box than they were to let these vital matters of personal conscience depend upon the succession of monarchs. The First Amendment was added to the Constitution to stand as a guarantee that neither the power nor the prestige of the Federal Government would be used to control, support or influence the kinds of prayer the American people can say—that the people's religions must not be subjected to the pressures of government for change each time a new political administration is elected to office. Under that Amendment's prohibition against governmental establishment of religion, as reinforced by the provisions of the Fourteenth Amendment, government in this country, be it state or federal, is without power to prescribe by law any particular form of prayer which is to be used as an official prayer in carrying on any program of governmentally sponsored religious activity.

There can be no doubt that New York's state prayer program officially establishes the religious beliefs embodied in the Regents' prayer. The respondents' argument to the contrary, which is largely based upon the contention that the Regents' prayer is "nondenominational" and the fact that the program, as modified and approved by state courts, does not require all pupils to recite the prayer, but permits those who wish to do so to remain silent or be excused from the room, ignores the essential nature of the program's constitutional defects. Neither the fact that the prayer may be denominationally neutral nor the fact that its observance on the part of the students is voluntary can serve to free it from the limitations of the Establishment Clause, as it might from the Free Exercise Clause, of the First Amendment, both of which are operative against the States by virtue of the Fourteenth Amendment. Although these two clauses may, in certain instances, overlap, they forbid two quite different kinds of governmental encroachment upon religious freedom. The Establishment Clause, unlike the Free Exercise Clause, does not depend upon any showing of direct governmental compulsion and is violated by the enactment of laws which establish an official religion whether those laws operate directly to coerce nonobserving individuals or not. This is not to say, of course, that laws officially prescribing a particular form of religious worship do not involve coercion of such individuals. When the power, prestige and financial support of government is placed behind a particular

religious belief, the indirect coercive pressure upon religious minorities to conform to the prevailing officially approved religion is plain. But the purposes underlying the Establishment Clause go much further than that. Its first and most immediate purpose rested on the belief that a union of government and religion tends to destroy government and to degrade religion. The history of governmentally established religion, both in England and in this country, showed that whenever government had allied itself with one particular form of religion, the inevitable result had been that it had incurred the hatred, disrespect and even contempt of those who held contrary beliefs. That same history showed that many people had lost their respect for any religion that had relied upon the support of government to spread its faith. The Establishment Clause thus stands as an expression of principle on the part of the Founders of our Constitution that religion is too personal, too sacred, too holy, to permit its "unhallowed perversion" by a civil magistrate.

Another purpose of the Establishment Clause rested upon an awareness of the historical fact that governmentally established religions and religious persecutions go hand in hand. The Founders knew that, only a few years after the Book of Common Prayer became the only accepted form of religious services in the established Church of England, an Act of Uniformity was passed to compel all Englishmen to attend those services and to make it a criminal offense to conduct or attend religious gatherings of any other kind—a law which was consistently flouted by dissenting religious groups in England and which contributed to widespread persecutions of people like John Bunyan who persisted in holding "unlawful [religious] meetings . . . to the great disturbance and distraction of the good subjects of this kingdom. . . ." And they knew that similar persecutions had received the sanction of law in several of the colonies in this country soon after the establishment of official religions in those colonies. It was in large part to get completely away from this sort of systematic religious persecution that the Founders brought into being our Nation, our Constitution, and our Bill of Rights, with its prohibition against any governmental establishment of religion. The New York laws officially prescribing the Regents' prayer are inconsistent both with the purposes of the Establishment Clause and with the Establishment Clause itself.

It has been argued that to apply the Constitution in such a way as to prohibit state laws respecting an establishment of religious services in public schools is to indicate a hostility toward religion or toward prayer. Nothing, of course, could be more wrong. The history of man is inseparable from the history of religion. And perhaps it is not too much to say that, since the beginning of that history, many people have devoutly believed that "More things are wrought by prayer than this world dreams of." It was doubtless largely due to men who believed this that there grew up a sentiment that caused men to leave the cross-currents of officially established state religions and religious persecution in Europe and come to this country filled with the hope that they could find a place in which they could pray when they pleased to the God of their faith in the language they chose. And there were men of this same faith in the power of prayer who led the fight for adoption of our Constitution and also for our Bill of Rights with the very guarantees of religious freedom that forbid the sort of governmental activity which New York has attempted here. These men knew that the First Amendment, which tried to put an end to governmental control of religion and of prayer, was not written to destroy either. They knew, rather, that it was written to quiet well justified fears which nearly all of them felt arising out of an awareness that governments of the past had shackled men's tongues to make them speak only the religious thoughts that government wanted them to speak and to pray only to the God that government wanted them to pray to. It is neither sacrilegious nor anti-religious to say that each separate government in this country should stay out of the business of writing or sanctioning official prayers and leave that purely religious function to the people themselves and to those the people choose to look to for religious guidance.

It is true that New York's establishment of its Regents' prayer as an officially approved religious doctrine of that State does not amount to a total establishment of one particular religious sect to the exclusion of all others—that, indeed, the governmental endorsement of that prayer seems relatively insignificant when compared to the governmental encroachments upon religion which were commonplace 200 years ago. To those who may subscribe to the view that, because the Regents' official prayer is so brief and general there can be no danger to religious freedom in its governmental establishment, however, it may be appropriate to say in the words of James Madison, the author of the First Amendment:

"[I]t is proper to take alarm at the first experiment on our liberties. . . . Who does not see that the same authority which can establish Christianity, in exclusion of all other Religions, may establish with the same ease any particular sect of Christians, in exclusion of all other Sects? That the same authority which can force a citizen to contribute three pence only of his property for the support of any one establishment may force him to conform to any other establishment in all cases whatsoever?"

The judgment of the Court of Appeals of New York is reversed, and the cause remanded for further proceedings not inconsistent with this opinion.

Reversed and remanded.

Glossary

atheist: a person who does not believe in gods or deities

establishment clause: a clause in the First Amendment that forbids Congress from establishing a state religion

free exercise clause: a clause in the First Amendment that prevents Congress from taking action that interferes with a person's ability to practice their religion

nondenominational: not adhering to a particular branch of a religion

Regents' prayer: a prayer that the New York State Board of Regents recommended be recited daily by students in the state's public schools

---

GIDEON V. WAINWRIGHT

DATE	**CITATION**
1963	372 U.S. 335
AUTHOR	**SIGNIFICANCE**
Hugo L. Black	Held that the Sixth Amendment's guarantee of a right to assistance of counsel applies to criminal defendants in state court by way of the Fourteenth Amendment
VOTE	
7–2	

Overview

 In the 1963 case of *Gideon v. Wainwright*, the Supreme Court ruled unanimously that under the terms of the Sixth Amendment to the U.S. Constitution, state courts are required to provide counsel in criminal cases to defendants who cannot afford their own attorneys. At the time, state courts were required to provide lawyers only for defendants accused of capital crimes. Clarence Gideon, a semiliterate indigent with a history of petty crime, had been arrested on suspicion of burglary and was denied his request for an attorney. He defended himself and, not surprisingly, was convicted of breaking and entering and sentenced to five years in jail. In their final decision, the Court held that the right to the assistance of counsel—whether in the case of capital or noncapital crimes—was fundamental and was necessary for due process of law.

Context

The factual background of *Gideon v. Wainwright* reads like a film script, and in fact, in 1980 the case was transformed into a made-for-television drama titled *Gide-*

on's Trumpet (the title borrowed from a 1964 book on the subject written by Anthony Lewis), starring Henry Fonda, José Ferrer, and John Houseman. Clarence Gideon, a semiliterate drifter with a history of petty crime, was picked up in Panama City, Florida, on the morning of June 4, 1961, on suspicion of burglary. The night before, a nearby pool hall had been broken into and robbed. A witness reported having seen Gideon in the pool room around 5:30 the next morning.

Gideon was indigent, but when he asked that the trial court assign him an attorney, his request was rejected. The Sixth Amendment requires that all indigent defendants being tried in federal courts be assigned a legal representative, but at the time state courts were required to provide lawyers only for defendants accused of capital crimes. Gideon was obliged to defend himself, and, not surprisingly, he performed poorly. Found guilty of the felony of breaking and entering, he was sentenced to serve five years in prison. While there, Gideon began to study law, and his study led him to believe that he had a right to petition the Florida Supreme Court for review of his case under a writ of habeas corpus, arguing that because he had been denied counsel, he had been illegally imprisoned. The Florida Supreme Court rejected Gideon's petition, after which Gideon drafted a handwritten petition for a writ of certiorari and forwarded it to the U.S. Supreme Court, asking the highest court in the land to review his case. The Court granted Gideon's wish and even assigned him a lawyer, the future justice Abe Fortas. Wainwright was Louie L. Wainwright, the secretary of the Florida Department of Corrections.

About the Author

Hugo Black was one of the most vivid and controversial personalities ever to occupy a seat on the Supreme Court bench. A onetime Ku Klux Klan member, he would seem an unlikely defender of the First Amendment, and yet Black became the very embodiment of a black-letter, literalist jurist, with his commitment to the rights established in the first eight amendments to the Constitution making him into one of the Court's intellectual leaders. He carried a dog-eared copy of the Constitution around in his right coat pocket and referred to it often. "That Constitution is my legal bible," he would declare. "I cherish every word of it from the first to the last." No part of the Constitution was more sacred to Black than the First Amendment, which, as he frequently—and pointedly—noted, begins with the words "Congress shall make no law." For Black, the framers of the Constitution meant what they wrote, and he demanded proof that laws being scrutinized by the Court were not in violation of any of the prohibitions that follow these words.

Hugo Lafayette Black was a son of the South, born in rural Harlan, Alabama, and raised in the town of Ashland, Alabama. His early legal career gave little indication of promise before politics afforded him a means of raising himself in the world. After holding a few local offices, Black decided to run for the U.S. Senate. The tactics he employed to get there were both practical and opportunistic. As a means of widening his base of support, Black used a populist orientation to appeal to organized labor, an alliance that led to him being called a "Bolshevik." During this same period, when acting as defense counsel during a notorious murder trial, Black appealed to racial and religious bias to win his client's acquittal. In 1923 he joined the Ku Klux Klan because, as he said later, most Alabama jurors were Klansmen.

Gideon's handwritten petition for certiorari to the U.S. Supreme Court
(U.S. National Archives)

It was a decision he came to regret, and he resigned from the Klan two years later. But Black's election to the Senate in 1926 was clearly aided by Klan support.

In the Senate, Black pursued a populist agenda, vigorously investigating improper ties between government and business and pushing for a thirty-hour workweek. His ardent support for the New Deal—and, in particular, for Franklin Delano Roosevelt's plan to pack the Supreme Court with devotees as a means of ousting the old guard—attracted the president's attention. In 1937 Black himself became one of Roosevelt's Court nominees. Black's nomination was approved handily, but it was followed almost immediately by public revelation of his history with the Klan. Black confronted the issue head on by making a public confession over the radio, declaring that he had had no connection with the Klan for more than a dozen years and that he had no intention of having any further association with the organization.

Soon Roosevelt had appointed enough justices to make a "second," more liberal Court than the one Chief Justice Charles Evans Hughes had led since 1930. Joined by such like-minded individuals as William O. Douglas and Frank Murphy, Black began his ascent as one of the Court's leading liberal thinkers by voting with a new coalition that upheld important New Deal legislation and emphasized individual rights, as in *Johnson v. Zerbst* (1938), a Sixth Amendment right-to-counsel case for which Black wrote the opinion of the Court. Black went on to lead the Court's so-called due process revolution, although one of the most significant cases for which he is remembered gave civil libertarians fresh reason to doubt his liberal credentials: He wrote the opinion of the Court in *Korematsu v. United States* (1944), the case upholding the internment of Japanese Americans during World War II.

Black's commitment to individual rights was an almost inevitable consequence of his fealty to the Bill of Rights. When his customary literalist approach to constitutional interpretation proved inapposite to certain aspects of his agenda, he turned instead to what the historical record could tell him about original intent. In *Adamson v. California* (1947), for example, Black famously argued in dissent that his reading of the Fourteenth Amendment's adoption indicated that the framers intended to incorporate the Bill of Rights, thus making these protections binding at the state as well as the federal level. Black refused, on the other hand, to support rights others read into the Constitution without literal, written evidence to support their position. He was, for example, ardently opposed to the majority's extension of a broad right of marital privacy in *Griswold v. Connecticut* (1965). Although he did support the right of the *New York Times* to publish the Pentagon Papers in *New York Times Co. v. United States* (1971), other opinions dating from the later period of his career reflect the same restraint and conservatism one detects in Black's vigorous *Griswold* dissent. Black always maintained that his was a consistent, disciplined approach to constitutional analysis. By the mid-1960s, Black had no stomach for the increasingly expansive reading of equal protection by the Court as headed by Earl Warren. The revolution he had set in motion seemed to have taken on a life of its own and passed him by. Black nonetheless hung on almost to the end. When he retired in 1971 after thirty-four years, he did so as one of the longest-serving justices the Court has ever known.

Explanation and Analysis of the Document

The question before the Court in *Gideon v. Wainwright* was whether to uphold its own precedent, *Betts v. Brady* (1942), wherein the Court had found that the Fourteenth Amendment did not make the Sixth Amendment right to counsel applicable to all state criminal proceedings. Justice Black had written a dissent for the minority in that case, and now, in *Gideon*, he had the opportunity to right what he clearly thought a wrong—and in so doing to write the opinion for a unanimous Court. Black, an advocate of what came to be known as the total incorporation theory, believed that the drafters of the Fourteenth Amendment had intended their work to incorporate all of the protections in the Bill of Rights, thus making the first eight amendments applicable at the state level. After reviewing those aspects of the Bill of Rights that the Court had already applied to the states, Black says that in *Gideon* the Court takes at face value the *Betts* assumption that, owing to the Fourteenth Amendment, state courts must observe any provision of the Bill of Rights that is "fundamental and essential to a fair trial." Unlike the *Betts* Court, however, the *Gideon* Court believes that the guarantee of counsel is a fundamental right. Black finds plenty of support for this proposition in other Court opinions, making the case that *Betts* is an anomaly that must be overturned.

The core of the Court's majority opinion is this:

> Reason and reflection require us to recognize that in our adversary system of criminal justice, any person haled into court, who is too poor to hire a lawyer, cannot be assured a fair trial unless counsel is provided for him. This seems to us to be an obvious truth. Governments, both state and federal, quite properly spend vast sums of money to establish machinery to try defendants accused of crime. Lawyers to prosecute are everywhere deemed essential to protect the public's interest in an orderly society. Similarly, there are few defendants charged with crime, few indeed, who fail to hire the best lawyers they can get to prepare and present their defenses.

Black concludes:

> From the very beginning, our state and national constitutions and laws have laid great emphasis on procedural and substantive safeguards designed to assure fair trials before impartial tribunals in which every defendant stands equal before the law. This noble ideal cannot be realized if the poor man charged with crime has to face his accusers without a lawyer to assist him.

Impact

Gideon contributed mightily to the due process revolution expanding individual rights. The public defender program was greatly expanded nationwide. The Court, in turn, expanded *Gideon* in *Argersinger v. Hamlin* (1972), making the right to counsel applicable to misdemeanor defendants facing the prospect of incarceration. Before long, the right to counsel was being read to imply a right to effective counsel. Still other cases drew on *Gideon* when addressing the issue of when in the course of legal proceedings a lawyer must be assigned. More recently, legal associations have been urging courts to assign attorneys to impoverished litigants pursuing civil actions concerning such matters as housing, health care, and child care.

A further impact of the case was the discarding of the previous "incorrect trial" rule, which gave the government latitude in criminal proceedings as long as there were no "shocking departures from fair procedure." This rule was replaced by a firm set of constitutionally based "procedural guarantees." The court adopted rules that did not require analysis on a case-by-case basis. Rather, they established the requirement of appointed counsel as a matter of right, without a defendant's having to show "special circumstances" that justified the need to have counsel appointed.

Questions for Further Study

1. Why did Gideon request an attorney from the state?

2. What rights did Abe Fortas (Gideon's attorney) argue were being violated?

3. What was the ruling of the Supreme Court?

4. What previous ruling did this overturn?

Further Reading

Books

Fridell, Ron. *Gideon v. Wainwright: The Right to Free Counsel.* Salt Lake City, UT: Benchmark Books, 2007.

Houppert, Karen. *Chasing Gideon: The Elusive Quest for Poor People's Justice.* New York: The New Press, 2015.

Articles

Green, Bruce. "Gideon's Amici: Why Do Prosecutors So Rarely Defend the Rights of the Accused?" *Yale Law Journal* 122, no. 8 (June 2013): 2336–57. https://www.yalelawjournal.org/pdf/1185_c2mdjexr.pdf.

Israel, Jerold H. "*Gideon v. Wainwright*—From a 1963 Perspective." *Iowa Law Review* 99 (2014): 2015–57.

Krash, Abe. "Right to a Lawyer: The Implications of *Gideon v. Wainwright*." *Notre Dame Law Review* 39, no. 2 (1964): 150–60. https://scholarship.law.nd.edu/cgi/viewcontent.cgi?article=3271&context=ndlr.

Uelmen, Gerald F. "2001: A Train Ride: A Guided Tour of the Sixth Amendment Right to Counsel." *Law and Contemporary Problems* 58, no. 1 (1995): 13–29. https://scholarship.law.duke.edu/lcp/vol58/iss1/2/.

Van Alstyne, William W. "In Gideon's Wake: Harsher Penalties and the 'Successful' Criminal Appellant." *Yale Law Journal* 74, no. 4 (1965): 606–39. https://scholarship.law.wm.edu/cgi/viewcontent.cgi?article=1812&context=-facpubs.

Websites

Fenton, Peter W., and Michael B. Shapiro. "Looking Back on *Gideon v. Wainwright*." *The Champion*, June 2012. Accessed March 10, 2023, https://www.nacdl.org/Article/June2012-LookingBackonGideonv-Wainwrigh.

—Commentary by Lisa Paddock and Michael J. O'Neal

GIDEON V. WAINWRIGHT

Document Text

MR. JUSTICE BLACK delivered the opinion of the Court

. . . The Sixth Amendment provides, "In all criminal prosecutions, the accused shall enjoy the right . . . to have the Assistance of Counsel for his defence." We have construed this to mean that in federal courts counsel must be provided for defendants unable to employ counsel unless the right is competently and intelligently waived.

We accept *Betts v. Brady*'s assumption, based as it was on our prior cases, that a provision of the Bill of Rights which is "fundamental and essential to a fair trial" is made obligatory upon the States by the Fourteenth Amendment. We think the Court in Betts was wrong, however, in concluding that the Sixth Amendment's guarantee of counsel is not one of these fundamental rights.

In light of these and many other prior decisions of this Court, it is not surprising that the *Betts* Court, when faced with the contention that "one charged with crime, who is unable to obtain counsel, must be furnished counsel by the State," conceded that "[e]xpressions in the opinions of this court lend color to the argument. . . ." The fact is that in deciding as it did—that "appointment of counsel is not a fundamental right, essential to a fair trial"—the Court in *Betts v. Brady* made an abrupt break with its own well-considered precedents. In returning to these old precedents,

sounder we believe than the new, we but restore constitutional principles established to achieve a fair system of justice. Not only these precedents but also reason and reflection require us to recognize that in our adversary system of criminal justice, any person haled into court, who is too poor to hire a lawyer, cannot be assured a fair trial unless counsel is provided for him. This seems to us to be an obvious truth. Governments, both state and federal, quite properly spend vast sums of money to establish machinery to try defendants accused of crime. Lawyers to prosecute are everywhere deemed essential to protect the public's interest in an orderly society. Similarly, there are few defendants charged with crime, few indeed, who fail to hire the best lawyers they can get to prepare and present their defenses. That government hires lawyers to prosecute and defendants who have the money hire lawyers to defend are the strongest indications of the widespread belief that lawyers in criminal courts are necessities, not luxuries. The right of one charged with crime to counsel may not be deemed fundamental and essential to fair trials in some countries, but it is in ours. From the very beginning, our state and national constitutions and laws have laid great emphasis on procedural and substantive safeguards designed to assure fair trials before impartial tribunals in which every defendant stands equal before the law. This noble ideal cannot be realized if the poor man charged with crime has to face his accusers without a lawyer to assist him.

Glossary

adversary system of criminal justice: a legal system in which individuals have the right to bring cases before a court

Assistance of Counsel: the help of a lawyer or other legal representative

but: only

haled: forced

impartial: fair and unbiased

lend color: give validity or believability

precedents: legal rulings in response to a particular situation that will serve as a guide to dealing with future occurrences of the same situation

procedural and substantive: relating to both the procedure by which cases are brought to trial and the methods by which the facts or substance will be reviewed in that trial

sounder: more sound; more logically justifiable

KATZENBACH V. MCCLUNG

<table>
<tr><td>DATE
1964</td><td>CITATION
379 U.S. 294</td></tr>
<tr><td>AUTHOR
Tom C. Clark</td><td>SIGNIFICANCE
Determined that the Civil Rights Act of 1964 provided protection against discrimination toward African Americans by a restaurant owner</td></tr>
<tr><td>VOTE
9–0</td><td></td></tr>
</table>

Overview

Argued on October 5, 1964, and decided on December 14, 1964, the case of *Katzenbach v. McClung* established the principle that a restaurant—even one that operated only in one state—was bound under the terms of the Civil Rights Act of 1964 to provide dine-in services to African American clients. The restaurant in question, Ollie's Barbecue, was owned by Ollie McClung and was in Birmingham, Alabama. Ollie McClung argued that Congress could not enforce the Civil Rights Act against him because his restaurant was a small business that was not directly involved in interstate commerce, so the federal government had no authority in the matter.

In a unanimous decision, authored by Associate Justice Tom C. Clark, the Supreme Court found the U.S. government did have an interest in the matter, and the restaurants that use food brought in from other states (such as Ollie's Barbecue) could not discriminate against African American customers. The case was a major step forward in the expansion of civil rights in the mid-1960s.

Context

Katzenbach v. McClung grew out of the civil rights movement of the 1950s and the early 1960s. Its main impetus was the Civil Rights Act of 1964, which guaranteed the right to vote, use public accommodations, attend desegregated schools, receive equal treatment in federally funded programs, and more. Title VII of the act, for instance, established the EEOC, the Equal Employment Opportunity Commission, that still enforces laws that prohibit race, sex, national origin, and other factors in terms and conditions of employment.

One of the earlier expansions of congressional power through the commerce clause, relied upon by the court in *Katzenbach v. McClung*, was *Wickard v. Filburn* (1942), In which an Ohio farmer sued the secretary of agriculture, Claude R. Wickard, over a provision in the Agricultural Adjustment Act of 1938, which regulated the amount of wheat farmers could grow and provided penalties if they exceeded the established amount. As in *Katzenbach v. McClung*, the Supreme Court found that Congress could use its power to regulate commerce, even on a hyper-local scale. The reasoning was that if other farmers followed Wickard's example and

Nicholas Katzenbach in 1968
(Yoichi R. Okamoto, White House Press Office)

broke the law, the resulting oversupply of wheat could have a significant impact on interstate commerce.

But the roots of the 1964 case lay in the struggle against racism and the "separate but equal" policies that characterized life for Black Americans from the 1890s through the 1950s. The Black experience during World War II strengthened the desire for equal treatment before the law. Many different factors accelerated this trend in the life of the nation. The breaking of the color bar in professional baseball by Jackie Robinson (1919–1972) in the spring of 1947 was one factor. Another was President Truman's desegregation of the U.S. armed forces in July of the same year. All these fostered a strong movement aimed at ending Jim Crow legislation and promoting civil rights across the United States, but especially in the Deep South.

The heart of the Deep South lay in the two states of Mississippi and Alabama, states with large (but also largely disenfranchised) Black populations. Since the late nineteenth century, racist white leaders had worked to suppress the rights that were due Black citizens in these states. Much of the early work centered on the ability of Black graduates to attend college. Supreme Court decisions in *Sipuel v. Board of Regents of the University of Oklahoma* (1948) and *Sweatt v. Painter* (1950) paved the way for the most groundbreaking decision in the civil rights movement: *Brown v. Board of Education of Topeka, Kansas* (1954). The *Brown* decision laid the framework for the Civil Rights Act of 1964 and for the cases that followed it.

Brown sparked fierce resistance from white racists across the South. Emmett Till, a fourteen-year-old Black boy visiting relatives in the small town of Money, Mississippi, was brutally tortured and murdered in the summer of 1955. In Montgomery, Alabama, in December of the same year, a seamstress and civil rights activist named Rosa Parks was arrested for refusing to surrender her seat on a city bus to a white man—an action that led to the Montgomery Bus Boycott.

Incidents such as these led Congress, during the second Eisenhower administration, to the Civil Rights Act of 1957, the first major civil rights legislation since the end of Reconstruction nearly ninety years earlier. As a symbol, the law was significant. In practice, however, it was weak. Black activists continued to campaign for racial equality through organizations such as the Student Nonviolent Coordinating Committee (SNCC). The SNCC organized confrontational but nonviolent ways of challenging racism. In 1961, the "Freedom Riders" disrupted racism in bus terminals in Mississippi and Alabama. By the end of the summer, more than 300 Freedom Riders had been arrested and sent to prison in Mississippi.

Events such as these concerned the new president, John F. Kennedy (1917–1963), a great deal. Kennedy owed his election in 1960 to the Black vote, and even though the core of his party was in the most racist part of the South, he was determined to further the cause of civil rights. In June of 1962, Kennedy sent U.S. Marshals to ensure that a Black student named James Meredith was admitted to the University of Mississippi. The following year, he took steps to ensure that Governor George Wallace would permit the desegregation of the University of Alabama.

The spring and summer of 1963 was marked by both increasing confrontation and increasing violence between civil rights workers and racist law enforcement in the South. Marches, demonstrations, and sit-ins across the region led to 20,000 arrests, ten deaths, and at least one open murder: Mississippi NAACP executive secretary Medgar Evers was shot in his own driveway in Jackson, Mississippi, by white extremist Byron de la Beckwith. In August a coalition of various civil rights organizations set up a march on Washington, bringing together a quarter of a million people. The capstone speech for the March was delivered by the Reverend Dr. Martin Luther King Jr.: his "I Have a Dream" speech.

Kennedy and his vice president, Lyndon Johnson, recognized that the grievances of the civil rights workers required a new civil rights act. Before it could be passed, however, President Kennedy was assassinated on November 22, 1963. The result, pushed through Congress by Lyndon Johnson, was the Civil Rights Act of 1964.

The 1964 act was designed to address all the issues raised by the civil rights movement up to that time. It effectively desegregated all public places, ranging from schools and playgrounds to hotels, gas stations, movie theaters, and restaurants. No longer was racial separation the law of the land.

Nicholas Katzenbach had been deputy attorney general under President Kennedy, and it was thanks to his work and the work of his colleagues that the Civil Rights Act of 1964 covered as many issues as it did. Following Kennedy's assassination, Katzenbach joined Johnson's administration as his attorney general. It was in that capacity that he became the plaintiff in *Katzenbach v. McClung*, one of the first challenges to the Civil Rights Act's attempt to regulate racist practices in public areas.

About the Author

Thomas Campbell Clark (1899–1977) was an associate justice of the U.S. Supreme Court from 1949 until his retirement in 1967. A Texas native, he fought with the Texas National Guard during World War I as an infantryman and then studied at the University of Texas School of Law, receiving his degree in 1922. In 1927, he became civil district attorney for Dallas, a position that he held until 1932. During World War II, he worked for the national government as an assistant attorney general and then as head of the Justice Department's criminal division. When Harry Truman took over the presidency after the death of Franklin Delano Roosevelt, he appointed Clark attorney general. In that capacity, Clark played a major role in supporting many of Truman's efforts to enforce civil rights.

The sudden death of Associate Justice Frank Murphy opened an opportunity for Clark. In August of 1949 he was confirmed by the Senate and, on August 24, sworn into office. His presence on the Court helped decide the increasing numbers of civil rights–related cases in favor of racial equality. Clark played an important, if largely unseen, role in the decisions of *Sweatt v. Painter* and *McLaurin v. Oklahoma State Regents* before he was chosen to speak for the entire Supreme Court in *Katzenbach v. McClung*.

Explanation and Analysis of the Document

Justice Clark begins the court's opinion with a summary of the progress of *Katzenbach v. McClung* through the judicial system. He notes several things. The first is that it is one of two cases argued together. The other, *Heart of Atlanta Motel v. United States*, also involved consideration of Title II of the Civil Rights Act of 1964. The question there was whether hotels, motels, and similar places of business were bound by the law to serve Black clients. Here, the question is whether small restaurants, like Ollie's Barbecue, were likewise bound under the same section of the law. Ollie's Barbecue said that it had not obeyed the requirements of Title II because seating Black customers in its restaurant would cause it to lose white customers, hurting its business. Clark notes that in the district court, a three-judge panel had ruled that Ollie's Barbecue was not bound by Title II.

The district court held that there was no relationship between the food that Ollie's Barbecue bought to cook (which came from out of state) and the place where it was prepared and sold. Because of that, the court held that the federal government had no jurisdiction over local restaurants, as opposed to national chains. Much of the defendant's argument, Clark notes, rests on the idea that Congress, when it created the Civil Rights Act, should have relied on direct evidence proving that restaurants that refuse to serve Black customers interfere with the flow of food between states. Plaintiffs asked the court to dismiss the case for lack of jurisdiction. Clark concludes the first section of the decision by noting that this case, along with the companion *Heart of Atlanta Motel* case, are significant because they affect the constitutionality of the Civil Rights Act.

Clark continues in the second section of the decision with an outline of the facts of the case. He describes Ollie's Barbecue as a family-owned restaurant with the ability to seat 220 customers. He notes that it is located on a state highway near, but not too near, an interstate route. He says that it offers dine-in service to families and professionals but provides only carry-out service for Black clients. The restaurant had never provided dine-in service for Black people since it was founded in 1927. He also notes that of the thirty-six people employed by the restaurant, two-thirds are Black.

In the last couple of paragraphs of Section 2, Clark examines the decision of the district court in some detail. The district court said that Congress had essentially made a mistake by assuming that restaurants affect interstate commerce (and therefore come under Congressional oversight under the Constitution) if they serve travelers who cross state borders or import food across state lines. Clark refers to the decision in *Heart of Atlanta Motel*, in which the Supreme Court decided that Congress could in fact regulate interstate commerce where it affected hotels and motels that refused service to Black Americans.

In the third section of the decision, Clark summarizes the way that section two of the Civil Rights Act impacts Ollie's Barbecue's business. He notes that section 201(a) of the act prohibits discrimination in any place of "public accommodation" based on race, color, religion, or national origin. The next sections, 201(b) (2) and Section 201(c), specifically single out dine-in restaurants that serve interstate travelers and import significant amounts of food across state borders. Clark notes that Ollie's Barbecue does not dispute that it falls under the jurisdiction of the act. Instead, the defendants say that Congress has no authority to place such restrictions on restaurants.

Clark's Section 4 analysis considers Congress's intent in the Civil Rights Act and the self-examination it went through to determine if in fact it had the right to establish the act's provisions. The justice notes that during the hearings Congress conducted prior to the act's passage, the body noted that racial discrimination restricted interstate commerce, primarily through racial segregation. In fact, Congress found that racial segregation was a form of "artificial restriction on the market" that was severe enough to constitute interfering with trade. It also depressed Black travel between states and kept businesses from opening new establishments in areas where discrimination was rampant.

The justice notes that the testimony before Congress shows that the district court was wrong in its suggestion that discrimination and interstate commerce were two separate issues. Even if Ollie's Barbecue only imported a fraction of the value of all food that crosses state lines, it would still be bound by federal law. Racial discrimination of any sort, whether in temporary housing or in the provision of food, is a problem of national interest, Clark says, and even as small a business as Ollie's Barbecue contributes to the problem when it refuses to serve Black customers.

In Section 5 of the Court's opinion, Clark considers Congress's ability to regulate affairs of local, as opposed to national, interest. He points out that the Constitution specifically gives Congress the power to regulate commerce between the states and to make laws "necessary and proper" to do so. The justice points out that the Supreme Court has, in its history, upheld Congress's power to regulate commerce that passes over state lines and that the defendant's contention—that Congress should have provided a case-by-case guide to when a restaurant is guilty of racial discrimination—is wrong. Clark says that Congress did not exceed its power when it established a broad plan for eliminating racial discrimination in restaurants and that Ollie's Barbecue is in fact covered by the provisions of the Civil Rights Act. Writing for the court, Clark says that the judgment of the district court is reversed.

Impact

Legal scholars agree that *Katzenbach v. McClung* accomplished its major goal: it helped reduce a major source of racial discrimination in the United States. It also established a precedent for Congress's ability to regulate local economic activity—an ability that many jurists in more recent times believe has been overextended. This expansion was part of the Court's oversight of Franklin Delano Roosevelt's New Deal program. From the mid-1930s on, the court generally found that the federal government under the Constitution had the right to pass broad-ranging regulations.

In terms of the Civil Rights movement, *Katzenbach v. McClung* provided a basis for further expansion of federal power against local prejudices—or in some cases, simple local interests. In recent times, the precedent established by *Katzenbach v. McClung* has begun to be challenged. As the makeup of the Supreme Court has become more conservative, Congress's power to regulate local issues through the commerce clause has been reduced. In *U.S. v. Lopez* (1995) and *U.S. v. Morrison* (2000), the Supreme Court rejected the idea that Congress had the power to regulate guns and acts of violence, striking down the Gun-Free School Zone Act of 1990 in the first case and the Violence Against Women Act of 1994 in the second. Those acts used the prec-edent of *Katzenbach* to prevent gun violence around schools and to prosecute rapists—both laudable goals but ones that, in the Court's opinion, were not protect-ed by the commerce clause. Does this mean that a conservative Supreme Court might at some point reverse its decision in *Katzenbach*? That remains to be seen.

Questions for Further Study

1. How did the civil rights movement benefit from the *Katzenbach* decision?

2. Should Congress have the power to regulate local affairs, even if there are questions about its power to do so?

3. One of the forms of discrimination that the Civil Rights Act of 1964 was meant to address was the refusal of a department store, Woolworth's, to seat and serve Black customers at its in-store restaurants. How was this different from Ollie's Barbecue?

4. Some early discrimination lawsuits centered on issues of higher education. Is being refused the ability to get a graduate degree different from being refused service in a restaurant?

5. The suit in *Katzenbach v. McClung* was brought not by Black customers who had been refused the right to be seated at Ollie's Barbecue but by the federal government in the person of Attorney General Nicholas Katzenbach. Would the case Katzenbach made have been stronger if a Black person who had been refused service at the restaurant had brought the suit?

Further Reading

Books

Brown, Steven Preston. *Alabama Justice: The Cases and Faces That Changed a Nation.* Tuscaloosa: University of Alabama Press, 2020.

Carson, Clayborne. *In Struggle: SNCC and the Black Awakening of the 1960s.* Cambridge, MA: Harvard University Press, 1981.

Dallek, Robert S. *Flawed Giant: Lyndon Johnson and His Times, 1961–1973.* New York: Oxford University Press, 1998.

Katzenbach, Nicholas deB. *Some of It Was Fun: Working with RFK and LBJ.* New York: Norton, 2008.

Lawson, Steven F. *Running for Freedom: Civil Rights and Black Politics in America since 1941.* 2nd edition. Philadelphia, PA: Temple University Press, 2008.

Articles

Jannetty, Carly, and Sharlene A. McEvoy. "Katzenbach v. McClung Revisited: How the Rehnquist and Roberts Courts Would Have Decided the Case." *North East Journal of Legal Studies* 30 (Fall 2013): 29–46.

McGoldrick, James M. "Katzenbach v. McClung: The Abandonment of Federalism in the Name of Rational Basis." *BYU Journal of Public Law* 14:1 (September 1999): 1.

Milazzo, Don. "Ollie's BBQ Closes, but the Sauce Will Live On." *Birmingham Business Journal*, September 23, 2001.

Websites

"The Papers of Justice Tom C. Clark." *Texas Law: Tarleton Law Library, Jamail Center for Legal Research.* October 5, 2022. Accessed March 9, 2023, https://tarlton.law.utexas.edu/clark.

—Commentary by Ken Shepherd

KATZENBACH V. MCCLUNG

Document Text

MR. JUSTICE CLARK delivered the opinion of the Court

This case was argued with No. 515, *Heart of Atlanta Motel v. United States,* decided this date, *ante,* p. 383 U. S. 241, in which we upheld the constitutional validity of Title II of the Civil Rights Act of 1964 against an attack by hotels, motels, and like establishments. This complaint for injunctive relief against appellants attacks the constitutionality of the Act as applied to a restaurant. The case was heard by a three-judge United States District Court and an injunction was issued restraining appellants from enforcing the Act against the restaurant. 233 F. Supp. 815. On direct appeal, 28 U.S.C. §§ 1252, 1253 (1958 ed.), we noted probable jurisdiction. 379 U. S. 802. We now reverse the judgment.

1. *The Motion to Dismiss*

The appellants moved in the District Court to dismiss the complaint for want of equity jurisdiction and that claim is pressed here. The grounds are that the Act authorizes only preventive relief; that there has been no threat of enforcement against the appellees and that they have alleged no irreparable injury. It is true that ordinarily equity will not interfere in such cases. However, we may and do consider this complaint as an application for a declaratory judgment under 28 U.S.C. §§ 2201 and 2202 (1958 ed.). In this case, of course, direct appeal to this Court would still lie under 28 U.S.C. § 1252 (1958 ed.). But even though Rule 57 of the Federal Rules of Civil Procedure permits declaratory relief although another adequate remedy exists, it should not be granted where a special statutory proceeding

has been provided. *See* Notes on Rule 57 of Advisory Committee on Rules, 28 U.S.C.App. 5178 (1958 ed.). Title II provides for such a statutory proceeding for the determination of rights and duties arising thereunder, §§ 204-207, and courts should, therefore, ordinarily refrain from exercising their jurisdiction in such cases.

The present case, however, is in a unique position. The interference with governmental action has occurred and the constitutional question is before us in the companion case of *Heart of Atlanta Motel* as well as in this case. It is important that a decision on the constitutionality of the Act as applied in these cases be announced as quickly as possible. For these reasons, we have concluded, with the above caveat, that the denial of discretionary declaratory relief is not required here.

2. *The Facts*

Ollie's Barbecue is a family owned restaurant in Birmingham, Alabama, specializing in barbecued meats and homemade pies, with a seating capacity of 220 customers. It is located on a state highway 11 blocks from an interstate one and a somewhat greater distance from railroad and bus stations. The restaurant caters to a family and white-collar trade with a take-out service for Negroes. It employs 36 persons, two-thirds of whom are Negroes.

In the 12 months preceding the passage of the Act, the restaurant purchased locally approximately $150,000 worth of food, $69,683 or 46% of which was meat that it bought from a local supplier who had procured it from outside the State. The District Court expressly found that a substantial portion of the food served in the restaurant had moved in interstate commerce. The restaurant has refused to serve Negroes in its dining accommodations since its original opening in 1927, and, since July 2, 1964, it has been operating in violation of the Act. The court below concluded that, if it were required to serve Negroes, it would lose a substantial amount of business.

On the merits, the District Court held that the Act could not be applied under the Fourteenth Amendment because it was conceded that the State of Alabama was not involved in the refusal of the restaurant to serve Negroes. It was also admitted that the Thirteenth Amendment was authority neither for validating nor for invalidating the Act. As to the Commerce Clause, the court found that it was

"an express grant of power to Congress to regulate interstate commerce, which consists of the movement of persons, goods or information from one state to another,"

and it found that the clause was also a grant of power

"to regulate intrastate activities, but only to the extent that action on its part is necessary or appropriate to the effective execution of its expressly granted power to regulate interstate commerce."

There must be, it said, a close and substantial relation between local activities and interstate commerce which requires control of the former in the protection of the latter. The court concluded, however, that the Congress, rather than finding facts sufficient to meet this rule, had legislated a conclusive presumption that a restaurant affects interstate commerce if it serves or offers to serve interstate travelers or if a substantial portion of the food which it serves has moved in commerce. This, the court held, it could not do, because there was no demonstrable connection between food purchased in interstate commerce and sold in a restaurant and the conclusion of Congress that discrimination in the restaurant would affect that commerce.

The basic holding in *Heart of Atlanta Motel* answers many of the contentions made by the appellees. There, we outlined the overall purpose and operational plan of Title II, and found it a valid exercise of the power to regulate interstate commerce insofar as it requires hotels and motels to serve transients without regard to their race or color. In this case, we consider its ap-

plication to restaurants which serve food a substantial portion of which has moved in commerce.

3. *The Act As Applied*

Section 201(a) of Title II commands that all persons shall be entitled to the full and equal enjoyment of the goods and services of any place of public accommodation without discrimination or segregation on the ground of race, color, religion, or national origin, and § 201(b) defines establishments as places of public accommodation if their operations affect commerce or segregation by them is supported by state action. Sections 201(b)(2) and (c) place any "restaurant . . . principally engaged in selling food for consumption on the premises" under the Act "if . . . it serves or offers to serve interstate travelers or a substantial portion of the food which it serves . . . has moved in commerce."

Ollie's Barbecue admits that it is covered by these provisions of the Act. The Government makes no contention that the discrimination at the restaurant was supported by the State of Alabama. There is no claim that interstate travelers frequented the restaurant. The sole question, therefore, narrows down to whether Title II, as applied to a restaurant annually receiving about $70,000 worth of food which has moved in commerce, is a valid exercise of the power of Congress. The Government has contended that Congress had ample basis upon which to find that racial discrimination at restaurants which receive from out of state a substantial portion of the food served does, in fact, impose commercial burdens of national magnitude upon interstate commerce. The appellees' major argument is directed to this premise. They urge that no such basis existed. It is to that question that we now turn.

4. *The Congressional Hearings*

As we noted in *Heart of Atlanta Motel,* both Houses of Congress conducted prolonged hearings on the Act. And, as we said there, while no formal findings were made, which, of course, are not necessary, it is well that we make mention of the testimony at these hearings the better to understand the problem before Congress and determine whether the Act is a reasonable and appropriate means toward its solution. The record is replete with testimony of the burdens placed on interstate commerce by racial discrimination in restaurants. A comparison of per capita spending by Negroes in restaurants, theaters, and like establishments indicated less spending, after discounting income differences, in areas where discrimination is widely practiced. This condition, which was especially aggravated in the South, was attributed in the testimony of the Under Secretary of Commerce to racial segregation. *See* Hearings before the Senate Committee on Commerce on S. 1732, 88th Cong., 1st Sess., 695. This diminutive spending springing from a refusal to serve Negroes and their total loss as customers has, regardless of the absence of direct evidence, a close connection to interstate commerce. The fewer customers a restaurant enjoys, the less food it sells, and consequently the less it buys. S.Rep. No. 872, 88th Cong., 2d Sess., at 19; Senate Commerce Committee Hearings at 207. In addition, the Attorney General testified that this type of discrimination imposed "an artificial restriction on the market," and interfered with the flow of merchandise. *Id.* at 18-19; also, on this point, *see* testimony of Senator Magnuson, 110 Cong.Rec. 7402-7403. In addition, there were many references to discriminatory situations causing wide unrest and having a depressant effect on general business conditions in the respective communities. *See, e.g.,* Senate Commerce Committee Hearings at 623-630, 695-700, 1384-1385.

Moreover, there was an impressive array of testimony that discrimination in restaurants had a direct and highly restrictive effect upon interstate travel by Negroes. This resulted, it was said, because discriminatory practices prevent Negroes from buying prepared food served on the premises while on a trip, except in isolated and unkempt restaurants and under most unsatisfactory and often unpleasant conditions. This obviously discourages travel and obstructs interstate commerce, for one can hardly travel without eating. Likewise, it was said that discrimination deterred professional as well as skilled people from moving into areas where such practices occurred, and thereby caused industry to be reluctant to establish there. S.Rep. No. 872, *supra,* at 18-19.

We believe that this testimony afforded ample basis for the conclusion that established restaurants in such areas sold less interstate goods because of the discrimination, that interstate travel was obstructed directly by it, that business in general suffered, and that many new businesses refrained from establishing there as a result of it. Hence, the District Court was in error in concluding that there was no connection between discrimination and the movement of interstate commerce.

The court's conclusion that such a connection is outside "common experience" flies in the face of stubborn fact.

It goes without saying that, viewed in isolation, the volume of food purchased by Ollie's Barbecue from sources supplied from out of state was insignificant when compared with the total foodstuffs moving in commerce. But, as our late Brother Jackson said for the Court in *Wickard v. Filburn,* 317 U. S. 111 (1942):

"That appellee's own contribution to the demand for wheat may be trivial by itself is not enough to remove him from the scope of federal regulation where, as here, his contribution, taken together with that of many others similarly situated, is far from trivial."

At 317 U. S. 127-128.

We noted in *Heart of Atlanta Motel* that a number of witnesses attested to the fact that racial discrimination was not merely a state or regional problem, but was one of nationwide scope. Against this background, we must conclude that, while the focus of the legislation was on the individual restaurant's relation to interstate commerce, Congress appropriately considered the importance of that connection with the knowledge that the discrimination was but

"representative of many others throughout the country, the total incidence of which, if left unchecked, may well become far-reaching in its harm to commerce."

Polish Alliance v. Labor Board, 322 U. S. 643, 322 U. S. 648 (1944).

With this situation spreading as the record shows, Congress was not required to await the total dislocation of commerce. As was said in *Consolidated Edison Co. v. Labor Board,* 305 U. S. 197 (1938):

"But it cannot be maintained that the exertion of federal power must await the disruption of that commerce. Congress was entitled to provide reasonable preventive measures and that was the object of the National Labor Relations Act."

At 305 U. S. 222.

5. The Power of Congress to Regulate Local Activities

Article I, § 8, cl. 3, confers upon Congress the power "[t]o regulate Commerce . . . among the several States" and

Clause 18 of the same Article grants it the power "[t]o make all Laws which shall be necessary and proper for carrying into Execution the foregoing Powers. . . ." This grant, as we have pointed out in *Heart of Atlanta Motel,*

"extends to those activities intrastate which so affect interstate commerce, or the exertion of the power of Congress over it, as to make regulation of them appropriate means to the attainment of a legitimate end, the effective execution of the granted power to regulate interstate commerce."

United States v. Wrightwood Dairy Co., 315 U. S. 110, 315 U. S. 119 (1942). Much is said about a restaurant business being local, but,

"even if appellee's activity be local, and though it may not be regarded as commerce, it may still, whatever its nature, be reached by Congress if it exerts a substantial economic effect on interstate commerce. . . ."

Wickard v. Filburn, supra, at 317 U. S. 125. The activities that are beyond the reach of Congress are

"those which are completely within a particular State, which do not affect other States, and with which it is not necessary to interfere, for the purpose of executing some of the general powers of the government."

Gibbons v. Ogden, 9 Wheat. 1, 22 U. S. 195 (1824). This rule is as good today as it was when Chief Justice Marshall laid it down almost a century and a half ago.

This Court has held time and again that this power extends to activities of retail establishments, including restaurants, which directly or indirectly burden or obstruct interstate commerce. We have detailed the cases in *Heart of Atlanta Motel,* and will not repeat them here.

Nor are the cases holding that interstate commerce ends when goods come to rest in the State of destination apposite here. That line of cases has been applied with reference to state taxation or regulation, but not in the field of federal regulation.

The appellees contend that Congress has arbitrarily created a conclusive presumption that all restaurants meeting the criteria set out in the Act "affect commerce." Stated another way, they object to the omission of a provision for a case-by-case determination—judicial or administrative—that racial discrimination in a particular restaurant affects commerce.

But Congress' action in framing this Act was not unprecedented. In *United States v. Darby,* 312 U. S. 100 (1941), this Court held constitutional the Fair Labor Standards Act of 1938. There, Congress determined that the payment of substandard wages to employees engaged in the production of goods for commerce, while not itself commerce, so inhibited it as to be subject to federal regulation. The appellees in that case argued, as do the appellees here, that the Act was invalid because it included no provision for an independent inquiry regarding the effect on commerce of substandard wages in a particular business. (Brief for appellees, pp. 76-77, *United States v. Darby,* 312 U. S. 100.) But the Court rejected the argument, observing that:

"[S]ometimes Congress itself has said that a particular activity affects the commerce, as it did in the present Act, the Safety Appliance Act, and the Railway Labor Act. In passing on the validity of legislation of the class last mentioned the only function of courts is to determine whether the particular activity regulated or prohibited is within the reach of the federal power."

At 312 U. S. 120-121.

Here, as there, Congress has determined for itself that refusals of service to Negroes have imposed burdens both upon the interstate flow of food and upon the movement of products generally. Of course, the mere fact that Congress has said when particular activity shall be deemed to affect commerce does not preclude further examination by this Court. But where we find that the legislators, in light of the facts and testimony before them, have a rational basis for finding a chosen regulatory scheme necessary to the protection of commerce, oar investigation is at an end. The only remaining question—one answered in the affirmative by the court below—is whether the particular restaurant either serves or offers to serve interstate travelers or serves food a substantial portion of which has moved in interstate commerce.

The appellees urge that Congress, in passing the Fair Labor Standards Act and the National Labor Relations Act, made specific findings which were embodied in those statutes. Here, of course, Congress has included no formal findings. But their absence is not fatal to the validity of the statute, *see United States v. Carolene Products Co.,* 304 U. S. 144, 304 U. S. 152 (1938), for the evidence presented at the hearings fully indicated the nature and effect of the burdens on commerce which Congress meant to alleviate.

Confronted as we are with the facts laid before Congress, we must conclude that it had a rational basis for finding that racial discrimination in restaurants had a direct and adverse effect on the free flow of interstate commerce. Insofar as the sections of the Act here relevant are concerned, §§ 201(b)(2) and (c), Congress prohibited discrimination only in those establishments having a close tie to interstate commerce, *i.e.,* those, like the McClungs', serving food that has come from out of the State. We think, in so doing, that Congress acted well within its power to protect and foster commerce in extending the coverage of Title II only to those restaurants offering to serve interstate travelers or serving food, a substantial portion of which has moved in interstate commerce.

The absence of direct evidence connecting discriminatory restaurant service with the flow of interstate food, a factor on which the appellees place much reliance, is not, given the evidence as to the effect of such practices on other aspects of commerce, a crucial matter.

The power of Congress in this field is broad and sweeping; where it keeps within its sphere and violates no express constitutional limitation it has been the rule of this Court, going back almost to the founding days of the Republic, not to interfere. The Civil Rights Act of 1964, as here applied, we find to be plainly appropriate in the resolution of what the Congress found to be a national commercial problem of the first magnitude. We find it in no violation of any express limitations of the Constitution and we therefore declare it valid.

The judgment is therefore

Reversed.

Glossary

commerce clause: a section of the Constitution (Article 1, Section 8, Clause 3) that grants Congress the power to regulate interstate business and trade

injunction: an order requiring one to do or to refrain from doing something; in this case, a district court order preventing the enforcement of Title II of the Civil Rights Act pf 1964 upon Ollie's Barbecue

interstate commerce: trading or transporting goods, services, or money across state borders

---

NEW YORK TIMES CO. v. SULLIVAN

DATE
1964

AUTHOR
William J. Brennan Jr.

VOTE
9–0

CITATION
376 U.S. 254

SIGNIFICANCE
Ruled that a newspaper cannot be held liable
for making false defamatory statements about
the official conduct of a public official unless the
statements were made with reckless disregard for
the truth

Overview

The U.S. Supreme Court case of *New York Times Co. v. Sullivan* revolutionized the law of libel, introducing a requirement for proof of "reckless disregard" for the truth of the statement in question. The case is considered key in the support of freedom of the press. In March of 1960, the *New York Times* featured an advertisement asking for donations to support the defense of Martin Luther King Jr. with respect to his civil rights activities in Alabama. The actions of the Alabama police were described inaccurately and in unflattering terms, leading the Montgomery public safety commissioner, L. B. Sullivan, to ask the *Times* for a retraction. The *Times*, believing that Sullivan did not represent the state and its employees, did not comply, and Sullivan later won a libel suit against the paper. The *Times* asked the Supreme Court to reconsider the decision. A unanimous Court sided with the *Times*, saying that Sullivan had not been named in the advertisement and thus had not been libeled. Moreover, factual error could not provide a cause of action for libel; proof of "actual malice" behind the error was required.

Context

New York Times Co. v. Sullivan arose in the context of the civil rights movement of the 1950s and 1960s. In early 1960, civil rights leader Martin Luther King Jr. was arrested on perjury charges—specifically, that he had signed fraudulent tax returns for 1956 and 1958. In response to the indictment, supporters who believed that the arrest was politically motivated met at the New York apartment of singer Harry Belafonte to form the Committee to Defend Martin Luther King and the Struggle for Freedom in the South. The committee, chaired by civil rights leader A. Philip Randolph, aimed to raise $200,000 in donations to be used for King's defense. In a press release dated March 3, the committee called the charges a "gross misrepresentation of fact." The committee then placed a full-page advertisement in the *New York Times* under the heading "Heed Their Rising Voices." The ad was signed by, among eighty-two others, baseball legend Jackie Robinson and former First Lady Eleanor Roosevelt.

Unfortunately, the ad contained some factual inaccuracies: the number of times King had been arrested, whether Alabama State University students had been expelled for participating in a protest held in response to King's arrest, and the name of the song that student protestors sang. Public officials throughout Alabama were incensed. Sullivan sued the newspaper as well as four African American clergymen affiliated with the committee. Even though Sullivan was not named in the ad, he claimed that he had been libeled by the ad's assertion that truckloads of armed police officers—men his office was charged with overseeing—had circled the Alabama State University campus in Montgomery. That assertion, combined with the errors, demonstrated the falsity of the ad, which damaged his reputation. Under Alabama law at the time, all Sullivan had to do was show that mistakes in the ad could harm his reputation. The state trial court agreed with Sullivan, calling the advertisement's claims false and misleading and the *Times* irresponsible. The jury awarded him $500,000, the equivalent of about $4.7 million in 2021 dollars. The *Times* appealed to the Supreme Court of Alabama, which affirmed the verdict of the lower court. The *Times* then appealed to the U.S. Supreme Court.

About the Author

William Brennan, U.S. Supreme Court justice, was one of the architects of the constitutional revolution that radically changed American life in the second half of the twentieth century. As Chief Justice Earl Warren's right-hand man, Brennan was responsible for crafting majority opinions such as *Baker v. Carr*, which helped to establish the principle of "one person, one vote" and which Warren always referred to as the most important decision handed down during his momentous tenure on the Court. Brennan, whose politics placed him squarely at the Warren Court's center, was also responsible for crafting majorities for opinions such as the one he wrote in *New York Times Co. v. Sullivan*, which managed to greatly expand the First Amendment while avoiding his more liberal colleagues' wish to make criticism of public officials immune to libel suits. During the Warren years (1953–1969), Brennan was the justice least likely to dissent from the majority's views, but later, during the tenures of Chief Justices Warren Burger and William Rehnquist, he frequently played the role of passionate dissenter, most notably in death penalty cases. Nonetheless, as late as a year before he retired from an increasingly conservative Court, Brennan marshaled a majority in *Texas v.*

The **New York Times** *advertisement at the center of the lawsuit*
(Wikimedia Commons)

Johnson and engineered an opinion that expanded the definition of protected speech. It is no accident that Brennan is remembered not only for the law he made but also for his skills as a coalition builder.

Born in Newark, New Jersey, on April 25, 1906, the son of Irish working-class parents, William Joseph Brennan Jr. could be said to have inherited the social activism he later exhibited on the high bench. His father worked as coal stoker at a brewery, hard labor that prompted him to become, first, a leader of the local labor union and, later, a reformer as member of the Newark Board of Commissioners. William Jr. shared many of his father's attitudes, but not—at least not overtly—his father's taste for politics. After graduating with an advanced business degree from the Wharton School at the University of Pennsylvania, Brennan attended Harvard Law School. He practiced law privately for only a short while before commencing a campaign to reform the New Jersey court system. Within a few years, he was sitting on the state supreme court bench, where, seemingly anticipating the role he would later play in connection to Earl Warren, Brennan became New Jersey Chief Justice Arthur Vanderbilt's closest associate.

Brennan arrived at the U.S. Supreme Court on October 16, 1956, appointed by President Dwight D. Eisenhower when Congress was in recess. When the Senate reconvened and voted on Brennan's appointment, only one voice was raised against him: that of Joseph McCarthy, who presumably objected not to Brennan's jurisprudence but to the latter's onetime comparison of McCarthy's Communist-hunting tactics to those employed at the Salem witch trials. Later, Eisenhower would come to regret his choice. Asked if he had made any mistakes as president, he responded, "Yes, two, and they are both sitting on the Supreme Court." Eisenhower grew to dislike Brennan's liberality on the Court almost as much as he disliked Warren's. And, indeed, Warren and Brennan worked together closely throughout Warren's tenure, meeting together privately to discuss strategies for bringing the other justices around to their view of current cases before each weekly judicial conference. Warren valued Brennan not only for his ability to parse and articulate a legal argument but also for his persuasiveness. Achieving unanimity—or, barring that, the clearest majority possible—was of the utmost importance to Warren, who sought to make his Court's precedents stick. Brennan was, in every sense, Warren's ambassador.

During the subsequent tenures of Chief Justices Burger and Rehnquist (respectively, 1969–1986 and 1986–2005), the politics of the Court shifted steadily rightward, and Brennan eventually lost both his leadership role and some of his optimism. Increasingly, he found himself in the minority, and whereas he had written few dissents during the Warren years, after 1969 the number rose steadily. Brennan's closest associate became Thurgood Marshall, one of the few other remaining members of the liberal voting bloc that had been responsible for so many of the Warren Court's momentous decisions. Brennan and Marshall frequently voted together—and they always voted together against imposing the death penalty, which both men believed to be inherently unconstitutional. In later years Brennan was, nonetheless, still an influential figure, drafting important opinions for the Court on gender discrimination and affirmative action, as well as First Amendment freedoms. He retired on July 20, 1990, having written 1,360 opinions, a number bested only by his fellow Warren Court liberal William O. Douglas.

Explanation and Analysis of the Document

Prior to *Sullivan*, libel had been a matter of state rather than federal law. The U.S. Supreme Court nonetheless granted the newspaper's application for reconsideration of the state courts' decision. After the case was argued before the Court on January 6, 1964, a majority of the justices felt that the libel verdict could be dismissed on narrow ground: because the advertisement had not named Sullivan, he had not been libeled. What is more, Sullivan had failed to demonstrate how the statements in the ad had harmed him. Justice Brennan, however, approached the case differently. The Court had an opportunity to preserve the constitutional ideals enshrined in the First Amendment by making the test of libel more rigorous. A mere showing of factual error should not, in itself, provide a cause of action for libel; what was required was proof of "actual malice" behind the error. Chief Justice Earl Warren assigned Brennan to write the opinion for what would in the end be a unanimous Court.

Brennan begins by quickly disposing of Sullivan's legalistic but misguided arguments, first that the Fourteenth Amendment does not mandate that the First Amendment be applied to a civil rather than a state action, and second that even if the First Amendment applies, the protections afforded to free speech and press freedom do not, because the alleged libel appeared in a "commercial" advertisement. Brennan is also obliged to dispense with the Court's prior holdings that libel is not an essential part of any expression of ideas and is not constitutionally protected speech. He does so by arguing that libel is not in a category by itself, with "talismanic immunity" from constitutional restraints; libel must, in fact, be measured against the requirements of the First Amendment. The background of this case is of the utmost importance, for it involves a national debate on public issues that needs to be uninhibited. Such debate can involve unpleasant attacks in public. Like the long-discredited Sedition Act of 1798, the civil law of libel as applied by the Alabama court has been invalidated by "the court of history," owing to the undue restrictions it imposes on criticism of the government and public officials.

The state rule of law cannot be saved just because it allows for a defense of truthfulness. Such a defense does not simply deter false speech but leads instead to the kind of self-censorship that is especially damaging to public debate. As such, the law is at odds with the intent of the First Amendment, even as it applies to the states through the Fourteenth Amendment. What the Constitution requires is a law that permits a public official to recover damages for an allegedly libelous statement not merely because it is false but also because he is able to prove that it was made with "reckless disregard" for whether or not it was false.

Sullivan revolutionized the law of libel, making it less dependent upon formulaic, often fine distinctions between protected and unprotected speech and upon muddy distinctions between truth and untruth. What mattered henceforth were the defendant's intent and, more important, the framers' intent as embodied in the First Amendment. *Sullivan* left unanswered the question of whether the actual malice standard extended to other libel plaintiffs. A few years later, in *Curtis Publishing Co. v. Butts* (1966) and *Associated Press v. Walker* (1967), the Court extended the standard to cases involving movie stars, athletes, high-profile business executives, and other individuals well known to the public. A decade after *Sullivan*, however, in *Gertz v. Robert Welch, Inc.*, the Court limited its prior holdings, ruling that the actual malice standard did not apply to cases brought by private individuals, even when the alleged libel concerned matters of public concern.

Sullivan cannot be properly understood unless it is viewed in the context of the times in which it was decided. As numerous commentators have noted, the case is as much about civil rights as it is about free speech. As previously applied, the law of libel had been used to curtail the civil rights movement; if the Warren Court had refused to hear *Sullivan* or had left the Alabama courts' argument unanswered, not only free speech but also racial equality would have been curtailed. *Sullivan* is one of those landmark cases that truly changed history.

Impact

Before *Sullivan*, state law governed libel and defamation. The rules governing the circumstances in which individuals could recover damages for injuries to their reputations varied widely from state to state. The Court's decision in *Sullivan* transformed the field of libel and defamation law by taking it out of the hands of the states and placing it under the purview of the First Amendment protection of freedom of the press. In later rulings the Court expanded the protection of the news media to include not just lawsuits by public officials but also by other public figures, such as celebrities. Oddly, however, the decision actually met with a measure of criticism from the media, which argued that the standard may have increased the costs of defending libel cases and that it made it too difficult for people to undo the damage to their reputation, for it was difficult to demonstrate actual malice. *New York Times* columnist Anthony Lewis wrote in 1983 that "it is not just judgments that worry publishers and reporters and others concerned with freedom of expression. It is the cost of defending libel actions: the cost not only in money but in time and in the psychological burden on editors and reporters."

Questions for Further Study

1. What was the central issue in *New York Times Co. v. Sullivan*?

2. What legal test did the *Sullivan* case establish?

3. In what way did the *Sullivan* case affect the civil rights movement?

4. What impact did the *Sullivan* case have on freedom of the press in the United States?

Further Reading

Books

Barbas, Samantha. *Actual Malice: Civil Rights and Freedom of the Press in New York Times v. Sullivan*. Berkeley: University of California Press, 2023.

Burnett, Nicholas F. "*New York Times v. Sullivan*." In *Free Speech on Trial: Communication Perspectives on Landmark Supreme Court Decisions*, edited by Richard A. Parker: 116–29. Tuscaloosa: University of Alabama Press, 2003.

Fireside, Harvey. *New York Times v. Sullivan: Affirming Freedom of the Press*. Berkeley Heights, NJ: Enslow Publishers, 1999.

Hall, Kermit L., and Melvin I. Urofsky. *New York Times v. Sullivan: Civil Rights, Libel Law, and the Free Press*. Lawrence: University Press of Kansas, 2011.

Hopkins, W. Wat. *New York Times Co. v. Sullivan Forty Years Later: Retrospective, Perspective, Prospective*. (Special Issue of *Communication Law and Policy*). New York: Routledge, 2017.

Levine, Lee, and Stephen Wermiel. *The Progeny: Justice William J. Brennan's Fight to Preserve the Legacy of New York Times v. Sullivan*. Chicago: American Bar Association, 2014.

Lewis, Anthony. *Make No Law: The Sullivan Case and the First Amendment*. New York: Random House, 1991.

Smolla, Rodney A. *Suing the Press: Libel, the Media, and Power*. New York: Oxford University Press, 1986.

Articles

Lewis, Anthony. "*New York Times v. Sullivan* Reconsidered: Time to Return to 'The Central Meaning of the First Amendment.'" *Columbia Law Review* 83, no. 3 (April 1983): 603–25. https://www.jstor.org/stable/1122305.

Schmidt, Christopher. "*New York Times v. Sullivan* and the Legal Attack on the Civil Rights Movement." *Alabama Law Review* 66 (2014): 293–335. https://www.law.ua.edu/pubs/lrarticles/Volume%2066/Issue%202/Schmidt%20.pdf.

Watson, John C. "*Times v. Sullivan*: Landmark or Land Mine on the Road to Ethical Journalism?" *Journal of Mass Media Ethics* 17, no. 1 (2002): 3–19. https://www.tandfonline.com/doi/abs/10.1207/S15327728JMME1701_02.

Websites

Wermiel, Stephen. "*New York Times Co. v. Sullivan* (1964)." *First Amendment Encyclopedia*. Accessed February 25, 2023. https://www.mtsu.edu/first-amendment/article/186/new-york-times-co-v-sullivan.

—Commentary by Lisa Paddock and Michael J. O'Neal

NEW YORK TIMES CO. V. SULLIVAN

Document Text

MR. JUSTICE BRENNAN delivered the opinion of the Court

The question before us is whether this rule of liability, as applied to an action brought by a public official against critics of his official conduct, abridges the freedom of speech and of the press that is guaranteed by the First and Fourteenth Amendments.

Respondent relies heavily, as did the Alabama courts, on statements of this Court to the effect that the Constitution does not protect libelous publications. Those statements do not foreclose our inquiry here. None of the cases sustained the use of libel laws to impose sanctions upon expression critical of the official conduct of public officials. . . . In deciding the question now, we are compelled by neither precedent nor policy to give any more weight to the epithet "libel" than we have to other "mere labels" of state law. . . . Like insurrection, contempt, advocacy of unlawful acts, breach of the peace, obscenity, solicitation of legal business, and the various other formulae for the repression of expression that have been challenged in this court, libel can claim no talismanic immunity from constitutional limitations. It must be measured by standards that satisfy the First Amendment.

The general proposition that freedom of expression upon public questions is secured by the First Amendment has long been settled by our decisions. The constitutional safeguard, we have said, "was fashioned to assure unfettered interchange of ideas for the bringing about of political and social changes desired by the people." . . . Thus we consider this case against the background of a profound national commitment to the principle that debate on public issues should be uninhibited, robust, and wide-open, and that it may well include vehement, caustic, and sometimes unpleasantly sharp attacks on government and public officials. . . . The present advertisement, as an expression of grievance and protest on one of the major public issues of our time, would seem clearly to qualify for the constitutional protection. The question is whether it forfeits that protection by the falsity of some of its factual statements and by its alleged defamation of respondent.

That erroneous statement is inevitable in free debate, and . . . it must be protected if the freedoms of expression . . . are to have the "breathing space" that they "need . . . to survive." . . . Injury to official reputation affords no more warrant for repressing speech that would otherwise be free than does factual error. . . . Criticism of their official conduct does not lose its constitutional protection merely because it is effective criticism and hence diminishes their official reputations.

If neither factual error nor defamatory content suffices to remove the constitutional shield from criticism of official conduct, the combination of the two elements is no less inadequate. This is the lesson to be drawn from the great controversy over the Sedition Act of 1798, 1 Stat. 596, which first crystallized a national awareness of the central meaning of the First Amendment.

These views reflect a broad consensus that the Act, because of the restraint it imposed upon criticism of government and public officials, was inconsistent with the First Amendment.

There is no force in respondent's argument that the constitutional limitations implicit in the history of the Sedition Act apply only to Congress and not to the States.

What a State may not constitutionally bring about by means of a criminal statute is likewise beyond the reach of its civil law of libel. The fear of damage awards under a rule such as that invoked by the Alabama courts here may be markedly more inhibiting than the fear of prosecution under a criminal statute....

A rule compelling the critic of official conduct to guarantee the truth of all his factual assertions—and to do so on pain of libel judgments virtually unlimited in amount—leads to a comparable "self-censorship." Allowance of the defense of truth, with the burden of proving it on the defendant, does not mean that only false speech will be deterred. Even courts accepting this defense as an adequate safeguard have recognized the difficulties of adducing legal proofs that the alleged libel was true in all its factual particulars.... Under such a rule, would-be critics of official conduct may be deterred from voicing their criticism, even though it is believed to be true and even though it is in fact true, because of doubt whether it can be proved in court or fear of the expense of having to do so. They tend to make only statements which "steer far wider of the unlawful zone."... The rule thus dampens the vigor and limits the variety of public debate. It is inconsistent with the First and Fourteenth Amendments.

The constitutional guarantees require, we think, a federal rule that prohibits a public official from recovering damages for a defamatory falsehood relating to his official conduct unless he proves that the statement was made ... with "actual malice"—that is, with knowledge that it was false or with reckless disregard of whether it was false or not.

We conclude that such a privilege is required by the First and Fourteenth Amendments.

Glossary

defamation: the communication of demonstrably false information concerning a party, thus giving that party legal standing to bring a lawsuit on the issue

foreclose: bring an end to

libelous: characterized by a demonstrable effort to bring libel, or the issuing, in the form of writing or some other physical representation, of deliberately false information about another party

precedent: a past case whose outcome provides a model for dealing with similar cases in the future

respondent: the party against whom a lawsuit is brought by another party, the petitioner

Sedition Act of 1798: one of the four Alien and Sedition Acts, a body of legislation issued under President John Adams that became notorious for its assault on civil liberties as a means of stifling disagreement with the administration

talismanic immunity: a legal "free pass" or "get-out-of-jail-free card"

GRISWOLD V. CONNECTICUT

DATE	CITATION
1965	381 U.S. 479
AUTHOR	**SIGNIFICANCE**
William O. Douglas	Paved the way for reproductive rights and established a constitutional right to privacy among married couples
VOTE	
7–2	

Overview

During Justice William O. Douglas's years on the Supreme Court bench, a variety of cases came before the Court that affected American life in fundamental ways, including in the areas of individual and civil rights. Justice Douglas sat on the Court during a tumultuous and pivotal time in American history that was marked by major international conflicts, such as World War II, the Cold War, and the Vietnam War, as well as major domestic movements, most notably the civil rights movement. His opinions demonstrate his judicial priorities—protection of civil and individual rights, including the right to privacy; near-absolute deference to the First Amendment; and environmental protection.

Douglas addressed cases not just from within the narrow confines of case-law precedent but also from what he saw as the social ramifications of the particular questions contested in the cases. The Supreme Court case *Griswold v. Connecticut* overturned the conviction of Estelle Griswold and C. Lee Buxton for violating an 1879 Connecticut law that prohibited the provision of contraceptive devices, medicines, or ad-

vice—even to married couples. The case definitively established a constitutional right to privacy among married couples.

Although Douglas found the Connecticut law offensive, in his dissent Hugo Black took issue with the concept that privacy was a right founded in any part of the Constitution. Although Black's dim view of unstated constitutional rights, such as the right to privacy he decries in *Griswold*, seemed out of step with the times in 1965, that opinion has since found favor with many who have been obliged to revisit one of the nation's most hotly contested issues: abortion and women's reproductive rights.

Context

Griswold remains a seminal case because it is seen as paving the way for reproductive rights. Most state laws in place at the time of the decision were drafted in the late 1800s and restricted the sale or advertisement of any type of contraception. At the time, the laws in both Connecticut and Massachusetts made the use of contraception illegal. The Connecticut law at issue penal-

Estelle Griswold
(Wikimedia Commons)

ized offenders with a fine of $50 and up to one year in jail. The law banned not only the individual who used contraception but also anyone who aided, abetted, or assisted another in using or obtaining contraception. Many such state laws were derived from Catholic religious canons on marriage. A bitter, forty-five-year battle attempted to eliminate Connecticut's birth-control statute, which was considered by many to be one of the most oppressive in the nation. The Connecticut state legislature had consistently been victorious until the decision in *Griswold*.

In 1961 Estelle Griswold, executive director of Planned Parenthood of Connecticut, and Dr. C. Lee Buxton, chair of the Department of Obstetrics at Yale School of Medicine, opened a clinic in New Haven, Connecticut, to challenge the state law banning contraception. Both were frustrated at the criminalization of a health issue. The clinic provided information and medical advice to married couples about contraception. Wives were also examined and given advice on various forms of contraception. After the clinic had been open for just ten days, both Griswold and Buxton were arrested and charged with violating the Connecticut anticontraception law. Both were found guilty and charged a fine of $100. The

lower courts affirmed their convictions, and the US Supreme Court accepted the matter for review.

Lawyers for Griswold and Buxton argued to the Supreme Court that the law violated the Fourteenth Amendment, which states in part, "No state shall make or enforce any law which shall abridge the privileges or immunities of citizens of the United States; nor shall any State deprive any person of life, liberty, or property, without due process of law; nor deny to any person the equal protection of the laws." After the hearing, the Supreme Court ruled in favor of Griswold and Buxton in a 7–2 vote.

The majority opinion held that there is a right to privacy in marriage that is included within the "penumbra" of the Bill of Rights. Since the justices could not find that a specific portion of the Bill of Rights applied, the majority had to determine whether an unexpressed, implied constitutional right was violated. The difficulty in reaching this determination is evidenced by the fact that there was a majority opinion written by Justice Douglas and a concurring opinion written by Justice Arthur Goldberg, in which he was joined by Chief Justice Earl Warren and Justice William J. Brennan. Justices John Marshall Harlan II and Byron White each wrote separate opinions concurring in the judgment. Justice Black and Justice Potter Stewart each wrote dissenting opinions. They both argued that the government has a right to invade an individual's privacy unless there is a specific constitutional provision that says they cannot and that there is no marital privacy right in the Constitution.

It is important to note that the *Griswold* opinion applied only to married couples and was not applied to unmarried people until the Court's decision in *Eisenstadt v. Baird* in 1972. However, *Griswold* opened the door to increasing court precedent establishing individual privacy rights.

About the Author

William O. Douglas

Douglas was born on October 16, 1898, in Maine, Minnesota, the son of Julia Fisk Douglas and the Reverend William Douglas. Following her husband's death in 1904, Julia moved the family to Yakima, Washington, where she purchased a small home before losing much of the family's money in a failed land investment. Growing up poor and working odd jobs from the age of seven, Douglas developed an appreciation for hard work and a strong sense of class justice that later influenced his belief that all citizens should be entitled to the same rights and privileges. Douglas went to nearby Whitman College, where he graduated in 1920. After spending time teaching, he enrolled at Columbia Law School in 1922. He graduated second in his class and began working at one of Wall Street's most prestigious law firms, Cravath, Henderson & de Gersdorff. After leaving Wall Street, Douglas taught at Columbia and then Yale Law School. He strongly supported President Franklin Roosevelt's New Deal program and left Yale to go to Washington to champion Roosevelt's policies, eventually becoming chairman of the Securities and Exchange Commission in 1937.

Douglas became the second-youngest Supreme Court justice in history when he was appointed by President Roosevelt and confirmed on April 4, 1939. Justice Douglas was one of the more competitive and naturally contrarian justices ever to serve on the Supreme Court. He set the record for the longest term on the Supreme Court bench and, in his more than thirty-five years at the Court, authored 531 dissents. His legal philosophy was strongly influenced by Underhill Moore, his professor at Columbia Law, and by Louis D. Brandeis, the justice whose place Douglas took on the Supreme Court. In his opinions, Douglas drew upon sources as varied as poetry, sociology, agricultural reports, and his own intuition to support his decisions, reflecting the realist belief that "real world" information needed to be considered in rendering legal decisions rather than relying exclusively on legal precedent.

Douglas is often said to have been an ecologist before there was such a thing, and his love of nature and the pristine wilderness was evident in several notable and even controversial opinions in major Supreme Court cases with respect to environmental concerns. Washington's William O. Douglas National Wilderness is named in his honor, in recognition of his efforts on behalf of the environment. Spending so much time in the outdoors sharpened Douglas's appreciation for unspoiled nature, which he maintained for the remainder of his life. He even intervened personally to save the Chesapeake and Ohio Canal from being turned into a highway.

Justice William O. Douglas
(Wikimedia Commons)

Douglas's Supreme Court opinions were typically short and, to the extent that they were influenced by personal beliefs rather than established case law, had very little precedential value. However, *Griswold v. Connecticut* stands out as one of the seminal cases with respect to individual privacy rights. Douglas died on January 19, 1980.

Hugo Black

Hugo Lafayette Black was a son of the South, born on February 27, 1886, in rural Harlan, Alabama, and raised in the town of Ashland, Alabama. After initially enrolling in medical school, Black instead attended the University of Alabama Law School. After graduating, he returned to Ashland and set up a law practice representing small businesses and individuals. After serving in the military briefly in World War I, he returned to Ashland, where his law practice began to thrive. Although he frequently represented African Americans in his practice, he joined the Ku Klux Klan in 1923, thinking that it would help him advance politically. He later regretted the decision and resigned two years later when he began his campaign to represent Alabama as a senator; he successfully won a seat in the US Senate in 1926 despite his lack of experience.

In the U.S. Senate, Black pursued a populist agenda, vigorously investigating improper ties between government and business and pushing for a thirty-hour workweek. His ardent support for the New Deal—and, in particular, for Franklin Roosevelt—attracted the president's attention. In 1937 Roosevelt nominated Black to the Supreme Court. His nomination led to the public revelation of his membership in the Ku Klux Klan. Black confronted the issue head on by making a public confession over the radio, declaring that he had had no connection with the Klan for more than a dozen years and that he had no intention of having any further association with the organization. Black was confirmed to the Supreme Court and sworn in on August 18, 1937.

Black's commitment to individual rights was based on his literalist approach to the historical intent of the framers of the Constitution. Despite this literalist approach, he joined a growing, more liberal majority on the Court that reversed previous vetoes of New Deal legislation. He also promoted free speech rights and dissented on cases that limited rights of core free speech liberties. In the 1960s he was one of the liberal majority that struck down mandatory school prayer in *Engel v. Vitale*. He was also in the majority in an opinion that guaranteed legal counsel to suspected criminals in *Gideon v. Wainwright*. Despite his more liberal views, he refused to support rights that others read into the Constitution without literal, written evidence to support their position. In *Griswold v. Connecticut*, Black was ardently opposed to the majority's extension of a broad right of marital privacy. Black became more conservative during his last years on the bench but did support the right of the *New York Times* to publish the *Pentagon Papers* in *New York Times Co. v. United States* (1971). Black retired in 1971 after thirty-four years on the bench, making him one of the longest-serving justices on the Court. He died just eight days after he retired, on September 25.

Explanation and Analysis of the Document

Majority Opinion written by Associate Justice William O. Douglas

In 1961 Estelle Griswold, executive director of the Planned Parenthood League of Connecticut, and Dr. C. Lee Buxton, a doctor and professor at Yale Medical School, opened a birth-control clinic in New Haven, Connecticut. The clinic faced controversy immediately and was shut down within days. Griswold and Buxton were arrested and convicted of breaking an 1879 Connecticut law that prohibited provision of contraceptive devices, medicines, or advice, including to married couples. The pair appealed their conviction to the Supreme Court, which decided by a vote of seven to two in their favor, striking down the Connecticut law and establishing a constitutional right to privacy among married couples.

Griswold is Douglas's most controversial opinion and his most enduring. It is frequently cited as a case of judicial activism, a charge somewhat buoyed by the fact that three concurring opinions were filed along with Douglas's majority opinion, all of which disagreed with Douglas's as to the extent of the right of privacy and where that right is located. Douglas's language is also particularly esoteric, finding the right to privacy in the "penumbras" (implications) created by the "emanations" of certain rights specifically articulated in the Bill of Rights.

Despite its esoteric language, however, *Griswold* represents a crystallization of Douglas's thought process with regard to privacy, a subject on which he had been writing for several years by this point. In 1958 Douglas had published *The Right of the People*, a collection of lectures he had given at Franklin and Marshall College in the spring of 1957. In "The Right to Privacy," he states that citizens have the right to privacy in matters of religion and conscience and within their own homes. In language foreshadowing the *Griswold* decision, he argues that "penumbras" of the Bill of Rights render these rights implicit, even though privacy is not mentioned explicitly. These penumbras form the basis for Douglas's articulation of the right to privacy in *Griswold*.

In the majority opinion, Douglas defines marriage as an "association" and argues that because the Supreme Court already had found a right to privacy in associations, marriage was likewise protected. The majority also held that the Third Amendment's prohibition against forced quartering of soldiers, the Fourth Amendment's protection against unreasonable searches and seizures, the Fifth Amendment's self-incrimination clause, and the Ninth Amendment's provision that rights not specifically named are reserved to the people combine to create a broad constitutional right to privacy. The Court was especially concerned with the right to privacy in one's own home and upheld the Court's decision in *Mapp v. Ohio* (1961).

Dissenting Opinion written by Justice Hugo Black

Like the majority of the Court, Justice Black thought the Connecticut law offensive and unwise. However, he did not think the statute unconstitutional. He disagreed with the notion that the statute violated the First Amendment, for what was at issue in the case was not speech but conduct. He also would not buy in to the notion that just as the First Amendment had been expanded to suggest a freedom of association not spelled out in the Constitution, other amendments implied a right to privacy.

In his dissent, Black expresses distaste for the majority's endorsement of a newfound right forged as an "emanation" from enumerated rights, a point he drives home by stating baldly, "I like my privacy as well as the next one, but I am nevertheless compelled to admit that government has a right to invade it unless prohibited by some specific constitutional provision."

Black reserves his most withering criticism for the due process, Ninth Amendment, and natural law arguments advanced in concurring opinions signed by Justices Harlan, White, and Goldberg. The various lines of argument are, Black says, essentially the same and suffer from the same fatal flaw: all are too broad, bereft of specificity. More to the point, the adoption of any of these arguments would lead to the Court's appropriation of the lawmaking power: "Surely it has to be admitted that no provision of the Constitution specifically gives such blanket power to courts to exercise such a supervisory veto over the wisdom and value of legislative policies and to hold unconstitutional those laws which they believe unwise or dangerous."

Finally, the Black dissent addresses those who argue for new rights as a means of keeping the Constitution up to date. Justice Black believed changes to the Constitution through the adoption of amendments was the province of the people through the legislature and not for the judiciary.

Impact

The majority in *Griswold* held that marriage is an intimate, sacred association, one that ideally will endure. Despite critics' condemnation of the holding as judicial activism, *Griswold* was a monumental decision, which provided the basis for later watershed right-to-privacy cases.

As *Griswold* applied only to married couples, birth control was still illegal for unmarried individuals. The Supreme Court in 1972 extended birth-control rights to unmarried people in *Eisenstadt v. Baird*. In *Eisenstadt*, the people charged with violating an anticontraception law argued that allowing married people to use contraception but not allowing unmarried people to prevent unwarranted pregnancies violated the equal protection clause of the Fourteenth Amendment. That clause provides that no state can "deny to any person within its jurisdiction the equal protection of the laws." *Griswold* is significant for having laid a foundation for privacy rights to be applied to reproductive freedom, moving the law away from its religious roots of promoting procreation and more toward the secular notion of being able to control one's reproductive health. The case opinion set the wheels in motion for the total legalization of birth control in *Eisenstadt*.

The argument in *Griswold* concerning the right to privacy in reproduction helped pave the way for a multitude of other cases involving privacy, including the legalization of abortion in *Roe v. Wade* (1973), which used Justice Harlan's "due process privacy" argument from his concurrence in *Griswold* to strike down laws prohibiting abortion. *Griswold* also was referenced in decisions to grant the right to contraception for juveniles at least sixteen years of age in *Carey v. Population Services International* (1977), the right to consensual sex between same-sex adults in *Lawrence v. Texas* (2003), and the right to same-sex marriage in *Obergefell v. Hodges* (2015). It is also important to note that this is not a settled area of the law, as states continue to pass antireproduction laws that are being brought to the Supreme Court to this day. Although it is still a controversial matter, the right to privacy articulated in *Griswold* continues to be an important judicial idea.

Questions for Further Study

1. According to Justice Douglas's majority opinion, how does the freedom to associate as held in *NAACP v. Alabama* relate to the privacy interests in *Griswold*?

2. How did Douglas's opinion discuss government action in the context of family privacy?

3. What are some of the ways family privacy rights set forth in *Griswold* can be applied to other individual privacy rights? Are there ways in which the state interferes with family privacy today?

Further Reading

Books

Douglas, William O. *The Right of the People*. Garden City, NY: Doubleday, 1958.

Haugeberg, Karissa. *Women against Abortion: Inside the Largest Moral Reform Movement of the Twentieth Century*. Champaign: University of Illinois Press, 2017.

Igo, Sarah E. *The Known Citizen: A History of Privacy in Modern America*. Boston: Harvard University Press, 2018.

Articles

Brown, Anne B. "The Evolving Definition of Marriage." *Suffolk University Law Review* 31 (1998): 917–944.

Katin, Ernest. "*Griswold v. Connecticut*: The Justices and Connecticut's Uncommonly Silly Law." *Notre Dame Law Review* 42, no. 5 (1967): 680–706.

Websites

Grossman, Joanna L. "*Griswold v. Connecticut*: The Start of the Revolution." Justia, June 8, 2015. https://verdict.justia.com/2015/06/08/griswold-v-connecticut-the-start-of-the-revolution.

—Commentary by David Simonelli

GRISWOLD V. CONNECTICUT

Document Text

William O. Douglas: Opinion

Appellant Griswold is Executive Director of the Planned Parenthood League of Connecticut. Appellant Buxton is a licensed physician and a professor at the Yale Medical School who served as Medical Director for the League at its Center in New Haven—a center open and operating from November 1 to November 10, 1961, when appellants were arrested.

They gave information, instruction, and medical advice to married persons as to the means of preventing conception. They examined the wife and prescribed the best contraceptive device or material for her use. Fees were usually charged, although some couples were serviced free....

The association of people is not mentioned in the Constitution nor in the Bill of Rights. The right to educate a child in a school of the parents' choice—whether public or private or parochial—is also not mentioned. Nor is the right to study any particular subject or any foreign language. Yet the First Amendment has been construed to include certain of those rights....

In *NAACP v. Alabama*, we protected the "freedom to associate and privacy in one's associations," noting that freedom of association was a peripheral First Amendment right.... In other words, the First Amendment has a penumbra where privacy is protected from governmental intrusion. In like context, we have protected forms of "association" that are not political in the customary sense, but pertain to the social, legal, and economic benefit of the members....

Those cases involved more than the "right of assembly"—a right that extends to all, irrespective of their race or ideology. The right of "association," like the right of belief, is more than the right to attend a meeting; it includes the right to express one's attitudes or philosophies by membership in a group or by affiliation with it or by other lawful means. Association in that context is a form of expression of opinion, and, while it is not expressly included in the First Amendment, its existence is necessary in making the express guarantees fully meaningful.

The foregoing cases suggest that specific guarantees in the Bill of Rights have penumbras, formed by emanations from those guarantees that help give them life and substance. Various guarantees create zones of privacy. The right of association contained in the penumbra of the First Amendment is one, as we have seen. The Third Amendment, in its prohibition against the quartering of soldiers "in any house" in time of peace without the consent of the owner, is another facet of that privacy. The Fourth Amendment explicitly affirms the "right of the people to be secure in their persons, houses, papers, and effects, against unreasonable searches and seizures." The Fifth Amendment, in its Self-Incrimination Clause, enables the citizen to create a zone of privacy which government may not force him to surrender to his detriment. The Ninth Amendment provides: "The enumeration in the Constitution, of certain rights, shall not be construed to deny or disparage others retained by the people."

The Fourth and Fifth Amendments were described in *Boyd v. United States* as protection against all governmental invasions "of the sanctity of a man's home and the privacies of life," ... the Fourth Amendment as creating a "right to privacy, no less important than any other right carefully and particularly reserved to the people."

We have had many controversies over these penumbral rights of "privacy and repose." ... These cases bear witness that the right of privacy which presses for recognition here is a legitimate one.

The present case, then, concerns a relationship lying within the zone of privacy created by several fundamental constitutional guarantees. And it concerns a law which, in forbidding the use of contraceptives, rather than regulating their manufacture or sale, seeks to achieve its goals by means having a maximum destructive impact upon that relationship. Such a law cannot stand in light of the familiar principle, so often applied by this Court, that a "governmental purpose to control or prevent activities constitutionally subject to state regulation may not be achieved by means which sweep unnecessarily broadly and thereby invade the area of protected freedoms [*NAACP v. Alabama*]."

Would we allow the police to search the sacred precincts of marital bedrooms for telltale signs of the use of contraceptives? The very idea is repulsive to the notions of privacy surrounding the marriage relationship.

We deal with a right of privacy older than the Bill of Rights—older than our political parties, older than our school system. Marriage is a coming together for better or for worse, hopefully enduring, and intimate to the degree of being sacred. It is an association that promotes a way of life, not causes; a harmony in living, not political faiths; a bilateral loyalty, not commercial or social projects. Yet it is an association for as noble a purpose as any involved in our prior decisions.

Hugo Black: Dissent

I agree with my Brother STEWART'S dissenting opinion. And like him I do not to any extent whatever base my view that this Connecticut law is constitutional on a belief that the law is wise or that its policy is a good one....

Had the doctor defendant here, or even the nondoctor defendant, been convicted for doing nothing more than expressing opinions to persons coming to the clinic that certain contraceptive devices, medicines or practices would do them good and would be desirable, or for telling people how devices could be used, I can think of no reasons at this time why their expressions of views would not be protected by the First and Fourteenth Amendments, which guarantee freedom of speech.... But speech is one thing; conduct and physical activities are quite another.... Strongly as I desire to protect all First Amendment freedoms, I am unable to stretch the Amendment so as to afford protection to the conduct of these defendants in violating the Connecticut law....

The Court talks about a constitutional "right of privacy" as though there is some constitutional provision or provisions forbidding any law ever to be passed which might abridge the "privacy" of individuals. But there is not. There are, of course, guarantees in certain specific constitutional provisions which are designed in part to protect privacy at certain times and places with respect to certain activities. Such, for example, is the Fourth Amendment's guarantee against "unreasonable searches and seizures." But I think it belittles that Amendment to talk about it as though it protects nothing but "privacy." To treat it that way is to give it a niggardly interpretation, not the kind of liberal reading I think any Bill of Rights provision should be given. The average man would very likely not have his feelings soothed any more by having his property seized openly than by having it seized privately and by stealth. He simply wants his property left alone. And a person can be just as much, if not more, irritated, annoyed and injured by an unceremonious public arrest by a policeman as he is by a seizure in the privacy of his office or home.

One of the most effective ways of diluting or expanding a constitutionally guaranteed right is to substitute for the crucial word or words of a constitutional guarantee another word or words, more or less flexible and more or less restricted in meaning. This fact is well illustrated by the use of the term "right of privacy" as a comprehensive substitute for the Fourth Amendment's guarantee against "unreasonable searches and seizures." "Privacy" is a broad, abstract and ambiguous concept which can easily be shrunken in meaning but which can also, on the other hand, easily be interpreted as a constitutional ban against many things other than searches and seizures. I have expressed the view many times that First Amendment freedoms, for example, have suffered from a failure of the courts to stick to the simple language of the First Amendment in construing it, instead of invoking multitudes of words substituted for those the Framers used.... For these reasons I get nowhere in this case by talk about a constitutional "right of privacy" as an emanation from one or more constitutional provisions. I like my privacy as well as the next one, but I am nevertheless compelled to admit that government has a right to invade it unless prohibited by some specific constitutional provision. For these reasons I cannot agree with the Court's judgment and the reasons it gives for holding this Connecticut law unconstitutional....

I have no doubt that the Connecticut law could be applied in such a way as to abridge freedom of speech and press and therefore violate the First and Fourteenth Amendments. My disagreement with the Court's opinion holding that there is such a violation here is a narrow one, relating to the application of the First Amendment to the facts and circumstances of this particular case. But my disagreement with Brothers HARLAN, WHITE and GOLDBERG is more basic. I think that if properly construed neither the Due Process Clause nor the Ninth Amendment, nor both together, could under any circumstances be a proper basis for invalidating the Connecticut law. I discuss the due process and Ninth Amendment arguments together because on analysis they turn out to be the same thing merely using different words to claim for this Court and the federal judiciary power to invalidate any legislative act which the judges find irrational, unreasonable or offensive.

The due process argument which my Brothers HARLAN and WHITE adopt here is based, as their opinions indicate, on the premise that this Court is vested with power to invalidate all state laws that it considers to be arbitrary, capricious, unreasonable, or oppressive, or on this Court's belief that a particular state law under scrutiny has no "rational or justifying" purpose, or is offensive to a "sense of fairness and justice." If these formulas based on "natural justice," or others which mean the same thing, are to prevail, they require judges to determine what is or is not constitutional on the basis of their own appraisal of what laws are unwise or unnecessary. The power to make such decisions is of course that of a legislative body. Surely it has to be admitted that no provision of the Constitution specifically gives such blanket power to courts to exercise such a supervisory veto over the wisdom and value of

legislative policies and to hold unconstitutional those laws which they believe unwise or dangerous. I readily admit that no legislative body, state or national, should pass laws that can justly be given any of the invidious labels invoked as constitutional excuses to strike down state laws. But perhaps it is not too much to say that no legislative body ever does pass laws without believing that they will accomplish a sane, rational, wise and justifiable purpose. While I completely subscribe to the holding of *Marbury v. Madison* and subsequent cases, that our Court has constitutional power to strike down statutes, state or federal, that violate commands of the Federal Constitution, I do not believe that we are granted power by the Due Process Clause or any other constitutional provision or provisions to measure constitutionality by our belief that legislation is arbitrary, capricious or unreasonable, or accomplishes no justifiable purpose, or is offensive to our own notions of "civilized standards of conduct." Such an appraisal of the wisdom of legislation is an attribute of the power to make laws, not of the power to interpret them. The use by federal courts of such a formula or doctrine or whatnot to veto federal or state laws simply takes away from Congress and States the power to make laws based on their own judgment of fairness and wisdom and transfers that power to this Court for ultimate determination—a power which was specifically denied to federal courts by the convention that framed the Constitution....

My Brother GOLDBERG has adopted the recent discovery that the Ninth Amendment as well as the Due Process Clause can be used by this Court as authority to strike down all state legislation which this Court thinks violates "fundamental principles of liberty and justice," or is contrary to the "traditions and [collective] conscience of our people." He also states, without proof satisfactory to me, that in making decisions on this basis judges will not consider "their personal and private notions." One may ask how they can avoid considering them. Our Court certainly has no machinery with which to take a Gallup Poll. And the scientific miracles of this age have not yet produced a gadget which the Court can use to determine what traditions are rooted in the "[collective] conscience of our people." Moreover, one would certainly have to look far beyond the language of the Ninth Amendment to find that the Framers vested in this Court any such awesome veto powers over lawmaking, either by the States or by the Congress. Nor does anything in the history of the Amendment offer any support for such a shocking doctrine. The whole history of the adoption of the Constitution and Bill of Rights points the other way, and the very material quoted by my Brother GOLDBERG shows that the Ninth Amendment was intended to protect against the idea that "by enumerating particular exceptions to the grant of power" to the Federal Government, "those rights which were not singled out, were intended to be assigned into the hands of the General Government [the United States], and were consequently insecure." That Amendment was passed, not to broaden the powers of this Court or any other department of "the General Government," but, as every student of history knows, to assure the people that the Constitution in all its provisions was intended to limit the Federal Government to the powers granted expressly or by necessary implication. If any broad, unlimited power to hold laws unconstitutional because they offend what this Court conceives to be the "[collective] conscience of our people" is vested in this Court by the Ninth Amendment, the Fourteenth Amendment, or any other provision of the Constitution, it was not given by the Framers, but rather has been bestowed on the Court by the Court. This fact is perhaps responsible for the peculiar phenomenon that for a period of a century and a half no serious suggestion was ever made that the Ninth Amendment, enacted to protect state powers against federal invasion, could be used as a weapon of federal power to prevent state legislatures from passing laws they consider appropriate to govern local affairs. Use of any such broad, unbounded judicial authority would make of this Court's members a day-to-day constitutional convention.

I repeat so as not to be misunderstood that this Court does have power, which it should exercise, to hold laws unconstitutional where they are forbidden by the Federal Constitution. My point is that there is no provision of the Constitution which either expressly or impliedly vests power in this Court to sit as a supervisory agency over acts of duly constituted legislative bodies and set aside their laws because of the Court's belief that the legislative policies adopted are unreasonable, unwise, arbitrary, capricious or irrational. The adoption of

such a loose, flexible, uncontrolled standard for holding laws unconstitutional, if ever it is finally achieved, will amount to a great unconstitutional shift of power to the courts which I believe and am constrained to say will be bad for the courts and worse for the country. Subjecting federal and state laws to such an unrestrained and unrestrainable judicial control as to the wisdom of legislative enactments would, I fear, jeopardize the separation of governmental powers that the Framers set up and at the same time threaten to take away much of the power of States to govern themselves which the Constitution plainly intended them to have.

I realize that many good and able men have eloquently spoken and written, sometimes in rhapsodical strains, about the duty of this Court to keep the Constitution in tune with the times. The idea is that the Constitution must be changed from time to time and that this Court is charged with a duty to make those changes. For myself, I must with all deference reject that philosophy. The Constitution makers knew the need for change and provided for it. Amendments suggested by the people's elected representatives can be submitted to the people or their selected agents for ratification. That method of change was good for our Fathers, and being somewhat old-fashioned I must add it is good enough for me. And so, I cannot rely on the Due Process Clause or the Ninth Amendment or any mysterious and uncertain natural law concept as a reason for striking down this state law. The Due Process Clause with an "arbitrary and capricious" or "shocking to the conscience" formula was liberally used by this Court to strike down economic legislation in the early decades of this century, threatening, many people thought, the tranquility and stability of the Nation. . . . That formula, based on subjective considerations of "natural justice," is no less dangerous when used to enforce this Court's views about personal rights than those about economic rights. I had thought that we had laid that formula, as a means for striking down state legislation, to rest once and for all. . . .

So far as I am concerned, Connecticut's law as applied here is not forbidden by any provision of the Federal Constitution as that Constitution was written, and I would therefore affirm.

Glossary

affirm: agree; in the language of the Supreme Court, to agree with the disputed judgment of a lower court

agents: elected representatives

appellant: the party appealing, or asking for a reconsideration of, a decision by a lower court

construing: interpreting

Due Process Clause: a guarantee in the Fifth and Fourteenth Amendments that an individual accused of a crime has a right to be formally charged and tried

emanations: things that arise from a particular source

HARLAN, WHITE and GOLDBERG: John Marshall Harlan (1899–1971), Byron White (1917–2002), and Arthur Goldberg (1908–1990)—associate justices of the Supreme Court (1955–1971, 1962–1993, and 1962–1965, respectively)

insecure: not guaranteed

liberal reading: open-minded interpretation

my Brother STEWART: Potter Stewart (1915–1985), associate justice of the Supreme Court from 1958 to 1981; "brother" being a term used to refer to colleagues on the Court

niggardly: stingy, small-minded

Ninth Amendment: the amendment that guarantees that the listing of specific rights in the Constitution does not mean that other rights are denied to citizens

parochial: related to a church

penumbra: body of rights considered to be guaranteed by implication

rhapsodical strains: tones of overwhelming and unthinking excitement

BOND V. FLOYD

DATE
1966

AUTHOR
Earl Warren

VOTE
9–0

CITATION
385 U.S. 116

SIGNIFICANCE
Held that legislators retain all of the First Amendment protections that citizens retain, including the right to dissent.

Overview

Argued on November 10, 1966, and decided on December 5, 1966, the case of *Bond v. Floyd* is probably best known for its result: stopping the Georgia House of Representatives from refusing to seat Julian Bond, an elected representative, based on his opposition to the Vietnam War. However, its import far outstrips its result. The opinion holds that legislators enjoy all of the First Amendment protections that citizens enjoy, including the right to dissent, and that their exercise of those rights allows constituents to know whether they are properly representing the constituents' interests. The U.S Supreme Court's conception of the role of the First Amendment in fostering a healthy relationship between legislator and constituent led to its judgment that legislatures are not allowed to refuse to seat a dissenter merely because the other members of the legislature do not like what the dissenting legislator says. This opinion guaranteed that candidates for office and elected legislators, including African Americans, who were just beginning to be elected in reasonable numbers at the time, could openly dissent on issues of foreign and domestic policy without worrying about whether they could be blocked from taking their seats because of their political views.

Context

The broad context of *Bond v. Floyd* involves the way in which dissent on American foreign policy by legislators is tolerated and how legislators may treat fellow legislators who dissent from the prevailing views. Legislators may be treated poorly by fellow legislators and by their constituents as a result of their dissenting views. However, it was unclear at the time whether a legislature could use its power to judge the qualifications of its members in order to refuse to seat a duly elected member merely for his or her opposition to war and dissent on foreign policy.

The narrow context of *Bond v. Floyd* involved the convergence of three powerful forces in 1960s America: the civil rights movement, anti–Vietnam War sentiment, and the push toward equally populous districts that would lead to the election of African American candidates in significant numbers for the first time since Reconstruction. Julian Bond, a leader in the Student Nonviolent Coordinating Committee (SNCC)—a major civil rights organization in the 1960s—endorsed SNCC's anti–Vietnam War statements and was consequently denied a seat in the Georgia legislature after being elected to a district that was created as a result.

War and civil rights had been linked for many generations prior to *Bond v. Floyd*. Whether the war at issue was the Civil War, World War I, or World War II, some discussion of the need for adequate civil rights for African American soldiers and African Americans in general had taken place. In these earlier wars, the demand for equal civil rights accompanied support for the war. The Vietnam War was different. Many who fought for civil rights at home questioned whether it made sense for African Americans to fight in the war when they did not have equal rights at home, particularly given that the Vietnam War was ostensibly being fought to keep or make Vietnam free. The linkage between support of civil rights and dissent on American war policy allowed some to renew their contempt for civil rights and for those who supported equality. Others thought that civil rights supporters should stick to advocating for civil rights and should not comment on war or foreign policy.

The struggle for Vietnam had been ongoing for years before the United States committed substantial emotional and physical resources in 1964. The escalation of America's role occurred in the wake of the Gulf of Tonkin resolution, which authorized President Lyndon Johnson to use force in Vietnam. Over the next year, President Johnson ordered significant aerial bombing of Vietnam, sent tens of thousands of troops to Vietnam, and authorized many tens of thousands more.

This escalation came at a momentous time for the civil rights movement. The Civil Rights Act of 1964, the most sweeping civil rights bill since Reconstruction, had been passed in no small measure because of President Johnson's support. Through a series of cases, the Supreme Court had declared that one-man, one-vote was required under the Constitution, leading to the redrawing of district lines to guarantee that districts would consist of equal populations. This redistricting promised that—if African Americans were allowed to vote—areas with high concentrations of African American citizens would be able to elect representatives to their liking for the first time in many years, if ever. The eventual passage of the Voting Rights Act of 1965 helped ensure that African Americans would be allowed to vote in areas of the country where their electoral voices had been stifled for years. American life was becoming relatively more equal and democratic. However, civil rights organizations, their leaders, and many others recognized that the United States had far to go before its citizens would become truly equal. This is why the

Julian Bond in 2000
(Wikimedia Commons)

U.S. claim that the war was being fought to guarantee freedom to the people of Vietnam struck a discordant note to some in civil rights organizations and triggered dissent. Some dissenters were philosophically opposed to war. Others were opposed to this particular war. In sum, the dissent was significant.

In August 1965 Martin Luther King, Jr., spoke out against U.S. involvement in the Vietnam War. Although some might have thought that the 1964 Nobel Peace Prize winner would understandably speak out against war, others argued that he should stick to civil rights rather than opine on American foreign policy. Nonetheless, King specifically linked civil rights and the war in Vietnam. His outspokenness was not appreciated by President Johnson or by some of his own supporters. Undaunted, King continued to oppose the war. Other civil rights leaders and organizations would speak out against the war when they deemed the time was right. In early 1966 SNCC did just that. It was their statement opposing the war that led directly to *Bond v. Floyd*.

When private citizens dissented with respect to the Vietnam War in particular and American foreign policy in general, legislators could do little to stop them.

Vietnam War protest in front of the White House
(Library of Congress)

The First Amendment clearly protected the right to dissent. Indeed, legislators arguably had little reason to pay attention to the dissenters as long as the dissent did not involve violence. However, legislators could take additional interest if those dissenters were going to become colleagues. Julian Bond's criticism of American foreign policy and the Vietnam War as he was about to take office put him in the category of potential legislator-dissenter.

Julian Bond was elected to the Georgia legislature in 1965 in a special election that was required when Georgia had to redraw its electoral districts as a result of the Supreme Court's one-man, one-vote jurisprudence. Before he was sworn in, he noted his support for an official statement made by SNCC in January 1966 regarding opposition to the Vietnam War. Bond was the communications director of SNCC and a supporter from the organization's early days, but he had not drafted the statement. The statement was issued in response to the murder of Samuel Younge, Jr. (misspelled "Young" in the document), a member of SNCC and a Tuskegee In-

stitute student who was killed in January 1966 for using the segregated bathroom at a Tuskegee gas station. The statement indicated SNCC's disapproval of American foreign policy as expressed in the country's involvement in the Vietnam War. The statement linked freedom at home with freedom abroad, suggesting that the U.S. government's claims to fight for freedom overseas appeared to be at odds with its refusal to fight for freedom at home. The statement also linked Younge's struggle for freedom and his ultimate death with the Vietnamese peasants' fight for freedom and potential death. SNCC's statement ultimately suggested that Americans ought to be allowed to avoid the military draft by working with organizations in the United States that sought to build democracy here.

A number of members of the Georgia legislature wanted to refuse to seat Bond because of his support for the statement and his opposition to the Vietnam War. It could be argued that the legislators merely claimed that Bond could not honestly take the oath of office and therefore could not be seated. However, whether Bond could profess support for the U.S. Constitution and the Georgia constitution, as required by the oath, was inextricably linked to the substance of the debate about the Vietnam War. The Court decided that whether a legislator could sincerely take an oath was to be decided by the legislator alone, not by the legislator's peers.

About the Author

Born on March 19, 1891, in Los Angeles, California, Earl Warren was chief justice of the United States from 1953 to 1969. Warren grew up in Bakersfield, California, the son of parents who were born in Scandinavia and raised in the United States. During his youth, Warren worked for the Southern Pacific Railroad as a call boy rounding up crews for the railroad. That experience exposed him to working men and labor issues in a way that some have suggested shaped his thoughts on the law, if not his entire outlook on life. After graduating from high school in 1908, he attended the University of California at Berkeley and its law school, Boalt Hall. Despite his discomfort with the narrowness of its curriculum, he graduated from Boalt Hall in 1914.

After practicing in the legal department of an oil company in San Francisco and with a small firm in Oakland, Warren joined the U.S. Army during World War I. He served stateside and left active duty at the end of the war. After clerking for the California legislature and working in Oakland's city attorney's office and as a deputy district attorney for Alameda County, California, Warren was appointed district attorney of the county. He was then elected to the post and served as district attorney for thirteen years before being elected attorney general of California in 1938. As attorney general, Warren played a significant role in the tragic and ill-conceived decision of the U.S. government to relocate Japanese and Japanese Americans during World War II. He later expressed regret for his role in the affair. After serving one term as attorney general of California, Warren was elected governor of California in 1942. He was reelected in 1946 and 1950, serving as governor until he was appointed to the Supreme Court in 1953.

Warren was also active in national politics. In 1948, during his second term as governor, Warren ran for the vice presidency as Republican Thomas Dewey's running mate. Warren sought the Republican Party's nomination for president in 1952, losing to Dwight Eisenhower. In early 1953, Warren accepted the post of solicitor general. However, following the death of Chief Justice Fred Vinson, Warren was appointed chief justice of the United States. After serving for several months, Warren was confirmed by the Senate on March 1, 1954. Although the Warren Court has been cheered by many and derided by others, the decisions issued during Warren's tenure as chief justice changed fundamental aspects of American law. Many of those seminal decisions were authored by Chief Justice Warren himself, including (1954) and its sequel, commonly called *Brown II* (1955); *Reynolds v. Sims* (1964); *Miranda v. Arizona* (1966); *Loving v. Virginia* (1967); and *Terry v. Ohio* (1968).

In the wake of the assassination of President John F. Kennedy, Warren served as the chair of the President's Commission on the Assassination of President Kennedy, commonly known as the Warren Commission. That commission's most famous conclusion—that Lee Harvey Oswald acted alone in assassinating President Kennedy—has been debated and challenged since the commission's report was issued in 1964. Earl Warren retired in 1969 at the close of the Court's term and died on July 9, 1974.

Explanation and Analysis of the Document

Chief Justice Warren begins the opinion by stating the question that the Court must answer: whether the Georgia House of Representatives could exclude Julian Bond based on statements Bond had made criticizing the war in Vietnam and the operation of the draft. In stating the question as such, Warren arguably asks simply whether elected officials enjoy the constitutional protection of freedom of speech. Warren suggests that the question might not be as straightforward as it seemed, but he ultimately would determine that the First Amendment fairly clearly protects Bond's right to free speech.

Before analyzing the issue, Warren sets the case in context. However, he omits some facts that might appear important to understanding the significance of the moment and precisely why Bond acted as he did. For example, Warren notes that Bond was elected from a district where more than 90 percent of the voters were African American, but he does not comment that the district and the election were direct results of the Court's one-man, one-vote jurisprudence.

SNCC's Statement in Opposition to Vietnam War and Bond's Statement of Support

Warren then provides the immediate circumstances that triggered the litigation: a statement issued by SNCC on January 6, 1966, opposing the war in Vietnam and remarks made by Bond, SNCC's communications director, in support of the statement. SNCC's statement noted that the organization opposed U.S. involvement in the Vietnam War and indicated the basis for its opposition: The U.S. government had neither sought nor supported freedom for people of color. The statement said that SNCC found a rough equivalence in the U.S. treatment of people of color in the southern United States and of people of color in Vietnam, with rights guaranteed by law ignored if enforcing those rights ran counter to U.S. interests. The killing of Samuel Younge, in Tuskegee, Alabama, was cited as proof that the United States was not willing to protect its citizens' rights any more than it was willing to protect the rights of the Vietnamese. In addition, the statement suggested that the right to free elections ensured by the Civil Rights Act of 1964 and the Voting Rights Act of 1965 was illusory, because those laws were not being fully implemented. Additionally, the U.S. government's commitment to free elections in other countries was questioned. The statement reasoned that, for many, it would not be sensible to fight for freedom abroad when freedom at home was impossible to achieve. Consequently, SNCC stated that "work[ing] in the civil rights movement and with other human rights organizations is a valid alternative to the draft" and urged those who agreed to embrace the alternative even though that embrace could cost them their lives.

SNCC's statement was issued the day after Samuel Younge, Jr., a member of the organization, a navy veteran, and a student at Tuskegee Institute, was murdered when he attempted to use a segregated restroom at a gas station in Tuskegee. After quoting portions of SNCC statement (but passing over the context in which it was made), the Court's opinion notes and quotes Bond's remarks. In an interview about the statement on the day it was released, Bond endorsed it, though he had not written it. Bond commented that as a pacifist he opposed all wars and felt it to be his

duty to encourage others to oppose war in general, the Vietnam War in particular, and the draft. He also observed that the statement correctly noted the hypocrisy of the U.S. government in encouraging freedom in foreign countries but not within its own borders. Consequently, Bond indicated that "as a second-class citizen" he did not feel compelled to support the war and that he did feel obliged to challenge situations he thought wrong. Bond's views on the war led to his belief "that people ought [not] to participate in it" and to his opposition to the draft. Nonetheless, Bond stated that he felt that his views on the war and American foreign policy did not conflict with his taking the oath of office under the Georgia constitution.

Bond's Exclusion from the Georgia Legislature

The opinion then details the firestorm that led to Bond's exclusion from the Georgia House of Representatives. In the wake of Bond's comments supporting SNCC's statement, many members of the Georgia legislature filed protests against Bond's taking his seat. The petitions claimed that "Bond's statements gave aid and comfort to the enemies of the United States and Georgia, violated the Selective Service laws, and tended to bring discredit and disrespect on the House." In addition, the petitions argued that Bond could not take the oath necessary to be seated, which required that the taker swear to support the Constitution of the United States. The clerk of the legislature refused to give Bond the oath until the challenge petitions were resolved.

Bond responded by arguing that the petitions were racially motivated and had been filed to restrict his First Amendment rights. Given how the Court resolved the case, it never reached the question of whether the petitions were racially motivated. A special committee of the Georgia legislature was convened to resolve the dispute, with the only testimony being Bond's, during which he defended his support for SNCC's statement. Bond explained that he had voiced support for those who had the courage to do what they believed to be right even when they faced serious harm for doing so. He denied that he ever had suggested that laws should be broken or draft cards should be burned, noting that he carried his own draft card in his pocket. The special committee also considered Bond's statements made after the clerk of the legislature refused to administer the oath. Bond indicated that he was being forced to defend his statements about a matter of public concern when others had not been asked to do so as a prerequisite to being seated. He spoke directly to his constituents, reiterating that he did not advocate violating the law but that he favored extending the recognized justifications for avoiding the draft to "building democracy at home." He explained that he had no plans to stop speaking out on matters of public concern as a legislator, even when his views were at odds with the views of others, and he reiterated that he planned to take the customary oath required of Georgia legislators.

The special legislative committee considered Bond's statements as proof that he could not honestly swear to support the constitutions of Georgia and the United States. In addition, it found that Bond's statements proved that he gave aid and comfort to the enemies of Georgia and the United States, violated the selective service laws, and would likely "bring discredit to and disrespect of" the legislature. Consequently, the committee determined that Bond would not be allowed to take the oath and would not be seated as a representative.

Procedural Background of the Case

The opinion next describes the legal proceedings that brought the case to the Supreme Court. In the wake of being excluded from the Georgia legislature, Bond filed suit seeking judgment that Georgia was not authorized to deny him a seat and that his First Amendment rights had been violated. The three-judge panel that heard the suit determined that Georgia law allowed the legislature to require qualifications of its members in addition to those specified in the Georgia constitution. The panel then determined that Bond's constitutional rights had not been violated. The legislature had satisfied procedural due process by providing a proper hearing in front of the special legislative committee. Similarly, according to the panel, substantive due process was satisfied because Bond's statements gave the legislature a reasonable basis for determining that Bond could not take the oath of office required of him. Two judges agreed that Bond's call to action to challenge the draft, rather than his dissent regarding policy, provided a basis for the legislature to believe that Bond "could not in good faith take an oath to support the State and Federal Constitutions." One judge dissented, arguing that barring Bond based on qualifications not in the Georgia constitution was beyond the legislature's authority under Georgia law.

The opinion notes that in the wake of the panel's decision and while Bond's appeal to the Supreme Court was pending, the governor of Georgia had ordered a special election to fill Bond's vacant seat. Bond won that election, and the legislature again refused to seat him. Bond also won the 1966 regular election to fill the seat.

Legal Analysis of Case

The opinion next analyzes the substance of the case, noting the specific qualifications listed in the Georgia constitution that could be required of its legislators without constitutional concern. Thus, the various eligibility requirements for Georgia's legislators, such as age and residency qualifications, were legitimate. In addition, the exclusion of those who have been convicted of various crimes or suffer from certain mental infirmities was acceptable. Indeed, even the requirement that legislators take an oath affirming support for the Georgia and U.S. constitutions and act in the best interests of Georgia was acceptable. However, the opinion then analyzes whether the Georgia legislature is limited to requiring that the oath be taken or whether it can opine on the sincerity of the legislator who takes the oath.

The opinion addresses the Georgia legislature's claim that the formal requirement of an oath allowed the House of Representatives to determine whether the legislator planned to take the oath "with sincerity" and that the sincerity requirement would merely qualify as an additional acceptable qualification for office. The legislature argued that it had the ability to establish the qualifications of its members under the Georgia constitution. Although it conceded that it could not exclude a member based on race or other unconstitutional bases, it argued that ascertaining the sincerity of a legislator in taking the required oath was at the core of determining a member's qualification and should not be subject to judicial review. The opinion rejects the suggestion that the Court did not have jurisdiction, noting that the issue was whether the decision violated Bond's First Amendment rights. That question, the opinion notes, was a matter for the Supreme Court to decide.

After noting its jurisdiction over the matter, the opinion reaches the key question: Did the Georgia legislature's action violate Bond's First Amendment rights? The Georgia House of Representatives claimed that

Bond's statements called for violations of the law and that even if a private citizen could have uttered those statements without repercussions, the state could hold its legislators to higher standards of loyalty than it held the public. The opinion agrees that Georgia could require that its legislators take an oath swearing fidelity to the U.S. Constitution and the Georgia constitution consistent with First Amendment principles, but it rejects the implications that the Georgia legislature suggested came with the oath requirement. The oath requirement did not limit the legislator's First Amendment rights. First, contrary to the Georgia legislature's claim, the Court found Bond's statements to be lawful expressions of dissent to American policy, rather than a call for lawless action. Any citizen would have been allowed to say what Bond said without repercussions. Second, the Court notes that the Constitution does not allow the state to restrict a legislator's rights to free expression any more than it can restrict an ordinary citizen's rights.

The Representative's Obligation of Open and Free Expression

The opinion takes the issue one step further in discussing the role of the First Amendment in public discourse. The Georgia legislature had sought to limit Bond's rights to free expression because he was to become a legislator. The Court suggested that Bond's rights needed to be protected precisely because he was about to become a legislator. Rather than being limited by their elected positions, legislators are supposed to be free to speak at least as broadly and forcefully about national policy as ordinary citizens are. Indeed, their role in deciding issues of public policy makes it necessary for legislators to communicate their positions to their constituents through expressions of opinions on matters of public interest. If that opinion is dissent regarding state or national policy, it ought to be known to those who elected a legislator, so they could take it into account when deciding whether that legislator is a proper representative. Consequently, the Court held "that the disqualification of Bond from membership in the Georgia House because of his statements violated Bond's right of free expression under the First Amendment."

Impact

Bond v. Floyd guaranteed that a legislator's admission to a legislature was to be validated by qualifications and election by the citizenry, not by that person's ability to convince other legislators that his or her views were sufficiently orthodox. Consequently, candidates for office were free to explain their views and encouraged to present those views to their constituents to ensure that those candidates would make appropriate representatives for their constituents. In addition, the decision freed candidates who might have come out of civil rights protest organizations and antiwar organizations to express themselves fully and run for office without fear that they might not be able to take the seats they had won. The list of legislators in state legislatures and the halls of Congress who fit this description is much longer than it would have been without *Bond v. Floyd*.

Questions for Further Study

1. How would you describe the relationship between the civil rights movement and the antiwar movement in the 1960s? How did the two movements overlap?

2. Why was opposition to the war in Vietnam so intense in the 1960s and early 1970s? What was different about this war and, say, World War I or World War II?

3. Compare this document with Martin Luther King, Jr.'s "Beyond Vietnam: A Time to Break Silence." Taken together, how do the two documents paint a picture of opposition to the Vietnam War and the intersection of race and national policy during this time period?

4. On what basis did the Warren Court conclude that the Georgia legislature had to seat Bond?

5. Very often, the outcome of a legal case affects only the parties involved and, by extension, others who could be involved in similar circumstances. What argument could be made that the Court's decision in *Bond v. Floyd* had very much a national audience and that the outcome of the case affected all Americans?

Further Reading

Books

Bond, Julian. *A Time to Speak, a Time to Act*. New York: Simon & Schuster, 1972.

Davidson, Chandler, and Bernard Grofman, eds. *Quiet Revolution in the South*. Princeton, NJ: Princeton University Press, 1994.

Forman, James. *The Making of Black Revolutionaries*. Seattle: University of Washington Press, 1997.

Lawson, Steven F. *Running for Freedom: Civil Rights and Black Politics in America since 1941*. 3rd ed. Chichester, UK: Wiley-Blackwell, 2008.

Maxwell, Jeremy P. *Brotherhood in Combat: How African Americans Found Equality in Korea and Vietnam*. Norman: University of Oklahoma Press, 2018.

Westheider, James E. *The African American Experience in Vietnam: Brothers in Arms*. Lanham, MD: Rowman & Littlefield, 2007.

Websites

"African-American Involvement in the Vietnam War." Accessed February 23, 2023, http://www.aavw.org.

Hudson, David L., Jr. "Bond v. Floyd." First Amendment Encyclopedia. Accessed February 23, 2023, https://www.mtsu.edu/first-amendment/article/182/bond-v-floyd.

"Six Years of the Student Nonviolent Coordinating Committee." SNCC 1960–1966 website. Accessed February 23, 2023, http://www.ibiblio.org/sncc/index.html.

—Commentary by Henry L. Chambers

BOND V. FLOYD

Document Text

Mr. Chief Justice Warren delivered the opinion of the Court

The question presented in this case is whether the Georgia House of Representatives may constitutionally exclude appellant Bond, a duly elected Representative, from membership because of his statements, and statements to which he subscribed, criticizing the policy of the Federal Government in Vietnam and the operation of the Selective Service laws. An understanding of the circumstances of the litigation requires a complete presentation of the events and statements which led to this appeal.

Bond, a Negro, was elected on June 15, 1965, as the Representative to the Georgia House of Representatives from the 136th House District. Of the District's 6,500 voters, approximately 6,000 are Negroes. Bond defeated his opponent, Malcolm Dean, Dean of Men at Atlanta University, also a Negro, by a vote of 2,320 to 487.

On January 6, 1966, the Student Nonviolent Coordinating Committee, a civil rights organization of which Bond was then the Communications Director, issued the following statement on American policy in Vietnam and its relation to the work of civil rights organizations in this country:

> The Student Nonviolent Coordinating Committee has a right and a responsibility to dissent with United States foreign policy on an issue when it sees fit. The Student Nonviolent Coordinating Committee now states its opposition to United States' involvement in Viet Nam on these grounds: [385 U.S. 119]

We believe the United States government has been deceptive in its claims of concern for freedom of the Vietnamese people, just as the government has been deceptive in claiming concern for the freedom of colored people in such other countries as the Dominican Republic, the Congo, South Africa, Rhodesia and in the United States itself.

We, the Student Nonviolent Coordinating Committee, have been involved in the black people's struggle for liberation and self-determination in this country for the past five years. Our work, particularly in the South, has taught us that the United States government has never guaranteed the freedom of oppressed citizens, and is not yet truly determined to end the rule of terror and oppression within its own borders.

We ourselves have often been victims of violence and confinement executed by United States government officials. We recall the numerous persons who have been murdered in the South because of their efforts to secure their civil and human rights, and whose murderers have been allowed to escape penalty for their crimes.

The murder of Samuel Young in Tuskegee, Ala., is no different than the murder of peasants in Viet Nam, for both Young and the Vietnamese sought, and are seeking, to secure the rights guaranteed them by law. In each case, the United States government bears a great part of the responsibility for these deaths.

Samuel Young was murdered because United States law is not being enforced. Vietnamese are murdered because the United States is pursuing an aggressive policy in violation of international law. The United States is no respecter of persons or law [385 U.S. 120] when such persons or laws run counter to its needs and desires.

We recall the indifference, suspicion and outright hostility with which our reports of violence have been met in the past by government officials.

We know that, for the most part, elections in this country, in the North as well as the South, are not free. We have seen that the 1965 Voting Rights Act and the 1964 Civil Rights Act have not yet been implemented with full federal power and sincerity.

We question, then, the ability and even the desire of the United States government to guarantee free elections abroad. We maintain that our country's cry of "preserve freedom in the world" is a hypocritical mask behind which it squashes liberation movements which are not bound, and refuse to be bound, by the expediencies of United States cold war policies.

We are in sympathy with, and support, the men in this country who are unwilling to respond to a military draft which would compel them to contribute their lives to United States aggression in Viet Nam in the name of the "freedom" we find so false in this country.

We recoil with horror at the inconsistency of a supposedly "free" society where responsibility to freedom is equated with the responsibility to lend oneself to military aggression. We take note of the fact that 16 percent of the draftees from this country are Negroes called on to stifle the liberation of Viet Nam, to preserve a "democracy" which does not exist for them at home.

We ask, where is the draft for the freedom fight in the United States? [385 U.S. 121]

We therefore encourage those Americans who prefer to use their energy in building democratic forms within this country. We believe that work in the civil rights movement and with other human relations organizations is a valid alternative to the draft. We urge all Americans to seek this alternative, knowing full well that it may cost their lives—as painfully as in Viet Nam.

On the same day that this statement was issued, Bond was interviewed by telephone by a reporter from a local radio station, and, although Bond had not par-

ticipated in drafting the statement, he endorsed the statement in these words:

> Why, I endorse it, first, because I like to think of myself as a pacifist, and one who opposes that war and any other war, and eager and anxious to encourage people not to participate in it for any reason that they choose, and secondly, I agree with this statement because of the reason set forth in it—because I think it is sorta hypocritical for us to maintain that we are fighting for liberty in other places and we are not guaranteeing liberty to citizens inside the continental United States.

Well, I think that the fact that the United States Government fights a war in Viet Nam, I don't think that I, as a second class citizen of the United States, have a requirement to support that war. I think my responsibility is to oppose things that I think are wrong if they are in Viet Nam or New York, or Chicago, or Atlanta, or wherever.

When the interviewer suggested that our involvement in Vietnam was because "if we do not stop Communism [385 U.S. 122] there, that it is just a question of where will we stop it next," Bond replied:

> Oh, no, I'm not taking a stand against stopping World Communism, and I'm not taking a stand in favor of the Viet Cong. What I'm saying is, first, that I don't believe in that war. That particular war. I'm against all war. I'm against that war in particular, and I don't think people ought to participate in it. Because I'm against war, I'm against the draft. I think that other countries in the World get along without a draft—England is one—and I don't see why we couldn't, too.

... I'm not about to justify that war, because it's stopping International Communism, or whatever—you know, I just happen to have a basic disagreement with wars for whatever reason they are fought ... fought to stop International Communism, to promote International Communism, or for whatever reason. I oppose the Viet Cong fighting in Viet Nam as much as I oppose the United States fighting in Viet Nam. I happen to live in the United States. If I lived in North Viet Nam, I might not have the same sort of freedom of expression, but it happens that I live here—not there.

The interviewer also asked Bond if he felt he could take the oath of office required by the Georgia Constitution, and Bond responded that he saw nothing inconsistent between his statements and the oath. Bond was also asked whether he would adhere to his statements if war were declared on North Vietnam and if his statements might become treasonous. He replied that he did not know "if I'm strong enough to place myself in a position where I'd be guilty of treason." [385 U.S. 123]

Before January 10, 1966, when the Georgia House of Representatives was scheduled to convene, petitions challenging Bond's right to be seated were filed by 75 House members. These petitions charged that Bond's statements gave aid and comfort to the enemies of the United States and Georgia, violated the Selective Service laws, and tended to bring discredit and disrespect on the House. The petitions further contended that Bond's endorsement of SNCC statement is totally and completely repugnant to and inconsistent with the mandatory oath prescribed by the Constitution of Georgia for a Member of the House of Representatives to take before taking his seat.

For the same reasons, the petitions asserted that Bond could not take an oath to support the Constitution of the United States. When Bond appeared at the House on January 10 to be sworn in, the clerk refused to administer the oath to him until the issues raised in the challenge petitions had been decided.

Bond filed a response to the challenge petitions in which he stated his willingness to take the oath and argued that he was not unable to do so in good faith. He further argued that the challenge against his seating had been filed to deprive him of his First Amendment rights, and that the challenge was racially motivated. A special committee was appointed to report on the challenge, and a hearing was held to determine exactly what Bond had said and the intentions with which he had said it.

At this hearing, the only testimony given against Bond was that which he himself gave the committee. Both the opponents Bond had defeated in becoming the Representative of the 136th District testified to his good character and to his loyalty to the United States. A recording of the interview which Bond had given to the reporter after SNCC statement was played, and Bond was called to the stand for cross-examination.

He there admitted his statements and elaborated his views. He [385 U.S. 124] stated that he concurred in SNCC statement "without reservation," and, when asked if he admired the courage of persons who burn their draft cards, responded:

I admire people who take an action, and I admire people who feel strongly enough about their convictions to take an action like that knowing the consequences that they will face, and that was my original statement when asked that question.

I have never suggested or counseled or advocated that any one other person burn their draft card. In fact, I have mine in my pocket, and will produce it if you wish. I do not advocate that people should break laws. What I simply tried to say was that I admired the courage of someone who could act on his convictions knowing that he faces pretty stiff consequences.

Tapes of an interview Bond had given the press after the clerk had refused to give him the oath were also heard by the special committee. In this interview, Bond stated:

I stand before you today charged with entering into public discussion on matters of National interest. I hesitate to offer explanations for my actions or deeds where no charge has been levied against me other than the charge that I have chosen to speak my mind and no explanation is called for, for no member of this House, has ever, to my knowledge, been called upon to explain his public statements for public postures as a prerequisite to admission to that Body. I therefore, offer to my constituents a statement of my views. I have not counseled burning draft cards, nor have I burned mine. I have suggested that congressionally outlined alternatives to military service be extended to [385 U.S. 125] building democracy at home. The posture of my life for the past five years has been calculated to give Negroes the ability to participate in formulation of public policies. The fact of my election to public office does not lessen my duty or desire to express my opinions even when they differ from those held by others. As to the current controversy, because of convictions that I have arrived at through examination of my conscience, I have decided I personally cannot participate in war.

I stand here with intentions to take an oath—that oath they just took in there—that will dispel any doubts about my convictions or loyalty.

The special committee gave general approval in its report to the specific charges in the challenge petitions that Bond's endorsement of SNCC statement and his supplementary remarks showed that he " does not and will not" support the Constitutions of the United States and of Georgia, that he "adheres to the enemies of the ... State of Georgia" contrary to the State Constitution, that he gives aid and comfort to the enemies of the United States, that his statements violated the Universal Military Training and Service Act, §12, 62 Stat. 622, 50 U.S.C. App. §462, and that his statements "are reprehensible, and are such as tend to bring discredit to and disrespect of the House." On the same day, the House adopted the committee report without findings and without further elaborating Bond's lack of qualifications, and resolved by a vote of 184 to 12 that

Bond shall not be allowed to take the oath of office as a member of the House of Representatives and that Representative-Elect Julian Bond shall not be seated as a member of the House of Representatives.

Bond then instituted an action in the District Court for the Northern District of Georgia for injunctive relief [385 U.S. 126] and a declaratory judgment that the House action was unauthorized by the Georgia Constitution and violated Bond's rights under the First Amendment. A three-judge District Court was convened under 28 U.S.C. §2281. All three members of the District Court held that the court had jurisdiction to decide the constitutionality of the House action because Bond had asserted substantial First Amendment rights. On the merits, however, the court was divided.

Judges Bell and Morgan, writing for the majority of the court, addressed themselves first to the question of whether the Georgia House had power under state law to disqualify Bond based on its conclusion that he could not sincerely take the oath of office. They reasoned that separation of powers principles gave the Legislature power to insist on qualifications in addition to those specified in the State Constitution. The majority pointed out that nothing in the Georgia Constitution limits the qualifications of the legislators to those expressed in the constitution.

Having concluded that the action of the Georgia House was authorized by state law, the court considered whether Bond's disqualification violated his constitutional right of freedom of speech. It reasoned that the

decisions of this Court involving particular state political offices supported an attitude of restraint in which the principles of separation of powers and federalism should be balanced against the alleged deprivation of individual constitutional rights. On this basis, the majority below fashioned the test to be applied in this case as being whether the refusal to seat Bond violated procedural or what it termed substantive due process. The court held that the hearing which had been given Bond by the House satisfied procedural due process. As for [385 U.S. 127] what it termed the question of substantive due process, the majority concluded that there was a rational evidentiary basis for the ruling of the House. It reasoned that Bond's right to dissent as a private citizen was limited by his decision to seek membership in the Georgia House. Moreover, the majority concluded, SNCC statement and Bond's related remarks went beyond criticism of national policy and provided a rational basis for a conclusion that the speaker could not in good faith take an oath to support the State and Federal Constitutions:

A citizen would not violate his oath by objecting to or criticizing this policy or even by calling it deceptive and false, as the statement did.

But the statement does not stop with this. It is a call to action based on race; a call alien to the concept of the pluralistic society which makes this nation. It aligns the organization with "... colored people in such other countries as the Dominican Republic, the Congo, South Africa, Rhodesia...." It refers to its involvement in the black people's "struggle for liberation and self-determination...." It states that "Vietnamese are murdered because the United States is pursuing an aggressive policy in violation of international law." It alleges that Negroes, referring to American servicemen, are called on to stifle the liberation of Viet Nam.

The call to action, and this is what we find to be a rational basis for the decision which denied Mr. Bond his seat, is that language which states that SNCC supports those men in this country who are unwilling to respond to a military draft.

Chief Judge Tuttle dissented. He reasoned that the question of the power of the Georgia House under the [385 U.S. 128] State Constitution to disqualify a Representative under these circumstances had never been decided by the state courts, and that federal courts should construe state law, if possible, so as to avoid unnecessary federal constitutional issues. Since Bond satisfied all the stated qualifications in the State Constitution, Chief Judge Tuttle concluded that his disqualification was beyond the power of the House as a matter of state constitutional law.

Bond appealed directly to this Court from the decision of the District Court under 28 U.S.C. §1253. While this appeal was pending, the Governor of Georgia called a special election to fill the vacancy caused by Bond's exclusion. Bond entered this election and won overwhelmingly. The House was in recess, but the Rules Committee held a hearing in which Bond declined to recant his earlier statements. Consequently, he was again prevented from taking the oath of office, and the seat has remained vacant. Bond again sought the seat from the 136th District in the regular 1966 election, and he won the Democratic primary in September, 1966, and won an overwhelming majority in the election of November 8, 1966.

The Georgia Constitution sets out a number of specific provisions dealing with the qualifications and eligibility of state legislators. These provide that Representatives shall be citizens of the United States, at least 21 years of age, citizens of Georgia for two years, and residents for one year of the counties from which elected. The [385 U.S. 129] Georgia Constitution further provides that no one convicted of treason against the State, or of any crime of moral turpitude, or of a number of other enumerated crimes, may hold any office in the State. Idiots and insane persons are barred from office, and no one holding any state or federal office is eligible for a seat in either house. The State Constitution also provides:

Election, returns, etc.; disorderly conduct.—Each House shall be the judge of the election, returns and qualifications of its members and shall have power to punish them for disorderly behavior, or misconduct, by censure, fine, imprisonment, or expulsion; but no member shall be expelled, except by a vote of two-thirds of the House to which he belongs.

These constitute the only stated qualifications for membership in the Georgia Legislature, and the State concedes that Bond meets all of them. The Georgia Constitution also requires Representatives to take an oath stated in the Constitution:

Oath of members.—Each senator and Representative, before taking his seat, shall take the following oath, or affirmation, to-wit: "I will support the Constitution of this State and of the United States, and on all questions and measures which may come before me, I will so conduct myself, as will, in my judgment, be most conducive to the interests and prosperity of this State." [385 U.S. 130]

The State points out in its brief that the latter part of this oath, involving the admonition to act in the best interests of the State, was not the standard by which Bond was judged.

The State does not claim that Bond refused to take the oath to support the Federal Constitution, a requirement imposed on state legislators by Art. VI, cl. 3, of the United States Constitution:

The Senators and Representatives before mentioned, and the Members of the several State Legislatures, and all executive and judicial Officers, both of the United States and of the several States, shall be bound by Oath or Affirmation, to support this Constitution; but no religious Tests shall ever be required as a Qualification to any Office or public Trust under the United States.

Instead, it argues that the oath provisions of the State and Federal Constitutions constitute an additional qualification. Because, under state law, the legislature has exclusive jurisdiction to determine whether an elected Representative meets the enumerated qualifications, it is argued that the legislature has power to look beyond the plain meaning of the oath provisions, which merely require that the oaths be taken. This additional power is said to extend to determining whether a given Representative may take the oath with sincerity. The State does not claim that it should be completely free of judicial review whenever it disqualifies an elected Representative; it admits that, if a State Legislature excluded a legislator on racial or other clearly unconstitutional grounds, the federal (or state) judiciary would be justified in testing the exclusion by federal constitutional standards. But the State argues that there can be no [385 U.S. 131] doubt as to the constitutionality of the qualification involved in this case, because it is one imposed on the State Legislatures by Article VI of the United States Constitution. Moreover, the State contends that no decision of this Court suggests that a State may not ensure the loyalty of its public servants by making the taking of an oath a qualification of office. Thus, the State argues that there should be no judicial review of the legislature's power to judge whether a prospective member may conscientiously take the oath required by the State and Federal Constitutions.

We are not persuaded by the State's attempt to distinguish, for purposes of our jurisdiction, between an exclusion alleged to be on racial grounds and one alleged to violate the First Amendment. The basis for the argued distinction is that, in this case, Bond's disqualification was grounded on a constitutional standard—the requirement of taking an oath to support the Constitution. But Bond's contention is that this standard was utilized to infringe his First Amendment rights, and we cannot distinguish, for purposes of our assumption of jurisdiction, between a disqualification under an unconstitutional standard and a disqualification which, although under color of a proper standard, is alleged to violate the First Amendment.

We conclude, as did the entire court below, that this Court has jurisdiction to review the question of whether the action of the Georgia House of Representatives deprived Bond of federal constitutional rights, and we now move to the central question posed in the case—whether Bond's disqualification because of his statements violated the free speech provisions of the First Amendment as applied to the States through the Fourteenth Amendment.

The State argues that the exclusion does not violate the First Amendment because the State has a right, under Article VI of the United States Constitution, to insist on loyalty to the Constitution as a condition of office. A legislator, of course, can be required to swear to support the Constitution of the United States as a condition of holding office, but that is not the issue in this case, as the record is uncontradicted that Bond has repeatedly expressed his willingness to swear to the oaths provided for in the State and Federal Constitutions. Nor is this a case where a legislator swears to an oath *pro forma* while declaring or manifesting his disagreement with or indifference to the oath. Thus, we do not quarrel with the State's contention that the oath provisions of the United States and Georgia Constitutions do not violate the First Amendment. But this requirement does not authorize a majority of state legislators to test the sincerity with which another duly elected legislator can swear to uphold the Constitution. Such a power could be utilized to restrict the right of legislators to dissent from national or state policy or that of a majority of their colleagues under the guise of judging their loyalty to the Constitution. Certainly there can be no question but that the First Amendment protects expressions in opposition to national foreign policy in Vietnam and to the Selective Service system. The State does not contend otherwise. But it argues that Bond went beyond expressions of opposition, and counseled violations of the Selective Service laws, and that advocating violation of federal law demonstrates a lack of support for the Constitution. The State declines to argue that Bond's statements would violate any law if made by a private citizen, but it does argue that, even though such [385 U.S. 133] a citizen might be protected by his First Amendment rights, the State may nonetheless apply a stricter standard to its legislators. We do not agree.

Bond could not have been constitutionally convicted under 50 U.S.C. App. §462(a), which punishes any person who "counsels, aids, or abets another to refuse or evade registration." Bond's statements were, at worst, unclear on the question of the means to be adopted to avoid the draft. While SNCC statement said "We are in sympathy with, and support, the men in this country who are unwilling to respond to a military draft," this statement alone cannot be interpreted as a call to unlawful refusal to be drafted. Moreover, Bond's supplementary statements tend to resolve the opaqueness in favor of legal alternatives to the draft, and there is no evidence to the contrary. On the day the statement was issued, Bond explained that he endorsed it because I like to think of myself as a pacifist and one who opposes that war and any other war and eager and anxious to [385 U.S. 134] encourage people not to participate in it for any reason that they choose.

In the same interview, Bond stated categorically that he did not oppose the Vietnam policy because he favored the Communists; that he was a loyal American citizen, and supported the Constitution of the United States. He further stated "I oppose the Viet Cong fighting in Viet Nam as much as I oppose the United States fighting in Viet Nam." At the hearing before the Special Committee of the Georgia House, when asked his position on persons who burned their draft cards, Bond replied that he admired the courage of persons who "feel strongly enough about their convictions to take an action like that knowing the consequences that they will face." When pressed as to whether his admiration was based on the violation of federal law, Bond stated:

I have never suggested or counseled or advocated that any one other person burn their draft card. In fact, I have mine in my pocket, and will produce it if you wish. I do not advocate that people should break laws. What I simply try to say was that I admired the courage of someone who could act on his convictions knowing that he faces pretty stiff consequences.

Certainly this clarification does not demonstrate any incitement to violation of law. No useful purpose would be served by discussing the many decisions of this Court which establish that Bond could not have been convicted for these statements consistently with the First Amendment. *See, e.g., Wood v. Georgia*, 370 U.S. 375 (1962); *Yates v. United States*, 354 U.S. 298 (1957); *Terminiello v. Chicago*, 337 U.S. 1 (1949). Nor does the fact that the District Court found the SNCC statement to have racial overtones constitute a reason for holding it outside [385 U.S. 135] the protection of the First Amendment. In fact, the State concedes that there is no issue of race in the case.

The State attempts to circumvent the protection the First Amendment would afford to these statements if made by a private citizen by arguing that a State is constitutionally justified in exacting a higher standard of loyalty from its legislators than from its citizens. Of course, a State may constitutionally require an oath to support the Constitution from its legislators which it does not require of its private citizens. But this difference in treatment does not support the exclusion of Bond, for while the State has an interest in requiring its legislators to swear to a belief in constitutional processes of government, surely the oath gives it no interest in limiting its legislators' capacity to discuss their views of local or national policy. The manifest function of [385 U.S. 136] the First Amendment in a representa-

tive government requires that legislators be given the widest latitude to express their views on issues of policy. The central commitment of the First Amendment, as summarized in the opinion of the Court in *New York Times Co. v. Sullivan*, 376 U.S. 254, 270 (1964), is that "debate on public issues should be uninhibited, robust, and wide-open." We think the rationale of the New York Times case disposes of the claim that Bond's statements fell outside the range of constitutional protection. Just as erroneous statements must be protected to give freedom of expression the breathing space it needs to survive, so statements criticizing public policy and the implementation of it must be similarly protected. The State argues that the *New York Times* principle should not be extended to statements by a legislator because the policy of encouraging free debate about governmental operations only applies to the citizen-critic of his government. We find no support for this distinction in the *New York Times* case or in any other decision of this Court. The interest of the public in hearing all sides of a public issue is hardly advanced by extending more protection to citizen critics than to legislators. Legislators have an obligation to take positions on controversial political questions so that their constituents can be fully informed by them, and be better able to assess their qualifications for office; also so they may be represented in governmental debates [385 U.S. 137] by the person they have elected to represent them. We therefore hold that the disqualification of Bond from membership in the Georgia House because of his statements violated Bond's right of free expression under the First Amendment. Because of our disposition of the case on First Amendment grounds, we need not decide the other issues advanced by Bond and the *amici*.

The judgment of the District Court is

Reversed.

Glossary

amici: a reference to *amici curiae* briefs, or "friends of the court" briefs filed by people who are not directly involved in the case but have an interest in supporting one side or the other

burning draft cards: a common, public way of opposing the Vietnam War in the 1960s

cold war: the state of tension between the United States and its allies and the Soviet Union and its satellite states in the decades following World War II

declaratory judgment: a judge's statement about someone's rights

Idiots: a clinical term used at the time to refer to a particular class of mentally disabled persons

injunctive relief: a court order requiring someone to do something or refrain from doing something

pro forma: from the Latin for "as a matter of form," used to describe something done in a perfunctory or purely formal way

procedural due process: the legal doctrine that ensures fairness in the application of rules, laws, and regulations

Samuel Young: Samuel Younge, Jr., a member of the Student Nonviolent Coordinating Committee and a Tuskegee Institute student killed in January 1966 for using the segregated bathroom at a Tuskegee gas station

Selective Service laws: the military draft, including the obligation to register for the draft

SNCC: an acronym for the Student Nonviolent Coordinating Committee, pronounced "snick"

substantive due process: the legal doctrine that ensures that the fundamental rights of people are protected in the outcome of a case

Viet Cong: a name derived from Vietnamese for "Vietnamese Communist" and referring to the National Liberation Front, which fought the United States and the South Vietnamese government in the Vietnam War

MIRANDA V. ARIZONA

DATE	CITATION
1966	384 U.S. 436

AUTHOR
Earl Warren

SIGNIFICANCE
Ruled that statements made by a person while in police custody may not be used as evidence unless the individual has been apprised of their right not to incriminate themselves or of the right to consult an attorney and have one present during an interrogation

VOTE
5–4

Overview

The U.S. Supreme Court dramatically reshaped the nation's criminal justice system in the 1960s. As presided over by Chief Justice Earl Warren until mid-1969, the Court broadly interpreted rights that the Fourth, Fifth, and Sixth Amendments afford persons accused of crimes. Through the process of selective incorporation, the Court used the Fourteenth Amendment to apply elements of these amendments, historically restricting federal but not state infringement of individual rights, to the states.

Miranda v. Arizona, decided in 1966, is a major landmark in the Warren Court's expansion of rights of the accused. The decision reversed criminal convictions and threw out statements made by the defendant while in police custody. The accused, the Court wrote, had not been apprised of his right not to incriminate himself or of his right to consult an attorney and have one present during interrogation. This violation of constitutional rights made his confession to the police, the major piece of evidence upon which the state relied for his conviction, inadmissible.

Context

The Constitution places value on both crime control and the rights of the accused. To the state and federal governments, the Constitution extends the authority to protect citizens' safety and to provide for the general security of the public. To an individual accused of crimes, it extends rights upon which governments may not infringe while investigating and prosecuting. The balance between government mandates and individual rights is delineated in the policies and practices employed by police and followed in court proceedings.

The Warren Court revolutionized the law of criminal procedure during the 1960s. Certain decisions increased the scope and reach of the constitutional rights of accused persons and established national standards for criminal procedures, applying across all states. Among the many cases that created this legacy, four stand out: *Mapp v. Ohio* (1961), *Gideon v. Wainwright* (1963), *Escobedo v. Illinois* (1964), and *Miranda v. Arizona* (1966). In the first three cases, the Court traveled a great distance in a very short time. These decisions spurred loud disapproval from advocates of crime control. In many quarters of the nation, the Court and especially the chief justice, Earl Warren,

Photograph of the Maricopa County Courthouse where Miranda was held
(Wikimedia Commons)

were roundly criticized, even vilified. But the decisions, as they piled up, also signaled to defendants convicted in lower courts and their attorneys that, where possible constitutional violations had occurred, the Warren Court was willing to hear pleas for reversal.

Ernesto Miranda was one of these defendants. The case unfolded as follows: A young woman in Phoenix reported to the police that she had been abducted and raped. Based on a description of the assailant's car, the police tracked down Miranda and, with his approval, brought him to the station at 10:30 AM for a lineup and questioning. At 1:30 PM, Miranda wrote and signed a statement admitting to the abduction and rape. The subsequent trial proceeded quickly, with the written confession entered as evidence. The jury quickly returned unanimous guilty verdicts for kidnapping and rape.

On appeal to the Arizona State Supreme Court, Miranda's convictions were upheld, but that decision caught the attention of attorneys in Phoenix, who then made an appeal to the U.S. Supreme Court on Miranda's behalf. In the spring of 1966, the case was argued before the Supreme

Court, as consolidated with appeals of three other lower-court decisions, all folded into the same case.

About the Author

Earl Warren, chief justice of the Supreme Court from 1953 to 1969, authored the Court's opinion in *Miranda v. Arizona*. Joining him were Justices Hugo Black, William O. Douglas, William Brennan, and Abe Fortas. These five formed a reliable liberal voting bloc that pushed for constitutional reforms in many areas during the 1960s. (Justice Fortas, replaced by Arthur Goldberg in 1965, and Thurgood Marshall, who joined the Court in 1967, were also members of this bloc.) By custom, the chief justice, when voting in the majority, assigns the authorship of the Court's opinion; in this case, to write an opinion sure to stir controversy, Warren chose himself.

President Dwight Eisenhower appointed Earl Warren as chief justice in 1953. A Republican, Warren had

Ernesto Miranda
(Wikimedia Commons)

served California as attorney general and three times was elected the state's governor. Eisenhower expressed surprise and disappointment when his choice for chief justice became the strong leader of a Court that boldly took American society in progressive directions in areas of race relations, legislative apportionment, free speech, and rights of the accused.

Dissenting opinions in *Miranda* were written by Tom Clark, appointed by President Harry Truman, for whom Clark had served as U.S. attorney general; by John Harlan, another Eisenhower appointee and grandson of Justice John Marshall Harlan, who famously dissented in *Plessy v. Ferguson* (1896); and by Byron White, appointed by President John F. Kennedy. These justices, along with Potter Stewart, who joined the dissents of Harlan and White—who also joined each other's dissents—often took conservative positions when casting votes in cases decided by the Warren Court.

Explanation and Analysis of the Document

Chief Justice Earl Warren's Majority Opinion

In the first paragraph of the majority opinion—which was joined by Black, Douglas, Brennan, and Fortas—

Warren places the four cases in question securely in the province of the constitutional rights of the accused, or "the restraints society must observe consistent with the Federal Constitution in prosecuting individuals for crime." The tone Warren adopts in this first paragraph foreshadows the Court's decision—it concerns not a suspected criminal who is questioned by the police but rather "an individual who is subjected to custodial police interrogation." In these cases the Court deals with "the necessity for procedures which assure that the individual is accorded his privilege under the Fifth Amendment to the Constitution not to be compelled to incriminate himself." At this point, the reader clearly may anticipate that Miranda has won on appeal.

Warren next aligns the cases in *Miranda* with the Court's decision two years earlier in *Escobedo v. Illinois*. In that case, the defendant, who had been arrested and was under interrogation at the police station, asked to see his lawyer. The police refused the request and subsequently obtained from Escobedo a confession that was used at trial to successfully prosecute him. Warren does not recount the basis on which the Supreme Court overturned this case on appeal: The Sixth Amendment right to counsel applies as soon as police focus on a particular suspect; the confession, because it was obtained in violation of this right, was inadmissible at trial.

The results in *Escobedo*, Warren explains, allowed for interpretation, debate, and speculation regarding issues on "applying the privilege of self-incrimination to in-custody interrogation." Thus, Warren fashions the ruling in *Escobedo* to play down the right to counsel (from the Sixth Amendment) and instead emphasizes self-incrimination (as addressed in the Fifth Amendment), the issue on which *Miranda* will turn. A holding based on the privilege against self-incrimination during in-custody interrogation, Warren assures, does not break new ground. It is "an application of principles long recognized and applied in other settings." (On this point, the dissenters to this decision strongly disagree.)

In part I, Warren writes that because the four cases under review all involve "incommunicado interrogation of individuals in a police-dominated atmosphere," this section will survey police methods in that setting. A factual study of police operations and police manuals is quoted at length. Warren stresses that "the modern practice of in-custody interrogation is psychologically rather than physically oriented." The manuals teach police to isolate the suspect in a setting chosen by authorities, to conduct extended questioning during which the suspect's guilt is assumed, and to deflect requests by the suspect for legal representation. In the cases under consideration, Warren admits, the records contain no evidence of "physical coercion or patent psychological ploys." The dissenting justices believe that the matter properly turns on whether evidence exists that a particular defendant's statements were made involuntarily. Warren, however, is building a more general case against in-custody questioning. To him, "the very fact of custodial interrogation exacts a heavy toll on individual liberty and trades on the weaknesses of individuals." He sees "an intimate connection between the privilege against self-incrimination and police custodial questioning."

The privilege against self-incrimination is lodged in venerable traditions of English law, Warren says in part II, and was given constitutional status by the framers. "We cannot depart from this noble heritage," he declares. In the third paragraph, Warren establishes this heritage further: Arising from a right to privacy and "founded on a complex of values," the privilege against self-incrimination strikes a fair balance between the individual and the state.

These are fine ideals, stated strongly. But because these ideals are expansive and general, it is difficult to make the argument that they require the highly specific *Miranda* rules that the Court is about to impose on police. These ideals could just as logically and reasonably support rules that do not go as far as those laid down in *Miranda* or rules that go even further. To support these particular practices, Warren examines the case law to determine "whether the privilege is fully applicable during a period of custodial interrogation." Predictably, the answer that he will arrive at is that it is applicable.

Warren writes that in *Bram v. United States* (1897), the Court reasoned that the Fifth Amendment requires that an admissible statement must be voluntary—that is, made by a defendant not compelled by improper influences to make the statement. In *Malloy v. Hogan* (1964), as Warren notes, the Court reasoned that the voluntariness doctrine "encompasses all interrogation practices which are likely to exert such pressure upon an individual as to disable him from making a free and rational choice." Finally, in *Escobedo v. Illinois*, when the defen-

dant chose to speak to the police, Warren writes, "the abdication of the constitutional privilege—the choice on his part to speak to the police—was not made knowingly or competently because of the failure to apprise him his rights; the compelling atmosphere of the in-custody interrogation, and not an independent decision on his part, caused the defendant to speak."

Thus, for the second time, Warren has cast the Court's holding in *Escobedo* in a way that smoothly anticipates the result to be arrived at in *Miranda*. The defendant in *Escobedo*, during custodial interrogation, asked for an attorney and was denied the request; the constitutional violation in question concerned the Sixth Amendment. As such, Fifth Amendment privilege as delineated in *Miranda* does not flow as directly from *Escobedo*, as Warren would have it. Still, the right to an attorney—what Warren calls "a protective device to dispel the compelling atmosphere of the interrogation"—does apply to both *Escobedo* and *Miranda*. The presence of counsel "would be the adequate protective device necessary to make the process of police interrogation conform to the dictates of the privilege."

In part III, Warren states the law that goes forward in *Miranda v. Arizona*. The first paragraph offers, in general terms, what the Court holds to be required by the Constitution. In the second paragraph, Warren writes that the Court encourages "Congress and the States to continue their laudable search for increasingly effective ways of protecting the rights of the individual while promoting efficient enforcement of our criminal laws." The invitation can be read two ways: It is modest and amenable but also, at the same time, critical and imperious. On one hand, under the Constitution, Congress and the States are recognized as having the power to pass laws governing police procedures. On the other hand, the Court's ruling in *Miranda* is intended to correct failures to observe the individual's privilege against self-incrimination, especially such failures by state police. In addition, the Court, because it exercises the power to interpret the Constitution, will pass judgment on any "possible alternatives for protecting the privilege which might be devised by Congress or the States in the exercise of their creative rule-making capacities."

The remainder of this section fleshes out the warnings that comprise the "*Miranda* warnings" that defendants are given by police. Warren emphasizes that these warnings are necessary anytime "a person in custody is to be subjected to interrogation." The capacity or background of the defendant does not matter; rather, the "warning is an absolute prerequisite in overcoming the inherent pressures of the interrogation process." The warning of the right to remain silent, "accompanied by the explanation that anything said can and will be used against the individual in Court," puts the defendant on alert "that he is faced with a phase of the adversary system." The presence of counsel at the interrogation is "indispensable to the protection of the Fifth Amendment privilege" and will sharpen the record of the interrogation to be reported at trial. A defendant may waive his right to counsel, but that waiver is effective only when "made after the warnings we here delineate have been given." Finally, "the financial ability of the individual has no relationship to the scope of the rights involved here." An express explanation to an indigent person that a lawyer will be appointed for him is necessary to assure that person that he is in a position to exercise the right to have counsel present during interrogation.

Warren next lays down additional ground rules: An individual, once given the warnings, may assert the rights at any time prior to or during questioning. If he waives his rights and speaks with the police, he may stop at any time and exercise his right to remain silent or his right to have counsel. In either instance, police are required to cease interrogation. Where an individual waives his rights and interrogation follows, "a heavy burden rests on the government to demonstrate that the defendant knowingly and intelligently waived" his rights. Silence from the defendant in response to any question does not constitute a waiver.

In part IV, Warren addresses critics who will claim—or who, in the case of justices dissenting to the decision, do claim—that with its holding in *Miranda*, the Court is hindering the ability of society, through the efforts of its police, to control crime. He cites the experiences of other law-enforcement agencies employing rules protecting against self-incrimination—the Federal Bureau of Investigation, criminal justice systems in other nations, and the U.S. military—to buttress his view that the *Miranda* warnings will not unduly hamper police.

Warren's opinion for the Court in *Miranda v. Arizona* is remarkable for many reasons. The discussion of the Fifth Amendment privilege is so expansive as to constitute an essay on the rights of the individual. The

warnings that the Court dictates must be given to defendants by police are highly specific; the Court rarely prescribes policy in such a detailed way. Regarding the actual cases under review, not until part V does Warren finally address the facts of the four cases collected under the rubric of *Miranda*.

In fact, discussion of the four cases may not appear until the final section for good reason. An important point *Miranda* makes is that the Court will not consider, case by case, whether a defendant's confession was voluntary. The intent of *Miranda* is that, absent the necessary warnings or a permissible equivalent, a Fifth Amendment violation has occurred, and statements made by the defendant are inadmissible. As time would tell, however, *Miranda* did not provide total resolution for questions about the privilege against self-incrimination during police questioning. To close the opinion, in quick order, the Court announces the findings in the four separate cases.

Justice Tom Clark's Dissenting Opinion

Justice Clark's dissent is short and focused. He objects to the majority's use of police manuals to explain its findings, as "not one is shown by the record here to be the official manual of any political department, much less in universal use in crime detection." Also, the Court has "not fairly characterized" the efforts made by city and state police to enforce the law. In part I, Clark criticizes the Court's innovation in *Miranda*, holding that the ruling goes "too far too fast." In part II, Clark criticizes the Court for "the promulgation of doctrinaire rules" that police must follow when conducting in-custody interrogation. The prior rule to determine whether a statement admitting guilt was voluntary, Clark writes, "depended upon 'a totality of circumstances.'" He declares in Part III, "I would continue to follow that rule." He does not object to having police inform detained persons, prior to custodial interrogation, that they have a right to counsel and that counsel will be appointed if they cannot afford one. "In the absence of warnings . . . the confession was clearly voluntary."

Justice John Marshall Harlan II's Dissenting Opinion

In this dissent, which was joined by Justices Potter Stewart and Byron White, Harlan expresses deep and fundamental disagreement with the Court's reasoning and results in *Miranda*. To Harlan, "the thrust of the new rules is to negate all pressures, to reinforce the nervous or ignorant suspect, and ultimately to discourage any confession at all." The decision, he says, is not supported by the Constitution, nor does it make good public policy.

With the *Miranda* rules, Harlan writes in part II, the Court travels far from the due process clause of the Fourteenth Amendment and its "voluntariness" test as a way to determine the admissibility of a statement made during police questioning. A string of Supreme Court cases had fine-tuned the "voluntariness" standard, resulting in "an elaborate, sophisticated, and sensitive approach to admissibility of confessions." Cases were considered one at a time, the standard was "flexible in its ability to respond to the endless mutations of fact presented," and lower courts knew how to use the standard. Furthermore, the cases attached ample value "to society's interest in suspect questioning as an instrument of law enforcement." For Harlan, no precedents exist in cases prior to *Miranda* supporting the view that the Fifth and Sixth Amendments protect defendants during police interrogation.

The *Miranda* rules, writes Harlan in part III, are not supported by concerns of public policy, such as by being "plainly desirable in the context of our society." The rules impair and may even frustrate police interrogation. He notes, "There can be little doubt that the Court's new code would markedly decrease the number of confessions." With this "hazardous experimentation," the Court is reaching far ahead of other societal forces that might lay claim to having a say in the determination of proper police practices. Harlan reasons that "this Court's too rapid departure from existing constitutional standards" will discourage criminal law reform that might otherwise occur elsewhere in the political system, particularly in the legislative branches, where the initiative "truly belongs."

Justice Byron White's Dissenting Opinion

White's dissent, which was joined by Justices Harlan and Stewart, differs in perspective and tone from Harlan's but comes to the same conclusions. White seemingly accepts the application of the Fifth Amendment privilege against self-incrimination during police questioning. However, he reasons that *Bram v. United States*, which is cited by Warren, supports only "whether a confession, obtained during custodial interrogation, had been compelled." White shares with Harlan the conviction that a version of the voluntariness standard, where the question becomes whether the confession was compelled, is better than the *Miranda* rules, where the question is whether the warnings were given. In part II, White does not dismiss out of hand the Court's innovation in *Miranda* but asserts that when the Court forges new law and policy, that act invites close examination.

The rules that the Court announces, writes White, are aimed at reducing confessions and guilty pleas. As such, the system of criminal law and "society's interest in the general security" will suffer. Although the Court's rules might appear to give clear-cut guidance as to when a statement is not admissible, White believes otherwise. He predicts that the decision will leave open questions as to whether the accused was in custody, whether his statements were spontaneous or the product of interrogation, whether the accused has effectively waived his rights, and whether nontestimonial evidence introduced at trial is the fruit of statements made during a prohibited interrogation, all of which are certain to prove productive of uncertainty during investigation and litigation during prosecution. White indeed writes presciently here; later Supreme Court cases on self-incrimination following *Miranda* probed exactly these issues.

Impact

The impact of *Miranda v. Arizona*, measured purely as a legal standard, began to dissipate shortly after it was handed down. Congress announced its displeasure with the *Miranda* rules in the Omnibus Crime Control and Safe Streets Act of 1968. As led by Chief Justice Warren Burger from 1969 to 1986, the Supreme Court never overruled *Miranda* but instead chipped away at it by developing, in cases where defendants claimed a *Miranda* violation, exceptions to the requirement that the warnings always be given. Other cases required the Court to confront issues created by *Miranda* but not settled there, including the questions raised by Justice White in his dissent. Clearly, *Miranda* was not the last word on the right against self-incrimination during in-custody interrogation.

Nonetheless, the general impact of the case cannot be denied, for, as noted in a *Los Angeles Times* editorial by the constitutional law scholar Akhil Reed Amar,

"*Miranda* has been woven into the fabric of daily life." Police departments incorporate the *Miranda* rules into their training and practices, sometimes printing the *Miranda* rights on cards for officers to hand to suspects. Americans are likely more familiar with the particulars of the holding in this case than in any other ever heard by the Supreme Court, for the *Miranda* warnings are common parlance on television and in crime fiction. Thus, the clamor trailing this case through American culture more than a half century after its disposition has instructed people, in a simplified manner, about important constitutional rights.

Dire predictions that *Miranda* would hinder or hobble efforts to fight crime, made by *Miranda*'s dissenters and repeated by law-enforcement officials when the decision became known, did not pan out. The legal scholar Stephen Schulhofer reviewed relevant empirical research and concluded that those studies show that *Miranda* did not seriously affect conviction rates or the ability of police to interrogate suspects and obtain statements that proved useful in convictions.

Overall, the Warren Court's decision in *Miranda*, as well as the decisions in prior cases that championed rights of the accused, undoubtedly set in motion political forces that helped shape the nation's future. Richard Nixon, accepting the Republican Party's presidential nomination on August 8, 1968, told delegates "that some of our courts in their decisions have gone too far in weakening the peace forces as against the criminal forces in this country and we must act to restore that balance." Nixon was elected that fall on a campaign that stressed "law and order." Meanwhile, Warren Burger, a U.S. appeals court judge, had become well known as a vocal critic of the Warren Court's expansion of the rights of the accused, especially the *Miranda* decision. Months after taking office, President Nixon selected Burger to replace the retiring Earl Warren as chief justice. The Burger Court (1969–1986) and the Court led by Chief Justice William Rehnquist (1986–2005) would try to undo the progressive steps taken by the Warren Court in many areas of the law.

Questions for Further Study

1. Review the standards set by the Court in *Miranda* for determining whether a defendant has "waived his privilege against self-incrimination and his right to retained or appointed counsel" (part III). Has the Court backed into another "voluntariness" standard here? Why did Chief Justice Warren not expressly rule that any in-custody interrogation require the presence of counsel? And why would a defendant agree to waive his rights? (In fact, many do.)

2. At retrial, Arizona convicted Miranda after presenting testimony by his common-law wife that he had confessed to her that he had committed the abduction and rape. She stated that the confession had been made to her when she visited Miranda in jail, three days after he confessed to the police, and after she confirmed, upon Miranda's inquiry, that police had informed her of his confession to them. Did the use of this evidence actually violate the Supreme Court's ruling in *Miranda*? Think carefully about Miranda's conversation with his common-law wife. Why did he confess to her?

3. The three dissenting opinions in *Miranda* criticize the Court for moving ahead of the rest of the political system. Does the Supreme Court's making new law and policy constitute a problem? Consider cases since *Miranda* in which courts have ruled in innovative ways, regarding, for example, abortion (*Roe v. Wade*, decided by the U.S. Supreme Court in 1973) or same-sex marriage (*Goodridge v. Department of Public Health*, decided by the Massachusetts Supreme Judicial Court in 2004).

4. Should the rights of the accused be applied on a sliding scale, based on the type of crime? Might, for example, a robbery suspect, undergoing police interrogation, deserve more rights than a murder suspect or than someone detained for suspicion of international terrorism? Why or why not?

Further Reading

Books

Baker, Liva. *Miranda: Crime, Law and Politics.* New York: Atheneum, 1983.

Belknap, Michal R. *The Supreme Court under Earl Warren, 1953–1969.* Columbia: University of South Carolina Press, 2004.

Horwitz, Morton J. *The Warren Court and the Pursuit of Justice: A Critical Issue.* New York: Hill and Wang, 1998.

LeMay, Michael C., and Alemayehu G. Mariam. *Civil Rights and Civil Liberties in America: A Reference Handbook.* Santa Barbara, CA: ABC-CLIO, 2020.

Rauf, Don. *Establishing the Rights of the Accused:* Miranda V. Arizona. Berkeley Heights, NJ: Enslow Publishing, 2017.

Schulhofer, Stephen. "*Miranda v. Arizona*: A Modest but Important Legacy." In *Criminal Procedure Stories,* ed. Carol Steiker. New York: Foundation Press/Thomson/West, 2006.

Stuart, Gary L. *Miranda: The Story of America's Right to Remain Silent.* Tucson: University of Arizona Press, 2004.

Articles

Amar, Akhil Reed. "OK, All Together Now: 'You Have the Right To . . .'" *Los Angeles Times,* December 12, 1999.

Schauer, Frederick. "The Miranda Warning." *Washington Law Review* 88 (2013): 155+.

Websites

"Gideon v. Wainwright." U.S. Supreme Court Media "Oyez" website. http://www.oyez.org/cases/1960-1969/1962/1962_155/.

"Mapp v. Ohio." U.S. Supreme Court Media "Oyez" website. http://www.oyez.org/cases/1960-1969/1960/1960_236/.

"Miranda v. Arizona—Oral Argument." U.S. Supreme Court Media "Oyez" website. http://www.oyez.org/cases/1960-1969/1965/1965_759/argument/.

"Richard M. Nixon: Presidential Nomination Acceptance Speech." 4President.org website. http://www.4president.org/speeches/nixon1968acceptance.htm.

—Commentary by Randy Wagner

MIRANDA V. ARIZONA

Document Text

Mr. Chief Justice Warren Delivered the Opinion of the Court

The cases before us raise questions which go to the roots of our concepts of American criminal jurisprudence: the restraints society must observe consistent with the Federal Constitution in prosecuting individuals for crime. More specifically, we deal with the admissibility of statements obtained from an individual who is subjected to custodial police interrogation and the necessity for procedures which assure that the individual is accorded his privilege under the Fifth Amendment to the Constitution not to be compelled to incriminate himself.

We dealt with certain phases of this problem recently in *Escobedo v. Illinois*, 378 U.S. 478 (1964). There, as in the four cases before us, law enforcement officials took the defendant into custody and interrogated him in a police station for the purpose of obtaining a confession. The police did not effectively advise him of his right to remain silent or of his right to consult with his attorney. Rather, they confronted him with an alleged accomplice who accused him of having perpetrated a murder. When the defendant denied the accusation and said "I didn't shoot Manuel, you did it," they handcuffed him and took him to an interrogation room. There, while handcuffed and standing, he was questioned for four hours until he confessed. During this interrogation, the police denied his request to speak to his attorney, and they prevented his retained attorney, who had come to the police station, from consulting with him. At his trial, the State, over his objection, introduced the confession against him. We held that the statements thus made were constitutionally inadmissible.

This case has been the subject of judicial interpretation and spirited legal debate since it was decided two years ago. Both state and federal courts, in assessing its implications, have arrived at varying conclusions. A wealth of scholarly material has been written tracing its ramifications and underpinnings. Police and prosecutor have speculated on its range and desirability. We granted certiorari in these cases, 382 U.S. 924, 925, 937, in order further to explore some facets of the problems, thus exposed, of applying the privilege against self-incrimination to in-custody interrogation, and to give concrete constitutional guidelines for law enforcement agencies and courts to follow.

We start here, as we did in Escobedo, with the premise that our holding is not an innovation in our jurisprudence, but is an application of principles long recognized and applied in other settings. We have undertaken a thorough re-examination of the Escobedo decision and the principles it announced, and we reaffirm it. That case was but an explication of basic rights that are enshrined in our Constitution—that "No person . . . shall be compelled in any criminal case to be a witness against himself," and that "the accused shall . . . have the Assistance of Counsel"—rights which were put in jeopardy in that case through official overbearing. These precious rights were fixed in our Constitution only after centuries of persecution and struggle. And in the words of Chief Justice Marshall, they were secured "for ages to come, and . . . designed to approach immortality as nearly as human institutions can approach it," *Cohens v. Virginia*, 6 Wheat. 264, 387 (1821).

Over 70 years ago, our predecessors on this Court eloquently stated:

"The maxim nemo tenetur seipsum accusare had its origin in a protest against the inquisitorial and manifestly unjust methods of interrogating accused persons, which [have] long obtained in the continental system, and, until the expulsion of the Stuarts from the British throne in 1688, and the erection of additional barriers for the protection of the people against the exercise of arbitrary power, [were] not uncommon even in England. While the admissions or confessions of the prisoner, when voluntarily and freely made, have always ranked high in the scale of incriminating evidence, if an accused person be asked to explain his apparent connection with a crime under investigation, the ease with which the questions put to him may assume an inquisitorial character, the temptation to press the witness unduly, to browbeat him if he be timid or reluctant, to push him into a corner, and to entrap him into fatal contradictions, which is so painfully evident in many of the earlier state trials, notably in those of Sir Nicholas Throckmorton, and Udal, the Puritan minister, made the system so odious as to give rise to a demand for its total abolition. The change in the English criminal procedure in that particular seems to be founded upon no statute and no judicial opinion, but upon a general and silent acquiescence of the courts in a popular demand. But, however adopted, it has become firmly embedded in English, as well as in American jurisprudence. So deeply did the iniquities of the ancient system impress themselves upon the minds of the American colonists that the States, with one accord, made a denial of the right to question an accused person a part of their fundamental law, so that a maxim, which in England was a mere rule of evidence, became clothed in this country with the impregnability of a constitutional enactment." Brown v. Walker, 161 U.S. 591, 596-597 (1896).

In stating the obligation of the judiciary to apply these constitutional rights, this Court declared in *Weems v. United States*, 217 U.S. 349, 373 (1910):

"... our contemplation cannot be only of what has been but of what may be. Under any other rule a constitution would indeed be as easy of application as it would be deficient in efficacy and power. Its general principles would have little value and be converted by precedent into impotent and lifeless formulas. Rights declared in words might be lost in reality. And this has been recognized. The meaning and vitality of the Constitution have developed against narrow and restrictive construction."

This was the spirit in which we delineated, in meaningful language, the manner in which the constitutional rights of the individual could be enforced against overzealous police practices. It was necessary in Escobedo, as here, to insure that what was proclaimed in the Constitution had not become but a "form of words," *Silverthorne Lumber Co. v. United States*, 251 U.S. 385, 392 (1920), in the hands of government officials. And it is in this spirit, consistent with our role as judges, that we adhere to the principles of Escobedo today.

Our holding will be spelled out with some specificity in the pages which follow but briefly stated it is this: the prosecution may not use statements, whether exculpatory or inculpatory, stemming from custodial interrogation of the defendant unless it demonstrates the use of procedural safeguards effective to secure the privilege against self-incrimination. By custodial interrogation, we mean questioning initiated by law enforcement officers after a person has been taken into custody or otherwise deprived of his freedom of action in any significant way. As for the procedural safeguards to be employed, unless other fully effective means are devised to inform accused persons of their right of silence and to assure a continuous opportunity to exercise it, the following measures are required. Prior to any questioning, the person must be warned that he has a right to remain silent, that any statement he does make may be used as evidence against him, and that he has a right to the presence of an attorney, either retained or appointed. The defendant may waive effectuation of these rights, provided the waiver is made voluntarily, knowingly and intelligently. If, however, he indicates in any manner and at any stage of the process that he wishes to consult with an attorney before speaking there can be no questioning. Likewise, if the individual is alone and indicates in any manner that he does not wish to be interrogated, the police may not question him. The mere fact that he may have answered some questions or volunteered some statements on his own does not deprive him of the right to refrain from answering any further inquiries until he has consulted with an attorney and thereafter consents to be questioned.

I

The constitutional issue we decide in each of these cases is the admissibility of statements obtained from a defendant questioned while in custody or otherwise deprived of his freedom of action in any significant way. In each, the defendant was questioned by police officers, detectives, or a prosecuting attorney in a room in which he was cut off from the outside world. In none of these cases was the defendant given a full and effective warning of his rights at the outset of the interrogation process. In all the cases, the questioning elicited oral admissions, and in three of them, signed statements as well which were admitted at their trials. They all thus share salient features—incommunicado interrogation of individuals in a police-dominated atmosphere, resulting in self-incriminating statements without full warnings of constitutional rights.

An understanding of the nature and setting of this in-custody interrogation is essential to our decisions today. The difficulty in depicting what transpires at such interrogations stems from the fact that in this country they have largely taken place incommunicado. From extensive factual studies undertaken in the early 1930's, including the famous Wickersham Report to Congress by a Presidential Commission, it is clear that police violence and the "third degree" flourished at that time. In a series of cases decided by this Court long after these studies, the police resorted to physical brutality—beating, hanging, whipping—and to sustained and protracted questioning incommunicado in order to extort confessions. The Commission on Civil Rights in 1961 found much evidence to indicate that "some policemen still resort to physical force to obtain confessions," 1961 Comm'n on Civil Rights Rep., Justice, pt. 5, 17. The use of physical brutality and violence is not, unfortunately, relegated to the past or to any part of the country. Only recently in Kings County, New York, the police brutally beat, kicked and placed lighted cigarette butts on the back of a potential witness under interrogation for the purpose of securing a statement incriminating a third party. *People v. Portelli*, 15 N.Y. 2d 235, 205 N.E. 2d 857, 257 N.Y. S. 2d 931 (1965).

The examples given above are undoubtedly the exception now, but they are sufficiently widespread to be the object of concern. Unless a proper limitation upon custodial interrogation is achieved—such as these decisions will advance—there can be no assurance that practices of this nature will be eradicated in the foreseeable future. The conclusion of the Wickersham Commission Report, made over 30 years ago, is still pertinent:

> "To the contention that the third degree is necessary to get the facts, the reporters aptly reply in the language of the present Lord Chancellor of England (Lord Sankey): 'It is not admissible to do a great right by doing a little wrong. . . . It is not sufficient to do justice by obtaining a proper result by irregular or improper means.' Not only does the use of the third degree involve a flagrant violation of law by the officers of the law, but it involves also the dangers of false confessions, and it tends to make police and prosecutors less zealous in the search for objective evidence. As the New York prosecutor quoted in the report said, 'It is a short cut and makes the police lazy and unenterprising.' Or, as another official quoted remarked: 'If you use your fists, you are not so likely to use your wits.' We agree with the conclusion expressed in the report, that 'The third degree brutalizes the police, hardens the prisoner against society, and lowers the esteem in which the administration of justice is held by the public.'" IV National Commission on Law Observance and Enforcement, Report on Lawlessness in Law Enforcement 5 (1931).

Again we stress that the modern practice of in-custody interrogation is psychologically rather than physically oriented. As we have stated before, "Since *Chambers v. Florida*, 309 U.S. 227, this Court has recognized that coercion can be mental as well as physical, and that the blood of the accused is not the only hallmark of an unconstitutional inquisition." *Blackburn v. Alabama*, 361 U.S. 199, 206 (1960). Interrogation still takes place in privacy. Privacy results in secrecy and this in turn results in a gap in our knowledge as to what in fact goes on in the interrogation rooms. A valuable source of information about present police practices, however, may be found in various police manuals and texts which document procedures employed with success in the past, and which recommend various other effective tactics. These texts are used by law enforcement agencies themselves as guides. It should be noted that these texts professedly present the most enlightened and effective means presently used to obtain statements through custodial interrogation. By considering these texts and other data, it is possible to describe procedures observed and noted around the country.

The officers are told by the manuals that the "principal psychological factor contributing to a successful interrogation is privacy—being alone with the person under interrogation." The efficacy of this tactic has been explained as follows:

> "If at all practicable, the interrogation should take place in the investigator's office or at least in a room of his own choice. The subject should be deprived of every psychological advantage. In his own home he may be confident, indignant, or recalcitrant. He is more keenly aware of his rights and more reluctant to tell of his indiscretions or criminal behavior within the walls of his home. Moreover his family and other friends are nearby, their presence lending moral support. In his own office, the investigator possesses all the advantages. The atmosphere suggests the invincibility of the forces of the law."

To highlight the isolation and unfamiliar surroundings, the manuals instruct the police to display an air of confidence in the suspect's guilt and from outward appearance to maintain only an interest in confirming certain details. The guilt of the subject is to be posited as a fact. The interrogator should direct his comments toward the reasons why the subject committed the act, rather than court failure by asking the subject whether he did it. Like other men, perhaps the subject has had a bad family life, had an unhappy childhood, had too much to drink, had an unrequited desire for women. The officers are instructed to minimize the moral seriousness of the offense, to cast blame on the victim or on society. These tactics are designed to put the subject in a psychological state where his story is but an elaboration of what the police purport to know already—that he is guilty. Explanations to the contrary are dismissed and discouraged.

The texts thus stress that the major qualities an interrogator should possess are patience and perseverance. One writer describes the efficacy of these characteristics in this manner:

> "In the preceding paragraphs emphasis has been placed on kindness and stratagems. The investigator will, however, encounter many situations where the sheer weight of his personality will be the deciding factor. Where emotional appeals and tricks are employed to no avail, he must rely on an oppressive atmosphere of dogged persistence. He must interrogate steadily and without relent, leaving the subject no prospect of surcease. He must dominate his subject and overwhelm him with his inexorable will to obtain the truth. He should interrogate for a spell of several hours pausing only for the subject's necessities in acknowledgment of the need to avoid a charge of duress that can be technically substantiated. In a serious case, the interrogation may continue for days, with the required intervals for food and sleep, but with no respite from the atmosphere of domination. It is possible in this way to induce the subject to talk without resorting to duress or coercion. The method should be used only when the guilt of the subject appears highly probable."

The manuals suggest that the suspect be offered legal excuses for his actions in order to obtain an initial admission of guilt. Where there is a suspected revenge-killing, for example, the interrogator may say:

> "Joe, you probably didn't go out looking for this fellow with the purpose of shooting him. My guess is, however, that you expected something from him and that's why you carried a gun—for your own protection. You knew him for what he was, no good. Then when you met him he probably started using foul, abusive language and he gave some indication that he was about to pull a gun on you, and that's when you had to act to save your own life. That's about it, isn't it, Joe?"

Having then obtained the admission of shooting, the interrogator is advised to refer to circumstantial evidence which negates the self-defense explanation. This should enable him to secure the entire story. One text notes that "Even if he fails to do so, the inconsistency between the subject's original denial of the shooting and his present admission of at least doing the shooting will serve to deprive him of a self-defense 'out' at the time of trial."

When the techniques described above prove unavailing, the texts recommend they be alternated with a show of some hostility. One ploy often used has been termed the "friendly-unfriendly" or the "Mutt and Jeff" act:

> ". . . In this technique, two agents are employed. Mutt, the relentless investigator, who knows the subject is guilty and is not going to waste any time. He's sent a dozen men away for this crime and he's going to send the subject away for the full term. Jeff, on the other hand, is obviously a kindhearted man. He has a family himself. He has a brother who was involved in a little scrape like this. He disapproves of Mutt and his tactics and will arrange to get him off the case if the subject will cooperate. He can't hold Mutt off for very long. The subject would be wise to make a quick decision. The technique is applied by having both investigators present while Mutt acts out his role. Jeff may stand by quietly and demur at some of Mutt's tactics. When Jeff makes his plea for cooperation, Mutt is not present in the room."

The interrogators sometimes are instructed to induce a confession out of trickery. The technique here is quite effective in crimes which require identification or which run in series. In the identification situation, the interrogator may take a break in his questioning to place the subject among a group of men in a line-up. "The witness or complainant (previously coached, if necessary) studies the line-up and confidently points out the subject as the guilty party." Then the questioning resumes "as though there were now no doubt about the guilt of the subject." A variation on this technique is called the "reverse line-up":

> "The accused is placed in a line-up, but this time he is identified by several fictitious witnesses or victims who associated him with different offenses. It is expected that the subject will become desperate and confess to the offense under investigation in order to escape from the false accusations."

The manuals also contain instructions for police on how to handle the individual who refuses to discuss the matter entirely, or who asks for an attorney or relatives. The examiner is to concede him the right to remain silent. "This usually has a very undermining effect. First of all, he is disappointed in his expectation of an unfavorable reaction on the part of the interrogator. Secondly, a concession of this right to remain silent impresses the subject with the apparent fairness of his interrogator." After this psychological conditioning, however, the officer is told to point out the incriminating significance of the suspect's refusal to talk:

> "Joe, you have a right to remain silent. That's your privilege and I'm the last person in the world who'll try to take it away from you. If that's the way you want to leave this, O. K. But let me ask you this. Suppose you were in my shoes and I were in yours and you called me in to ask me about this and I told you, 'I don't want to answer any of your questions.' You'd think I had something to hide, and you'd probably be right in thinking that. That's exactly what I'll have to think about you, and so will everybody else. So let's sit here and talk this whole thing over."

Few will persist in their initial refusal to talk, it is said, if this monologue is employed correctly.

In the event that the subject wishes to speak to a relative or an attorney, the following advice is tendered:

> "[T]he interrogator should respond by suggesting that the subject first tell the truth to the interrogator himself rather than get anyone else involved in the matter. If the request is for an attorney, the interrogator may suggest that the subject save himself or his family the expense of any such professional service, particularly if he is innocent of the offense under investigation. The interrogator may also add, 'Joe, I'm only looking for the truth, and if you're telling the truth, that's it. You can handle this by yourself.'"

From these representative samples of interrogation techniques, the setting prescribed by the manuals and observed in practice becomes clear. In essence, it is this: To be alone with the subject is essential to prevent distraction and to deprive him of any outside support. The aura of confidence in his guilt undermines his will to resist. He merely confirms the preconceived story the police seek to have him describe. Patience and persistence, at times relentless questioning, are employed. To obtain a confession, the interrogator must "patiently maneuver himself or his quarry into a position from which the desired objective may be attained." When normal procedures fail to produce the needed result, the police may resort to deceptive stratagems such as giving false legal advice. It is important to keep the subject off balance, for example, by trading on his insecurity about himself or his surroundings. The police then persuade, trick, or cajole him out of exercising his constitutional rights.

Even without employing brutality, the "third degree" or the specific stratagems described above, the very fact of custodial interrogation exacts a heavy toll on individual liberty and trades on the weakness of individuals. This fact may be illustrated simply by referring to three confession cases decided by this Court in the Term immediately preceding our Escobedo decision. In *Townsend v. Sain*, 372 U.S. 293 (1963), the defendant was a 19-year-old heroin addict, described as a "near mental defective," id., at 307-310. The defendant in *Lynumn v. Illinois*, 372 U.S. 528 (1963), was a woman who confessed to the arresting officer after being importuned to "cooperate" in order to prevent her children from being taken by relief authorities. This Court as in those cases reversed the conviction of a defendant in *Haynes v. Washington*, 373 U.S. 503 (1963), whose persistent request during his interrogation was to phone his wife or attorney. In other settings, these individuals might have exercised their constitutional rights. In the incommunicado police-dominated atmosphere, they succumbed.

In the cases before us today, given this background, we concern ourselves primarily with this interrogation atmosphere and the evils it can bring. In No. 759, *Miranda v. Arizona*, the police arrested the defendant and took him to a special interrogation room where they secured a confession. In No. 760, *Vignera v. New York*, the defendant made oral admissions to the police after interrogation in the afternoon, and then signed an inculpatory statement upon being questioned by an assistant district attorney later the same evening. In No. 761, *Westover v. United States*, the defendant was handed over to the Federal Bureau of Investigation by local authorities after they had detained and interrogated him for a lengthy period, both at night and the following morning. After some two hours of questioning, the federal officers had obtained signed statements from the defendant. Lastly, in No. 584, *California v. Stewart*, the local police held the defendant five days in the station and interrogated him on nine separate occasions before they secured his inculpatory statement.

In these cases, we might not find the defendants' statements to have been involuntary in traditional terms. Our concern for adequate safeguards to protect precious Fifth Amendment rights is, of course, not lessened in the slightest. In each of the cases, the defendant was thrust into an unfamiliar atmosphere and run through menacing police interrogation procedures. The potentiality for compulsion is forcefully apparent, for example, in Miranda, where the indigent Mexican defendant was a seriously disturbed individual with pronounced sexual fantasies, and in Stewart, in which the defendant was an indigent Los Angeles Negro who had dropped out of school in the sixth grade. To be sure, the records do not evince overt physical coercion or patent psychological ploys. The fact remains that in none of these cases did the officers undertake to afford appropriate safeguards at the outset of the interrogation to insure that the statements were truly the product of free choice.

It is obvious that such an interrogation environment is created for no purpose other than to subjugate the individual to the will of his examiner. This atmosphere carries its own badge of intimidation. To be sure, this is not physical intimidation, but it is equally destructive of human dignity. The current practice of incommunicado interrogation is at odds with one of our Nation's most cherished principles—that the individual may not be compelled to incriminate himself. Unless adequate protective devices are employed to dispel the compulsion inherent in custodial surroundings, no statement obtained from the defendant can truly be the product of his free choice.

From the foregoing, we can readily perceive an intimate connection between the privilege against self-incrimination and police custodial questioning. It is fitting to turn to history and precedent underlying the Self-Incrimination Clause to determine its applicability in this situation.

II

We sometimes forget how long it has taken to establish the privilege against self-incrimination, the sources from which it came and the fervor with which it was defended. Its roots go back into ancient times. Perhaps the critical historical event shedding light on its origins and evolution was the trial of one John Lilburn, a vocal anti-Stuart Leveller, who was made to take the Star Chamber Oath in 1637. The oath would have bound him to answer to all questions posed to him on any subject. The Trial of John Lilburn and John Wharton, 3 How. St. Tr. 1315 (1637). He resisted the oath and declaimed the proceedings, stating:

> "Another fundamental right I then contended for, was, that no man's conscience ought to be racked by oaths imposed, to answer to questions concerning himself in matters criminal, or pretended to be so." Haller & Davies, The Leveller Tracts 1647-1653, p. 454 (1944).

On account of the Lilburn Trial, Parliament abolished the inquisitorial Court of Star Chamber and went further in giving him generous reparation. The lofty principles to which Lilburn had appealed during his trial gained popular acceptance in England. These sentiments worked their way over to the Colonies and were implanted after great struggle into the Bill of Rights. Those who framed our Constitution and the Bill of Rights were ever aware of subtle encroachments on individual liberty. They knew that "illegitimate and unconstitutional practices get their first footing . . . by silent approaches and slight deviations from legal modes of procedure." *Boyd v. United States*, 116 U.S. 616, 635 (1886). The privilege was elevated to constitutional status and has always been "as broad as the mischief against which it seeks to guard." *Counselman v. Hitchcock*, 142 U.S. 547, 562 (1892). We cannot depart from this noble heritage.

Thus we may view the historical development of the privilege as one which groped for the proper scope of governmental power over the citizen. As a "noble principle often transcends its origins," the privilege has come rightfully to be recognized in part as an individual's substantive right, a "right to a private enclave where he may lead a private life. That right is the hallmark of our democracy." *United States v. Grunewald*, 233 F.2d 556, 579, 581-582 (Frank, J., dissenting), rev'd, 353 U.S. 391 (1957). We have recently noted that the privilege against self-incrimination—the essential mainstay of our adversary system—is founded on a complex of values, *Murphy v. Waterfront Comm'n*, 378 U.S. 52, 55-57, n. 5 (1964); *Tehan v. Shott*, 382 U.S. 406, 414-415, n. 12 (1966). All these policies point to one overriding thought: the constitutional foundation underlying the privilege is the respect a government—state or federal—must accord to the dignity and integrity of its citizens. To maintain a "fair state-individual balance," to require the government "to shoulder the entire load," 8 Wigmore, Evidence 317 (McNaughton rev. 1961), to respect the inviolability of the human personality, our accusatory system of criminal justice demands that the government seeking to punish an individual produce the evidence against him by its own independent labors, rather than by the cruel, simple expedient of compelling it from his own mouth. *Chambers v. Florida*, 309 U.S. 227, 235-238 (1940). In sum, the privilege is fulfilled only when the person is guaranteed the right "to remain silent unless he chooses to speak in the unfettered exercise of his own will." *Malloy v. Hogan*, 378 U.S. 1, 8 (1964).

The question in these cases is whether the privilege is fully applicable during a period of custodial interrogation. In this Court, the privilege has consistently been accorded a liberal construction. *Albertson v. SACB*, 382 U.S. 70, 81 (1965); *Hoffman v. United States*, 341 U.S. 479, 486 (1951); *Arndstein v. McCarthy*, 254 U.S. 71, 72-73 (1920); *Counselman v. Hitchock*, 142 U.S. 547, 562 (1892). We are satisfied that all the principles embodied in the privilege apply to informal compulsion exerted by law-enforcement officers during in-custody questioning. An individual swept from familiar surroundings into police custody, surrounded by antagonistic forces, and subjected to the techniques of persuasion described above cannot be otherwise than under compulsion to speak. As a practical matter, the compulsion to speak in the isolated setting of the police station may well be greater than in courts or other official investigations, where there are often impartial observers to guard against intimidation or trickery.

This question, in fact, could have been taken as settled in federal courts almost 70 years ago, when, in *Bram v. United States*, 168 U.S. 532, 542 (1897), this Court held:

> "In criminal trials, in the courts of the United States, wherever a question arises whether a confession is incompetent because not voluntary, the issue is controlled by that portion of the Fifth Amendment . . . commanding that no person 'shall be compelled in any criminal case to be a witness against himself.'"

In Bram, the Court reviewed the British and American history and case law and set down the Fifth Amendment standard for compulsion which we implement today:

"Much of the confusion which has resulted from the effort to deduce from the adjudged cases what would be a sufficient quantum of proof to show that a confession was or was not voluntary, has arisen from a misconception of the subject to which the proof must address itself. The rule is not that in order to render a statement admissible the proof must be adequate to establish that the particular communications contained in a statement were voluntarily made, but it must be sufficient to establish that the making of the statement was voluntary; that is to say, that from the causes, which the law treats as legally sufficient to engender in the mind of the accused hope or fear in respect to the crime charged, the accused was not involuntarily impelled to make a statement, when but for the improper influences he would have remained silent...." 168 U.S., at 549. And see, id., at 542.

The Court has adhered to this reasoning. In 1924, Mr. Justice Brandeis wrote for a unanimous Court in reversing a conviction resting on a compelled confession, *Wan v. United States*, 266 U.S. 1. He stated:

"In the federal courts, the requisite of voluntariness is not satisfied by establishing merely that the confession was not induced by a promise or a threat. A confession is voluntary in law if, and only if, it was, in fact, voluntarily made. A confession may have been given voluntarily, although it was made to police officers, while in custody, and in answer to an examination conducted by them. But a confession obtained by compulsion must be excluded whatever may have been the character of the compulsion, and whether the compulsion was applied in a judicial proceeding or otherwise. Bram v. United States, 168 U.S. 532." 266 U.S., at 14-15.

In addition to the expansive historical development of the privilege and the sound policies which have nurtured its evolution, judicial precedent thus clearly establishes its application to incommunicado interro-

gation. In fact, the Government concedes this point as well established in No. 761, *Westover v. United States*, stating: "We have no doubt ... that it is possible for a suspect's Fifth Amendment right to be violated during in-custody questioning by a law-enforcement officer."

Because of the adoption by Congress of Rule 5 (a) of the Federal Rules of Criminal Procedure, and this Court's effectuation of that Rule in *McNabb v. United States*, 318 U.S. 332 (1943), and *Mallory v. United States*, 354 U.S. 449 (1957), we have had little occasion in the past quarter century to reach the constitutional issues in dealing with federal interrogations. These supervisory rules, requiring production of an arrested person before a commissioner "without unnecessary delay" and excluding evidence obtained in default of that statutory obligation, were nonetheless responsive to the same considerations of Fifth Amendment policy that unavoidably face us now as to the States. In McNabb, 318 U.S., at 343-344, and in Mallory, 354 U.S., at 455-456, we recognized both the dangers of interrogation and the appropriateness of prophylaxis stemming from the very fact of interrogation itself.

Our decision in *Malloy v. Hogan*, 378 U.S. 1 (1964), necessitates an examination of the scope of the privilege in state cases as well. In Malloy, we squarely held the privilege applicable to the States, and held that the substantive standards underlying the privilege applied with full force to state court proceedings. There, as in *Murphy v. Waterfront Comm'n*, 378 U.S. 52 (1964), and *Griffin v. California*, 380 U.S. 609 (1965), we applied the existing Fifth Amendment standards to the case before us. Aside from the holding itself, the reasoning in Malloy made clear what had already become apparent—that the substantive and procedural safeguards surrounding admissibility of confessions in state cases had become exceedingly exacting, reflecting all the policies embedded in the privilege, 378 U.S., at 7-8. The voluntariness doctrine in the state cases, as Malloy indicates, encompasses all interrogation practices which are likely to exert such pressure upon an individual as to disable him from making a free and rational choice. The implications of this proposition were elaborated in our decision in *Escobedo v. Illinois*, 378 U.S. 478, decided one week after Malloy applied the privilege to the States.

Our holding there stressed the fact that the police had not advised the defendant of his constitutional privilege to remain silent at the outset of the interrogation, and we drew attention to that fact at several points in the decision, 378 U.S., at 483, 485, 491. This was no isolated factor, but an essential ingredient in our decision. The entire thrust of police interrogation there, as in all the cases today, was to put the defendant in such an emotional state as to impair his capacity for rational judgment. The abdication of the constitutional privilege—the choice on his part to speak to the police—was not made knowingly or competently because of the failure to apprise him of his rights; the compelling atmosphere of the in-custody interrogation, and not an independent decision on his part, caused the defendant to speak.

A different phase of the Escobedo decision was significant in its attention to the absence of counsel during the questioning. There, as in the cases today, we sought a protective device to dispel the compelling atmosphere of the interrogation. In Escobedo, however, the police did not relieve the defendant of the anxieties which they had created in the interrogation rooms. Rather, they denied his request for the assistance of counsel, 378 U.S., at 481, 488, 491. This heightened his dilemma, and made his later statements the product of this compulsion. Cf. *Haynes v. Washington*, 373 U.S. 503, 514 (1963). The denial of the defendant's request for his attorney thus undermined his ability to exercise the privilege—to remain silent if he chose or to speak without any intimidation, blatant or subtle. The presence of counsel, in all the cases before us today, would be the adequate protective device necessary to make the process of police interrogation conform to the dictates of the privilege. His presence would insure that statements made in the government-established atmosphere are not the product of compulsion.

It was in this manner that Escobedo explicated another facet of the pre-trial privilege, noted in many of the Court's prior decisions: the protection of rights at trial. That counsel is present when statements are taken from an individual during interrogation obviously enhances the integrity of the fact-finding processes in court. The presence of an attorney, and the warnings delivered to the individual, enable the defendant under otherwise compelling circumstances to tell his story without fear, effectively, and in a way that eliminates the evils in the interrogation process. Without the protections flowing from adequate warnings and the rights of counsel, "all the careful safeguards erected around the giving of testimony, whether by an accused or any other witness, would become empty formalities in a procedure where the most compelling possible evidence of guilt, a confession, would have already been obtained at the unsupervised pleasure of the police." *Mapp v. Ohio*, 367 U.S. 643, 685 (1961) (HARLAN, J., dissenting). Cf. *Pointer v. Texas*, 380 U.S. 400 (1965).

III

Today, then, there can be no doubt that the Fifth Amendment privilege is available outside of criminal court proceedings and serves to protect persons in all settings in which their freedom of action is curtailed in any significant way from being compelled to incriminate themselves. We have concluded that without proper safeguards the process of in-custody interrogation of persons suspected or accused of crime contains inherently compelling pressures which work to undermine the individual's will to resist and to compel him to speak where he would not otherwise do so freely. In order to combat these pressures and to permit a full opportunity to exercise the privilege against self-incrimination, the accused must be adequately and effectively apprised of his rights and the exercise of those rights must be fully honored.

It is impossible for us to foresee the potential alternatives for protecting the privilege which might be devised by Congress or the States in the exercise of their creative rule-making capacities. Therefore we cannot say that the Constitution necessarily requires adherence to any particular solution for the inherent compulsions of the interrogation process as it is presently conducted. Our decision in no way creates a constitutional straitjacket which will handicap sound efforts at reform, nor is it intended to have this effect. We encourage Congress and the States to continue their laudable search for increasingly effective ways of protecting the rights of the individual while promoting efficient enforcement of our criminal laws. However, unless we are shown other procedures which are at least as effective in apprising accused persons of their right of silence and in assuring a continuous opportunity to exercise it, the following safeguards must be observed.

At the outset, if a person in custody is to be subjected to interrogation, he must first be informed in clear and unequivocal terms that he has the right to remain silent. For those unaware of the privilege, the warning is needed simply to make them aware of it—the threshold requirement for an intelligent decision as to its exercise. More important, such a warning is an absolute prerequisite in overcoming the inherent pressures of the interrogation atmosphere. It is not just the subnormal or woefully ignorant who succumb to an interrogator's imprecations, whether implied or expressly stated, that the interrogation will continue until a confession is obtained or that silence in the face of accusation is itself damning and will bode ill when presented to a jury. Further, the warning will show the individual that his interrogators are prepared to recognize his privilege should he choose to exercise it.

The Fifth Amendment privilege is so fundamental to our system of constitutional rule and the expedient of giving an adequate warning as to the availability of the privilege so simple, we will not pause to inquire in individual cases whether the defendant was aware of his rights without a warning being given. Assessments of the knowledge the defendant possessed, based on information as to his age, education, intelligence, or prior contact with authorities, can never be more than speculation; a warning is a clearcut fact. More important, whatever the background of the person interrogated, a warning at the time of the interrogation is indispensable to overcome its pressures and to insure that the individual knows he is free to exercise the privilege at that point in time.

The warning of the right to remain silent must be accompanied by the explanation that anything said can and will be used against the individual in court. This warning is needed in order to make him aware not only of the privilege, but also of the consequences of forgoing it. It is only through an awareness of these consequences that there can be any assurance of real understanding and intelligent exercise of the privilege. Moreover, this warning may serve to make the individual more acutely aware that he is faced with a phase of the adversary system—that he is not in the presence of persons acting solely in his interest.

The circumstances surrounding in-custody interrogation can operate very quickly to overbear the will of one merely made aware of his privilege by his interrogators. Therefore, the right to have counsel present at the interrogation is indispensable to the protection of the Fifth Amendment privilege under the system we delineate today. Our aim is to assure that the individual's right to choose between silence and speech remains unfettered throughout the interrogation process. A once-stated warning, delivered by those who will conduct the interrogation, cannot itself suffice to that end among those who most require knowledge of their rights. A mere warning given by the interrogators is not alone sufficient to accomplish that end. Prosecutors themselves claim that the admonishment of the right to remain silent without more "will benefit only the recidivist and the professional." Brief for the National District Attorneys Association as amicus curiae, p. 14. Even preliminary advice given to the accused by his own attorney can be swiftly overcome by the secret interrogation process. Cf. *Escobedo v. Illinois*, 378 U.S. 478, 485, n. 5. Thus, the need for counsel to protect the Fifth Amendment privilege comprehends not merely a right to consult with counsel prior to questioning, but also to have counsel present during any questioning if the defendant so desires.

The presence of counsel at the interrogation may serve several significant subsidiary functions as well. If the accused decides to talk to his interrogators, the assistance of counsel can mitigate the dangers of untrustworthiness. With a lawyer present the likelihood that the police will practice coercion is reduced, and if coercion is nevertheless exercised the lawyer can testify to it in court. The presence of a lawyer can also help to guarantee that the accused gives a fully accurate statement to the police and that the statement is rightly reported by the prosecution at trial. See *Crooker v. California*, 357 U.S. 433, 443-448 (1958) (DOUGLAS, J., dissenting).

An individual need not make a pre-interrogation request for a lawyer. While such request affirmatively secures his right to have one, his failure to ask for a lawyer does not constitute a waiver. No effective waiver of the right to counsel during interrogation can be recognized unless specifically made after the warnings we here delineate have been given. The accused who does not know his rights and therefore does not make a request may be the person who most needs counsel. As the California Supreme Court has aptly put it:

> "Finally, we must recognize that the imposition of the requirement for the request would discriminate against the defendant who does not know his rights. The defendant who does not ask for counsel is the very defendant who most needs counsel. We cannot penalize a defendant who, not understanding his constitutional rights, does not make the formal

request and by such failure demonstrates his helplessness. To require the request would be to favor the defendant whose sophistication or status had fortuitously prompted him to make it." People v. Dorado, 62 Cal. 2d 338, 351, 398 P.2d 361, 369-370, 42 Cal. Rptr. 169, 177-178 (1965) (Tobriner, J.).

In *Carnley v. Cochran*, 369 U.S. 506, 513 (1962), we stated: "[I]t is settled that where the assistance of counsel is a constitutional requisite, the right to be furnished counsel does not depend on a request." This proposition applies with equal force in the context of providing counsel to protect an accused's Fifth Amendment privilege in the face of interrogation. Although the role of counsel at trial differs from the role during interrogation, the differences are not relevant to the question whether a request is a prerequisite.

Accordingly we hold that an individual held for interrogation must be clearly informed that he has the right to consult with a lawyer and to have the lawyer with him during interrogation under the system for protecting the privilege we delineate today. As with the warnings of the right to remain silent and that anything stated can be used in evidence against him, this warning is an absolute prerequisite to interrogation. No amount of circumstantial evidence that the person may have been aware of this right will suffice to stand in its stead: Only through such a warning is there ascertainable assurance that the accused was aware of this right.

If an individual indicates that he wishes the assistance of counsel before any interrogation occurs, the authorities cannot rationally ignore or deny his request on the basis that the individual does not have or cannot afford a retained attorney. The financial ability of the individual has no relationship to the scope of the rights involved here. The privilege against self-incrimination secured by the Constitution applies to all individuals. The need for counsel in order to protect the privilege exists for the indigent as well as the affluent. In fact, were we to limit these constitutional rights to those who can retain an attorney, our decisions today would be of little significance. The cases before us as well as the vast majority of confession cases with which we have dealt in the past involve those unable to retain counsel. While authorities are not required to relieve the accused of his poverty, they have the obligation not to take advantage of indigence in the administration of justice. Denial

of counsel to the indigent at the time of interrogation while allowing an attorney to those who can afford one would be no more supportable by reason or logic than the similar situation at trial and on appeal struck down in *Gideon v. Wainwright*, 372 U.S. 335 (1963), and *Douglas v. California*, 372 U.S. 353 (1963).

In order fully to apprise a person interrogated of the extent of his rights under this system then, it is necessary to warn him not only that he has the right to consult with an attorney, but also that if he is indigent a lawyer will be appointed to represent him. Without this additional warning, the admonition of the right to consult with counsel would often be understood as meaning only that he can consult with a lawyer if he has one or has the funds to obtain one. The warning of a right to counsel would be hollow if not couched in terms that would convey to the indigent—the person most often subjected to interrogation—the knowledge that he too has a right to have counsel present. As with the warnings of the right to remain silent and of the general right to counsel, only by effective and express explanation to the indigent of this right can there be assurance that he was truly in a position to exercise it.

Once warnings have been given, the subsequent procedure is clear. If the individual indicates in any manner, at any time prior to or during questioning, that he wishes to remain silent, the interrogation must cease. At this point he has shown that he intends to exercise his Fifth Amendment privilege; any statement taken after the person invokes his privilege cannot be other than the product of compulsion, subtle or otherwise. Without the right to cut off questioning, the setting of in-custody interrogation operates on the individual to overcome free choice in producing a statement after the privilege has been once invoked. If the individual states that he wants an attorney, the interrogation must cease until an attorney is present. At that time, the individual must have an opportunity to confer with the attorney and to have him present during any subsequent questioning. If the individual cannot obtain an attorney and he indicates that he wants one before speaking to police, they must respect his decision to remain silent.

This does not mean, as some have suggested, that each police station must have a "station house lawyer" present at all times to advise prisoners. It does mean, however, that if police propose to interrogate a person they must make known to him that he is entitled to a lawyer and that if he cannot afford one, a lawyer will be provided for him prior to any interrogation. If authorities conclude that they will not provide counsel during a reasonable period of time in which investigation in the field is carried out, they may refrain from doing so without violating the person's Fifth Amendment privilege so long as they do not question him during that time.

If the interrogation continues without the presence of an attorney and a statement is taken, a heavy burden rests on the government to demonstrate that the defendant knowingly and intelligently waived his privilege against self-incrimination and his right to retained or appointed counsel. *Escobedo v. Illinois*, 378 U.S. 478, 490, n. 14. This Court has always set high standards of proof for the waiver of constitutional rights, *Johnson v. Zerbst*, 304 U.S. 458 (1938), and we re-assert these standards as applied to in-custody interrogation. Since the State is responsible for establishing the isolated circumstances under which the interrogation takes place and has the only means of making available corroborated evidence of warnings given during incommunicado interrogation, the burden is rightly on its shoulders.

An express statement that the individual is willing to make a statement and does not want an attorney followed closely by a statement could constitute a waiver. But a valid waiver will not be presumed simply from the silence of the accused after warnings are given or simply from the fact that a confession was in fact eventually obtained. A statement we made in *Carnley v. Cochran*, 369 U.S. 506, 516 (1962), is applicable here:

> "Presuming waiver from a silent record is impermissible. The record must show, or there must be an allegation and evidence which show, that an accused was offered counsel but intelligently and understandingly rejected the offer. Anything less is not waiver."

See also *Glasser v. United States*, 315 U.S. 60 (1942). Moreover, where in-custody interrogation is involved, there is no room for the contention that the privilege is waived if the individual answers some questions or gives some information on his own prior to invoking his right to remain silent when interrogated.

Whatever the testimony of the authorities as to waiver of rights by an accused, the fact of lengthy interrogation or incommunicado incarceration before a statement is made is strong evidence that the accused did not validly waive his rights. In these circumstances the fact that the individual eventually made a statement is consistent with the conclusion that the compelling influence of the interrogation finally forced him to do so. It is inconsistent with any notion of a voluntary relinquishment of the privilege. Moreover, any evidence that the accused was threatened, tricked, or cajoled into a waiver will, of course, show that the defendant did not voluntarily waive his privilege. The requirement of warnings and waiver of rights is a fundamental with respect to the Fifth Amendment privilege and not simply a preliminary ritual to existing methods of interrogation.

The warnings required and the waiver necessary in accordance with our opinion today are, in the absence of a fully effective equivalent, prerequisites to the admissibility of any statement made by a defendant. No distinction can be drawn between statements which are direct confessions and statements which amount to "admissions" of part or all of an offense. The privilege against self-incrimination protects the individual from being compelled to incriminate himself in any manner; it does not distinguish degrees of incrimination. Similarly, for precisely the same reason, no distinction may be drawn between inculpatory statements and statements alleged to be merely "exculpatory." If a statement made were in fact truly exculpatory it would, of course, never be used by the prosecution. In fact, statements merely intended to be exculpatory by the defendant are often used to impeach his testimony at trial or to demonstrate untruths in the statement given under interrogation and thus to prove guilt by implication. These statements are incriminating in any meaningful sense of the word and may not be used without the full warnings and effective waiver required for any other statement. In Escobedo itself, the defendant fully intended his accusation of another as the slayer to be exculpatory as to himself.

The principles announced today deal with the protection which must be given to the privilege against self-incrimination when the individual is first subjected to police interrogation while in custody at the station or otherwise deprived of his freedom of action in any significant way. It is at this point that our adversary system of criminal proceedings commences, distinguishing itself at the outset from the inquisitorial system recognized in some countries. Under the system of warnings we delineate today or under any other system which may be devised and found effective, the safeguards to be erected about the privilege must come into play at this point.

Our decision is not intended to hamper the traditional function of police officers in investigating crime. See *Escobedo v. Illinois*, 378 U.S. 478, 492. When an individual is in custody on probable cause, the police may, of course, seek out evidence in the field to be used at trial against him. Such investigation may include inquiry of persons not under restraint. General on-the-scene questioning as to facts surrounding a crime or other general questioning of citizens in the fact-finding process is not affected by our holding. It is an act of responsible citizenship for individuals to give whatever information they may have to aid in law enforcement. In such situations the compelling atmosphere inherent in the process of in-custody interrogation is not necessarily present.

In dealing with statements obtained through interrogation, we do not purport to find all confessions inadmissible. Confessions remain a proper element in law enforcement. Any statement given freely and voluntarily without any compelling influences is, of course, admissible in evidence. The fundamental import of the privilege while an individual is in custody is not whether he is allowed to talk to the police without the benefit of warnings and counsel, but whether he can be interrogated. There is no requirement that police stop a person who enters a police station and states that he wishes to confess to a crime, or a person who calls the police to offer a confession or any other statement he desires to make. Volunteered statements of any kind are not barred by the Fifth Amendment and their admissibility is not affected by our holding today.

To summarize, we hold that when an individual is taken into custody or otherwise deprived of his freedom by the authorities in any significant way and is subjected to questioning, the privilege against self-incrimination is jeopardized. Procedural safeguards must be employed to protect the privilege, and unless other fully effective means are adopted to notify the person of his right of silence and to assure that the exercise of the right will be scrupulously honored, the following measures are required. He must be warned prior to any questioning that he has the right to remain silent, that anything he says can be used against him in a court of law, that he has the

right to the presence of an attorney, and that if he cannot afford an attorney one will be appointed for him prior to any questioning if he so desires. Opportunity to exercise these rights must be afforded to him throughout the interrogation. After such warnings have been given, and such opportunity afforded him, the individual may knowingly and intelligently waive these rights and agree to answer questions or make a statement. But unless and until such warnings and waiver are demonstrated by the prosecution at trial, no evidence obtained as a result of interrogation can be used against him.

IV

A recurrent argument made in these cases is that society's need for interrogation outweighs the privilege. This argument is not unfamiliar to this Court. See, e.g., *Chambers v. Florida*, 309 U.S. 227, 240-241 (1940). The whole thrust of our foregoing discussion demonstrates that the Constitution has prescribed the rights of the individual when confronted with the power of government when it provided in the Fifth Amendment that an individual cannot be compelled to be a witness against himself. That right cannot be abridged. As Mr. Justice Brandeis once observed:

> "Decency, security and liberty alike demand that government officials shall be subjected to the same rules of conduct that are commands to the citizen. In a government of laws, existence of the government will be imperilled if it fails to observe the law scrupulously. Our Government is the potent, the omnipresent teacher. For good or for ill, it teaches the whole people by its example. Crime is contagious. If the Government becomes a lawbreaker, it breeds contempt for law; it invites every man to become a law unto himself; it invites anarchy. To declare that in the administration of the criminal law the end justifies the means . . . would bring terrible retribution. Against that pernicious doctrine this Court should resolutely set its face." Olmstead v. United States, 277 U.S. 438, 485 (1928) (dissenting opinion).

In this connection, one of our country's distinguished jurists has pointed out: "The quality of a nation's civilization can be largely measured by the methods it uses in the enforcement of its criminal law."

If the individual desires to exercise his privilege, he has the right to do so. This is not for the authorities to decide. An attorney may advise his client not to talk to police until he has had an opportunity to investigate the case, or he may wish to be present with his client during any police questioning. In doing so an attorney is merely exercising the good professional judgment he has been taught. This is not cause for considering the attorney a menace to law enforcement. He is merely carrying out what he is sworn to do under his oath—to protect to the extent of his ability the rights of his client. In fulfilling this responsibility the attorney plays a vital role in the administration of criminal justice under our Constitution.

In announcing these principles, we are not unmindful of the burdens which law enforcement officials must bear, often under trying circumstances. We also fully recognize the obligation of all citizens to aid in enforcing the criminal laws. This Court, while protecting individual rights, has always given ample latitude to law enforcement agencies in the legitimate exercise of their duties. The limits we have placed on the interrogation process should not constitute an undue interference with a proper system of law enforcement. As we have noted, our decision does not in any way preclude police from carrying out their traditional investigatory functions. Although confessions may play an important role in some convictions, the cases before us present graphic examples of the overstatement of the "need" for confessions. In each case authorities conducted interrogations ranging up to five days in duration despite the presence, through standard investigating practices, of considerable evidence against each defendant. Further examples are chronicled in our prior cases. See, e.g., *Haynes v. Washington*, 373 U.S. 503, 518-519 (1963); *Rogers v. Richmond*, 365 U.S. 534, 541 (1961); *Malinski v. New York*, 324 U.S. 401, 402 (1945).

It is also urged that an unfettered right to detention for interrogation should be allowed because it will often redound to the benefit of the person questioned. When police inquiry determines that there is no reason to believe that the person has committed any crime, it is said, he will be released without need for further formal procedures. The person who has committed no offense, however, will be better able to clear himself after warnings with counsel present than without. It can be assumed that in such circumstances a lawyer would advise his client to talk freely to police in order to clear himself.

Custodial interrogation, by contrast, does not necessarily afford the innocent an opportunity to clear themselves. A serious consequence of the present practice of the interrogation alleged to be beneficial for the innocent is that many arrests "for investigation" subject large numbers of innocent persons to detention and interrogation. In one of the cases before us, No. 584, *California v. Stewart*, police held four persons, who were in the defendant's house at the time of the arrest, in jail for five days until defendant confessed. At that time they were finally released. Police stated that there was "no evidence to connect them with any crime." Available statistics on the extent of this practice where it is condoned indicate that these four are far from alone in being subjected to arrest, prolonged detention, and interrogation without the requisite probable cause.

Over the years the Federal Bureau of Investigation has compiled an exemplary record of effective law enforcement while advising any suspect or arrested person, at the outset of an interview, that he is not required to make a statement, that any statement may be used against him in court, that the individual may obtain the services of an attorney of his own choice and, more recently, that he has a right to free counsel if he is unable to pay. A letter received from the Solicitor General in response to a question from the Bench makes it clear that the present pattern of warnings and respect for the rights of the individual followed as a practice by the FBI is consistent with the procedure which we delineate today. It states:

> "At the oral argument of the above cause, Mr. Justice Fortas asked whether I could provide certain information as to the practices followed by the Federal Bureau of Investigation. I have directed these questions to the attention of the Director of the Federal Bureau of Investigation and am submitting herewith a statement of the questions and of the answers which we have received.

> "'(1) When an individual is interviewed by agents of the Bureau, what warning is given to him?

> "'The standard warning long given by Special Agents of the FBI to both suspects and persons under arrest is that the person has a right to say nothing and a right to counsel, and that any statement he does make

may be used against him in court. Examples of this warning are to be found in the Westover case at 342 F.2d 684 (1965), and *Jackson v. U.S.*, 337 F.2d 136 (1964), cert. den. 380 U.S. 935.

"After passage of the Criminal Justice Act of 1964, which provides free counsel for Federal defendants unable to pay, we added to our instructions to Special Agents the requirement that any person who is under arrest for an offense under FBI jurisdiction, or whose arrest is contemplated following the interview, must also be advised of his right to free counsel if he is unable to pay, and the fact that such counsel will be assigned by the Judge. At the same time, we broadened the right to counsel warning to read counsel of his own choice, or anyone else with whom he might wish to speak.

"'(2) When is the warning given?

"'The FBI warning is given to a suspect at the very outset of the interview, as shown in the Westover case, cited above. The warning may be given to a person arrested as soon as practicable after the arrest, as shown in the Jackson case, also cited above, and in *U.S. v. Konigsberg*, 336 F.2d 844 (1964), cert. den. 379 U.S. 933, but in any event it must precede the interview with the person for a confession or admission of his own guilt.

"'(3) What is the Bureau's practice in the event that (a) the individual requests counsel and (b) counsel appears?

"'When the person who has been warned of his right to counsel decides that he wishes to consult with counsel before making a statement, the interview is terminated at that point, *Shultz v. U.S.*, 351 F.2d 287 (1965). It may be continued, however, as to all matters other than the person's own guilt or innocence. If he is indecisive in his request for counsel, there may be some question on whether he did or did not waive counsel. Situations of this kind must necessarily be left to the judgment of the interviewing Agent. For example, in *Hi-*

ram v. U.S., 354 F.2d 4 (1965), the Agent's conclusion that the person arrested had waived his right to counsel was upheld by the courts.

"'A person being interviewed and desiring to consult counsel by telephone must be permitted to do so, as shown in *Caldwell v. U.S.*, 351 F.2d 459 (1965). When counsel appears in person, he is permitted to confer with his client in private.

"'(4) What is the Bureau's practice if the individual requests counsel, but cannot afford to retain an attorney?

"'If any person being interviewed after warning of counsel decides that he wishes to consult with counsel before proceeding further the interview is terminated, as shown above. FBI Agents do not pass judgment on the ability of the person to pay for counsel. They do, however, advise those who have been arrested for an offense under FBI jurisdiction, or whose arrest is contemplated following the interview, of a right to free counsel if they are unable to pay, and the availability of such counsel from the Judge.'"

The practice of the FBI can readily be emulated by state and local enforcement agencies. The argument that the FBI deals with different crimes than are dealt with by state authorities does not mitigate the significance of the FBI experience.

The experience in some other countries also suggests that the danger to law enforcement in curbs on interrogation is overplayed. The English procedure since 1912 under the Judges' Rules is significant. As recently strengthened, the Rules require that a cautionary warning be given an accused by a police officer as soon as he has evidence that affords reasonable grounds for suspicion; they also require that any statement made be given by the accused without questioning by police. The right of the individual to consult with an attorney during this period is expressly recognized.

The safeguards present under Scottish law may be even greater than in England. Scottish judicial decisions bar use in evidence of most confessions obtained through police interrogation. In India, confessions made to police not in the presence of a magistrate have been excluded by rule of evidence since 1872, at a time when it operated under British law. Identical provisions appear in the Evidence Ordinance of Ceylon, enacted in 1895. Similarly, in our country the Uniform Code of Military Justice has long provided that no suspect may be interrogated without first being warned of his right not to make a statement and that any statement he makes may be used against him. Denial of the right to consult counsel during interrogation has also been proscribed by military tribunals. There appears to have been no marked detrimental effect on criminal law enforcement in these jurisdictions as a result of these rules. Conditions of law enforcement in our country are sufficiently similar to permit reference to this experience as assurance that lawlessness will not result from warning an individual of his rights or allowing him to exercise them. Moreover, it is consistent with our legal system that we give at least as much protection to these rights as is given in the jurisdictions described. We deal in our country with rights grounded in a specific requirement of the Fifth Amendment of the Constitution, whereas other jurisdictions arrived at their conclusions on the basis of principles of justice not so specifically defined.

It is also urged upon us that we withhold decision on this issue until state legislative bodies and advisory groups have had an opportunity to deal with these problems by rule making. We have already pointed out that the Constitution does not require any specific code of procedures for protecting the privilege against self-incrimination during custodial interrogation. Congress and the States are free to develop their own safeguards for the privilege, so long as they are fully as effective as those described above in informing accused persons of their right of silence and in affording a continuous opportunity to exercise it. In any event, however, the issues presented are of constitutional dimensions and must be determined by the courts. The admissibility of a statement in the face of a claim that it was obtained in violation of the defendant's constitutional rights is an issue the resolution of which has long since been undertaken by this Court. See *Hopt v. Utah*, 110 U.S. 574 (1884). Judicial solutions to problems of constitutional dimension have evolved decade by decade. As courts have been presented with the need to enforce constitutional rights, they have found means of doing so. That was our responsibility when Escobedo was before us and it is our responsibility today. Where rights secured

by the Constitution are involved, there can be no rule making or legislation which would abrogate them.

V

Because of the nature of the problem and because of its recurrent significance in numerous cases, we have to this point discussed the relationship of the Fifth Amendment privilege to police interrogation without specific concentration on the facts of the cases before us. We turn now to these facts to consider the application to these cases of the constitutional principles discussed above. In each instance, we have concluded that statements were obtained from the defendant under circumstances that did not meet constitutional standards for protection of the privilege.

No. 759. *Miranda v. Arizona.*

On March 13, 1963, petitioner, Ernesto Miranda, was arrested at his home and taken in custody to a Phoenix police station. He was there identified by the complaining witness. The police then took him to "Interrogation Room No. 2" of the detective bureau. There he was questioned by two police officers. The officers admitted at trial that Miranda was not advised that he had a right to have an attorney present. Two hours later, the officers emerged from the interrogation room with a written confession signed by Miranda. At the top of the statement was a typed paragraph stating that the confession was made voluntarily, without threats or promises of immunity and "with full knowledge of my legal rights, understanding any statement I make may be used against me."

At his trial before a jury, the written confession was admitted into evidence over the objection of defense counsel, and the officers testified to the prior oral confession made by Miranda during the interrogation. Miranda was found guilty of kidnapping and rape. He was sentenced to 20 to 30 years' imprisonment on each count, the sentences to run concurrently. On appeal, the Supreme Court of Arizona held that Miranda's constitutional rights were not violated in obtaining the confession and affirmed the conviction. 98 Ariz. 18, 401 P.2d 721. In reaching its decision, the court emphasized heavily the fact that Miranda did not specifically request counsel.

We reverse. From the testimony of the officers and by the admission of respondent, it is clear that Miranda was not in any way apprised of his right to consult with an attorney and to have one present during the interrogation, nor was his right not to be compelled to incriminate himself effectively protected in any other manner. Without these warnings the statements were inadmissible. The mere fact that he signed a statement which contained a typed-in clause stating that he had "full knowledge" of his "legal rights" does not approach the knowing and intelligent waiver required to relinquish constitutional rights. Cf. *Haynes v. Washington*, 373 U.S. 503, 512-513 (1963); *Haley v. Ohio*, 332 U.S. 596, 601 (1948) (opinion of MR. JUSTICE DOUGLAS).

No. 760. *Vignera v. New York.*

Petitioner, Michael Vignera, was picked up by New York police on October 14, 1960, in connection with the robbery three days earlier of a Brooklyn dress shop. They took him to the 17th Detective Squad headquarters in Manhattan. Sometime thereafter he was taken to the 66th Detective Squad. There a detective questioned Vignera with respect to the robbery. Vignera orally admitted the robbery to the detective. The detective was asked on cross-examination at trial by defense counsel whether Vignera was warned of his right to counsel before being interrogated. The prosecution objected to the question and the trial judge sustained the objection. Thus, the defense was precluded from making any showing that warnings had not been given. While at the 66th Detective Squad, Vignera was identified by the store owner and a saleslady as the man who robbed the dress shop. At about 3 p.m. he was formally arrested. The police then transported him to still another station, the 70th Precinct in Brooklyn, "for detention." At 11 p.m. Vignera was questioned by an assistant district attorney in the presence of a hearing reporter who transcribed the questions and Vignera's answers. This verbatim account of these proceedings contains no statement of any warnings given by the assistant district attorney. At Vignera's trial on a charge of first degree robbery, the detective testified as to the oral confession. The transcription of the statement taken was also introduced in evidence. At the conclusion of the testimony, the trial judge charged the jury in part as follows:

> "The law doesn't say that the confession is void or invalidated because the police officer didn't advise the defendant as to his rights. Did you hear what I said? I am telling you what the law of the State of New York is."

Vignera was found guilty of first degree robbery. He was subsequently adjudged a third-felony offender and sentenced to 30 to 60 years' imprisonment. The conviction was affirmed without opinion by the Appellate Division, Second Department, 21 App. Div. 2d 752, 252 N.Y.S. 2d 19, and by the Court of Appeals, also without opinion, 15 N.Y. 2d 970, 207 N.E. 2d 527, 259 N.Y.S. 2d 857, remittitur amended, 16 N.Y. 2d 614, 209 N.E. 2d 110, 261 N.Y.S. 2d 65. In argument to the Court of Appeals, the State contended that Vignera had no constitutional right to be advised of his right to counsel or his privilege against self-incrimination.

We reverse. The foregoing indicates that Vignera was not warned of any of his rights before the questioning by the detective and by the assistant district attorney. No other steps were taken to protect these rights. Thus he was not effectively apprised of his Fifth Amendment privilege or of his right to have counsel present and his statements are inadmissible.

No. 761. *Westover v. United States.*

At approximately 9:45 p.m. on March 20, 1963, petitioner, Carl Calvin Westover, was arrested by local police in Kansas City as a suspect in two Kansas City robberies. A report was also received from the FBI that he was wanted on a felony charge in California. The local authorities took him to a police station and placed him in a line-up on the local charges, and at about 11:45 p.m. he was booked. Kansas City police interrogated Westover on the night of his arrest. He denied any knowledge of criminal activities. The next day local officers interrogated him again throughout the morning. Shortly before noon they informed the FBI that they were through interrogating Westover and that the FBI could proceed to interrogate him. There is nothing in the record to indicate that Westover was ever given any warning as to his rights by local police. At noon, three special agents of the FBI continued the interrogation in a private interview room of the Kansas City Police Department, this time with respect to the robbery of a savings and loan association and a bank in Sacramento, California. After two or two and one-half hours, Westover signed separate confessions to each of these two robberies which had been prepared by one of the agents during the interrogation. At trial one of the agents testified, and a paragraph on each of the statements states, that the agents advised Westover that he did not have to make a statement, that any statement he made could be used against him, and that he had the right to see an attorney.

Westover was tried by a jury in federal court and convicted of the California robberies. His statements were introduced at trial. He was sentenced to 15 years' imprisonment on each count, the sentences to run consecutively. On appeal, the conviction was affirmed by the Court of Appeals for the Ninth Circuit. 342 F.2d 684.

We reverse. On the facts of this case we cannot find that Westover knowingly and intelligently waived his right to remain silent and his right to consult with counsel prior to the time he made the statement. At the time the FBI agents began questioning Westover, he had been in custody for over 14 hours and had been interrogated at length during that period. The FBI interrogation began immediately upon the conclusion of the interrogation by Kansas City police and was conducted in local police headquarters. Although the two law enforcement authorities are legally distinct and the crimes for which they interrogated Westover were different, the impact on him was that of a continuous period of questioning. There is no evidence of any warning given prior to the FBI interrogation nor is there any evidence of an articulated waiver of rights after the FBI commenced its interrogation. The record simply shows that the defendant did in fact confess a short time after being turned over to the FBI following interrogation by local police. Despite the fact that the FBI agents gave warnings at the outset of their interview, from Westover's point of view the warnings came at the end of the interrogation process. In these circumstances an intelligent waiver of constitutional rights cannot be assumed.

We do not suggest that law enforcement authorities are precluded from questioning any individual who has been held for a period of time by other authorities and interrogated by them without appropriate warnings. A different case would be presented if an accused were taken into custody by the second authority, removed both in time and place from his original surroundings, and then adequately advised of his rights and given an opportunity to exercise them. But here the FBI interrogation was conducted immediately following the state interrogation in the same police station—in the same compelling surroundings. Thus, in obtaining a confession from Westover the federal authorities were the beneficiaries of the pressure applied by the local in-custody interrogation. In these circumstances the giving of warnings alone was not sufficient to protect the privilege.

In the course of investigating a series of purse-snatch robberies in which one of the victims had died of injuries inflicted by her assailant, respondent, Roy Allen Stewart, was pointed out to Los Angeles police as the endorser of dividend checks taken in one of the robberies. At about 7:15 p.m., January 31, 1963, police officers went to Stewart's house and arrested him. One of the officers asked Stewart if they could search the house, to which he replied, "Go ahead." The search turned up various items taken from the five robbery victims. At the time of Stewart's arrest, police also arrested Stewart's wife and three other persons who were visiting him. These four were jailed along with Stewart and were interrogated. Stewart was taken to the University Station of the Los Angeles Police Department where he was placed in a cell. During the next five days, police interrogated Stewart on nine different occasions. Except during the first interrogation session, when he was confronted with an accusing witness, Stewart was isolated with his interrogators.

During the ninth interrogation session, Stewart admitted that he had robbed the deceased and stated that he had not meant to hurt her. Police then brought Stewart before a magistrate for the first time. Since there was no evidence to connect them with any crime, the police then released the other four persons arrested with him.

Nothing in the record specifically indicates whether Stewart was or was not advised of his right to remain silent or his right to counsel. In a number of instances, however, the interrogating officers were asked to recount everything that was said during the interrogations. None indicated that Stewart was ever advised of his rights.

Stewart was charged with kidnapping to commit robbery, rape, and murder. At his trial, transcripts of the first interrogation and the confession at the last interrogation were introduced in evidence. The jury found Stewart guilty of robbery and first degree murder and fixed the penalty as death. On appeal, the Supreme Court of California reversed. 62 Cal. 2d 571, 400 P.2d 97, 43 Cal. Rptr. 201. It held that under this Court's decision in Escobedo, Stewart should have been advised of his right to remain silent and of his right to counsel and that it would not presume in the face of a silent record that the police advised Stewart of his rights.

We affirm. In dealing with custodial interrogation, we will not presume that a defendant has been effectively apprised of his rights and that his privilege against self-incrimination has been adequately safeguarded on a record that does not show that any warnings have been given or that any effective alternative has been employed. Nor can a knowing and intelligent waiver of these rights be assumed on a silent record. Furthermore, Stewart's steadfast denial of the alleged offenses through eight of the nine interrogations over a period of five days is subject to no other construction than that he was compelled by persistent interrogation to forgo his Fifth Amendment privilege.

Therefore, in accordance with the foregoing, the judgments of the Supreme Court of Arizona in No. 759, of the New York Court of Appeals in No. 760, and of the Court of Appeals for the Ninth Circuit in No. 761 are reversed. The judgment of the Supreme Court of California in No. 584 is affirmed.

It is so ordered.

Mr. Justice Clark, Dissenting in Nos. 759, 760, and 761, and Concurring in the Result in No. 584

It is with regret that I find it necessary to write in these cases. However, I am unable to join the majority because its opinion goes too far on too little, while my dissenting brethren do not go quite far enough. Nor can I join in the Court's criticism of the present practices of police and investigatory agencies as to custodial interrogation. The materials it refers to as "police manuals" are, as I read them, merely writings in this field by professors and some police officers. Not one is shown by the record here to be the official manual of any police department, much less in universal use in crime detection. Moreover, the examples of police brutality mentioned by the Court are rare exceptions to the thousands of cases that appear every year in the law reports. The police agencies—all the way from municipal and state forces to the federal bureaus—are responsible for law enforcement and public safety in this country. I am proud of their efforts, which in my view are not fairly characterized by the Court's opinion.

I

The ipse dixit of the majority has no support in our

cases. Indeed, the Court admits that "we might not find the defendants' statements [here] to have been involuntary in traditional terms." Ante, p. 457. In short, the Court has added more to the requirements that the accused is entitled to consult with his lawyer and that he must be given the traditional warning that he may remain silent and that anything that he says may be used against him. *Escobedo v. Illinois*, 378 U.S. 478, 490-491 (1964). Now, the Court fashions a constitutional rule that the police may engage in no custodial interrogation without additionally advising the accused that he has a right under the Fifth Amendment to the presence of counsel during interrogation and that, if he is without funds, counsel will be furnished him. When at any point during an interrogation the accused seeks affirmatively or impliedly to invoke his rights to silence or counsel, interrogation must be forgone or postponed. The Court further holds that failure to follow the new procedures requires inexorably the exclusion of any statement by the accused, as well as the fruits thereof. Such a strict constitutional specific inserted at the nerve center of crime detection may well kill the patient. Since there is at this time a paucity of information and an almost total lack of empirical knowledge on the practical operation of requirements truly comparable to those announced by the majority, I would be more restrained lest we go too far too fast.

II

Custodial interrogation has long been recognized as "undoubtedly an essential tool in effective law enforcement." *Haynes v. Washington*, 373 U.S. 503, 515 (1963). Recognition of this fact should put us on guard against the promulgation of doctrinaire rules. Especially is this true where the Court finds that "the Constitution has prescribed" its holding and where the light of our past cases, from *Hopt v. Utah*, 110 U.S. 574, (1884), down to *Haynes v. Washington*, supra, is to the contrary. Indeed, even in Escobedo the Court never hinted that an affirmative "waiver" was a prerequisite to questioning; that the burden of proof as to waiver was on the prosecution; that the presence of counsel—absent a waiver—during interrogation was required; that a waiver can be withdrawn at the will of the accused; that counsel must be furnished during an accusatory stage to those unable to pay; nor that admissions and exculpatory statements are "confessions." To require all those things at one gulp should cause the Court to choke over more cases than *Crooker v. California*, 357 U.S. 433

(1958), and *Cicenia v. Lagay*, 357 U.S. 504 (1958), which it expressly overrules today.

The rule prior to today—as Mr. Justice Goldberg, the author of the Court's opinion in Escobedo, stated it in *Haynes v. Washington*—depended upon "a totality of circumstances evidencing an involuntary . . . admission of guilt." 373 U.S., at 514. And he concluded:

"Of course, detection and solution of crime is, at best, a difficult and arduous task requiring determination and persistence on the part of all responsible officers charged with the duty of law enforcement. And, certainly, we do not mean to suggest that all interrogation of witnesses and suspects is impermissible. Such questioning is undoubtedly an essential tool in effective law enforcement. The line between proper and permissible police conduct and techniques and methods offensive to due process is, at best, a difficult one to draw, particularly in cases such as this where it is necessary to make fine judgments as to the effect of psychologically coercive pressures and inducements on the mind and will of an accused. . . . We are here impelled to the conclusion, from all of the facts presented, that the bounds of due process have been exceeded." Id., at 514-515.

III

I would continue to follow that rule. Under the "totality of circumstances" rule of which my Brother Goldberg spoke in Haynes, I would consider in each case whether the police officer prior to custodial interrogation added the warning that the suspect might have counsel present at the interrogation and, further, that a court would appoint one at his request if he was too poor to employ counsel. In the absence of warnings, the burden would be on the State to prove that counsel was knowingly and intelligently waived or that in the totality of the circumstances, including the failure to give the necessary warnings, the confession was clearly voluntary.

Rather than employing the arbitrary Fifth Amendment rule which the Court lays down I would follow the more pliable dictates of the Due Process Clauses of the Fifth and Fourteenth Amendments which we are accustomed to administering and which we know from our cases are effective instruments in protecting persons in police custody. In this way we would not be acting in the dark nor in one full sweep changing the traditional rules of custodial interrogation which this Court has for so long recognized as a justifiable and proper tool in balancing individual rights against the rights of society. It will be soon enough to go further when we are able to appraise with somewhat better accuracy the effect of such a holding.

I would affirm the convictions in *Miranda v. Arizona*, No. 759; *Vignera v. New York*, No. 760; and *Westover v. United States*, No. 761. In each of those cases I find from the circumstances no warrant for reversal. In *California v. Stewart*, No. 584, I would dismiss the writ of certiorari for want of a final judgment, 28 U.S.C. 1257 (3) (1964 ed.); but if the merits are to be reached I would affirm on the ground that the State failed to fulfill its burden, in the absence of a showing that appropriate warnings were given, of proving a waiver or a totality of circumstances showing voluntariness. Should there be a retrial, I would leave the State free to attempt to prove these elements.

Mr. Justice Harlan, whom Mr. Justice Stewart and Mr. Justice White Join, Dissenting

I believe the decision of the Court represents poor constitutional law and entails harmful consequences for the country at large. How serious these consequences may prove to be only time can tell. But the basic flaws in the Court's justification seem to me readily apparent now once all sides of the problem are considered.

I. Introduction

At the outset, it is well to note exactly what is required by the Court's new constitutional code of rules for confessions. The foremost requirement, upon which later admissibility of a confession depends, is that a fourfold warning be given to a person in custody before he is questioned, namely, that he has a right to remain silent, that anything he says may be used against him, that he has a right to have present an attorney during the questioning, and that if indigent he has a right to a lawyer without charge. To forgo these rights, some affirmative statement of rejection is seemingly required, and threats, tricks, or cajolings to obtain this waiver are forbidden. If before or during questioning the suspect seeks to invoke his right to remain silent, interrogation must be forgone or cease; a request for counsel brings about the same result until a lawyer is procured. Finally, there are a miscellany of minor directives, for example, the burden of proof of waiver is on the State, admissions and exculpatory statements are treated just like confessions, withdrawal of a waiver is always permitted, and so forth.

While the fine points of this scheme are far less clear than the Court admits, the tenor is quite apparent. The new rules are not designed to guard against police brutality or other unmistakably banned forms of coercion. Those who use third-degree tactics and deny them in court are equally able and destined to lie as skillfully about warnings and waivers. Rather, the thrust of the new rules is to negate all pressures, to reinforce the nervous or ignorant suspect, and ultimately to discourage any confession at all. The aim in short is toward "voluntariness" in a utopian sense, or to view it from a different angle, voluntariness with a vengeance.

To incorporate this notion into the Constitution requires a strained reading of history and precedent and a disregard of the very pragmatic concerns that alone may on occasion justify such strains. I believe that reasoned examination will show that the Due Process Clauses provide an adequate tool for coping with confessions and that, even if the Fifth Amendment privilege against self-incrimination be invoked, its precedents taken as a whole do not sustain the present rules. Viewed as a choice based on pure policy, these new rules prove to be a highly debatable, if not one-sided, appraisal of the competing interests, imposed over widespread objection, at the very time when judicial restraint is most called for by the circumstances.

II. Constitutional Premises

It is most fitting to begin an inquiry into the constitutional precedents by surveying the limits on confessions the Court has evolved under the Due Process Clause of the Fourteenth Amendment. This is so because these cases show that there exists a workable and effective means of dealing with confessions in a judicial manner; because the cases are the baseline from which the Court now departs and so serve to measure the actual as opposed to the professed distance it travels; and because examination of them helps reveal how the Court has coasted into its present position.

The earliest confession cases in this Court emerged from federal prosecutions and were settled on a nonconstitutional basis, the Court adopting the common-law rule that the absence of inducements, promises, and threats made a confession voluntary and admissible. *Hopt v. Utah*, 110 U.S. 574; *Pierce v. United States*, 160 U.S. 355. While a later case said the Fifth Amendment privilege controlled admissibility, this proposition was not itself developed in subsequent decisions. The Court did, however, heighten the test of admissibility in federal trials to one of voluntariness "in fact," *Wan v. United States*, 266 U.S. 1, 14 (quoted, ante, p. 462), and then by and large left federal judges to apply the same standards the Court began to derive in a string of state court cases.

This new line of decisions, testing admissibility by the Due Process Clause, began in 1936 with *Brown v. Mississippi*, 297 U.S. 278, and must now embrace somewhat more than 30 full opinions of the Court. While the voluntariness rubric was repeated in many instances, e.g., *Lyons v. Oklahoma*, 322 U.S. 596, the Court never pinned it down to a single meaning but on the contrary infused it with a number of different values. To travel quickly over the main themes, there was an initial emphasis on reliability, e.g., *Ward v. Texas*, 316 U.S. 547, supplemented by concern over the legality and fairness of the police practices, e.g., *Ashcraft v. Tennessee*, 322 U.S. 143, in an "accusatorial" system of law enforcement, *Watts v. Indiana*, 338 U.S. 49, 54, and eventually by close attention to the individual's state of mind and capacity for effective choice, e.g., *Gallegos v. Colorado*, 370 U.S. 49. The outcome was a continuing re-evaluation on the facts of each case of how much pressure on the suspect was permissible.

Among the criteria often taken into account were threats or imminent danger, e.g., *Payne v. Arkansas*, 356 U.S. 560, physical deprivations such as lack of sleep or food, e.g., *Reck v. Pate*, 367 U.S. 433, repeated or extended interrogation, e.g., *Chambers v. Florida*, 309 U.S. 227, limits on access to counsel or friends, *Crooker v. California*, 357 U.S. 433; *Cicenia v. Lagay*, 357 U.S. 504, length and illegality of detention under state law, e.g., *Haynes v. Washington*, 373 U.S. 503, and individual weakness or incapacities, *Lynumn v. Illinois*, 372 U.S. 528. Apart from direct physical coercion, however, no single default or fixed combination of defaults guaranteed exclusion, and synopses of the cases would serve little use because the overall gauge has been steadily changing, usually in the direction of restricting admissibility. But to mark just what point had been reached before the Court jumped the rails in *Escobedo v. Illinois*, 378 U.S. 478, it is worth capsulizing the then-recent case of *Haynes v. Washington*, 373 U.S. 503. There, Haynes had been held some 16 or more hours in violation of state law before signing the disputed confession, had received no warnings of any kind, and despite requests had been refused access to his wife or to counsel, the police indicating that access would be allowed after a confession. Emphasizing especially this last inducement and rejecting some contrary indicia of voluntariness, the Court in a 5-to-4 decision held the confession inadmissible.

There are several relevant lessons to be drawn from this constitutional history. The first is that with over 25 years of precedent the Court has developed an elaborate, sophisticated, and sensitive approach to admissibility of confessions. It is "judicial" in its treatment of one case at a time, see *Culombe v. Connecticut*, 367 U.S. 568, 635 (concurring opinion of THE CHIEF JUSTICE), flexible in its ability to respond to the endless mutations of fact presented, and ever more familiar to the lower courts. Of course, strict certainty is not obtained in this developing process, but this is often so with constitutional principles, and disagreement is usually confined to that borderland of close cases where it matters least.

The second point is that in practice and from time to time in principle, the Court has given ample recognition to society's interest in suspect questioning as an instrument of law enforcement. Cases countenancing quite significant pressures can be cited without difficulty, and the lower courts may often have been yet more tolerant. Of course the limitations imposed today were rejected by necessary implication in case after case, the right to warnings having been explicitly rebuffed in this Court many years ago. *Powers v. United States*, 223 U.S. 303; *Wilson v. United States*, 162 U.S. 613. As recently as *Haynes v. Washington*, 373 U.S. 503, 515, the Court openly acknowledged that questioning of witnesses and suspects "is undoubtedly an essential tool in effective law enforcement." Accord, *Crooker v. California*, 357 U.S. 433, 441.

Finally, the cases disclose that the language in many of the opinions overstates the actual course of decision. It has been said, for example, that an admissible confession must be made by the suspect "in the unfettered exercise of his own will," *Malloy v. Hogan*, 378 U.S. 1, 8, and that "a prisoner is not 'to be made the deluded instrument of his own conviction,'" *Culombe v. Connecticut*, 367 U.S. 568, 581 (Frankfurter, J., announcing the Court's judgment and an opinion). Though often

repeated, such principles are rarely observed in full measure. Even the word "voluntary" may be deemed somewhat misleading, especially when one considers many of the confessions that have been brought under its umbrella. See, e.g., supra, n. 5. The tendency to overstate may be laid in part to the flagrant facts often before the Court; but in any event one must recognize how it has tempered attitudes and lent some color of authority to the approach now taken by the Court.

I turn now to the Court's asserted reliance on the Fifth Amendment, an approach which I frankly regard as a trompe l'oeil. The Court's opinion in my view reveals no adequate basis for extending the Fifth Amendment's privilege against self-incrimination to the police station. Far more important, it fails to show that the Court's new rules are well supported, let alone compelled, by Fifth Amendment precedents. Instead, the new rules actually derive from quotation and analogy drawn from precedents under the Sixth Amendment, which should properly have no bearing on police interrogation.

The Court's opening contention, that the Fifth Amendment governs police station confessions, is perhaps not an impermissible extension of the law but it has little to commend itself in the present circumstances. Historically, the privilege against self-incrimination did not bear at all on the use of extra-legal confessions, for which distinct standards evolved; indeed, "the history of the two principles is wide apart, differing by one hundred years in origin, and derived through separate lines of precedents. . . ." 8 Wigmore, Evidence 2266, at 401 (McNaughton rev. 1961). Practice under the two doctrines has also differed in a number of important respects. Even those who would readily enlarge the privilege must concede some linguistic difficulties since the Fifth Amendment in terms proscribes only compelling any person "in any criminal case to be a witness against himself." Cf. Kamisar, Equal Justice in the Gatehouses and Mansions of American Criminal Procedure, in Criminal Justice in Our Time 1, 25-26 (1965).

Though weighty, I do not say these points and similar ones are conclusive, for, as the Court reiterates, the privilege embodies basic principles always capable of expansion. Certainly the privilege does represent a protective concern for the accused and an emphasis upon accusatorial rather than inquisitorial values in law enforcement, although this is similarly true of other limitations such as the grand jury requirement

---

and the reasonable doubt standard. Accusatorial values, however, have openly been absorbed into the due process standard governing confessions; this indeed is why at present "the kinship of the two rules [governing confessions and self-incrimination] is too apparent for denial." McCormick, Evidence 155 (1954). Since extension of the general principle has already occurred, to insist that the privilege applies as such serves only to carry over inapposite historical details and engaging rhetoric and to obscure the policy choices to be made in regulating confessions.

Having decided that the Fifth Amendment privilege does apply in the police station, the Court reveals that the privilege imposes more exacting restrictions than does the Fourteenth Amendment's voluntariness test. It then emerges from a discussion of Escobedo that the Fifth Amendment requires for an admissible confession that it be given by one distinctly aware of his right not to speak and shielded from "the compelling atmosphere" of interrogation. See ante, pp. 465-466. From these key premises, the Court finally develops the safeguards of warning, counsel, and so forth. I do not believe these premises are sustained by precedents under the Fifth Amendment.

The more important premise is that pressure on the suspect must be eliminated though it be only the subtle influence of the atmosphere and surroundings. The Fifth Amendment, however, has never been thought to forbid all pressure to incriminate one's self in the situations covered by it. On the contrary, it has been held that failure to incriminate one's self can result in denial of removal of one's case from state to federal court, *Maryland v. Soper*, 270 U.S. 9 ; in refusal of a military commission, *Orloff v. Willoughby*, 345 U.S. 83; in denial of a discharge in bankruptcy, *Kaufman v. Hurwitz*, 176 F.2d 210; and in numerous other adverse consequences. See 8 Wigmore, Evidence 2272, at 441-444, n. 18 (McNaughton rev. 1961); Maguire, Evidence of Guilt 2.062 (1959). This is not to say that short of jail or torture any sanction is permissible in any case; policy and history alike may impose sharp limits. See, e.g., *Griffin v. California*, 380 U.S. 609. However, the Court's unspoken assumption that any pressure violates the privilege is not supported by the precedents and it has failed to show why the Fifth Amendment prohibits that relatively mild pressure the Due Process Clause permits.

The Court appears similarly wrong in thinking that precise knowledge of one's rights is a settled prerequisite under the Fifth Amendment to the loss of its protections. A number of lower federal court cases have held that grand jury witnesses need not always be warned of their privilege, e.g., *United States v. Scully*, 225 F.2d 113, 116, and Wigmore states this to be the better rule for trial witnesses. See 8 Wigmore, Evidence 2269 (McNaughton rev. 1961). Cf. *Henry v. Mississippi*, 379 U.S. 443, 451-452 (waiver of constitutional rights by counsel despite defendant's ignorance held allowable). No Fifth Amendment precedent is cited for the Court's contrary view. There might of course be reasons apart from Fifth Amendment precedent for requiring warning or any other safeguard on questioning but that is a different matter entirely. See infra, pp. 516-517.

A closing word must be said about the Assistance of Counsel Clause of the Sixth Amendment, which is never expressly relied on by the Court but whose judicial precedents turn out to be linchpins of the confession rules announced today. To support its requirement of a knowing and intelligent waiver, the Court cites *Johnson v. Zerbst*, 304 U.S. 458, ante, p. 475; appointment of counsel for the indigent suspect is tied to *Gideon v. Wainwright*, 372 U.S. 335, and *Douglas v. California*, 372 U.S. 353, ante, p. 473; the silent-record doctrine is borrowed from *Carnley v. Cochran*, 369 U.S. 506, ante, p. 475, as is the right to an express offer of counsel, ante, p. 471. All these cases imparting glosses to the Sixth Amendment concerned counsel at trial or on appeal. While the Court finds no pertinent difference between judicial proceedings and police interrogation, I believe the differences are so vast as to disqualify wholly the Sixth Amendment precedents as suitable analogies in the present cases.

The only attempt in this Court to carry the right to counsel into the station house occurred in Escobedo, the Court repeating several times that that stage was no less "critical" than trial itself. See 378 U.S., 485-488. This is hardly persuasive when we consider that a grand jury inquiry, the filing of a certiorari petition, and certainly the purchase of narcotics by an undercover agent from a prospective defendant may all be equally "critical" yet provision of counsel and advice on that score have never been thought compelled by the Constitution in such cases. The sound reason why this right is so freely extended for a criminal trial is the severe injustice risked by confronting an untrained defendant with a range of technical points of law, evidence, and tactics familiar to the prosecutor but not to himself. This danger shrinks markedly in the police station where indeed the lawyer in fulfilling his professional responsibilities of necessity may become an obstacle to truthfinding. See infra, n. 12. The Court's summary citation of the Sixth Amendment cases here seems to me best described as "the domino method of constitutional adjudication . . . wherein every explanatory statement in a previous opinion is made the basis for extension to a wholly different situation." Friendly, supra, n. 10, at 950.

III. Policy Considerations

Examined as an expression of public policy, the Court's new regime proves so dubious that there can be no due compensation for its weakness in constitutional law. The foregoing discussion has shown, I think, how mistaken is the Court in implying that the Constitution has struck the balance in favor of the approach the Court takes. Ante, p. 479. Rather, precedent reveals that the Fourteenth Amendment in practice has been construed to strike a different balance, that the Fifth Amendment gives the Court little solid support in this context, and that the Sixth Amendment should have no bearing at all. Legal history has been stretched before to satisfy deep needs of society. In this instance, however, the Court has not and cannot make the powerful showing that its new rules are plainly desirable in the context of our society, something which is surely demanded before those rules are engrafted onto the Constitution and imposed on every State and county in the land.

Without at all subscribing to the generally black picture of police conduct painted by the Court, I think it must be frankly recognized at the outset that police questioning allowable under due process precedents may inherently entail some pressure on the suspect and may seek advantage in his ignorance or weaknesses. The atmosphere and questioning techniques, proper and fair though they be, can in themselves exert a tug on the suspect to confess, and in this light "[t]o speak of any confessions of crime made after arrest as being 'voluntary' or 'uncoerced' is somewhat inaccurate, although traditional. A confession is wholly and incontestably voluntary only if a guilty person gives himself up to the law and becomes his own accuser." *Ashcraft v. Tennessee*, 322 U.S. 143, 161 (Jackson, J., dissenting). Until today, the role of the Constitution has been only to sift out undue pressure, not to assure spontaneous confessions.

The Court's new rules aim to offset these minor pressures and disadvantages intrinsic to any kind of police interrogation. The rules do not serve due process interests in preventing blatant coercion since, as I noted earlier, they do nothing to contain the policeman who is prepared to lie from the start. The rules work for reliability in confessions almost only in the Pickwickian sense that they can prevent some from being given at all. In short, the benefit of this new regime is simply to lessen or wipe out the inherent compulsion and inequalities to which the Court devotes some nine pages of description. Ante, pp. 448-456.

What the Court largely ignores is that its rules impair, if they will not eventually serve wholly to frustrate, an instrument of law enforcement that has long and quite reasonably been thought worth the price paid for it. There can be little doubt that the Court's new code would markedly decrease the number of confessions. To warn the suspect that he may remain silent and remind him that his confession may be used in court are minor obstructions. To require also an express waiver by the suspect and an end to questioning whenever he demurs must heavily handicap questioning. And to suggest or provide counsel for the suspect simply invites the end of the interrogation. See, supra, n. 12.

How much harm this decision will inflict on law enforcement cannot fairly be predicted with accuracy. Evidence on the role of confessions is notoriously incomplete, see Developments, supra, n. 2, at 941-944, and little is added by the Court's reference to the FBI experience and the resources believed wasted in interrogation. See infra, n. 19, and text. We do know that some crimes cannot be solved without confessions, that ample expert testimony attests to their importance in crime control, and that the Court is taking a real risk with society's welfare in imposing its new regime on the country. The social costs of crime are too great to call the new rules anything but a hazardous experimentation.

While passing over the costs and risks of its experiment, the Court portrays the evils of normal police questioning in terms which I think are exaggerated. Albeit stringently confined by the due process standards interrogation is no doubt often inconvenient and unpleasant for the suspect. However, it is no less so for a man to be arrested and jailed, to have his house searched, or to stand trial in court, yet all this may properly happen to the most innocent given probable cause, a warrant, or an indictment. Society has always paid a stiff price for law and order, and peaceful interrogation is not one of the dark moments of the law.

This brief statement of the competing considerations seems to me ample proof that the Court's preference is highly debatable at best and therefore not to be read into the Constitution. However, it may make the analysis more graphic to consider the actual facts of one of the four cases reversed by the Court. *Miranda v. Arizona* serves best, being neither the hardest nor easiest of the four under the Court's standards.

On March 3, 1963, an 18-year-old girl was kidnapped and forcibly raped near Phoenix, Arizona. Ten days later, on the morning of March 13, petitioner Miranda was arrested and taken to the police station. At this time Miranda was 23 years old, indigent, and educated to the extent of completing half the ninth grade. He had "an emotional illness" of the schizophrenic type, according to the doctor who eventually examined him; the doctor's report also stated that Miranda was "alert and oriented as to time, place, and person," intelligent within normal limits, competent to stand trial, and sane within the legal definition. At the police station, the victim picked Miranda out of a lineup, and two officers then took him into a separate room to interrogate him, starting about 11:30 a.m. Though at first denying his guilt, within a short time Miranda gave a detailed oral confession and then wrote out in his own hand and signed a brief statement admitting and describing the crime. All this was accomplished in two hours or less without any force, threats or promises and—I will assume this though the record is uncertain, ante, 491-492 and nn. 66-67—without any effective warnings at all.

Miranda's oral and written confessions are now held inadmissible under the Court's new rules. One is entitled to feel astonished that the Constitution can be read to produce this result. These confessions were obtained during brief, daytime questioning conducted by two officers and unmarked by any of the traditional indicia of coercion. They assured a conviction for a brutal and unsettling crime, for which the police had and quite possibly could obtain little evidence other than the victim's identifications, evidence which is frequently unreliable. There was, in sum, a legitimate purpose, no perceptible unfairness, and certainly little risk of injustice in the interrogation. Yet the resulting confessions, and the responsible course of police practice they represent, are to be sacrificed to the Court's own finespun conception of fairness which I seriously doubt is shared by many thinking citizens in this country.

The tenor of judicial opinion also falls well short of supporting the Court's new approach. Although Escobedo has widely been interpreted as an open invitation to lower courts to rewrite the law of confessions, a significant heavy majority of the state and federal decisions in point have sought quite narrow interpretations. Of the courts that have accepted the invitation, it is hard to know how many have felt compelled by their best guess as to this Court's likely construction; but none of the state decisions saw fit to rely on the state privilege against self-incrimination, and no decision at all has gone as far as this Court goes today.

It is also instructive to compare the attitude in this case of those responsible for law enforcement with the official views that existed when the Court undertook three major revisions of prosecutorial practice prior to this case, *Johnson v. Zerbst*, 304 U.S. 458, *Mapp v. Ohio*, 367 U.S. 643, and *Gideon v. Wainwright*, 372 U.S. 335. In Johnson, which established that appointed counsel must be offered the indigent in federal criminal trials, the Federal Government all but conceded the basic issue, which had in fact been recently fixed as Department of Justice policy. See Beaney, Right to Counsel 29-30, 36-42 (1955). In Mapp, which imposed the exclusionary rule on the States for Fourth Amendment violations, more than half of the States had themselves already adopted some such rule. See 367 U.S., at 651. In Gideon, which extended *Johnson v. Zerbst* to the States, an amicus brief was filed by 22 States and Commonwealths urging that course; only two States besides that of the respondent came forward to protest. See 372 U.S., at 345. By contrast, in this case new restrictions on police questioning have been opposed by the United States and in an amicus brief signed by 27 States and Commonwealths, not including the three other States which are parties. No State in the country has urged this Court to impose the newly announced rules, nor has any State chosen to go nearly so far on its own.

The Court in closing its general discussion invokes the practice in federal and foreign jurisdictions as lending weight to its new curbs on confessions for all the States. A brief resume will suffice to show that none of these jurisdictions has struck so one-sided a balance as the Court does today. Heaviest reliance is placed on the FBI practice. Differing circumstances may make this comparison quite untrustworthy, but in any event the FBI falls sensibly short of the Court's formalistic rules. For example, there is no indication that FBI agents must obtain an affirmative "waiver" before they pursue their questioning. Nor is it clear that one invoking his right to silence may not be prevailed upon to change his mind. And the warning as to appointed counsel apparently indicates only that one will be assigned by the judge when the suspect appears before him; the thrust of the Court's rules is to induce the suspect to obtain appointed counsel before continuing the interview. See ante, pp. 484-486. Apparently American military practice, briefly mentioned by the Court, has these same limits and is still less favorable to the suspect than the FBI warning, making no mention of appointed counsel. Developments, supra, n. 2, at 1084-1089.

The law of the foreign countries described by the Court also reflects a more moderate conception of the rights of the accused as against those of society when other data are considered. Concededly, the English experience is most relevant. In that country, a caution as to silence but not counsel has long been mandated by the "Judges' Rules," which also place other somewhat imprecise limits on police cross-examination of suspects. However, in the court's discretion confessions can be and apparently quite frequently are admitted in evidence despite disregard of the Judges' Rules, so long as they are found voluntary under the common-law test. Moreover, the check that exists on the use of pretrial statements is counterbalanced by the evident admissibility of fruits of an illegal confession and by the judge's often-used authority to comment adversely on the defendant's failure to testify.

India, Ceylon and Scotland are the other examples chosen by the Court. In India and Ceylon the general ban on police-adduced confessions cited by the Court is subject to a major exception: if evidence is uncovered by police questioning, it is fully admissible at trial along with the confession itself, so far as it relates to the evidence and is not blatantly coerced. See Developments, supra, n. 2, at 1106-1110; *Reg. v. Ramasamy* 1965. A.C. 1 (P.C.). Scotland's limits on interrogation do measure up to the Court's; however, restrained comment at trial on the defendant's failure to take the stand is allowed the judge, and in many other respects Scotch law redresses the prosecutor's disadvantage in ways not permitted in this country. The Court ends its survey by imputing added strength to our privilege against self-incrimination since, by contrast to other countries, it is embodied in a written Constitution.

Considering the liberties the Court has today taken with constitutional history and precedent, few will find this emphasis persuasive.

In closing this necessarily truncated discussion of policy considerations attending the new confession rules, some reference must be made to their ironic untimeliness. There is now in progress in this country a massive re-examination of criminal law enforcement procedures on a scale never before witnessed. Participants in this undertaking include a Special Committee of the American Bar Association, under the chairmanship of Chief Judge Lumbard of the Court of Appeals for the Second Circuit; a distinguished study group of the American Law Institute, headed by Professors Vorenberg and Bator of the Harvard Law School; and the President's Commission on Law Enforcement and Administration of Justice, under the leadership of the Attorney General of the United States. Studies are also being conducted by the District of Columbia Crime Commission, the Georgetown Law Center, and by others equipped to do practical research. There are also signs that legislatures in some of the States may be preparing to re-examine the problem before us.

It is no secret that concern has been expressed lest long-range and lasting reforms be frustrated by this Court's too rapid departure from existing constitutional standards. Despite the Court's disclaimer, the practical effect of the decision made today must inevitably be to handicap seriously sound efforts at reform, not least by removing options necessary to a just compromise of competing interests. Of course legislative reform is rarely speedy or unanimous, though this Court has been more patient in the past. But the legislative reforms when they come would have the vast advantage of empirical data and comprehensive study, they would allow experimentation and use of solutions not open to the courts, and they would restore the initiative in criminal law reform to those forums where it truly belongs.

IV. Conclusions

All four of the cases involved here present express claims that confessions were inadmissible, not because of coercion in the traditional due process sense, but solely because of lack of counsel or lack of warnings concerning counsel and silence. For the reasons stated in this opinion, I would adhere to the due process test and reject the new requirements inaugurated by the Court. On this premise my disposition of each of these cases can be stated briefly.

In two of the three cases coming from state courts, *Miranda v. Arizona* (No. 759) and *Vignera v. New York* (No. 760), the confessions were held admissible and no other errors worth comment are alleged by petitioners. I would affirm in these two cases. The other state case is *California v. Stewart* (No. 584), where the state supreme court held the confession inadmissible and reversed the conviction. In that case I would dismiss the writ of certiorari on the ground that no final judgment is before us, 28 U.S.C. 1257 (1964 ed.); putting aside the new trial open to the State in any event, the confession itself has not even been finally excluded since the California Supreme Court left the State free to show proof of a waiver. If the merits of the decision in Stewart be reached, then I believe it should be reversed and the case remanded so the state supreme court may pass on the other claims available to respondent.

In the federal case, *Westover v. United States* (No. 761), a number of issues are raised by petitioner apart from the one already dealt with in this dissent. None of these other claims appears to me tenable, nor in this context to warrant extended discussion. It is urged that the confession was also inadmissible because not voluntary even measured by due process standards and because federal-state cooperation brought the McNabb-Mallory rule into play under *Anderson v. United States*, 318 U.S. 350. However, the facts alleged fall well short of coercion in my view, and I believe the involvement of federal agents in petitioner's arrest and detention by the State too slight to invoke Anderson. I agree with the Government that the admission of the evidence now protested by petitioner was at most harmless error, and two final contentions—one involving weight of the evidence and another improper prosecutor comment—seem to me without merit. I would therefore affirm Westover's conviction.

In conclusion: Nothing in the letter or the spirit of the Constitution or in the precedents squares with the heavy-handed and one-sided action that is so precipitously taken by the Court in the name of fulfilling its constitutional responsibilities. The foray which the Court makes today brings to mind the wise and farsighted words of Mr. Justice Jackson in *Douglas v. Jeannette*, 319 U.S. 157, 181 (separate opinion): "This Court is forever adding new stories to the temples of constitutional law, and the temples have a way of collapsing when one story too many is added."

Mr. Justice White, with Whom Mr. Justice Harlan and Mr. Justice Stewart Join, Dissenting

I

The proposition that the privilege against self-incrimination forbids in-custody interrogation without the warnings specified in the majority opinion and without a clear waiver of counsel has no significant support in the history of the privilege or in the language of the Fifth Amendment. As for the English authorities and the common-law history, the privilege, firmly established in the second half of the seventeenth century, was never applied except to prohibit compelled judicial interrogations. The rule excluding coerced confessions matured about 100 years later, "[b]ut there is nothing in the reports to suggest that the theory has its roots in the privilege against self-incrimination. And so far as the cases reveal, the privilege, as such, seems to have been given effect only in judicial proceedings, including the preliminary examinations by authorized magistrates." Morgan, The Privilege Against Self-Incrimination, 34 Minn. L. Rev. 1, 18 (1949).

Our own constitutional provision provides that no person "shall be compelled in any criminal case to be a witness against himself." These words, when "[c]onsidered in the light to be shed by grammar and the dictionary . . . appear to signify simply that nobody shall be compelled to give oral testimony against himself in a criminal proceeding under way in which he is defendant." Corwin, The Supreme Court's Construction of the Self-Incrimination Clause, 29 Mich. L. Rev. 1, 2. And there is very little in the surrounding circumstances of the adoption of the Fifth Amendment or in the provisions of the then existing state constitutions or in state practice which would give the constitutional provision any broader meaning. Mayers, The Federal Witness' Privilege Against Self-Incrimination: Constitutional or Common-Law? 4 American Journal of Legal History 107 (1960). Such a construction, however, was considerably narrower than the privilege at common law, and when eventually faced with the issues, the Court extended the constitutional privilege to the compulsory production of books and papers, to the ordinary witness before the grand jury and to witnesses generally. *Boyd v. United States*, 116 U.S. 616, and *Counsel-*

man v. Hitchcock, 142 U.S. 547. Both rules had solid support in common-law history, if not in the history of our own constitutional provision.

A few years later the Fifth Amendment privilege was similarly extended to encompass the then well-established rule against coerced confessions: "In criminal trials, in the courts of the United States, wherever a question arises whether a confession is incompetent because not voluntary, the issue is controlled by that portion of the Fifth Amendment to the Constitution of the United States, commanding that no person 'shall be compelled in any criminal case to be a witness against himself.'" *Bram v. United States*, 168 U.S. 532, 542. Although this view has found approval in other cases, *Burdeau v. McDowell*, 256 U.S. 465, 475; *Powers v. United States*, 223 U.S. 303, 313; *Shotwell v. United States*, 371 U.S. 341, 347, it has also been questioned, see *Brown v. Mississippi*, 297 U.S. 278, 285; *United States v. Carignan*, 342 U.S. 36, 41; *Stein v. New York*, 346 U.S. 156, 191, n. 35, and finds scant support in either the English or American authorities, see generally *Regina v. Scott*, Dears. & Bell 47; 3 Wigmore, Evidence 823 (3d ed. 1940), at 249 ("a confession is not rejected because of any connection with the privilege against self-crimination"), and 250, n. 5 (particularly criticizing Bram); 8 Wigmore, Evidence 2266, at 400-401 (McNaughton rev. 1961). Whatever the source of the rule excluding coerced confessions, it is clear that prior to the application of the privilege itself to state courts, *Malloy v. Hogan*, 378 U.S. 1, the admissibility of a confession in a state criminal prosecution was tested by the same standards as were applied in federal prosecutions. Id., at 6-7, 10.

Bram, however, itself rejected the proposition which the Court now espouses. The question in Bram was whether a confession, obtained during custodial interrogation, had been compelled, and if such interrogation was to be deemed inherently vulnerable the Court's inquiry could have ended there. After examining the English and American authorities, however, the Court declared that:

> "In this court also it has been settled that the mere fact that the confession is made to a police officer, while the accused was under arrest in or out of prison, or was drawn out by his questions, does not necessarily render the confession involuntary, but, as one of the circumstances, such imprisonment or inter-

rogation may be taken into account in determining whether or not the statements of the prisoner were voluntary." 168 U.S., at 558.

In this respect the Court was wholly consistent with prior and subsequent pronouncements in this Court.

Thus prior to Bram the Court, in *Hopt v. Utah*, 110 U.S. 574, 583-587, had upheld the admissibility of a confession made to police officers following arrest, the record being silent concerning what conversation had occurred between the officers and the defendant in the short period preceding the confession. Relying on Hopt, the Court ruled squarely on the issue in Sparf and *Hansen v. United States*, 156 U.S. 51, 55:

> "Counsel for the accused insist that there cannot be a voluntary statement, a free open confession, while a defendant is confined and in irons under an accusation of having committed a capital offence. We have not been referred to any authority in support of that position. It is true that the fact of a prisoner being in custody at the time he makes a confession is a circumstance not to be overlooked, because it bears upon the inquiry whether the confession was voluntarily made or was extorted by threats or violence or made under the influence of fear. But confinement or imprisonment is not in itself sufficient to justify the exclusion of a confession, if it appears to have been voluntary, and was not obtained by putting the prisoner in fear or by promises. Wharton's Cr. Ev. 9th ed. 661, 663, and authorities cited."

Accord, *Pierce v. United States*, 160 U.S. 355, 357.

And in *Wilson v. United States*, 162 U.S. 613, 623, the Court had considered the significance of custodial interrogation without any antecedent warnings regarding the right to remain silent or the right to counsel. There the defendant had answered questions posed by a Commissioner, who had failed to advise him of his rights, and his answers were held admissible over his claim of involuntariness. "The fact that [a defendant] is in custody and manacled does not necessarily render his statement involuntary, nor is that necessarily the effect of popular excitement shortly preceding. . . . And it is laid down that it is not essential to the admissibility of a confession that it should appear that the person was warned that what he said would be used against him, but on the contrary, if the confession was voluntary, it is sufficient though it appear that he was not so warned."

Since Bram, the admissibility of statements made during custodial interrogation has been frequently reiterated. *Powers v. United States*, 223 U.S. 303, cited Wilson approvingly and held admissible as voluntary statements the accused's testimony at a preliminary hearing even though he was not warned that what he said might be used against him. Without any discussion of the presence or absence of warnings, presumably because such discussion was deemed unnecessary, numerous other cases have declared that "[t]he mere fact that a confession was made while in the custody of the police does not render it inadmissible," *McNabb v. United States*, 318 U.S. 332, 346; accord, *United States v. Mitchell*, 322 U.S. 65, despite its having been elicited by police examination, *Wan v. United States*, 266 U.S. 1, 14; *United States v. Carignan*, 342 U.S. 36, 39. Likewise, in *Crooker v. California*, 357 U.S. 433, 437, the Court said that "the bare fact of police 'detention and police examination in private of one in official state custody' does not render involuntary a confession by the one so detained." And finally, in *Cicenia v. Lagay*, 357 U.S. 504, a confession obtained by police interrogation after arrest was held voluntary even though the authorities refused to permit the defendant to consult with his attorney. See generally *Culombe v. Connecticut*, 367 U.S. 568, 587-602 (opinion of Frankfurter, J.); 3 Wigmore, Evidence 851, at 313 (3d ed. 1940); see also Joy, Admissibility of Confessions 38, 46 (1842).

Only a tiny minority of our judges who have dealt with the question, including today's majority, have considered in-custody interrogation, without more, to be a violation of the Fifth Amendment. And this Court, as every member knows, has left standing literally thousands of criminal convictions that rested at least in part on confessions taken in the course of interrogation by the police after arrest.

II

That the Court's holding today is neither compelled nor even strongly suggested by the language of the Fifth Amendment, is at odds with American and English legal history, and involves a departure from a long line of precedent does not prove either that the Court has exceeded its powers or that the Court is wrong or unwise in its present reinterpretation of the Fifth Amendment. It does, however, underscore the obvious—that the Court has not discovered or found the law in making today's decision, nor has it derived it from some irrefutable sources; what it has done is to make new law and new public policy in much the same way that it has in the course of interpreting other great clauses of the Constitution. This is what the Court historically has done. Indeed, it is what it must do and will continue to do until and unless there is some fundamental change in the constitutional distribution of governmental powers.

But if the Court is here and now to announce new and fundamental policy to govern certain aspects of our affairs, it is wholly legitimate to examine the mode of this or any other constitutional decision in this Court and to inquire into the advisability of its end product in terms of the long-range interest of the country. At the very least the Court's text and reasoning should withstand analysis and be a fair exposition of the constitutional provision which its opinion interprets. Decisions like these cannot rest alone on syllogism, metaphysics or some ill-defined notions of natural justice, although each will perhaps play its part. In proceeding to such constructions as it now announces, the Court should also duly consider all the factors and interests bearing upon the cases, at least insofar as the relevant materials are available; and if the necessary considerations are not treated in the record or obtainable from some other reliable source, the Court should not proceed to formulate fundamental policies based on speculation alone.

III

First, we may inquire what are the textual and factual bases of this new fundamental rule. To reach the result announced on the grounds it does, the Court must stay within the confines of the Fifth Amendment, which forbids self-incrimination only if compelled. Hence the core of the Court's opinion is that because of the "compulsion inherent in custodial surroundings, no statement obtained from [a] defendant [in custody] can truly be the product of his free choice," ante, at 458, absent the use of adequate protective devices as described by the Court. However, the Court does not point to any sudden inrush of new knowledge requiring the rejection of 70 years' experience. Nor does it assert that its novel conclusion reflects a changing consensus among state courts, see *Mapp v. Ohio*, 367 U.S. 643, or that a succession of cases had steadily eroded the old rule and proved it unworkable, see *Gideon v. Wainwright*, 372 U.S. 335. Rather than asserting new knowledge, the Court concedes that it cannot truly know what occurs during custodial questioning, because of the innate secrecy of such proceedings. It extrapolates a picture of what it conceives to be the norm from police investigatorial manuals, published in 1959 and 1962 or earlier, without any attempt to allow for adjustments in police practices that may have occurred in the wake of more recent decisions of state appellate tribunals or this Court. But even if the relentless application of the described procedures could lead to involuntary confessions, it most assuredly does not follow that each and every case will disclose this kind of interrogation or this kind of consequence. Insofar as appears from the Court's opinion, it has not examined a single transcript of any police interrogation, let alone the interrogation that took place in any one of these cases which it decides today. Judged by any of the standards for empirical investigation utilized in the social sciences the factual basis for the Court's premise is patently inadequate.

Although in the Court's view in-custody interrogation is inherently coercive, the Court says that the spontaneous product of the coercion of arrest and detention is still to be deemed voluntary. An accused, arrested on probable cause, may blurt out a confession which will be admissible despite the fact that he is alone and in custody, without any showing that he had any notion of his right to remain silent or of the consequences of his admission. Yet, under the Court's rule, if the police ask him a single question such as "Do you have anything to say?" or "Did you kill your wife?" his response, if there is one, has somehow been compelled, even if the accused has been clearly warned of his right to remain silent. Common sense informs us to the contrary. While one may say that the response was "involuntary" in the sense the question provoked or was the occasion for the response and thus the defendant was induced to speak out when he might have remained silent if not arrested and not questioned, it is patently unsound to say the response is compelled.

Today's result would not follow even if it were agreed that to some extent custodial interrogation is inherently coercive. See *Ashcraft v. Tennessee*, 322 U.S. 143,

161 (Jackson, J., dissenting). The test has been whether the totality of circumstances deprived the defendant of a "free choice to admit, to deny, or to refuse to answer," *Lisenba v. California*, 314 U.S. 219, 241, and whether physical or psychological coercion was of such a degree that "the defendant's will was overborne at the time he confessed," *Haynes v. Washington*, 373 U.S. 503, 513; *Lynumn v. Illinois*, 372 U.S. 528, 534. The duration and nature of incommunicado custody, the presence or absence of advice concerning the defendant's constitutional rights, and the granting or refusal of requests to communicate with lawyers, relatives or friends have all been rightly regarded as important data bearing on the basic inquiry. See, e.g., *Ashcraft v. Tennessee*, 322 U.S. 143; *Haynes v. Washington*, 373 U.S. 503. But it has never been suggested, until today, that such questioning was so coercive and accused persons so lacking in hardihood that the very first response to the very first question following the commencement of custody must be conclusively presumed to be the product of an overborne will.

If the rule announced today were truly based on a conclusion that all confessions resulting from custodial interrogation are coerced, then it would simply have no rational foundation. Compare *Tot v. United States*, 319 U.S. 463, 466; *United States v. Romano*, 382 U.S. 136. A fortiori that would be true of the extension of the rule to exculpatory statements, which the Court effects after a brief discussion of why, in the Court's view, they must be deemed incriminatory but without any discussion of why they must be deemed coerced. See *Wilson v. United States*, 162 U.S. 613, 624. Even if one were to postulate that the Court's concern is not that all confessions induced by police interrogation are coerced but rather that some such confessions are coerced and present judicial procedures are believed to be inadequate to identify the confessions that are coerced and those that are not, it would still not be essential to impose the rule that the Court has now fashioned. Transcripts or observers could be required, specific time limits, tailored to fit the cause, could be imposed, or other devices could be utilized to reduce the chances that otherwise indiscernible coercion will produce an inadmissible confession.

On the other hand, even if one assumed that there was an adequate factual basis for the conclusion that all confessions obtained during in-custody interrogation are the product of compulsion, the rule propounded by the Court would still be irrational, for, apparently, it is only if the accused is also warned of his right to counsel and waives both that right and the right against self-incrimination that the inherent compulsiveness of interrogation disappears. But if the defendant may not answer without a warning a question such as "Where were you last night?" without having his answer be a compelled one, how can the Court ever accept his negative answer to the question of whether he wants to consult his retained counsel or counsel whom the court will appoint? And why if counsel is present and the accused nevertheless confesses, or counsel tells the accused to tell the truth, and that is what the accused does, is the situation any less coercive insofar as the accused is concerned? The Court apparently realizes its dilemma of foreclosing questioning without the necessary warnings but at the same time permitting the accused, sitting in the same chair in front of the same policemen, to waive his right to consult an attorney. It expects, however, that the accused will not often waive the right; and if it is claimed that he has, the State faces a severe, if not impossible burden of proof.

All of this makes very little sense in terms of the compulsion which the Fifth Amendment proscribes. That amendment deals with compelling the accused himself. It is his free will that is involved. Confessions and incriminating admissions, as such, are not forbidden evidence; only those which are compelled are banned. I doubt that the Court observes these distinctions today. By considering any answers to any interrogation to be compelled regardless of the content and course of examination and by escalating the requirements to prove waiver, the Court not only prevents the use of compelled confessions but for all practical purposes forbids interrogation except in the presence of counsel. That is, instead of confining itself to protection of the right against compelled self-incrimination the Court has created a limited Fifth Amendment right to counsel—or, as the Court expresses it, a "need for counsel to protect the Fifth Amendment privilege. . . ." Ante, at 470. The focus then is not on the will of the accused but on the will of counsel and how much influence he can have on the accused. Obviously there is no warrant in the Fifth Amendment for thus installing counsel as the arbiter of the privilege.

In sum, for all the Court's expounding on the menacing atmosphere of police interrogation procedures, it has failed to supply any foundation for the conclusions it draws or the measures it adopts.

IV

Criticism of the Court's opinion, however, cannot stop with a demonstration that the factual and textual bases for the rule it propounds are, at best, less than compelling. Equally relevant is an assessment of the rule's consequences measured against community values. The Court's duty to assess the consequences of its action is not satisfied by the utterance of the truth that a value of our system of criminal justice is "to respect the inviolability of the human personality" and to require government to produce the evidence against the accused by its own independent labors. Ante, at 460. More than the human dignity of the accused is involved; the human personality of others in the society must also be preserved. Thus the values reflected by the privilege are not the sole desideratum; society's interest in the general security is of equal weight.

The obvious underpinning of the Court's decision is a deep-seated distrust of all confessions. As the Court declares that the accused may not be interrogated without counsel present, absent a waiver of the right to counsel, and as the Court all but admonishes the lawyer to advise the accused to remain silent, the result adds up to a judicial judgment that evidence from the accused should not be used against him in any way, whether compelled or not. This is the not so subtle overtone of the opinion—that it is inherently wrong for the police to gather evidence from the accused himself. And this is precisely the nub of this dissent. I see nothing wrong or immoral, and certainly nothing unconstitutional, in the police's asking a suspect whom they have reasonable cause to arrest whether or not he killed his wife or in confronting him with the evidence on which the arrest was based, at least where he has been plainly advised that he may remain completely silent, see *Escobedo v. Illinois*, 378 U.S. 478, 499 (dissenting opinion). Until today, "the admissions or confessions of the prisoner, when voluntarily and freely made, have always ranked high in the scale of incriminating evidence." *Brown v. Walker*, 161 U.S. 591, 596; see also *Hopt v. Utah*, 110 U.S. 574, 584-585. Particularly when corroborated, as where the police have confirmed the accused's disclosure of the hiding place of implements or fruits of the crime, such confessions have the highest reliability and significantly contribute to the certitude with which we may believe the accused is guilty. Moreover, it is by no means certain that the process of confessing is injurious to the accused. To the contrary it may provide psychological relief and enhance the prospects for rehabilitation.

This is not to say that the value of respect for the inviolability of the accused's individual personality should be accorded no weight or that all confessions should be indiscriminately admitted. This Court has long read the Constitution to proscribe compelled confessions, a salutary rule from which there should be no retreat. But I see no sound basis, factual or otherwise, and the Court gives none, for concluding that the present rule against the receipt of coerced confessions is inadequate for the task of sorting out inadmissible evidence and must be replaced by the per se rule which is now imposed. Even if the new concept can be said to have advantages of some sort over the present law, they are far outweighed by its likely undesirable impact on other very relevant and important interests.

The most basic function of any government is to provide for the security of the individual and of his property. *Lanzetta v. New Jersey*, 306 U.S. 451, 455. These ends of society are served by the criminal laws which for the most part are aimed at the prevention of crime. Without the reasonably effective performance of the task of preventing private violence and retaliation, it is idle to talk about human dignity and civilized values.

The modes by which the criminal laws serve the interest in general security are many. First the murderer who has taken the life of another is removed from the streets, deprived of his liberty and thereby prevented from repeating his offense. In view of the statistics on recidivism in this country and of the number of instances in which apprehension occurs only after repeated offenses, no one can sensibly claim that this aspect of the criminal law does not prevent crime or contribute significantly to the personal security of the ordinary citizen.

Secondly, the swift and sure apprehension of those who refuse to respect the personal security and dignity of their neighbor unquestionably has its impact on others who might be similarly tempted. That the criminal law is wholly or partly ineffective with a segment of the population or with many of those who have been apprehended and convicted is a very faulty basis for concluding that it is not effective with respect to the great bulk of our citizens or for thinking that without the criminal laws, or in the absence of their enforcement, there would be no increase in crime. Arguments of this nature are not borne out by any kind of reliable evidence that I have seen to this date.

Thirdly, the law concerns itself with those whom it has confined. The hope and aim of modern penology, fortunately, is as soon as possible to return the convict to society a better and more law-abiding man than when he left. Sometimes there is success, sometimes failure. But at least the effort is made, and it should be made to the very maximum extent of our present and future capabilities.

The rule announced today will measurably weaken the ability of the criminal law to perform these tasks. It is a deliberate calculus to prevent interrogations, to reduce the incidence of confessions and pleas of guilty and to increase the number of trials. Criminal trials, no matter how efficient the police are, are not sure bets for the prosecution, nor should they be if the evidence is not forthcoming. Under the present law, the prosecution fails to prove its case in about 30% of the criminal cases actually tried in the federal courts. See Federal Offenders: 1964, supra, note 4, at 6 (Table 4), 59 (Table 1); Federal Offenders: 1963, supra, note 4, at 5 (Table 3); District of Columbia Offenders: 1963, supra, note 4, at 2 (Table 1). But it is something else again to remove from the ordinary criminal case all those confessions which heretofore have been held to be free and voluntary acts of the accused and to thus establish a new constitutional barrier to the ascertainment of truth by the judicial process. There is, in my view, every reason to believe that a good many criminal defendants who otherwise would have been convicted on what this Court has previously thought to be the most satisfactory kind of evidence will now, under this new version of the Fifth Amendment, either not be tried at all or will be acquitted if the State's evidence, minus the confession, is put to the test of litigation.

I have no desire whatsoever to share the responsibility for any such impact on the present criminal process.

In some unknown number of cases the Court's rule will return a killer, a rapist or other criminal to the streets and to the environment which produced him, to repeat his crime whenever it pleases him. As a consequence, there will not be a gain, but a loss, in human dignity. The real concern is not the unfortunate consequences of this new decision on the criminal law as an abstract, disembodied series of authoritative proscriptions, but the impact on those who rely on the public authority for protection and who without it can only engage in violent self-help with guns, knives and the help of their neighbors similarly inclined. There is, of course, a saving factor: the next victims are uncertain, unnamed and unrepresented in this case.

Nor can this decision do other than have a corrosive effect on the criminal law as an effective device to prevent crime. A major component in its effectiveness in this regard is its swift and sure enforcement. The easier it is to get away with rape and murder, the less the deterrent effect on those who are inclined to attempt it. This is still good common sense. If it were not, we should posthaste liquidate the whole law enforcement establishment as a useless, misguided effort to control human conduct.

And what about the accused who has confessed or would confess in response to simple, noncoercive questioning and whose guilt could not otherwise be proved? Is it so clear that release is the best thing for him in every case? Has it so unquestionably been resolved that in each and every case it would be better for him not to confess and to return to his environment with no attempt whatsoever to help him? I think not. It may well be that in many cases it will be no less than a callous disregard for his own welfare as well as for the interests of his next victim.

There is another aspect to the effect of the Court's rule on the person whom the police have arrested on probable cause. The fact is that he may not be guilty at all and may be able to extricate himself quickly and simply if he were told the circumstances of his arrest and were asked to explain. This effort, and his release, must now await the hiring of a lawyer or his appointment by the court, consultation with counsel and then a session with the police or the prosecutor. Similarly, where probable cause exists to arrest several suspects, as where the body of the victim is discovered in a house having several residents, compare *Johnson v. State*, 238 Md. 140, 207 A. 2d 643 (1965), cert. denied, 382 U.S. 1013, it will often be true that a suspect may be cleared only through the results of interrogation of other suspects. Here too the release of the innocent may be delayed by the Court's rule.

Much of the trouble with the Court's new rule is that it will operate indiscriminately in all criminal cases, regardless of the severity of the crime or the circum-

stances involved. It applies to every defendant, whether the professional criminal or one committing a crime of momentary passion who is not part and parcel of organized crime. It will slow down the investigation and the apprehension of confederates in those cases where time is of the essence, such as kidnapping, see *Brinegar v. United States*, 338 U.S. 160, 183 (Jackson, J., dissenting); *People v. Modesto*, 62 Cal. 2d 436, 446, 398 P.2d 753, 759 (1965), those involving the national security, see *United States v. Drummond*, 354 F.2d 132, 147 (C.A. 2d Cir. 1965) (en banc) (espionage case), pet. for cert. pending, No. 1203, Misc., O.T. 1965; cf. *Gessner v. United States*, 354 F.2d 726, 730, n. 10 (C.A. 10th Cir. 1965) (upholding, in espionage case, trial ruling that Government need not submit classified portions of interrogation transcript), and some of those involving organized crime. In the latter context the lawyer who arrives may also be the lawyer for the defendant's colleagues and can be relied upon to insure that no breach of the organization's security takes place even though the accused may feel that the best thing he can do is to cooperate.

At the same time, the Court's per se approach may not be justified on the ground that it provides a "bright line" permitting the authorities to judge in advance whether interrogation may safely be pursued without jeopardizing the admissibility of any information obtained as a consequence. Nor can it be claimed that judicial time and effort, assuming that is a relevant consideration, will be conserved because of the ease of application of the new rule. Today's decision leaves open such questions as whether the accused was in custody, whether his statements were spontaneous or the product of interrogation, whether the accused has effectively waived his rights, and whether nontestimonial evidence introduced at trial is the fruit of statements made during a prohibited interrogation, all of which are certain to prove productive of uncertainty during investigation and litigation during prosecution. For all these reasons, if further restrictions on police interrogation are desirable at this time, a more flexible approach makes much more sense than the Court's constitutional straitjacket which forecloses more discriminating treatment by legislative or rule-making pronouncements.

Applying the traditional standards to the cases before the Court, I would hold these confessions voluntary. I would therefore affirm in Nos. 759, 760, and 761, and reverse in No. 584.

Glossary

adversary system: legal system, as in the United States, in which opposing parties contest each other before an independent judge

amicus curiae: literally, "friend of the court," a nonparty in the proceedings who files a brief arguing issues to be settled in the case

certiorari: a writ issued by an appellate court calling up a lower court case for review; the way most cases reach the U.S. Supreme Court

exculpatory: regarding evidence, tending to establish innocence

inculpatory: regarding evidence, tending to show guilt or involvement in a crime

inquisitorial system: legal system used in much of the world outside the United States and Britain, in which the judge directs most facets of the inquiry, including the collection of evidence and the questioning of witnesses

Solicitor General: Justice Department official who conducts all litigation on behalf of the United States in the Supreme Court

SOUTH CAROLINA V. KATZENBACH

<table>
<tr><td>

DATE
1966

AUTHOR
Earl Warren

VOTE
8–1

</td><td>

CITATION
383 U.S. 301

SIGNIFICANCE
Confirmed the legality of the landmark Voting Rights Act of 1965, which gave the federal government sweeping powers to combat disenfranchisement of African Americans in the South

</td></tr>
</table>

Overview

 The case of *South Carolina v. Katzenbach* constituted the first time the U.S. Supreme Court ruled on the Voting Rights Act of 1965. Passed in March 1965, the Voting Rights Act gave the federal government sweeping new powers to combat the pervasive disenfranchisement of African Americans perpetuated by southern government officials. Many across the South denied Congress's power to pass such sweeping legislation. They argued that Congress had overstepped the bounds of the Fifth and Fifteenth Amendments to the U.S. Constitution. They also objected to the act's wider social and political objectives as a piece of civil rights legislation.

In South Carolina, the state attorney general, Daniel R. McCleod, quickly filed a bill of complaint directly with the Supreme Court attacking the constitutionality of the act and asking for an injunction against enforcement by the attorney general of the United States, Nicholas Katzenbach. McCleod challenged the Voting Rights Act as an unconstitutional encroachment on states' rights, as a violation of the principle of equality

between the states, and as an illegal bill of attainder (a legislative punishment enforced without due process of law). More specifically, the complaint directly challenged the "triggering mechanism" in Section 4 of the act, which brought South Carolina under the act's provisions, and argued that Section 5's preclearance provisions (under which any changes to South Carolina's election laws or procedures had to be cleared in advance by the Department of Justice) exceeded Congress's constitutional powers.

South Carolina was joined in its attack on the Voting Rights Act by five other southern states: Georgia, Alabama, Louisiana, Virginia, and Mississippi. Twenty states, among them Illinois, Massachusetts, and California, filed amicus curiae (friend of the court) briefs in support of the act's provisions and powers. As a consequence, the case of *South Carolina v. Katzenbach* took on an even wider significance than normal in a state challenge to a new federal law. At issue in this case was the constitutional legitimacy not only of the Voting Rights Act but, indeed, of the entire federal effort to defend, uphold, and enhance minority civil rights.

President Lyndon B. Johnson signing the Voting Rights Act of 1965. **South Carolina v. Katzenbach** *marked the first time the Supreme Court ruled on the Act.*
(Lyndon Baines Johnson Library and Museum)

Context

In the years following the Civil War, hope dawned for the nation's millions of African Americans that freedom would bring with it a full entry into American public life—an entry best represented by the right to vote. Most Americans understood the Thirteenth Amendment's requirement (1865) that "neither slavery nor involuntary servitude ... shall exist within the United States" to mean that newly freed Blacks would acquire all aspects of freedom, including the right to vote. The Fourteenth Amendment's promise (1868) of equal protection and its defense of the "privileges or immunities of citizens of the United States" added support to newly freed African Americans' claims to the right to vote. Finally the Fifteenth Amendment (1870) declared: "The right of citizens of the United States to vote shall not be denied or abridged by the United States or by any State on account of race, color, or previous condition of servitude." It seemed that the path to the polls would be a clear and simple one for African Americans.

Events proved otherwise. Most white southerners disliked the federally mandated program of postwar "Reconstruction" and opposed the Republican- and Black-led governments organized under this process. As early as 1866, white terrorist organizations—the Ku Klux Klan being the best known—instituted waves of race-based violence and terror that soon spread across the South. In the worst instances, white mobs attacked entire groups of Blacks, terrorizing most and killing many. Bad economic times, well-publicized political scandals, and heavy campaigning by Democrats among the region's white voters added to the Republicans' woes. The chilling effects of violence on Black voting, not to mention election fraud by Democratic-leaning local white officials, led by the mid-1870s to the rise of Democratic "redeemer" governments opposed to all Black civil and political rights.

Once in power, these white Democratic officials began a slow, steady, and ultimately successful campaign of race-based disenfranchisement. Among the techniques used to exclude Black voters were the use of unfairly applied literacy or understanding tests in which voters had to read, understand, or interpret any section of the state constitution to the satisfaction of a white (and usually hostile) election official; complicated registration requirements that excluded minority voters on technical grounds; and financial barriers such as poll taxes. Intimidation and threats of violence were also effective means of keeping southern Blacks from the polls. One of the simplest ways of undermining the Black vote involved setting up polling places in areas inconvenient for Blacks. Many polling places, for instance, were placed at distant locations or in the middle of white sections of the town or county. Similarly, some polls were established in businesses owned by known opponents of African American voting. Finally, in an effort to exclude all possibility that southern Blacks could have a voice in government through the election process, state legislatures across the South implemented rules prohibiting Blacks from voting in the politically dominant Democratic Party primaries. Since the Democratic candidate almost always won in the general election, this exclusion denied southern Blacks a chance to participate in the one election that mattered most.

The results of such efforts were immediate and drastic. By 1896 Black voter participation in Mississippi had declined to fewer than nine thousand out of a potential one hundred forty-seven thousand voting-age Blacks. In Louisiana registered Black voting had declined by 99 percent. Alabama had only three thousand registered black voters in 1902. Texas saw Black voting decline to a mere five thousand votes by 1906. In Georgia, only 4 percent of Black males were registered to vote as of 1910. In fact, across the entire region voter turnout fell from a high of 85 percent of all voters during Reconstruction to less than 50 percent for whites and single-digit percentages for Blacks by the early twentieth century. Mid-twentieth-century attacks on a number of disenfranchising techniques in the federal courts resulted only in the revision and modification of these methods, not their abandonment. As late as 1940, only 3 percent of voting-age southern Blacks were registered to vote. Fewer still were actually able to cast a meaningful ballot.

In the 1950s this situation began to change. By 1956, 25 percent of voting-age Blacks were registered to vote; by 1964 this number had increased to 43.3 percent across the South. Raw numbers can be deceiving, however. Most registered Black voters lived in the border states or in Florida; in the Deep South, where most Blacks lived, African American voter registration stood at only 22.5 percent as late as 1964, with Mississippi setting the lowest standard at 6.7 percent (itself an increase from a rate of 1.98 percent a mere two years earlier). Worse yet, the application of such vote-dilution techniques as voting-list purges, at-large elections, and full-slate and majority-vote requirements—not to mention the ever-present threat of economic reprisals and physical violence against any Black trying to vote—meant that, even in those areas where Blacks could vote, actual African American voting rates were much lower.

The Voting Rights Act of 1965 was designed to directly combat this race-specific, regionally based disenfranchisement. Previous federal efforts to end southern Black disenfranchisement in the courts had been ineffectual and even counterproductive. Civil rights legislation passed in 1957, 1960, and 1964 had expanded the federal government's role in minority vote protection, but with few concrete results to show for the effort. The problem lay with the enforcement tools available to the federal courts. Litigation as an enforcement mechanism was a slow and unwieldy process. It offered recalcitrant southern election officials (not to mention segregationist federal judges) numerous opportunities for delay and obstructionism. Every time the courts overturned laws aimed at disenfranchising southern Black voters, southern election officials simply turned to new or different techniques to achieve the same discriminatory end—techniques not covered by the courts' orders and thus still permissible until invalidated by another court proceeding. In consequence, opponents of Black vote denial were forced to initiate case after case in their efforts to gain the vote—with very little practical gain.

Expressly designed to attack the sources of delay in the case-by-case litigation approach, the nineteen sections of the Voting Rights Act imposed a completely new enforcement methodology for voting-rights violations. Not only did the act outlaw vote denial based on race or color in Section 2, it also gave both the executive branch and the federal courts a powerful new set of approaches for voting-rights enforcement. Among them were the power to appoint federal examiners and observers in whatever numbers the president felt necessary, prohibitions on literacy tests and poll taxes, and rules outlawing any action "under color of the law" that prevented qualified voters from voting or having their votes fairly counted. Most important of all, the act froze all southern election laws in place as of November 1, 1964. If local or state officials wanted to change an election law or procedure, they were required first to receive clearance from the Justice Department or the federal courts before acting. In this way, the southern strategy of using ever-shifting techniques of voter denial to derail election reforms was effectively ended. These enforcement provisions—along with the more general issue of congressional authority to adopt such extreme and powerful provisions—were what South Carolina challenged in *South Carolina v. Katzenbach*.

About the Author

The majority opinion in *South Carolina v. Katzenbach* was written by Chief Justice Earl Warren. He was joined in this majority by seven of his colleagues. One justice, Hugo L. Black, concurred as to the bulk of the opinion but dissented as to those sections upholding the constitutionality of Section 5 of the Voting Rights Act.

Warren had been appointed as chief justice in 1953 by President Dwight D. Eisenhower. A former state attorney general and governor of California, Warren had the reputation of being a fundamentally conservative, yet bipartisan Republican politician. Once on the Court, however, Warren swung quickly to the left on such key civil rights and liberties issues as school desegregation, the rights of the accused, and freedom of religion. He was joined in this shift by a majority of his brethren on the bench. Hence, by the time he wrote the opinion in *South Carolina v. Katzenbach*, Warren (who would retire in 1969) and the Court were approaching the end of a period of sweeping judicial activity that had transformed the constitutional status of individual civil rights and liberties in America.

The dissenting justice, Hugo Black, served on the Supreme Court for thirty-four years (1937–1971). Appointed to the Court by President Franklin D. Roosevelt, Black's judicial philosophy centered on a close textual reading of the U.S. Constitution, a reading that stressed the idea that the liberties guaranteed in the Bill of Rights were "incorporated" on the states by the Fourteenth Amendment. While this belief led Black to be a leader in the Warren Court's expansion of civil liberties and rights in most instances, in certain cases,

such as *Katzenbach*, it pushed Black to oppose legislation that he felt exceeded the textual reach of the Constitution. As Black explained in his *Katzenbach* dissent, he saw "no reason to read into the Constitution meanings it did not have when it was adopted and which have not been put into it since."

Explanation and Analysis of the Document

The central question in *South Carolina v. Katzenbach* was the power of Congress to pass the Voting Rights Act of 1965, with all of its sweeping and transformative powers—powers that the federal government had never before claimed or applied in the realm of voting rights. In its complaint, South Carolina had attacked the Voting Rights Act as an unconstitutional encroachment on "an area reserved to the States by the Constitution," as a violation of the principle of equality between the states, and as an illegal bill of attainder (a legislative punishment enforced without due process of law). More specifically, the complaint directly challenged the "triggering mechanism" in Section 4 that brought South Carolina under the act's provisions, objected to that section's "temporary suspension of a State's voting tests or devices," and argued that Section 5's preclearance provisions exceeded Congress's constitutional powers. Also receiving special notice was the act's use of examiners to supervise state electoral procedures.

The federal government had responded to these charges by noting the long history of race-based discrimination as practiced in South Carolina and other southern states, stressing the pressing need for reform, and showing the failure of the case-by-case litigation approach in combating voting discrimination under the Civil Rights Acts of 1957, 1960, and 1964. More generally, the government lawyers stressed Congress's supreme authority to act in these matters under its inherent legislative powers.

"Mr. Chief Justice Warren Delivered the Opinion of the Court"

In responding to these arguments, Chief Justice Warren began the Court's opinion with the recognition that any ruling as to "the constitutional propriety of the Voting Rights Act of 1965" had to be "judged with reference to the historical experience which it reflected." That context was the extensive record of race-based discrimination found throughout the South. The Court identified "an insidious and pervasive evil which had been perpetuated in certain parts of our country through unremitting and ingenious defiance of the Constitution." Noting also the history of "unsuccessful remedies," it accepted the need for "sterner and more elaborate measures in order to satisfy the clear commands of the Fifteenth Amendment."

The Voting Rights Act of 1965 thus reflected "Congress' firm intention to rid the country of racial discrimination in voting." The crucial question before the Court, therefore, was the constitutional legitimacy of this "complex scheme of stringent remedies aimed at areas where voting discrimination has been most flagrant." Did Congress have the power to pass such laws? And assuming that Congress had such broad powers, were such new and innovative enforcement techniques as preclearance a legitimate application of Congress's powers under the Fifteenth Amendment? Moreover, did these new powers come into conflict with other fundamental constitutional rights and doctrines, such as that of "the equality of States," "due process," and the ban on federal courts issuing "advisory opinions"?

In terms of the general question of Congress's power to legislate, the Court's answer was short and direct: In light of the many years of southern obstruction, Congress had every right to decide "to shift the advantage of time and inertia from the perpetrators of the evil to its victims." The Fifteenth Amendment, combined with established constitutional interpretation, clearly authorized Congress to "effectuate the prohibition of racial discrimination in voting." Besides, noted Warren, the act's provisions strictly applied to those states where discrimination was most prevalent, which clearly constituted "a permissible method of dealing with the problem."

But what of the specific provisions of the act? The Court again came down fully in support of Congress's powers to act as it saw fit. In the case of the coverage formula, which limited the scope of the act to certain southern states and counties, the Court held that the formula was relevant to the specific problem. That was enough to justify congressional intervention under the "express powers under the Fifteenth Amendment."

The Court endorsed the act's temporary suspension of existing voting qualifications on the ground that Congress "knew that continuance of the tests and devices in use … , no matter how fairly administered in the future, would freeze the effect of past discrimination in favor of unqualified white registrants." Given this fact, Congress's determination that such tests were in violation of the Fifteenth Amendment was "a legitimate response to the problem, for which there is ample precedent under other constitutional provisions."

Perhaps most important, Warren found that the imposition of a preclearance requirement for any changes to existing or new election laws and procedures was constitutionally permissible. "This may have been an uncommon exercise of congressional power," explained Warren, "but the Court has recognized that exceptional conditions can justify legislative measures not otherwise appropriate." For years southern states had avoided the intent of the law by "the extraordinary stratagem" of devising ad hoc regulations to frustrate "adverse federal court decrees." Congress knew this and properly acted to put a stop to future evasions of the law. Given such "unique circumstances," Warren concluded, "Congress responded in a permissibly decisive manner."

In conclusion, Warren noted how "after enduring nearly a century of widespread resistance to the Fifteenth Amendment, Congress has marshalled an array of potent weapons against the evil, with authority in the Attorney General to employ them effectively." This was a good and necessary thing, one that should be applauded. "We here hold that the portions of the Voting Rights Act properly before us are a valid means for carrying out the commands of the Fifteenth Amendment." The opinion concludes by expressing hope for true equality of democratic participation for all: "We may finally look forward to the day when truly 'the right of citizens of the United States to vote shall not be denied or abridged by the United States or by any State on account of race, color, or previous condition of servitude.'"

"Mr. Justice Black, Concurring and Dissenting"

Only one justice dissented from this opinion, and he did so only in response to a single aspect of the ruling. Justice Hugo Black agreed with "substantially all of the Court's opinion sustaining the power of Congress under §2 of the Fifteenth Amendment." His only concern was with Section 5 and preclearance.

First, on purely technical ground, Black argued that "the Constitution gives federal courts jurisdiction over cases and controversies only." Such was not the case with preclearance. Black found it hard "to believe that a justiciable controversy can arise in the constitutional sense from a desire by the United States Government or some of its officials to determine in advance what legislative provisions a State may enact or what constitutional amendments it may adopt." This was regulation, not litigation.

Second, and much more important, Section 5 distorted "our constitutional structure of government as to render any distinction drawn in the Constitution between state and federal power almost meaningless." The federal government was a limited government under a constitution that reserved all powers not explicitly granted to the federal government to the states or the people. Such was not the case with Section 5. Black feared that forcing local laws to be preapproved in Washington could "create the impression that the State or States treated in this way are little more than conquered provinces."

Despite Justice Black's worries and concerns, *South Carolina v. Katzenbach* was a sweeping endorsement of the Voting Rights Act of 1965. Notwithstanding that act's innovative—and to some, constitutionally radical—enforcement approaches, the justices concluded that the scope of the problem demanded extreme action and thus gave the act their full support.

Impact

As with most landmark civil rights opinions, the Supreme Court's ruling in *South Carolina v. Katzenbach* is an important document. As a statement of intent by the Supreme Court that race-based disenfranchisement was not constitutionally permissible, the opinion made clear the Court's willingness to act (or, alternatively, to accept action on the part of the other branches of the federal government) in defense of African American voting rights. One cannot overstate the importance that this willingness of the Court to act had in the ongoing civil rights process in America. Although the Voting Rights Act shifted much of the enforcement from the courts to the executive branch of the federal government, the Justice Department (not to mention oppressed minority groups) was still going to need the willing assistance of the federal courts. Had the courts proved unwilling to help in these matters, the Justice Department's lawyers would have faced a much more difficult task in implementing what the voting-rights scholars Chandler Davidson and Bernard Grofman called the "Quiet Revolution" in their landmark book on this process.

Of course, *South Carolina v. Katzenbach* cannot be viewed in isolation. It was the first ruling by the Supreme Court on the constitutionality of the Voting Rights Act of 1965, but it was not the last. In the next few years, the Court would often return to elements of the act, upholding its provisions time and again. In some instances, such as *Allen v. State Board of Elections* (1969), which addressed race-based vote dilution as well as vote denial, the Court would significantly expand the reach of the Voting Rights Act. None of this would have happened if the Court had not first upheld the act's basic constitutionality in *Katzenbach*.

Questions for Further Study

1. On what constitutional basis did some states and individuals oppose the Voting Rights Act of 1965? How did other states respond to these objections?

2. In what ways did some states, particularly in the South, disenfranchise Black voters? How did the Voting Rights Act attempt to correct this situation?

3. The Voting Rights Act was one piece of civil rights legislation passed in the 1960s. What other bills were passed during this era, and what effect did they have on the condition of African Americans?

4. What was the relationship between the Voting Rights Act and the Fifteenth Amendment to the Constitution? What role did this relationship play in *South Carolina v. Katzenbach*?

5. In the modern era, an increasing number of people object to gerrymandering, or the creation of bizarrely shaped electoral districts with a view to grouping together racial or ethnic groups into a single district. To what extent, if any, do you believe that this practice is a violation of the spirit of the Voting Rights Act and *South Carolina v. Katzenbach*?

Further Reading

Books

Bickel, Alexander M. "The Voting Rights Cases." In *The Supreme Court Review*. Chicago: University of Chicago Press, 1966.

Davidson, Chandler, and Bernard Grofman, eds. *Quiet Revolution in the South: The Impact of the Voting Rights Act, 1965–1990*. Princeton, N.J.: Princeton University Press, 1994.

Hasen, Richard L. *The Supreme Court and Election Law: Judging Equality from "Baker v. Carr" to "Bush v. Gore."* New York: New York University Press, 2003.

Zelden, Charles L. *The Supreme Court and Elections: Into the Political Thicket*. Washington, D.C.: CQ Press, 2009.

Articles

Lichtman, Allan. "The Federal Assault against Voting Discrimination in the Deep South 1957–1967." *Journal of Negro History* 54, no. 4 (October 1969): 346–367.

—Commentary by Charles L. Zelden

SOUTH CAROLINA V. KATZENBACH

Document Text

Mr. Chief Justice Warren delivered the opinion of the Court

The Voting Rights Act was designed by Congress to banish the blight of racial discrimination in voting, which has infected the electoral process in parts of our country for nearly a century. The Act creates stringent new remedies for voting discrimination where it persists on a pervasive scale, and in addition the statute strengthens existing remedies for pockets of voting discrimination elsewhere in the country. Congress assumed the power to prescribe these remedies from §2 of the Fifteenth Amendment, which authorizes the National Legislature to effectuate by "appropriate" measures the constitutional prohibition against racial discrimination in voting. We hold that the sections of the Act which are properly before us are an appropriate means for carrying out Congress' constitutional responsibilities and are consonant with all other provisions of the Constitution. We therefore deny South Carolina's request that enforcement of these sections of the Act be enjoined.

I

The constitutional propriety of the Voting Rights Act of 1965 must be judged with reference to the historical experience which it reflects....

Two points emerge vividly from the voluminous legislative history of the Act.... First: Congress felt itself confronted by an insidious and pervasive evil which had been perpetuated in certain parts of our country through unremitting and ingenious defiance of the Constitution. Second: Congress concluded that the unsuccessful remedies which it had prescribed in the past would have to be replaced by sterner and more elaborate measures in order to satisfy the clear commands of the Fifteenth Amendment....

According to the evidence in recent Justice Department voting suits, [discriminatory application of voting tests] ... is now the principal method used to bar Negroes from the polls. Discriminatory administration of voting qualifications has been found in all eight Alabama cases, in all nine Louisiana cases, and in all nine Mississippi cases which have gone to final judgment. Moreover, in almost all of these cases, the courts have held that the discrimination was pursuant to a widespread "pattern or practice." White applicants for registration have often been excused altogether from the literacy and understanding tests or have been given easy versions, have received extensive help from voting officials, and have been registered despite serious errors in their answers. Negroes, on the other hand, have typically been required to pass difficult versions of all the tests, without any outside assistance and without the slightest error. The good-morals requirement is so vague and subjective that it has constituted an open invitation to abuse at the hands of voting officials. Negroes obliged to obtain vouchers from registered voters have found it virtually impossible to comply in areas where almost no Negroes are on the rolls.

In recent years, Congress has repeatedly tried to cope with the problem by facilitating case-by-case litigation against voting discrimination....

Despite the earnest efforts of the Justice Department and of many federal judges, these new laws have done little to cure the problem of voting discrimination. According to estimates by the Attorney General during hearings on the Act, registration of voting-age Negroes in Alabama rose only from 14.2% to 19.4% between 1958 and 1964; in Louisiana it barely inched ahead from 31.7% to 31.8% between 1956 and 1965; and in Mississippi it increased only from 4.4% to 6.4% between 1954 and 1964. In each instance, registration of voting-age whites ran roughly 50 percentage points or more ahead of Negro registration.

The previous legislation has proved ineffective for a number of reasons. Voting suits are unusually onerous to prepare, sometimes requiring as many as 6,000 manhours spent combing through registration records in preparation for trial. Litigation has been exceedingly slow, in part because of the ample opportunities for delay afforded voting officials and others involved in the proceedings. Even when favorable decisions have finally been obtained, some of the States affected have merely switched to discriminatory devices not covered by the federal decrees or have enacted difficult new tests designed to prolong the existing disparity between white and Negro registration. Alternatively, certain local officials have defied and evaded court orders or have simply closed their registration offices to freeze the voting rolls. The provision of the 1960 law authorizing registration by federal officers has had little impact on local maladministration because of its procedural complexities....

II

The Voting Rights Act of 1965 reflects Congress' firm intention to rid the country of racial discrimination in voting. The heart of the Act is a complex scheme of stringent remedies aimed at areas where voting discrimination has been most flagrant. Section 4 (a)–(d) lays down a formula defining the States and political subdivisions to which these new remedies apply. The first of the remedies, contained in §4 (a), is the suspension of literacy tests and similar voting qualifications for a period of five years from the last occurrence of substantial voting discrimination. Section 5 prescribes a second remedy, the suspension of all new voting regulations pending review by federal authorities to determine whether their use would perpetuate voting discrimination. The third remedy, covered in §§6 (b), 7, 9, and 13 (a), is the assign-

ment of federal examiners on certification by the Attorney General to list qualified applicants who are thereafter entitled to vote in all elections ....

III

These provisions of the Voting Rights Act of 1965 are challenged on the fundamental ground that they exceed the powers of Congress and encroach on an area reserved to the States by the Constitution. South Carolina and certain of the *amici curiae* also attack specific sections of the Act for more particular reasons. They argue that the coverage formula prescribed in §4 (a)-(d) violates the principle of the equality of States, denies due process by employing an invalid presumption and by barring judicial review of administrative findings, constitutes a forbidden bill of attainder, and impairs the separation of powers by adjudicating guilt through legislation. They claim that the review of new voting rules required in §5 infringes Article III by directing the District Court to issue advisory opinions. They contend that the assignment of federal examiners authorized in 6 (b) abridges due process by precluding judicial review of administrative findings and impairs the separation of powers by giving the Attorney General judicial functions; also that the challenge procedure prescribed in §9 denies due process on account of its speed. Finally, South Carolina and certain of the *amici curiae* maintain that §§4 (a) and 5, buttressed by §14 (b) of the Act, abridge due process by limiting litigation to a distant forum.

Some of these contentions may be dismissed at the outset. The word "person" in the context of the Due Process Clause of the Fifth Amendment cannot, by any reasonable mode of interpretation, be expanded to encompass the States of the Union, and to our knowledge this has never been done by any court.... Likewise, courts have consistently regarded the Bill of Attainder Clause of Article I and the principle of the separation of powers only as protections for individual persons and private groups, those who are peculiarly vulnerable to nonjudicial determinations of guilt.... Nor does a State have standing as the parent of its citizens to invoke these constitutional provisions against the Federal Government, the ultimate parens patriae of every American citizen.... The objections to the Act which are raised under these provisions may therefore be considered only as additional aspects of the basic question presented by the case: Has Congress exercised its powers under the Fifteenth Amendment in an appropriate manner with relation to the States?

The ground rules for resolving this question are clear. The language and purpose of the Fifteenth Amendment, the prior decisions construing its several provisions, and the general doctrines of constitutional interpretation, all point to one fundamental principle. As against the reserved powers of the States, Congress may use any rational means to effectuate the constitutional prohibition of racial discrimination in voting.... We turn now to a more detailed description of the standards which govern our review of the Act.

Section 1 of the Fifteenth Amendment declares that "the right of citizens of the United States to vote shall not be denied or abridged by the United States or by any State on account of race, color, or previous condition of servitude." This declaration has always been treated as self-executing and has repeatedly been construed, without further legislative specification, to invalidate state voting qualifications or procedures which are discriminatory on their face or in practice.... These decisions have been rendered with full respect for the general rule, reiterated last Term in Carrington v. Rash ... that States "have broad powers to determine the conditions under which the right of suffrage may be exercised." The gist of the matter is that the Fifteenth Amendment supersedes contrary exertions of state power. "When a State exercises power wholly within the domain of state interest, it is insulated from federal judicial review. But such insulation is not carried over when state power is used as an instrument for circumventing a federally protected right." ...

South Carolina contends that the cases cited above are precedents only for the authority of the judiciary to strike down state statutes and procedures—that to allow an exercise of this authority by Congress would be to rob the courts of their rightful constitutional role. On the contrary, §2 of the Fifteenth Amendment expressly declares that "Congress shall have power to enforce this article by appropriate legislation." By adding this authorization, the Framers indicated that Congress was to be chiefly responsible for implementing the rights created in §1. "It is the power of Congress which has been enlarged. Congress is authorized to enforce the prohibitions by appropriate legislation. Some legislation is contemplated to make the [Civil War] amendments fully effective." Ex parte Virginia....

Accordingly, in addition to the courts, Congress has full remedial powers to effectuate the constitutional prohibition against racial discrimination in voting.

Congress has repeatedly exercised these powers in the past, and its enactments have repeatedly been upheld. For recent examples, see the Civil Rights Act of 1957, which was sustained in United States v. Raines, ... United States v. Thomas, ... and Hannah v. Larche, ... and the Civil Rights Act of 1960, which was upheld in Alabama v. United States, ... Louisiana v. United States, ... and United States v. Mississippi.... On the rare occasions when the Court has found an unconstitutional exercise of these powers, in its opinion Congress had attacked evils not comprehended by the Fifteenth Amendment....

The basic test to be applied in a case involving §2 of the Fifteenth Amendment is the same as in all cases concerning the express powers of Congress with relation to the reserved powers of the States. Chief Justice Marshall laid down the classic formulation, 50 years before the Fifteenth Amendment was ratified:

"Let the end be legitimate, let it be within the scope of the constitution, and all means which are appropriate, which are plainly adapted to that end, which are not prohibited, but consist with the letter and spirit of the constitution, are constitutional."...

The Court has subsequently echoed his language in describing each of the Civil War Amendments:

"Whatever legislation is appropriate, that is, adapted to carry out the objects the amendments have in view, whatever tends to enforce submission to the prohibitions they contain, and to secure to all persons the enjoyment of perfect equality of civil rights and the equal protection of the laws against State denial or invasion, if not prohibited, is brought within the domain of congressional power." ...

This language was again employed, nearly 50 years later, with reference to Congress' related authority under §2 of the Eighteenth Amendment....

We therefore reject South Carolina's argument that Congress may appropriately do no more than to forbid violations of the Fifteenth Amendment in general terms—that the task of fashioning specific remedies or of applying them to particular localities must necessarily be left entirely to the courts. Congress is not circumscribed by any such artificial rules under §2 of the Fifteenth Amendment. In the oft-repeated words of Chief Justice Marshall, referring to another specific legislative authorization in the Constitution, "This power, like all others vested in Congress, is complete in itself, may be exercised to its utmost extent, and acknowledges no limitations, other than are prescribed in the constitution." ...

IV

Congress exercised its authority under the Fifteenth Amendment in an inventive manner when it enacted the Voting Rights Act of 1965. First: The measure prescribes remedies for voting discrimination which go into effect without any need for prior adjudication. This was clearly a legitimate response to the problem, for which there is ample precedent under other constitutional provisions.... Congress had found that case-by-case litigation was inadequate to combat widespread and persistent discrimination in voting, because of the inordinate amount of time and energy required to overcome the obstructionist tactics invariably encountered in these lawsuits. After enduring nearly a century of systematic resistance to the Fifteenth Amendment, Congress might well decide to shift the advantage of time and inertia from the perpetrators of the evil to its victims. The question remains, of course, whether the specific remedies prescribed in the Act were an appropriate means of combating the evil, and to this question we shall presently address ourselves.

Second: The Act intentionally confines these remedies to a small number of States and political subdivisions which in most instances were familiar to Congress by name. This, too, was a permissible method of dealing with the problem. Congress had learned that substantial voting discrimination presently occurs in certain sections of the country, and it knew no way of accurately forecasting whether the evil might spread elsewhere in the future. In acceptable legislative fashion, Congress chose to limit its attention to the geographic areas where immediate action seemed necessary. The doctrine of the equality of States, invoked by South Carolina, does not bar this approach, for that doctrine applies only to the terms upon which States are admitted to the Union, and not to the remedies for local evils which have subsequently appeared.

Coverage formula.

We now consider the related question of whether the specific States and political subdivisions within §4 (b) of the Act were an appropriate target for the new remedies. South Carolina contends that the coverage formula is awkwardly designed in a number of respects and that it disregards various local conditions which have nothing to do with racial discrimination. These arguments, however, are largely beside the point. Congress began work with reliable evidence of actual voting discrimination in a great majority of the States and political subdivisions affected by the new remedies of the Act. The formula eventually evolved to describe these areas was relevant to the problem of voting discrimination, and Congress was therefore entitled to infer a significant danger of the evil in the few remaining States and political subdivisions covered by §4 (b) of the Act. No more was required to justify the application to these areas of Congress' express powers under the Fifteenth Amendment....

To be specific, the new remedies of the Act are imposed on three States—Alabama, Louisiana, and Mississippi—in which federal courts have repeatedly found substantial voting discrimination. Section 4 (b) of the Act also embraces two other States—Georgia and South Carolina—plus large portions of a third State—North Carolina—for which there was more fragmentary evidence of recent voting discrimination mainly adduced by the Justice Department and the Civil Rights Commission. All of these areas were appropriately subjected to the new remedies. In identifying past evils, Congress obviously may avail itself of information from any probative source....

The areas listed above, for which there was evidence of actual voting discrimination, share two characteristics incorporated by Congress into the coverage formula: the use of tests and devices for voter registration, and a voting rate in the 1964 presidential election at least 12 points below the national average. Tests and devices are relevant to voting discrimination because of their long history as a tool for perpetrating the evil; a low voting rate is pertinent for the obvious reason that widespread disenfranchisement must inevitably affect the number of actual voters. Accordingly, the coverage formula is rational in both practice and theory. It was therefore permissible to impose the new remedies on the few remaining States and political subdivisions covered by the formula, at least in the absence of proof that they have been free of substantial voting discrimination in recent years. Congress is clearly not bound by the rules relating to statutory presumptions in criminal cases when it prescribes civil remedies against other organs of government under §2 of the Fifteenth Amendment....

It is irrelevant that the coverage formula excludes certain localities which do not employ voting tests and devices but for which there is evidence of voting discrimination by other means. Congress had learned that widespread and persistent discrimination in voting during recent years has typically entailed the misuse of tests and devices, and this was the evil for which the new remedies were specifically designed. At the same time, through §§3, 6 (a), and 13 (b) of the Act, Congress strengthened existing remedies for voting discrimination in other areas of the country. Legislation need not deal with all phases of a problem in the same way, so long as the distinctions drawn have some basis in practical experience.... There are no States or political subdivisions exempted from coverage under §4 (b) in which the record reveals recent racial discrimination involving tests and devices. This fact confirms the rationality of the formula.

Acknowledging the possibility of overbreadth, the Act provides for termination of special statutory coverage at the behest of States and political subdivisions in which the danger of substantial voting discrimination has not materialized during the preceding five years. Despite South Carolina's argument to the contrary, Congress might appropriately limit litigation under this provision to a single court in the District of Columbia, pursuant to its constitutional power under Art. III, §1, to "ordain and establish" inferior federal tribunals.... At the present time, contractual claims against the United States for more than $10,000 must be brought in the Court of Claims, and, until 1962, the District of Columbia was the sole venue of suits against federal officers officially residing in the Nation's Capital. We have discovered no suggestion that Congress exceeded constitutional bounds in imposing these limitations on litigation against the Federal Government, and the Act is no less reasonable in this respect.

South Carolina contends that these termination procedures are a nullity because they impose an impossible burden of proof upon States and political subdivisions entitled to relief. As the Attorney General pointed out during hearings on the Act, however, an area need do no more than submit affidavits from voting officials, asserting that they have not been guilty of racial discrimination through the use of tests and devices during the past five years, and then refute whatever evidence to the contrary may be adduced by the Federal Government. Section 4 (d) further assures that an area need not disprove each isolated instance of voting discrimination in order to obtain relief in the termination proceedings. The burden of proof is therefore quite bearable, particularly since the relevant facts relating to the conduct of voting officials are peculiarly within the knowledge of the States and political subdivisions themselves....

The Act bars direct judicial review of the findings by the Attorney General and the Director of the Census which trigger application of the coverage formula. We reject the claim by Alabama as amicus curiae that this provision is invalid because it allows the new remedies of the Act to be imposed in an arbitrary way. The Court has already permitted Congress to withdraw judicial review of administrative determinations in numerous cases involving the statutory rights of private parties. For example, see United States v. California Eastern Line, ... Switchmen's Union v. National Mediation Bd.... In this instance, the findings not subject to review consist of objective statistical determinations by the Census Bureau and a routine analysis of state statutes by the Justice Department. These functions are unlikely to arouse any plausible dispute, as South Carolina apparently concedes. In the event that the formula is improperly applied, the area affected can always go into court and obtain termination of coverage under §4 (b), provided of course that it has not been guilty of voting discrimination in recent years. This procedure serves as a partial substitute for direct judicial review.

Suspension of tests.

We now arrive at consideration of the specific remedies prescribed by the Act for areas included within the coverage formula. South Carolina assails the temporary suspension of existing voting qualifications, reciting the rule laid down by Lassiter v. Northampton County Bd. of Elections, ... that literacy tests and related devices are not in themselves contrary to the Fifteenth Amendment. In that very case, however, the Court went on to say, "Of course a literacy test, fair on its face, may be employed to perpetuate that discrimination which the Fifteenth Amendment was designed to uproot." ...

The record shows that in most of the States covered by the Act, including South Carolina, various tests and devices have been instituted with the purpose of disenfranchising Negroes, have been framed in such a way as to facilitate this aim, and have been administered in a discriminatory fashion for many years. Under these circumstances, the Fifteenth Amendment has clearly been violated....

The Act suspends literacy tests and similar devices for a period of five years from the last occurrence of substantial voting discrimination. This was a legitimate response to the problem, for which there is ample precedent in Fifteenth Amendment cases. Underlying the response was the feeling that States and political subdivisions which had been allowing white illiterates to vote for years could not sincerely complain about "dilution" of their electorates through the registration of Negro illiterates. Congress knew that continuance of the tests and devices in use at the present time, no matter how fairly administered in the future, would freeze the effect of past discrimination in favor of unqualified white registrants. Congress permissibly rejected the alternative of requiring a complete re-registration of all voters, believing that this would be too harsh on many whites who had enjoyed the franchise for their entire adult lives.

Review of new rules.

The Act suspends new voting regulations pending scrutiny by federal authorities to determine whether their use would violate the Fifteenth Amendment. This may have been an uncommon exercise of congressional power, as South Carolina contends, but the Court has recognized that exceptional conditions can justify legislative measures not otherwise appropriate.... Congress knew that some of the States covered by §4 (b) of the Act had resorted to the extraordinary stratagem of contriving new rules of various kinds for the sole purpose of perpetuating voting discrimination in the face of adverse federal court decrees. Congress had reason to suppose that these States might try similar maneuvers in the future in order to evade the remedies for voting discrimination contained in the Act itself. Under the compulsion of these unique circumstances, Congress responded in a permissibly decisive manner.

For reasons already stated, there was nothing inappropriate about limiting litigation under this provision to the District Court for the District of Columbia, and in putting the burden of proof on the areas seeking relief. Nor has Congress authorized the District Court to issue advisory opinions, in violation of the principles of Article III invoked by Georgia as amicus curiae. The Act automatically suspends the operation of voting regulations enacted after November 1, 1964, and furnishes mechanisms for enforcing the suspension. A State or political subdivision wishing to make use of a recent amendment to its voting laws therefore has a concrete and immediate "controversy" with the Federal Government.... An appropriate remedy is a judicial determination that continued suspension of the new rule is unnecessary to vindicate rights guaranteed by the Fifteenth Amendment.

Federal examiners.

The Act authorizes the appointment of federal examiners to list qualified applicants who are thereafter entitled to vote, subject to an expeditious challenge procedure. This was clearly an appropriate response to the problem, closely related to remedies authorized in prior cases.... In many of the political subdivisions covered by §4 (b) of the Act, voting officials have persistently employed a variety of procedural tactics to deny Negroes the franchise, often in direct defiance or evasion of federal court decrees. Congress realized that merely to suspend voting rules which have been misused or are subject to misuse might leave this localized evil undisturbed. As for the briskness of the challenge procedure, Congress knew that in some of the areas affected, challenges had been persistently employed to harass registered Negroes. It chose to forestall this abuse, at the same time providing alternative ways for removing persons listed through error or fraud. In addition to the judicial challenge procedure, §7 (d) allows for the removal of names by the examiner himself, and §11 (c) makes it a crime to obtain a listing through fraud.

In recognition of the fact that there were political subdivisions covered by §4 (b) of the Act in which the appointment of federal examiners might be unnecessary, Congress assigned the Attorney General the task of determining the localities to which examiners should be sent. There is no warrant for the claim, asserted by Georgia as amicus curiae, that the Attorney General is free to use this power in an arbitrary fashion, without regard to the purposes of the Act. Section 6 (b) sets adequate standards to guide the exercise of his discretion, by directing him to calculate the registration ratio of non-whites to whites, and to weigh evidence of good-faith efforts to avoid possible voting discrimination. At the same time, the special termination procedures of §13 (a) provide indirect judicial review for the political subdivisions affected, assuring the withdrawal of federal examiners from areas where they are clearly not needed....

After enduring nearly a century of widespread resistance to the Fifteenth Amendment, Congress has marshalled an array of potent weapons against the evil, with authority in the Attorney General to employ them effectively. Many of the areas directly affected by this development have indicated their willingness to abide by any restraints legitimately imposed upon them. We here hold that the portions of the Voting Rights Act properly before us are a valid means for carrying out the commands of the Fifteenth Amendment. Hopefully, millions of non-white Americans will now be able to participate for the first time on an equal basis in the government under which they live. We may finally look forward to the day when truly "[t]he right of citizens of the United States to vote shall not be denied or abridged by the United States or by any State on account of race, color, or previous condition of servitude."

The bill of complaint is Dismissed.

Mr. Justice Black, concurring and dissenting

I agree with substantially all of the Court's opinion sustaining the power of Congress under §2 of the Fifteenth Amendment to suspend state literacy tests and similar voting qualifications and to authorize the Attorney General to secure the appointment of federal examiners to register qualified voters in various sections of the country. Section 1 of the Fifteenth Amendment provides that "The right of citizens of the United States to vote shall not be denied or abridged by the United States or by any State on account of race, color, or previous condition of servitude."

In addition to this unequivocal command to the States and the Federal Government that no citizen shall have his right to vote denied or abridged because of race or color, §2 of the Amendment unmistakably gives Congress specific power to go further and pass appropriate legislation to protect this right to vote against any

method of abridgment no matter how subtle. Compare my dissenting opinion in Bell v. Maryland.... I have no doubt whatever as to the power of Congress under §2 to enact the provisions of the Voting Rights Act of 1965 dealing with the suspension of state voting tests that have been used as notorious means to deny and abridge voting rights on racial grounds. This same congressional power necessarily exists to authorize appointment of federal examiners. I also agree with the judgment of the Court upholding §4 (b) of the Act which sets out a formula for determining when and where the major remedial sections of the Act take effect. I reach this conclusion, however, for a somewhat different reason than that stated by the Court, which is that "the coverage formula is rational in both practice and theory." I do not base my conclusion on the fact that the formula is rational, for it is enough for me that Congress by creating this formula has merely exercised its hitherto unquestioned and undisputed power to decide when, where, and upon what conditions its laws shall go into effect. By stating in specific detail that the major remedial sections of the Act are to be applied in areas where certain conditions exist, and by granting the Attorney General and the Director of the Census unreviewable power to make the mechanical determination of which areas come within the formula of §4 (b), I believe that Congress has acted within its established power to set out preconditions upon which the Act is to go into effect....

Though, as I have said, I agree with most of the Court's conclusions, I dissent from its holding that every part of §5 of the Act is constitutional. Section 4 (a), to which §5 is linked, suspends for five years all literacy tests and similar devices in those States coming within the formula of §4 (b). Section 5 goes on to provide that a State covered by §4 (b) can in no way amend its constitution or laws relating to voting without first trying to persuade the Attorney General of the United States or the Federal District Court for the District of Columbia that the new proposed laws do not have the purpose and will not have the effect of denying the right to vote to citizens on account of their race or color. I think this section is unconstitutional on at least two grounds.

(a) The Constitution gives federal courts jurisdiction over cases and controversies only. If it can be said that any case or controversy arises under this section which gives the District Court for the District of Columbia jurisdiction to approve or reject state laws or constitutional amendments, then the case or controversy must be between a State and the United States Government. But it is hard for me to believe that a justiciable controversy can arise in the constitutional sense from a desire by the United States Government or some of its officials to determine in advance what legislative provisions a State may enact or what constitutional amendments it may adopt. If this dispute between the Federal Government and the States amounts to a case or controversy it is a far cry from the traditional constitutional notion of a case or controversy as a dispute over the meaning of enforceable laws or the manner in which they are applied. And if by this section Congress has created a case or controversy, and I do not believe it has, then it seems to me that the most appropriate judicial forum for settling these important questions is this Court acting under its original Art. III, §2, jurisdiction to try cases in which a State is a party. At least a trial in this Court would treat the States with the dignity to which they should be entitled as constituent members of our Federal Union.

The form of words and the manipulation of presumptions used in §5 to create the illusion of a case or controversy should not be allowed to cloud the effect of that section. By requiring a State to ask a federal court to approve the validity of a proposed law which has in no way become operative, Congress has asked the State to secure precisely the type of advisory opinion our Constitution forbids. As I have pointed out elsewhere, ... some of those drafting our Constitution wanted to give the federal courts the power to issue advisory opinions and propose new laws to the legislative body. These suggestions were rejected. We should likewise reject any attempt by Congress to flout constitutional limitations by authorizing federal courts to render advisory opinions when there is no case or controversy before them. Congress has ample power to protect the rights of citizens to vote without resorting to the unnecessarily circuitous, indirect and unconstitutional route it has adopted in this section.

(b) My second and more basic objection to §5 is that Congress has here exercised its power under §2 of the Fifteenth Amendment through the adoption of means that conflict with the most basic principles of the Constitution. As the Court says the limitations of the power granted under §2 are the same as the limitations imposed on the exercise of any of the powers expressly granted Congress by the Constitution. The

classic formulation of these constitutional limitations was stated by Chief Justice Marshall when he said in McCulloch v. Maryland, 4 Wheat.... "Let the end be legitimate, let it be within the scope of the constitution, and all means which are appropriate, which are plainly adapted to that end, which are not prohibited, but consist with the letter and spirit of the constitution, are constitutional."

Section 5, by providing that some of the States cannot pass state laws or adopt state constitutional amendments without first being compelled to beg federal authorities to approve their policies, so distorts our constitutional structure of government as to render any distinction drawn in the Constitution between state and federal power almost meaningless. One of the most basic premises upon which our structure of government was founded was that the Federal Government was to have certain specific and limited powers and no others, and all other power was to be reserved either "to the States respectively, or to the people." Certainly if all the provisions of our Constitution which limit the power of the Federal Government and reserve other power to the States are to mean anything, they mean at least that the States have power to pass laws and amend their constitutions without first sending their officials hundreds of miles away to beg federal authorities to approve them. Moreover, it seems to me that §5 which gives federal officials power to veto state laws they do not like is in direct conflict with the clear command of our Constitution that "The United States shall guarantee to every State in this Union a Republican Form of Government." I cannot help but believe that the inevitable effect of any such law which forces any one of the States to entreat federal authorities in far-away places for approval of local laws before they can become effective is to create the impression that the State or States treated in this way are little more than conquered provinces. And if one law concerning voting can make the States plead for this approval by a distant federal court or the United States Attorney General, other laws on different subjects can force the States to seek the advance approval not only of the Attorney General but of the President himself or any other chosen members of his staff. It is inconceivable to me that such a radical degradation of state power was intended in any of the provisions of our Constitution or its Amendments. Of course I do not mean to cast any doubt whatever upon the indisputable power of the Federal Government to invalidate a state law once enacted and operative on the ground that it intrudes into the area of supreme federal power. But the Federal Government has heretofore always been content to exercise this power to protect federal supremacy by authorizing its agents to bring lawsuits against state officials once an operative state law has created an actual case and controversy. A federal law which assumes the power to compel the States to submit in advance any proposed legislation they have for approval by federal agents approaches dangerously near to wiping the States out as useful and effective units in the government of our country. I cannot agree to any constitutional interpretation that leads inevitably to such a result.

I see no reason to read into the Constitution meanings it did not have when it was adopted and which have not been put into it since. The proceedings of the original Constitutional Convention show beyond all doubt that the power to veto or negative state laws was denied Congress. On several occasions proposals were submitted to the convention to grant this power to Congress. These proposals were debated extensively and on every occasion when submitted for vote they were overwhelmingly rejected. The refusal to give Congress this extraordinary power to veto state laws was based on the belief that if such power resided in Congress the States would be helpless to function as effective governments. Since that time neither the

Fifteenth Amendment nor any other Amendment to the Constitution has given the slightest indication of a purpose to grant Congress the power to veto state laws either by itself or its agents. Nor does any provision in the Constitution endow the federal courts with power to participate with state legislative bodies in determining what state policies shall be enacted into law. The judicial power to invalidate a law in a case or controversy after the law has become effective is a long way from the power to prevent a State from passing a law. I cannot agree with the Court that Congress—denied a power in itself to veto a state law—can delegate this same power to the Attorney General or the District Court for the District of Columbia. For the effect on the States is the same in both cases—they cannot pass their laws without sending their agents to the City of Washington to plead to federal officials for their advance approval.

In this and other prior Acts Congress has quite properly vested the Attorney General with extremely broad power to protect voting rights of citizens against discrimination on account of race or color. Section 5 viewed in this context is of very minor importance and in my judgment is likely to serve more as an irritant to the States than as an aid to the enforcement of the Act. I would hold §5 invalid for the reasons stated above with full confidence that the Attorney General has ample power to give vigorous, expeditious and effective protection to the voting rights of all citizens.

Glossary

amici curiae: Latin for "friends of the court"; persons or organizations with an interest in a case but who are not party to it and who file court briefs with a view to influencing a case's outcome

bill of attainder: a law that punishes a person or group of persons without benefit of trial

Chief Justice Marshall: John Marshall, the chief justice of the United States in the early nineteenth century, whose decisions tended to enforce the power of the federal government

Civil War Amendments: the Thirteenth, Fourteenth, and Fifteenth Amendments to the U.S. Constitution, passed in the wake of the Civil War

Constitutional Convention: the convention in Philadelphia in 1787 at which the U.S. Constitution was drafted

ex parte: Latin for "by (or for) one party," used in the law to refer to a legal proceeding brought by one party without the presence of the other being required

justiciable: able to come under the authority of the court

literacy tests: written tests administered to potential voters to determine, as a condition for voting, whether they can read

McCulloch v. Maryland: a landmark 1819 U.S. Supreme Court decision in which Chief Justice John Marshall held that states could not impede the power of the federal government

nullity: legal ineffectiveness or invalidity

parens patriae: Latin for "parents of the nation," referring to the power of the state to intervene to protect people from an abuse

LOVING V. VIRGINIA

DATE 1967	**CITATION** 388 U.S. 1
AUTHOR Earl Warren	**SIGNIFICANCE** Struck down laws banning interracial marriage
VOTE 9–0	

Overview

 In 1967 in *Loving v. Virginia*, Chief Justice Earl Warren wrote on behalf of a unanimous Supreme Court to declare antimiscegenation laws in violation of the Fourteenth Amendment to the U.S. Constitution. Laws against interracial marriage were widespread in the United States into the 1960s. An interracial couple from Virginia, wanting to be "Mr. and Mrs. Richard Loving," found themselves taken to jail in 1958 and then to court because he was white and she was not. They were convicted of the crime of marrying each other, but eventually they appealed their convictions, and the case went to the U.S. Supreme Court. There, the Fourteenth Amendment, which had been in the Constitution for almost exactly a century, was for the first time interpreted to declare unconstitutional all state laws against interracial marriage. As a result, more than three hundred years after the first of such laws was passed, none could any longer be enforced. States retained their authority over the law of marriage in other respects but no longer as regarded racial classifications.

Thus, thirteen years after the Warren Court overturned segregated public schooling, all laws against interracial marriage—the last refuge for state-mandated segregation—were overturned as well. As with the Montgomery bus boycott, some citizens had protested the segregation laws, and their resistance led to the Supreme Court's ruling against those laws. The Lovings, then, can be seen as important actors in the civil rights movement. At the same time, Chief Justice Warren's decision to throw out the case against them can be seen as a crucial document, akin to President Harry S. Truman's Executive Order 9981 in 1948 against segregation in the U.S. armed forces, the Supreme Court's ruling in *Brown v. Board of Education of Topeka* in 1954, and the congressional passage of the Civil Rights Act of 1964 and the Voting Rights Act of 1965. *Loving v. Virginia* brought down the last of the Jim Crow laws that had segregated so much of American life for so long.

Context

Laws against interracial marriage were on the books of most of the American colonies before the Revolution. The term *miscegenation*, referring to sex or marriage between people of two different races, was coined

Mildred and Richard Loving
(Wikimedia Commons)

in the course of President Abraham Lincoln's bid for reelection in 1864, when David Goodman Croly and George Wakeman, two Democratic newspapermen, produced a hoax pamphlet with that term as the title designed to give the impression that Lincoln favored interracial marriage. A majority of states retained their antimiscegenation laws through the nineteenth century and even beyond World War II. Those laws varied widely, however, in how they chose to define *interracial*, in whether they made interracial marriage a crime, and in whether they would recognize an interracial marriage that took place outside their borders. Some states repealed their laws and never restored them, while seven southern states, including Louisiana and Arkansas, dropped such laws in the 1870s but then restored them by the 1890s. As of 1895, interracial marriage was banned throughout the South. In 1912 the Georgia congressman Seaborn Roddenbery proposed an amendment to the U.S. Constitution to ban Black-white marriages everywhere in the nation, but it did not pass. Nonetheless, between 1913 and 1948, thirty of the forty-eight states maintained laws

against interracial marriage. Then, beginning with a four-to-three decision in *Perez v. Sharp* by the Supreme Court of California in 1948, followed by a series of legislative repeals, all the states outside the South shed those laws; after 1965 only the seventeen states of the South retained them. A newly reapportioned Maryland legislature passed a repeal measure in early 1967, to be effective on June 1, leaving sixteen states with antimiscegenation laws.

Over the years, the Supreme Court had addressed various matters related to marriage. The majority opinion in the 1857 *Dred Scott* case cited northern laws against interracial marriage as evidence that whites outside the South shared a common disinclination to recognize their African American neighbors as full citizens. In a major precedent, the Court ruled unanimously in *Pace v. Alabama* (1883) that, where a Black man and a white woman had been convicted of living together outside marriage—and under Alabama law at the time, they could not have legally married—it was no violation of their rights that the punishment for their crime was greater than it would have been had they shared a racial identity, white or Black. In the 1888 case *Maynard v. Hill*, the Court stated that marriage has "always been subject to the control of the legislature." In *Plessy v. Ferguson* (1896), the Court made passing note of segregation statutes governing marriage on its way to upholding a segregation statute governing railway travel. Between 1954 and 1956 the Supreme Court refused to hear two cases, *Jackson v. State of Alabama* and the Virginia case *Naim v. Naim*, regarding antimiscegenation statutes, leaving the statutes intact. And in 1964 the Court expressly chose not to address interracial marriage in a case, *McLaughlin v. Florida*, that resembled *Pace v. Alabama*—except that here the Court did throw out as unconstitutional Florida's statute against interracial cohabitation.

Virginia's first law against interracial marriage dated from 1691, when a white person who married a nonwhite was subject to exile from the colony—though back in 1614, the marriage between the Native American Pocahontas and the Englishman John Rolfe had brought a peaceful respite to the awful warfare that had been going on between the two peoples. In 1878, following the Civil War and the end of slavery, the legislature overhauled the rules to now subject both parties in a Black-white marriage to two to five years in the penitentiary as well as to provide that if a Virginia couple, seeking to evade the statute, went out of state to get married and then returned, the penalties would be the same. Throughout the nineteenth century, a person in Virginia was legally white if less than one-quarter Black; that is, a person with three white grandparents and one Black grandparent was Black, but a person with seven white great-grandparents was white. That law was changed in 1910, so that a person as much as one-sixteenth Black was "colored," and again in 1924, with the Racial Integrity Act, so that any traceable African ancestry resulted in classification as a colored person. Thus the "one-drop" rule of Black racial identity came to Virginia's law of marriage in 1924. The one material change to the law thereafter reduced the minimum prison term to a single year for each party to a marriage between a "white" person and a "colored" person.

In Caroline County, a rural portion of eastern Virginia, Richard Perry Loving was born a white man in 1933, and Mildred Delores Jeter, of African and Native American descent, was born a "colored" woman in 1939. They drove to Washington, D.C., in June 1958 to get married, returned to Caroline County, and were living with her parents about a month later when three law enforcement officers walked into the unlocked house late one night, awoke them, and arrested them for their unlawful marriage. At trial the following January, they pled guilty in accordance with the terms of a plea bargain. Instead of being sent to prison for a year, they were exiled from Virginia; reluctantly, they moved to Washington, D.C.

In 1963, however, Mrs. Loving wrote to Attorney General Robert F. Kennedy at the U.S. Department of Justice for help, and her plea made its way to Bernard S. Cohen, a young lawyer for the American Civil Liberties Union with an office in Alexandria, Virginia. Subsequently joined by another young lawyer, Philip J. Hirschkop, Cohen appealed the 1959 outcome at trial to the original judge, Leon M. Bazile. At issue under the Constitution were the due process and equal protection clauses of the Fourteenth Amendment, according to which governments must not intervene arbitrarily in people's lives or treat one racial group differently from another. In January 1965, Bazile wrote out a long opinion explaining why the law was constitutional and its application to the Lovings just; he remarked (as Warren would cite in *Loving*),

> Almighty God created the races white, Black, yellow, malay and red, and he placed them on separate continents. And but for the interference with his arrangement there would be no cause for such marriages. The fact that he separated the races shows that he did not intend for the races to mix.

The case went next to the Virginia Supreme Court, which in 1966 upheld the trial judge, and then to the U.S. Supreme Court.

Under Chief Justice Warren, the Court had been relying on the equal protection clause to chip away at the edifice of Jim Crow all the way back to the 1954 *Brown v. Board* case (with considerable preliminary work along those lines having been accomplished even before Warren came on the Court). Even aside from race, the Warren Court had been attacking impediments to human freedom that state authorities often imposed, whether state failure to provide defense lawyers to indigent defendants in criminal proceedings or state laws restricting access to birth control for married couples. The decision in *Loving v. Virginia* reflected both impulses, as the case was resolved with the Court's landmark 1967 ruling striking down laws against interracial marriage.

About the Author

As chief justice, Earl Warren assigned to himself the task of writing the Court's opinion in *Loving v. Virginia*. In the way that law clerks often do much of the actual drafting, however, Warren's clerk Benno Schmidt did the heavy lifting in the *Loving* case, following his boss's directions as to the reasoning and also some of the content. For example, Warren directed Schmidt to center the opinion on racial discrimination and the right to marry and to definitely cite Judge Bazile's language about how God had created the separate races and wanted to keep them separate.

Earl Warren was born in Los Angeles, California, in 1891. The son of a railroad-car repairman, the young Warren also worked for a time on railroads. He went to college and law school at the University of California, Berkeley; served briefly in World War I; and then went to work in the office of the district attorney for Alameda County, California. He would work there for eighteen years, thirteen as district attorney himself, gaining extensive experience as a prosecutor; in a 1931 survey he was voted the best district attorney in the nation. Beyond prosecuting defendants, on their behalf he urged that they each, if necessary, have a public defender so as to be fairly represented in criminal court proceedings. In 1938 he was elected attorney general of California, to serve a four-year term. In 1942 he ran as a Republican for the governorship of California and was elected to the first of three four-year terms. He was nominated for the vice presidency in 1948 as Thomas Dewey's running mate, but the presidency instead went to Harry Truman. Warren helped Dwight Eisenhower win their party's nomination for the presidency in 1952 and was offered the position of solicitor general in the new administration, but he was then nominated as chief justice of the United States when Chief Justice Fred Vinson died in September 1953. Warren was quickly confirmed and took the helm of the Supreme Court the following month.

In joining the Court, Warren was not new to issues related to the laws of race and marriage. As California's attorney general back in 1939, he was obligated to interpret the state's racial restrictions on marriage. And in 1948 he was serving as governor when the Supreme Court of California struck down that state's law against interracial marriages. Within three years of his appointment as chief justice, two cases regarding the constitutionality of laws against interracial marriage came to the Court, and in each—one from Virginia, one from Alabama—he was in the minority as to whether the Court would hear the case and potentially overturn the law that had given rise to it. As late as 1964, in *McLaughlin v. Florida*, though ruling in favor of an unmarried interracial couple, the Court had not been prepared to overturn laws against interracial marriage. In *Loving* in 1967, Warren had the perfect case and the perfect occasion for ruling against such laws everywhere.

While serving as chief justice, Warren reluctantly accepted the chairmanship of a special commission set up by Congress to investigate the 1963 assassination of President John F. Kennedy. The Warren Commission, as it became known, found that Lee Harvey Oswald acted alone in his assassination, a controversial conclusion. In June 1968, one year after the ruling in *Loving v. Virginia*, Warren informed President Lyndon B. Johnson that he wished to retire as soon as his successor could be confirmed. Johnson chose the associate Supreme Court justice Abe Fortas, whose nomination ran into such trouble toward the end of Johnson's presidency that he eventually withdrew his name; Warren's successor, Warren E. Burger, was an appointee of the new president, Richard M. Nixon. Earl Warren was working on his memoirs when he died in 1974.

Explanation and Analysis of the Document

Chief Justice Warren declares in the opening sentence of his opinion, "This case presents a constitutional question never addressed by this Court." While he is pointing out the novelty of the question, and certainly of the position the Court took that day, at the same time the chief justice may be apologizing for the Court's failure to address the question of interracial marriage at any of several earlier opportunities, including three on his watch. He specifies the question of whether state laws against interracial marriage violate the equal protection and due process clauses of the Fourteenth Amendment. He does not reserve the punch line: indeed, those laws do conflict with the Fourteenth Amendment; so they must fall. He then recounts the long journey the Lovings had taken, from their wedding nine years earlier up until their triumph achieved as he then read the Court's unanimous ruling that their convictions could not stand. And he quotes the trial judge's language about how God had "created the races"—five are listed—and wanted them not "to mix," though Warren misdates the trial judge's comments as coming from the original trial in 1959 rather than the actual occasion, the rehearing in 1965.

The chief justice quotes in full the statutory provisions that made it a crime for an interracial couple in Virginia to marry, not only inside the state but also outside of it if they planned to return to Virginia and live as a married couple there, as the Lovings had. He also supplies (in a lengthy footnote not reproduced here) the exact language that defined "white persons" and "colored persons" in Virginia. He notes that the Lovings had never contested their being classified, one as white and the other as colored, under those legal provisions (an approach sometimes taken by other interracial couples, who claimed to be both white or both nonwhite and therefore not subject to prosecution under the law). Warren mentions the extraordinary antiquity of Virginia's law, where "penalties for miscegenation arose as an incident to slavery and have been common in Virginia since the colonial period." But, as he observes, "the present statutory scheme dates from the adoption of the Racial Integrity Act of 1924," whose key provisions he recounts. A footnote (not provided here) lists the statutory provisions of the fifteen other states, all in the South, that still had such laws as Virginia's, and it also lists the fourteen states that, in the previous two decades, had repealed their antimiscegenation laws.

Part I

In part I of the opinion, the chief justice reviews the charges against the Lovings and the leading arguments that the state of Virginia offered in its defense of its laws, and he rebuts each in turn. The Supreme Court of Appeals of Virginia, whose ruling was under appeal in this case, had, as one of its arguments in support of the constitutionality of the state's antimiscegenation laws, reached for a ruling by that same court a decade earlier, *Naim v. Naim* (1955), regarding a Chinese man

and a white woman. As Warren forthrightly assesses, the Virginia court had declared that the state's "legitimate purposes" in enacting, enforcing, and upholding such laws "were 'to preserve the racial integrity of its citizens,' and to prevent 'the corruption of blood,' 'a mongrel breed of citizens,' and 'the obliteration of racial pride,' obviously an endorsement of the doctrine of White Supremacy." As the chief justice notes a little later, Virginia had banned not all interracial marriages but "only interracial marriages involving white persons." He goes on, in a footnote (not reproduced here), to condemn racial classifications in criminal statutes regardless of whether the "integrity" of all races or only that of whites is to be protected. So from the Court's perspective, neither white supremacy nor concern for racial integrity passed muster as a defense of the Virginia laws.

In the opening sentence of the second paragraph, Chief Justice Warren seriously undercuts the state's reliance on the Tenth Amendment's declaration regarding the legitimate powers of the states, and thus the rightful limits on federal authority, to deflect arguments based upon the Fourteenth Amendment and the limits on state powers. But such arguments still had to be addressed. In presenting its case to the Supreme Court, the state of Virginia drew upon a ruling from 1888, *Maynard v. Hill*, in which the Court baldly stated that marriage, "having more to do with the morals and civilization of a people than any other institution, has always been subject to the control of the legislature." Warren chides the state of Virginia for mounting such an argument in support of its laws of race and marriage: "While the state court is no doubt correct in asserting that marriage is a social relation subject to the State's police power,... the State does not contend in its argument before this Court that its powers to regulate marriage are unlimited notwithstanding the commands of the Fourteenth Amendment. Nor could it do so," the chief justice goes on, in view of some important cases from long before the 1960s but long after the 1880s, including *Meyer v. Nebraska* (1923), in which the Court had spoken expressly of "the right ... to marry."

The state also argued that the equal protection clause should be understood as reflecting an intent by the Framers that, so long as punishments visited upon people, both Black and white, were the same for violating a given law, such as Virginia's against interracial marriage, then the requirements of equal protection were satisfied. Indeed, the Supreme Court had accepted that very argument in 1883 in *Pace v. Alabama*, a case that arose when a man classified as Black and a woman classified as white had, upon conviction for living together without being married, suffered a more severe sentence than they would have had they both been white or both Black. Judge Bazile, in writing his opinion in 1965 in support of the original outcome for the Lovings at trial six years before, called upon a wide range of precedents that supported him, but he ignored a 1964 ruling by the Supreme Court to the contrary—viewing it as no more legitimate than he had perceived *Brown v. Board of Education* to be a decade earlier. That 1964 ruling, *McLaughlin v. Florida*, Chief Justice Warren now invokes, quoting the remark that "*Pace* represents a limited view of the Equal Protection Clause which has not withstood analysis in the subsequent decisions of this Court." Thus, *Pace v. Alabama* helped the state's case no more than did *Maynard v. Hill*. As to whether the Fourteenth Amendment protects against "classifications drawn by any statute" that "constitute an arbitrary and invidious discrimination," the Court had so held in *McLaughlin v. Florida*, and it is ruling so again in *Loving v. Virginia*. Warren has established that the equal protection clause sufficed to strike the Virginia laws and therefore the Lovings' convictions under those laws.

Part II

The Lovings' attorneys had also argued on the basis of the due process clause, and this portion of the Fourteenth Amendment the Court also considers. To do so, the Court cites the 1942 case *Skinner v. State of Oklahoma* (which was primarily concerned with sterilization as legal punishment) as well as *Maynard v. Hill*, one of the key props in the state's case. That long-ago case from 1888, which on its face had nothing to do with race, spoke in very strong terms not only of legislative prerogative in the law of marriage but also of the supreme importance of marriage as an institution. So in the short final section on the due process clause, the chief justice speaks of "this fundamental freedom" and notes with reproof how antimiscegenation laws serve to "deprive all the State's citizens of liberty without due process of law." In short, though the Court does not use this precise language, Richard Loving had been denied—not despite his being a white man but indeed because he was a white man—the right to marry Mildred Jeter, and she had been similarly deprived of the right to marry him. In sum, this dual deprivation, and the Lovings' punishment for the crime of trying to be a married couple, constituted a denial of both equal protection and due process of law. So, the Court concludes, "These convictions must be reversed."

Impact

The ruling's impact was immediate for the Lovings, who found themselves free to live openly together with their children in Virginia. There the children would grow to adulthood, and their parents would live out the rest of their lives. Richard Loving, among whose many occupations was that of bricklayer, symbolically heralded the family's newfound freedom by building a permanent new home of brick for them all.

Elsewhere, throughout the nation, public authorities could no longer enforce miscegenation laws. Interracial couples in Delaware, Arkansas, Louisiana, and many other states thus suddenly found that the key obstacle to their marrying had been taken down. *Loving*'s impact also extended to different dimensions of the law of marriage. The outcome of litigation in Oklahoma, for example, took a new turn after *Loving v. Virginia*, since a 1939 marriage between a white man and an African American woman, under which the widow's daughter and granddaughter had sought to inherit property in the 1960s, was suddenly valid; thus it could not be successfully contested by a son from his father's earlier marriage who did not wish to share his father's estate. Some years later, in 1984, the Supreme Court had occasion to revisit the *Loving* case and expand its reach after a local court in Florida removed a white child from the custody of her divorced mother, Linda Sidoti, on the grounds that she had married a Black man, Clarence Palmore Jr. The Court decided that race could not be grounds for reassigning child custody when a parent remarries across racial lines.

Within four years of *Loving v. Virginia*, same-sex couples were going to court seeking to obtain marriage licenses, arguing on the basis of the language and logic of *Loving* that they should not be denied the right to marry. In state after state, beginning with Minnesota in 1971 in *Baker v. Nelson*, such arguments were rebuffed. State legislatures thus yet retained the authority to define marriage and to continue, on grounds other than race, to restrict people's freedom to marry. In the 1990s, however, state judges began to prove receptive to such arguments if couched in terms of the provisions of state constitutions rather than those of the Fourteenth Amendment. In Hawaii and Alaska, voters subsequently approved a change in the language of their respective state constitutions to undo rulings based upon judicial interpretation of the former language. But in Vermont, "civil unions" resulted from a state supreme court ruling in favor of same-sex litigants, *Baker v. State of Vermont.* And in Massachusetts even that degree of change was deemed too small, an unconstitutional infringement of a constitutional right to marry. In *Goodrich v. Department of Public Health* (2003), the Supreme Judicial Court of Massachusetts, relying in part on *Loving v. Virginia*, interpreted the Massachusetts state constitution to require that same-sex couples enjoy the full right to marry that heterosexual couples do. Finally, in *Obergefell v. Hodges* (2015), the Court approved same-sex marriage nationwide.

Questions for Further Study

1. The Commonwealth of Virginia had a long legal history pertaining to African Americans. Compare this document with Virginia's Act III: Baptism Does Not Exempt Slaves from Bondage (1667) and the Virginia Slave Code (1860). How were the antimiscegenation laws in effect in Virginia as late as the 1960s an outgrowth of the commonwealth's history?

2. What was the "one drop rule"? Why was this "rule" important in the nation's racial history?

3. On what fundamental constitutional basis did the Warren Court negate Virginia's laws against interracial marriage? Did the Court use the same principle in its decision in *Brown v. Board of Education* (1954)? Explain.

4. What impact did the Court's decision in *Loving v. Virginia* have on the debate involving same-sex couples? According to some people, how does the logic of the decision extend to such couples?

5. According to the entry, the "last wall in the edifice of American apartheid had been taken down" through the Court's decision in this case. Do you agree with this conclusion?

Further Reading

Books

Cashin, Sheryll. *Loving: Interracial Intimacy in America and the Threat to White Supremacy.* Boston: Beacon Press, 2018.

Cray, Ed. *Chief Justice: A Biography of Earl Warren.* New York: Simon & Schuster, 1997.

Kennedy, Randall. *Interracial Intimacies: Sex, Marriage, Identity, and Adoption.* New York: Pantheon, 2003.

Newbeck, Phyl. *Virginia Hasn't Always Been for Lovers: Interracial Marriage Bans and the Case of Richard and Mildred Loving.* Carbondale: Southern Illinois University Press, 2004.

Pascoe, Peggy. *What Comes Naturally: Miscegenation Law and the Making of Race in America.* New York: Oxford University Press, 2009.

Wallenstein, Peter. *Tell the Court I Love My Wife: Race, Marriage, and Law—An American History.* New York: Palgrave Macmillan, 2002.

Wallenstein, Peter. *Race, Sex, and the Freedom to Marry: Loving v. Virginia.* Lawrence: University Press of Kansas, 2014.

Websites

"Loving Day." Loving Day website. Accessed April 6, 2023. http://www.lovingday.org/.

—Commentary by Peter Wallenstein

LOVING V. VIRGINIA

Document Text

Mr. Chief Justice Warren delivered the opinion of the Court

This case presents a constitutional question never addressed by this Court: whether a statutory scheme adopted by the State of Virginia to prevent marriages between persons solely on the basis of racial classifications violates the Equal Protection and Due Process Clauses of the Fourteenth Amendment. For reasons which seem to us to reflect the central meaning of those constitutional commands, we conclude that these statutes cannot stand consistently with the Fourteenth Amendment.

In June 1958, two residents of Virginia, Mildred Jeter, a Negro woman, and Richard Loving, a white man, were married in the District of Columbia pursuant to its laws. Shortly after their marriage, the Lovings returned to Virginia and established their marital abode in Caroline County. At the October Term, 1958, of the Circuit Court of Caroline County, a grand jury issued an indictment charging the Lovings with violating Virginia's ban on interracial marriages. On January 6, 1959, the Lovings pleaded guilty to the charge and were sentenced to one year in jail; however, the trial judge suspended the sentence for a period of 25 years on the condition that the Lovings leave the State and not return to Virginia together for 25 years. He stated in an opinion that:

> "Almighty God created the races white, Black, yellow, malay and red, and he placed them on separate continents. And but for the interference with his arrangement there would be no cause for such marriages. The fact that he separated the races shows that he did not intend for the races to mix."

After their convictions, the Lovings took up residence in the District of Columbia. On November 6, 1963, they filed a motion in the state trial court to vacate the judgment and set aside the sentence on the ground that the statutes which they had violated were repugnant to the Fourteenth Amendment. The motion not having been decided by October 28, 1964, the Lovings instituted a class action in the United States District Court for the Eastern District of Virginia requesting that a three-judge court be convened to declare the Virginia antimiscegenation statutes unconstitutional and to enjoin state officials from enforcing their convictions. On January 22, 1965, the state trial judge denied the motion to vacate the sentences, and the Lovings perfected an appeal to the Supreme Court of Appeals of Virginia. On February 11, 1965, the three-judge District Court continued the case to allow the Lovings to present their constitutional claims to the highest state court.

The Supreme Court of Appeals upheld the constitutionality of the antimiscegenation statutes and, after modifying the sentence, affirmed the convictions. The Lovings appealed this decision, and we noted probable jurisdiction on December 12, 1966, 385 U.S. 986.

The two statutes under which appellants were convicted and sentenced are part of a comprehensive statutory scheme aimed at prohibiting and punishing interracial marriages. The Lovings were convicted of violating § 20–58 of the Virginia Code:

"Leaving State to evade law.—If any white person and colored person shall go out of this State, for the purpose of being married, and with the intention of returning, and be married out of it, and afterwards return to and reside in it, cohabiting as man and wife, they shall be punished as provided in § 20–59, and the marriage shall be governed by the same law as if it had been solemnized in this State. The fact of their cohabitation here as man and wife shall be evidence of their marriage."

Section 20–59, which defines the penalty for miscegenation, provides:

"Punishment for marriage.—If any white person intermarry with a colored person, or any colored person intermarry with a white person, he shall be guilty of a felony and shall be punished by confinement in the penitentiary for not less than one nor more than five years."

Other central provisions in the Virginia statutory scheme are §20–57, which automatically voids all marriages between "a white person and a colored person" without any judicial proceeding, and §§20–54 and 1–14 which, respectively, define "white persons" and "colored persons and Indians" for purposes of the statutory prohibitions. The Lovings have never disputed in the course of this litigation that Mrs. Loving is a "colored person" or that Mr. Loving is a "white person" within the meanings given those terms by the Virginia statutes.

Virginia is now one of 16 States which prohibit and punish marriages on the basis of racial classifications. Penalties for miscegenation arose as an incident to slavery and have been common in Virginia since the colonial period. The present statutory scheme dates from the adoption of the Racial Integrity Act of 1924, passed during the period of extreme nativism which followed the end of the First World War. The central features of this Act, and current Virginia law, are the absolute prohibition of a "white person" marrying other than another "white person," a prohibition against issuing marriage licenses until the issuing official is satisfied that the applicants' statements as to their race are correct, certificates of "racial composition" to be kept by both local and state registrars, and the carrying forward of earlier prohibitions against racial intermarriage.

I

In upholding the constitutionality of these provisions in the decision below, the Supreme Court of Appeals of Virginia referred to its 1955 decision in *Naim v. Naim*, 197 Va. 80, 87 S.E. 2d 749, as stating the reasons supporting the validity of these laws. In *Naim*, the state court concluded that the State's legitimate purposes were "to preserve the racial integrity of its citizens," and to prevent "the corruption of blood," "a mongrel breed of citizens," and "the obliteration of racial pride," obviously an endorsement of the doctrine of White Supremacy. *Id.*, at 90, 87 S.E. 2d, at 756. The court also reasoned that marriage has traditionally been subject to state regulation without federal intervention, and, consequently, the regulation of marriage should be left to exclusive state control by the Tenth Amendment.

While the state court is no doubt correct in asserting that marriage is a social relation subject to the State's police power, *Maynard v. Hill*, 125 U.S. 190 (1888), the State does not contend in its argument before this Court that its powers to regulate marriage are unlimited notwithstanding the commands of the Fourteenth Amendment. Nor could it do so in light of *Meyer v. Nebraska*, 262 U.S. 390 (1923), and *Skinner v. Oklahoma*, 316 U.S. 535 (1942). Instead, the State argues that the meaning of the Equal Protection Clause, as illuminated by the statements of the Framers, is only that state penal laws containing an interracial element as part of the definition of the offense must apply equally to whites and Negroes in the sense that members of each race are punished to the same degree. Thus, the State contends that, because its miscegenation statutes punish equally both the white and the Negro participants in an interracial marriage, these statutes, despite their reliance on racial classifications, do not constitute an invidious discrimination based upon race. The second argument advanced by the State assumes the validity of its equal application theory. The argument is that, if the Equal Protection Clause does not outlaw miscegenation statutes because of their reliance on racial classifications, the question of constitutionality would thus become whether there was any rational basis for a State to treat interracial marriages differently from other marriages. On this question, the State argues, the scientific evidence is substantially in doubt and, consequently, this Court should defer to the wisdom of the state legislature in adopting its policy of discouraging interracial marriages.

Because we reject the notion that the mere "equal application" of a statute containing racial classifications is enough to remove the classifications from the Fourteenth Amendment's proscription of all invidious racial discriminations, we do not accept the State's contention that these statutes should be upheld if there is any possible basis for concluding that they serve a rational purpose. The mere fact of equal application does not mean that our analysis of these statutes should follow the approach we have taken in cases involving no racial discrimination where the Equal Protection Clause has been arrayed against a statute discriminating between the kinds of advertising which may be displayed on trucks in New York City, *Railway Express Agency, Inc. v. New York*, 336 U.S. 106 (1949), or an exemption in Ohio's ad valorem tax for merchandise owned by a nonresident in a storage warehouse, *Allied Stores of Ohio, Inc. v. Bowers*, 358 U.S. 522 (1959). In these cases, involving distinctions not drawn according to race, the Court has merely asked whether there is any rational foundation for the discriminations, and has deferred to the wisdom of the state legislatures. In the case at bar, however, we deal with statutes containing racial classifications, and the fact of equal application does not immunize the statute from the very heavy burden of justification which the Fourteenth Amendment has traditionally required of state statutes drawn according to race.

The State argues that statements in the Thirty-ninth Congress about the time of the passage of the Fourteenth Amendment indicate that the Framers did not intend the Amendment to make unconstitutional state miscegenation laws. Many of the statements alluded to by the State concern the debates over the Freedmen's Bureau Bill, which President Johnson vetoed, and the Civil Rights Act of 1866, 14 Stat. 27, enacted over his veto. While these statements have some relevance to the intention of Congress in submitting the Fourteenth Amendment, it must be understood that they pertained to the passage of specific statutes and not to the broader, organic purpose of a constitutional amendment. As for the various statements directly concerning the Fourteenth Amendment, we have said in connection with a related problem, that although these historical sources "cast some light" they are not sufficient to resolve the problem; "[a]t best, they are inconclusive. The most avid proponents of the post-War Amendments undoubtedly intended them to remove all legal distinctions among 'all persons born or naturalized in the United States.' Their opponents, just as certainly, were antagonistic to both the letter and the spirit of the Amendments and wished them to have the most limited effect." *Brown v. Board of Education*, 347 U.S. 483, 489 (1954). See also *Strauder v. West Virginia*, 100 U.S. 303, 310 (1880). We have rejected the proposition that the debates in the Thirty-ninth Congress or in the state legislatures which ratified the Fourteenth Amendment supported the theory advanced by the State, that the requirement of equal protection of the laws is satisfied by penal laws defining offenses based on racial classifications so long as white and Negro participants in the offense were similarly punished. *McLaughlin v. Florida*, 379 U.S. 184 (1964).

The State finds support for its "equal application" theory in the decision of the Court in *Pace v. Alabama*, 106 U.S. 583 (1883). In that case, the Court upheld a conviction under an Alabama statute forbidding adultery or fornication between a white person and a Negro which imposed a greater penalty than that of a statute proscribing similar conduct by members of the same race. The Court reasoned that the statute could not be said to discriminate against Negroes because the punishment for each participant in the offense was the same. However, as recently as the 1964 Term, in rejecting the reasoning of that case, we stated " *Pace* represents a limited view of the Equal Protection Clause which has not withstood analysis in the subsequent decisions of this Court." *McLaughlin v. Florida, supra*, at 188. As we there demonstrated, the Equal Protection Clause requires the consideration of whether the classifications drawn by any statute constitute an arbitrary and invidious discrimination. The clear and central purpose of the Fourteenth Amendment was to eliminate all official state sources of invidious racial discrimination in the States. *Slaughter-House Cases*, 16 Wall. 36, 71 (1873); *Strauder v. West Virginia*, 100 U.S. 303, 307–308 (1880); *Ex parte Virginia*, 100 U.S. 339, 344–345 (1880); *Shelley v. Kraemer*, 334 U.S. 1 (1948); *Burton v. Wilmington Parking Authority*, 365 U.S. 715 (1961).

There can be no question but that Virginia's miscegenation statutes rest solely upon distinctions drawn according to race. The statutes proscribe generally accepted conduct if engaged in by members of different races. Over the years, this Court has consistently repudiated "[d]istinctions between citizens solely because of their ancestry" as being "odious to a free people whose institutions are founded upon the doctrine of equality." *Hirabayashi v. United States*, 320 U.S. 81, 100 (1943). At the very least, the Equal Protection Clause demands that racial classifications, especially suspect in criminal statutes, be subjected to the "most rigid scrutiny," *Korematsu v. United States*, 323 U.S. 214, 216 (1944), and, if they are ever to be upheld, they must be shown to be necessary to the accomplishment of some permissible state objective, independent of the racial discrimination which it was the object of the Fourteenth Amendment to eliminate. Indeed, two members of this Court have already stated that they "cannot conceive of a valid legislative purpose ... which makes the color of a person's skin the test of whether his conduct is a criminal offense." *McLaughlin v. Florida, supra*, at 198 (Stewart, J., joined by Douglas, J., concurring).

There is patently no legitimate overriding purpose independent of invidious racial discrimination which justifies this classification. The fact that Virginia prohibits only interracial marriages involving white persons demonstrates that the racial classifications must stand on their own justification, as measures designed to maintain White Supremacy. We have consistently denied the constitutionality of measures which restrict the rights of citizens on account of race. There can be no doubt that restricting the freedom to marry solely because of racial classifications violates the central meaning of the Equal Protection Clause.

II

These statutes also deprive the Lovings of liberty without due process of law in violation of the Due Process Clause of the Fourteenth Amendment. The freedom to marry has long been recognized as one of the vital personal rights essential to the orderly pursuit of happiness by free men.

Marriage is one of the "basic civil rights of man," fundamental to our very existence and survival. *Skinner v. Oklahoma*, 316 U.S. 535, 541 (1942). See also *Maynard v. Hill*, 125 U.S. 190 (1888). To deny this fundamental freedom on so unsupportable a basis as the racial classifications embodied in these statutes, classifications so directly subversive of the principle of equality at the heart of the Fourteenth Amendment, is surely to deprive all the State's citizens of liberty without due process of law. The Fourteenth Amendment requires that the freedom of choice to marry not be restricted by invidious racial discriminations. Under our Constitution, the freedom to marry, or not marry, a person of another race resides with the individual and cannot be infringed by the State.

These convictions must be reversed.

It is so ordered.

Glossary

ad valorem tax: a tax on goods computed on the basis of their value

case at bar: the case that the Court is presently hearing (used in preference to "this case," which can be mis-interpreted to have a more general meaning)

class action: a lawsuit brought by one or more persons on behalf of a large group

Framers: the writers of the Constitution

Freedmen's Bureau Bill: the bill that established the Bureau of Refugees, Freedmen, and Abandoned Lands in 1865 to aid newly emancipated African Americans

nativism: any policy or viewpoint that favors the interests of the present inhabitants of a country over those of newcomers; opposition to immigration

post-War Amendments: the Thirteenth, Fourteenth, and Fifteenth Amendments to the U.S. Constitution, passed in the immediate aftermath of the Civil War to abolish slavery and protect the rights of African Americans

President Johnson: Andrew Johnson, Abraham Lincoln's successor as president in the years immediately following the Civil War

Tenth Amendment: the amendment to the U.S. Constitution, contained in the Bill of Rights, that says that powers not expressly conferred on the federal government are reserved to the states

TINKER V. DES MOINES INDEPENDENT COMMUNITY SCHOOL DISTRICT

DATE	CITATION
1969	393 U.S. 503
AUTHOR	**SIGNIFICANCE**
Abe Fortas	Affirmed the rights of legal minors—in this case, high school students—to freedom of speech in the school classroom
VOTE	
7–2	

Overview

 Argued on November 12, 1968, and decided on February 24, 1969, *Tinker v. Des Moines Independent Community School District* established the principle that students had a right to self-expression, even within the context of the classroom. The case, which involved two high school students and one junior high school student, grew out of a protest the group—with the support of their parents—organized against the Vietnam War. Principals of the affected schools in the Des Moines school district learned about the planned protest and adopted a policy that threatened students participating in it with suspension.

On December 16, 1965, Christopher Eckhardt, sixteen, and Mary Beth Tinker, thirteen, wore black armbands to school. They were sent home. The following day Mary Beth's brother John wore a similar armband. He was sent home as well. When school opened again the next year, the students' fathers filed suit, alleging that the schools' policy violated the students' constitutional rights. Three other students—Ross Peterson, Bruce Clark, and Chris Singer—were also involved in the protest, but they did not become part of the lawsuit.

The U.S. district court found in favor of the defendants. The 8th Circuit Court of Appeals had a split verdict, which allowed that decision to stand. Finally, however, the Supreme Court found in favor of the students. For the first time in the history of American jurisprudence, minors were included among the groups that could exercise First Amendment rights.

Context

The contest that led to *Tinker v. Des Moines Independent Community School District* grew out of increasing American involvement in the Vietnam War in the mid-1960s. The U.S. had maintained troops in Vietnam since the 1950s, but they were euphemistically called "advisors" rather than troops. The problem centered on questions of how to treat Vietnam, part of a former French colony that had been known as French Indochina. The Vietnamese, under their charismatic Communist leader Ho Chi Minh (1890–1969), fought a long and arduous war of liberation against colonial French forces. They won a significant victory at Dienbienphu in 1954, but negotiations broke down when the United States, an ally of France, supported the European country over the anticolonial forces in Vietnam. As a result, the United States pushed for division of Vietnam into two separate countries, North and South.

In 1956, North and South Vietnam were supposed to be united by referendum. However, the leader of South Vietnam, Ngo Dinh Diem, refused to hold the referendum and sought American support for his anticommunist regime. After the assassination of President John Fitzgerald Kennedy in November of 1963, his successor, Lyndon Baines Johnson (1908–1973), had planned to remove Americans from the war-torn country.

But Johnson was faced with a quandary. He wanted to advance a domestic civil rights agenda and to win the election of 1964. To do both, he needed support from both the opponent Republican Party and from as much of his Democratic Party as he could muster. Republicans were, for the most part, in favor of a strong response to what they saw as communist influence in Vietnam. Johnson's fellow Democrats from the Deep South were mostly opposed to expanding civil rights to Black Americans. To pass his civil rights reform agenda, Johnson needed to cultivate Republican votes, and to do that he had to appear strongly anticommunist.

After he won the election of 1964, Johnson was ready to act. In the summer of that year, the north Vietnamese army invaded South Vietnam. At the same time, North Vietnamese torpedo boats attacked the U.S. destroyer *Maddox* in the Gulf of Tonkin. As a result, Congress effectively awarded Johnson the power to wage war in Vietnam through the Gulf of Tonkin Resolution. By the end of 1965, more than 184,000 U.S. troops had already been deployed in Vietnam, and another 200,000 were set to be deployed at the beginning of the year.

Opposition to American involvement in the war was already beginning to solidify. On December 10, 1965, Senator Robert Kennedy—the brother of assassinated president John F. Kennedy, and the attorney general during his administration—publicly endorsed a twelve-hour Christmas truce that had been suggested by the Vietcong. Kennedy saw this as a first step toward a permanent peace.

The Tinker family agreed with Kennedy. The Tinkers' father, Leonard Tinker, was a Methodist minister who supported the civil rights movement, and both their

Mary Beth Tinker in 2014
(Eli Hiller)

parents had participated in freedom summer in 1964, any event coordinated by the Student Nonviolent Coordinating Committee (SNCC) to register Black Americans to vote in Mississippi. With that sort of background, the young people had no difficulty in deciding to express their opposition to the Vietnam War by donning black armbands at school during the last days of the fall semester. The armbands were meant to express solidarity with Kennedy's call for a truce but also to express sorrow and regret for the casualties the war had already claimed on both sides of the conflict.

But the school had learned about the plans several days before. On December 14, school principals of the Des Moines school district had met together and decided to adopt a policy that threatened students who participated in the protest with suspension. When Mary Beth Tinker and Christopher Eckhardt wore the armbands on December 16, they were sent home. When John Tinker did the same thing the following day, he was sent home as well. All three were suspended.

Early in the new year, the school board met and affirmed the policy adopted by the school principals by a vote of five to two. Three months later, on March 14, 1966, the Tinkers, Eckhardt, and their fathers, Leonard Tinker and William Eckhardt, with the support of the Iowa Civil Liberties Union, filed a formal complaint in the U.S. District Court for the Southern District of Iowa.

This was not just an academic question for the Tinkers and Eckhardt. The U.S. district court, where their petition was first heard, noted that the war had become a dividing force in the community. The district court's presiding judge said that discussion of the war had been marked by the very public burning of draft cards. The school principals felt that the subject of the war was too heated to be introduced into the classroom without adequate preparation. But the justices, led by Fortas, in the end found that this was no excuse for violating the peaceful expression of a political opinion, regardless of the age of the protester.

About the Author

Tennessee-born Abraham Fortas (1910–1982) spent only four years as an associate justice of the Supreme Court before resigning because of allegations of corruption. He was a graduate of Rhodes College and Yale University, and he served as a law professor for the Yale Law School and as an advisor for the Securities and Exchange Commission before joining the U.S. Department of the Interior as undersecretary during the Franklin Roosevelt administration. Toward the end of World War II, President Harry Truman enlisted his help as a member of the delegations that created the United Nations in 1945.

Fortas's route to the bench came via his association with President Lyndon Johnson. Fortas had first met Johnson when the future president was still a congressman from Texas in the early 1940s. In 1948, however, Johnson was involved in a runoff election for the Democratic nomination to one of Texas's two U.S. Senate seats. Johnson's opponent had Johnson's name removed from the ballot, but Fortas, appealing to Supreme Court Associate Justice Hugo Black, had it reinstated. Johnson never forgot that favor, and when an opening appeared on the Supreme Court in 1965, he nominated Fortas for the position.

In the summer of 1968, President Johnson nominated Fortas to take the position of Chief Justice Earl Warren once he retired. Because 1968 was an election year, however, the nomination was delayed, and by the time it came before the Judiciary Committee, opposition had solidified against Fortas. Some of the opposition was racist; Fortas was a Jew and a well-known liberal who supported Johnson's civil rights platform, and

after four days of questioning by the Senate, his nomination was effectively killed by Senator Strom Thurmond, who threatened a filibuster.

Fortas left the bench in 1969 following a threat of impeachment by Attorney General John Mitchell (1913–1988). Fortas had accepted a $20,000 retainer from Wall Street magnate Louis Wolfson (1912–2007) at a time when Wolfson was under investigation by the Securities and Exchange Commission for securities fraud. Fortas returned the retainer, but the fact that he had accepted it in the first place allowed Mitchell to threaten both Fortas and his wife. Fortas resigned to protect his wife's reputation. He reentered private practice and continued to work as a lawyer until his death.

Although Fortas and his wife never had children of their own, he is best remembered today for the legal protections he championed for them. He helped extend due process and procedure to minors, and he argued for extending the Fourteenth Amendment's guarantees of rights to juveniles in *In re Gault* (1967). *Tinker v. Des Moines Independent Community School District*, issued two years later, extended First Amendment rights to young people for the first time ever.

Explanation and Analysis of the Document

Fortas begins the Court's opinion by summarizing the history and the findings in the case. He traces the case's journey through the federal district court and court of appeals, and he concludes the first section with a summary of the Supreme Court's findings. He asserts that wearing armbands is a form of free speech, "quiet and passive," that did not disrupt school proceedings and did not interfere with other students exercising their rights. As such, he says, the way the students behaved is protected by both the First Amendment and by the due process clause of the Fourteenth Amendment. In addition, Fortas continues, the First Amendment protects the exercise of free speech among both teachers and students as long as those rights do not interfere with the proper functioning of their school. Finally, he concludes, since the school issued its prohibition on the armbands as a proactive measure rather than in response to a disruptive event, the action it took by banning armbands was not covered by protections under either the First or the Fourteenth Amendments.

Associate Justice Fortas continues in the first section following his introduction by giving details about the case and explaining a bit about the court's process of investigating the facts of the matter. He notes that none of the three young people interfered in any way with the business of their schools or with the rights of their fellow students. In addition, out of some 18,000 students in the schools involved, only a few were suspended for wearing the armbands.

Then the associate justice points out that key element in the Tinkers' case is one of free speech. The students were not accused of wearing inappropriate clothing or behaving in a disruptive manner. Instead, they were expressing a political opinion and doing so in a way that did not directly affect the school or their fellow students.

The district court based its opinion on the idea that the school principals' actions were reasonable because they were afraid that the armbands might cause a disturbance. But Fortas points out that a person cannot be stripped of their First Amendment rights simply because someone is afraid of what might result. In addition, he says, "Under our Constitution, free speech is not a right that is given only to be so circumscribed that it exists in principle but not in fact. . . . [W]e do not confine the permissible exercise of First Amendment rights to a telephone booth or the four corners of a pamphlet, or to supervised and ordained discussion in a school classroom." Accordingly, he states, the decision of the 8th Circuit Court in this matter is reversed and the case is remanded.

Although Fortas spoke for the Court's majority, two justices concurred with him but offered slightly different interpretations of the case. Potter Stewart (1915–1985) agreed with the judgment, but he held that extending the rights conferred by the First Amendment to children in all cases was too great a stretch. Byron White (1917–2002) drew a distinction between First Amendment rights in spoken speech and other forms of communication; actions and modes of dress, he felt, fell into another category.

In addition to the seven justices who offered the majority opinion, two justices dissented. Justice John Marshall Harlan II (1899–1971) felt that the school officials were acting in good faith when they banned armbands. Therefore, they should be given considerable leeway in issuing orders that are designed to maintain discipline. He suggests that in future cases like this one, plaintiffs be required to show that school rules were specifically designed to suppress freedom of speech rather than to maintain school order.

The longest dissent was filed by Hugo Black (1886–1971). Justice Black felt that although the form of speech was protected by the First and Fourteenth Amendments, the students were exercising their right in ways that were disruptive, even if that was not their intention. As Justice Fortas had noted, the protest against the Vietnam War had provoked comment, and although comment and discussion were legitimate educational exercises, the ways in which that comment was expressed disrupted regular school activities. He pointed out that a mathematics teacher complained that Mary Beth Tinker's armband effectively "wrecked" his lesson plans. In that sense, Justice Black said, the protest was disruptive, and the principals were acting appropriately when they tried to ban the wearing of armbands.

Much of the rest of Black's dissent involves looking at individual cases in which freedom of speech was restricted by law. But in his summary, Black brings up another important point: the question of order within public schools. He suggests that freedom of speech could be used as a tool to disrupt learning by students' "whims and caprices." "It is a myth," Black asserts, "to say that any person has a constitutional right to say what he pleases, where he pleases, and when he pleases."

Impact

Tinker v. Des Moines Independent Community School District had an almost-immediate impact on the extension of political speech to students. At a time when college students were already mobilizing to protest injustices against Black Americans in support of the civil rights movement and against the Vietnam War, the Court's decision extended free speech protections to high school, junior high school, and even elementary students. The decision continues to be cited in questions of student free-speech rights. Sometimes the rulings extend the rights, while in other cases free speech is limited. In *Papish v. Board of Curators of the University of Missouri* (1973), a court found that the university violated the rights of a student who was expelled after distributing a newspaper with language the university found objectionable. In *Bethel School District v. Fras-*

er (1986), however, the courts found that a student's use of vulgar speech in a school assembly was not protected by First Amendment guarantees. As recently as 2013, the 3rd Circuit Court of Appeals heard a case concerning students wearing bracelets in school that supported breast cancer awareness.

One of the most significant ways the *Tinker* decision is applied in the twenty-first century is over the question of internet speech. In 2017, a Pennsylvania high school student filed suit against her school district after she was reprimanded for social media posts she had made outside of school. In 2021, the Supreme Court passed down a decision in that case, *Mahanoy Area School District v. B.L.* Writing for the majority, Justice Stephen Breyer reaffirmed *Tinker*'s basic principles. However, Breyer did note that schools might have a compelling interest in restricting students' free speech even out-side of school in cases where students were harassing or bullying other students through social media.

Christopher Eckhardt died of cancer in 2013, but Mary Beth and John Tinker, his fellow plaintiffs, continue to advocate for rights of free speech more than half a century after their case was decided. Mary Beth in particular has become an important advocate for the rights of young people, including freedom of speech. A retired pediatric nurse with master's degrees in public health and nursing, she has become a public speaker about children's rights. In 2000, Washington College of Law's Marshall–Brennan Project, named after two Supreme Court justices, named its youth advocacy award in honor of Mary Beth Tinker. In 2014, with the support of the Student Press Law Center (SPLC), she embarked on a nationwide speaking tour called "Tinker Tour USA" to bring questions about children's rights to the attention of all Americans.

Questions for Further Study

1. What is the relationship between the civil rights movement of the 1960s, the protests against the Vietnam War, and the *Tinker* case? How did they influence one another?

2. *Tinker* is important in part because it recognizes children as persons under American law. What does that mean for the rights of young people, related both to free speech and to other constitutionally guaranteed rights?

3. Justice Hugo Black, in his dissent, emphasizes the testimony of a math teacher who claimed he was unable to teach because of the disruption Mary Beth Tinker's armband caused in his class. Should that have been a consideration in the majority opinion?

4. Several justices noted that although the students voluntarily joined in the Vietnam War protests, they were following the examples of their parents, who were experienced protestors. Does that undercut Justice Black's statement about the "whims and caprices" of students?

5. Justice Fortas asserts in his opinion that freedom of speech overrides considerations based on fear. But the years since *Tinker* was decided have seen the rise of internet bullying and hate speech. Should these new means of communication be restricted, or should *Tinker*'s definition of free speech still be used?

Further Reading

Books

Johnson, John W. *The Struggle for Student Rights: Tinker v. Des Moines and the 1960s.* Lawrence: University Press of Kansas, 1997.

McPherson, Stephanie Sammartino. *Tinker v. Des Moines and Students' Right to Free Speech: Debating Supreme Court Decisions.* Berkeley Heights, NJ: Enslow, 2006.

Patterson, Nancy C., and Prentice T. Chandler, eds. *At the Schoolhouse Gate: Stakeholder Perceptions of First Amendment Rights and Responsibilities in US Public Schools.* Charlotte, NC: Information Age, 2022.

Articles

Bohannan, Christina. "On the 50th Anniversary of Tinker v. Des Moines: Toward a Positive View of Free Speech on College Campuses." *Iowa Law Review* 105, no. 5 (July 2020): 2233–72.

Corn-Revere, Robert. "The Anti-Free Speech Movement." *Brooklyn Law Review* 87 (Fall 2021): 145–93.

Krafte, Jill H. "Tinker's Legacy: Freedom of the Press in Public High Schools." *DePaul Law Review* 28 (1979): 387–428.

Russo, Charles J. "The Supreme Court and Student Free Speech: A Retrospective Look at Tinker v. Des Moines Independent Community School District and Its Progeny." *University of Dayton Law Review* 45, no. 2 (Spring 2020): 189–228.

Schmidt, Kara A. "Out of Bounds: Reviving Tinker's Territorial Nexus to Constrain Schools' Disciplinary Power over Student Internet Speech." *George Mason Law Review* 28, no. 2 (Winter 2021): 853–83.

Websites

"Tinker v. Des Moines (1969)." *CSPAN: Landmark Cases: Historic Supreme Court Decisions.* Accessed February 20, 2023, https://landmarkcases.c-span.org/Case/24/Tinker-v.-Des-Moines.

"Tinker v. Des Moines Podcast." *United States Courts.* Accessed February 20, 2023, https://www.uscourts.gov/about-federal-courts/educational-resources/supreme-court-landmarks/tinker-v-des-moines-podcast.

—Commentary by Kenneth R. Shepherd

TINKER V. DES MOINES INDEPENDENT COMMUNITY SCHOOL DISTRICT

Document Text

MR. JUSTICE FORTAS delivered the opinion of the Court

Petitioner John F. Tinker, 15 years old, and petitioner Christopher Eckhardt, 16 years old, attended high schools in Des Moines, Iowa. Petitioner Mary Beth Tinker, John's sister, was a 13-year-old student in junior high school.

In December, 1965, a group of adults and students in Des Moines held a meeting at the Eckhardt home. The group determined to publicize their objections to the hostilities in Vietnam and their support for a truce by wearing black armbands during the holiday season and by fasting on December 16 and New Year's Eve. Petitioners and their parents had previously engaged in similar activities, and they decided to participate in the program.

The principals of the Des Moines schools became aware of the plan to wear armbands. On December 14, 1965, they met and adopted a policy that any student wearing an armband to school would be asked to remove it, and, if he refused, he would be suspended until he returned without the armband. Petitioners were aware of the regulation that the school authorities adopted.

On December 16, Mary Beth and Christopher wore black armbands to their schools. John Tinker wore his armband the next day. They were all sent home and suspended from school until they would come back without their armbands. They did not return to school until after the planned period for wearing armbands had expired—that is, until after New Year's Day.

This complaint was filed in the United States District Court by petitioners, through their fathers, under § 1983 of Title 42 of the United States Code. It prayed for an injunction restraining the respondent school officials and the respondent members of the board of directors of the school district from disciplining the petitioners, and it sought nominal damages. After an evidentiary hearing, the District Court dismissed the complaint. It upheld the constitutionality of the school authorities' action on the ground that it was reasonable in order to prevent disturbance of school discipline. 258 F. Supp. 971 (1966). The court referred to, but expressly declined to follow, the Fifth Circuit's holding in a similar case that the wearing of symbols like the armbands cannot be prohibited unless it "materially and substantially interfere[s] with the requirements of appropriate discipline in the operation of the school." *Burnside v. Byars*, 363 F.2d 744, 749 (1966).

On appeal, the Court of Appeals for the Eighth Circuit considered the case en banc. The court was equally divided, and the District Court's decision was accordingly affirmed without opinion. 383 F.2d 988 (1967). We granted certiorari. 390 U.S. 942 (1968).

IThe District Court recognized that the wearing of an armband for the purpose of expressing certain views is the type of symbolic act that is within the Free Speech Clause of the First Amendment. *See West Virginia v. Barnette*, 319 U. S. 624 (1943); *Stromberg v. California*, 283 U. S. 359 (1931). *Cf. Thornhill v. Alabama*, 310 U. S. 88 (1940); *Edwards v. South Carolina*, 372 U. S. 229 (1963); *Brown v. Louisiana*, 383 U. S. 131 (1966). As we shall discuss, the wearing of armbands in the circumstances of this case was entirely divorced from actually or potentially disruptive conduct by those participating in it. It was closely akin to "pure speech" which, we have repeatedly held, is entitled to comprehensive protection under the First Amendment. *Cf. Cox v. Louisiana*, 379 U. S. 536, 555 (1965); *Adderley v. Florida*, 385 U. S. 39 (1966).

First Amendment rights, applied in light of the special characteristics of the school environment, are available to teachers and students. It can hardly be argued that either students or teachers shed their constitutional rights to freedom of speech or expression at the schoolhouse gate. This has been the unmistakable holding of this Court for almost 50 years. In *Meyer v. Nebraska*, 262 U. S. 390 (1923), and *Bartels v. Iowa*, 262 U. S. 404 (1923), this Court, in opinions by Mr. Justice McReynolds, held that the Due Process Clause of the Fourteenth Amendment prevents States from forbidding the teaching of a foreign language to young students. Statutes to this effect, the Court held, unconstitutionally interfere with the liberty of teacher, student, and parent. *See also Pierce v. Society of Sisters,* 268 U.S. 510 (1925); *West Virginia v. Barnette,* 319 U. S. 624 (1943); *McCollum v. Board of Education,* 333 U. S. 203 (1948); *Wieman v. Updegraff,* 344 U. S. 183, 195 (1952) (concurring opinion); *Sweezy v. New Hampshire,* 354 U. S. 234 (1957); *Shelton v. Tucker,* 364 U. S. 479, 487 (1960); *Engel v. Vitale,* 370 U. S. 421 (1962); *Keyishian v. Board of Regents,* 385 U. S. 589, 603 (1967); *Epperson v. Arkansas, ante*, p. 97 (1968).

In *West Virginia v. Barnette, supra*, this Court held that, under the First Amendment, the student in public school may not be compelled to salute the flag. Speaking through Mr. Justice Jackson, the Court said:

"The Fourteenth Amendment, as now applied to the States, protects the citizen against the State itself and all of its creatures—Boards of Education not excepted. These have, of course, important, delicate, and highly discretionary functions, but none that they may not perform within the limits of the Bill of Rights. That they are educating the young for citizenship is reason for scrupulous protection of Constitutional freedoms of the individual, if we are not to strangle the free mind at its source and teach youth to discount important principles of our government as mere platitudes."319 U.S. at 637.

On the other hand, the Court has repeatedly emphasized the need for affirming the comprehensive authority of the States and of school officials, consistent with fundamental constitutional safeguards, to prescribe and control conduct in the schools. *See Epperson v. Arkansas, supra*, at 104; *Meyer v. Nebraska, supra*, at 402. Our problem lies in the area where students in the exercise of First Amendment rights collide with the rules of the school authorities.

II

The problem posed by the present case does not relate to regulation of the length of skirts or the type of clothing, to hair style, or deportment. *Cf. Ferrell v. Dallas Independent School District*, 392 F.2d 697 (1968); *Pugsley v. Sellmeyer*, 158 Ark. 247, 250 S.W. 538 (1923). It does not concern aggressive, disruptive action or even group demonstrations. Our problem involves direct, primary First Amendment rights akin to "pure speech."

The school officials banned and sought to punish petitioners for a silent, passive expression of opinion, unaccompanied by any disorder or disturbance on the part of petitioners. There is here no evidence whatever of petitioners' interference, actual or nascent, with the schools' work or of collision with the rights of other students to be secure and to be let alone. Accordingly, this case does not concern speech or action that intrudes upon the work of the schools or the rights of other students.

Only a few of the 18,000 students in the school system wore the black armbands. Only five students were suspended for wearing them. There is no indication that the work of the schools or any class was disrupted. Outside the classrooms, a few students made hostile remarks to the children wearing armbands, but there were no threats or acts of violence on school premises.

The District Court concluded that the action of the school authorities was reasonable because it was based upon their fear of a disturbance from the wearing of the armbands. But, in our system, undifferentiated fear or apprehension of disturbance is not enough to overcome the right to freedom of expression. Any departure from absolute regimentation may cause trouble. Any variation from the majority's opinion may inspire fear. Any word spoken, in class, in the lunchroom, or on the campus, that deviates from the views of another person may start an argument or cause a disturbance. But our Constitution says we must take this risk, *Terminiello v. Chicago*, 337 U. S. 1 (1949); and our history says that it is this sort of hazardous freedom—this kind of openness—that is the basis of our national strength and of the independence and vigor of Americans who grow up and live in this relatively permissive, often disputatious, society.

In order for the State in the person of school officials to justify prohibition of a particular expression of opinion, it must be able to show that its action was caused by something more than a mere desire to avoid the discomfort and unpleasantness that always accompany an unpopular viewpoint. Certainly where there is no finding and no showing that engaging in the forbidden conduct would "materially and substantially interfere with the requirements of appropriate discipline in the operation of the school," the prohibition cannot be sustained. *Burnside v. Byars, supra* at 749.

In the present case, the District Court made no such finding, and our independent examination of the record fails to yield evidence that the school authorities had reason to anticipate that the wearing of the armbands would substantially interfere with the work of the school or impinge upon the rights of other students. Even an official memorandum prepared after the suspension that listed the reasons for the ban on wearing the armbands made no reference to the anticipation of such disruption.

On the contrary, the action of the school authorities appears to have been based upon an urgent wish to avoid the controversy which might result from the expression, even by the silent symbol of armbands, of opposition to this Nation's part in the conflagration in Vietnam. It is revealing, in this respect, that the meeting at which the school principals decided to issue the contested regulation was called in response to a student's statement to the journalism teacher in one of the schools that he wanted to write an article on Vietnam and have it published in the school paper. (The student was dissuaded.)

It is also relevant that the school authorities did not purport to prohibit the wearing of all symbols of political or controversial significance. The record shows that students in some of the schools wore buttons relating to national political campaigns, and some even wore the Iron Cross, traditionally a symbol of Nazism. The order

prohibiting the wearing of armbands did not extend to these. Instead, a particular symbol—black armbands worn to exhibit opposition to this Nation's involvement in Vietnam—was singled out for prohibition. Clearly, the prohibition of expression of one particular opinion, at least without evidence that it is necessary to avoid material and substantial interference with schoolwork or discipline, is not constitutionally permissible.

In our system, state-operated schools may not be enclaves of totalitarianism. School officials do not possess absolute authority over their students. Students in school, as well as out of school, are "persons" under our Constitution. They are possessed of fundamental rights which the State must respect, just as they themselves must respect their obligations to the State. In our system, students may not be regarded as closed-circuit recipients of only that which the State chooses to communicate. They may not be confined to the expression of those sentiments that are officially approved. In the absence of a specific showing of constitutionally valid reasons to regulate their speech, students are entitled to freedom of expression of their views. As Judge Gewin, speaking for the Fifth Circuit, said, school officials cannot suppress "expressions of feelings with which they do not wish to contend." *Burnside v. Byars, supra*, at 749.

In *Meyer v. Nebraska, supra*, at 402, Mr. Justice McReynolds expressed this Nation's repudiation of the principle that a State might so conduct its schools as to "foster a homogeneous people." He said:

> In order to submerge the individual and develop ideal citizens, Sparta assembled the males at seven into barracks and intrusted their subsequent education and training to official guardians. Although such measures have been deliberately approved by men of great genius, their ideas touching the relation between individual and State were wholly different from those upon which our institutions rest; and it hardly will be affirmed that any legislature could impose such restrictions upon the people of a State without doing violence to both letter and spirit of the Constitution.

This principle has been repeated by this Court on numerous occasions during the intervening years. In *Keyishian v. Board of Regents*, 385 U. S. 589, 603, MR. JUSTICE BRENNAN, speaking for the Court, said:

'The vigilant protection of constitutional freedoms is nowhere more vital than in the community of American schools.' Shelton v. Tucker, [364 U.S. 479,] at 487. The classroom is peculiarly the 'marketplace of ideas.' The Nation's future depends upon leaders trained through wide exposure to that robust exchange of ideas which discovers truth 'out of a multitude of tongues, [rather] than through any kind of authoritative selection.'

The principle of these cases is not confined to the supervised and ordained discussion which takes place in the classroom. The principal use to which the schools are dedicated is to accommodate students during prescribed hours for the purpose of certain types of activities. Among those activities is personal intercommunication among the students. This is not only an inevitable part of the process of attending school; it is also an important part of the educational process. A student's rights, therefore, do not embrace merely the classroom hours. When he is in the cafeteria, or on the playing field, or on the campus during the authorized hours, he may express his opinions, even on controversial subjects like the conflict in Vietnam, if he does so without "materially and substantially interfer[ing] with the requirements of appropriate discipline in the operation of the school" and without colliding with the rights of others. *Burnside v. Byars, supra*, at 749. But conduct by the student, in class or out of it, which for any reason—whether it stems from time, place, or type of behavior—materially disrupts classwork or involves substantial disorder or invasion of the rights of others is, of course, not immunized by the constitutional guarantee of freedom of speech. *Cf. Blackwell v. Issaquena County Board of Education.*, 363 F.2d 740 (C.A. 5th Cir.1966).

Under our Constitution, free speech is not a right that is given only to be so circumscribed that it exists in principle, but not in fact. Freedom of expression would not truly exist if the right could be exercised only in an area that a benevolent government has provided as a safe haven for crackpots. The Constitution says that Congress (and the States) may not abridge the right to free speech. This provision means what it says. We properly read it to permit reasonable regulation of speech-connected activities in carefully restricted circumstances. But we do not confine the permissible exercise of First Amendment rights to a telephone booth or the four corners of a pamphlet, or to supervised and ordained discussion in a school classroom.

If a regulation were adopted by school officials forbidding discussion of the Vietnam conflict, or the expression by any student of opposition to it anywhere on school property except as part of a prescribed classroom exercise, it would be obvious that the regulation would violate the constitutional rights of students, at least if it could not be justified by a showing that the students' activities would materially and substantially disrupt the work and discipline of the school. *Cf. Hammond v. South Carolina State College*, 272 F. Supp. 947 (D.C.S.C.1967) (orderly protest meeting on state college campus); *Dickey v. Alabama State Board of Education*, 273 F. Supp. 613 (D.C.M.D. Ala. 967) (expulsion of student editor of college newspaper). In the circumstances of the present case, the prohibition of the silent, passive "witness of the armbands," as one of the children called it, is no less offensive to the Constitution's guarantees.

As we have discussed, the record does not demonstrate any facts which might reasonably have led school authorities to forecast substantial disruption of or material interference with school activities, and no disturbances or disorders on the school premises in fact occurred. These petitioners merely went about their ordained rounds in school. Their deviation consisted only in wearing on their sleeve a band of black cloth, not more than two inches wide. They wore it to exhibit their disapproval of the Vietnam hostilities and their advocacy of a truce, to make their views known, and, by their example, to influence others to adopt them. They neither interrupted school activities nor sought to intrude in the school affairs or the lives of others. They caused discussion outside of the classrooms, but no interference with work and no disorder. In the circumstances, our Constitution does not permit officials of the State to deny their form of expression.

We express no opinion as to the form of relief which should be granted, this being a matter for the lower courts to determine. We reverse and remand for further proceedings consistent with this opinion.

Reversed and remanded.

Glossary

freedom of speech: one of the rights contained in the First Amendment to the Constitution, which states, in part: "Congress shall make no law respecting an establishment of religion, or prohibiting the free exercise thereof; or abridging the freedom of speech, or of the press"

symbolic speech: nonverbal and nonwritten form of communication, such as wearing an armband or political pin, picketing, or flag burning

totalitarianism: absolute control by an authority

NEW YORK TIMES CO. V. UNITED STATES

DATE 1971	**CITATION** 403 U.S. 713
AUTHOR Six concurring opinions: Hugo L. Black, Byron R. White, William J. Brennan Jr., William O. Douglas, Potter Stewart, Thurgood Marshall	**SIGNIFICANCE** Ruled that the Nixon administration violated the First Amendment when it tried to prevent the New York Times (and, in a related case, the Washington Post) from publishing material about the Vietnam War
VOTE 6–3	

Overview

The case, which was argued on June 26, 1971, and decided on June 30, 1971, was based on the release of a set of government documents that became known as the Pentagon Papers. Formally titled *Report of the Office of the Secretary of Defense Vietnam Task Force*, the Pentagon Papers provided a history of the United States' involvement in the Vietnam War, commissioned in 1967 by Secretary of Defense Robert McNamara. The report not only gave a history of the United States' relationship with Vietnam but also showed that Lyndon Johnson's administration systematically misled or lied to Congress and the American public about the progress and aims of the war. When the *New York Times* began publishing excerpts from the report that had been leaked by military analyst Daniel Ellsberg, Nixon's attorney general, John Mitchell, sought an injunction against the *Times* to stop publication.

The administration filed a separate suit at the same time against the *Washington Post*, which had also begun publishing excerpts, and the case of *United States v. The Washington Post Company et al.* was decided concurrently with *New York Times Company v. United States*.

The Court found that in both cases, the government failed to show that it had a compelling reason for blocking publication of the Pentagon Papers. The decision was hailed as a significant victory for First Amendment rights of the press and for freedom of speech.

Context

The Pentagon Papers traced the history of U.S. involvement in Vietnam from before World War II to 1967, the point at which the report was commissioned. Since the nineteenth century, France had occupied Vietnam, Cambodia, and Laos in an imperial organization known as French Indochina. Resistance to French control of the region stretched back to immediately after World War I, when a Vietnamese Communist named Ho Chi Minh sought recognition for his native land in the meetings leading up to the Treaty of Versailles (1919). By 1941, Ho Chi Minh had led a small group to create the League for Vietnamese Independence, or Vietminh. Ho Chi Minh and the Vietminh joined the Allies in fighting against the Japanese during World War II, and in 1945 Japanese forces in the region sur-

President Richard Nixon
(Wikimedia Commons)

rendered to the Vietminh rather than to the French. Ho Chi Minh proclaimed Vietnamese independence on September 2, 1945.

Ho Chi Minh expected support from the United States. He had modeled his proclamation on the U.S. Declaration of Independence, and he believed the United States would rally behind a fellow country fighting against an imperial overlord. But he was mistaken. President Truman, confronted with the political realities of the early Cold War, chose instead to back France. By 1946, France was at war with its former colony, and the struggle persisted through the spring of 1954.

To Ho Chi Minh, the final victory over French forces at Dienbienphu on May 7, 1954, represented a victory for Vietnamese statehood. What the United States saw, however, was a Communist leader stepping in and taking control of what had been the colony of a Western nation. Truman's government responded by pushing for a division of Vietnam at 17 degrees of latitude into a North and a South. North Vietnam, called the Democratic Republic of Vietnam, would be a Communist state with its capital at Hanoi and Ho Chi Minh as pres-

ident, and South Vietnam, under the rule of a native monarch, Bao Dai, would have its capital at Saigon.

North and South Vietnam were supposed to be united by a referendum in 1956, but Bao Dai was deposed by his prime minister, Ngo Dinh Diem. Diem's family was originally from North Vietnam, and he was adamantly opposed to Communism. As a result, with backing from the United States, he refused to hold the referendum called for by the Geneva Convention. After he came to power, he used dictatorial powers to suppress opposition and to arrest and execute enemies. He also refused to reform land policies, which helped alienate the 85 percent of the population that lived on the land.

Diem's policies helped alienate a sizeable number of veterans of the anti-colonial struggle living in South Vietnam, and with encouragement from Ho's successors Le Duan and Pham Van Dong, they organized a resistance. As a result, violence, by both the Vietminh and the South Vietnamese government, escalated in the late 1950s and early 1960s. In December 1960, the anti-government forces organized their resistance into the National Liberation Front (NLF), sometimes called the Viet Cong. Diem responded by herding suspected militants into compounds that were rather like concentration camps. In November 1963, Diem was overthrown in an army coup and murdered. Three weeks later U.S. President John F. Kennedy was shot and killed.

The deaths of two heads of state within weeks of one another threw both South Vietnam and the United States into confusion. In Washington, Kennedy's vice president, Lyndon Johnson, now president himself, wanted to find a way to advance his domestic civil rights agenda, and to win the upcoming 1964 election. To promote civil rights, Johnson needed Republican votes—he could not count upon the racists in his own party. As a result, he had to take a strong line against international Communism. That in turn meant that he had to show leadership against the Communists in North Vietnam.

Johnson did not want to get further involved in Vietnam. In an October 1964 speech he said that the United States would not send American men to fight so far away from home. But the politics of the moment required him to modify his position. One of his first actions as president was to reverse a secret directive by President Kennedy, issued less than two weeks before he was killed, to withdraw 1,000 U.S. military advisors from South Vietnam. Johnson hoped that by doing so he could contain the Communists and mollify the Republicans without escalating the conflict into open war—and without alienating anti-war senators whose support he needed for his social programs.

The North Vietnamese government in Hanoi made Johnson's decision easier when, in August of 1964, it sent North Vietnamese army (NVA) units into South Vietnam. Around the same time, according to U.S. reports, the destroyer U.S.S. *Maddox* was attacked by North Vietnamese torpedo boats in international waters. This was not altogether true. The *Maddox* was in Vietnamese water and was using electronic surveillance to spy on the North Vietnamese and to report that information to South Vietnam. But Johnson seized the moment and asked Congress for the right to use military force against North Vietnam in Southeast Asia. The result was the Gulf of Tonkin Resolution—an effective declaration of war without doing so.

Once Johnson won the 1964 election, he was ready to use those powers. In February 1965, following an attack on U.S. military advisors at Pleiku, he authorized sustained bombing raids against targets in North Vietnam—an operation that became infamous as "Rolling Thunder." If anything, however, the bombing had the reverse effect of boosting North Vietnamese morale. Early in 1965, a threat to the U.S. air base at Danang convinced General William Westmoreland and President Johnson to commit two battalions of marines: the first American troops committed to combat in the Vietnam War. By the end of the year, 184,300 U.S. troops were deployed in the country, and another 200,000 were set to enter the region early the following year.

The escalation of U.S. involvement in Vietnam posed significant problems for Johnson. He had promised the American public that he would not commit U.S. troops to fight in a land war in Asia. At the same time, he concealed the extent to which American troops were involved. In addition, another South Vietnamese coup in June 1965 brought General Nguyen Van Thieu into power as head of a military junta. The result of this was more and more U.S. commitment of arms and forces to the war in Vietnam. By the end of 1967, the United States was both paying for and fighting the war.

It was at this point that Secretary of Defense Robert McNamara commissioned the report that would be-

come the Pentagon Papers. McNamara ordered the report produced without consulting either President Johnson or Secretary of State Dean Rusk, and it was rumored that he did so to support Robert Kennedy in a potential bid for the presidency. The report was produced internally, under the direction of Defense Department official Leslie H. Gelb and thirty-six analysts, using material taken from the Office of the Secretary of Defense. It was completed only five days before Richard Nixon was inaugurated president.

The Pentagon Papers ran to some 3,000 pages of historical analysis, plus 4,000 additional pages of government documents. The entire work took up forty-seven volumes. Only fifteen copies of the original work were produced. Two of those went to the RAND Corporation, a global policy think tank that rose to prominence during the Cold War.

Daniel Ellsberg had worked for Assistant Secretary of Defense John McNaughton in the early years of the Vietnam escalation, and he had been one of the analysts who contributed to the Pentagon Papers. By 1969, however, anti-war protests had convinced him that the Vietnam War was both immoral and unwinnable. He copied the report with the intention of releasing it to the media, but he could not interest either members of Nixon's administration or members of Congress to be part of the disclosure. It was only in February 1971 that Ellsberg, while talking to a *New York Times* reporter named Neil Sheehan, found an interested party. He supplied Sheehan with a portion of the report, and the *New York Times* began publishing excerpts from that portion on June 13, 1971.

This presented the Nixon administration with a dilemma. The report had been ordered and produced under the aegis of the previous administration. If anything, releasing it would embarrass the Johnson administration rather than the Nixon administration. But Nixon had inherited the war that Johnson had escalated, and it was not clear how Nixon could fulfill his promises to end the war while still appearing tough on Communism to appease his anticommunist supporters. Nixon's national security advisor, Henry Kissinger, convinced the president and his cabinet that making the report public would undermine peace talks Kissinger was undertaking in Paris. As a result, the Nixon administration claimed a prior restraint—a blanket refusal of permission to publish the document—in the name of national security. When the *Times* and the *Post* rejected the administration's claims, the case went into federal court.

About the Author

New York Times v. United States is an unusual case because no one justice spoke for the court. Instead, the six justices in the majority released separate concurring opinions, agreeing on the verdict—that the government had not shown that it was justified in claiming a prior restraint on the Pentagon Papers—but not on the reasons for it.

The first of the concurring justices whose opinion appears in the decision is Hugo L. Black (1885–1971). Black was a native Alabamian and a former U.S. senator appointed to the Supreme Court by Franklin Delano Roosevelt in 1937. In a juridical career that lasted for more than three decades, Black became well known for his liberal views, emphasizing the liberties guaranteed by the Bill of Rights. He was an especially strong defender of First Amendment rights, which may be why his opinion appears first among the concurring opinions in this case.

Explanation and Analysis of the Document

The Majority Opinions

The vote in *New York Times v. United States* was split 6–3, with the majority defending the *Times*.

Hugo L. Black's opinion appears first, but Justice William O. Douglas concurs with it. Black's view, stated in the first few paragraphs of his opinion, is that the government's attempts to suppress publication constitutes a flagrant violation of the First Amendment. In his second paragraph, Black uses constitutional history to emphasize the importance of the First Amendment in securing unwarranted restrictions on government power. Central to his argument is the idea that government security is too vague a restriction to be used as a restraint on First Amendment rights. Justice William O. Douglas concurs with Justice Black in his understanding of the intent of the Founders about the First Amendment, but he adds details based on prec-

edent and case law. William J. Brennan also concurs with Black and Douglas but stresses in his opinion that the injunction that tried to stop publication of the Pentagon Papers was a violation of the First Amendment and never should have been issued in the first place.

Justices Potter Stewart and Byron White, in concurring opinions, point out that the government's position suggests that the president could stop publication of any newspaper story simply by claiming that revealing the information would hurt the public interest. It is not enough to claim, as the government has, that the document the *Times* published was obtained illegally. Stewart points out that the Criminal Code contains many ways of addressing complaints such as the one addressed in this case. But the United States, he says, is not making this a criminal trial. There are many ways of protecting information that threatens national security, Justice Stewart concludes, but an injunction is not one of them.

Thurgood Marshall, the last of the concurring justices, points out that by seeking an injunction to stop publication of the material, the executive branch of the government is effectively trying to make law without going through Congress. By doing so, Marshall says, the executive is making things easier for itself but is violating the principle of separation of powers that is basic to American government. Congress, he says, has provided numerous remedies for keeping state secrets secure, and since the administration is not arguing that a crime has been committed, an injunction is not an appropriate step to take.

The Dissenting Opinions

The three dissenting judges also issued separate opinions in the case. The first to appear is that of Chief Justice Warren E. Burger. He begins his dissent by rejecting the idea that the First Amendment is absolute in all circumstances, as presented in the arguments of the concurring justices. Burger believes that the case is more complicated than it seems and that the court is not in possession of all the facts surrounding the matter. He says that this is because the case has been brought to the Supreme Court in a rush, without respect for thought and judicial process. He also disapproves of the way the *Times* received the published report in the first place; he refers to it as a "purloined" document. Chief Justice Burger concludes by recommending that the trial be returned to the district court to be decided there with due consideration.

Justice John M. Harlan II begins his dissent with an outline of seven different points that he feels the Court is being asked to consider. Like Chief Justice Burger, Harlan believes that the case has been rushed into court without the time needed to verify questions of fact and law. Harlan also states that he feels the publicity surrounding the *Times* case has adversely affected the Court's consideration.

The final dissenting opinion comes from Justice Harry A. Blackmun. Like the two other dissenters, Blackmun says that the case came before the Court too quickly for the justices to reach a considered opinion. But he also adds that he has had a chance to review some of the material published by the *Times*, and he fears, he says, that the release of the information might cause harm to American soldiers, delays in freeing prisoners of war, and overall, a delay in ending the war itself. He concludes by expressing the hope that the two newspapers—the *New York Times* and the *Washington Post*—will carefully consider their responsibility not only in reporting information to the public but in considering what making that information public might do.

Impact

New York Times v. United States was significant on many levels. It reinvigorated protests against the Vietnam War, which dragged on for several more years before the Nixon administration negotiated an exit in January 1973. It exposed the extent to which the Johnson administration was prepared to mislead and lie to the American people—and that revelation, coupled with the 1974 Watergate revelations, severely eroded trust in the U.S. government. It also served as a reaffirmation of the importance of the First Amendment and freedom of the press.

The Supreme Court's support for the First Amendment, however, was obscured by the fact that the Court's decision was expressed in so many different voices. There is no single majority opinion that gives a clear and unmistakable guide to the use of prior restraint and injunctions. The Court does not indicate that prior restraint can never be used. On the other hand, it does not say that it can be used even if Congress authorizes it. The result could potentially allow government censorship within the confines of the First Amendment.

Questions for Further Study

1. What is an injunction, and why was the Court focused on the Nixon administration's attempts to use one to stop publication of the Pentagon Papers?

2. What were President Johnson's reasons for escalating the war in Vietnam?

3. The doctrine of "prior restraint" allows the government to stop publication of sensitive news without revealing what that news might be. Should a democratic government have such a power?

4. The three dissenting justices in New York Times v. United States all complained that the case was brought before the Supreme Court too quickly. The case came before the Court and was decided in less than a week. Is that too short a time?

5. One matter that many of the dissenting justices brought up in their opinions was that the New York Times might have obtained the Pentagon Papers illegally. Why was that not part of the majority opinion?

Further Reading

Books

Bollinger, Lee C., and Geoffrey R Stone. *National Security Leaks and Freedom of the Press: The Pentagon Papers Fifty Years On.* New York: Oxford University Press, 2021.

Ellsberg, Daniel. *Secrets: A Memoir of Vietnam and the Pentagon Papers.* New York: Viking, 2002.

Goodale, James C. *Fighting for the Press: The Inside Story of the Pentagon Papers and Other Battles.* New York: CUNY Journalism Press, 2013.

Rudenstine, David. *The Day the Presses Stopped: A History of the Pentagon Papers Case.* Berkeley: University of California Press, 1996.

Articles

Altschuler, Bruce E. "Is the Pentagon Papers Case Relevant in the Age of WikiLeaks?" *Political Science Quarterly* 130, no. 3 (Fall 2015): 401–23.

Kitrosser, Heidi. "What If Daniel Ellsberg Hadn't Bothered?" *Indiana Law Review* 45 (2011): 89–129.

Websites

"51st Anniversary of the Release of the Pentagon Papers." *Richard M. Nixon Presidential Library*, June 6, 2022. Accessed February 19, 2023, https://www.nixonlibrary.gov/news/51st-anniversary-release-pentagon-papers.

"The Complete Pentagon Papers." *New York Times.* Accessed February 19, 2023, http://archive.nytimes.com/www.nytimes.com/interactive/us/2011_PENTAGON_PAPERS.html?ref=us.

—Commentary by Kenneth R. Shepherd

NEW YORK TIMES CO. V. UNITED STATES

Document Text

MR. JUSTICE BLACK, with whom MR. JUSTICE DOUGLAS joins, concurring

I adhere to the view that the Government's case against the Washington Post should have been dismissed, and that the injunction against the New York Times should have been vacated without oral argument when the cases were first presented to this Court. I believe that every moment's continuance of the injunctions against these newspapers amounts to a flagrant, indefensible, and continuing violation of the First Amendment. Furthermore, after oral argument, I agree completely that we must affirm the judgment of the Court of Appeals for the District of Columbia Circuit and reverse the judgment of the Court of Appeals for the Second Circuit for the reasons stated by my Brothers DOUGLAS and BRENNAN. In my view, it is unfortunate that some of my Brethren are apparently willing to hold that the publication of news may sometimes be enjoined. Such a holding would make a shambles of the First Amendment.

Our Government was launched in 1789 with the adoption of the Constitution. The Bill of Rights, including the First Amendment, followed in 1791. Now, for the first time in the 182 years since the founding of the Republic, the federal courts are asked to hold that the First Amendment does not mean what it says, but rather means that the Government can halt the publication of current news of vital importance to the people of this country.

In seeking injunctions against these newspapers, and in its presentation to the Court, the Executive Branch seems to have forgotten the essential purpose and his-

tory of the First Amendment. When the Constitution was adopted, many people strongly opposed it because the document contained no Bill of Rights to safeguard certain basic freedoms. They especially feared that the new powers granted to a central government might be interpreted to permit the government to curtail freedom of religion, press, assembly, and speech. In response to an overwhelming public clamor, James Madison offered a series of amendments to satisfy citizens that these great liberties would remain safe and beyond the power of government to abridge. Madison proposed what later became the First Amendment in three parts, two of which are set out below, and one of which proclaimed:

"The people shall not be deprived or abridged of their right to speak, to write, or to publish their sentiments, *and the freedom of the press, as one of the great bulwarks of liberty, shall be inviolable.*"

(Emphasis added.) The amendments were offered to curtail and restrict the general powers granted to the Executive, Legislative, and Judicial Branches two years before in the original Constitution. The Bill of Rights changed the original Constitution into a new charter under which no branch of government could abridge the people's freedoms of press, speech, religion, and assembly. Yet the Solicitor General argues and some members of the Court appear to agree that the general powers of the Government adopted in the original Constitution should be interpreted to limit and restrict the specific and emphatic guarantees of the Bill of Rights adopted later. I can imagine no greater perversion of history. Madison and the other Framers of the First Amendment, able men that they were, wrote in language they earnestly believed could never be misunderstood: "Congress shall make no law . . . abridging the freedom . . . of the press. . . ." Both the history and language of the First Amendment support the view that the press must be left free to publish news, whatever the source, without censorship, injunctions, or prior restraints.

In the First Amendment, the Founding Fathers gave the free press the protection it must have to fulfill its essential role in our democracy. The press was to serve the governed, not the governors. The Government's power to censor the press was abolished so that the press would remain forever free to censure the Government. The press was protected so that it could bare the secrets of government and inform the people. Only a free and unrestrained press can effectively expose deception in government. And paramount among the responsibilities of a free press is the duty to prevent any part of the government from deceiving the people and sending them off to distant lands to die of foreign fevers and foreign shot and shell. In my view, far from deserving condemnation for their courageous reporting, the New York Times, the Washington Post, and other newspapers should be commended for serving the purpose that the Founding Fathers saw so clearly. In revealing the workings of government that led to the Vietnam war, the newspapers nobly did precisely that which the Founders hoped and trusted they would do.

The Government's case here is based on premises entirely different from those that guided the Framers of the First Amendment. The Solicitor General has carefully and emphatically stated:

"Now, Mr. Justice [BLACK], your construction of . . . [the First Amendment] is well known, and I certainly respect it. You say that no law means no law, and that should be obvious. I can only say, Mr. Justice, that to me it is equally obvious that 'no law' does not mean 'no law,' and I would seek to persuade the Court that that is true. . . . [T]here are other parts of the Constitution that grant powers and responsibilities to the Executive, and . . . the First Amendment was not intended to make it impossible for the Executive to function or to protect the security of the United States."

And the Government argues in its brief that, in spite of the First Amendment,

"[t]he authority of the Executive Department to protect the nation against publication of information whose disclosure would endanger the national security stems from two interrelated sources: the constitutional power of the President over the conduct of foreign affairs and his authority as Commander-in-Chief."

In other words, we are asked to hold that, despite the First Amendment's emphatic command, the Executive Branch, the Congress, and the Judiciary can make laws enjoining publication of current news and abridging freedom of the press in the name of "national security." The Government does not even attempt to rely on any act of Congress. Instead, it makes the bold and dangerously far-reaching contention that the courts should take it upon themselves to "make" a law abridging freedom of the press in the name of equity, presidential power and national security, even when the representatives of the people in Congress have adhered to the command of the First Amendment and refused to make such a law. *See* concurring opinion of MR. JUSTICE DOUGLAS, *post* at 403 U. S. 721-722. To find that the President has "inherent power" to halt the publication of news by resort to the courts would wipe out the First Amendment and destroy the fundamental liberty and security of the very people the Government hopes to make "secure." No one can read the history of the adoption of the First Amendment without being convinced beyond any doubt that it was injunctions like those sought here that Madison and his collaborators intended to outlaw in this Nation for all time.

The word "security" is a broad, vague generality whose contours should not be invoked to abrogate the fundamental law embodied in the First Amendment. The guarding of military and diplomatic secrets at the expense of informed representative government provides no real security for our Republic. The Framers of the First Amendment, fully aware of both the need to defend a new nation and the abuses of the English and Colonial governments, sought to give this new society strength and security by providing that freedom of speech, press, religion, and assembly should not be abridged. This thought was eloquently expressed in 1937 by Mr. Chief Justice Hughes—great man and great Chief Justice that he was—when the Court held a man could not be punished for attending a meeting run by Communists.

"The greater the importance of safeguarding the community from incitements to the overthrow of our institutions by force and violence, the more imperative is the need to preserve inviolate the constitutional rights of free speech, free press and free assembly in order to maintain the opportunity for free political discussion, to the end that government may be responsive to the will of the people and that changes, if desired, may be obtained by peaceful means. Therein lies the security of the Republic, the very foundation of constitutional government."

MR. JUSTICE BRENNAN, concurring

I

I write separately in these cases only to emphasize what should be apparent: that our judgments in the present cases may not be taken to indicate the propriety, in the future, of issuing temporary stays and restraining orders to block the publication of material sought to be suppressed by the Government. So far as I can determine, never before has the United States sought to enjoin a newspaper from publishing information in its possession. The relative novelty of the questions presented, the necessary haste with which decisions were reached, the magnitude of the interests asserted, and the fact that all the parties have concentrated their arguments upon the question whether permanent restraints were proper may have justified at least some of the restraints heretofore imposed in these cases. Certainly it is difficult to fault the several courts below for seeking to assure that the issues here involved were preserved for ultimate review by this Court. But even if it be assumed that some of the interim restraints were proper in the two cases before us, that assumption has no bearing upon the propriety of similar judicial action in the future. To begin with, there has now been ample time for reflection and judgment; whatever values there may be in the preservation of novel questions for appellate review may not support any restraints in the future. More important, the First Amendment stands as an absolute bar to the imposition of judicial restraints in circumstances of the kind presented by these cases.

II

The error that has pervaded these cases from the outset was the granting of any injunctive relief whatsoever, interim or otherwise. The entire thrust of the Government's claim throughout these cases has been that publication of the material sought to be enjoined "could," or "might," or "may" prejudice the national interest in various ways. But the First Amendment tolerates absolutely no prior judicial restraints of the press predicated upon surmise or conjecture that untoward consequences may result.* Our cases, it is true, have indicated that there is a single, extremely narrow class of cases in which the First Amendment's ban on prior judicial restraint may be overridden. Our cases have thus far indicated that such cases may arise only when the Nation "is at war," *Schenck v. United States,* 249 U. S. 47, 249 U. S. 52 (1919), during which times

"[n]o one would question but that a government might prevent actual obstruction to its recruiting service or the publication of the sailing dates of transports or the number and location of troops."

Near v. Minnesota, 283 U. S. 697, 283 U. S. 716 (1931). Even if the present world situation were assumed to be tantamount to a time of war, or if the power of presently available armaments would justify even in peacetime the suppression of information that would set in motion a nuclear holocaust, in neither of these actions has the Government presented or even alleged that publication of items from or based upon the material at issue would cause the happening of an event of that nature. "[T]he chief purpose of [the First Amendment's] guaranty [is] to prevent previous restraints upon publication." *Near v. Minnesota, supra,* at 283 U. S. 713. Thus, only governmental allegation and proof that publication must inevitably, directly, and immediately cause the occurrence of an event kindred to imperiling the safety of a transport already at sea can support even the issuance of an interim restraining order. In no event may mere conclusions be sufficient, for if the Executive Branch seeks judicial aid in preventing publication, it must inevitably submit the basis upon which that aid is sought to scrutiny by the judiciary. And, therefore, every restraint issued in this case, whatever its form, has violated the First Amendment—and not less so because that restraint was justified as necessary to afford the courts an opportunity to examine the claim more thoroughly. Unless and until the Government has clearly made out its case, the First Amendment commands that no injunction may issue.

* *Freedman v. Maryland,* 380 U. S. 51 (1965), and similar cases regarding temporary restraints of allegedly obscene materials are not in point. For those cases rest upon the proposition that "obscenity is not protected by the freedoms of speech and press." *Roth v. United*

States, 354 U. S. 476, 354 U. S. 481 (1957). Here there is no question but that the material sought to be suppressed is within the protection of the First Amendment; the only question is whether, notwithstanding that fact, its publication may be enjoined for a time because of the presence of an overwhelming national interest. Similarly, copyright cases have no pertinence here: the Government is not asserting an interest in the particular form of words chosen in the documents, but is seeking to suppress the ideas expressed therein. And the copyright laws, of course, protect only the form of expression, and not the ideas expressed.

MR. JUSTICE STEWART, with whom MR. JUSTICE WHITE joins, concurring

In the governmental structure created by our Constitution, the Executive is endowed with enormous power in the two related areas of national defense and international relations. This power, largely unchecked by the Legislative and Judicial branches, has been pressed to the very hilt since the advent of the nuclear missile age. For better or for worse, the simple fact is that a President of the United States possesses vastly greater constitutional independence in these two vital areas of power than does, say, a prime minister of a country with a parliamentary form of government.

In the absence of the governmental checks and balances present in other areas of our national life, the only effective restraint upon executive policy and power in the areas of national defense and international affairs may lie in an enlightened citizenry—in an informed and critical public opinion which alone can here protect the values of democratic government. For this reason, it is perhaps here that a press that is alert, aware, and free most vitally serves the basic purpose of the First Amendment. For, without an informed and free press, there cannot be an enlightened people.

Yet it is elementary that the successful conduct of international diplomacy and the maintenance of an effective national defense require both confidentiality and secrecy. Other nations can hardly deal with this Nation in an atmosphere of mutual trust unless they can be assured that their confidences will be kept. And, within our own executive departments, the development of considered and intelligent international policies would be impossible if those charged with their formulation could not communicate with each other freely, frankly, and in confidence. In the area of basic national defense, the frequent need for absolute secrecy is, of course, self-evident.

I think there can be but one answer to this dilemma, if dilemma it be. The responsibility must be where the power is. If the Constitution gives the Executive a large degree of unshared power in the conduct of foreign affairs and the maintenance of our national defense, then, under the Constitution, the Executive must have the largely unshared duty to determine and preserve the degree of internal security necessary to exercise that power successfully. It is an awesome responsibility, requiring judgment and wisdom of a high order. I should suppose that moral, political, and practical considerations would dictate that a very first principle of that wisdom would be an insistence upon avoiding secrecy for its own sake. For when everything is classified, then nothing is classified, and the system becomes one to be disregarded by the cynical or the careless, and to be manipulated by those intent on self-protection or self-promotion. I should suppose, in short, that the hallmark of a truly effective internal security system would be the maximum possible disclosure, recognizing that secrecy can best be preserved only when credibility is truly maintained. But, be that as it may, it is clear to me that it is the constitutional duty of the Executive—as a matter of sovereign prerogative, and not as a matter of law as the courts know law—through the promulgation and enforcement of executive regulations, to protect the confidentiality necessary to carry out its responsibilities in the fields of international relations and national defense.

This is not to say that Congress and the courts have no role to play. Undoubtedly, Congress has the power to enact specific and appropriate criminal laws to protect government property and preserve government secrets. Congress has passed such laws, and several of them are of very colorable relevance to the apparent circumstances of these cases. And if a criminal prosecution is instituted, it will be the responsibility of the courts to decide the applicability of the criminal law under which the charge is brought. Moreover, if Congress should pass a specific law authorizing civil proceedings in this field, the courts would likewise have the duty to decide the constitutionality of such a law, as well as its applicability to the facts proved.

But in the cases before us, we are asked neither to construe specific regulations nor to apply specific laws.

We are asked, instead, to perform a function that the Constitution gave to the Executive, not the Judiciary. We are asked, quite simply, to prevent the publication by two newspapers of material that the Executive Branch insists should not, in the national interest, be published. I am convinced that the Executive is correct with respect to some of the documents involved. But I cannot say that disclosure of any of them will surely result in direct, immediate, and irreparable damage to our Nation or its people. That being so, there can under the First Amendment be but one judicial resolution of the issues before us. I join the judgments of the Court.

MR. JUSTICE WHITE, with whom MR. JUSTICE STEWART joins, concurring

I concur in today's judgments, but only because of the concededly extraordinary protection against prior restraints enjoyed by the press under our constitutional system. I do not say that in no circumstances would the First Amendment permit an injunction against publishing information about government plans or operations. Nor, after examining the materials the Government characterizes as the most sensitive and destructive, can I deny that revelation of these documents will do substantial damage to public interests. Indeed, I am confident that their disclosure will have that result. But I nevertheless agree that the United States has not satisfied the very heavy burden that it must meet to warrant an injunction against publication in these cases, at least in the absence of express and appropriately limited congressional authorization for prior restraints in circumstances such as these.

The Government's position is simply stated: the responsibility of the Executive for the conduct of the foreign affairs and for the security of the Nation is so basic that the President is entitled to an injunction against publication of a newspaper story whenever he can convince a court that the information to be revealed threatens "grave and irreparable" injury to the public interest; and the injunction should issue whether or not the material to be published is classified, whether or not publication would be lawful under relevant criminal statutes enacted by Congress, and regardless of the circumstances by which the newspaper came into possession of the information. At least in the absence of legislation by Congress, based on its own investigations and findings, I am quite unable to agree that the inherent powers of the Executive and the courts reach so far as to authorize remedies having such sweeping potential for inhibiting publications by the press. Much of the difficulty inheres in the "grave and irreparable danger" standard suggested by the United States. If the United States were to have judgment under such a standard in these cases, our decision would be of little guidance to other courts in other cases, for the material at issue here would not be available from the Court's opinion or from public records, nor would it be published by the press. Indeed, even today, where we hold that the United States has not met its burden, the material remains sealed in court records and it is properly not discussed in today's opinions. Moreover, because the material poses substantial dangers to national interests, and because of the hazards of criminal sanctions, a responsible press may choose never to publish the more sensitive materials. To sustain the Government in these cases would start the courts down a long and hazardous road that I am not willing to travel, at least without congressional guidance and direction.

It is not easy to reject the proposition urged by the United States, and to deny relief on its good faith claims in these cases that publication will work serious damage to the country. But that discomfiture is considerably dispelled by the infrequency of prior-restraint cases. Normally, publication will occur and the damage be done before the Government has either opportunity or grounds for suppression. So here, publication has already begun, and a substantial part of the threatened damage has already occurred. The fact of a massive breakdown in security is known, access to the documents by many unauthorized people is undeniable, and the efficacy of equitable relief against these or other newspapers to avert anticipated damage is doubtful, at best.

What is more, terminating the ban on publication of the relatively few sensitive documents the Government now seeks to suppress does not mean that the law either requires or invites newspapers or others to publish them, or that they will be immune from criminal action if they do. Prior restraints require an unusually heavy justification under the First Amendment, but failure by the Government to justify prior restraints does not measure its constitutional entitlement to a conviction for criminal publication. That the Government mistakenly chose to proceed by injunction does not mean that it could not successfully proceed in another way.

When the Espionage Act was under consideration in 1917, Congress eliminated from the bill a provision that would have given the President broad powers in time of war to proscribe, under threat of criminal penalty, the publication of various categories of information related to the national defense. Congress at that time was unwilling to clothe the President with such far-reaching powers to monitor the press, and those opposed to this part of the legislation assumed that a necessary concomitant of such power was the power to "filter out the news to the people through some man." 55 Cong.Rec. 2008 (remarks of Sen. Ashurst). However, these same members of Congress appeared to have little doubt that newspapers would be subject to criminal prosecution if they insisted on publishing information of the type Congress had itself determined should not be revealed. Senator Ashurst, for example, was quite sure that the editor of such a newspaper

"should be punished if he did publish information as to the movements of the fleet, the troops, the aircraft, the location of powder factories, the location of defense works, and all that sort of thing."

Id. at 2009.

The Criminal Code contains numerous provisions potentially relevant to these cases. Section 797 makes it a crime to publish certain photographs or drawings of military installations. Section 798, also in precise language, proscribes knowing and willful publication of any classified information concerning the cryptographic systems or communication intelligence activities of the United States, as well as any information obtained from communication intelligence operations. If any of the material here at issue is of this nature, the newspapers are presumably now on full notice of the position of the United States, and must face the consequences if they publish. I would have no difficulty in sustaining convictions under these sections on facts that would not justify the intervention of equity and the imposition of a prior restraint.

The same would be true under those sections of the Criminal Code casting a wider net to protect the national defense. Section 793(e) makes it a criminal act for any unauthorized possessor of a document "relating to the national defense" either (1) willfully to communicate or cause to be communicated that document to any person not entitled to receive it or (2)

willfully to retain the document and fail to deliver it to an officer of the United States entitled to receive it. The subsection was added in 1950 because preexisting law provided no penalty for the unauthorized possessor unless demand for the documents was made.

"The dangers surrounding the unauthorized possession of such items are self-evident, and it is deemed advisable to require their surrender in such a case, regardless of demand, especially since their unauthorized possession may be unknown to the authorities who would otherwise make the demand."

S.Rep. No. 2369, pt. 1, 81st Cong., 2d Sess., 9 (1950). Of course, in the cases before us, the unpublished documents have been demanded by the United States, and their import has been made known at least to counsel for the newspapers involved. In *Gorin v. United States,* 312 U. S. 19, 312 U. S. 28 (1941), the words "national defense" as used in a predecessor of § 793 were held by a unanimous Court to have "a well understood connotation"—a "generic concept of broad connotations, referring to the military and naval establishments and the related activities of national preparedness"—and to be "sufficiently definite to apprise the public of prohibited activities" and to be consonant with due process. 312 U.S. at 312 U. S. 28. Also, as construed by the Court in *Gorin,* information "connected with the national defense" is obviously not limited to that threatening "grave and irreparable" injury to the United States.

It is thus clear that Congress has addressed itself to the problems of protecting the security of the country and the national defense from unauthorized disclosure of potentially damaging information. *Cf. Youngstown Sheet & Tube Co. v. Sawyer,* 343 U. S. 579, 343 U. S. 585-586 (1952); *see also id.* at 343 U. S. 593-628 (Frankfurter, J., concurring). It has not, however, authorized the injunctive remedy against threatened publication. It has apparently been satisfied to rely on criminal sanctions and their deterrent effect on the responsible, as well as the irresponsible, press. I am not, of course, saying that either of these newspapers has yet committed a crime, or that either would commit a crime if it published all the material now in its possession. That matter must await resolution in the context of a criminal proceeding if one is instituted by the United States. In that event, the issue of guilt or innocence would be determined by procedures and standards quite different from those that have purported to govern these injunctive proceedings.

MR. CHIEF JUSTICE BURGER, dissenting

So clear are the constitutional limitations on prior restraint against expression that, from the time of *Near v. Minnesota,* 283 U. S. 697 (1931), until recently in *Organization for a Better Austin v. Keefe,* 402 U. S. 415 (1971), we have had little occasion to be concerned with cases involving prior restraints against news reporting on matters of public interest. There is, therefore, little variation among the members of the Court in terms of resistance to prior restraints against publication. Adherence to this basic constitutional principle, however, does not make these cases simple. In these cases, the imperative of a free and unfettered press comes into collision with another imperative, the effective functioning of a complex modern government, and, specifically, the effective exercise of certain constitutional powers of the Executive. Only those who view the First Amendment as an absolute in all circumstances—a view I respect, but reject—can find such cases as these to be simple or easy.

These cases are not simple for another and more immediate reason. We do not know the facts of the cases. No District Judge knew all the facts. No Court of Appeals judge knew all the facts. No member of this Court knows all the facts.

Why are we in this posture, in which only those judges to whom the First Amendment is absolute and permits of no restraint in any circumstances or for any reason, are really in a position to act?

I suggest we are in this posture because these cases have been conducted in unseemly haste. MR. JUSTICE HARLAN covers the chronology of events demonstrating the hectic pressures under which these cases have been processed, and I need not restate them. The prompt setting of these cases reflects our universal abhorrence of prior restraint. But prompt judicial action does not mean unjudicial haste.

Here, moreover, the frenetic haste is due in large part to the manner in which the Times proceeded from the date it obtained the purloined documents. It seems reasonably clear now that the haste precluded reasonable and deliberate judicial treatment of these cases, and was not warranted. The precipitate action of this Court aborting trials not yet completed is not the kind of judicial conduct that ought to attend the disposition of a great issue.

The newspapers make a derivative claim under the First Amendment; they denominate this right as the public "right to know"; by implication, the Times asserts a sole trusteeship of that right by virtue of its journalistic "scoop." The right is asserted as an absolute. Of course, the First Amendment right itself is not an absolute, as Justice Holmes so long ago pointed out in his aphorism concerning the right to shout "fire" in a crowded theater if there was no fire. There are other exceptions, some of which Chief Justice Hughes mentioned by way of example in *Near v. Minnesota.* There are no doubt other exceptions no one has had occasion to describe or discuss. Conceivably, such exceptions may be lurking in these cases and, would have been flushed had they been properly considered in the trial courts, free from unwarranted deadlines and frenetic pressures. An issue of this importance should be tried and heard in a judicial atmosphere conducive to thoughtful, reflective deliberation, especially when haste, in terms of hours, is unwarranted in light of the long period the Times, by its own choice, deferred publication.

It is not disputed that the Times has had unauthorized possession of the documents for three to four months, during which it has had its expert analysts studying them, presumably digesting them and preparing the material for publication. During all of this time, the Times, presumably in its capacity as trustee of the public's "right to know," has held up publication for purposes it considered proper, and thus public knowledge was delayed. No doubt this was for a good reason; the analysis of 7,000 pages of complex material drawn from a vastly greater volume of material would inevitably take time, and the writing of good news stories takes time. But why should the United States Government, from whom this information was illegally acquired by someone, along with all the counsel, trial judges, and appellate judges be placed under needless pressure? After these months of deferral, the alleged "right to know" has somehow and suddenly become a right that must be vindicated instanter.

Would it have been unreasonable, since the newspaper could anticipate the Government's objections to release of secret material, to give the Government an opportunity to review the entire collection and determine whether agreement could be reached on publication? Stolen or not, if security was not, in fact, jeopardized, much of the material could no doubt have been declassified, since it spans a period ending in 1968. With such an approach—one that great newspapers have in the past practiced and stated editorially to be the duty of an honorable press—the newspapers and Government might well have narrowed the area of disagreement as to what was and was not publishable, leaving the remainder to be resolved in orderly litigation, if necessary. To me, it is hardly believable that a newspaper long regarded as a great institution in American life would fail to perform one of the basic and simple duties of every citizen with respect to the discovery or possession of stolen property or secret government documents. That duty, I had thought—perhaps naively—was to report forthwith, to responsible public officers. This duty rests on taxi drivers, Justices, and the New York Times. The course followed by the Times, whether so calculated or not, removed any possibility of orderly litigation of the issue. If the action of the judges up to now has been correct, that result is sheer happenstance.

Our grant of the writ of certiorari before final judgment in the *Times* case aborted the trial in the District Court before it had made a complete record pursuant to the mandate of the Court of Appeals for the Second Circuit.

The consequence of all this melancholy series of events is that we literally do not know what we are acting on. As I see it, we have been forced to deal with litigation concerning rights of great magnitude without an adequate record, and surely without time for adequate treatment either in the prior proceedings or in this Court. It is interesting to note that counsel on both sides, in oral argument before this Court, were frequently unable to respond to questions on factual points. Not surprisingly, they pointed out that they had been working literally "around the clock," and simply were unable to review the documents that give rise to these cases and were not familiar with them. This Court is in no better posture. I agree generally with MR. JUSTICE HARLAN and MR. JUSTICE BLACKMUN, but I am not prepared to reach the merits.

I would affirm the Court of Appeals for the Second Circuit and allow the District Court to complete the trial aborted by our grant of certiorari, meanwhile preserving the *status quo* in the *Post* case. I would direct that the District Court, on remand, give priority to the *Times* case to the exclusion of all other business of that court, but I would not set arbitrary deadlines.

I should add that I am in general agreement with much of what MR. JUSTICE WHITE has expressed with respect to penal sanctions concerning communication or retention of documents or information relating to the national defense.

We all crave speedier judicial processes, but, when judges are pressured, as in these cases, the result is a parody of the judicial function.

Glossary

censorship: suppression from publication

freedom of the press: one of the rights contained in the First Amendment to the Constitution, which states, in part: "Congress shall make no law respecting an establishment of religion, or prohibiting the free exercise thereof; or abridging the freedom of speech, or of the press"

inherent powers: powers of an office or branch of government not expressly outlined in the Constitution; in this case, the power claimed by the U.S. president to prevent the newspapers from publishing the Pentagon Papers

Pentagon Papers: a forty-seven-volume report commissioned by the U.S. secretary of defense in 1967, excerpts of which were published by the *New York Times* and the *Washington Post* beginning in June 1971, that provided a history of the United States' involvement in the Vietnam War